State *and* Local Government

Politics and Public Policies

NINTH EDITION

David C. Saffell
Ohio Northern University

Harry Basehart
Salisbury University

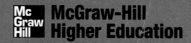
McGraw-Hill
Higher Education

Boston   Burr Ridge, IL   Dubuque, IA   New York   San Francisco   St. Louis
Bangkok   Bogotá   Caracas   Kuala Lumpur   Lisbon   London   Madrid   Mexico City
Milan   Montreal   New Delhi   Santiago   Seoul   Singapore   Sydney   Taipei   Toronto

McGraw-Hill
Higher Education

Published by McGraw-Hill, an imprint of The McGraw-Hill Companies, Inc., 1221 Avenue of the Americas, New York, NY 10020. Copyright © 2009, 2005, 2001, 1998, 1993, 1990, 1987, 1982, 1978.

This book is printed on acid-free paper.

2 3 4 5 6 7 8 9 0 DOC/DOC 0 9 8

ISBN: 978-0-07-352632-4
MHID: 0-07-352632-0

Editor in Chief: *Michael Ryan*
Publisher: *Lisa Moore*
Sponsoring Editor: *Mark Georgiev*
Development Editor: *Larry Goldberg*
Editorial Assistant: *Briana Porco*
Marketing Manager: *Simon Heathcote*
Production Editor: *Alison Meier*
Design Coordinator: *Margarite Reynolds*
Interior Design: *Kay Lieberherr*

Cover Design: *Asylum Studios*
Art Editor: *Ayelet Arbel*
Photo Researcher: *Brian J. Pecko*
Production Supervisor: *Richard DeVitto*
Composition: *10/12 Times Roman by ICC Macmillan Inc.*
Printing: *45# New Era Matte Plus, R. R. Donnelley & Sons*

Photo Credits

Library of Congress Cataloging-in-Publication Data

Saffell, David C., 1941–
    State and local government: politics and public policies / David
C. Saffell and Harry Basehart. — 9th ed.
        p. cm.
    Includes bibliographical references and index.
    ISBN-13: 978-0-07-352632-4 (alk. paper)
    ISBN-10: 0-07-352632-0 (alk. paper)
    1. State governments—United States. 2. Local government—United States. I. Basehart, Harry. II. Title.

JK2408.S17 2009
320.80973—dc22

                                                                    2007037986

The Internet addresses listed in the text were accurate at the time of publication. The inclusion of a Web site does not indicate an endorsement by the authors or McGraw-Hill, and McGraw-Hill does not guarantee the accuracy of the information presented at these sites.

www.mhhe.com

To our wives, Ainsley and Priscilla

Brief Contents

Contents

3 Political Parties and Interest Groups   75

4 Political Participation and Elections   117

Case Studies

Preface

Beginning with the first edition in 1978, *State and Local Government: Politics and Public Policy* has presented up-to-date, readable analysis of the structure and operation of state and local government. Although the book has remained a concise treatment of subnational politics, we have always included discussion of a wide range of policy issues and have made extensive references to the current academic research in the field.

Our discussion of political parties, interest groups, political participation, elections, and the legislative, executive, and judicial branches centers on state government, but it also includes considerable analysis of political behavior and government structure in cities, counties, and other units of local government. At all levels, readers are reminded about the impact of political culture, tradition, and levels of economic development on governmental structure and policy making.

We have chronicled the evolution of state and local governments beginning in a period of serious financial difficulties in the early 1980s. That was followed by a resurgence of the states in the 1990s, marked by budget surpluses, and then a return to several years of serious financial problems, strongly influenced by cuts in federal assistance following the events of 9/11. In this edition we describe the recent upturn in state financial fortunes and renewed policy making activity, during a period when Congress often has been paralyzed by strong partisan division and the president's focus has largely been on fighting terrorism. During these financial ups and downs, we have remained impressed with the continuing vitality of state governments.

We hope that student readers will come to appreciate better how their everyday lives are directly impacted by policies made in their state capitals and city halls and implemented by employees at all levels of government and that they will become active participants in the affairs of their communities. Committed individuals can "fight city hall" and they can, and often do, get subnational governments to create new policies or stop some of what they have been doing.

A variety of pedagogical devises are employed in all chapters. These include all new chapter-opening Case Studies, Points to Consider, Key Terms in bold with definitions in the text, Chapter Summaries, Brief Comparisons of State/Local Differences, and expanded Interesting Web Sites.

The Web sites are user-friendly and have a wealth of current information that will enable you to easily pursue an in-depth analysis of some of the topics in the chapters. In addition, we strongly recommend that students acquaint themselves with Stateline.org at www.stateline.org, the single best Web site for state government. This site is one of several sponsored by The Pew Research Center, a nonpartisan "fact tank" that provides information on issues, attitudes, and trends shaping America and the world. Once you are at the home page of Stateline.org, you will find the "Top Stories" for the day. "Additional Stories" will have news arranged by states. If you want to look at specific issues, click on one that you are interested in such as "Environment" or "Crimes & Courts" to find recent stories on these topics in almost every state. Please consider registering for "News Alerts" so that you can stay up-to-date with the latest state government news. You can register for a daily news alert or a weekly newsletter. You can even select the type of news alerts that you would like to receive. Finally, Governing.com at www.governing.com, Web site for the magazine *Governing,* is especially good for up-to-the-minute news for both state and local governments. The existence of these Web sites and others makes the study of state and local government more exciting than ever. It has never been easier to study the politics of the fifty states, and even hundreds of cities and counties.

In addition to updating statistics in graphs, maps, and tables and information about how voters behaved in the 2006 elections, including governors, legislators, mayors, and ballot propositions, this edition contains new or expanded material on a wide range of subjects. These include the myth of a polarized America; intergovernmental responses to immigration, Hurricane Katrina, and homeland security; decisions of the Roberts Court dealing with federalism; the development and expansion of a hybrid system of city government; recent changes in voting behavior in suburbs and rural areas; controversy regarding the use of eminent domain; the continuing trend toward competitive political parties and divided government; civic engagement as an alternative to political participation; college students and voter registration laws; early voting and instant runoff voting; clean election laws; the role of staff in state legislatures; constituency service and casework as a way of viewing representation; the effect of term limits on legislators and legislatures; city council member characteristics and causes of high turnover; taxpayers' bill of rights; the expansion of legalized gambling in the states and on American Indian tribal lands; structural deficits and revenue shortfalls; state programs for children; and greenhouse gas emission initiatives.

A password-protected, instructors-only Web site contains the instructor's manual and test bank at www.mhhe.com/saffell9.

ACKNOWLEDGMENTS

Preparation of this text was greatly aided by the thoughtful comments of the reviewers of the ninth edition, who pointed out factual errors and made more general suggestions regarding organization, emphasis, and style. They are John David Briley, East Tennessee State University, Johnson City; Cynthia Carter, Florida Community College at Jacksonville; Theophilus Herrington, Texas Southern University; Joel Lieske, Cleveland State University; Gregory P. Rabb, Jamestown Community College; Gary D. Wekkin, University of Central Arkansas; and John Wood, Rose State College.

Others who provided valuable advice and who helped us acquire information include Timothy G. O'Rourke, Dean of the Fulton School of Liberal Arts, Salisbury University, and David A. Warner, of the Maryland Department of Legislative Services, who assisted Harry Basehart. In Eugene, staff at the Knight Library and the John E. Jaqua Law Library of the University of Oregon were very generous with their time, helping Dave Saffell locate materials. We would especially like to thank Professor Deil S. Wright of the University of North Carolina at Chapel Hill for sharing with us much of his recent research and for comments about his classic discussion of picket fence federalism.

As with several past editions of this book, Monica Eckman provided excellent editorial direction. Also in Boston, Jessica Badiner skillfully attended to a host of details regarding reviewer comments, scheduling, and preparation of the manuscript. Larry Goldberg's careful manuscript preparation and suggestions improved the content and appearance of this edition. Meticulous copyediting by Margaret Moore significantly improved the clarity and accuracy of the text. Alison Meier in San Francisco efficiently managed the last stages in the production process. As always, we were impressed with the high quality of work done by everyone at McGraw-Hill who played a role in the production of this book. Equally important to us was the fact that we enjoyed very much our personal contact with each person noted above.

David C. Saffell

Harry Basehart

About the Authors

DAVID C. SAFFELL is professor emeritus of political science at Ohio Northern University. He received his Ph.D. in political science from The University of Minnesota. He is the coauthor (with Harry Basehart) of *Governing States and Cities* (1997); the coeditor (with Harry Basehart) of *Readings in State and Local Government: Problems and Prospects* (1994); and the author of several other textbooks on American government. He helped manage a successful campaign for the Oregon legislature in 2006.

HARRY BASEHART is professor of political science and codirector of the Institute for Public Affairs and Civic Engagement at Salisbury University in Salisbury, Maryland. He received his Ph.D. in political science from The Ohio State University. Professor Basehart is the author or coauthor of articles on state legislatures that have appeared in *American Politics Quarterly* and *Legislative Studies Quarterly.* As a participant in the American Democracy Project of the American Association of State Colleges and Universities, he has worked to find new ways of engaging college students in elections through voter registration, voter education, and voter participation.

THE SETTING OF STATE AND LOCAL GOVERNMENT

COMMANDING NATIONAL GUARD TROOPS

In May 2006, President Bush called for 6,000 National Guard troops to be deployed along the Mexican border to assist the U.S. Border Patrol largely by providing logistical, rather than law enforcement, functions. This was a response to growing political pressure to secure the southern border of the country, both to fight terrorism and to keep illegal immigrants from entering.

Of the four governors whose states border Mexico, only Arizona's Janet Napolitano, a Democrat, received a courtesy call from the Bush administration about a week before the announcement.[1] Although the call was merely notification, not consultation, the president's announcement regarding the use of National Guard troops came as a complete surprise to the other three governors.

As commanders of state National Guard units, governors have considerable power regarding their deployment. Although the president does not have the ability to mobilize the Guard for routine law enforcement, governors can mobilize the Guard for a variety of functions, including protection of roads and bridges.

California Governor Arnold Schwarzenegger, a Republican and a supporter of the president, initially opposed the administration's request that California supply 1,500 of the troops. The governor called the plan a "Band-Aid" solution to the problem of immigration and complained that to comply would spread California's National Guard troops too thin to be able to respond effectively to natural disasters that were certain to occur during the summer. Three months earlier all fifty governors had signed a letter telling President Bush that deployment in Afghanistan and Iraq was stripping the National Guard of equipment and personnel needed to respond to natural disasters in their states.

After a seventeen-day standoff with federal officials, agreement was reached that California would provide about 1,000 troops. Governor Schwarzenegger drafted his own plan of deployment to preserve the Guard's response capacity in California. It was agreed that the federal government would pay for the cost of the deployment. Schwarzenegger said most of the troops would be volunteers, not troops on short-term summer duty, as suggested by the federal government. And the governor issued an executive order that the National Guard troops would not be authorized to assist Guard patrol after the end of 2008. Perhaps giving consideration to the California gubernatorial election in November, Schwarzenegger said, "It's not my preference to send National Guard troops, but there's an important need to protect the border."

As will be discussed in this chapter and in Chapter 2, the process of deploying the National Guard to the Mexican border illustrates how immigration policy is being made on a piecemeal basis by Congress, the president, and the states, with little or no coordination among the governmental units. It is curious that as the former governor of Texas, President Bush did not reach out to the governors of border states, including the Republican governor of Texas.

POINTS TO CONSIDER

- How state government activities recently have been affected by the national economy, the threat of terrorism, and the war in Iraq.
- How state policy is influenced by economic factors, physical setting, political culture, sectionalism, and racial/ethnic diversity.

- Do large numbers of immigrants hurt low-income American workers a little or lot?
- How have states responded to the lack of congressional action regarding immigration?
- The nature of population change in states and cities, especially in the Sunbelt, and how this has affected public policy in the past fifty years.
- Is there a "culture war" going on in the United States?
- In what ways do public policies move, or diffuse, from state to state?
- The composition of state constitutions and their historical evolution.
- The legal position of cities and how this affects their policy making.
- The process by which state constitutions are amended. What is the best way to accomplish significant constitutional change?
- To what extent are states similar to and different from each other, and what factors account for the differences?
- How do state constitutions differ from the U.S. Constitution?

STATES IN THE TWENTIETH CENTURY

The states dominated American government in the nineteenth century and the first decade of the twentieth century. However, several events in the first half of the twentieth century relegated the states to a position of secondary importance. Ratification of the Sixteenth Amendment (relating to income tax) in 1913 gave the federal government much greater ability to raise money and to centralize policy making. The Depression showed the weaknesses of the states in responding to the nation's economic problems and led to greater focus on the president as the center of government. World War II further strengthened the authority of the president and the centralization of power in Washington, D.C.

State reform has been taking place since the early twentieth century, but the negative image of corrupt and incompetent state government persisted (and with good reason) into the early 1960s.[2] Since the mid-1960s, nearly all states have ratified new constitutions or made significant changes in existing ones. Governors' terms have been lengthened and their powers increased. Legislatures have become more professional (see Chapter 5) and more representative of urban interests, and nearly all meet in annual sessions. Court systems have been unified (see Chapter 7), and intermediate appellate courts have been added in many states. State bureaucrats are more professional, and the number of state employees under some form of merit system has increased from 50 percent in 1960 to nearly 80 percent, with nearly all state employees covered by merit systems in nearly three-fourths of the states (see Chapter 6). An increase in party competition in the states, followed by the election of energetic governors and the relaxation of federal directives, has led to more innovative state policies. In addition, cuts in federal aid have caused local governments to look more to the states for financial help (see Chapter 2).

This resurgence of the states was well under way when Ronald Reagan was elected president in 1980. Reagan believed that the federal government had been too involved in state issues and that more responsibility for policy making should be turned over to the states. In addition, federal categorical grants-in-aid (see Chapter 2) were criticized by congressional conservatives and by state and local officials for their red tape and insensitivity to local problems. The timing of Reagan's changes in policy and philosophy thus caught the states at a point at which they were the most capable of assuming new policy making responsibilities. Unfortunately, the states also found themselves without some of the financial assistance they had come to expect from the national government. By 1990, states and localities faced severe financial pressures brought on by the recession and cuts in federal funds. A majority of states raised taxes, spending was cut, and employees were furloughed or fired in the early 1990s.

By the mid-1990s the financial position of most states and cities had improved as the national economy rebounded. Many states cut taxes and boosted spending for social services and infrastructure, and some put money away for a "rainy day." But the boom years for virtually all governments ended with the dawn of the new century. As the bubble burst on high-technology companies, stock values plummeted, unemployment rose, and state and federal budget surpluses turned to deficits (see Chapter 9).

Following federal tax cuts in 2001, dozens of states that tied their tax codes to federal rates had to make major code changes to avoid the loss of tax revenue. States also have had to absorb increases of about 10 percent annually in Medicaid costs. When they turned to the federal government, whose policies were adding to their woes, for financial help, states found that the Bush administration was preoccupied by its war on terrorism and that the federal budget surplus of 2000 had disappeared. When the war in Iraq began in 2003, financial pressures on the federal government made increased assistance to states even less likely. At the same time, state and local security expenses grew, and many local police were called up to military service.

After five years of economic hard times, most states experienced better than expected revenue in 2005, as the national economy improved. Many states had cut spending and raised taxes in the preceding years, and, as a result, they experienced a short-term financial windfall. Most of those states began to restore funding for education and infrastructure repairs, and in 2006 a few considered significant tax cuts. But having drawn down their **rainy day funds** (revenue set aside to cover some expenses during economic hard times), some states had serious carryover economic problems with which to deal. Many governors tended to be cautious, emphasizing long-range planning and balance, rather than responding to new spending initiatives.

As we would expect, the recovery has not been equally distributed across the states. Great Lakes states continue to suffer from declining manufacturing jobs and stagnant populations, and Gulf Coast states will take several years to recover from the devastation of Hurricane Katrina.

STATE VITALITY

Current state vitality is part of a long history of innovative policy making by state governments. Wisconsin serves as a classic example. During the period 1910–1914 Wisconsin initiated the direct primary, civil service regulations, a state income tax, conservation laws, and a variety of state regulatory commissions. Political scientist John Kincaid notes that much of the New Deal legislation enacted by Congress in the 1930s was modeled after action already taken in the states.[3] For example, several states already had old-age pension systems that were similar to what became Social Security, and they had workers' compensation plans that predated federal plans. We have noted that state reforms in the 1950s and 1960s strengthened the powers of governors and legislators and put states in a position to be active policy makers in the 1970s and 1980s. Historically, state policy activism often has come at times when Congress refused to deal with social problems. Clearly this has been true in several periods since 1980.

When Congress and the president chose to cut federal programs in the 1980s, states responded with a burst of innovation that included creating charter schools, welfare-to-work programs, and expanded environmental protection. Many of those programs were continued in the face of an economic downturn at the turn of the twenty-first century and a lack of support from the Bush administration, which was preoccupied with fighting a war on terrorism.

As their financial position improved in 2006, states passed bills dealing with issues such as immigration, health care, and the minimum wage that were bogged down in Congress.[4] When President Bush vetoed a bill to expand federal financing for embryonic stem cell research in 2006, the governors of California and Illinois responded the next day by allocating additional state grants to pay for stem cell research. Congress rejected an increase in the federal minimum wage in 2006, while six states, bringing the total to twenty-nine states, raised their minimum wage above the federal level. As we will discuss later in this chapter, more than half the states passed immigration laws in 2006, while Congress remained deadlocked on the issue. In Massachusetts, Republican Governor Mitt Romney, with help from Democratic Senator Edward Kennedy, persuaded the state's Democratic legislature to pass a groundbreaking bill, with near unanimity, to provide health insurance to the state's uninsured residents. In 2007 several states, including California, announced plans to work toward implementing a form of universal health care. In 2006 a dozen states brought suit seeking to require the U.S. Environmental Protection Agency to impose limits on various greenhouse gases emitted by new cars.

When Democrats gained control of Congress in the 2006 elections, many observers believed that states might get a better response from the new Congress than had been the case in recent years. That was because many issues, such as support for stem cell research and crackdowns on greenhouse gases that had been supported in the states, were issues Democrats touted in the 2006 campaign. There also was hope that Congress would provide states some relief from mandates and preemptions. In particular, states were looking for changes in federal mandates under the No Child Left Behind Act.

State vitality was evident in the ways in which states and local governments across the country quickly responded to the terrorist attacks of September 11, 2001. Although state-local cooperation worked well, there often was an absence of effective coordination among federal agencies and between federal officials and state and local officials. Despite the creation of the Department of Homeland Security, little improvement has been evident in coordination among governmental agencies fighting terrorism.

State attorneys general, led by New York's Eliot Spitzer, have been especially active in pursuit of consumer protection, and they have secured judgments against major corporations. Before his election in 2006 as governor of New York, Spitzer successfully prosecuted corruption in investment banking, insurance, pharmaceuticals, and energy. In part, he acted because the underfunded and unmotivated federal Securities and Exchange Commission had not responded to growing corruption in those industries. Although Spitzer's prosecutions involved business in New York State, they have had an impact on business procedures around the country. As we will see in Chapter 6, Spitzer's actions were reminiscent of lawsuits brought by state attorneys general against tobacco companies in the 1990s that resulted in the payout of billions of dollars to the states.

Of course, not all state policy is innovative, or even adequate. In Chapter 2 we will discuss the breakdown in federal-state-local cooperation in the aftermath of Hurricane Katrina, four years after the events of 9/11. Despite accurate warnings three or four days before landfall, officials at all levels of government paid too little attention to the predicted hurricane damage. No level of government performed even satisfactorily. Within a day after the hurricane hit the Gulf Coast, the mayor of New Orleans and the governor of Louisiana were criticizing the Federal Emergency Management Agency and President Bush.

Studies done in the 1960s found that larger, wealthier, industrialized states were the most innovative in policy making. Still, states that were innovative in one area were not necessarily innovative in other areas. More recently, political scientists have found that innovation often comes in response to financial crisis. Other factors affecting state innovation include the influence of other states in the region and response to federal financial incentives.

In pioneering research, political scientist Jack L. Walker and others defined innovation as the adoption of laws modeled after those in other states.[5] Other definitions of innovation look at the creation of new programs, and they go beyond the enactment of legislation to consider gubernatorial and administrative actions.

While recognizing that there is a certain amount of follow-the-leader **diffusion of policy innovation**—that is, spreading of new policies from one state to another, often within regions of the country—political scientists have suggested that the pattern of diffusion more often resembles a convoy in which states as a group head in a common direction. Some states may break away from the convoy, but no state wants to fall too far behind those states in front of it. Even among states that adopt a broadly defined type of innovation, specific differences may exist, and some states may never adopt a given policy. For example, thirty-seven states created a wide variety of charter school programs in the 1990s, while thirteen states did not make any serious effort to adopt this innovation (see chapter 10).[6] When convoys become very compact, that is, when many states have nearly identical policy, the pattern is said to resemble a "pack."

Policies diffuse across the American states because states observe what works in neighboring states and because they seek competitive economic advantages over their neighbors. Diffusion tends to be regional whereby states with similar cultural and political characteristics can observe what policies are likely to be effective for them. For example, William Berry and Brady Baybeck found that the adoption of state lotteries has been due more to economic competition than to learning from neighboring states.[7] States fear losing revenue when their residents travel to other states to play lotteries. On the other hand, they found no evidence that people move to neighboring states in order to get higher welfare benefits. Thus welfare innovations are largely a matter of observing and learning from what works in other states.

As we will see in Chapter 6, a host of cities and counties across the country have been busy "reinventing government" by changing their budget processes; moving to prevent problems, such as crime and pollution, instead of treating symptoms; empowering citizens to manage public housing; privatizing public services; and establishing enterprises that make money. For example, some sewerage facilities are transforming sludge into fertilizer and selling it at a profit.

Much more so than federal government policy, what states and localities do directly affects everyday life. These governments not only have the major responsibility for education, crime, AIDS and other health problems, and welfare administration, but they also determine public university tuition, the price of subway fares, where and when we can purchase alcoholic beverages, whether soda bottles are returnable, and how much we pay for electricity. Most of these issues, even those that may appear trivial, generate strong political reactions from groups that have economic or ideological interests in public policy outcomes.

Political activity within the states is another indication of vitality. The activities of political parties and the management of campaigns and elections occur mainly in state and local settings. All elected public officials, except the president, are selected by voters within the states. Political parties have their organizational base in the states, with their power lodged most firmly in county committees and city organizations. Many members of the U.S. Congress initially held state or local office. Once elected, many senators and representatives devote much of their time (and the time of their staff members) to "casework"—that is, representing the interests of their local constituents in dealing with federal agencies. In election campaigns they often focus their attention on local issues. In electing a multitude of state and local officials (plus participating in federal elections) and in deciding special ballot issues, such as higher tax rates for schools, voters experience a nearly continuous process of campaigns and elections. By holding the first presidential primary, New Hampshire exerts a disproportionate influence on national politics. In the 2000 presidential election, Republican governors played a major role in the nomination of fellow-governor George W. Bush.

Vitality also can be seen in the actions of people of all ages taking advantage of the wide variety of opportunities for participation in local government. Obviously, it is easier for individuals and groups to get a government to do something at the city or county level than at the state and national levels. Neighborhood associations are flourishing in many cities across the country, and there are uncounted opportunities for individuals to do volunteer work for schools and nearly all public service agencies. Residents attend a wide variety of public hearings, and even in fairly large cities they often address the city council during its regularly scheduled meetings. Cities often advertise for residents to serve on city boards, commissions, and committees, such as budget, planning, and human rights.

PUBLIC POLICY IN THE STATES

Economic Factors

Public policy making is affected by a variety of factors operating outside the formal structure of state and local governments. A state's economic characteristics—including levels of urbanization, personal income, and education—influence political decision making as well as the nature of political participation and party competition.[8]

One example of the effects of economic factors on policy making is funding for education. Wealthy, urbanized states, such as Michigan, New Jersey, and New York, spend considerably more per capita on K–12 education than do less prosperous, rural, southern states. Although wealthy states can obviously afford to spend more money per capita on social services than can poor states, their willingness to spend should be differentiated from their ability to spend. In education, some relatively poor states, such as New Mexico and Vermont, make a stronger effort to assist their schools than do some rich states (i.e., their educational spending as a proportion of personal income is greater than that of wealthier states). Still, those poor states with relatively high tax rates are unable to match the per-pupil expenditures of wealthier states where the tax effort (or burden) is less. The term **tax burden** refers to taxes as a percentage of personal income; it expresses a relation between total taxes and total income in a state. The tax burden is lower than the national average in New Jersey because personal income is high and tax rates are relatively low.

The willingness to spend money on social services often is tied to such political factors as the role of political parties, the influence of public opinion, and the leadership of the governor. These political factors help to explain why differences in spending levels exist among rich states and why some poor states make substantially greater efforts than other poor states. As we will see later in this chapter, willingness to spend money also is related to political culture and state tradition.

As far as political participation is concerned, party competition usually is stronger in the wealthy, urbanized states, and voter turnout tends to be higher in those states as well. A few interest groups are more likely to dominate government in poor states, such as South Carolina and West Virginia, whereas in wealthy states a variety of interest groups tend to balance one another. The economically well-developed states also have been the most likely to adopt new policy ideas. Although there are many exceptions to economic explanations (see the sections that follow), they do provide us with one of several useful approaches to understanding state politics.

Physical Setting

In a country as diverse as the United States, the physical environment affects the decisions of the state governments in many ways. Geographically large states have huge rural legislative and congressional districts that make political campaigning and representation much different from those of the small districts of New Hampshire. Large states, such as Wyoming and Montana, often spend significantly more per capita to maintain their highways than do smaller states, such as Maryland and Massachusetts. In addition, the presence of natural resources may affect state policies significantly. Oil and natural gas interests have had a major impact on government in Oklahoma and Texas. Alaska and Wyoming have no income tax and rely heavily on revenue from severance taxes, which are placed on the extraction of natural resources such as oil and coal (see Chapter 9). For many years, fluctuations in the price of oil and other resources have created boom-and-bust economies in several western states. For example, in recent years the economy of Wyoming has boomed as the state benefits from high energy costs. For most of the twentieth century the Anaconda Company (copper) was the dominant political force in Montana. When it was unable to comply with new environmental standards in the 1970s, Anaconda ended all mining operations in Montana.[9]

The distribution of water rights has had a tremendous influence on politics in such western states as Arizona and California. Water shortage is a permanent circumstance in Los Angeles, where the annual rainfall is a scant nine inches. Farms and cities from Salt Lake City to San Diego are literally drinking the Colorado River dry. In many western states nearly 90 percent of water is used by agricultural interests. This can create strong conflict when, as in Arizona, growing urban populations outnumber traditionally powerful rural interests. The existence of such geographical features as mountains, deserts, and lakes within a state may cause special problems and influence the allocation of state resources. Historically, physical features influenced the flow of migration and helped shape political institutions. For example, Utah is one of the most geographically isolated states, and Mormons chose to settle there largely for that reason.

Alaska is as large as the combined area of the twenty-two smallest states. Large, sparsely populated states such as Alaska, Montana, Wyoming, and the Dakotas have state legislative districts that are much larger than congressional districts in most states. While their representatives must travel great distances to see their constituents, state legislators in New England states practice a kind of neighborhood, personal style of politics.

Consider some of the physical features of California—features that subject its political decision makers to contrasting pressures from interest groups as well as force them to acquire knowledge about a wide array of technical matters. The state stretches for 650 miles, from the Mexican border to the Oregon state line. The Sierra Nevada Mountains extend for about 400 miles along the eastern border of the state. Temperatures range from harsh cold and deep snow in the High Sierras to unbearable heat in Death Valley. Northern California has ample water, but southern California must import its water. The same state that has produced the Los Angeles freeway system also has the agriculturally rich Central Valley where 90 percent of all fresh vegetables consumed in the U.S. are grown.

California is so physically and culturally diverse that since it achieved statehood in 1850, propositions repeatedly have been made in its state legislature to split up the state. The most recent, in 1992, called for three states: a predominantly rural Northern California, Central California with San Francisco and Sacramento, and Southern California with Los Angeles and San Diego.[10] Rural, northern Californians argue that unfunded state mandates and unfair legislative districting have helped push their counties toward bankruptcy. They also contend that their political power has been weakened by legislative redistricting that strengthened urban areas. The 1992 proposal by Assemblyman Stan Statham of Shasta County passed in the Assembly, but died in the Senate Rules Committee.

At California's first legislative session in 1852, a group of northern legislators proposed the creation of a separate state, combining several California counties with the southern part of the Oregon territory. Since the 1930s, this area has been referred to as the "State of Jefferson." In both states, residents of rural counties contend they often are forgotten by remote legislators in their state capitals.

Another secessionist movement in California has involved residents of the San Fernando Valley who want to split from the city of Los Angeles. Separated from the rest of the city by the Santa Monica Mountains, the Valley has nearly 1.8 million people and about half the land area of Los Angeles. Its residents contend that they have been shortchanged on a variety of city services and that with Los Angeles sprawling over 467 square miles the city is just too big for a single government to be effective. After years of complaining, secessionists succeeded in getting the issue on the 2002 ballot, and at the same time there was a separate vote for Hollywood to secede from Los Angeles. Under California law, a vote to secede must be approved by a majority of the area that wants to secede *and* by a majority of the entire city.[11] The San Fernando Valley vote failed when 66 percent of the total city voters said no (among Valley residents the secessionist vote was split nearly 50-50). Sixty-eight percent of the residents of Hollywood voted against secession. Before the election, the city built new parks and roads in the Valley and pushed a program to give more policy making power to neighborhood councils. Following the vote, the *Los Angeles Times* suggested in its lead editorial that Valley residents "claim victory and come home" to Los Angeles.

In 2005, one of eight Americans lived in California, whose population is over 36 million. About 40 percent are racial/ethnic minorities. In addition, there are an estimated 2.5 million illegal immigrants living in California. Census Bureau estimates are that California will have 46 million people in 2030, an increase of 13 million (the size of Illinois) since 2000. Politicians and scholars are asking if California has become so large and complex that it is unmanageable. We have noted periodic calls to divide the state. As we will see in the next section, much of California's population is fueled by immigration, which places heavy demands on health, education, and welfare services.

Under the U.S. Constitution, a state can be divided if its legislature and Congress agree. Historically, Vermont, Maine, Massachusetts, and Kentucky were carved out of existing states. Because Texas was an independent nation when it was annexed to the United States, it was given the right to divide itself into as many as five states.

Population size and the presence of large metropolitan areas also have important effects on state politics. In the mid-1970s, the financial problems of New York City threatened the fiscal stability of New York State and involved the governor in extended negotiations with private bankers and the federal government to help "save" New York City. In the early 1990s the state's budget deficit led to cuts for projects in New York City. City dwellers demand more services—health care, welfare, sanitation, recreation, slum clearance, public housing—than do residents of small towns. These demands are transmitted to state legislative and gubernatorial candidates, who cannot ignore city voters as they campaign for office. In New York, Illinois, Pennsylvania, and Michigan, to name a few, serious conflicts between major cities and the rest of the state have long existed within state government. In Illinois nearly two-thirds of the state's population lives in the Chicago metropolitan area.

The Impact of Immigration on the States

In 2003 Hispanics officially became the largest minority group, 14 percent, in the United States. The Hispanic population has more than doubled since 1980, accounting for 40 percent of the entire country's population growth. By 2010, Hispanics are estimated to comprise about one-third of the United States population. Of course, they are not evenly distributed across the country. Ten states, led by California, Texas, New York, and Florida, contain nearly 80 percent of the Hispanic population. New Mexico has the highest percentage of Hispanics, about 44 percent. Whites who are not Hispanic make up less than half the population in Hawaii, New Mexico, California, and Texas.

But there is increasing dispersion of Hispanics beyond border states and larger cities in the North. The Census Bureau reported in 2006 that minority groups, led by Hispanics, make up an increasing percentage of the population in every state except West Virginia. For example, Colorado had a 73 percent increase in its Hispanic population in the 1990s. The Pew Hispanic Center estimates that the illegal immigrant population of South Carolina increased 1,000 percent from 1990 to 2004. As a result of the geographic diffusion of Hispanics, more states and cities are affected by the costs associated with immigrant populations, especially for education and health care, as well as by the political impact of new voters.

Although the federal government makes and enforces immigration policy, it is state and city governments that must respond to most of the social, economic, and cultural problems associated with the nation's estimated 12 million **illegal immigrants.** They include those who entered the country legally as temporary visitors, but never left; those who were refused permission for legal entry; and those who never applied for permission because of various factors. The number of illegal, or undocumented, immigrants is up about 250 percent since 1990, with an estimated 850,000 arriving each year since 2000. They make up about 30 percent of the total foreign-born population of the United States. Nearly 60 percent of all undocumented immigrants come from Mexico, and another 23 percent come from other Latin American countries. About 13 percent are Asian. Curiously, recent successful efforts to reduce illegal entry have not reduced the illegal population because undocumented persons already here are staying due to the difficulty of moving back and forth across the border.

What to do about the large number of undocumented immigrants has sparked a national debate, dividing political parties in Congress, academics, and the American public. After failing to resolve House-Senate differences in separate immigration bills in 2006, immigration legislation collapsed again in 2007. The 2007 bill would have created the most significant change in immigration law in over twenty years, but a fragile bipartisan coalition fell apart despite personal appeals by President Bush. The bill would have created a complicated way for many in the country illegally to gain citizenship. This was a key goal for Democrats, but it was opposed by many Republicans, and some Democrats, as "amnesty." The bill's provisions to shift the emphasis on the entry of future immigrants from family ties to applicants' skills and education levels was supported by Republicans, but opposed by Democrats who feared the breakup of families. Only twelve of forty-nine Republican senators voted for the bill.

In 2006 Congress approved building 700 miles of metal fence on the U.S.-Mexican border, but a year later funding had not been provided. At the time the bill was passed, there was about 75 miles of metal fence on the 1,951-mile border.

The inability of Congress to pass immigration legislation has left states to foot the bill for a host of services used by immigrants. In response to rising costs and voter displeasure, hundreds of immigration bills were introduced in states across the country in 2006 and 2007. While the majority of laws and initiatives have provisions to deny noncitizens state-funded services, some states have acted to guarantee access to services regardless of citizenship. New Mexico prints all state documents in English and Spanish, but since 1980 over half the states have approved English-only laws. More than half the states have considered prohibiting undocumented immigrants from obtaining driver's licenses.[12] On the other hand, Nebraska, which faces a population drain and a need for meatpacking workers, passed legislation in 2006 to allow illegal immigrants in-state tuition at state universities. In some states, businesses have been pressured not to employ illegal immigrants, while in other states day-labor centers have been built for immigrant workers.[13] In 2007 Arizona passed an illegal worker law calling for suspension and then permanent revocation of business licenses for repeat-offender employers who hire undocumented workers. While 74 percent of Arizonans approved an English-as-the-official-language initiative in 2006, two incumbent Republican members of Congress who were hard-liners on immigration were defeated. In 2007 Georgia approved the nation's most stringent law requiring government agencies to verify the legal residency of recipients of state social service benefits.

Many of the recent bills passed relating to illegal immigrants are likely to be challenged in court because it is unlikely the federal government will stand by while states enact their own competing laws. A 1996 bill forbids states from enacting stricter criminal or civil penalties for illegal immigration than those passed by Congress. Still, states continue to enact tough immigration laws.

Political Culture

Although explanations based on economics and physical characteristics are helpful in understanding state politics, there remain a significant number of exceptions to the rule. Economic conditions do not explain the high levels of voter turnout in Montana, Idaho, Wyoming, and Utah, where levels of income and urbanization are below the national average. Some states with low levels of personal income, such as West Virginia and Kentucky, provide surprisingly high welfare benefits. In contrast, while Nevada ranked fifteenth in personal income per capita in 2004, it ranked fiftieth in welfare spending as a percentage of income and forty-third in education spending as a percentage of income. In this section, we note some of the vast differences that exist even among states within the same geographical area.

Sometimes states that have similar economic and demographic characteristics are very different politically. A case in point is the adjacent states of Michigan and Ohio. They are alike in terms of population, industrialization, and urbanization. Both have many small towns and rich farmland. In both states, there is significant party competition. In both, organized labor is a strong political force. Yet Michigan has been a much more progressive state than Ohio. It has allocated proportionately greater expenditures for social welfare services, and it has experienced significantly less corruption in government. In Ohio, on the other hand, the **spoils system,** in which political parties give public jobs to their supporters, has been more prevalent than in Michigan.

Another example is the neighboring states of Vermont and New Hampshire. Both are small and predominantly rural. Yet Vermont, the poorer of the two states, ranks among the highest in terms of tax burden, whereas New Hampshire ranks among the lowest. Vermont has been a center of public-spirited activism, but New Hampshire is characterized as a stronghold of stingy government. The former Socialist mayor of Burlington, Bernie Sanders, has been Vermont's Independent U.S. Representative since

1991. Much of the reason for these differences appears to lie in the political cultures of the two states.

Political culture is defined by Daniel Elazar as "the particular pattern of orientation to political action in which each political system is embedded." Elazar notes that "the study of political culture is related to the study of culture as a whole."[14] Culture refers to a "way of life": It is learned behavior based on communication within a society. Political culture, says Elazar, sets limits on political behavior and provides subtle direction for political action. In the following analysis, political culture is understood to encompass political tradition and the rules governing political behavior. For students of state government, political culture helps explain differences in political attitudes and government concerns from state to state. In large part, political culture determines what policies can be expected from state government, the kinds of people who become active in political affairs, and the way in which the political game is played in particular states and their communities.

Each state has its own history and traditions that are reflected in differences in its population's concerns and attitudes toward political life. In many states, differences among nationalities are important to understanding politics. For example, Irish Catholics in Massachusetts and Jews in New York have played major roles in forming distinctive patterns of political participation in those states. The Civil War and Reconstruction left a lasting mark on the political systems of southern and border states. The **Progressive movement** early in this century had a major impact on the political processes in Wisconsin, Minnesota, and the Dakotas. In particular, Progressivism created an intense distrust of party organizations, and it encouraged reliance on widespread citizen participation. Alaska and Hawaii have truly unique histories and cultures because of their geographic isolation and their mixtures of racial and ethnic groups. Residents of some states have a strong sense of identity with their state, but it has been suggested that the dominant fact of political life in New Jersey is that residents do not and never did identify with their state.[15]

Elazar identifies three political cultures that can be found throughout the United States—**individualistic, traditionalistic, and moralistic.**[16] These cultures have their roots in the three geographic regions of colonial America. The individualistic culture developed in the business centers of New York, Philadelphia, and Baltimore; the traditionalistic culture developed in the plantation society of the Old South; and the moralistic culture arose out of the tradition of Puritanism and town meetings in New England. As waves of settlers moved westward, these three cultures spread throughout the United States. In many instances, two or three cultures met, meshed together, and produced a variety of state and sectional cultural strains. In Illinois, Indiana, and Ohio, this mixing of political cultures produced complex politics and caused conflicts that have persisted over decades.

Political scientist Daniel Elazar uses the concept of cultural "geology" to illustrate how the three political subcultures (moralistic, traditionalistic, and individualistic) spread across the United States and subsequently were modified by local conditions.[17] In Elazar's descriptive words, as great streams of immigrants moved west and stopped in various places, they deposited their relatively clear-cut political cultures. In many cases, other populations stopped in the same locations and deposited their cultures. Sometimes these "deposits" were side by side; in other cases they were on top of each other; and in some cases they overlapped. Over time, external events, such as economic depressions, eroded these cultural traditions, or they may have modified or strengthened them. At any rate, the result was something like strata in exposed rock that's been blasted out for an interstate highway—a look into the past and present.

Politics in the three political cultures can be described with respect to (1) degree of political participation, (2) development of government bureaucracy, and (3) amount of government intervention in society. Of the three dimensions, degree of political participation (i.e., voter turnout and suffrage regulations) is the most consistent indicator of political culture. In individualistic political cultures, participation is limited because politics is viewed as just another means by which individuals may improve their economic and social position. Because corruption is accepted as a natural part of politics, its disclosure is unlikely to produce public protest. In moralistic cultures, political participation is regarded as the duty of each citizen in a political setting where government seeks to promote the public welfare of all persons. In traditionalistic cultures, voter turnout is low and voting regulations are restrictive. Here government is controlled by an elite whose family and social position give it a "right" to govern. In many cases, citizens are not even expected to vote. Corruption tends to be even more widespread in traditional than in individualistic states because politics is not oriented toward the **public interest,** that is, for the good of the whole community; rather, it is expected that public payoffs will be made to support private interests.

In regard to the development of government bureaucracy, individualistic cultures limit government functions and provide only those few basic services demanded by the public. Bureaucracy is distrusted because of its potential to encroach on private matters, but it often is used to advance the personal goals of public officials, and in the past the spoils system provided government jobs to political supporters. In moralistic cultures, bureaucracy typically is permitted to expand to provide the public with the wide range of services it demands. Here government commitment to the public good, honesty, and selflessness leads to low levels of corruption. Traditionalistic cultures tend to be anti-bureaucratic, because a professional bureaucracy would interfere with the established pattern of personal relations developed by politicians.

In regard to government intervention into community affairs, both individualistic and traditional political cultures strive to protect private activities by limiting government intrusions. Government action in the individualistic political culture is largely limited to encouraging private economic initiative. In traditionalistic cultures, government's role is limited to maintaining the existing social order. The moralistic culture, in contrast, fosters a definite commitment to government intervention; government is viewed as a positive force.

Those who represent the moralistic political culture may oppose federal aid to some local projects because they favor community responsibility for local problem solving. **Communitarianism** (communal activism) often results in innovative new approaches to problems that may not be perceived by the general population. Communitarians are both liberal *and* conservative. Although they favor liberal programs, such as public housing, that support equality, they also favor conservative programs, such as mandatory testing for AIDS, that seek to impose social order in communities.

The moralistic political culture also differs from the other two cultures in that its political campaigns are marked by an emphasis on issues rather than personalities. Parties and interest groups are organized to direct policy in the public interest.

Each culture has made both positive and negative contributions. Elazar notes that the moralistic culture, although it has been a significant force in the American quest for the good society, tends toward fanaticism and narrow-mindedness—roughly parallel to groups that claim to have found the "true religion." In spite of widespread corruption, the individualistic culture of the Northeast and many large midwestern cities did facilitate the assimilation of immigrant groups into American society. Moreover, some corruption occurs in all states, and it does not necessarily affect the delivery of public services. Although the predominant traditional culture in the South has helped sustain racial discrimination and second-rate demagogues, it also has produced a significant number of first-rate national leaders and effective governors.

As we would expect, southern states with traditional political cultures rank at the bottom of states in terms of policy liberalism. An index of **policy liberalism** created by political scientist Virginia Gray that examined five indicators of liberalism: strong gun-control laws, pro-choice abortion laws, generous welfare benefits, tax progressivity, and support of unionization. Gray's data showed southern states and some Rocky Mountain and Plains states clustered at the bottom.[18] Still, most states are not consistently liberal or conservative across the range of issues. For example, Louisiana, which ranks forty-eighth on abortion laws, favoring strict limitations, also ranks tenth in terms of eligibility for major welfare programs. In general, women have more economic and political opportunities in individualistic and moralistic states, where there is more support for everyone getting involved in the political process, than in traditionalistic states.

Elazar's theory has been subjected to vigorous investigation from critics who charge that it is static and impressionistic. But most of his conclusions linking policy to political culture have been confirmed. Political scientist Joel Lieske has refined Elazar's three categories, using race, ethnicity, and religion to identify a number of subcultures within a single state.[19] Other researchers have found greater policy innovation in moralistic states than in states with individualistic or traditionalistic political cultures. When people move, those raised as moralists tend to remain moralistic, whereas those raised as traditionalists or individualists are more likely to adapt to their new cultures.[20]

One significant departure from Elazar's work is a study by political scientists Rodney E. Hero and Caroline J. Tolbert that argues that much of state politics and policy is a product of racial/ethnic diversity.[21] They suggest that Elazar's categories may be largely a function of diversity. For example, moralistic states are the least ethnically diverse and individualistic states are the most ethnically diverse. Hero and Tolbert found a number of strong relationships between diversity and policy. For example, as state minority diversity increases, African Americans have higher school graduation rates and state Medicaid expenditures are lower.

As we have noted, political culture has been found to have a strong impact on political participation: It is higher in moralistic states. Moralistic states also are more likely to support social programs that are generous to the poor, and public officials in those states are less corrupt than in traditionalistic and individualistic states. Although there is independent evidence linking political culture with policy making and citizen participation, other factors that we explain in this chapter—economic factors, physical setting, sectionalism, and immigration—also affect state politics. Often it is difficult to isolate the impact of any one factor. Because economic factors are easier to quantify (that is, we have lots of economic data to examine), political culture often is used to explain state political behavior when social or economic factors are inadequate.

There is some evidence to suggest that distinctive state and local cultures are weakening because of population mobility, especially in the **Sunbelt** states—the fifteen states extending from southern California through Arizona, Texas, Florida, and up the Atlantic coast to Virginia. The change has arisen because of the growing importance of the news media, especially television, nationwide and because federal grants have encouraged states to enact a variety of programs under which they can receive matching funds.

Although population mobility dilutes political cultures, many states continue to have a dominant culture. This is helped by the fact that nearly 60 percent of Americans live in the state where they were born. Many states have long contained mixtures of political cultures, depending on patterns of early population settlement. In his research, Elazar did not find a single dominant political culture in many states because states with dominant moralistic and traditionalistic cultures often had strong individualistic strains.

Sectionalism

Adjacent states tend to share some persistent political similarities. States within particular areas, sharing a common cultural, economic, and historical background, exhibit clearly identifiable political tendencies. This is known as **sectionalism.** Major sections as defined by the U.S. Bureau of the Census are the Northeast, the North Central states, the South, and the West. Within each section we can identify several regions, such as the Southwest (West) and the Middle Atlantic (Northeast). The component states of the various sections and regions define problems and formulate public policy in a similar manner.

The *South,* which includes the eleven former Confederate states plus the border states of West Virginia, Kentucky, Delaware, Oklahoma, and Maryland, has long been the most clearly identifiable section of America. Throughout most of the South, there is widespread poverty, levels of educational attainment are generally low, and government functions are centralized at the state level. In the South, state governments often perform many of the government functions typically carried out by cities and counties in other sections of the country. As in other sections, it often is difficult to tell whether policy is influenced more by geographic location or by economic factors. Moreover, as in other sections, major exceptions to the general rule can be identified. For example, West Virginia has had a high level of interparty competition; considerable wealth exists in parts of Texas, Virginia, and Florida; and politics in Atlanta is vastly different from politics in Yazoo County, Mississippi. Florida's large Cuban population and its high percentage of northern-born whites make it different from other southern states.

From the Civil War until after World War II, the South remained solidly Democratic. Southern states began to vote for Republican presidential candidates in the 1950s and steadily elected more Republican governors, state legislators, and U.S. Congress members during the next three decades. In 1994 Republicans first won a majority of U.S. House and Senate seats in the South. Republicans also have made unprecedented gains in southern state legislatures since 1994. Except for Democratic gains in 1998, Republicans continued to gain strength in the South through the 2004 elections. In 2002 a political shift in power was evident as Georgia elected a Republican governor for the first time since Reconstruction. In 1965 there was only one Republican governor (in

Oklahoma) in the sixteen census-defined southern states; following elections in 2005 there were nine Republican governors. In 2003 Republicans gained control of both houses of the Texas legislature and the governor's office for the first time since 1870. In 2006 Democrats added one southern governor, in Arkansas. In the eight southern states with gubernatorial elections, Republicans won five. As a result, there were nine Republican and seven Democratic governors in the South.

Although the South has undergone dramatic political and social change, "the Southern way of life" continues to bind southerners, black and white, together. Despite great urban growth, traditional courthouse politics in small-town county seats continues to characterize the South more than any other section of the country.[22]

In the *Northeast* (the six New England states plus the Middle Atlantic states of New York, Pennsylvania, and New Jersey), most states share problems of congestion and industrialization. Levels of party competition and voter turnout are comparatively high. There is an emphasis on local government decision making stemming from the New England tradition of town meetings. As a result, government functions are much less centralized than in the South. On a regional basis, Boston continues to be the economic and educational hub of New England, and New York City dominates the Middle Atlantic states in terms of culture and business. In many northeastern states a substantial number of children attend parochial schools. Yet major differences exist between the northern northeastern states, which have been predominantly rural and Protestant (Maine, New Hampshire, and Vermont), and the southern northeastern states, which have been predominantly urban and Catholic (Rhode Island, New York, Connecticut, Massachusetts, Pennsylvania, and New Jersey). There is a great contrast between the wealth of suburban Connecticut and the poverty of rural Maine and Vermont. Without military installations or large public works projects, northeastern states lack a highly visible federal presence.

The eleven states of the *West* (including the Mountain and Pacific states, but excluding Alaska and Hawaii), which comprise nearly 60 percent of the land mass of the continental United States, share problems of natural resource development, population diffusion, and water distribution. Most western states have relied heavily on resource extraction with little economic diversity. This has produced a history of boom-and-bust economic cycles. Despite their political conservatism and dislike of the federal government, the western states have depended heavily on federal aid, and government is the major employer in several of these states.[23] In fact, no other section of the country is more dependent on federal aid, which provides water, rangeland, and fire control assistance that keeps much of the West from becoming a desert. In each of the eleven western states, the federal government owns at least 29 percent of the land. The federal government owns 79 percent of the land in Nevada and 45 percent in California. As noted, there can be great geographic diversity in just one state, such as California, and there are vast cultural differences between residents of San Francisco and those of Salt Lake City. Geographically, California is about the same size as Japan and its population is comparable to that of Argentina. As with other sections of the country, we need to be careful about stereotyping the West. Although there have been great population increases in metropolitan areas, such as Los Angeles, Las Vegas, Phoenix, and Seattle, other parts of the West have experienced population decline since the 1970s. For example, Wyoming lost 3.4 percent of its population in the 1980s and became the nation's least populous state, and in the 1990s its population increased by less than the national average.

Typically, the western states are marked by high levels of voter turnout and relatively weak party organizations. Although Democratic–Republican competition is keen in state elections, these states have been strongly Republican in presidential elections. In the 1968 and 1972 presidential elections, Richard Nixon carried every western state (except Washington in 1968). In 1976, Gerald Ford lost only Texas and Hawaii among all states west of Minnesota. In 1980 and 1984, Ronald Reagan carried all the western states. And in 1988, George Bush carried all the western states except Washington and Oregon. Bill Clinton broke the trend by carrying a majority of the eleven Mountain and Pacific states in 1996, but in 2000 George W. Bush won seven of those eleven states, and he carried the same states, plus New Hampshire and New Mexico, in 2006.

The *North Central* (Great Lakes and Great Plains) states each have a blend of agricultural, industrial, and urban areas. There is strong two-party competition and above-average wealth, particularly in the Great Lakes states. However, the twelve North Central states are the least homogeneous of the four sections. Because the North Central section borders on each of the other three sections, some of its regional areas share the characteristics found in other sections. As with the other sections, there are major internal contradictions. Politics in Indiana, Ohio, and Missouri often has centered on patronage, jobs, and personalities (a reflection of their Southern heritage), but in Minnesota, Wisconsin, and Michigan it has been issue-oriented and government has been essentially corruption-free.[24]

The Great Plains region includes parts of ten West and North Central states, extending south from Montana and North Dakota to New Mexico and Texas. It is where rainfall begins to lessen and the tall grasses of the prairies become shorter. This area, with very hot summers and cold winters, has been called the Empty Quarter. The population of North Dakota peaked in 1930 and by 2005 it had declined by nearly 50,000. Of the twenty-five counties in the United States with the greatest population loss in the 1990s, twenty-two were in North Dakota, where forty-seven of the state's fifty-seven counties lost population. The northwestern part of the state seems on the verge of emptying out. Some towns have responded by giving away free land, but few people want to move to this cold, isolated part of the country.[25]

The Great Plains comprises about 20 percent of the territory of the lower forty-eight states, with a population of about 6.5 million people. Nearly 40 percent of the counties in this region have been losing population continuously since 1950. In 1990 Kansas had more "frontier land"—counties with less than six people per square mile—than it had in 1890. Ninety percent of Nebraska and South Dakota was frontier in 1890 and remained that way in 2000.

Although the Great Plains are emptying and many counties are becoming nearly all white (all but three of the 767 residents of Slope County, North Dakota, were white in 2000), there are more American Indians and bison in the Plains than at any time since the 1870s.[26] In the 1990s the Indian populations in North Dakota, South Dakota, and Nebraska grew by 12 to 23 percent. Even as Indians return, they still comprise less than 10 percent of the population in South Dakota and Oklahoma, the states with the highest percentages of Indians.

POPULATION SHIFTS

Americans are a highly mobile people, moving among regions of the country and becoming increasingly urban and suburban. But not until 1920 did more than half the population live in **urban areas,** that is, in places with more than 2,500 people. As recently as 1950, the nation was 40 percent rural. Barely half, 56 percent, of the population lived in metropolitan areas in 1950.

Although census definitions and terms have changed over the years, **metropolitan statistical areas** (MSAs) have a central city, or contiguous cities, of 50,000 or more people and include the county containing the central city plus adjacent cities that are metropolitan in character and are economically and socially integrated with the central county. In 2005 there were 361 MSAs, containing about 80 percent of the United States population. Nearly 90 percent of the nation's growth since 1990 has been in MSAs.

Combined statistical areas (CSAs) are composed of adjacent metropolitan areas and micropolitan statistical areas, in various combinations. They have a high degree of employment interchange plus common labor and media markets. At the end of 2005, there were 125 CSAs. The New York CSA, for example, had about 3 million more people than the New York MSA and was composed of people in New York State, New Jersey, Connecticut, and Pennsylvania. **Micropolitan statistical areas,** created in 2003, are based around core cities of 10,000 to 49,999 and include surrounding populations that share demographic characteristics. In 2005 there were nearly 600 micropolitan areas, some as large as 200,000 people.

The density, heterogeneity, and interdependence of urban life have created obvious political problems in the areas of health, housing, and crime. The spread of the suburbs (in extreme cases creating vast, sprawling developments—as along the East Coast, southern California, and southern Lake Michigan)—has fragmented government and made metropolitan planning and coordination extremely difficult. There are fifty MSAs that have more than 1 million population and two with populations that exceed 10 million (Table 1-1). The increasing metropolitanization of the U.S. population masks the fact that Americans in the twentieth century became less likely to live in large cities. For example, the percentage of our population living in cities over 1 million peaked in 1930. Currently a smaller percentage of people live in cities over 1 million than was the case in 1900.

While Las Vegas struggles to build new schools and keep up with its fast-growing population, several states, led by Pennsylvania, West Virginia, Iowa, and North Dakota, are dealing with how to provide nursing homes and other services to their aging populations. In Utah and New Mexico there is demand to build new schools and, at the same time, provide services for the growing numbers of retirees who are moving there. Surprisingly, federalism expert John Kincaid points out that dealing with aging populations is "the states' most formidable challenge." As the country's population is getting older, states can expect less financial help from the federal government, and many of those senior citizens who are on fixed incomes strongly resist tax increases.

Particularly during the 1950s and 1960s, great numbers of lower-income southern blacks and Appalachian whites moved into northern cities such as Chicago, Detroit, and New York, greatly compounding the financial problems of those city governments.

TABLE 1-1 The 25 Largest Metropolitan Areas, 2000–2004

Rank	Metropolitan Area	Population in 2004 (in thousands)	Population in 2000 (in thousands)	Percent change 2000–2004
1.	New York-Northern N.J.-Long Island, N.Y.-N.J.-Pa.	18,710	18,323	2.1
2.	Los Angeles-Long Beach- Santa Ana	12,925	12,333	4.5
3.	Chicago-Naperville-Joliet, Ill.-Ind.-Wisc.	9,392	9,098	3.2
4.	Philadelphia-Camden- Wilmington, Pa.- N.J.-Del.-Md.	5,801	5,687	2.0
5.	Dallas-Fort Worth-Arlington	5,700	5,162	10.4
6.	Miami-Fort Lauderdale- Miami Beach	5,362	5,008	7.1
7.	Houston-Sugarland- Baytown	5,180	4,715	9.9
8.	Washington-Arlington- Alexandria, D.C.-Va.-Md.-W.Va.	5,140	4,122	7.2
9.	Atlanta-Shady Springs-Marietta	4,708	4,248	10.8
10.	Detroit-Warren-Livonia	4,493	4,453	0.9
11.	Boston-Cambridge- Quincy, Mass.-N.H.	4,425	4,391	0.7
12.	San Francisco- Oakland-Fremont	4,154	4,124	0.7
13.	Riverside-San Bernardino-Ontario	3,793	3,255	16.5
14.	Phoenix-Mesa-Scottsdale	3,715	3,252	14.3
15.	Seattle-Tacoma-Bellevue	3,167	3,044	4.0
16.	Minneapolis-St.Paul- Bloomington	3,116	2,969	5.0
17.	San Diego-Carlsbad- San Marcos	2,932	2,814	4.2
18.	St. Louis	2,764	2,699	2.4
19.	Baltimore-Towson	2,639	2,553	3.4
20.	Tampa-St. Petersburg-Clearwater	2,588	2,396	8.0

21.	Pittsburgh	2,402	2,431	−1.2
22.	Denver-Aurora	2,330	2,179	6.9
23.	Cleveland-Elyria-Mentor	2,137	2,148	−0.5
24.	Portland-Vancouver- Beaverton, Ore.-Wash.	2,064	1,928	7.1
25.	Cincinnati-Middleton, Ohio-Ky.-Ind.	2,058	2,010	2.4

Source: U.S. Bureau of the Census, 2006.

Since the 1980s there has been a large increase in the number of Asians and Hispanics in many American cities. About two-thirds of immigrants to the United States from 1980 to 2000 settled in ten metropolitan areas. The population of New York City increased by 685,000 in the 1990s, but without immigrants it would have lost over 350,000 people. In eighteen of the twenty-five largest metropolitan areas, from 2000 to 2004 more people moved out than moved in. These figures did not consider people moving in from other countries. The New York metropolitan area had a net loss of about 210,000 residents each of those years, and the Los Angeles area lost nearly 118,000 annually. Demographers cite the flight of the middle class—white, black, and Hispanic—looking for more affordable housing as the major cause of out-migration. Metropolitan areas that attracted more people, such as Phoenix, Atlanta, and Dallas-Fort Worth, have less-expensive, if not cheap, housing. Job availability also affected mobility.

In the 1990s there was a record black migration to the South. Atlanta led all the metropolitan areas in total black population gains in the 1990s, and there were large black increases in Miami, Houston, and Dallas. The so-called Great Migration of African Americans who left the rural South began early in the twentieth century and ended in the late 1960s. Blacks began returning to the rural South in the 1980s and the rate has increased since 1990. Nearly 95 percent of the nation's rural African American population lives in the South.

In 1976 the Census Bureau reported for the first time that a majority of the U.S. population lived in the South and the West, and by the 2000 census nearly 60 percent of the nation's population lived in southern and western states. Nevada has been the fastest-growing state in every decade since 1970. From 1990 to 2000 it had by far the fastest growth of any state—66 percent. After being the fastest-growing state for nineteen consecutive years, Nevada was replaced at the top by Arizona during the period July 2005 to July 2006. Like Nevada's, much of Arizona's population gain came from people moving there from California. Demographer William Fry noted that across the country much of the population movement was by people moving inward, away from "unaffordable America." Following Hurricane Katrina, Louisiana lost 5 percent of its population, much of it to Texas and Georgia, as New Orleans suffered the loss of about half its population from July 2005 to July 2006. New York, Rhode Island, and Michigan each lost about 1 percent of its population during the same twelve-month period. Across the southern part of the United States, from California to Virginia, only two states in the nation's Sunbelt grew by less than 10 percent in the 1990s (Figure 1-1).

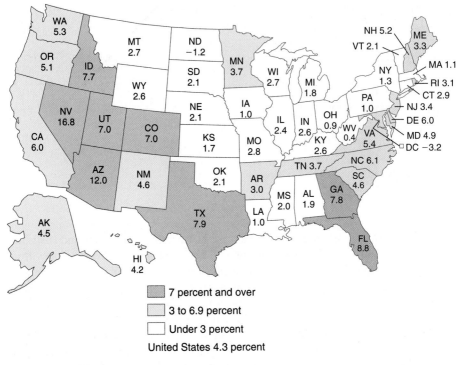

7 percent and over

3 to 6.9 percent

Under 3 percent

United States 4.3 percent

FIGURE 1-1 Percent population change: 2000–2004.

Source: Statistical Abstract of the United States: 2006 (Washington, D.C.: U.S. Government Printing Office, 2006), p. 22.

From 1940 through 2000, the population of Houston grew from 385,000 to 1,954,000; that of Phoenix from 65,000 to 1,321,000; San Diego and San Antonio each have gained more than one million people in the past sixty years. At the same time, Chicago lost nearly 800,000 people and St. Louis saw its population cut in half. In 2000 Detroit became the nation's first city to have lost more than 1 million people. Its population peaked in 1950 with nearly 2 million. Philadelphia has lost over 500,000 people since 1950 and recently had an inventory of 31,000 vacant lots and 26,000 abandoned residential structures.[27] Five of the nation's twenty-five largest cities lost population in the 1990s, and all of them except Washington, D.C., were in the Midwest and Northeast (Table 1-2).

Many of the fastest-growing cities since 1970 have been midsize suburbs, close to interstate highways, located in the Sunbelt. For example, from 1970 to 2000 the population of Coral Springs, Florida, ballooned from 1,000 to 118,000; Gilbert, Arizona, from 2,000 to 110,000. The population of Las Vegas, now the nation's twenty-ninth largest city, increased about 15 percent from 2000 to 2004. Of the fifteen cities that grew by more than 20 percent in those years, five were in California. Gilbert, Arizona, 42.6 percent, was the fastest-growing city and North Las Vegas grew by 37.5 percent. All large cities that grew by more than 10 percent in the 1990s were in the Sunbelt. Still, some Sunbelt cities, such as New Orleans and Jackson, Mississippi, lost population in the last decade. As we

	TABLE 1-2 The 25 Largest Cities, 2000–2004			
Rank	Population in 2004 (in thousands)	Population in 2000 (in thousands)	Percent Change 2000–2004	Rank in 2000
1. New York	8,104	8,008	1.2%	1
2. Los Angeles	3,846	3,695	4.1	2
3. Chicago	2,862	2,896	−1.2	3
4. Houston	2,013	1,954	2.8	4
5. Philadelphia	1,470	1,518	−3.1	5
6. Phoenix	1,418	1,321	7.3	6
7. San Diego	1,269	1,223	3.3	7
8. San Antonio	1,236	1,145	7.4	9
9. Dallas	1,210	1,189	1.8	8
10. San Jose	905	895	1.0	11
11. Detroit	900	951	−5.4	10
12. Indianapolis*	784	782	0.3	12
13. Jacksonville*	778	736	5.7	14
14. San Francisco	744	777	−4.2	13
15. Columbus	730	711	2.5	15
16. Austin	682	657	3.3	16
17. Memphis	672	650	3.4	18
18. Baltimore	636	651	−2.3	17
19. Fort Worth	603	535	11.5	27
20. Charlotte	594	541	6.5	26
21. El Paso	592	564	5.0	23
22. Milwaukee	584	597	−2.2	19
23. Seattle	571	563	1.4	24
24. Boston	569	589	−3.4	20
25. Denver	557	555	0.6	25

Source: U.S. Bureau of the Census, 2006.

*Consolidated city-counties.

will discuss in Chapter 2, the population of New Orleans declined dramatically after Hurricane Katrina hit in 2005.

Population growth has been especially strong in state capitals and in university towns across the country. Sunbelt state capitals with large state universities, such as Austin and Tallahassee, have had especially strong growth. In many cases, state government generates jobs and helps the economy of an entire metropolitan area. In several instances, urban public universities have spurred economic growth and have become community social leaders. For example, the University of Alabama at Birmingham is the largest employer in the state.

In his groundbreaking book, *Power Shift,* Kirkpatrick Sale described the political implications of the major population shift to the South and West.[28] Sale argued that by the early 1970s America's southern rim, or Sunbelt, had come to dominate American politics as population, manufacturing, and capital moved from the North to the South. From 1960 to 2002, New York lost twelve seats in Congress and Florida gained thirteen. In 1960 California had thirty-two electoral votes, the same number as Pennsylvania; in 2002 California had fifty-five electoral votes, Pennsylvania only twenty-one. Congressional re-districting for 2002 resulted in a switch of twelve seats. All the gainers, except Colorado (one seat), were in the Sunbelt, and most of the losers were concentrated in a nearly un-broken line from Massachusetts west to Illinois. Arizona, Georgia, Texas, and Florida each gained two seats.

Population growth in the South and West combined accounted for about 80 percent of United States growth between 2000 and 2025. Texas passed New York to become the nation's second largest state in the mid-1990s, and Florida has replaced New York as the third largest state. New York was the nation's largest state until the mid-1960s. California, Texas, and Florida contain nearly one-fourth the total United States population. Nevada's population gain in the 1990s exceeded the population of each of the six smallest states, and California's gain of about 6 million people in the 1990s was greater than the popula-tion of about half the states.

THE MYTH OF A POLARIZED AMERICA?

Much has been made of a blue-state–red-state divide in the United States. It is alleged that there is a **culture war** in which moral and religious issues have replaced traditional economic issues as the driving force in American politics. **Red states,** those that vote Republican, cover the vast interior of the United States, and **blue states,** those that vote Democratic, are on the Pacific Coast, in the uppper Midwest, and in New England. In 2004 President Bush won the same states as he did in 2000, with the addition of New Mexico and New Hampshire.

As evidence of a divide based on cultural issues, advocates point out that in 2004 anti–gay marriage initiatives passed in all eleven states where they were on the ballot, and they were approved in seven of eight states in 2006. Voters in Arizona became the first in twenty-eight statewide initiatives on the ballot since 1998 to defeat an initiative to prohibit same-sex marriages. Forty-five states have taken legislative action to pro-hibit same-sex marriages. On the other hand, by 2007 eight states, all in the Northeast and on the Pacific coast, had approved either civil unions or domestic partnerships. Only Massachusetts has legalized same-sex marriage. While the state of Kansas called for the teaching of "intelligent design" as an alternative to evolution and South Dakota in 2006 banned all abortions except those necessary to save the life of the mother, several other states have approved financing for stem cell research. In a 2006 vote, 56 percent of South Dakotans rejected the state ban on abortions.

Political scientist Morris P. Fiorina contends that the so-called culture war is a myth. There is, he says, little evidence that Americans' policy positions are more polarized than they were twenty or thirty years ago.[29] What has changed, he believes, is that political leaders have become more polarized, and, as a result, Americans are given electroal choices that force them to vote for candidates who espouse increasingly extreme ideological positions.

To illustrate the lack of polarization, Fiorina gives the example of Montana where, in 2004, voters overwhelmingly approved a gay-marriage prohibition, as well as an initiative to legalize the medical use of marijuana. While Bush got 59 percent of their votes, Montanans also elected a Democratic governor and turned control of the state legislature over to Democrats.[30] Montana's incumbent Republican senator lost in 2006. Voters in Colorado elected a Democratic governor in 2006, and both houses of their state legislature are controlled by Democrats. But Coloradans also approved a constitutional ban on same-sex marriages and rejected an initiative to legalize marijuana in 2006.

In many states, voters see their governors in less ideological terms than they view members of Congress, believing that state issues such as education, crime, and transportation need pragmatic solutions. As a result, successful candidates often are political moderates. Fiorina believes that the reason voters appear to be more partisan and issues are more polarized in congressional and presidential elections is that the parties run ideological candidates and this limits voters' choices. In 2006 nearly half of all voters across the country described themselves as "moderates." Helped by widespread disapproval of the war in Iraq and the Democratic Party's strategy of recruiting moderate candidates in a number of swing districts, Democrats regained control of Congress in 2006. The party also added six governors to give Democrats a 28 to 22 advantage over Republicans.

CONSTITUTIONAL AND LEGAL LIMITS ON STATE ACTION

The U.S. Constitution on the one hand provides certain guarantees to the states and on the other hand imposes certain restrictions on state actions. For example, political integrity is protected by federal constitutional provisions that states cannot be divided or consolidated without state legislative consent. In addition, amendments to the Constitution must be ratified by three-fourths of the states. The Constitution limits state action by denying to the states the power to coin money or pass **ex post facto laws,** which allow a person to be punished for an action that was not a crime when it was committed. Treaties with foreign nations are binding on the states as the law of the land; and the Constitution and all laws made under it are the supreme law of the land.

The American system of federalism (discussed in detail in Chapter 2) distributes power in such a way as to deny the central government authority in only a few areas. However, the central government must rely on the cooperation of state and local governments to achieve most of its objectives. As a result, there is a great deal of sharing in policy making between the states and the federal government. Because the constitutional division of power between the states and the federal government is not precise, a dynamic relationship exists that allowed the federal government to move into many areas traditionally reserved to the states. Federal administrative actions, congressional statutes, and court decisions have imposed national standards that in some instances replace previously controlling local standards. Specifically, federal grants-in-aid (see Chapter 2) have given the national government the means to exercise powers concurrent with the states in many areas of policy making.

Federal court decisions have limited state action from the earliest days of the republic. In *McCulloch v. Maryland* (1819) and *Gibbons v. Ogden* (1824), the Supreme Court supported the supremacy of national law and broadly interpreted congressional power in interstate commerce (these decisions are discussed in Chapter 2). In the 1960s, decisions in the areas of civil rights, school integration, rights of criminal defendants, and voting qualifications expanded federal authority while limiting that of the states. As an instrument of the national government, the Supreme Court, under Chief Justice John Marshall and in most instances from the late 1930s through the 1980s, broadly construed the implied powers of Congress vis-à-vis the states and ignored the **Tenth Amendment,** which says that "powers not given to the federal government, nor denied to the states, are reserved to the states, or to the people." However, as we will see in Chapter 2, the Court rediscovered the Tenth Amendment in the 1990s and consistently ruled against federal intrusion into state affairs.

STATE CONSTITUTIONS

Historical Development

State constitutions prescribe the structure of government, the powers granted various public officials, terms of office and means of election, and the way in which constitutional amendments shall be enacted.[31] Of course, provisions of the U.S. Constitution take precedence over state laws that may conflict with them. Some powers granted to the national government, such as regulation of interstate commerce, are denied to the states. However, other powers are reserved to the states and, as we will see in Chapter 2, many powers are shared by the states and the federal government.

In some cases, state constitutions give their residents more rights than are provided in the U.S. Constitution. As we will see in Chapter 7, several assertive state supreme courts in recent years have interpreted their states' constitutions to add protections that have not been extended in more conservative interpretations of the Constitution by the U.S. Supreme Court. In this way, changes are made to the meaning of constitutions without the use of the formal amendments.

It is difficult to generalize among the fifty state constitutions (Table 1-3). The oldest is that of Massachusetts, adopted in 1780; Georgia, Illinois, Louisiana, Montana, and Virginia have adopted new constitutions since 1970. The 1982 constitution in Georgia replaced a document well known for its excessive length and excessive amendments. The new Georgia constitution eliminated approximately 1,200 local amendments added by voters over the years. Georgia has had ten constitutions and Louisiana has had eleven. The charters of the thirteen original states, which in most cases were extended into their constitutions, were only about five pages long. The U.S. Constitution has about 8,700 words. Among the states, only New Hampshire's is less than 10,000 words (9,200).

Alabama's constitution is more than three times longer than any other state's. Vermont has added fifty-three amendments to its 1793 constitution, and California has added over 500. The typical unamended state constitution is over three times longer than the federal constitution and has an average of 120 amendments.[32] Although nineteen states have their original constitution, most have had three or more.

Most state constitutions were written in the nineteenth century, when government power was distrusted. In the period of Reconstruction that followed the Civil War, strong governors, backed by federal troops, centralized power in the former Confederate states. After the troops left, southern states rewrote their constitutions to give little power to either their governors or their legislators. As a result, states such as Texas continue to have governors with weak formal powers.

Only eighteen state constitutions are twentieth-century documents. The reform movement of the early twentieth century focused on rooting out political corruption and bringing more popular participation through the initiative, recall, referendum, and direct primary.

Framework of Constitutions

In spite of their differences, a general framework of state constitutions can be presented. Most constitutions have a separate section that affirms the doctrine of separation of powers. All state constitutions have a preamble and a bill of rights. Like the United States Constitution, state preambles identify the source of authority (the people) and the purposes the constitution is intended to serve. Although preambles do not have legal authority, they serve as concise statements of basic principles envisioned by the state's founders. Often these sections contain obsolete provisions. For example, according to the Pennsylvania and Tennessee preambles, a state officeholder must believe not only in God but also in a future state of rewards and punishments. And in seven of the bills of rights, the honorable art of dueling is at issue. Many of these provisions, such as a belief in God, have been declared unconstitutional by the Supreme Court and others have been overturned by state law. Because of that, and because most of these provisions have not been enforced for many years, state legislators feel little political pressure to clean up obsolete language.

The newer constitutions, such as Alaska's and Hawaii's, omit any specific reference to the mutual exclusiveness of legislative and executive functions. Legislative articles have been strengthened since the 1960s so that most legislatures are considered to be in continuous session and empowered to meet annually. Executive articles limited the power of governors by creating large numbers of boards and commissions whose members often were independent of the governor. For example, before Michigan wrote a new constitution in 1963, the executive branch consisted of the governor, six major elected officials, twenty-three executive departments, four elected boards, sixty-four appointed boards and commissions, six ex officio boards, and five retirement boards. Judicial articles typically have been marked by detail, multiplicity of courts, and overlapping jurisdictions. Here, too, many amendments have been added to establish new courts, alter the way in which judges are selected, and create a unified state judicial system.

TABLE 1-3 General Information on State Constitutions, as of January 1, 2006

State or Other Jurisdiction	Number of Constitutions*	Dates of Adoption	Effective Date of Present Constitution	Estimated Length (Number of Words)	Number of Amendments Submitted to Voters	Number of Amendments Adopted
Alabama	6	1819, 1861, 1865, 1868, 1875, 1901	Nov. 28, 1901	340,136 (a)(b)(c)	1,063	766
Alaska	1	1956	Jan. 3, 1959	15,988 (b)	41	29
Arizona	1	1911	Feb. 14, 1912	28,876	246	136
Arkansas	5	1836, 1861, 1864, 1868, 1874	Oct. 30, 1874	59,500 (b)	189	91 (d)
California	2	1849, 1879	July 4, 1879	54,645	863	513
Colorado	1	1876	Aug. 1, 1876	74,522 (b)	304	145
Connecticut	4	1818 (f), 1965	Dec. 30, 1965	17,256 (b)	30	29
Delaware	4	1776, 1792, 1831, 1897	June 10, 1897	19,000	(e)	138
Florida	6	1839, 1861, 1865, 1868, 1886, 1968	Jan. 7, 1969	51,456 (b)	135	104
Georgia	10	1777, 1789, 1798, 1861, 1865, 1868, 1877, 1945, 1976, 1982	July 1, 1983	39,526 (b)	83 (g)	63 (g)
Hawaii	1 (h)	1950	Aug. 21, 1959	20,774 (b)	123	104
Idaho	1	1889	July 3, 1890	24,232 (b)	204	117
Illinois	4	1818, 1848, 1870, 1970	July 1, 1971	16,510 (b)	17	11
Indiana	2	1816, 1851	Nov. 1, 1851	10,379 (b)	78	46
Iowa	2	1846, 1857	Sept. 3, 1857	12,616 (b)	57	52 (i)
Kansas	1	1859	Jan. 29, 1861	12,296 (b)	123	93 (i)
Kentucky	4	1792, 1799, 1850, 1891	Sept. 28, 1891	23,911 (b)	75	41
Louisiana	11	1812, 1845, 1852, 1861, 1864, 1868, 1879, 1898, 1913, 1921, 1974	Jan. 1, 1975	54,112 (b)	189	129

State						
Maine	1	1819	March 15, 1820	16,276 (b)	202	170 (j)
Maryland	4	1776, 1851, 1864, 1867	Oct. 5, 1867	46,600 (b)	254	218 (k)
Massachusetts	1	1780	Oct. 25, 1780	36,700 (l)	148	120
Michigan	4	1835, 1850, 1908, 1963	Jan. 1, 1964	34,659 (b)	63	25
Minnesota	1	1857	May 11, 1858	11,547 (b)	213	118
Mississippi	4	1817, 1832, 1869, 1890	Nov. 1, 1890	24,323 (b)	158	123
Missouri	4	1820, 1865, 1875, 1945	March 30, 1945	42,600 (b)	165	105
Montana	2	1889, 1972	July 1, 1973	13,145 (b)	53	30
Nebraska	2	1866, 1875	Oct. 12, 1875	20,048	336 (m)	222 (m)
Nevada	1	1864	Oct. 31, 1864	31,377 (b)	220	132
New Hampshire	2	1776, 1784	June 2, 1784	9,200	285 (n)	143
New Jersey	3	1776, 1844, 1947	Jan. 1, 1948	22,956 (b)	71	38
New Mexico	1	1911	Jan. 6, 1912	27,200	280	151
New York	4	1777, 1822, 1846, 1894	Jan. 1, 1895	51,700	291	216
North Carolina	3	1776, 1868, 1970	July 1, 1971	16,532 (b)	42	34
North Dakota	1	1889	Nov. 2, 1889	19,130 (b)	258	145 (o)
Ohio	2	1802, 1851	Sept. 1, 1851	48,521 (b)	272	162
Oklahoma	1	1907	Nov. 16, 1907	74,075 (b)	336 (p)	171 (p)
Oregon	1	1857	Feb. 14, 1859	54,083 (b)	473 (q)	238 (q)
Pennsylvania	5	1776, 1790, 1838, 1873, 1968 (r)	1968 (r)	27,711 (b)	36 (r)	30 (r)
Rhode Island	3	1842 (f), 1986 (s)	Dec. 4, 1986	10,908 (b)	8 (s)	8 (s)
South Carolina	7	1776, 1778, 1790, 1861, 1865, 1868, 1895	Jan. 1, 1896	22,300	672 (t)	485 (t)
South Dakota	1	1889	Nov. 2, 1889	27,675 (b)	219	212
Tennessee	3	1796, 1835, 1870	Feb. 23, 1870	13,300	59	36
Texas	5 (u)	1845, 1861, 1866, 1869, 1876	Feb. 15, 1876	90,000	614 (v)	439
Utah	1	1895	Jan. 4, 1896	11,000	157	106
Vermont	3	1777, 1786, 1793	July 9, 1793	10,286 (b)	211	53

(Continued)

TABLE 1-3 (*Continued*)

State or Other Jurisdiction	Number of Constitutions*	Dates of Adoption	Effective Date of Present Constitution	Estimated Length (Number of Words)	Number of Amendments Submitted to Voters	Adopted
Virginia	6	1776, 1830, 1851, 1869, 1902, 1970	July 1, 1971	21,319 (b)	48	40
Washington	1	1889	Nov. 11, 1889	33,564 (b)	169	96
West Virginia	2	1863, 1872	April 9, 1872	26,000	121	71
Wisconsin	1	1848	May 29, 1848	14,392 (b)	182	134 (i)
Wyoming	1	1889	July 10, 1890	31,800	120	94
America Samoa	2	1960, 1967	July 1, 1967	6,000	14	7
No. Mariana Islands	1	1977	Jan. 9, 1978	11,000	55	51 (w)(x)
Puerto Rico	1	1952	July 25, 1952	9,281	6	6

Source: The Book of the States 2006 (Lexington, Ky.: Council of State Governments, 2006), pp. 9–10. Based on surveys conducted in previous years by Janice May and updated by John Dinan in January 2006.

*The constitutions referred to in this table include those Civil War documents customarily listed by the individual states.

(a) The Alabama constitution includes numerous local amendments that apply to only one county. An estimated 70 percent of all amendments are local. A 1982 amendment provides that after proposal by the legislature to which special procedures apply, only a local vote (with exceptions) is necessary to add them to the constitution.

(b) Computer word count.

(c) The total number of Alabama amendments includes one that is commonly overlooked.

(d) Eight of the approved amendments have been superseded and are not printed in the current edition of the constitution. The total adopted does not include five amendments proposed and adopted since statehood.

(e) Proposed amendments are not submitted to the voters in Delaware.

(f) Colonial charters with some alterations served as the first constitutions in Connecticut (1638, 1662) and in Rhode Island (1663).

(g) The Georgia constitution requires amendments to be of "general and uniform application throughout the state," thus eliminating local amendments that accounted for most of the amendments before 1982.

(h) As a kingdom and republic, Hawaii had five constitutions.

(i) The figure includes amendments approved by the voters and later nullified by the state supreme court in Iowa (three), Kansas (one), Nevada (six), and Wisconsin (two).

(j) The figure does not include one amendment approved by the voters in 1967 that is inoperative until implemented by legislation.

(k) Two sets of identical amendments were on the ballot and adopted in the 1992 Maryland election. The four amendments are counted as two in the table.

(l) The printed constitution includes many provisions that have been annulled. The length of effective provisions is an estimated 24,122 words (12,400 annulled) in Massachusetts, and in Rhode Island before the "rewrite" of the constitution in 1986, it was 11,399 words (7,627 annulled).

(m) The 1998 and 2000 Nebraska ballots allowed the voters to vote separately on "parts" of propositions. In 1998, 10 of 18 separate propositions were adopted; in 2000, 6 of 9.

(n) The constitution of 1784 was extensively revised in 1792. Figure shows proposals and adoptions since the constitution was adopted in 1784.

(o) The figures do not include submission and approval of the constitution of 1889 itself and of Article XX; these are constitutional questions included in some counts of constitutional amendments and would add two to the figure in each column.

(p) The figures include five amendments submitted to and approved by the voters which were, by decisions of the Oklahoma or U.S. Supreme Courts, rendered inoperative or ruled invalid, unconstitutional, or illegally submitted.

(q) One Oregon amendment on the 2000 ballot was not counted as approved because canvassing was enjoined by the courts.

(r) Certain sections of the constitution were revised by the limited convention of 1967–68. Amendments proposed and adopted are since 1968.

(s) Following approval of the eight amendments and a "rewrite" of the Rhode Island Constitution in 1986, the constitution has been called the 1986 Constitution. Amendments since 1986 total eight proposed and eight adopted. Otherwise, the total is 106 proposals and 60 adopted.

(t) In 1981 approximately two-thirds of 626 proposed and four-fifths of the adopted amendments were local. Since then the amendments have been statewide propositions.

(u) The Constitution of the Republic of Texas preceded five state constitutions.

(v) The number of proposed amendments to the Texas Constitution excludes three proposed by the legislature but not placed on the ballot.

(w) By 1992, 49 amendments had been proposed and 47 adopted. Since then, one was proposed but rejected in 1994, all three proposals were ratified in 1996, and in 1998, of two proposals one was adopted.

(x) The total excludes one amendment ruled void by a federal district court.

Other constitutional articles deal with suffrage and elections, local government, particular economic interests (such as farming), and amendments. Although most rules and regulations regarding voting have been established by the states, a series of amendments to the U.S. Constitution (Fifteenth, Seventeenth, Nineteenth, Twenty-third, Twenty-fourth, and Twenty-sixth) have provided a degree of uniformity throughout the nation. Nevertheless, a few interesting examples may be cited. In Vermont, for example, the constitution requires "quiet and peaceable behavior" as a voting qualification. In some southern states before 1965, a person of "good character" might have been excused by the local voting registrar from taking a literacy test or complying with other regulations specifically established to disenfranchise African Americans.

Most newer state constitutions have separate articles on policy areas, such as education and welfare. In the 1980s and 1990s, several states made changes to eliminate gender bias language in their constitutions. Most constitutions have a miscellaneous or general provisions article to lay out provisions that do not fit elsewhere or that apply to more than one section of the constitution. Eighteen states have an equal rights amendment, similar to the national amendment that failed to be ratified.

There were fewer constitutional amendments in the 1990s than in the 1970s and 1980s, but the number of changes brought out by the initiative process was at a record high. Mississippi became the eighteenth state to permit the constitutional initiative, and Rhode Island and New Jersey authorized the recall in the 1990s.

In contrast to the U.S. Constitution, most state constitutions are long, detailed, and heavily amended. There is a strong feeling among academics that much of their detail should have been left to legislatures to determine by passing bills. Although length and detail are not necessarily bad, these characteristics have had great political significance in the operation of state government. Excessive detail is due in part to the successful efforts of interest groups to have constitutions specifically recognize and protect their economic concerns. Indeed, constitutions are longest in those states with the strongest interest groups. Unless amended, these provisions may hinder government regulation as changes in society occur. Political scientist Duane Lockard notes that the complexity of state constitutions invites litigation and thus plays into the hands of those resisting change.[33] Opponents can often challenge new laws on the grounds that some detail of constitutional procedure was not properly followed. State courts have often tended toward a narrow interpretation of state constitutions, particularly limiting legislative and executive authority. Indeed, Lockard suggests that courts often have been so opposed to change that they reach beyond specific to general provisions to invalidate laws.

Constitutions also are detailed because they include very specific provisions defining what local governments can do and what is taught in public schools. Political scientist Christopher Hammons estimates that 39 percent of state constitutions deal with matters that most observers consider to be extraneous. An example would be a provision in the South Dakota constitution to establish a twine and cordage plant at the state prison. In comparison, Hammons says that about 6 percent of the U.S. Constitution is devoted to particularistic issues.[34]

Since the 1970s, state supreme courts have been forces for change, not obstruction. In what is referred to as judicial federalism (see Chapter 2), many state courts have interpreted their own constitutions independently of the U.S. Constitution, especially in civil rights cases to support reformist goals. We need to remember that state constitutions are changed by judicial interpretation as well as by amendments. Very detailed constitutions make it more likely that amendments will be added as circumstances change and explicit provisions leave less leeway for change through interpretation. As a result, length and detail beget greater length through amendments.

Model Constitutions

Many state constitutions reveal a strong suspicion of government power, and they act as roadblocks to change. In particular, constitutional restrictions on gubernatorial power made activist government in the twentieth century difficult. In many of the constitutions written in the nineteenth century, governors were limited to two-year terms; legislatures met as infrequently as every other year and only for a limited period (sixty to ninety days); legislative salaries were specified; most state officials, such as the attorney general and auditor, were elected rather than appointed by the governor; significant restraints were placed on borrowing; many special interests were exempt from taxation; and reapportionment in some cases required constitutional amendment. As we will see in Chapter 6, much of the history of state governors can be written in terms of constitutional amendments to give them powers comparable to those of the president of the United States.

An effective state constitution—that is, one allowing government to take an active role in the initiation and implementation of policy—should include these three fundamental characteristics:[35]

1. It should be brief and to the point. Constitutions are not legislative codes; all they should do is establish the basic framework within which state officials can act.
2. It should make direct grants of authority so that the governor and legislators can be held accountable by the voters for their actions.
3. It should be receptive to orderly change. The amendment process should not be too cumbersome, and the constitution should include enforceable provisions on redrawing legislative districts. Unfortunately, legislators often have a built-in resistance to change, and voters often defeat new constitutions at the polls when they are asked to accept or reject in total a new constitution.

To most people, state constitutions are painfully boring documents. They are not read by those seeking examples of stirring phrases or eloquent prose style. However, as we shall see throughout this book, there are few, if any, problems of state government for which the suggested solution will not sooner or later run headlong into constitutional prohibitions, restrictions, or obstructions. Constitutions are necessarily conservative documents that limit the exercise of political power. Because of the nature of state constitutions, there was a strong movement in the twentieth century to pass constitutional amendments aimed at increasing the power of legislators, governors, and judges and at providing an independent basis of power for local governments.

Probably the most unusual of all state constitutions was a proposal for the new state of New Columbia, which was approved by voters of the District of Columbia in 1982; a revised document was submitted to Congress in 1987. The proposed government structure called for a unicameral legislature, permitted public employees to strike, guaranteed a right to employment, and gave state benefits to persons unable to work because of pregnancy. It was rejected by Congress.

Constitutional Status of Cities

Because cities and counties are not mentioned in the U.S. Constitution, they fall under the control of states. This means that local powers are provided by state constitutions or by acts of state legislatures and that cities and counties are not given any protection against state interference.

Local governments are clearly subordinate to the state. In a classic statement, Judge John F. Dillon formulated **Dillon's Rule** (1868), which says that municipal corporations can exercise only those powers expressly granted by state constitutions and laws and those necessarily implied from granted powers. If there is any question about the exercise of power, it should be resolved in favor of the state. Guided by Dillon's Rule, many state legislatures passed legislation that affected only one or two cities, and they often enacted policy that concerned minor local matters. Although this rule has been accepted by the U.S. Supreme Court, Daniel Elazar notes that more than 80 percent of the states have rejected Dillon's Rule or have changed it to recognize the residual powers of local government.[36]

The powers that cities have under state law are spelled out under general statutes or in **city charters.** Until the 1850s, legislatures issued a special act or specific charter to explain the structure of government for individual cities. Because this was a time-consuming process, state legislatures moved to establish classified charters in which cities are put in general classes according to population. Under this system larger cities typically have a broader range of powers than smaller cities. Many states use optional charters in which voters can choose among several plans—mayor-council, manager-council, or commission—when a new city is incorporated.

Most states now provide **home-rule charters** for cities (in 48 states) and counties (in 37 states), and two-thirds of cities with populations over 2,500 have adopted home-rule charters. Home rule modifies the traditional subordinate relationship of cities to states by permitting cities to draft and approve their own charters, and it limits the ability of states to act on certain local matters. Home-rule cities are free to enact their own laws so long as they are not contrary to state law. There also is the recognition of implied powers for cities to do anything so long as it is not prohibited by state law. Variations in home-rule provisions among the states mean that in some states there is extensive local discretion and in others local choices are very limited. In states with constitutional home rule, cities can adopt whatever form of charter they wish without getting legislative approval to spell out details. In other states, legislative home rule can be withdrawn or amended by a vote of the legislature. A few states have "self-enforcing" home-rule provisions that permit cities to bypass state legislatures and enact home rule for themselves. In the other cases, cities must get legislative approval to have home rule. Broader grants of local self-rule mean that long, detailed provisions for cities in state constitutions can be shortened. In response to the passage of abusive nineteenth-century legislation aimed at a specific city, forty-one states prohibit passage of special laws unless a local government requests it.[37]

Curiously, in some states home rule has been resisted. Political scientist David R. Berman notes that interest groups often oppose grants of power to local governments, preferring to deal with a single state legislature.[38] There also are regional differences; for example, the tradition of local authority in the South has limited the use of home rule. Home-rule cities typically have more authority than do home-rule counties. Only one in ten cities eligible to adopt a home-rule charter has done so.

Amending Constitutions

There are four methods of changing state constitutions: legislative proposal, constitutional initiative, constitutional commission, and constitutional convention. **Legislative proposal** is available in all states, and it is by far the most commonly used means of change. In most states, a two-thirds or three-fifths vote of the legislature is required as the first step in approving an amendment. In seventeen states, only a majority vote is necessary. Although most states require approval in only one legislative session, twelve require approval in two consecutive sessions. Following legislative approval, the amendment is typically placed on the ballot, where a majority vote is needed for ratification. Only Delaware does not require voter approval of amendments. State legislators initiate nearly 90 percent of all proposed amendments. Voters approve about 75 percent of legislative proposals submitted to them.

The **constitutional initiative** can be used in eighteen states. It allows proponents of reform to have suggestions for limited change placed on the ballot. The process is time-consuming and often expensive for reform groups, especially in large states. Still, the number of constitutional initiatives rose to all-time highs during the 1980s and 1990s. Proponents must first get signatures on an initiative proposal. In California, for example, the number required is 8 percent of the total number of voters for governor in the last election. In a few states, the signatures must come from people distributed across the state. In Massachusetts no more than one-fourth can come from any one county. As a final step, there is a referendum vote, in which most states require a majority vote on the amendment for it to be approved.

Eighteen states use a constitutional initiative in which citizens by petition propose amendments that go directly to the voters. Only Massachusetts and Mississippi employ an indirect initiative, which is submitted to the legislature before it is placed on the ballot. Thirteen of the states employing the initiative are west of the Mississippi River. The initiative process is discussed in more detail in Chapter 3.

In the mid-1990s two state constitutional amendments approved by the initiative process were struck down by the Supreme Court. In *Romer v. Evans* (1996) a six-member majority overruled a Colorado amendment that nullified existing civil rights protection for homosexuals and barred passage of new laws by the state or localities that protected homosexuals. In 1995 the Court ruled against state-imposed term limits on U.S. Congress members.

Constitutional commissions, available in all fifty states, may be formed to study the state constitution and make recommendations for change, or their purpose may be to make arrangements for a constitutional convention. Only in Florida can a constitutional commission initiate and refer amendments to the voters. Most commissions have acted as study groups that turn their work over to state legislatures. As a result, they operate under less media and public scrutiny than do constitutional conventions. Commission size varies from as few as five members to as many as fifty. Members are usually appointed by the governor, legislative leaders, and chief justice of the highest court in the state.

Constitutional conventions, where delegates meet to amend or completely rewrite state constitutions, are the oldest method of changing state constitutions. In most cases, conventions must be authorized by the voters, but in six states the legislatures can call them without approval by voters in a statewide referendum. In Alaska and Iowa, conventions are held automatically every ten years. Delegates to conventions can amend, revise, or completely rewrite their state's constitution. Whatever changes are approved at conventions must also be approved by the voters. Not surprisingly, less extreme changes in constitutions are more likely to be approved by voters than are extensive changes. The most recently adopted new constitution was in Georgia in 1982, where a constitutional convention was employed.

If constitutions were extensively changed even every ten years (which they aren't), it might reflect dangerous short-term responses to shifts in public opinion. Delegates to conventions usually are elected on a nonpartisan basis from state legislative districts. In most instances, delegates have been white, middle-aged, professional men. In some cases the state legislature convenes as a constitutional convention.

Rhode Island was the last state to hold a constitutional convention in 1986. Its delegates were selected in nonpartisan elections in each of the state's 100 House districts. One delegate was elected governor four years later and several were elected to the legislature. The convention made structural changes, deleted old language, and included as constitutional provisions material that had been added as amendments. Before this it was said that the only way to read the Rhode Island constitution was backwards, starting with the amendments. Following the convention, voters approved eight of fourteen proposals made by the delegates. A different approach was taken in 1967 when New York's constitutional convention met for six months and in an up-or-down vote the state's voters defeated a new constitution. The Rhode Island constitution requires that, at least every ten years, there will be a popular vote on holding a convention. Thirteen other states require the question of a convention to be put before the voters periodically.

Since 2000 there has been a downturn in the number of amendments proposed and adopted in the states. Banning same-sex marriage, approved in twenty-one states since 2004, has been the most popular subject for successful amendments. In 2006 ten states had amendments on the ballot to limit the ability of local governments to use the power of eminent domain to take property for private use. This is discussed in Chapter 8. In 2004 and 2005, all amendments were by legislative proposal or constitutional initiative. Not since 1982 have any new constitutions been proposed or adopted.[39]

THE STATES CONTRASTED AND COMPARED

This chapter has pointed out the great diversity among the states in terms of culture, socioeconomic characteristics, population, and geography. In the chapters that follow, the reader should develop a clearer picture of *similarities* among the states. Most states have virtually the same patterns of government structure—they have bicameral (two-house) legislatures organized by parties and by committees; their governors exercise similar constitutional powers in such areas as the budget and veto; and their judicial systems are organized in a common three- or two-tier arrangement of trial and appellate courts. Still, there are significant differences in the powers given to governors and legislatures in state constitutions. As we have noted, historical circumstances at the time constitutions were written and the impact of political culture, among other factors, have strongly affected the willingness of some states, especially in the South, to create the legal framework for **activist government**—that is, government that will support generous spending for a variety of social programs and will protect the civil rights of its residents.

Although elections proceed in the same general pattern in all states, personalities and tradition have helped create unique styles of campaigning and supported various means of campaign financing in different parts of the country. While states confront relatively common problems in education, housing transportation, health, and safety, how they respond to those problems varies greatly across the country. Some states fund government well and provide generous public services; others, because of limited resources or limited will, provide only bare-bones public services. For example, in some states the quality of public universities is comparable to that of the best private institutions, whereas in others state universities are barely adequate. In-state tuition rates also vary greatly among the states.

Because the states are alike in many ways, they offer social scientists the opportunity to make a wide range of comparisons. Because there also is great variety among the states and the thousands of local governments, it gives us the opportunity to study why structural and behavioral differences occur at particular times and under particular conditions.

Comparative state politics provides an excellent means to introduce the study of political science by examining differences and similarities among the states and attempting to provide some of the answers to help explain why these differences exist.[40] Moreover, state and local governments are primarily responsible for those public issues that most directly affect our lives—education, public safety, and transportation. For example, about 80 percent of college students attend public institutions and about 70 percent of elementary and secondary students attend public schools. Because most students come to their first course on state government with a considerable amount of general information, the study of comparative state politics is much more manageable than the study of international relations.

As noted at the beginning of this chapter, states have been policy innovators even in financially troubled times. All of us should pay more attention to state governments because they determine most issues, big and small, that affect our daily lives. These include "whether customers can smoke in restaurants and bars, whether children can be tried as adults . . . how many minority students will be admitted to state universities, how difficult it will be for women to get abortions, (whether) dog groomers (or) veterinarians (have) the right to brush a dog's teeth, . . . how much you will pay to get your car insured, how fast you can drive it, . . . whether your 10-year-old child legally can buy an assault weapon (yes in Arkansas)." And states control much of what cities can do. "Albany decides whether New York City subway trains have one crew member or two . . . and New Jersey has seized control of . . . schools (in Newark, Jersey City, and Paterson) and begun running them itself."[41]

SUMMARY

There has been a resurgence of state government, beginning with constitutional reform in the 1960s and extending into the twenty-first century, as the predominant political mood in the country has favored the return of power to the states. Helped by a strong national economy and their own reform initiatives, states experienced budget surpluses in the late 1990s. In the period 2001–2005, state finances suffered as the national economy declined. At the same time, federal aid and attention to states and localities dropped as the attention of government in Washington turned to fighting terrorism. Since the national economy began to improve in 2006, many states have seen an improvement in their financial positions. This has helped lead to a situation in which states have been much more innovative than the national government in developing policies to respond to a variety of pressing social and economic issues.

Faced with a deadlocked Congress, states have passed legislation aimed at both assisting immigrants and denying them access to state services. Although immigration is a particularly strong issue in states such as California and Texas, with large Hispanic populations, it also has become a significant issue, with controversial political implications, in states across the country.

The nature of public policy varies greatly among the fifty states. Even states with similar economic and geographic circumstances may differ markedly in the amount of money they devote to particular policy areas. Differences in public policy making are explained by examining the impact of the following factors on the states: level of economic development, physical setting, political culture, sectionalism, public opinion, and race and ethicity.

Shifts in population—to metropolitan areas, to suburbs, and to the South and West—have had major impacts on state policy making since the end of World War II. Projections are that these population trends will continue well into this century.

Public policy making also is affected by state constitutions, which are conservative documents that have hindered change. Constitutional change mainly comes from legislative proposals for amendments and from direct initiatives in which the general public may recommend and approve amendments.

KEY TERMS

rainy day funds (p. 4)
diffusion of policy innovation (p. 6)
tax burden (p. 8)
illegal immigrants (p. 11)
spoils system (p. 12)
political culture (p. 13)
Progressive movement (p. 13)
individualistic culture (p. 13)
traditionalistic culture (p. 13)
moralistic culture (p. 13)
public interest (p. 14)
communitarianism (p. 14)
policy liberalism (p. 15)
Sunbelt (p. 16)
sectionalism (p. 16)
urban areas (p. 19)

metropolitan statistical areas (MSAs) (p. 19)
combined statistical areas (CSAs) (p. 19)
micropolitan statistical areas (p. 19)
culture war (p. 24)
red states (p. 24)
blue states (p. 24)
ex post facto laws (p. 25)
Tenth Amendment (p. 26)
Dillon's Rule (p. 34)
city charters (p. 34)
home-rule charters (p. 34)
legislative proposal (p. 35)
constitutional initiative (p. 35)
constitutional commissions (p. 35)
constitutional conventions (p. 36)
activist government (p. 37)

BRIEF COMPARISONS OF STATE/LOCAL DIFFERENCES

Issue	States	Local Governments
Vitality	Innovations in education, health care, and welfare	Innovations in policing, controlling sprawl, and fighting illegal drugs
Political culture	Traditionalistic in the South, moralistic in the Northeast, individualistic in Mid-Atlantic states and spreading across the country	Individualistic culture tends to flourish in cities that are business centers
Population shifts	Gains in the Sunbelt, losses in the Great Plains, little change in the Midwest and Northeast	Gains in most Sunbelt cities, large losses in many Midwest cities, such as Detroit
Legal documents	Constitutions that prescribe the structure of state government	Cities and counties are legal creatures of the states, which control the kinds of charters they can have

INTERESTING WEB SITES

www.census.gov. U.S. Census Bureau's Web site. Lots of information: Click on "Quick Facts" to find demographic statistics on states, counties, and cities. Also, find "Subjects A to Z" and click on the letter "G" to find the "Census of Governments" and other reports on state and local governments.

www.loc.gov/rr/news/stategov/stategov.html. "Internet Resources" page of the Library of Congress with links to Web sites for general information about state and local governments and to several Web sites in each state.

www.law.cornell.edu/statutes.html. This Web site has links to the fifty state constitutions. Scroll down to "Constitutions, Statutes, and Legislative Information—By State."

http://camlaw.rutgers.edu/statecon. Research reports on state constitutions and subnational constitutions in other federal systems are available at the Center for State Constitutional Studies.

NOTES

1. Jonathan Walters, "Bordering on Disaster," *Governing* (July 2006), p. 24.
2. Larry Sabato, *Goodbye to Goodtime Charlie,* 2d ed. (Washington, D.C.: Congressional Quarterly Press, 1983), p. 8.

3. Noted in Pam Bulluck, "The Not-So United States," *New York Times* (April 23, 2006), sec. 4, p. 2.
4. Pamela M. Prah, "States Step in to Fill Fed's Role," *Stateline.org* (July 25, 2006).
5. Jack L. Walker, Jr., "The Diffusion of Innovations in the American States," *American Political Science Review* (September 1973), pp. 880–899.
6. Greg M. Shaw and Tari Renner, "Patterns of State Policy Diffusion: Convoys, Packs, and Clusters." Paper presented at the Midwest Political Science Convention, Chicago, April 2002, p. 3.
7. William D. Berry and Brady Baybeck, "Using Geographic Information Systems to Study Interstate Competition," *American Political Science Review* (November 2005), p. 505.
8. See Thomas R. Dye, *Understanding Public Policy,* 9th ed. (Englewood Cliffs, N.J.: Prentice-Hall, 1998).
9. Thomas Payne, "Montana: From Copper Fiefdom to Pluralist Polity," in *Interest Group Politics in the American West,* Ronald J. Hrebenar and Clive S. Thomas, eds. (Salt Lake City: University of Utah Press, 1987), p. 77.
10. Charles Price, "The Longshot Bid to Split California," *California Journal* (August 1992), pp. 387–391. Also see Margo Price and Stephen Birdsall, *Regional Landscapes of the United States and Canada* (New York: John Wiley, 1999).
11. Joseph Kahn, "Valley Girls (and Guys) Push to Secede from Los Angeles," *New York Times* (April 20, 2002), pp. A1, 14.
12. Donald F. Ketti, "Border Wars," *Governing* (December 2005), p. 20.
13. Jonathan Walters, "Bordering on Disaster," *Governing* (July 2006), p. 24.
14. Daniel J. Elazar, *American Federalism: A View from the States,* 3d ed. (New York: Harper & Row, 1984), p. 109.
15. Maureen Moakley, "New Jersey," in *The Political Life of the American States,* Alan Rosenthal and Maureen Moakley, eds. (New York: Praeger, 1984), pp. 219–220.
16. Elazar, *American Federalism,* pp. 114–122.
17. Elazar, *American Federalism,* pp. 122–141; and Elazar, *The American Mosaic* (Boulder, Colo.: Westview Press, 1994), pp. 237–252.
18. Virginia Gray and Russell L. Hanson, *Politics in the American States,* 8th ed. (Washington, D.C.: Congressional Quarterly Press, 2004), pp. 4–5.
19. Joel Lieske, "Regional Subcultures of the United States," *Journal of Politics* (November 1993), pp. 888–913.
20. Russell L. Hanson, "The Political Acculturation of Migrants in the American States," *Western Political Quarterly* (June 1992), pp. 355–384.
21. Rodney E. Hero and Caroline J. Tolbert, "A Racial/Ethnic Diversity Interpretation of Politics and Policy in the States of the U.S.," *American Journal of Political Science* (August 1996), p. 853. Also see Rodney E. Hero, *Faces of Inequality: Social Diversity in American Politics* (New York: Oxford University Press, 1998).
22. Elazar, *The American Mosaic,* p. 140.
23. Ronald J. Hrebenar and Clive S. Thomas, eds., *Interest Group Politics in the American West* (Salt Lake City: University of Utah Press, 1987), p. 144.
24. See John H. Fenton, *Midwest Politics* (New York: Holt, Rinehart and Winston, 1966).
25. Richard Rubin, "Not Far From Forsaken," *New York Times Magazine* (April 9, 2006), pp. 49–55.
26. Timothy Egan, "Indians and Bison Returning to Plains Others Abandoned," *New York Times* (May 27, 2001), p. A1.
27. Rob Gurwitt, "Betting on the Bulldozer," *Governing* (July 2002), p. 30.
28. Kirkpatrick Sale, *Power Shift: The Rise of the Southern Rim* (New York: Random House, 1975).
29. Morris P. Fiorina, *Culture War?* 2nd ed. (New York: Pearson Longman, 2006), p. 8.
30. Ibid., p. 30.

31. See Albert L. Strum, "The Development of American State Constitutions," *Publius* (Winter 1982).

32. G. Alan Tarr, *Understanding State Constitutions* (Princeton, N.J.: Princeton University Press, 1998), p. 10.

33. Duane Lockard, *The Politics of State and Local Government,* 3d ed. (New York: Macmillan, 1983), chap. 4.

34. Christopher Hammons, "Was James Madison Wrong? Rethinking the American Preference for Short, Framework-Oriented Constitutions," *American Political Science Review* (December 1999), p. 840.

35. See National Municipal League, *Model State Constitution,* 6th ed. (New York: National Municipal League, 1968).

36. Elazar, *American Federalism,* p. 203.

37. Joseph F. Zimmerman, "Evolving State-Local Relations," *The Book of the States 2002* (Lexington, Ky.: Council of State Governments, 2002), p. 33.

38. David R. Berman, "State-Local Relations: Authority, Finances, Partnerships," *Municipal Year Book 2001* (Washington: International City Management Association, 2001), p. 63.

39. John Dinan, "State Constitutional Developments in 2005," *The Book of the States 2006* (Lexington, KY.: Council of State Governments, 2006), pp. 3–8.

40. Christopher Z. Mooney, "Why Do They Tax Dogs in West Virginia? Teaching Political Science Through Comparative State Politics," *PS: Political Science and Politics* (June 1998), pp. 199–203.

41. All quotes from Charles S. Layton and Mary Walton, "Missing the Story at the Statehouse," *American Journalism Review* (July/August 1998), p. 46.

chapter
2

INTERGOVERNMENTAL RELATIONS

CASE STUDY

INTERGOVERNMENTAL RESPONSE TO HURRICANE KATRINA

In the immediate aftermath of Hurricane Katrina in September 2005, levees broke and pumps failed and then nearly every public service in New Orleans failed—electricity, water, sewers, telephones, fire protection, police, hospitals, even the disposal of corpses. The hurricane displaced about 1 million people in the Gulf Coast region and led to the deaths of more than 1,800 people. Within a few hours, 75 percent of metropolitan New Orleans was covered with up to 15 feet of water. Damages stretched 100 miles inland across Louisiana and Mississippi. New Orleans lost more than 200,000 homes and 43,000 rental units.

Catastrophes bring out the worst and best in people. While there were heroic individual acts, there was widespread chaos, including looting and violence, in New Orleans. In December 2004, a draft report by state and federal officials, as directed by the Federal Emergency Management Agency (FEMA), predicted that floodwaters from a Category 3 Hurricane would surge over levees, create high casualties, and force mass evacuation. Local officials, the report noted, would quickly be overwhelmed.

There was blame all around as each party in the intergovernmental system failed and effective cooperation among governments never took place. The inability to respond effectively was particularly troublesome considering the reforms that supposedly had been acted since the 9/11 disaster.

FEMA underestimated the strength of the storm, despite accurate predictions from the National Hurricane Center. No one at FEMA or the Department of Homeland Security took charge to carry out the federal government's role of coordination in the face of a disaster after the storm struck. At the state level, where there was responsibility for evacuation planning in the region, as well as control of the National Guard, there were critical delays in issuing evacuation orders. While the Bush administration wanted Louisiana Governor Kathleen Blanco to issue an official request for the feds to take control, she refused. Apparently the Democratic governor mistrusted the administration and wanted to maintain control in her office. In New Orleans, Mayor Ray Nagin eventually issued the city's first ever mandatory evacuation order, but as many as 100,000 people, mostly African Americans, remained in the city as buses were slow getting to New Orleans. Crime was rampant, after the city's police force was overwhelmed and thousands of people waited in the dark inside the Superdome. Later, a House of Representatives report titled "A Failure of Initiative" said that multiple communication breakdowns had "paralyzed effective response."

We are left with a classic "textbook example" of how not to respond to an emergency. As federalism expert Deil Wright notes, complexities tilt "the American intergovernmental system of governance toward devolution, deference, and delay. In emergencies, local officials are first responders, state actors are secondary, and nationals provide 'last resort' resources. Caution is favored over action. Risk and uncertainty prevail over active search for certainty."[1] Still, most of the time, public services get provided in a satisfactory manner.

In Katrina, failure occurred, in large part, due to federal ineptitude and to problems endemic to New Orleans. City government long has been one of the most corrupt in the country, and New Orleans ranks near the bottom nationwide in every measure of civic health. Not surprisingly, repair of hurricane damage, as we will see later in this chapter, has gone slowly.

POINTS TO CONSIDER

- How has the United States system of federalism evolved since its creation?
- How should power be divided among levels of government? Is devolution a good thing? What domestic responsibilities should be the primary responsibility of the federal government?
- Compare and contrast the positions on federalism taken by presidents since the 1960s.
- Why has coercive federalism become dominant since 2001?
- Are block grants better than categorical grants? If so, why aren't there proportionately more block grants?
- How do we explain the Supreme Court's recent pull back in supporting states in federalism cases?
- Should the national government and the states be permitted to approve *any* unfunded mandates?
- What factors lead to a willingness on the part of states to cooperate, and what factors lead to conflict?
- Is the intergovernmental system better prepared to deal with major emergencies than it was in 2001?

FEDERALISM AS A POLITICAL CONCEPT

Most textbooks in the past discussed federalism in terms of structure and legal principles. This approach stressed the constitutional division of authority and functions between the national government and the states. As such, it was a static view of power being assigned to units of government and remaining fixed over a long time. The current approach suggests a much more dynamic notion of intergovernmental relations. Thus interpretation focuses not on *structure* but on *politics*. According to this view, levels of government share authority and power in an interdependent and constantly changing relationship of joint action. Federalism is regarded, in part, as a state of mind. For example, although the national government has the *legal* authority to take a wide range of actions, it is constrained by political and social forces that support state autonomy and resist centralization. As we will see in the chapters that deal with education, welfare, crime, and economic development, the decentralized nature of our system has a powerful impact on how money is spent and how problems are addressed.

We need to be reminded that there never was a time when federal, state, and local government affairs were completely separate. The traditional analogy of the American federal system as a "layer cake," with clear divisions between layers of government, was never true. Instead, it is more accurate to speak of the federal system as a "marble cake," in which government functions are shared by all levels.[2] Cooperative efforts by federal, state, and local governments have become increasingly necessary since the 1960s. A vast system of over 87,000 local governments works to serve a wide variety of functions. In 2002 there were 3,034 counties, 19,429 municipalities, 16,505 townships, 13,506 school districts, and 35,052 special districts.[3] The typical suburban resident in any metropolitan area across the country is likely to be under the jurisdiction of and pay taxes to nearly a dozen governments. In 2002 the number of local governmental units per state ranged from 6,903 in Illinois to 19 in Hawaii.

In many ways, states are at the center of an elaborate web of relationships among governments in our federal system.[4] States mediate differences among local governments and the national government. They manage affairs among their local governments. And through trade missions, states act as intermediaries between private businesses and foreign governments.

This sharing of functions is most clearly seen in federal grants-in-aid (which are discussed in detail later in this chapter). Most Americans favor the decentralization of power. At the same time, they want to solve problems. Grants-in-aid are a practical solution: The programs are funded by the national government but administered by state and local governments and even by nonprofit business firms. Virtually every function of local government has a counterpart federal program. As we shall see in this chapter, fiscal federalism provides the means by which the congressional majority's sense of basic policy needs directs and shapes public policy making in states and cities.

The Reagan administration believed that the expansion of grants-in-aid in the 1960s and 1970s represented a serious overreaching of federal authority. It was concerned that the state and local governments had become too dependent on federal funds and that federal regulations had become too intrusive. The Reagan administration also was convinced that state and local aid was taking too high a percentage of the federal budget (it had reached an all-time high of 17 percent of all federal spending in 1978). Although President George H. W. Bush continued to support the Reagan philosophy of limiting federal expenditures and giving more management responsibility to states and cities, funding for grants-in-aid increased substantially while he was in office.

Under President Clinton and a Republican-controlled Congress, power continued to flow to the states. New block grants, begun in the 1980s, gave states more flexibility to manage their affairs. In particular, the conversion of the nation's welfare system (formerly known as Aid to Families with Dependent Children) into a block grant (Temporary Assistance to Needy Families) signaled a major change away from power in Washington, D.C. The welfare system could be changed more easily than some other social programs because it had never been fully centralized.

Although the George W. Bush administration came to office talking about continuing support for greater state flexibility and less federal control, it has, as we will see later in this chapter, repeatedly supported programs that have expanded federal involvement. This has been particularly true in education and law enforcement, policy making areas that traditionally have been left to the states. What has emerged is what federalism and public administration expert Paul L. Posner calls "opportunistic federalism where the federal role is defined with little regard to traditional notions of propriety or appropriateness."[5] Increasingly, it is Democrats, not Republicans, who support state power to override national authority.

As noted in Chapter 1, the reemergence of a federal budget deficit and preoccupation with fighting terrorism and the war in Iraq have led both Congress and the president to shortchange states since 2001. States are developing strategies to adapt to the reality of *less* federal financial assistance with *more* federal control of public policy.[6] Still, states continue to play a major role in the *implementation* of federal policy. Moreover, as noted in Chapter 1, helped by the economic recovery that began in 2005, many states have asserted leadership in a variety of policy areas, such as immigration, in which Congress has been unwilling or unable to act.

CREATION OF THE AMERICAN FEDERAL SYSTEM

The decision by the framers of the Constitution in 1787 to create a **federal system** of government may be viewed as a compromise between those who wanted to continue with a confederate form of government and those who wanted to change to a centralized system as existed in England. In the United States federal system, the national and state governments share power and can act with authority over the same people and same territory. Under the Articles of Confederation, the national government lacked the authority to manage effectively the economic and international affairs of the nation. The population had strong loyalties to the states, and there was a general fear of centralized authority as it had been manifested in colonial America. A federal system offered unity without uniformity. By reserving to the states considerable power, it lessened the likelihood of centralized tyranny. A federal system seems appropriate for many developing countries because it is flexible and permits changes in the distribution of power among government units and in the balance of power without changing the fundamental charter of government.

A federal system may be distinguished from a confederacy in the following ways: (1) In a federal system, the central government is stronger than its member states in regard to the size of its budget and the scope of its jurisdiction; (2) in a federal system, national law is supreme; (3) in a federal system, the central government acts directly upon individuals in such matters as taxation and raising an army, whereas in a confederacy, the central government must act indirectly through the states when dealing with individual citizens; and (4) in a federal system, states may not withdraw from the union, but in a confederacy, they may secede.

A **confederacy** is a voluntary association of independent governments in which the central government depends on regional governments to give it power. There are only a handful of confederacies in existence. Most are regional organizations, such as the European Union, created for limited purposes. The most basic problem faced by confederacies is that they must rely on member states to provide revenue voluntarily to the central government.

But federal systems often face many of the problems confronted by confederacies. Since 1990 several federal systems, most notably the Soviet Union and Yugoslavia, have been pulled apart by regional conflict. Canada has faced a strong secessionist movement in Quebec for several decades.

A less flexible sort of system is the **unitary nation-state,** in which local governments can exercise only those powers given them by the central government. Unitary government exists in such nations as Great Britain, France, and Israel, as well as in African and Middle East monarchies. In physically small countries, a unitary structure provides efficiency in dealing with national problems and ensures that national values will prevail. Because most nondemocratic nations have unitary systems, it means that only about thirty nations in the world are federal systems. Curiously, as American federalism has devolved power to the states since the early 1980s, so too have British and French unitary systems given more power to their subgovernments.

As political scientist Joseph F. Zimmerman points out, the U.S. Constitution incorporated both unitary and confederate elements in a federal system.[7] There is unitary control over the District of Columbia and overseas territories and elements of confederacy in that states retain regulatory powers, as well as providing most public services within their boundaries. As noted in Chapter 1, the Tenth Amendment underlines the limits of federal authority, by reserving powers to the states.

The relationship between states and cities in the United States is unitary. Legally, cities are creatures of the states, meaning that states have much greater control over cities than the federal government has over states. For example, state legislatures determine which taxes cities can impose and what the rate will be and what forms of government cities can have. Among the fifty states there are vast differences in how much authority cities are permitted to exercise.

Relations among states are **confederal,** meaning that all states are equal to each other. In a real sense their relations with each other are like relations among sovereign nations. As a result, when state representatives interact with each other they proceed diplomatically, recognizing others as their legal equals.

As discussed in Chapter 1, the U.S. Constitution provides guarantees to the states and imposes limits on their actions. The powers of the states are limited because substantial powers are delegated to Congress, and the supremacy clause makes very clear the subordinate relationship of the states to the national government:

> This constitution, and the laws of the United States which shall be made in pursuance thereof; and all treaties made or which shall be made under the authority of the United States shall be the supreme law of the land; and the judges in every state shall be bound thereby, anything in the constitution or laws of any state to the contrary notwithstanding.

The Constitution created a system of **dual sovereignty** in which the national government has the exclusive power to act in its sphere of influence, for example, in interstate commerce. At the same time, certain constitutional powers are reserved to the states. These include ownership of property, regulation of domestic relations, prosecution of most crimes, and control of local government. As we will see later in this chapter, the line between national and state authority is not clearly drawn. This has led to disagreement among Supreme Court justices as to what is "truly local" and what is within the proper sphere of the national government.

THE EVOLUTION OF AMERICAN FEDERALISM

Relationships among governments in the United States have been dynamic, rather than stable. As conceived by the framers of the Constitution, federal authority was limited largely to foreign affairs, whereas state authority was relatively broad, and there was little overlap or cooperation between the two levels of government. Over time, both federal and state authority have expanded, and increasingly there has been an overlap in powers exercised by both states and the federal government.

As noted earlier, federal power expanded greatly in the 1960s. In some cases, states encouraged Congress to enact national standards to prevent unfair economic competition. In the area of civil rights, Congress enacted legislation and presidents supported broad federal enforcement of those laws. Expanded government regulation in such areas as environmental control and occupational safety limited the authority of private persons and businesses. Although this led to a reaction against federal power in the 1980s, the national government has reasserted leadership in domestic policy making since the events of September 11, 2001. At various times in history, assertions of federal power have led to challenges in federal courts, as we will see later in this chapter.

As a result of the increase in federal authority, federal courts (especially the Supreme Court) have acted as umpires in the federal system to decide where power should reside. As part of the national government, the Supreme Court most often in United States history has supported federal power over state power. However, in a series of decisions the Court since the early 1990s has limited the reach of federal law, restricting the ability of Congress to pass laws that were binding on the states. At the same time, the Supreme Court in recent years has supported strong assertions of power by the president into areas traditionally controlled by the states.

Early Nineteenth-Century Federalism

McCulloch v. Maryland (1819) was the first examination by the Supreme Court of state-federal relations. The background of the case is as follows: Maryland had levied a tax on notes issued by all banks not chartered by the state of Maryland. McCulloch, the cashier in the Baltimore branch of the United States Bank, refused to pay the tax, and Maryland brought suit against him. After losing in Maryland state courts, McCulloch (as directed by the secretary of the treasury) appealed and the case was reviewed by the Supreme Court, headed by Chief Justice John Marshall.

Regarding the first issue—"Does Congress have the authority to charter a bank?"—the Court ruled that although this was not among the enumerated powers of Congress, it could be implied from the **"necessary and proper" clause** of the Constitution, which states that Congress has the power "to make all laws which shall be necessary and proper for carrying into Execution" the seventeen congressional powers that are specifically mentioned immediately preceding the clause. Marshall reasoned that although the chartering of a bank was not absolutely indispensable in the performance of delegated congressional responsibilities, it was, nevertheless, "convenient or useful to another objective." On the second issue—"Can the states tax an instrument of the national government?"—the Court ruled no. The power to tax, said the chief justice, is the power to destroy, and states cannot interfere with operations of the national government.

Shortly after *McCulloch,* the Marshall Court had another opportunity to rule in favor of a broad interpretation of national authority. *Gibbons v. Ogden* (1824) concerned the desire of New York and New Jersey to control shipping on the lower Hudson River. The states argued that the definition of *commerce* should be narrowly construed so as to include only direct dealings in commodities. Thus the regulation of shipping on inland waterways would be beyond the constitutional power of Congress. Marshall, however, ruled that the power of the national government to regulate commerce included all commercial activity. The Court stated: "This power, like all others vested in Congress, is complete in itself, may be exercised to its utmost extent, and acknowledges no limitations other than are prescribed in the Constitution."

The first federal money grants to states were made in 1837, when surplus funds were sent to the states with no restrictions regarding their use. Before that, federal land grants had been made to assist in the construction of schools, canals, roads, and railroads. The first Morrill Act, passed in 1862, provided land to states to establish agricultural colleges; these institutions became land-grant universities. Terms of the legislation foreshadowed more modern grants-in-aid because they required colleges to make annual reports and required governors to account for the use of federal funds.

Of course, the most serious threat to national authority came with the Civil War. Prior to 1860, John C. Calhoun proposed the concept of **concurrent majority.** In Calhoun's model each interest group (or state) had the right to decide independently whether to accept or reject national policy affecting it. Calhoun's idea was similar to the doctrine of **nullification,** under which each state could veto national legislation with which it disagreed. Ultimately, the Southern states seceded from the Union. After the issue had been decided on the battlefield, the Supreme Court ruled in *Texas v. White* (1869) that "[o]urs is an indestructible union, composed of indestructible states."

Dual Federalism

Dual federalism is the concept that the distribution of powers between the federal government and the states is fixed and clearly separated. Within their spheres of authority, each level of government is free to act independently of the other. As noted earlier, such a system is analogous to a "layer cake" in which there are clear divisions between powers exercised by the federal government and the states. It was a doctrine supported by the Supreme Court between the Civil War and 1937. The Court's opinions discouraged joint federal-state programs, and they kept the federal government out of most areas of domestic policy making.

Dual federalism had its roots in the **compact theory of federalism** that was used as an argument for states' rights in the pre–Civil War period. As formulated by John C. Calhoun, this theory stated that the framers had created a system in which the United States was composed of sovereign states united through a compact. Power was given to the national government by the states, but the states could reclaim power by nullifying, or vetoing, laws passed by Congress that affected them. Thus the states operated separately from the national government. Although dual federalism dominated from early in the nineteenth century, Joseph F. Zimmerman notes that the framers of the Constitution had assumed there would be cooperation between the national and state governments when they included provisions that authorized the states to determine qualifications of voters in congressional elections and gave them the power to ratify or reject constitutional amendments approved by Congress.

Acting under the theory of dual federalism, the federal government in the 1920s turned away from social concerns supported by President Wilson, and the states were left to take action regarding such problems as care of dependent children. Federal domestic programs in the late 1920s were so limited that state spending was double federal spending.[8] States also were dominant over cities as policy makers, spending about three times as much money as local governments.

From 1860 until 1932 only two Democrats, Grover Cleveland and Woodrow Wilson, were elected president. When Franklin D. Roosevelt became president in 1932, the Supreme Court was dominated by conservative justices who had been appointed by Republican presidents. With a majority of its members continuing to apply the theory of dual federalism, the Supreme Court repeatedly overturned New Deal legislation from 1933 to 1937.

Cooperative Federalism

President Roosevelt's transformation of the Supreme Court began with his first appointment of a justice in 1937 (he ultimately appointed eight justices). With new members and a change of heart by some moderate justices, the Court reverted to the views of the Marshall era that the national government has broad authority under its implied powers and that the reserved powers under the Tenth Amendment do not limit national action. As a result the Court approved New Deal legislation that supported social and economic regulation, such as the federally prescribed minimum wage and a very broad interpretation of the power of Congress over interstate commerce. By the early 1940s, says political scientist Martin Shapiro, "The New Deal Court had effectively announced the constitutional demise of federalism as a limit on the power of the national government."[9]

State dominance quickly changed with the coming of the Great Depression. Cities, states, and private charities were overwhelmed by high unemployment rates that led to the homeless constructing tent cities and out-of-work men trying to sell apples on street corners. Faced with depleted budgets and fearing social rebellions, governors and mayors begged the federal government to come to their assistance. The election of Franklin D. Roosevelt in 1932, and the beginning of New Deal programs the next year, ushered in a new era in intergovernmental relations. Federal domestic spending tripled in the years leading up to World War II.

The size of state bureaucracy also increased from the 1930s through the 1960s.[10] This was because much of the increased federal aid was transferred to the states. In turn, state aid to cities (much of it federal aid passed on to local governments) stimulated a growth in city bureaucracy.

This era in intergovernmental relations has become known as **cooperative federalism.** Unlike dual federalism, in which there were differences between state and federal power and responsibilities, under cooperative federalism the system looked more like a "marble cake" in which federal power and responsibilities were intermingled. State and federal agencies undertook joint projects and power was shared, even as the role of the federal government expanded. In most cases Congress has described the basic direction for programs and provided funds, but it has given states and localities responsibility for administrating them.

As we will see later in this chapter, over time academics have identified a variety of subsets of cooperative federalism. In some cases these subsets have faded out and then returned under future presidential administrations.

The modern-day structure of categorical grants-in-aid came into being in the 1930s when federal aid was provided almost exclusively to states.[11] Congress required states to submit plans for the use of the funds, to provide matching funds, and to allow federal audit and review of the programs. Under President Harry Truman, proportionately more federal aid went directly to local governments than was the case under President Roosevelt. Federal grants continued to expand under President Dwight Eisenhower, although there was some concern about the proper division of responsibility between Washington and the states. Federal aid tripled from 1952 to 1961 (reaching $7.3 billion), but dramatic change in the federal system did not occur until the mid-1960s.

In the 1960s and 1970s the Supreme Court became a nationalizing power itself, upholding provisions of the Voting Rights Act of 1965 that called for federal registrars to replace state officials in several southern states. It ordered apportionment of both houses of state legislatures on the basis of population; and it ordered busing to achieve racial integration of public schools where segregation had been imposed by state law.

From 1965 to 1969, federal aid to state and local governments nearly doubled. Under President Lyndon Johnson, more than 200 new grant programs were created. Johnson, who saw himself as a protégé of Franklin D. Roosevelt, wanted to be remembered as the health, education, and welfare president. His War on Poverty program significantly increased the federal presence among the states. In many cases, states were bypassed and aid went directly to cities, counties, school districts, and nonprofit organizations.

By the late 1960s, political scientists were using the term **coercive federalism** to refer to the fact that as the number of federal grants grew, so too did federal rules attached to them. As a result, the national government often was forcing states to comply with regulations that they found unduly restrictive in order to receive federal funds. While the system remained cooperative in many ways, especially in the administration of programs, federal rules dictated how states would act. When state and local governments accepted federal grants, it often skewed their priorities, causing them to ignore more pressing problems in order to do projects for which federal money was available. As we will see later in this chapter, coercion increasingly was accomplished by means of mandates and preemptions that did not include receipt of federal funds.

In the 1968 presidential campaign, Richard Nixon stressed his commitment to return power to the states and to cut administrative red tape. This became known as **new federalism.** It promised more flexibility to states, with block grants and revenue sharing and more money. The value of federal grants doubled from 1970 to 1975. As part of the new federalism program, **revenue sharing** awarded money to state and local governments on the basis of a complicated formula that included population and per capita income. Recipients had broad discretion over how they spent the money. Revenue sharing began in 1972 and ended in 1986. In another move to reduce federal control, the Nixon administration replaced three major categorical grant programs with block grants, which are designed with few strings attached. They are discussed later in this chapter.

The 1970s were marked by several significant changes in intergovernmental relations. We have noted the continued growth of federal grants. Grant eligibility was extended to virtually all local governments and many nonprofit organizations. As a result, by 1980 about 30 percent of all federal aid bypassed state governments, compared with 8 percent in 1960. Federal aid became available for a host of projects (e.g., libraries, historic preservation, snow removal, and development of bikeways) that had previously been state and local responsibilities. Thus state and local reliance on the federal government grew significantly. More procedural strings were attached to grants-in-aid, and more substantive strings were added to block grants. As a result, a coercive federal presence persisted and Nixon's new federalism failed to alter the relative power of the federal governments and the states.

As president, Jimmy Carter spoke of a "new partnership" in referring to intergovernmental relations. This was a return to Johnson's policies and a retreat from Nixon's new federalism. There was a clear shift in federal aid policy in the second half of Carter's term. Carter pulled back from his earlier proposals for expanded federal aid to cities, and the national political mood (as evidenced in "tax revolts" across the country) began to call for cuts in government programs. This shift became a focal point of the Reagan administration.

Under Ronald Reagan's new federalism plan, the first substantial effort was made to reduce the tide of centralization that had been growing since the 1930s. After his first year in office, Reagan cut federal aid to state and local governments by about $6.5 billion. About sixty categorical aid programs were dropped, and more than seventy-seven others were consolidated into block grants. Essentially, the administration sought to retrench by cutting the federal budget and to "devolve" domestic programs back to state and local governments.

At the beginning of his second year in office, President Reagan announced plans to shift most domestic programs to state and local governments by 1990. Reagan's "new" new federalism program, if enacted, would have given the federal system its most dramatic change since the New Deal brought big government to Washington in the 1930s. A key part of Reagan's proposal was a swap in which the federal government would have taken complete responsibility for Medicaid and states would have taken over welfare programs. Both state officials and Congress opposed the swap and it was quickly dropped. States soon assumed the major responsibility for both welfare and Medicaid. While recent reform has helped reduce state welfare expenses, Medicaid costs have soared, leaving some state officials to wish they had accepted Reagan's swap when it was offered.[12]

Despite the abandonment of his comprehensive plan for the federal system, Reagan brought an end to the expansion of federal welfare programs that had begun in the mid-1960s. His policies led to basic changes in federal grants and to welfare reform in 1996.

Another major legacy of the Reagan and Bush administrations was the huge federal debt. Although the federal budget had a deficit every year since 1969, the rate of growth was particularly steep in the 1980s. The size of the debt and the anti-tax sentiment of the Reagan and Bush years made it very difficult to initiate new domestic programs in the 1990s. In response to these financial and political restraints, Congress effected change largely through unfunded mandates that required spending by state and local governments. At the same time, states were willing to fund programs cut by Congress, and they have become more assertive than Congress in dealing with pressing domestic issues, such as health care and environmental protection.

A Devolution Revolution?

As a former governor and personal friend of many sitting governors, President Bill Clinton was expected to identify closely with the intergovernmental problems faced by states. During his first year in office President Clinton met frequently with state and local officials, and he placed Vice President Al Gore in charge of a review of relations between the federal government and the states. In his 1996 State of the Union Address, President Clinton seemed to align himself with the **"devolution revolution"** when he stated, "The era of big government is over." This policy of voluntary transfers of power and programs from the national government to state and local governments was an extension of the new federalism approach begun under President Nixon.

Although President Clinton issued an executive order on unfunded mandates shortly after he took office, he found mandates and preemptions (coercive federalism) convenient ways to support his domestic programs when the federal deficit made it difficult to find additional funding. For example, the Handgun Violence Prevention Act of 1993 (the Brady Act) requires local law-enforcement officers to conduct background checks on handgun purchasers, but it does not provide any money to cover the added expense. That provision was struck down by the Supreme Court. The Americans with Disabilities Act of 1993 requires state and local governments to make all new and renovated facilities accessible to the disabled, but it is an underfunded mandate that provides only part of the cost of compliance.

Vice President Gore's National Performance Review (NPR) proposed more than 100 recommendations for change in federal-state relations in 1993. The broad goals of the NPR sounded a definite "reinventing government" theme (see Chapter 6) that included "cutting red tape, putting customers first, empowering employees to get results, cutting back to basics."[13] The NPR noted, "In a perfect world, we would consolidate the 600 federal grant programs into broad funding pools, organized around major goals and desired outcomes—for example, safe and secure communities."

The NPR called for improved management and performance with federal monitoring of states and more state flexibility. But it did not envision a basic restructuring of intergovernmental relations.[14] In fact, the number of categorical grants increased in 1993–94, and proposals were made by the president to expand the federal role in areas such as health care and education. This haphazard reform, which also occurred under President Bush, is referred to by David B. Walker, who served on the U.S. Advisory Commission on Intergovernmental Relations, as "slouching toward Washington."[15]

During the 1994 congressional election campaign, public support for devolution grew and the Republican Party's Contract With America supported several changes, including reform of unfunded mandates (the first item). The newly elected Republican majority in Congress acted quickly to devolve much more power to the states than had occurred under President Reagan in the 1980s. An early Republican plan would have consolidated nearly 350 existing programs into ten broad block grants. Had that been approved, it would have brought about a true "devolution revolution." Still, Congress approved and Clinton signed into law several significant measures, beginning with the Unfunded Mandates Act (1995) and including a package of block grants plus welfare reform in 1996. Mandate reform will be discussed later in this chapter and welfare reform is discussed in detail in Chapter 10.

Evaluating the Clinton administration's reinventing government programs, federalism expert John Kincaid concluded that it produced little increased discretion for state and local governments.[16] Although cooperation continued between the states and the federal government, Kincaid suggested that it was "under conditions often dictated by Congress and presidents."[17] Thus the era of coercive, or regulatory, federalism continued.

Later in this chapter we will look at mandates, preemptions, and conditions attached to federal grants. All of them have been used recently at historically high levels by Congress and the president to regulate state governments.

Waivers of federal regulations for welfare policy by the Clinton administration did permit state experimentation, but rules attached to the major welfare reform program, Temporary Assistance for Needy Families (TANF), have meant that devolution has delivered less than expected.[18] The Unfunded Mandates Reform Act slowed mandates, but Congress has continued to attach them to legislation.

Like President Clinton, President Bush, as a former governor, philosophically supports devolution of power to the states. He supports block grants and has placed several former governors in top administration positions. However, Bush's education program, the No Child Left Behind Act, supports *more* federal intervention in setting standards for curriculum, testing, and teacher qualifications than was made in any other proposals since President Lyndon B. Johnson. The 2001 federal tax cut, as noted in Chapter 1, hurt those states whose tax systems were tied to the federal system. And preoccupation with fighting terrorism and the war in Iraq have resulted in making federalism issues a low priority for the Bush administration.

In 2006, John Kincaid noted, "Although state-activism generates a kind of competitive state-federal federalism, coercive federalism is the system's dominant motif."[19] Most academics believe that under President Bush, who does not have a defined federalism agenda, there has been the greatest expansion of federal involvement in areas traditionally controlled by the states since the 1960s. Beyond law enforcement and education, this includes support by President Bush and social conservatives in Congress for national legislation that would override state laws that are supportive of a right to abortion, same-sex marriage, the medical use of marijuana, and the right to end one's life. This is a reversal of the historical roles of liberals and conservatives in which liberals favored the use of federal power to achieve social goals and conservatives opposed it.

In several states, liberals have succeeded in enacting legislation to protect Medicaid, clean up the environment, equalize school aid, raise the minimum wage, fund sex education and stem cell research, and support end-of-life decisions. Richard P. Nathan, who helped develop President Nixon's new federalism program, says there will always be a "new federalism."[20] The newest new federalism supports a liberal, or progressive, agenda with activist state government leading the way to support change. Nathan notes that state-level spending has grown steadily since 1980 and, as a percentage of gross domestic product (GDP), federal domestic spending has fallen.[21] Since 2001, the federal and state-local shares have been about equal—now each is about 18 percent of GDP. The growing state share is an indication, says Nathan, of "liberals on the march."

As we will see in the following section, even after more than a decade of Supreme Court decisions that often have supported the states against the federal government, the devolution picture as framed in Court opinions is far from clear.

SUPREME COURT FEDERALISM SINCE THE 1970s

Federalism cases, involving interpretation of the historically obscure Tenth and Eleventh Amendments, may not seem very exciting when compared to more controversial cases on abortion or criminal rights that regularly are decided by the Supreme Court. But since the 1990s, the Supreme Court has become strongly polarized in a series of 5–4 opinions that brought federalism to the forefront of constitutional issues. As a result, the Court placed states outside the reach of several federal laws.

As noted earlier, the Tenth Amendment reserves to states all powers not specifically granted to the national government or prohibited to the states. It has been resurrected from its earlier obscurity to serve as the legal basis for striking down federal laws that the Court majority believes interfere with powers reserved to the states. The **Eleventh Amendment** prohibits suits against states by citizens of another state. Recently, it has been interpreted to shield states from being sued by their citizens in federal and state courts for alleged violations of federal law.

Since the mid-1970s, the Supreme Court has decided several significant cases involving interpretation of the Tenth Amendment. In *National League of Cities v. Usery* (1976) the Court overturned congressional action that had extended federal minimum wage and overtime provisions to state and local government employees. Citing the Tenth Amendment, the Court held that federal laws could not impinge on traditional state functions. After struggling to define "traditional state functions," the Court reversed itself in *Garcia v. San Antonio Metropolitan Area Transit Authority* (1985), stating that "the Constitution does not carve out express elements of state sovereignty that Congress may not employ its delegated powers to displace." Although *Garcia* has not been overruled, the Court often has ignored it in decisions since the early 1990s that limit federal authority.

When Congress passed the National Minimum Drinking Age Act in 1985, it included a provision that states would get reductions in federal highway funds if they did not raise the legal age for purchasing alcoholic beverages to 21. This was challenged as a violation of the Twenty-first Amendment (repeal of Prohibition), which some constitutional scholars contended returned absolute control of alcoholic beverages to the states. In *South Dakota v. Dole* (1987) the Supreme Court held that, even though Congress lacked the authority to raise the drinking age, it could attach an age requirement to a grant proposal because state participation was voluntary. To others it seemed coercive because states could not afford to give up sizable federal revenue. Although South Dakota would have lost $8 million in 1988, Texas would have forfeited $100 million in highway aid. All states raised their drinking age to 21. In dissent, Justice Sandra Day O'Connor believed the legislation violated the Twenty-first Amendment, and she stated that the drinking age was not "sufficiently related to highway construction to justify conditioning funds appropriated for that purpose." This was the last time Justice O'Connor found herself in the minority in a major federalism decision.

Using a "state autonomy" argument based on the Tenth Amendment and the Constitution's guarantee to the states of a "republican form of government," O'Connor authored the Court's opinion in *Gregory v. Ashcroft* (1991), upholding a mandatory retirement age for judges in Missouri, despite the federal Age Discrimination in Employment Act. In another approach to the Tenth Amendment, the Court in *New York v. United States* (1992) struck down a federal law governing the disposal of radioactive waste. In that opinion Justice O'Connor noted that the federal government could not "commandeer" the states "into the service of Federal regulatory purposes." The commandeering or conscription argument was used by the Supreme Court to strike down the provisions of the Brady gun-control law that required local sheriffs to perform background checks on would-be gun purchasers. In *Printz v. United States* (1997) the Court extended its prohibition on commandeering beyond federally mandated policy to a statute that obligated state law enforcement officials to "make a reasonable effort" to determine if pending gun purchases would be illegal.

In *United States v. Lopez* (1995) a five-person majority for the first time since 1936 overturned a federal law on the ground that it exceeded the Constitution's grant of authority to Congress to regulate interstate commerce. In *Lopez* the Court declared unconstitutional the Gun-Free School Zones Act of 1990 that made it a federal crime to possess a gun in close proximity to a school. The majority held that this was the responsibility of states, noting that many states already had approved gun-free zones around schools and that the law had "nothing to do with commerce." With Justice Clarence Thomas now on the Court, a definite shift occurred as conservatives had a majority on most issues, including federalism. In *United States v. Morrison* (2000) the Court invalidated a provision of the Violence Against Women Act as an overreach of the commerce clause. Here Congress had based the law on the idea that violence against women has effects on the nation's economy.

Employing yet another pro–states' rights strategy, in 1996 the Supreme Court turned to the obscure Eleventh Amendment to strike down part of the Indian Gaming Regulatory Act, which set terms by which Indian tribes could conduct gambling on their reservations. Despite the nearly complete power Congress has to control Indian affairs, the decision in *Seminole Tribe v. Florida* (1986) overturned part of a federal law that permitted Indian tribes to sue states to bring them to the bargaining table over terms to open casinos. Four years later, in *Kimel v. Florida Board of Regents,* the Court ruled that states could not be sued in federal court by state employees who claimed they were victims of age discrimination.

The same concept of states' **sovereign immunity,** protection against lawsuits without their consent, was used to prevent private parties from suing states for monetary damages under the Americans with Disabilities Act (*Board of Trustees of the University of Alabama v. Garrett,* 2001). And in *Federal Maritime Commission v. South Carolina* (2002), the Court held that sovereign immunity under the Eleventh Amendment means that state governments are not subject to the jurisdiction of the Federal Maritime Commission. Justice Thomas argued that the opinion upheld the "dignity" of the states as dual sovereigns with the federal government.

In a series of decisions from 1995 to 2005, the Court's "Federalism Five"—Justices O'Connor, Rehnquist, Scalia, Kennedy, and Thomas—frequently prevailed in 5–4 opinions that supported states' rights by striking down laws passed by Congress that had expanded federal authority. Linda Greenhouse, who reports on the Supreme Court for the *New York Times,* observed that often the majority seemed more concerned about the balance of power between Congress and the Court than between states and the federal government.[22] Greenhouse suggested that, contrary to popular belief, the Court's actions should be viewed more as waging "war" on Congress than as supporting a "devolution revolution."

The same 5–4 majority that had been ruling in favor of state governments in federalism cases overruled the Florida supreme court's interpretation of its state's law in *Bush v. Gore* in 2000. That decision, handed down thirty-five days after election day, ended the recount and, in effect, gave the election to Bush. The U.S. Supreme Court rejected the option of remanding the case to the Florida supreme court and then waiting to see if the manual recount of votes could be completed within the specified time of six days. By intervening the Court also removed Congress from ruling in what might have been defined as a political dispute.

Members of the "Federalism Five" did not always vote as a block in federalism cases, and, as a result, the Court ruled against the exercise of state power in several high-profile cases and consistently ruled against states in challenges to federal preemptions. For example, in the 2000–2001 term the Court struck down a Massachusetts law that regulated the advertising of tobacco products, by upholding a federal law that preempts state laws on that issue. In 2003 the Court held that provisions of the Family Medical Leave Act apply to state employees, and in 2004 in a 5–4 opinion it upheld the power of Congress to subject states to lawsuits under the Americans with Disabilities Act *(Tennessee v. Lane)*. In 2005 the Court upheld the power of Congress to enforce the Controlled Substances Act's ban on the medical use of marijuana in California and the other nine states that permitted such use.

In several cases decided in 2000 and 2003 the Court seemed to say that any state activity that touches foreign affairs, such as banning state agencies from doing business with a particular foreign country, is presumed to be preempted by federal authority.

In *Gonzales v. Oregon* (2006) the Court voted 6–3 that former Attorney General John Ashcroft had acted without legal authority when he ruled in 2001 that physicians would lose their federal prescription-writing privileges if they prescribed lethal doses of medication under Oregon's Death with Dignity law. The opinion stated that Ashcroft had acted "contrary to the background principles of our federal system." However, it did not directly address the constitutionality of Oregon's law, focusing instead on the attorney general's interpretation of the Controlled Substances Act of 1970. Also in 2006 the Court held 5–4 that states are not immune from private lawsuits under federal bankruptcy laws. Chief Justice Roberts dissented in both cases, and Justice O'Connor voted with the majority in two of her last opinions before leaving the Court.

John Kincaid argued in 2005 that since 2001 the Supreme Court had not advanced the state-friendly federalism position that started in 1991. This held true through the 2005–2006 term as the "Roberts conservative Court" was put on hold. Curiously, in *Gonzales v. Oregon* it was the Court's liberal members who supported the state of Oregon, while the conservatives backed the use of national power. Of course, this was another example of how liberals and conservatives view socially conservative issues.

The headline for *New York Times* reporter Linda Greenhouse's annual review of Supreme Court decisions for 2006–2007—the first full year with both John Roberts (as Chief Justice) and Samuel Alito (replacing Sandra Day O'Connor) on the Court—was "In Steps Big and Small the Supreme Court Moved Right." In Chapter 7 we will see how the Court moved to the political right in criminal cases. Although there were few federalism cases in 2006–2007, one major opinion stands out. In *Parents Involved in Community Schools v. Seattle School District, No. 1* (this decision was decided together with a similar case from Louisville, Kentucky), the Supreme Court voted 5–4 to limit the use of race in a voluntary school assignment plan for the purpose of preventing resegregation. The opinion, written by Roberts, stated that the school district had not shown that there was a compelling state interest in creating racial balance in schools and therefore the plan was unconstitutional. An effect of the decision was that the former Federalism Five, now including Roberts and Alito, scaled back the power of local officials to determine school policy. Once again, the Court's conservative bloc supported national over local authority and the effect was to support a policy goal favored by political conservatives.

FEDERAL-STATE FUNDING ARRANGEMENTS

The evolution of American federalism shows that the nation has moved from separate levels of government, acting almost as sovereign entities, to levels of government that interact and cooperate in an increasingly interdependent system. Intergovernmental relations involve interactions between the federal government and the states, between states, and between states and their localities.

Grants-in-Aid

The bulk of assistance that the national government provides to states is in the form of **grants-in-aid.** These payments made to states and localities have been central to the system of cooperative federalism. They have helped lead to increased national power since the 1960s because of the large number of grants and the regulations attached to most of them. As a result **fiscal federalism,** by which the federal government threatens to withhold grants if states do not comply with regulations attached to grants, is at the center of intergovernmental relations and enables Congress to exert considerable influence over the states. For example, the threat of withholding funds from the states allowed Congress to set such national standards as the 55 mph speed limit and led to increasing the legal age for drinking alcoholic beverages. These so-called crossover sanctions give Congress substantial power over the states. Despite concerns about devolving power, since the 1960s Congress has continued to increase conditions attached to grants.

One argument for increased federal involvement in traditional state and local activities has been that it provides a degree of national uniformity (in the form of minimal standards) in a system divided by interstate competition. Also, because of great differences in state wealth, spending for such programs as education and public assistance varies greatly from one part of the country to another. Federal aid can make things more equal and provide more nearly uniform benefits by transferring money from rich states to poor states (the "Robin Hood effect"). As a result, the federal grants-in-aid program has provided a politically acceptable way of providing needed money to state and local governments while keeping the formal structure of federalism.

Increasingly in the 1950s and 1960s, both state and local governments were faced with pressing demands to solve social problems at a time when their financial base was either dwindling or expanding only a little. Cities often found state legislatures unwilling or unable to come to their aid. As a result, they turned directly to Congress for help. Congress responded to cities and states by greatly expanding the grants-in-aid programs already existing while keeping state and local administration of government programs. Grants provide the means by which the federal government exerts some effect on state

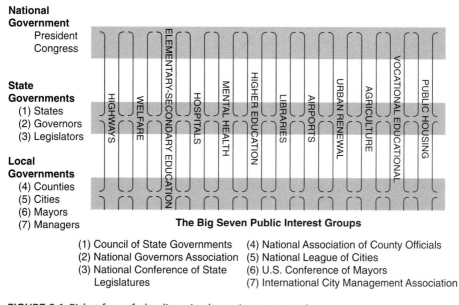

National Government
President
Congress

State Governments
(1) States
(2) Governors
(3) Legislators

Local Governments
(4) Counties
(5) Cities
(6) Mayors
(7) Managers

The Big Seven Public Interest Groups

(1) Council of State Governments
(2) National Governors Association
(3) National Conference of State Legislatures
(4) National Association of County Officials
(5) National League of Cities
(6) U.S. Conference of Mayors
(7) International City Management Association

FIGURE 2-1 Picket fence federalism: A schematic representation.

Source: Deil Wright, *Understanding Intergovernmental Relations,* 3rd ed. (Brooks/Cole, Pacific Grove, Calif.: 1988), p. 63.

programs without taking over the entire function and removing it from state or local control. Grants have been maintained and expanded even in the face of budget deficits.

Grants also have been supported by alliances of bureaucrats (program specialists) at the national, state, and local levels of government. At each level, bureaucrats have a self-interest in the continuation of programs. These ties that run between levels of government have classically been described and diagrammed by political scientist Deil S. Wright as **picket fence federalism** (see Figure 2-1).[23] The interrelationships often lead to situations in which local bureaucrats become closely tied to their federal counterparts and resist control by locally elected officials. However, national administrators seldom "order" their state counterparts to make specific decisions. The vertical pickets in Figure 2-1 refer only to very broad categories. Wright says there are over 500 pickets, plus at least another 500 nonmonetary technical assistance programs. Often the pickets are in competition with each other for federal and state funding.

Grants-in-aid are by no means new. They began with the Land Ordinance Act of 1785, which provided land grants for public schools in the developing Western territory. Early grants did not have conditions attached to acceptance. Throughout the nineteenth century, grants were made available for railroads and canals. However, they did not become politically significant until after World War II. In 1950, federal grants to state and local governments amounted to only $2 billion annually. By 1970, there were 530 grants-in-aid programs paying out about $24 billion every year. In spite of President Nixon's campaign oratory about decentralizing government, about 100 grant programs were created by the Nixon and Ford administrations. The federal grant program continued to increase sharply under the Carter administration.

In fiscal 1982, federal grants had their first absolute decline in more than twenty-five years. As noted, this was consistent with President Reagan's desire to cut federal spending and reduce government regulation. However, total grants-in-aid outlays doubled in the 1990s. Still, as a percentage of all state revenues, money from the federal government remained steady at about 25 percent through the 1990s, after dropping to the low 20s in the 1980s. Local governments received about 4 percent of their revenue in the 1980s from federal grants, down from nearly 15 percent in the late 1970s.

While total aid to state and local governments increased during President George W. Bush's first term, federal aid as a percentage of total revenues declined. By 2006, states were receiving 22 percent of their revenues from the national government. For fiscal year 2007, the Bush administration proposed cutting or reducing more than 140 domestic discretionary programs. Under the Bush administration, federal aid has shifted significantly from places to people. Nearly two-thirds of aid now is in the form of social welfare that goes directly to individuals. Place aid—for infrastructure, education, and economic development—has decreased sharply.[24] This means that states and cities often are treated just like other interest groups seeking funds from the federal government. Indeed, local governments often are encouraged to hire Washington lobbyists to contact their U.S. representatives.

Grants have become increasingly coercive as Congress uses "conditions of aid" to force states and cities to spend more to help achieve federal objectives and to set standards for states to meet. The No Child Left Behind Act, with its costly testing and performance standards, has been especially troublesome to states (see Chapter 10).

Crosscutting requirements and crossover sanctions are other ways in which federal aid is coercive. **Crosscutting requirements** are applied to all federal grants as conditions of acceptance. For example, states must prepare environmental impact assessments to receive most federal grants. **Crossover sanctions** require recipients to pass certain laws as conditions of acceptance. For example, to receive federal highway funds, states must have a drinking age of twenty-one. As we will see later in this chapter, coercion also is applied by the use of mandates and preemptions.

As reported in *Governing's State & Local Sourcebook 2007,* the states receiving the highest per capita federal aid in 2005 were Wyoming ($5,373) and Alaska ($3,849). New York was third with $2,366 and the District of Columbia received $4,836 per capita. Only two states received less than $1,000 per capita, Virginia ($917) and Nevada ($929). Among the other states there was relatively little variation (the national average was $1,478), and no clear regional differences in amount of aid can be seen.

There are several ways in which the federal government sends money to the states, and some ways give states more control than others. **Categorical grants** are made for specific purposes, such as job training, highway safety, prevention of juvenile delinquency, and agricultural extension. The recipient of such a grant has little choice about how the money is to be spent, so the federal government retains more control.

Block grants are provided for general categories of expenditures. They allow greater choice by the recipient, and they reduce or end matching requirements. For example, Community Development Small Cities Block Grants create a "package" of grants to deal with a series of problems previously covered by separate, categorical grants. Block grants began in the last year of the Nixon administration as a means of lessening the requirements attached to categorical grants. Recipients had more administrative control over programs, but they got less money. As noted earlier, block grants were a central part of President Reagan's new federalism program. Initially Reagan sought to combine over 100 categorical grants into block grants, but he settled for a plan that combined fifty-seven categorical grants in nine block grants. Some sixty other categorical grants were eliminated.

The Clinton administration consolidated several categorical grants into block grants in the 1990s. The best-known example was the Welfare Reform Act of 1996 that ended AFDC and replaced it with a block grant. (This will be discussed in Chapter 10.) A study by Chung-Lea Cho and Deil Wright found that there was more evolution than revolution in federal-state relations in the 1990s, as levels of perceived national intrusiveness among local officials remained high in the 1990s.[25]

When George W. Bush became president, he initially set out to find ways to lessen the strings attached to categorical grants. But much of his domestic program was side-tracked by the war on terrorism. What was enacted, such as the No Child Left Behind Act, often increased federal control over states and localities.

While members of Congress like to talk about giving more power and flexibility to states and localities, the number of block grants has remained stable—about twenty-five—for many years. In large part, this is because members of Congress like to take credit when categorical grants are awarded to governments and private institutions within their districts. With hundreds of grants available, each member can be assured that there will be many photo opportunities available when new buildings, roads, or educational programs are initiated in his or her district. Paul L. Posner notes that increasingly the relationship between members of Congress and elected state and local officials is not one of allies, but of competitors seeking "money, visibility, and votes."[26] In 2006 there were ten former governors in Congress and more than half the House members had served in state legislatures. But this didn't make them particularly state-friendly.

Beginning with Jimmy Carter in 1972, four of the last five presidents have been governors. With each new administration there was early optimism that the president would push programs to give states more power, but in each case the results were largely disappointing to the states.

Another way of categorizing grants is according to their terms for distribution. **Formula grants** are distributed automatically to all eligible recipients on the basis of established guidelines. For example, a formula grant in a highway bill might provide for funds to be distributed on the basis of the number of miles of highway in a state. Controversy with this type of grant involves what formula should be used.

When Congress creates **project grants** it makes funds available for a specific purpose, and state or local governments must apply to the agency in charge of administering the grant to get approval. This introduces competition among potential recipients, and it may be that governments with the ability to write the best proposals are the ones that are funded. As a result, "grantsmanship"—knowing what grants are available and how best to complete the application forms—may determine who gets the money.

More recently, combined **formula/project grants** have been developed. These grants are competitive, but they also are based on a formula. For example, only so much money may be awarded to a state or region.

A balance sheet evaluating the grants-in-aid system would contain the following advantages and disadvantages:

Advantages	Disadvantages
1. Provide funds needed by state and local governments.	1. Large number and complexity of grants imposes administrative burdens on recipients and leads to the development of large bureaucracies.
2. Help equalize resources in rich and poor states.	2. Uncoordinated grants often overlap or are at odds with one another.
3. Encourage local initiative and experimentation.	3. They discourage local initiative and distort planning by directing attention to available grants rather than proposing solutions for problems in fields not covered by grants.
4. Are based on the progressive tax structure of the federal government.	4. Duration of grants is often too long or too short.
5. Can concentrate attention in a problem area and provide valuable technical assistance.	5. They encourage "grantsmanship"—the ability to fill out the forms in a way that pleases federal officials.
6. Allow introduction into the federal system of national values and standards.	6. Categorical grants leave little room for state and local discretion regarding expenditures and require increased federal supervision. Local elected officials have little control of the programs.

Although states have the option of *not* participating in the grants-in-aid programs, there is strong pressure to take advantage of the opportunity to get programs for half cost or less. This, in turn, places a great financial burden on states (particularly poor ones) to earmark much of their discretionary money as matching funds for grants-in-aid. This fiscal federalism also puts strong pressure (some would say coercion) on the states to comply with federal regulations. Earlier we said that states were pressured by Congress into raising the drinking age to 21.

Let us now look at the *economic rationales* that support the entire grants-in-aid system. As noted, it is easier to raise revenue at the national level than at the state and local levels because the federal tax structure is more elastic than that of the state and local governments. Federal revenues rise in direct proportion to overall economic growth in the United States. As a result, federal revenue expands greatly without any increase in tax rates. In contrast, state and local taxes are less elastic; they do not respond well to economic growth. Thus city councils and state legislatures must create new taxes or raise existing tax rates to get added funds necessary to respond to their constituents' demands for more services. In addition, federal taxes are more progressive than state and local taxes. (Chapter 9 deals more specifically with state and local financing.)

A second economic rationale for grants-in-aid is what some observers refer to as **spillover benefits.** This means that the benefits obtained from a program administered in one government area may extend into other government areas. Thus it seems fair that all who benefit should share in the cost. Education is an example of how spillover benefits work. If a person educated in New York or New Jersey, where per capita spending is far greater than the national average, moves to a state such as Tennessee, where per capita spending for education is lower, the second state benefits from educational programs for which it has not paid. Federal grants that support education make certain that all states share in the cost of any single program by the national government.

An additional benefit of federal grants is that they have helped reduce corruption by requiring review of state and local financial records by federal auditors. A final economic rationale is that grants reduce unnecessary administrative expense by requiring recipients to improve their administrative structures.

Regarding *political expediency,* it may be easier to mount a national campaign for a mixed federal-state program than to manage campaigns throughout the fifty states. Labor, for example, has its membership centered in about one-third of the states. It therefore has little effect in many of the other state capitals. Yet labor's strong influence in urban, industrial states gives it a great deal of bargaining power with Congress and the president. Because there are so many categorical grants, all congressional districts receive some federal assistance, allowing members of Congress to claim credit for helping their constituents. This is a major reason why most incumbents get reelected.

More and more, traditional state and local political problems can be viewed as having national implications. With an interdependent economy, including transportation and communications systems, most problems do not have a purely local impact. As a result, the federal system involves plans in which federal and state officials join in fighting such problems as air pollution and urban decay. Federal grants allow Congress to form national objectives, which are put into effect through cooperation between federal officials and state and local governments. Such grants also have been an effective way for strong presidents, such as Franklin D. Roosevelt and Lyndon Johnson, to centralize their political aims.

Federal Mandates and Preemptions

Federal mandates are legal orders from Congress or administrative agencies that require state or local governments to perform a certain activity or to provide a service. Condition-of-aid provisions in categorical grants can be avoided by states and localities by simply not applying for the grant, but mandates legally cannot be avoided, and they can be enforced in court. Nearly all mandates in United States history have been enacted since 1969.

A mandate problem began to occur in the late 1980s because of the cumulative effect of an increased number of mandates since the mid-1960s and because an increasing percentage of mandates were unfunded. Cities got a double hit from mandates imposed by Congress and by state legislatures. In addition, some federal mandates were placed on states that, in turn, passed them through to local governments. Environmental mandates have placed especially heavy financial burdens on states and localities. Mandates are appealing to members of Congress and presidents because in times of budget deficits they allow the federal government to impose its objectives without spending money.

Two bills passed by Congress in 1993 show the financial impact of mandates on state and local governments. First, the Family and Medical Leave Act requires private and public employers with fifty or more employees to allow up to twelve weeks of unpaid leave in any twelve-month period. Second, the National Voter Registration Act ("Motor-Voter Bill") mandates that state and local governments establish procedures to permit voter registration where individuals apply for drivers' licenses or by mail. It also permits, but doesn't require, state and local governments to use offices that provide public assistance, unemployment compensation, and services to the disabled at voter registration locations. As noted earlier, a mandate in the Brady Handgun Control Act, also passed in 1993, was struck down by the Supreme Court.

Unfunded mandates were the biggest source of conflict between states and the federal government in the 1980s. By the early 1990s, nearly twenty pieces of federal legislation imposed mandates on states and localities. In response to widespread criticism from state officials about mandates, President Clinton issued an executive order on unfunded mandates that provided limited relief to states soon after taking office. Mandate reform was part of the Republican Party's Contract with America in 1994. Soon after gaining control of Congress in the 1994 elections, the Unfunded Mandates Reform Act of 1995 was passed with broad support among Republicans and Democrats. This legislation forced Congress to define the costs and vote on individual mandates, but it did not prohibit Congress from imposing new mandates, nor did it apply to existing legislation or to bills, such as the Clean Water Act, when they come up for reauthorization. New mandates that will cost the states more than $50 million must be approved by majority vote in both the House and Senate.

The Unfunded Mandates Reform Act has not prevented Congress from imposing many new mandates, although only five intergovernmental mandates with costs above $50 million were enacted from 1995 through 2005. New mandates have been less demanding and less expensive than before 1995. The most recent mandate that seriously irked states was the Real ID law of 2005. It was intended to make it more difficult for terrorists to obtain driver's licenses and for people without proper identification to board planes and enter federal buildings. At issue for states is the cost of meeting a 2008 deadline to use sources such as birth certificates and national immigration databases to verify that people are citizens or legal residents before issuing them driver's licenses. The New Hampshire legislature overwhelmingly passed a bill to opt out of Real ID, citing both costs and privacy issues.[27]

In addition to mandates, restraints, and restrictions in federal grants, **preemption** is another means of federal intervention into state and local affairs. Here Congress nullifies certain state and local laws totally or partially in order to assert its own control over a policy area. Congress enacted only thirty preemption statutes before 1900, and the number remained low until the mid-1960s. From 1965 through 2004 Congress enacted 356 preemptions.[28]

Congress passed an increasing number of regulatory laws after 1965 that often included preemptions, especially in dealing with air and water pollution, In many cases, interest groups that were unsuccessful at the state level turned to Congress for protection against state regulation. For example, Joseph Zimmerman notes that the motor vehicle industry lobbied successfully for Congress to completely preempt state regulatory power over safety equipment when it passed the National Traffic and Motor Vehicle

Safety Act of 1966. The Clean Air Act of 1967 totally preempts state regulation of motor vehicle emissions. California, with its large House membership, was able to negotiate an exemption from this provision.

To illustrate the complexity of preemptions, Zimmerman identifies eighteen subtypes of complete preemptions and twelve subtypes of partial preemptions. The situation is further complicated by "contingent" preemptions that come into effect only under certain conditions. Often the line between preemptions and mandates is unclear. What is technically a preemption, for example, forbidding state taxation of Internet access, also is a form of mandate with a financial impact on states.[29]

Although federal aid as a percentage of all state and local expenditures has declined from an all-time high in 1978, the federal government actually has become *more* intrusive in state and local affairs. This is due to the increase in mandates and preemptions plus the fact, as noted, that federal aid increasingly has bypassed state and local governments to go directly to individuals. Earlier we noted the strong tendency of the Supreme Court in recent years to support federal preemptions.

HORIZONTAL FEDERALISM: INTERSTATE COOPERATION

As noted earlier, relations among states are confederal, meaning that states must negotiate with each other as political equals.

The U.S. Constitution attempts to encourage cooperation among the states in the following ways:

1. States are to give "**full faith and credit** . . . to the public acts, records, and judicial proceedings of every other state." This clause requires a state to recognize the validity of actions among private citizens, such as a contract for sale of property, which originate in another state. In the area of domestic relations—divorce, child custody, alimony—the situation is complicated by state refusal on occasion to accept as binding civil judgments of other states. Recent same-sex marriages and civil unions performed in several states raise the question of whether the full faith and credit clause should make them binding in other states.

2. States are to extend to residents of other states all "**privileges and immunities**" granted their own residents, meaning they must extend the same legal rights to residents of other states that are enjoyed by their own residents. This includes allowing residents of one state to acquire property, enter into contracts, and have access to the courts in a second state. It does not include the extension of political rights such as voting and jury service. The Supreme Court has held that some kinds of discrimination against nonresidents, such as charging them higher tuition at state universities and higher hunting and fishing fees, does not violate the privileges and immunities clause.

3. The interstate rendition clause requires states to return to another state fugitives who have fled from justice. It is the governor who signs **extradition** papers to deliver a fugitive to the state having jurisdiction over the criminal act. Although governors usually comply with requests for extradition, the Supreme Court during the Civil War ruled that this was a matter of executive discretion and that a governor may refuse to deliver a fugitive upon request from another state. More recently the

Court held that states must return fugitives. In 1934, Congress made it a federal crime to cross state lines to avoid prosecution or imprisonment.

4. States may enter into **interstate compacts,** which are formal agreements among states to cooperate in solving a common problem. They must be approved by the U.S. Senate. There has been only one case in which congressional approval of a proposed interstate compact was denied. A state cannot withdraw from a compact unless the other-party states agree. The provisions of compacts take precedence over any state laws that conflict with their provisions.

The most significant use of interstate compacts has developed since World War II. Only thirty-six compacts were created between 1783 and 1920, most dealing with boundary disputes between states.[30] Since then, states have enacted over 160 compacts and many old compacts have been updated. Compacts deal with the management of problems that cross state lines, such as transportation, environmental protection, taxes, and health care. In recent years there has been a decline in the number of compacts enacted, but an increase in interstate administrative agreements. The latter are entered into by administrative officials as a way to improve interstate cooperation in areas such as criminal identification and motor vehicle law enforcement.

The best-known interstate compact is the Port Authority of New York, established in 1920 between New York and New Jersey. The Port Authority controls much of the transportation in greater New York City. It manages marine terminals and tunnels, leases airports, and is responsible for the rapid transit system.

Beginning with the Delaware Basin Commission in 1961, the federal government has joined with states—here Delaware, New York, New Jersey, and Pennsylvania—in "federal-interstates." More than thirty compacts are open to participation nationwide, and others are organized on a regional basis. An example of a compact open to all fifty states is the Interstate Compact on Juveniles that currently is being considered by state legislatures and has been approved by over half the states. It permits youth offenders to transfer their supervision from one state to another. Although the growth of interstate compacts has slowed, new compacts have been formed since 1980 dealing with such areas as hazardous waste and natural resources management. In most instances, compacts are viewed as a way to improve problem solving without involving the federal government.

States also cooperate by exchanging information. An ever-growing number of associations—governors, attorneys general, welfare officials, lieutenant governors— hold regular conferences. Many of these organizations are associated with the Council of State Governments, which provides a framework of organization and also publishes materials (including *The Book of the States*) on a wide range of state government issues. State and local police cooperate with each other and with the FBI in the exchange of information regarding criminals. Some states have developed reciprocal programs in higher education. For example, residents of northwestern Ohio can attend Eastern Michigan University and pay Michigan in-state tuition. In turn, residents of southeastern Michigan can attend the University of Toledo and pay Ohio in-state tuition.

In spite of the availability of formal means of cooperation, interstate relations often are marked by *competition* and *conflict,* rather than by accommodation. In the field of taxation, states sometimes cite their low tax rates as a means of luring businesses from other states. Increasingly, environmental issues are causing interstate conflict. These include disposal of hazardous waste, dumping of pollutants in waterways, and acid rain in New England that is caused by air pollution in the Midwest.

Although there is greater uniformity in state laws now than there was in the mid-twentieth century, significant differences in areas such as child support remain. Even though legislators and attorneys general attend regular conferences, and even though the National Conference of the Commissioners on Uniform Law has existed since 1892, there remains a significant lack of uniformity in commercial law. Differences also exist in divorce laws, legal marriage age, and voting residency requirements. At one time, California legislators attempted (unsuccessfully) to bar paupers from moving into their state. In 1999 the Supreme Court rejected a California plan to limit first-year residents to the welfare benefits they would have received had they stayed in their former states. Truckers are confronted with a variety of state rules regulating lights, load limits, and licensing as they travel cross-country. One might expect that in a "reasonable" system such confusion would have been eliminated by now. However, in the name of federalism, Americans continue to support state and local autonomy and are therefore willing to live with the inconveniences that inevitably result.

STATE-LOCAL RELATIONS

As seen, states and cities in the United States exist in a unitary relationship. Thus, unlike the federal government's relations with the states, each state can coerce its cities to comply with policy objectives. While states often can resist national directives, local governments are legally bound to follow state policy. This is especially true regarding finances. In most cases, forms of local taxation are set by state legislatures, as well as rates of increase. Local borrowing limits are established, and in a few states entire city budgets must be approved by a state agency. Increased state financial control began in the 1930s when local governments were overwhelmed by the effects of the Depression. More recently, state financial control has come in the form of measures aimed at reducing taxes at the state and local level. As noted in Chapter 1, many states, especially in the South, have constitutions that spell out in detail what local governments can do. Legislatures that meet annually and in fairly long sessions have more time to devote to local matters.

There are many more state mandates to local governments than there are federal mandates to the states. And some expensive federal mandates are passed on to localities by states. Many mandates are enacted to promote uniformity across the state, and there is general agreement that they are beneficial. For example, the length of the public school year and the permissible number of bad-weather days off generate little controversy. Problems arise because local governments may disagree with the goals of state legislators and, like the states' reactions to federal mandates, they object to the cost imposed on them to implement the programs. Whenever one level of government can push a costly responsibility down to another level, it nearly always does so.

As in Congress, a majority of states have enacted laws restricting mandates by requiring extramajority votes in the legislature or, as in California and New Hampshire, requiring the state to pay the full cost of mandates. Still, as in Congress, although the number of unfunded mandates has declined, they are far from being eliminated.

As in Congress, state legislatures also preempt and prohibit local governments from taking certain actions. Preemptions are especially prevalent in the areas of smoking bans, rent control, and gun control. Tobacco interests often have successfully pressured legislatures to enact state clean-indoor-air regulations that are less stringent than city ordinances. In about a dozen states the National Rifle Association has succeeded in getting legislatures to prohibit cities from suing gun makers to recover the costs of gun-related violence.

Although state legislators criticize federal control of states, both Republican and Democratic legislators resist turning over political power to cities and counties, in part because business groups (refer to preemptions) prefer to deal with one government rather than fight battles across the state.

Federal *and* state mandates illustrate the mistrust between levels of government in our federal system. Federal officials mistrust the ability of the states to make good decisions, especially when it comes to protecting the interests of the poor, and, in turn, state officials don't trust city and county governments to act in the best interests of the public. States criticize the federal government, and cities and counties criticize the states, both arguing that remote officials in Washington and in state capitals do not understand what it is like to govern on a daily basis.

Local governments turn to their states for help because limited resources make them unable to respond to local demands for more and better services. And, as we have noted, state mandates put additional financial pressure on local governments. Currently, localities provide about 60 percent of their own revenues, 35 percent comes from the states, and 5 percent from the federal government.[31] Since 1975 the bulk of state aid to localities has been for education (ranging from 60 to 64 percent of all state aid) and for welfare, now about 12 percent of aid. From 1980 to 2000, state aid to local governments increased nearly fourfold, in part due to the reduction of federal aid in the 1980s.

As we would expect, there is wide variation among the states in levels of aid to localities. According to data from Morgan Quitno, Hawaii ranks last in per capita aid, far below the forty-ninth state, South Dakota. In large part, this is because Hawaii administers and finances its elementary and secondary educational system. California, New York, and Wyoming provide the greatest amount of aid to localities. Wyoming and Alaska rank high in per capita state aid for education, reflecting the need to serve widely dispersed populations and the availability of severance tax revenue from the extraction of natural resources, such as coal and oil, to fund programs. Among southern states, only North Carolina provides aid above the national per capita amount. Still, southern states are not clustered at the bottom. While some poor states, such as South Dakota, give little aid, other poor states, such as New Mexico, rank high in giving aid.

Much of the difference in levels of state aid is explained by the degree of state centralization of services. Some states historically have centralized services with state legislative control; others have permitted services to be decentralized at the local level and have provided aid to assist localities in delivering those services. Regardless of the degree of centralization, there tends to be a common division of policy responsibility across the country. States build highways, provide welfare, and regulate businesses. Local governments provide law enforcement and fire protection, attend to sanitation and water, and organize recreational opportunities. School districts manage education.

Many governors have opposed local autonomy if that means mayors could ignore the state's general strategy, even as they decry centralization of power in Washington. Still, many governors and legislators respond to public opinion that favors local delivery of services. As a result, in a way similar to federal-state relations, states have enacted programs that rely on cooperation in administration between state and local officials. States also provide revenue sharing that returns a portion of state taxes, with few strings attached, to the jurisdictions in which they were raised.[32]

States also interact with more than 500 federally recognized Native American tribes. In many ways, tribes are independent of state control. Tribes pass, enforce, and adjudicate criminal laws; they impose taxes and do not pay state sales, property, or income taxes from on-reservation activities; and tribes cannot be sued by states. However, non-Indians committing crimes on reservation land are tried in state or federal courts.

While states cannot tax reservation gambling, they have negotiated compacts with tribal governments that define conditions under which gambling takes place.[33] As the number of Indian-run gambling casinos has mushroomed around the country, there have been increased conflicts between them and state authorities. States typically receive a share of gambling profits, in part, to recover costs of upgrading roads into reservations (see Chapter 9 for more discussion about gambling revenue).

FEDERALISM EVALUATED

Critics of federalism offer a number of serious charges. Some suggest that, because it gave southern states independent power, federalism helped foster racism in America;[34] that the states cannot deal effectively with social problems that cross state boundaries; that relations between states are marked more by conflict than by cooperation; that the unequal distribution of wealth among the states creates a system in which social benefits vary greatly from state to state; and that with more than 80,000 units of government, duplication of effort is unavoidable and makes it difficult for citizens to hold officials accountable for their actions.

In this chapter we have examined the lack of cooperation and the unequal distribution of social services among the states. We have noted that states have delayed and often obstructed national policy directions. Perhaps federalism means that too much attention is directed to local matters. What level of government should address specific societal problems has been the most persistent and divisive fundamental political issue throughout American history.

There is a need to sort out responsibilities between the states and the federal government. During the Clinton transition period of 1992–1993, management expert David Osborne argued that the federal government should not act unless (1) the problem needs an interstate solution, (2) uniform national standards are required, (3) the absence of national standards would lead to "destructive competition" among the states, or (4) redistribution across state lines is required to solve local problems.[35] Osborne's recommendation to eliminate 100 federal aid programs and devolve control over 400 others was not acted upon by the Clinton administration.

As we have noted, coercive federalism has increased under the Bush administration. The war on terrorism at home (discussed more in Chapter 10) has raised questions about the effectiveness of intergovernmental cooperation and about the abuse of civil liberties by federal officials acting under provisions of the USA Patriot Act and direction from the president. The Department of Homeland Security (DHS) must rely on states and localities to provide the first responders in virtually all emergency situations. But too often there has been reluctance by federal agents to share critical information with local law-enforcement officials. Many states, led by New York, have been critical of the allotment of federal anti-terrorism funds that has sent more money per capita to small western states than to states with large cities that are most likely to be terrorist targets. In 2006 the DHS identified Indiana as the national center of terrorism, with 8,591 potential targets.

As noted in the case study at the beginning of this chapter, the response to Hurricane Katrina showed a near total breakdown in intergovernmental cooperation and the inability of any level of government to respond in an adequate manner. Things did not go much better in the first year of reconstruction of the damaged coastal area. Large amounts of debris remained, tens of thousands of families lived in trailers, and little had been done about the welfare of poor people in the Gulf Coast area. In June 2007 the Brookings Institution's "Katrina Index" reported that compared to pre-storm levels, 64 percent of state-licensed hospitals were open and 45 percent of schools were open.

It should be noted that hurricane recovery efforts have gone much better in Mississippi. Governor Haley Barbour, former chair of the National Republican Committee and a former Washington lobbyist, has provided the strong leadership that centralized decision making. In contrast to recovery efforts in Louisiana, Barbour communicated calm to the public, and services, for the most part, were quickly restored. All of the state's public schools were open by November 2005.

Federal systems offer a number of benefits.[36] These include the flexibility to respond to regional differences; the prevention of abuse of power because no single group is likely to gain control of government at the state and local levels; the encouragement of innovation by testing new ideas at the local level; the creation of many centers of power to resolve conflict and to handle administrative burdens; the stimulation of competition among levels of government that encourages policy innovation; and, as James Madison predicted, the prevention of abuse of power because it is nearly impossible for a single group to gain control of government at all levels. As noted in Chapter 1, with their many levels of government, federal systems provide multiple opportunities for citizen participation. Often, state elected officials begin their careers by serving on city councils or county commissions.

Of course, most of these benefits will occur only if state and local governments are energetic and respond to public demands. As we shall see throughout this book, there is strong evidence that the states have made the necessary structural changes and that elected officials have sufficient personal commitment to enable them to respond effectively to policy needs, but only if they have sufficient revenue and citizen support for expanded programs.

SUMMARY

American federalism has evolved from a decentralized (state-centered) system at the time of its creation until the first part of the twentieth century, to a much more centralized system. This expansion of power in Washington reached its high point in the 1960s and 1970s. President Reagan's call for a "new federalism" in the 1980s and the Clinton administration's efforts at devolution of power led to a shift of government responsibilities to the states. Still, a "devolution revolution" has not occurred because federal control has been expanded by such coercive measures as categorical grant rules, mandates, and preemptions. We have noted the centralization of authority in education policy and the support of the Bush administration to prevent states from regulating social conduct in areas such as abortion, marriage, and the medical use of marijuana.

Since the early 1990s, the Supreme Court most often has ruled against Congress in cases where states have resisted federal authority. Interpretation of the Tenth and Eleventh Amendments by the Court has been applauded by political conservatives and criticized by liberals, who fear the balance of power in the federal system will be pushed too far in favor of the states. However, in recent years several major federalism cases have been decided in favor of the national government and conservative justices have been strong supporters of federal preemptions.

Much of the increase in federal power in the 1960s and 1970s was accomplished by the expansion of federal grants-in-aid. Since then, the use of mandates and preemptions has helped expand federal power.

The Constitution provides several means of encouraging cooperation among the states. Still, there is a lack of uniformity in many areas of state law, and interstate relations often are marked by conflict as states seek economic advantages.

States exercise unitary power over cities, often controlling their forms of taxation and how they spend money. States may provide services directly to individuals, or they may rely on indirect methods to provide funding to localities, which then administer programs. Over the past twenty-five years the amount of state aid to localities has greatly increased.

Although we have identified numerous disadvantages of our federal system, including the failure of intergovernmental cooperation in the aftermath of Hurricane Katrina, federal systems offer many advantages, including flexibility to respond to regional differences in geographically large countries and the opportunity for political participation in many local governments. In many ways, states have been "laboratories of democracy" where new ideas can be tried on a limited basis and then expanded to other parts of the country.

KEY TERMS

federal system (p. 46)
confederacy (p. 46)
unitary nation-state (p. 46)
confederal (p. 47)
dual sovereignty (p. 47)
necessary and proper clause (p. 48)
concurrent majority (p. 49)
nullification (p. 49)
dual federalism (p. 49)
compact theory of federalism (p. 49)
cooperative federalism (p. 50)
coercive federalism (p. 51)
new federalism (p. 51)
revenue sharing (p. 51)
devolution revolution (p. 53)
Eleventh Amendment (p. 55)
sovereign immunity (p. 56)

grants-in-aid (p. 58)
fiscal federalism (p. 58)
picket fence federalism (p. 59)
crosscutting requirements (p. 60)
crossover sanctions (p. 60)
categorical grants (p. 60)
block grants (p. 60)
formula grants (p. 61)
project grants (p. 61)
formula/project grants (p. 61)
spillover benefits (p. 62)
federal mandates (p. 63)
preemptions (p. 64)
full faith and credit (p. 65)
privileges and immunities (p. 65)
extradition (p. 65)
interstate compacts (p. 66)

BRIEF COMPARISONS OF STATE/LOCAL DIFFERENCES

Issue	States	Local Governments
U.S. Constitutional status	Certain powers are reserved to the states and others are shared with the national government (a federal relationship)	No mention is made of cities or counties
State constitutional status	Free to write and amend their constitutions	Forms of government are prescribed by the state; home rule charters give some autonomy (a unitary relationship)
Grants-in-aid	Categorical and block federal grants to states	Categorical state grants to localities
Mandates	States have gotten some relief from unfunded federal mandates	Localities have gotten some relief from state mandates
Devolution	Some responsibilities have been transferred to states, but coercion continues by using mandates and preemptions	Some relief for cities from unfunded mandates, but state coercion continues

INTERESTING WEB SITES

www.oyez.org. Federal-state issues are frequently resolved by the U.S. Supreme Court, and this is a good site to access the Court's decisions. If you don't know the name of a case, go to "Browse Cases" and click on "By Issue."

www.ncsl.org. Click on "State and Federal Issues," then "State-Federal Relations." You will find a number of current issues and even a "Mandate Monitor."

www.nga.org. Click on "Federal Relations" and learn the NGA's position on a host of intergovernmental issues.

NOTES

1. Deil S. Wright, "How Did Intergovernmental Relations Fail in the USA After Hurricane Katrina?" *Federations* (November 2005), pp. 11–12.
2. See Morton Grodzins, "Centralization and Decentralization in the American Federal System," in *A Nation of States,* Robert A. Goldwin, ed. (Chicago: Rand McNally, 1963).
3. *Statistical Abstract of the United States, 2006* (Washington, D.C.: U.S. Government Printing Office, 2006), p. 272.
4. Russell L. Hanson, "Intergovernmental Relations," in *Politics in the American States,* 7th ed., Virginia Gray and Herbert Jacob, eds. (Washington, D.C.: Congressional Quarterly Press, 1999), p. 34.

5. Paul L. Posner, "The Politics of Preemption: Prospects for the States," *PS: Political Science and Politics* (July 2005), p. 373.

6. John Kincaid, "State-Federal Relations: Federal Dollars Down, Federal Power Up," *The Book of the States 2005* (Lexington, Ky.: Council of State Governments, 2006), pp. 19–25.

7. Joseph F. Zimmerman, "The Nature and Political Significance of Preemption," *PS: Political Science and Politics* (July 2005), p. 359.

8. Hanson, "Intergovernmental Relations," p. 40.

9. Martin Shapiro, "The Supreme Court from Early Burger to Early Rehnquist," in *The New American Political System,* 2d version, Anthony King, ed. (Washington, D.C.: American Enterprise Press, 1990), p. 66.

10. John E. Chubb, "Federalism and the Bias for Centralization," in *The New Direction in American Politics,* John E. Chubb and Paul E. Peterson, eds. (Washington, D.C.: Brookings Institution, 1995).

11. Richard P. Nathan, Fred C. Doolittle, et al., *Reagan and the States* (Princeton, N.J.: Princeton University Press, 1987), p. 31.

12. Donald F. Kettl, "Radical Federalist," *Governing* (August 2004), p. 14.

13. *Creating a Government That Works Better and Costs Less* (Washington, D.C.: U.S. Government Printing Office, 1993), p. 1. Also see Bill Clinton and Al Gore, *Putting People First* (New York: Times Books, 1992); and William A. Galston and Geoffrey L. Tibbets, "Reinventing Federalism: The Clinton/Gore Program for a New Partnership Among the Federal, State, Local, and Tribal Governments," *Publius* (Summer 1994), pp. 23–48.

14. Timothy J. Conlon, *From New Federalism to Devolution: Twenty-Five Years of Intergovernmental Reform* (Washington, D.C.: Brookings Institution, 1998), p. 224.

15. David B. Walker, *The Rebirth of Federalism: Slouching Toward Washington,* 2d ed. (Chatham, N.J.: Chatham House, 1999).

16. John Kincaid, "The State of U.S. Federalism 2000–2001: Continuity and Crisis," *Publius* (Summer 2001), p. 20.

17. John Kincaid, "State-Federal Relations: Continuing Regulatory Federalism," *The Book of the States 2002* (Lexington, Ky.: Council of State Governments, 2002), pp. 26–28.

18. Ann O'M Bowman, "American Federalism on the Horizon," *Publius* (Spring 2002), p. 12.

19. Kincaid, "State-Federal Relations," p. 24.

20. Richard P. Nathan, "There Will Always Be New Federalism," *Journal of Public Administration Research and Theory* (2006), www.rockinst.org.

21. Richard P. Nathan, "Rethinking the Politics of Federalism" (August 9, 2006), www.governing.com.

22. Linda Greenhouse, "The High Court's Target: Congress," *New York Times* (February 25, 2001), sec. 4, p. 3.

23. Deil S. Wright, *Understanding Intergovernmental Relations,* 3d ed. (Pacific Grove, Calif.: Brooks/Cole, 1988), p. 64.

24. Kincaid, "State-Federal Relations," p. 21.

25. Chung-Lea Cho and Deil Wright, "Managing Carrots and Sticks," *Publius* (Spring 2001), p. 80.

26. Posner, "The Politics of Preemption," p. 372.

27. Pam Belluck, "Mandate for ID Meets Resistance From States," *New York Times* (May 6, 2006), p. A11.

28. Zimmerman, "The Nature and Political Significance of Preemption," p. 361.

29. Posner, "The Politics of Preemption," p. 371.

30. Jack Penchoff, "Compacts Are Contracts," *State News* (August 2005), p. 22.

31. Daniel R. Berman, "State-Local Relations: Partnership, Conflict, and Autonomy," *Municipal Year Book 2005* (Washington, D.C.: International City/Country Management Association, 2005), p. 52.

32. Russell L. Hanson, "Intergovernmental Relations," in *Politics in the American States,* 8th ed., Virginia Gray and Russell L. Hanson, eds. (Washington, D.C.: Congressional Quarterly Press, 2004), p. 55.

33. Ibid., p. 48.

34. William H. Riker, *Federalism: Origin, Operation, Significance* (Boston: Little, Brown, 1964), p. 155.

35. David Osborne, "A New Federal Compact: Sorting Out Washington's Proper Role," in *Mandate for Change,* Will Marshall and Martin Schram, eds. (New York: Berkley Books, 1993).

36. See David C. Nice and Patricia Fredericksen, *The Politics of Intergovernmental Relations,* 2d ed. (Chicago: Nelson-Hall, 1995), pp. 15–20.

POLITICAL PARTIES AND INTEREST GROUPS

IS THERE ANYONE ELSE I CAN VOTE FOR?

CASE STUDY   When voting on Election Day in November we are accustomed to choosing between two candidates, one a Democrat and the other a Republican. Many citizens, both voters and nonvoters, believe that candidates of the two major parties do not represent their political philosophies. Consequently, voters frequently feel that they are voting for "the lesser of two evils" and other citizens simply decide not to vote.

In 2006, Texans did not face this problem because they had more than enough candidates to choose from in the governor's race. Rick Perry, the incumbent governor, decided to seek reelection but first he had to win the Republican Party's primary election, which he did. Chris Bell, a former U.S. congressman, won the Democratic Party's primary to become the Democratic nominee for governor. And this is where it becomes interesting, not only because of the colorful names of the two independent candidates—Richard "Kinky" Friedman and Carole "One Tough Grandma" Strayhorn—but the procedures they had to follow to get on the ballot.

Friedman and Strayhorn both saw themselves as serious candidates "with enough support—and populist spark—to shake up the outcome in November."[1] Friedman, clearly a political outsider, had a varied career as country musician, mystery book writer, and founder of the Utopia Rescue Ranch for abused and abandoned dogs. His black cowboy hat, ever-present cigar, and slogans such as "Why the hell not?" and "How hard could it be?" earned him media attention beyond Texas. But there was more to Friedman than his one-liners; he talked about immigration and school reform, urging cooperation among southwest border states on immigration and a 1 percent tax on Texas oil and gas companies to pay for improved teacher salaries and school resources.[2]

Strayhorn was not the outsider candidate that Friedman was. She was a political veteran, elected mayor of Austin three times and elected as state comptroller in 1998. In 2002 she was reelected with the highest vote total of any statewide elected official in Texas. Although a Republican, she believed that it was time to end Rick Perry's "uninspired" time in office.[3] She did not challenge Perry in the Republican primary because she thought she would lose; she decided to run as an independent.

How do independents get on a general election ballot? Do they just tell someone at the board of elections? As you might expect, it is not that easy, and in Texas it is more difficult than in most states. Here's what Friedman and Strayhorn had to do. Texas law gives independents a sixty-day window, beginning after the two major parties hold their primaries in March, to gather signatures equal to 1 percent (45,540) of voter turnout in the previous gubernatorial election. The signatures must be of registered voters who did not vote in the primary elections. These are the toughest requirements in the nation; nevertheless, both Friedman and Strayhorn were successful in gathering the signatures and getting their names on the ballot.

But in the general election, Friedman and Strayhorn could not overcome the name recognition, financial resources, and voter loyalties that go to the two major-party candidates. Perry won with 39 percent of the vote, Bell followed with 30 percent; Strayhorn and Friedman had 18 percent and 12 percent, respectively. This election reminds us of the important role Democratic and Republican Parties continue to play in political campaigns and elections. As we will discuss in this chapter, their importance also extends to governing and policy making, especially at the state level.

POINTS TO CONSIDER

- Are political parties private associations?
- How did the reform movement affect urban political machines?
- Describe the activities of today's Democratic and Republican Parties at the state and local level.
- What types of primaries are used in the states?
- Are the Democratic and Republican Parties becoming more competitive in state elections?
- What is the effect of party competition and divided government on state policies?
- How do political parties differ from interest groups?
- What tactics do interest groups use in state capitals?
- Can lobbyists buy influence?
- What interest groups are found in cities?
- What are the approaches to the study of community power?

POLITICAL PARTIES AS ORGANIZATIONS

Legal Basis of Parties

The U.S. Constitution does not mention political parties, and Congress has made little effort to pass laws affecting them. As a result, states are relatively free to regulate party organizations and activities by provisions in their constitutions and laws. On occasion, however, the U.S. Supreme Court has found some of these regulations unconstitutional.

State regulation of parties can be divided into three periods. The first period, from the adoption of the U.S. Constitution through the beginning of the 1880s, contained no regulation. Parties were considered to be private political associations. Early national leaders such as George Washington and James Madison feared the effects of parties and viewed them as necessary evils, at best. Nevertheless, parties developed quickly because they were effective in mobilizing voters to elect their candidates.

By the 1880s, with state and local parties increasingly under the control of corrupt party bosses, state governments began a period of extensive regulation. This second period of state regulation of parties proceeded at different speeds in different states and eventually became an important part of the Progressive movement (1900–1920). Fraudulent voting was frequent because votes were cast by depositing in the ballot box, in full public view, a ballot that had been printed by one of the parties and contained only the names of its candidates. The earliest laws provided for voter registration and the Australian ballot, and were designed to prevent abuses such as fictitious voters and "repeaters" who voted several times in the same election.[4] **Voter registration** is a process that identifies and lists eligible voters in advance of election day; only voters on the list are permitted to vote. The **Australian ballot system** consists of a single official ballot that is prepared by the state and lists all recognized parties and their candidates; voters are provided a booth so that they can mark their ballot in secret. Other laws were directed at regulating the parties' internal structures and procedures, requiring, among other things, the use of primary elections to nominate candidates.[5] These laws will be discussed in more detail in the section on the reform movement later in this chapter.

The third period of state regulation began in the 1970s and offers examples of deregulation. This period has been strongly influenced by several U.S. Supreme Court decisions; it does not represent a complete return to the earlier view of parties as private political associations, but it does reflect some of this thinking. The Supreme Court declared some state laws unconstitutional because they violate a party's First Amendment right of freedom of association. A Connecticut law that limited participation in a party's primary election to voters registered only with that party is a good example. The Republican Party of Connecticut challenged the law because it wanted to allow voters registered as independents to vote in Republican primaries. Republicans hoped that if independents voted in their party's primary they would also vote for Republican candidates in the general election and that some of these voters might eventually join the party, resulting in a stronger organization. The Court concluded in 1986 that the Republican Party's decision on who could vote in its primary was a private matter, and not one that could be overturned by state law.[6] In another important Court decision (1989), a major obstacle to party activity in California was eliminated when laws prohibiting parties from endorsing candidates in primary elections and regulating various details of internal governance of the parties were overturned.[7]

How far will this deregulation trend go? Will political parties be completely deregulated? This seems unlikely because party officials have frequently persuaded state legislatures to enact laws that give some protection to the two major parties, even though the general thrust of state laws, as described above, was designed to restrict parties. Sore-loser laws, for example, help the Democratic and Republican Parties by prohibiting a candidate who loses in a primary election from running in the general election as an independent or as the nominee of another party. And the Supreme Court recently upheld a Minnesota law that prohibits fusion candidacies; it was challenged by the Twin Cities Area New Party, a minor party. A **fusion candidate** is a person who is nominated for an elected office by two or more political parties, usually a major party and minor party. Supporters of minor parties believe that fusion candidates will help them gain an electoral foothold because minor party voters can point to their votes for the fusion candidate and, consequently, expect the winning candidate to be responsive to some of their policy views. But the Court majority decided that Minnesota had a valid state interest in preserving the stability of its political system by enacting laws that may favor the existing two-party system.[8] It appears that even the Supreme Court does not want to invalidate all state laws regulating parties.

Urban Political Machines

Perhaps the best example of traditional party organizations occurred not at the state level but at the local level. Around the middle of the nineteenth century, party organizations known as political machines spread rapidly among many cities, primarily those in the Northeast and Midwest. An **urban political machine** was a cohesive and unified party organization led by a strong leader usually called the boss. The machine controlled city or county government because voters loyal to the machine voted for its candidates on election day. The machine gained and kept the loyalty of voters mainly through patronage.[9] **Patronage** refers to the distribution of material rewards, especially public

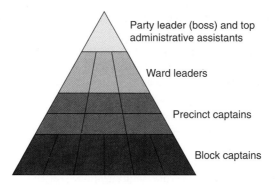

FIGURE 3-1 Political machine organization chart.

Source: Bernard H. Ross and Myron A. Levine, *Urban Politics*: *Power in Metropolitan America,* 7th ed. (Belmont, Calif.: Thomson Wadsworth, 2006), p. 177. Reproduced with permission of the publisher.

jobs, to the politically faithful. Control of public payroll jobs and influence over hiring for some jobs in private business was always the machine's greatest source of power.

In terms of organizational structure, the political machine was based on city blocks, precincts, and wards. (A **precinct** is the smallest unit for voting in elections and usually contains up to 1,000 people and one polling place. To elect members to the city council, precincts frequently were joined together to form election districts called **wards.**) Each precinct was headed by a precinct captain and each ward by a ward leader. Precinct captains were responsible for delivering the votes for the boss; they frequently held city jobs and could lose those jobs if the vote was lower than expected.[10] (See Figure 3-1.)

Council elections by wards helped machines by focusing elections on small areas where an ethnic group beholden to the machine often constituted a majority of the population. Although the boss was often the mayor and ward leaders were often members of the city council, sometimes they were party officials who operated behind the scenes to control local government.

But why did political machines emerge and thrive? Political scientists Fred I. Greenstein and Frank Feigert state that their development in the second half of the nineteenth century was caused by a number of factors, including the following:

1. The population of American cities experienced dramatic growth as the nation's economy shifted from agriculture to industry. In 1850, only one American city had a population over 250,000; in 1890 eleven cities had more than 250,000 and three had over a million.
2. The structure of city government, marked by mayors with little power and many elected officials, made it almost impossible to manage the challenges of urban growth.
3. More than 25 million immigrants came to the United States, and most of them settled in cities. They were an important source of cheap labor for American industry. Local governments, however, were ill-equipped to aid in their transition to a new culture.
4. Businesses increasingly needed services from government in the form of construction permits, roads paved, and water and sewerage services, among others. Also, utility producers and transit companies were interested in obtaining city franchises that gave them the exclusive right to provide a service within the city's boundaries.[11]

It was city political machines that rushed to fill many of these needs. The machine centralized public decision making and provided much needed social services at a time when government assumed little responsibility for social welfare. Most importantly, in terms of votes that the machine needed to survive, it assisted immigrants. As political scientist William J. Crotty puts it, the machine "figuratively and literally met people at their boats, helped them settle in ethnic neighborhoods, provided them with gift baskets of food or clothing or coal at Christmas and Thanksgiving . . . occasionally got them jobs, and acted as an intermediary with government agencies."[12] The machine saw to it that immigrants became naturalized citizens and voters. In some cities, machines created new voters almost as needed because the clerk of a local court, an office easily influenced by the machine, could certify naturalization.[13]

Although immigrants were important to political machines, it should be remembered that machines dominated many southern and midwestern cities early in the twentieth century where there were relatively few new immigrants. In these cases, machines relied on the working-class poor for much of their support.

For city policies to be carried out, it was absolutely critical that the boss put his stamp of approval on them. Bosses were usually brokers who chose among alternatives developed by others. They had little interest in political ideology and seldom developed broad policy goals. An exception to this general rule was in Boston where Mayor James M. Curley's machine went beyond providing basic services to build parks, modernize roads, and redevelop the city. (Curley, first elected mayor in 1914, served three more nonconsecutive terms.)

Reform Movement

Although there was much that was positive about political machines, a negative side existed, also, namely, election fraud, kickbacks and payoffs in city contracts, and, of course, patronage. Early in the twentieth century, the Progressive movement was in full swing and citizens in many communities organized reform groups called good-government organizations. **Good-government organizations** (also called goo-goos) advocated and eventually won structural reforms of local government. These reforms included merit systems for hiring city employees (civil service), professional city managers, nonpartisan elections, and at-large elections. The National Municipal League was formed and held national conferences at which local reform leaders would meet and discuss ways of changing city government.[14] The National Municipal League is still in existence, now known as the National Civic League.

All of these reforms were direct attempts to eliminate, or at least reduce, the influence of political machines. The change to a merit system (civil service) for hiring most public employees hit the machines especially hard because it reduced their most important source of patronage. George Washington Plunkett, a member of New York City's machine known as Tammany Hall, denounced civil service as "the curse of the nation." Still, some patronage jobs continued to be available for decades, especially in cities such as Chicago. Beginning in the 1970s, three Supreme Court decisions dealt a serious blow to a party's ability to reward its supporters with jobs. The Court held that non–civil service employees in the sheriff's office in Cook County (Illinois) could not be fired simply because they did not support the party of the newly elected sheriff.[15] In another case from Illinois, the Court also decided that party affiliation could not be a factor in hiring, promoting, or transferring state employees.[16] This decision affected the treatment of 60,000 employees in Illinois and caused changes in personnel practices in several states and cities. In *O'Hare Truck Service v. City of Northlake* (1996) the Court extended this protection from jobs to businesses that contract their services to a city. The case came from the city of Northlake, Illinois, where O'Hare Truck Service was taken off the city's list of towing contractors because its owner refused to contribute to the incumbent mayor's reelection campaign and displayed at his place of business a campaign poster supporting the mayor's opponent. In all of these cases ruling against patronage, the Court has argued that it is supporting the individual's right of political association.[17]

The creation of city manager positions meant the hiring of professional, nonpolitical administrators who were not dependent on the machine. Nonpartisan and at-large elections also reduced the influence of machines to elect their favorite candidates. In **nonpartisan elections,** candidates are prohibited from listing their party affiliation on the ballot. The machine cannot officially select or formally endorse a candidate. (Informally, of course, parties could still try to influence elections.) Over 70 percent of all cities in the United States use nonpartisan elections. In **at-large elections,** *all* council members are elected by voters of the entire city. There are no wards or districts from which individual council members are elected. Reformers hoped that the switch to at-large elections would elevate the tone of elections, produce better candidates, break the local bias of ward elections, and eliminate the "building blocks of the machines."[18] Today about 60 percent of all cities have at-large elections.

Although these changes in the structure of local government had significant adverse effects on political machines, several other factors combined to weaken them. In the 1920s, federal government policy severely limited immigration. Without new arrivals, machines lost their supply of new voters. Meanwhile, second- and third-generation immigrants moved into the middle class and lost their ties to the machines. Even among lower-class residents, the availability of federal welfare programs, beginning in the 1930s, eliminated another machine resource. No longer able to attract voters by giving out food baskets, the most machines could do was to help people apply for public assistance or to take political credit for government programs.[19]

In many instances the "goo-goo" reformers had little faith in the ability of the people to make good judgments about their government. They wanted cities to be run by an educated, upper-class elite. Only a few reformers at the beginning of the twentieth century were social reformers who sought to help the working class. Social reformers included two colorful mayors: Samuel "Golden Rule" Jones in Toledo, Ohio, advocated an eight-hour day for city employees and services for poor citizens that included playgrounds, public baths, and free kindergartens. Hazen Pingree, mayor of Detroit, Michigan, battled the privately owned phone, gas, and light utilities in an effort to keep prices low and initiated work-relief programs for the city's poor.

Years later, reforms frequently have unanticipated consequences, and this is the case with the switch from ward or district elections of city council members to at-large elections. Researchers agree that minorities have better representation in the unreformed district election system. A study of ten Texas cities concludes that under district systems more Mexican Americans seek and win election to city councils. The presence of Mexican

Americans on the councils, at least in these cities, had a policy impact in that more Mexican Americans were hired as city employees, salaries of Mexican Americans were increased, and more Mexican Americans were appointed to city boards and commissions.[20]

A few machines continued their influence, even with the reforms of the good-government organizations, well into the twentieth century. The most notable example was the Democratic Party organization of Chicago, known as the Daley Machine (1955–1976). As mayor of Chicago and chairman of the Cook County Democratic Party, Richard J. Daley controlled as many as 30,000 public jobs and perhaps 10,000 private jobs. Chicago's civil service was notoriously weak, with many permanent jobs filled with "temporary" employees, which allowed the hiring process to bypass civil service procedures. Not only was Mayor Daley powerful in Chicago, Democratic presidential candidates visited him on a regular basis seeking his support in their quest for the Democratic nomination. Although several of his associates went to jail in the 1970s for graft, Daley did not fall victim to personal greed. Still, the Daley machine eventually lost power. While Chicago won national praise as "the city that works," a growing African American population, representing almost 35 percent of Chicago's residents in 1977, believed that their needs were being ignored in favor of policies that favored the older white ethnic wards. African Americans were demanding "open housing" policies that would attack Chicago's segregated housing market.

Mayor Daley's son, Richard M. Daley, was elected mayor in 1989, after the city's first African American mayor, Harold Washington, died early in his second term. As mayor, Daley has received national attention for innovative quality-of-life concerns such as creating more green space, implementing a citywide recycling plan, and developing affordable housing. Still, the Daley administration has been bedeviled by investigations and trials that have produced evidence of a lingering machine politics. Recently, one of his top aides was convicted of rigging hiring decisions so that jobs would go to the politically faithful.[21] (It appears that ways were found to continue patronage even after the Supreme Court decisions mentioned previously.) In 2007 Daley was reelected for the sixth time, equaling his father's record, receiving more than 70 percent of the vote.

Party Organization Today

An example of how one state party (Kansas Democrats) is organized is found in Figure 3-2. Precinct committees are at the bottom, county committees are in the middle, and the state committee and chairperson are at the top. The Kansas Democratic Party also has congressional district committees and members on the Democratic National Committee. Although all state parties have members on their national committees, congressional district party organization is not found in all states. State party organization is not a true hierarchical structure, in which power flows from the top to the bottom; instead, each level operates somewhat independently of those units above and below it.

Most political scientists agree that it is the local party organizational units, especially county committees, that are vital to a strong party. Sarah McCally Morehouse and Malcolm E. Jewell suggest that the county committee is important because the county as a governmental unit elects a large number of public officials; its officials still control some patronage, although significantly less than in the past; the boundaries of many

DNC Representatives

The state chair, vice chair, committeeman and committeewoman represent Kansas at the Democratic National Committee.

Kansas Democratic State Committee

State committee elects officers. Members of the state executive committee are indicated with a red line. (The Hispanic Caucus is an example of an affiliated organization.)

Congressional District Committees

Each of the four district committees elects officers and additional delegates to represent the district on the state committee.

County Central Committees

Central committees elect officers (chair, vice chair, secretary, and treasurer). Additional delegates may be elected to represent the county on their congressional district committee.

Election of Precinct Committeepersons

At the statewide primary Democrats vote to elect one man and one woman to the county central committee.

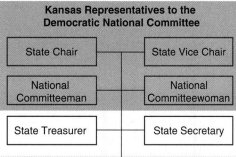

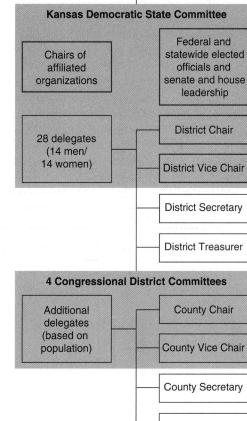

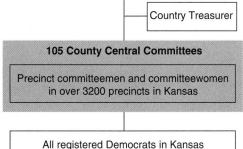

FIGURE 3-2 Democratic party organization in Kansas.

Source: Based on the *Bylaws of the Kansas Democratic State Committee*, available at www.ksdp.org/files/bylaws.pdf (accessed February 1, 2007). The authors wish to thank Mike Gaughan, executive director, Kansas Democratic Party for his assistance.

larger electoral units, such as congressional and state legislative districts, frequently follow county lines; and county chairpersons usually serve as members of the state committee.[22] The structure of parties at the county level varies among the states. In most states a precinct committeeperson (or captain or chair) is elected by voters in the primary election or by a precinct caucus. (A **precinct caucus** refers to a meeting where voters registered with the party get together and as a group elect the committeeperson.) The committeeperson becomes a member of the county committee, which elects the county party chairperson. In another pattern, members of a county committee are the lowest level of elected party officials, and if precincts are organized it is done by the appointment of the county chairperson.

Great variation is found in the actual strength and activity of county party organizations. A very few are well funded with a paid executive director and permanent headquarters, but almost all are part-time, voluntary operations without even a telephone listing.[23] Sometimes just finding an intelligent and energetic person to become Republican or Democratic county chairperson is a difficult task. Activity is cyclical, peaking in the years of election campaigns. Table 3-1 identifies the frequency at which local Democratic and Republican parties in southern states engage in certain campaign activities.

TABLE 3-1 Campaign Activity Levels of Local Party Organizations in Southern States (*Percentages*)

	DEMOCRATS		REPUBLICANS	
Activity	Chair	Member	Chair	Member
Organized canvassing	29.7	25.8	31.9	30.6
Organized campaign events	66.7	29.9	70.0	33.8
Arranged fundraising	57.2	25.4	60.6	28.1
Sent mailings	40.5	33.0	53.8	47.1
Distributed literature	72.9	60.5	78.7	71.4
Organized phone banks	45.6	29.1	56.8	38.6
Purchased billboards	8.4	4.5	9.2	5.4
Distributed posters	70.8	52.2	79.7	65.3
Contributed money	77.2	59.8	85.4	72.9
Registration drives	35.1	20.3	33.6	23.0
Utilized surveys	12.8	9.1	16.5	12.5
Dealt with media	60.9	18.0	64.0	22.6
(N)	(619)	(4981)	(611)	(4246)

Source: John A. Clark, Brad Lockerbie, and Peter W. Wielhouwer, "Campaign Activities," in *Party Organization and Activism in the American South,* Robert P. Steed, John A. Clark, Lewis Bowman, and Charles D. Hadley, eds. (Tuscaloosa, Ala.: The University of Alabama Press, 1998), p. 123. Reproduced with permission of The University of Alabama Press.

Turning to the state level, state party chairs and committees are selected according to state laws or, in the absence of such laws, party rules. In more than forty states, members of state committees are selected by committee members at local levels or by delegates to party conventions. The remaining states select state committee members in primary elections. The formal means of selecting state party chairs are by the state committee or by state conventions; however, the state's governor frequently influences the actual choice.

A general revitalization of state-level party organization started in the 1980s; however, it is important to keep this heralded revitalization in the context of history and region. There is little doubt that both the Democratic and Republican state parties are stronger in southern states where previously the Republicans were a hopeless minority and the dominance of the Democratic Party "produced a politics of faction rather than party, and state party organizations were largely irrelevant."[24] The same is true in states where the Progressive movement was strong; from the upper midwestern states of Wisconsin and Minnesota extending to Pacific Coast states, party organizations were typically weak. On the other hand, in older industrial states, reaching from New England to Illinois, most state party organizations are stronger today than they were at their low point in the early 1970s, but they will probably never be as strong at the state or local level as they were in the later part of the nineteenth century.

State parties in almost all states now have permanent headquarters, annual budgets in election years that average more than $2 million, and a professional staff organized into several sections such as finance, political, communications, field operations, and clerical. In addition to the position of state party chair, which is usually not a paid position, there is a paid, full-time executive director in all of the state parties.

Political scientist John Bibby calls today's state parties "service-oriented" organizations that provide important services to local parties and candidates.[25] Party-building activities include regular programs to raise money, maintaining voter identification lists, and conducting public opinion polls for the development of campaign strategy. Money is particularly important for organizational vitality, and fundraising events along with direct-mail fundraising are used by almost every party. Wisconsin Republicans have their own computerized marketing center with thirty-five telemarketers who work to expand the number of donors who make small contributions to the party.[26] Candidates' personal campaign organizations, especially in statewide races, make most of the day-to-day decisions about individual campaigns, but state parties are increasingly providing services to candidates: training of campaign volunteers, assistance in polling, and get-out-the-vote drives. Morehouse and Jewell report that Republican parties in several southern states have helped their candidates make major gains in state legislatures by developing techniques to target legislative districts where they have the best chance of winning rather than spreading themselves too thin by contesting every district.[27]

How many and how well these activities are performed by a state party depend in part on the relationship between the party chairperson and the governor, when they are of the same party. Frequently, a governor will be responsible for the election of a chairperson, and when this happens, he or she serves as the governor's agent and tries to control the party and have it fight the governor's battles.[28] Sometimes the chairperson is more independent of the governor, especially if the office was achieved on his or her own efforts. Although this chairperson may cooperate with the governor, he or she will devote more time to broad-based party activities. Of course, half of the chairpersons are members of the party that does not control the governor's office (the outparty) and also tend to concentrate on party-building activities.

Activities presently performed by state and local parties appear to be routine, and one may wonder whether they affect the outcomes of elections. Overall, studies show that a well-organized county party has a positive, though minor, effect on the share of the vote received by its candidates. However, in certain situations a well-organized party can make a greater difference. This is true in counties where the party occupies a minority status, that is, a party that wins few or no elections. In these counties, the better organized parties will run candidates for every elected office on the ballot (a full slate of candidates), resulting in an increase in the number of votes their candidates receive, even at the congressional level. Also, it is likely that a minority party with a strong organization may have a greater effect on election results when longtime incumbents retire or a sudden swing in the mood of the voters goes against the dominant party.[29] A well-organized minority party is capable of taking advantage of these situations. Finally, party organization is an important factor in determining how close the parties are in contesting statewide offices: The better organized the parties, the more competition there is between the Democratic and Republican Parties.[30]

People active in a political party, from precinct committeepersons to state party chairs, often are classified as professionals or amateurs. **Amateurs** are more reform-minded, more interested in advocating certain issue positions and supporting candidates who take the same positions. They enter politics because of their desire to further particular political causes. **Professionals** are more interested in winning elections and are therefore more willing to compromise issue positions if that is what it takes to win. They are less concerned about their parties' candidates taking clear positions on the issues. (See Table 3-2.)

The Christian Right, especially state chapters of the Christian Coalition, is a recent example of issue-oriented activists winning control or at least substantial influence in state and local party organizations to advance a particular policy agenda—in this case, conservative positions on social and moral issues such as prayer in schools, same-sex marriage, and abortion. The Texas Christian Coalition, for example, trained and mobilized its members to vote in Republican primary elections and then attend precinct caucuses held the day after the primary; at these caucuses, Republican precinct chairs are selected along with delegates to the county convention who in turn select delegates to the state convention. The coalition's success in Texas has been called a textbook example of how to win control of a party organization, and, of course, this control provides leverage to influence party nominees for political office and the issue positions they espouse during the campaign and the policy decisions they make if elected.[31] The Christian Coalition, although its influence has ebbed in the past couple of years, is still important in Florida, Iowa, and Kansas, among others.

Because the amateur style emphasizes issues over party, there has been speculation that it might severely weaken party organizations, but there is no real evidence that this has occurred.[32] In fact, politically active groups would not try to gain control of party organizations if they didn't think they were important in the political process. Nevertheless, differing styles are a source of tension and conflict within party organizations.

TABLE 3-2 Professionals and Amateurs: A Typology		
	Professionals	Amateurs
Political style	Pragmatic	Purist
What do they want?	Material rewards (patronage, preferments)	Purposive rewards (issues, ideology)
Their loyalty is to:	Party organization	Officeholders, other political groups
They want the party to focus on:	Candidates, elections	Issues, ideology
The party should choose candidates on the basis of:	Their electability	Their principles
The style of party governance should be:	Hierarchical	Democratic
Their support of party candidates is:	Automatic	Conditional on candidates' principles
They were recruited into politics through:	Party work	Issue or candidate organizations
Their socioeconomic status is:	Average to above average	Well above average

Source: Marjorie Randon Hershey, *Party Politics in America,* 11th ed. (New York: Pearson Education, 2005), p. 90. Reprinted by permission of Pearson Longman.

PARTIES AND THE NOMINATION OF CANDIDATES

The importance of the nomination process to political parties is summed up by the statement "Who can make nominations is the owner of the party."[33] During the latter half of the nineteenth century, statewide nominations were formally made by state party conventions composed of delegates selected earlier at county conventions. And, as mentioned previously, party bosses frequently controlled nominations that were made at the local level. Primary elections changed forever the role of party organizations in the nomination of candidates.

The Direct Primary

In 1903 Wisconsin adopted the first direct primary law to nominate candidates for statewide offices, and by 1917 a majority of states had adopted it. The **direct primary** is an election in which voters decide the parties' nominees for the general election. In other words, voters are directly involved in the nomination process, unlike party conventions, where only delegates to the convention vote on nominees. The spread of the direct primary weakened party organizations. Of course, this is just what its advocates, members of the Progressive movement, intended. They wanted to open the nominating process by removing the monopoly of power held by party leaders to handpick candidates and even to direct their behavior once they were elected to office. Today, no state uses only the convention method to nominate candidates. State nominating conventions, however, have not completely disappeared; for example, in Alabama and Virginia the party may choose to hold a convention rather than a primary. A handful of states use primaries to nominate top statewide offices and conventions for lesser offices such as attorney general, and a few states use conventions to screen candidates before their names are placed on the primary ballot.[34]

Types of Primaries

Who is allowed to vote in primary elections? One might think all registered voters, but this is usually not the case. One view is that voters who participate in the Democratic primary must be registered as Democrats in advance of the primary election and voters who participate in the Republican primary must be registered as Republicans, again in advance of the primary election. This view is based on the idea that political parties are organizations and before people participate in organizational decision making they should "join" the organization. To be considered a member of the Democratic, Republican, or some other political party, citizens simply have to indicate their party preference when they register to vote. Others argue that voters should have the freedom to vote for the person they perceive as the best candidate, and that the party affiliation of the voter and candidate is immaterial. In devising primary laws, states have sided with one or the other of these two views, and some have managed to fall in between. Political scientists have developed elaborate schemes to classify state primaries. Nevertheless, the familiar terms of closed primary and open primary, along with the less familiar blanket primary and open elections, make for the simplest presentation.

Closed primaries are used in twenty-eight states. In a **closed primary,** voters declare a party preference in advance and can vote only in that party's primary. States vary in terms of how far in advance voters need to declare their party preference or affiliation. Most require voters who want to change their party to do so several months in advance of the primary. Others have more flexibility in changing parties. Iowa, for example, allows voters to switch registration on the day of the election, although a record is kept of the party a voter registers with. States that allow voters to change registration on Election Day are very similar to open primaries.

Open primaries are used in twenty-one states. (Today, open primaries are frequently called "pick-a-party" primaries.) In an **open primary,** voters do not declare a party preference in advance and may choose either a Republican or a Democratic ballot, that is, vote in either party's primary. In other words, they should be able to choose either party's ballot at the precinct voting place. Although some states require voters to express publicly a preference for the ballot of a party at the polls, in other states voters can decide which party's primary they will vote in in the privacy of the voting booth. (Either way it is possible for the supporters of one party to vote in the other party's primary. When this happens it is called crossover voting.)

A **blanket primary** gives registered voters maximum choice in selecting candidates. It goes a step further than open primaries by allowing voters to decide office by office which party's primary they will vote in. A voter can vote in the Democratic primary for governor and then in the Republican primary for attorney general, for example, moving back and forth between the parties by office; however, it is not permissible to vote in both parties' primary for the same office. In 1996 California switched from a closed primary to a blanket primary when voters approved a ballot initiative titled the "Open Primary Initiative." (Although it was called an open primary, it was actually a blanket primary.) At the present time, the continued use of the blanket primary is problematic. The U.S. Supreme Court in *California Democratic Party v. Jones* (2000)[35] concluded that a political party has a right, protected by the First Amendment, to determine which voters may participate in the nomination of its candidates for public office. As in the Connecticut case mentioned earlier, the Court is saying that state laws cannot mandate the type of primary a party must use. In 2001 California returned to the closed primary, which it had used prior to 1996. For several decades, a blanket primary was used in Alaska and Washington. As a result of further federal court decisions, Alaska has modified its primary and Washington, where the blanket primary was popular with voters and almost a state institution, has moved to an open primary.[36]

A unique open elections procedure,[37] adopted in 1975, is used in Louisiana. In **open elections** all candidates for an office, regardless of party affiliation, are required to appear on the same ballot. Candidates may, and usually do, list their party affiliation. If one of the candidates receives a majority of the votes cast, that candidate is declared elected and the general election is canceled. If no one has a majority, the general election is held and the top two candidates run against each other. This allows for the possibility that the two candidates could be affiliated with the same party, two Democrats or two Republicans. The effect of this system in state legislative races has been to help incumbents, who, because of their name recognition, frequently win a majority in the first election. Also, at least initially, the law resulted in fewer Republicans—the minority party in Louisiana—contesting state legislative contests. More recently, the Republican Party has done better in gubernatorial races, with Republican Mike Foster elected twice in the 1990s, including once with a majority vote in the primary election. Nevertheless, the strong possibility that a minority party may not have a chance to run its candidates in the general election makes the open elections a bad choice because it hinders the development of a strong second party. In 2006 Louisiana adopted a law that will allow closed primaries in U.S. Senate and House elections, but open elections for state and local offices.[38]

In most states the winner of the primary is the candidate who receives the most votes (plurality), even if it is not a majority. In many southern states, however, a majority vote is required. This has led to **runoff primaries,** a second primary between the top two candidates if no one received a majority in the first primary. The runoff primary was instituted in the South when the Democratic Party was dominant and winning the Democratic primary was tantamount to winning the general election. The runoff required a candidate to receive support of a majority of the Democrats. The rise of the Republican Party has put more importance on the general election and decreased participation in the Democratic primary.[39] Some civil rights organizations have claimed that runoff primaries discriminate. They argue that fewer whites voting in the Democratic primary has increased the importance of the African American vote. And if there is one African American candidate and several white candidates on the ballot, it is possible for the African American candidate to win a plurality, but not a majority, of the votes in the *first* primary if white voters split their votes among all of the white candidates. In the ensuing runoff primary, with an African American candidate facing a white candidate, white voters may coalesce around the white candidate, who will then have a majority to win the nomination. A study of a number of primary elections in the South found that the number of African American candidates who led in the first primary fell by 50 percent in the runoff primary, giving some support to the belief that runoff primaries have a discriminatory effect.[40] Thus far, courts have not declared runoff primaries unconstitutional.

At the local level, elections are frequently nonpartisan, and when that is the case, the primary election is nonpartisan and the two candidates receiving the most votes in the primary will face each other in the general election. In some cities and towns, the general election is canceled if a candidate receives a majority of votes in the primary.

Access to the Primary Ballot

Candidates normally gain access to the primary ballot by obtaining signatures on a petition or paying a modest filing fee. In about half of the states, this stage is also viewed as an opportunity for parties to try to gain back some influence over nominations that they lost with the adoption of the direct primary. **Preprimary endorsements** refer to a process whereby political parties attempt to influence who is nominated in a primary election by endorsing the candidate they prefer in advance of the primary. Endorsements can be made at state party conventions or by state party committees. In a few states, these endorsements have a firm footing in state law and can, for example, benefit candidates by giving them easier access to the primary ballot. In other states, endorsements are made informally under party rules and grant no advantage in ballot access. Either way, endorsed candidates can benefit from campaign workers and financial contributions that may come from party endorsements.[41]

Occasionally, endorsed candidates have no primary opposition, which is called an uncontested primary. This almost always happens when an incumbent governor seeks renomination, and it can also occur when party leaders negotiate an agreement among several contenders to support the nomination of the person who appears to be the most electable. Those not receiving the endorsement would agree to support the endorsee in exchange, for example, for an appointment in the new governor's administration or the promise of a future endorsement. How successful are endorsed candidates in winning the primary and the nomination? In contested primaries, the success rate has fallen from 75 percent in the 1960s and 1970s to 50 percent in recent years.[42] Malcolm Jewell suggests there is no single explanation for this decline. Some endorsed candidates lost to opponents who had little political experience, which is not usually considered a qualification for office, but can be appealing to voters at certain times. Others lost to candidates who had ample campaign funds and spent heavily on television ads.[43]

It also has happened that a well-organized faction in a party will elect a majority of state convention delegates and endorse a candidate whose policy positions are too extreme for voters who normally support the party. (Occasionally, as few as 12,000 voters will participate in the convention delegate selection process.) This happened in Minnesota in 1994, when the Republican state convention did *not* endorse the incumbent Republican governor, Arne Carlson. The convention endorsed a candidate with more conservative political views, Allen Quist, who lost to Carlson in the primary.[44] In 1998, in Minnesota, the candidate endorsed by the Democrat-Farmer-Labor (DFL) Party lost in the primary to Hubert H. Humphrey, III. Stephen I. Frank and Steven C. Wagner suggest that one reason independent Jesse Ventura was elected governor was that he was able to "capitalize on the dissatisfaction of the voters with the Republican and DFL endorsement and primary process and made a successful appeal to them."[45] Preprimary endorsements of candidates by convention delegates that are unrepresentative of a party's supporters will be of little help to them in winning the primary.

PARTY COMPETITION IN THE STATES

Political scientists have devoted considerable attention to the level of party competition in the states. **Party competition** is present when candidates of the two major parties (Democrats and Republicans) have an almost equal chance of winning the governor's office and a majority of seats in the state legislature.

Classifying the States

Regardless of measurement techniques employed to determine the degree of competition, states are usually grouped into a number of categories that identify those where Republicans dominate elections, those with competitive elections, and those where Democrats dominate elections. Our classification is for 1992 through 2006 elections and is based on definitions developed by Malcolm Jewell and David Olson that we have modified to take into account the large number of competitive states that have emerged recently.[46] Jewell and Olson, analyzing the 1965–1988 time period, identified thirty-two states as competitive. Because the competitive category is so large, Jewell and Olson's single competitive category has been expanded to three categories so that we can classify states as competitive or as leaning to one party or the other. Fewer one-party dominant and one-party majority states allow the merger of these two categories into one. For Figure 3-3, states were classified as follows:

Dominant/majority. In majority party states, one party is consistently more successful in winning elections to state offices. Both parties seriously contest elections for the governor's office and for control of the legislature. However, the majority party controls the governor's office more than two-thirds of the time, and its candidates usually receive approximately 60 percent of the vote. The majority party also controls the senate and house more than two-thirds of the time, and the proportion of the seats it wins is usually less than three-fourths of the total. Also in this category are a few states labeled "one-party dominant." In these states, one party always or almost always wins the election for governor with more than two-thirds of the total vote cast and always wins control of the state legislature with a majority that frequently exceeds three-fourths of the total number of seats.

Competitive leaning. Both parties win elections to state offices, but one party does just slightly better. Typically, in these states the Democratic and Republican Parties divide control of the governor's office, but one is more consistent in winning control of the legislature. Competitive leaning states are classified as competitive

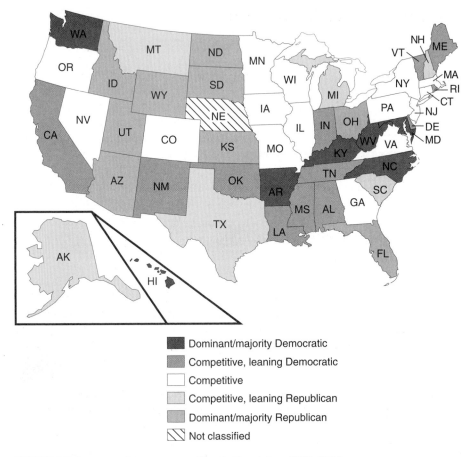

FIGURE 3-3 Patterns of party competition in the states, 1992–2006.

Source: Authors' update of a map of party competition that appeared in Malcolm E. Jewell and David M. Olson, *Political Parties and Elections in American States,* 3d ed. (Chicago: The Dorsey Press, 1988), p. 29.

Note: Nebraska is not classified because its state legislative elections are nonpartisan.

Democratic or competitive Republican to indicate which party has a slight advantage.

Competitive. Both parties come close to sharing equally the winning of state offices. Democratic and Republican Parties divide control of the governor's office close to one-half of the time. Even control of both houses of the legislature is frequently divided between the parties, as is the membership in each chamber. Also labeled as competitive are states in which the parties split control of the executive and legislative branches, with one party consistently winning the governor's office and one party consistently winning control of both houses of the legislature.

Generally, competitive and competitive leaning states are described as two-party states and states in the dominant/majority category are called one-party states.

The Trends Toward Competition

Today, competition between the two major parties at the state level is widespread. A close look at Figure 3–3 reveals fifteen states that are classified as competitive. New Jersey may be the best example, with the two major parties equally dividing the governor's office during this fourteen-year period; the Democrats were slightly ahead in control of the state legislature. On two occasions, membership in the senate was evenly divided between the two parties, requiring co-presidents, one from each party, to serve as presiding officers. An additional eighteen states are in the slightly less competitive category because they tilt toward the Democratic Party (twelve states) or the Republican Party (six states). Texas is a competitive, Republican-leaning state, winning the governor's office during almost all of the period covered in Figure 3–3; control of the legislature was more split with Republicans doing better in the senate and Democrats doing better in the house. In Indiana, a competitive, Democratic-leaning state, Democrats were strong in winning the governor's office and the house while Republicans controlled the senate. At the opposite end of competitive states are those where one party dominates; for example, the Democratic Party is strongest in Maryland and West Virginia and the Republicans are strongest in Utah and the two Dakotas.

The process by which party competition develops in a state can be described as follows: (1) Voters who consistently supported the dominant party begin to split their tickets and vote for some minority party candidates in national and state elections; (2) voters (especially younger persons) begin to shift their party identification, perhaps first to independent and then to the minority party; and (3) voters shift their party registration. This is not an automatic process, and a wide variety of factors may work to retard change. Republicans have been frequently frustrated in the South because Democratic incumbents compile fairly conservative records, giving the people little incentive to switch parties. Political scientists Earl Black and Merle Black, who specialize in southern politics, note that southern Democratic candidates for statewide office try to distance themselves from the liberal image of the national Democratic Party. They campaign on platforms that are both conservative (support of budgetary restraint and school prayer) and progressive (support for improving the educational system and environmental protection).[47]

However, the 1994 midterm elections reduced the Republican Party's frustration in winning congressional and state-level offices in the South. The **Republican Revolution** was a stunning electoral victory with the Republican Party winning a majority of seats in the U.S. Senate and House of Representatives, controlling both houses of Congress for the first time in forty years. The revolution's leader was Congressman Newt Gingrich (Georgia), with his Contract with America campaign theme of reducing government that was too big, too intrusive, and too easy with the public's money. The Republican tide at the national level carried over to the states, where the party had equally historic gains, winning control of a majority of governors' offices in the South for the first time in the twentieth century. Although Democrats still controlled almost all of the state legislatures, the Republicans won a majority of the seats in North Carolina's House of Representatives and the Florida Senate, again for the first time in the twentieth century. Another indication of growing Republican strength was that two of the Republican governors elected in 1994 were previously members of the Democratic Party. In fact, both had been elected as Democrats: Fob James, Jr., was Democratic governor of Alabama (1979–1983), and David Beasley was a Democratic member of the South Carolina state legislature.

Republicans continued their success in 2002, winning the Georgia governor's office and a majority of seats in the state senate. John H. Aldrich, who has written extensively on political parties, concludes that in the South, "The Republican Party has become a serious and sustained competitor to the Democrats for essentially all national and state-level offices, and quite often at lower levels as well."[48] Research by Robert Erickson, Gerald Wright, and John McIver confirms that the trend in southern states is of citizens slowly moving away from a long tradition of Democratic partisanship. While this has been occurring, however, the conservative ideology of southerners has remained stable; the change has been one of conservative Democrats becoming conservative Republicans. The correlation between ideology and partisanship in the South is much stronger than it was thirty years ago, it now more clearly resembles states outside the South where liberals tend to be Democrats and conservatives tend to be Republicans.[49]

Among all fifty states, from 1994 to 2006, the Republican Party dominated governors' offices and maintained at least parity with the Democrats in control of state legislatures. With an unpopular Republican president, George W. Bush, an unpopular war in Iraq, and ethics lapses in Congress, the midterm elections of 2006 were almost a mirror image of 1994; the national tide of electoral politics ran heavily against the Republican Party. Democrats regained control of the U.S. Senate and House of Representatives. As in 1994, voters' views of the national parties and leaders affected, to some extent, state elections. (For further discussion of the role of national events in state elections, see Chapter 4.) Democratic candidates won governors' offices in six additional states bringing their total to twenty-eight, with Republican governors in twenty-two states. Democratic gains were not restricted to one region of the country, but included states from different regions: Arkansas, Colorado, Maryland, Massachusetts, New York, and Ohio. The Democratic Party also did well in state legislative races, picking up more than 300 legislative seats nationwide, giving it new majorities in ten legislative chambers including the New Hampshire House for the first time since 1922. Overall, the Democratic Party won control of both legislative chambers in twenty-three states (up from nineteen); Republicans control both chambers in fifteen states and eleven states have split control of the legislature.[50]

In recent election years, it has been possible for the Republicans or the Democrats to gain a temporary advantage in the number of governors' offices and legislative seats they control; nevertheless, the general pattern is clear: Competition between the parties in the states is alive and well.

Third Parties

The Democratic and Republican parties have a near monopoly on state politics, but it is not a complete monopoly as noted in the chapter opener on the 2006 gubernatorial election in Texas. Third-party candidates and independents, candidates not affiliated with any party, have occasionally been elected. During the 1990s, four states had independent or third-party governors: Alaska, Connecticut, Maine, and Minnesota. Some states have a history of active minor parties. Minnesota's Farmer-Labor Party won gubernatorial elections early in the twentieth century and eventually merged with the Democratic Party. The official name of the Democratic Party in Minnesota is still the Democrat-Farmer-Labor (DFL) Party. Currently, Minnesota has an active Independence Party, and its candidate, Jesse Ventura, was elected governor in 1998. It had a full slate of statewide candidates in 2006, but won only 6 percent of the vote in the governor's race. More states than usual had third-party or independent candidates on the ballot in 2006; still, it is difficult to compete with the two major parties in any particular election and difficult to keep a third-party movement viable from election to election. Barbara Merrill, an independent candidate for governor of Maine, with 22 percent of the vote, received the largest share of the vote for third-party or independent candidates. The Green Party gubernatorial candidate in Illinois received 10 percent of the vote, and the Libertarian candidate in Georgia received less than 5 percent. The Green Party of New Mexico was active in the 2002 elections,[51] but failed to run a candidate for governor or any statewide office in 2006.

PARTY COMPETITION AND PUBLIC POLICIES

Two-Party States

Although it is generally taken for granted that competitive, two-party states are preferable to one-party states, political scientists disagree regarding the effects of competition on government performance. V. O. Key, a pioneer in the modern study of state politics, framed the debate in his classic book, *Southern Politics in State and Nation.*[52] Key analyzed the politics of southern states in the late 1940s, noting that the South's one-party politics did not raise important issues during election campaigns, discouraged voter participation, and resulted in governments adopting policies that ignored the needs of the "have-nots" (lower socioeconomic groups).[53] Two-party politics, Key believed, would raise more important issues because the parties would tend to represent different socioeconomic classes. The presence of these issues in elections and governing would increase voter participation. In addition, close electoral competition between the parties would force one of the parties to offer some policies favored by the "have-nots" so as to win their votes.

Some political scientists adapted Key's framework by using interparty competition to study all fifty states, but they did not always agree with his conclusions. Studies by Thomas R. Dye indicate that education, welfare, taxation, and highway programs appear to be more closely related to economic factors in the states than the degree of party competition. In other words, states with greater wealth spend more money on various programs regardless of levels of competition. Dye concludes, "Party competition itself does not necessarily cause more liberal welfare policies."[54] In fact, some observers even went so far as to argue that politics was really unimportant in the making of policy.

Unfortunately, analyzing all fifty states, although a good idea, frequently pushes researchers to rely on a few statistical indicators of each state's politics and policies that in all likelihood do not accurately reflect its political history and perhaps not even the current context of policy making. And in doing so they underestimate the important role of political parties. However, additional research is providing new evidence that parties do affect policy making.

Robert D. Brown concludes that greater state policy benefits for the have-nots are found in states where the electoral base of the Democratic Party tends to be a coalition of low-income persons, union members, and Catholics.[55] Using a similar approach in a study of California and New York, Diana Dwyre and associates add more evidence for the importance of parties in policy making when they have different electoral bases. This study concludes that the "disorganized" decision-making process in California is the principal cause of policies that have placed a greater state and local tax burden on low-income groups (have-nots) than in New York, where the process is more "organized." California's decision-making process is one where parties are minor actors. Many decisions are made through the use of ballot initiatives (see Chapter 4) with temporary coalitions forming around them. These coalitions are composed of various interests but not political parties; they exist for that single issue and then disappear. In New York's decision-making process, parties are major actors having clear differences in their electoral bases, with the Democratic Party representing the interests of the have-nots.[56] Party members in the legislature are reasonably cohesive in advancing the interests of their electoral base. Brown and Dwyre and associates, by examining the electoral bases of parties, are focusing on a crucial and frequently neglected part of Key's arguments.

Another problem with studies that have found economic factors of prime importance in policy making is that they were usually cross-sectional; that is, the data were collected for fifty states at one point in time and then the states were compared with each other. James Garand utilized a longitudinal approach, collecting data on each state at different points. In other words, the data reflect characteristics of each state at several points during a twenty-year period. As a result, he was able to examine the effect of political changes on policy within states. Garand finds, for example, that a change in the party that controls state government does have a substantial impact on spending priorities, especially on the money spent for education.[57] Further evidence of parties affecting state budgets comes from research by James E. Alt and Robert C. Lowery. They conclude that when Democrats win state elections they will use, especially when they take control of the governor's office and both houses of the legislature, a larger share of a state's aggregate personal income for the state budget than Republicans. When Republicans have success in state elections, they will take a smaller share than Democrats.[58]

Further evidence that parties matter in the making of policy comes from a study that finds state party elites have different **ideologies,** beliefs about the purpose and role of government. Although it is frequently claimed that there is not a "dime's worth" of difference between the Democratic and Republican Parties, this bit of conventional wisdom appears to be wrong. Robert Erikson, Gerald Wright, and John McIver have developed a "party elite ideology" score for both parties in forty-six states.[59] The term "party elite" refers to Democrats and Republicans who occupy reasonably high-level positions such as national convention delegates, local party chairpersons, and state legislators.

The attitudes of state party elites were classified on a liberal/conservative dimension. Liberals have been defined as favoring an active role for government in solving problems in society and conservatives as favoring a limited role for government. These definitions are not sufficient for the assortment of issues today; nevertheless, the proper role of government is still a key difference between conservatives and liberals, but it is no longer as clearly defined as it once was. Today's **liberals** generally believe government should act to assist the economically disadvantaged and minority groups but are less willing than conservatives to have government intervene on moral and social issues. Abortion and school prayer are examples of moral and social issues. **Conservatives** generally oppose government acting on economic issues and assisting minority groups but favor government action on many moral and social issues.

Erikson, Wright, and McIver conclude that Republican Party elites tend to be conservative and Democrats tend to be liberal. The largest concentration of "most liberal" Democratic Party elites is in the Northeast. In the Republican Party, the "most conservative" are found in the South and West. No state Republican Party is classified as liberal, not even in the more liberal Northeast. Although these variations are important, it should be remembered that in each state the Republican Party is always more conservative than the Democratic Party. State Democratic and Republican Party elites do have different beliefs on public policy issues.[60]

The Question of Divided Government

Divided government at the national level—when the presidency and the Congress are controlled by opposite political parties—is a frequent occurrence. For example, while Bill Clinton was president the Democratic Party controlled both houses of Congress for only two of eight years (1993 and 1994). **Divided government** in the states occurs when one or both houses of the legislature is controlled by the opposite party of the governor. **Unified government** occurs when one party controls the governor's office and both houses of the state legislature. (Control in each house of a legislature is determined by identifying the party to which a majority of its members belong. The importance of political parties in state legislatures is discussed in Chapter 5.)

Since the 1980s, divided government has become as common as unified government, and after some elections it has occurred even more frequently. Divided government was especially prominent in the late 1980s and early 1990s as more Republicans were elected governors. After the 1994 elections, the trend of divided government states continued and, among unified states, Republican states outnumbered Democratic states. This was still apparent after the 2004 elections when thirty-one states had divided government. Another trend at this time was an increase in the number of states with split control of the legislature—one party controls one house and the other party controls the other house. After the Democratic victories in 2006, the number of unified government states increased; overall, the number of unified and divided states was almost equal, as can be seen in Table 3-3. The most significant changes from 2004 are the increase in the number of unified Democratic states (they doubled from 2004 to 2006) and the decrease in the number of divided government states with a Republican governor and split legislature.

Is it of any importance that a state has divided government rather than unified government? The most often suggested negative consequence is that divided government will make it impossible for the governor and the legislature, since they represent different parties, to get anything accomplished—in other words, gridlock. However, a number of studies at the national level conclude that the prevalence of gridlock has been exaggerated and that a close look at legislative accomplishments indicates that unified governments were

TABLE 3-3 **Unified and Divided Party Government in the States, 2007**		
UNIFIED GOVERNMENT	25 STATES	
Republican governor and legislature	10 states	Alaska, Florida, Georgia, Idaho, Missouri, North Dakota, South Carolina, South Dakota, Texas, Utah
Democratic governor and legislature	15 states	Arkansas, Colorado, Illinois, Iowa, Louisiana, Maine, Maryland, Massachusetts, New Hampshire, New Jersey, New Mexico, North Carolina, Oregon, Washington, West Virginia
DIVIDED GOVERNMENT	24 STATES	
Republican governor and Democratic legislature	8 states	Alabama, California, Connecticut, Hawaii, Minnesota, Mississippi, Rhode Island, Vermont
Republican governor and split legislature	3 states	Indiana, Kentucky, Nevada
Democratic governor and Republican legislature	6 states	Arizona, Kansas, New York, Ohio, Virginia, Wyoming
Democratic governor and split legislature	7 states	Delaware, Michigan, Montana, Oklahoma, Pennsylvania, Tennessee, Wisconsin

Source: The authors collected the data for this table.

Note: Nebraska is not included in this table because of its nonpartisan legislature.

no more likely than divided governments to produce important or significant laws.[61] It needs to be pointed out that no consensus exists among scholars as to the exact effect of divided government in national politics.

A number of political scientists have studied the effects of divided government in the states. Generally, they conclude that divided government has important consequences for a state's politics. Cynthia J. Bowling and Margaret R. Ferguson take a comprehensive look at all fifty states. They discover that gridlock from divided government is unlikely to occur on every type of issue; rather, it is most likely to occur on those issues that have a high potential for partisan conflict, such as welfare, education, crime, and the environment. Divided government encourages "gridlock as the two parties wrestle with the difficult policy challenges or ideological symbolism surrounding these high conflict areas."[62] Another important finding is that the normal way of thinking about divided government—one party controlling the governor's office and the other party controlling the legislature—has the least impact on gridlock. Gridlock is more likely to occur when one party controls *one* house of the legislature and the other party has the other legislative chamber and the governor's office. (Table 3-3 shows that this kind of divided government happened in ten states after the 2006 elections.)

In another useful study, Laura A. van Assendelft looks at the politics of four southern states, two with divided government (Mississippi and South Carolina) and two with unified government (Georgia and Tennessee). She concludes that the principal effect of divided government is not on the number of bills passed by the legislature, but on what the governors place on their agendas, that is, the priorities they establish from among numerous competing policy alternatives. Governors in unified states are more likely to place controversial issues on their agendas. For example, Ned McWherter, Democratic governor of Tennessee (1987–1995), hoped to advance major educational reforms to create the "21st Century Classroom." He proposed to pay for the reforms with the adoption of an individual income tax; this was so controversial that even with a Democratic legislature McWherter had to back down. The legislature eventually approved a one-half-cent increase in the sales tax to help in equalizing funding among Tennessee's school districts. Although McWherter did not achieve everything he wanted, he was partly successful. Governors in divided states probably would not have attempted what he did; they are less likely to pursue controversial issues. A legislator from South Carolina described the effect of divided government on the governor's agenda this way:

> . . . a lot of times you may think about introducing something, but you know good and well that it is never going to pass. So to keep from being publicly defeated you just don't introduce it. That's what the difference is. You temper what you put out based on the audience that is there.[63]

Finally, Robert C. Lowry, James E. Alt, and Karen E. Ferree, researching gubernatorial and state legislative elections, determine that voters are more likely to hold elected officials responsible for taxing and spending policies in states with unified government than in states with divided government.[64] In other words, divided government makes it harder for voters to figure out who is responsible for, in particular, budget deficits and surpluses. This improved accountability is an important benefit of unified government.

INTEREST GROUPS IN THE STATES

Do interest groups differ from political parties? The answer is yes and no. They are similar in that both are important links between citizens and their government. For example, both seek to influence who is nominated and elected to public office (although only political parties can officially nominate candidates and have their names on the election ballot). The principal difference between parties and interest groups revolves around the emphasis given to furthering a specific interest or policy versus winning elections. Jeffrey M. Berry puts it this way: **Interest groups** are *policy maximizers;* they offer citizens "a direct, focused, and undiluted way of supporting advocacy on the issue they care most about."[65] **Political parties,** are *vote maximizers;* their primary concern is to win elections so that their candidates can control important positions in state and local governments. Interest groups are concerned about a single policy or at most a very limited number of policy areas, whereas the Democratic and Republican Parties take positions on a large number of social and economic issues. Frequently, in attempting to appeal to a broad spectrum of the electorate, political parties will have weak or even ambiguous policy positions, just the opposite of interest groups. Finally, organized group activity is

TABLE 3-4 Examples of Types of Interest Groups in California	
AIDS Project Los Angeles	California Professional Firefighter
Asian Pacific American Legal Center	California Teachers Association
California Association of Non-profits	Christian Coalition of California
California Bicycle Association	Community College League of California
California Chamber of Commerce	Family Winemakers of California
California Clean Money Campaign	Nature Conservancy of California

Source: California Voter Foundation, "California Interest Groups," www.calvoter.org/voter/politics/groups.html (accessed January 29, 2007).

more important to the average person. Only around 10 percent of American adults have attended political meetings or made political donations. In contrast, 27 percent indicate belonging to a group involved in politics or public issues.[66]

Since the 1960s, there has been a significant expansion in virtually all states in the number of groups that are politically active. Although interest groups representing business, labor, and agriculture continue to be important, new groups are becoming active and influential; the interests they represent "range from environmentalists to women's groups to gay rights and victims' rights groups to hunting and fishing groups to antipoverty and senior citizens' lobbies."[67] Greater economic diversity in the states (such as the growth of the telecommunications industry) also has caused the creation of new groups in the private economic sector. People in jobs such as public school teaching have become much more politically active and influential through their state professional associations. A sample of interest groups in California is listed in Table 3-4. Similar listings could be compiled for all fifty states.

Power of Interest Groups

No state today is run by one or two interests, as once was the case in Montana with the Anaconda Copper Company. Nevertheless, Clive S. Thomas and Ronald J. Hrebenar believe that the increased number of interest groups and the fragmentation of the business community have not lessened the overall power of interest groups. In addition, the need for more campaign money, and the rise of PACs to furnish it, have increased the power of interest groups.

One way to look at interest group power is to compare interest groups to political parties. In other words, are interest groups or political parties dominant in making policy in a state? It should be assumed that interest groups are always important; and the real question is the extent of their power, or dominance. Strong political parties can exert some control over the process of making policy and reduce the ability of interest groups to dominate it. Because parties represent broader constituencies than interest groups, they provide a way for the public to have a voice in policy deliberations. Table 3-5 classifies the states according to the impact on policy making by interest groups. In states with the "dominant" classification, groups as a whole are the overwhelming influence

TABLE 3-5 Classification of the States According to the Overall Impact of Interest Groups in 2002, with Comparison to 1985 Classification

Dominant (5)	Dominant/ complementary (26)	Complementary (16)	Complementary/ subordinate (3)	Subordinate (0)
Alabama	−Alaska	Colorado	−Michigan	
Florida	Arizona	+Connecticut	Minnesota	
+Montana	Arkansas	+Delaware	−South Dakota	
+Nevada	California	−Hawaii		
West Virginia	Georgia	Indiana		
	Idaho	Maine		
	+Illinois	Massachusetts		
	+Iowa	New Hampshire		
	+Kansas	New Jersey		
	Kentucky	New York		
	−Louisiana	North Carolina		
	+Maryland	North Dakota		
	−Mississippi	Pennsylvania		
	+Missouri	+Rhode Island		
	Nebraska	+Vermont		
	−New Mexico	Wisconsin		
	Ohio			
	Oklahoma			
	Oregon			
	−South Carolina			
	−Tennessee			
	Texas			
	Utah			
	Virginia			
	Washington			
	Wyoming			

Source: Clive S. Thomas and Ronald J. Hrebenar, "Interest Groups in the States," in *Politics in the American States: A Comparative Analysis,* 8th ed., Virginia Gray and Russell L. Hanson, eds. (Washington, D.C.: CQ Press, 2004), p. 122. Reproduced by permission of CQ Press.

Note: + or − indicates movement one category up or down since the first survey in 1985.

on policy making. Interest groups in "complementary" states have to work with other participants, most notably political parties; otherwise, they are constrained in their influence. Groups in the "subordinate" category consistently have little impact on policies; no state fits this category. States in the mixed categories ("dominant/complementary" and "complementary/subordinate") alternate between the two categories over time or are evolving from one category to the next.[68]

Interest Group Tactics

To achieve their goals, interest groups go anywhere they need to go—including the executive and judicial branches—but they usually focus on state legislatures where they work to pass or defeat bills or have money appropriated in the amounts they consider necessary. Before discussing specific tactics, it should be noted that in many instances the most successful interest groups are those that can use a defensive strategy: They wish to preserve the status quo against those who are trying to bring about change. Many legislators live by the adage "If it ain't broke, don't fix it." The status quo represents previous political compromises. As a consequence, interest groups advocating a new policy must first show that something is so wrong that it must be fixed before they can effectively argue for their proposed solution. For convenience, interest group tactics may be divided into three categories: public relations campaigns, electioneering, and lobbying.

Public Relations Campaigns

Interest groups can use public relations campaigns to help create a favorable image of themselves and to generate support on specific issues. These campaigns include press conferences, advertising, radio and television interviews, and news releases. Because there is a close connection between public relations campaigns and commercial advertising, groups representing the business community have an advantage in expertise and available personnel, not to mention money. The advantage of money is partially offset because the media frequently give favorable coverage to groups that take positions—such as protecting the environment—that are popular with the public. A little creativity can also help. Alan Rosenthal reports that an environmental group in New Jersey received considerable media attention when it announced the results of pollution studies at contaminated waste sites rather than in an office conference room.[69]

Electioneering

Interest groups may participate in political campaigns by providing assistance to political parties or individual candidates. Some groups may assume a position of neutrality and support candidates from both parties if they support the group's goals. Others may be closely tied to partisan politics. Labor unions, for example, are usually connected to the Democratic Party in most of the large, industrial states, such as California, Illinois, Michigan, New Jersey, New York, Ohio, and Pennsylvania.

Interest groups provide an opportunity for candidates to acquire friendships and build reputations. Most candidates are members of several groups, and they believe they can translate friendship into votes. Candidates may be invited to appear before the group, or they may respond to questionnaires that seek to identify candidates' positions on issues that are of concern to the group. More directly, interest groups may provide staff assistance in running a campaign. Mailing lists of members, office material, and equipment also can be made available for candidates' use.

Money is an important resource that an interest group can provide candidates. Many states still allow corporations and labor unions to contribute money legally to campaigns. **Political action committees (PACs),** frequently sponsored by interest groups, are created specifically to raise and distribute money to candidates running for political office. State PACs have quickly grown in number just as they have at the national level. Every state has hundreds of PACs, and they have become the dominant source of campaign funds as election campaigns have become more and more expensive. According to Rosenthal, PACs contribute money to political campaigns to (1) help elect candidates who are considered friends; (2) show support for those who are likely to be reelected, especially if they are in a legislative leadership position such as committee chair; and (3) gain or improve access to legislators.[70]

PACs raise money through personal contact and direct-mail appeals. Some corporations and labor unions even use voluntary payroll deduction; teachers' unions are particularly good at raising money. Education Minnesota, a professional association of 70,000 public school teachers, includes with its annual membership dues a $10 donation for political activity. It is considered a voluntary donation because members can request that it be refunded to them.[71] Incumbents are the prime beneficiaries of PAC money, sometimes receiving up to 80 percent of PAC contributions. Frequently, PACs ignore party labels, give money to incumbents of both parties, and "go with the power."

Lobbying

Lobbying communicates specific policy goals directly to legislators. Communication may be in the form of testimony before legislative committees or, more indirectly, by establishing contacts in a social setting. In state legislatures with a large professional staff, it is often as important to communicate with the members of the legislator's staff as it is with the legislator. If lobbyists can convince a staff member that their policy position is the correct one, then the staff member may be able to convince his or her boss.

According to the Center for Public Integrity, in 2005 there were 40,000 registered lobbyists paid to advance the agendas of almost 50,000 interest groups. Among the fifty states, that averages to approximately five lobbyists for every one legislator. In New York, the ratio is 20 to 1; in Florida 13 to 1. And a lot of money was spent; in 2005, for the forty-two states that report lobbying expenditures, the total was $1.16 billion. Most of this money goes to pay for lobbyists' salaries and fees. Often a single issue will cause a large amount of money to be spent. Efforts to find a new source of revenue for public school funding in Texas resulted in two special legislative sessions and $9.3 million paid to lobbyists. Every proposal for a new tax to increase revenue caused lobbying by those who strongly opposed it.[72]

Thomas and Hrebenar have identified five categories of lobbyists in the states:[73]

1. *In-house.* Employees of organizations who have titles such as vice president of public affairs or director of government relations and as part of their job devote at least some of their time to lobbying. They represent only one client, and that is their employer. Examples are state chambers of commerce or large corporations. This category represents nearly 40 to 50 percent of all state lobbyists.

2. *Government or legislative liaisons.* Employees of state, local, and federal agencies that, as part of their job, represent their agencies to the legislature. These are sometimes called the "hidden lobbies" because many states do not require government employees to register as lobbyists. State universities, for example, usually have a vice president of state relations (or a similar title) whose real job is to lobby the legislature. This category contains 25 to 40 percent of all lobbyists.

3. *Contract.* Also known as independent lobbyists or "hired guns." They are hired for a fee to lobby and will represent a number of clients, ranging from fewer than ten to thirty or forty. Contract lobbyists sometimes work by themselves or with partners in law firms; either way they are a growing presence in state capitals. They represent 15 to 25 percent of all lobbyists.

4. *Citizen, cause, or volunteer.* These lobbyists represent citizen or community organizations on a part-time and volunteer basis. They rarely represent more than one organization at a time. Perhaps 10 to 20 percent of all lobbyists fit into this category.

5. *"Hobbyists."* These are self-styled lobbyists, private individuals, who act on their own behalf to support pet projects and are not designated to act on the behalf of any organization. The number of "hobbyists" (perhaps 5 percent) is hard to estimate because few are required to register by law.

After laws are passed, interest group activity continues as lobbyists contact executive branch administrators, who are usually given considerable discretion in executing the law. Administrators interact very little with the general public, and they have a tendency to identify very closely with the goals of the groups they are supposed to oversee. As noted in Chapter 1, detailed state constitutions invite litigation by opponents charging that a new law violates part of the constitution. This provides yet another tactic for interest groups that hope to negate laws or render their provisions meaningless through narrow judicial interpretation. Since the 1980s, interest groups have increased their participation in state court litigation, and a greater variety of interest groups are using litigation as a means of shaping policy. Business, religious, and civil rights organizations are continuing to use litigation strategies, and educational and health groups are using it more than they have in the past.[74] In some states, pro-smoking groups have gone to court to challenge the legality of government regulations banning smoking in places such as work areas. In a continuing legal battle that began in 1999, the Brady Center to Prevent Gun Violence joined Gary, Indiana, and other cities in suing sixteen gun manufacturers and six northern Indiana gun dealers. The Indiana suit alleged that the gun dealers, in particular, engaged in "gross misconduct" in supplying guns to an underground market and eventually to criminals. To prevent these lawsuits, the U.S. Congress passed a law limiting the legal liability of the gun industry; in response, lawyers from the Brady Center, representing the City of Gary, challenged the constitutionality of the federal law and won an initial victory in a lower Indiana state court.[75]

Ethics of Lobbying

Given the large number of individuals who are lobbyists and the large amounts of money spent on lobbying, an important question is this: Can lobbyists buy an elected official's support or vote? Unfortunately, during the 1990s, there were a number of incidents of legislators taking money from a lobbyist in exchange for official actions. Many of these were the result of federal investigations and led to indictments and convictions. In 2006, as part of an FBI sting, an Alaska state representative was indicted for agreeing to use his committee positions to secure favorable legislation in exchange for payments that totaled $26,000.[76] The indictment of several state and local legislators in Tennessee resulted from similar undercover federal investigation. Still, given the 40,000 lobbyists and 7,400 legislators, the actual number of examples of bribery is very small. However, this is not to underestimate the importance of influence buying because its effect on public confidence and trust in government can be devastating. After a corruption probe in Arizona was made public, a statewide survey found that more than 70 percent of the people interviewed believed that a legislator would take a bribe if offered one![77]

If the actual buying of influence is infrequent, lobbying activities that have the *appearance* of buying influence are widespread, at least in the public's perception. One of the more dominant images of lobbying is that of legislators accepting gifts and free entertainment from lobbyists; these may include dinners and drinks during the legislative session, tickets to sporting events, and hunting and golf trips. And this image certainly has a basis in reality. Restrictions on gifts and entertainment in many states have reduced gifts and free entertainment, which will be discussed below. But the question of what was actually being "bought," if anything, needs to be considered.

One view is that lobbyists are only buying access to legislators; they want to ensure that when they need five minutes with a legislator, they can get it. Or when a legislator has twenty phone messages, their call is one of the three that will actually be returned. Tickets to games and free food and drinks at receptions, it is argued, are not given with the expectation that lobbyists are actually buying a vote; they are only buying access. An alternative view is that access is close to influence. And if money is needed to have access, then interest groups that can mount a well-financed lobbying operation have an advantage over groups with less money. According to Common Cause, the "result is that public policy decisions may be based solely on who has money and access to government officials, rather than on whether the policy is in the public's interest."[78]

For over two decades, most state legislatures have adopted more and more laws that cover many aspects of the lobbyist-legislator relationship. As might be expected, one important factor in explaining new ethics laws and regulations is the occurrence of a scandal within a state. More recently, public interest groups such as Common Cause and Council on Governmental Ethics Laws have affected the actual content of these laws.[79] Lobbying activities can be regulated, but they cannot be eliminated because lobbying falls under the right of the people to "petition the Government for a redress of grievances," guaranteed by the First Amendment to the U.S. Constitution and provisions in state constitutions as well. All states and the District of Columbia require lobbyists to register with a state ethics commission or a similar agency; accompanying registration will be the requirement to report lobbying expenditures. This type of regulation provides "public information and illuminate[s] group activities."[80] Approximately half of the states require lobbyists to identify legislative and administrative actions that the lobbyists seek to influence. Lobbying on a contingency fee basis, which means that lobbyists are paid only if they are successful, is prohibited in almost all states; it is believed that lobbyists are more likely to attempt to exert "improper influence" if they have to win to be paid. All but a few states prohibit lobbyists from making campaign contributions during the legislative sessions.[81]

FIGURE 3-4 State laws regulating lobbyist giving/reporting gifts to legislators.

Source: The Center for Public Integrity, "Lobbying Disclosure Comparisons 2003," www.publicintegrity.org/hiredguns/
comparisons.aspx (accessed April 17, 2007).

Note: The Center did not classify Pennsylvania because its lobbying law had been held unconstitutional by the Pennsylvania Supreme Court at
the time of the Center's report. A new law was passed in 2006 and the authors have classified Pennsylvania in the "lobbyist required to report
gifts" category.

Regulation of gifts from lobbyists to legislators has received the greatest attention
in the states. As can be seen in Figure 3-4, states are taking different approaches. The
most restrictive states are those that have "zero tolerance." These states also are called
"no cup of coffee states" because a lobbyist cannot give *anything* to a legislator, including a cup of coffee. A number of states allow gifts up to a certain dollar value, for example, $3 per day in Iowa; dollar limits vary considerably among the states. Quite a few
states restrict gifts but allow exceptions for food and entertainment under certain conditions such as inviting all members of the legislature to a reception. Finally, a number of
states have no monetary limits and require only that gifts be reported.[82] Unfortunately,
this is not enough guidance for lobbyists and legislators and does little to reduce the appearance of buying influence.

Of course, more laws and rules lead to more questions: How will these rules be enforced? And who will enforce them? All fifty state legislatures either have a permanent ethics committee or the leadership can appoint a special committee to investigate complaints of
legislators' misconduct. In other words, legislators police themselves. This approach would
appear to have inherent problems. Beth A. Rosenson quotes a New Jersey legislator who
sees the difficulty: "A lot of legislators believe they are appointed to these ethics committees
to protect their own. I'm sure many legislators think 'I might be in this situation someday

myself' and take it easy on their fellow lawmakers."[83] A minority of states have gone beyond this approach and created additional independent commissions that are not composed of legislators. The appointing process varies in the states, ranging from the governor appointing all members to the legislature appointing at least a few and sometimes a majority; of course, the latter commissions would not be considered truly independent.

Can ethics be legislated? Laws frequently have loopholes, either by design or by creative, or devious, thinking. For example, as noted above, in some states lobbyists are prohibited from buying dinner for an individual legislator, but are allowed to buy dinner for members of a committee or a delegation or for the entire membership for that matter. Maryland is a state where lobbyists cannot buy dinner for individual legislators, but the prohibition does not apply out-of-state; this allowed a prominent Maryland lobbyist to invite a number of Maryland legislators, attending a conference in San Francisco, to dinner and a cruise on a chartered boat around San Francisco Bay.[84] Even with independent commissions, observers have noticed that they are not always fully staffed or funded; of course, authorization for staff positions and appropriated money for operations come from the legislature.[85] Clearly, ethics cannot be legislated. Still, these laws and rules serve as important guidelines for legislators in their day-to-day activities, and they serve as standards for the public to judge legislators' behavior. It is also important to remember that all but a few legislators behave ethically; they recognize their moral obligations as an elected representative of their constituents and as a member of one of the key institutions of representative democracy.[86]

URBAN INTEREST GROUPS

Interest groups operate in much the same way in large cities as in state legislatures. The difference is that the same groups are not equally active in state capitols and city halls. Real estate groups and downtown merchants have been more influential at the city level than at the state level.

Types and Tactics

Major urban interest groups may be classified as follows:

Business and economic interests. Groups are organized on the basis of common economic interests. Examples of specific interests are boards of realtors, downtown merchants associations, and local manufacturing associations. Active and influential in almost all cities and towns are local chamber of commerce associations; with membership open to all businesses, they seek to represent business interests generally. Although the interests of labor organizations tend to be with national and state issues (occupational safety and minimum wage, for example), the presence of a large, unionized workforce in the private sector in many cities in the Midwest and East does lead to more labor union activity in local politics. Individual labor unions in a city usually come together to form a labor council to represent labor's interests much in the same way that a chamber of commerce represents business interests.

Neighborhood interests. A neighborhood is usually thought of as the houses in the immediate vicinity of one's own house. At a more general level, a neighborhood can be thought of as an area where housing is of a similar type and market value. It is at this more general level that neighborhood organizations and homeowner associations form for political action. Neighborhood organizations frequently form, as Terry Christensen says, when they "find themselves trying to prevent something from happening to their area that they perceive as a threat, either to their local quality of life or to property values."[87] While these groups primarily emerge in middle- and upper-class neighborhoods, the Association of Community Organizations for Reform Now (ACORN) is active in low-income areas. It has 850 neighborhood chapters in 80 cities that are linked with a national office.[88] Local chapters have worked for affordable housing and a living minimum wage and are active in voter registration and voter turnout drives.

Good-government interests. As noted, the municipal reform movement that started in the late nineteenth century was aided by a number of so-called good-government groups. The desire for local government reform is still alive and so are some of the original reform groups. The League of Women Voters, for example, is active in many cities and towns and emphasizes contemporary reforms such as ethics in public service, campaign financing, and opening government meetings to the public. Other, more conservative groups have advocated for term limits for elected political leaders and for limits on property tax increases.

The strength of interest groups comes from their willingness to take action and their resources (organization, leadership, number of members, and money), all factors that are found in abundance in the business community. And there are plenty of local issues for businesses to be concerned with, including taxes, parking, zoning restrictions, building and housing regulations, and policies toward economic development and growth.

Many interest groups adopt the tactics of state-level interest groups and apply them to the local level, such as providing testimony at public hearings of the city council or some other governing body, lobbying elected and appointed officials in private meetings, and supporting favored candidates in their election campaigns. Citizens without traditional political resources may adopt different tactics. African Americans, other minority groups, and low-income neighborhood associations frequently use nonviolent protests such as demonstrations, rallies, and marches to influence decision makers. (See Chapter 4.)

Neighborhood groups are frequently criticized for manifesting a Not in My Backyard (NIMBY) syndrome. **NIMBY** refers to neighborhood opposition to a government-sponsored project designed to benefit the welfare of the whole community, but one that also could have a negative impact on the particular neighborhood where the project is to be located. Examples include controversies concerning where to locate (usually called siting) halfway houses, landfills, and even Wal-Marts. NIMBY citizens are frequently characterized as being motivated by narrow self-interest, overly emotional, and uninformed in their opposition to these facilities. More recently, researchers realize that the wisdom of government experts arguing for a particular site should not be assumed and that citizen input is valuable.[89]

Community Power Studies

Another approach by scholars seeking to understand the various groups that compete for influence in cities and towns, especially those representing economic interests, is to ask this important question: Who really has power? This seemingly simple question has been looked at from a number of perspectives and has stirred decades of debate. Political scientists and sociologists have studied community power structures, and their conclusions are nearly as numerous as the individual cities and towns studied. Generally speaking, conclusions fall into two categories: the **elitist theory** that a few top leaders form a power structure that dominates decision making, and the **pluralist theory** that views power as being shared by a variety of competing groups with no single group dominating on every issue. Research by sociologists usually has supported the elite theory, and political scientists have tended to support the pluralist theory.

In the classic elitist studies, such as Robert and Helen Lynd's work on Middletown[90] (actually Muncie, Indiana) and Floyd Hunter's examination of Regional City[91] (actually Atlanta, Georgia), power is believed to be concentrated in the hands of a few old families and business leaders. Community leadership is viewed as a rigid system in which those at the top are a relatively permanent group. There is a one-way flow of power, with the elite dictating policy to subordinates. In many cases, the "power elite" does not exercise control openly but operates by manipulating more visible public officials. Although there are occasional disagreements among the elite membership, their common economic interests unite them on most basic issues. In such a system, public opinion and elections have little effect on policy making.

Critics charge that there is more conflict among top business leaders than the Lynds or Hunter suggest.[92] Still, at the time these studies were made (Middletown, 1929 and 1937; Regional City, 1953), their conclusions, if a bit exaggerated, may have been correct. Many U.S. cities—such as Pittsburgh, Atlanta, and Gary, Indiana—early in this century were dominated by a single industry or small group of businesspersons, or even by a single family. As urban populations have become more heterogeneous, we would expect power relationships to change.

Pluralist studies such as Robert Dahl's analysis of New Haven, Connecticut (1961), conclude that power is shared by a variety of groups that are in conflict with one another.[93] The groups are often short-lived—they form around an issue and then disappear. Thus pluralists do not see a stable power structure; rather, they perceive a fluid system of leadership. Persons or groups who dominate decision making in one area are seldom equally effective in other areas. In the pluralist model, public decisions are influenced by public opinion, and elections are an important means of transferring power from one group to another.

As one might expect, elitists and pluralists are critical of each other's methodology. Pluralists charge that elitists begin by assuming the existence of power relations. Elitists often rely on an interview method in which the respondents are asked, "Who has power in Gotham City?" Such a *reputational* approach, suggest the pluralists, often results in confusing groups with high potential for power (i.e., groups that have high status) with groups that actually exercise power. A great many people believe that "they"—bankers, merchants, old families—run cities, so the elitist argument has strong appeal: It is simple, dramatic, and "realistic."

Elitists argue that the pluralist method of focusing on decision making has some major drawbacks. They contend that "key decisions" are not easily selected for analysis. Furthermore, elitists note that political influence is not always seen in the public decision-making process. Those with power may be able to exclude an issue from public discussion altogether and thus exercise control by blocking decision making.

For example, wealthy landlords might prevent a city council from proposing laws that would require landlords to maintain their rental property and expose them to fines if they violate the law. The ability to keep issues off local political agendas is, of course, the ultimate power that individuals or groups can exercise.

No definitive answer that applies to all cities can be given to the question "Who has power?" Particular mixtures of social, economic, and cultural patterns clearly influence the distribution of power in different cities. Furthermore, current research shows that cities characterized by citizen activism on community issues are less likely to have power concentrated in the hands of a few.[94] We turn to the topic of political participation in the next chapter.

SUMMARY

Political parties and interest groups are important to democratic societies because they help to link citizens to their government. Political parties are regulated by the states, but the U.S. Supreme Court has declared some of these regulations unconstitutional. Urban political machines, the best example of traditional party organizations, dominated many cities in the last half of the nineteenth century. Through the use of patronage they won voter support and controlled who was elected as mayor and members of the city council. Machines became corrupt and structural changes in local government advocated by good-government organizations in the early part of the twentieth century made it difficult for them to continue. However, the Daley Machine in Chicago survived into the 1970s, and the use of patronage still occurs but has been further limited by recent Supreme Court decisions.

State party organizations were never as strong as urban political machines, but today they are a vital component of political parties. They provide more services to candidates running for elected offices, even though they may never again control the nominating process the way traditional party organizations did. Local party organizations still vary a great deal in terms of organizational strength and level of activity. In almost every state, some type of primary election is used to nominate their candidates for elected state-level positions, but only the closed primary requires a voter to register with a party before voting in its primary. Primaries tend to weaken party influence over nominations and, in a few states, parties have tried to regain influence through preprimary endorsements.

Fewer states are dominated by one party; the trend is toward two competitive parties in an increasing number of states. Republican Party strength in the South has increased dramatically as Democratic strength has waned. Political scientists have debated whether or not which party controls state government makes any difference in state policy. Recent research concludes that it does make a difference. For example, the Democratic Party tends to take a larger share of a state aggregate personal income for the state budget than Republicans.

Divided government in the states, when one or both houses of the legislature are not controlled by the governor's party, is as common as unified government. Under divided government, governors must compromise with legislative leaders and they may not place controversial issues on their agenda; sometimes gridlock occurs. In addition, the accountability of elected leaders to the voters is weakened in divided government.

Accompanying the growth of state government in policy making has been the growth in the number of interest groups and the variety of interests they represent. Interest groups use various tactics to present their views to legislators in the hope of having favorable policies enacted. Often, groups find that having their own lobbyist or hiring one may be the most effective way to influence decisions. The ethics of lobbyists attempting to influence state legislators has caused many states to enact new laws regulating the lobbyist-legislator relationship.

Local interest groups primarily reflect business and economic interests, along with neighbor-hood and good-government interests. Community power studies look beyond the more visible as-pects of local politics and ask the question: Who really has power? Some researchers find an elite power structure and others find a pluralist one. Recent research concludes that the amount of citizen activism on community issues can affect the extent to which power is concentrated in the hands of an elite.

KEY TERMS

voter registration (p. 77)
Australian ballot system (p. 77)
fusion candidate (p. 78)
urban political machine (p. 78)
patronage (p. 78)
precinct (p. 79)
wards (p. 79)
good-government organizations (p. 80)
nonpartisan elections (p. 81)
at-large elections (p. 81)
precinct caucus (p. 84)
amateurs (p. 86)
professionals (p. 86)
direct primary (p. 87)
closed primary (p. 88)
open primary (p. 88)
blanket primary (p. 88)

open elections (p. 89)
runoff primaries (p. 89)
preprimary endorsements (p. 90)
party competition (p. 91)
Republican Revolution (p. 93)
ideologies (p. 96)
liberals (p. 97)
conservatives (p. 97)
divided government (p. 97)
unified government (p. 97)
interest groups (p. 99)
political parties (p. 99)
political action committees (PACs) (p. 103)
lobbying (p. 103)
NIMBY (p. 108)
elitist theory (p. 109)
pluralist theory (p. 109)

BRIEF COMPARISONS OF STATE/LOCAL DIFFERENCES

Issue	State Level	Local Level
Political parties	Paid executive director and staff at headquarters, conduct opinion polls and party-building activities	Volunteers serve on party committees, distribute campaign literature, and conduct get-out-the-vote drives
Nominations	Voters choose a party's nominee in a primary election	Nonpartisan primaries are used more frequently
Interest groups	Great diversity in interests that are represented in state capitals	Groups representing business are more active and influential

INTERESTING WEB SITES

www.ballot-access.org. This is a nonpartisan Web site that focuses on the difficulties independent and third-party candidates have in placing their names on national, state, and local ballots.

www.commoncause.org. Common Cause is a national organization that is committed to "honest, open and accountable government." Click on "State Organizations" to find out what is going on with state chapters or take a look at "Our Issues," which includes "Ethics in Government."

www.democrats.org. Official Web site for the Democratic National Committee. Click on "Local" for links to state Democratic parties.

www.ncsl.org/ethics. The Center for Ethics in Government is sponsored by the National Conference of State Legislatures. Up-to-date information on ethics issues in government generally, and state legislatures in particular.

www.gop.org. Official Web site for the Republican National Committee. Click on "State Parties" for information on state Republican parties.

NOTES

1. Kris Axtman, "Two Lone Stars Ride into Texas State Race," *Christian Science Monitor* (May 16, 2006), www.csmonitor.com/2006/0516/p02s01-uspo.htm.
2. Jordan Smith, "Kinky Friedman Lights up His Campaign," *Austin Chronicle* (February 16, 2006), www.austinchronicle.com/gyrobase/Issue/print?oid=oid%3A339272.
3. Axtman, "Two Lone Stars."
4. A. James Reichley, *The Life of the Parties: A History of American Political Parties* (New York: Free Press, 1992), pp. 207–209.
5. An excellent analysis of the effect of state laws on political parties can be found in Kay Lawson, "How State Laws Undermine Parties," in *Elections American Style,* A. James Reichley, ed. (Washington, D.C.: Brookings Institution, 1987), pp. 240–260.
6. *Tashjian v. Republican Party of Connecticut,* 479 U.S. 208 (1986).
7. *Eu v. San Francisco County Democratic Central Committee,* 489 U.S. 214 (1989).
8. *Timmons v. Twin Cities Area New Party,* 520 U.S. 351 (1997); a defense of fusion candidacies can be found in Adam Morse and J. J. Gass, *More Choices, More Voices: A Primer on Fusion,* Voting Rights & Elections Series, October 2006, www.brennancenter.org.
9. William J. Crotty, "Urban Political Machines," in *Parties and Politics in American History: A Reader,* L. Sandy Maisel and William G. Shade, eds. (New York: Garland Publishing, 1994), p. 134.
10. Samuel J. Eldersveld, *Political Parties in American Society* (New York: Basic Books, 1982), pp. 150–152.
11. Fred I. Greenstein and Frank Feigert, *The American Party System and the American People,* 3d ed. (Englewood Cliffs, N.J.: Prentice-Hall, 1985), pp. 60–63.
12. Crotty, "Urban Political Machines," p. 137.
13. John Allswang, *Bosses, Machines and Urban Voters,* rev. ed. (Baltimore: Johns Hopkins University Press, 1986), p. 52.
14. Dennis R. Judd and Todd Swanstrom, *City Politics: Private Power & Public Policy* (New York: HarperCollins College Publishers, 1994), p. 79.
15. *Elrod v. Burns,* 427 U.S. 347 (1976).
16. *Rutan v. Illinois Republican Party,* 497 U.S. 62 (1990).
17. See *O'Hare Truck Service v. City of Northlake,* 518 U.S. 712 (1996). A good review of these patronage cases can be found in Cynthia Grant Bowman, "The Supreme Court's Patronage

Decisions and the Theory and Practice of Politics," in *The U.S. Supreme Court and the Electoral Process,* 2d ed., David K. Ryden, ed. (Washington, D.C.: Georgetown University Press, 2002), pp. 126–143.

18. Terry Christensen and Tom Hogen-Esch, *Local Politics: A Practical Guide to Local Politics at the Grassroots,* 2d ed. (Armonk, N.Y.: M. E. Sharpe, 2006), pp. 130–133.

19. Bernard H. Ross and Myron A. Levin, *Urban Politics: Power in Metropolitan America,* 7th ed. (Belmont, Calif.: Thomson Wadsworth, 2006), pp. 183–185.

20. J. L. Polinard, Robert D. Wrinkle, Tomas Longoria, and Norma E. Binder, *Electoral Structure and Urban Policy: The Impact in Mexican American Communities* (Armonk, N.Y.: M. E. Sharpe, 1994).

21. Peter Slevin, "Favoritism Trial Hurts Chicago Mayor," *Washington Post* (July 7, 2006, p. A6), www.washingtonpost.com/wp-dyn/content/article/2006/07/06/AR2006070601563_pf.html; Amanda Paulson, "Chicago Fights Corruption's Long Shadow—Again," *Christian Science Monitor,* (February 4, 2005), p. 2, www.csmonitor.com/2005/0204/p02s01-ussc.htm.

22. Sarah McCally Morehouse and Malcolm E. Jewell, *State Politics, Parties, & Policy,* 2d ed. (Lanham, Md.: Rowman & Littlefield, 2003), pp. 116–117.

23. John F. Bibby, *Politics, Parties, and Elections in America,* 3d ed. (Chicago: Nelson-Hall, 1996), pp. 111–113.

24. Reichley, *Life of the Parties,* p. 382.

25. John F. Bibby, "State Party Organizations: Coping and Adapting," in *The Parties Respond: Changes in American Parties and Campaigns,* 2d ed., L. Sandy Maisel, ed. (Boulder, Colo.: Westview Press, 1994), p. 30; Reichley, *The Life of the Parties,* p. 388.

26. Marjorie Random Hershey, *Party Politics in America,* 11th ed. (New York: Pearson Longman, 2005), p. 59.

27. Sarah M. Morehouse and Malcolm E. Jewell, "The Future of Political Parties in the States," *The Book of the States 2005* (Lexington, Ky.: Council of State Governments, 2006), p. 337.

28. Robert J. Huckshorn, "State Party Leaders," in *Political Parties and Elections in the United States: An Encyclopedia,* L. Sandy Maisel and Charles Bassett, eds. (New York: Garland Publishing, 1991), pp. 1059–1060.

29. John P. Frendreis, James L. Gibson, and Laura L. Vertz, "The Electoral Relevance of Local Party Organizations," *American Political Science Review* 84 (March 1990), pp. 228–233.

30. Samuel C. Patterson and Gregory A. Calderia, "The Etiology of Partisan Competition," *American Political Science Review* 78 (September 1984), pp. 701–703.

31. James W. Lamare, Jerry L. Polinard, and Robert D. Wrinkle, "Texas: Religion and Politics in God's Country," in *The Christian Right in American Politics: Marching to the Millennium* (Washington, D.C.: Georgetown University Press, 2003), pp. 67–70. This book has excellent case studies of the Christian Right in thirteen states.

32. Bibby, *Politics, Parties, and Elections,* pp. 116–118.

33. E. E. Schattschneider, *Party Government* (New York: Holt, Rinehart and Winston, 1942), p. 1, quoted in Bibby, *Politics, Parties, and Elections,* p. 8.

34. Hershey, *Party Politics in America,* p. 159.

35. *California Democratic Party v. Jones,* 530 U.S. 567 (2000).

36. Secretary of State, Washington, *History of Washington State Primary Systems,* www.secstate.wa.gov/documentvault/HistoryofWashingtonStatePrimarySystems-920.pdf.

37. Louisiana's nomination process is sometimes classified as "nonpartisan," meaning no party names are on the ballot. (Also, "nonpartisan" is placed in quotes indicating that it is somehow different from the normal nonpartisan election.) This seems incorrect for Louisiana because party names are allowed in both the first and second elections. The open elections name has been used by Kazee and Hadley and is more appropriate. See Charles D. Hadley, "The Impact

of the Louisiana Open Elections System Reform," *State Government* 58, no. 4 (1986), pp. 152–156; Thomas A. Kazee, "The Impact of Electoral Reform: 'Open Elections' and the Louisiana Party System," *Publius* 13 (Winter 1983), pp. 131–139.

38. Meghan Gordon, "Saturday Is Last Hurrah for Open Primaries," *Times-Picayune* (December 3, 2006), www.nola.com/newslogs/tpupdates/index.ssf?/mtlogs/nola_tpupdates/archives/2006_12_03.html.

39. Bibby, *Politics, Parties, and Elections,* p. 137.

40. Ibid., p. 139.

41. Morehouse and Jewell, "Future of Political Parties," p. 335.

42. Ibid., p. 336.

43. Morehouse and Jewell, *State Politics, Parties, & Policy,* p. 137.

44. James P. Melcher, "Party Endorsements in Minnesota in the Wake of the 1994 Elections: Reform Strikes Out," *Comparative State Politics* 16 (December 1995), pp. 1–13.

45. Stephen I. Frank and Steven C. Wagner, *"We Shocked the World!" A Case Study of Jesse Ventura's Election as Governor of Minnesota* (New York: Harcourt College Publishers, 1999), p. 6.

46. Malcolm Jewell and David Olson, *Political Parties and American States,* 3d ed. (Chicago: The Dorsey Press, 1988), pp. 28–30.

47. Earl Black and Merle Black, *Politics and Society in the South* (Cambridge, Mass.: Harvard University Press, 1987), p. 287.

48. John H. Aldrich, "Southern Parties in State and Nation," *Journal of Politics* 62 (August 2000), p. 647.

49. Robert S. Erickson, Gerald C. Wright, and John P. McIver, "Public Opinion in the States: A Quarter Century of Change and Stability," in *Public Opinion in State Politics,* Jeffrey E. Cohen, ed. (Stanford, Calif.: Stanford University Press, 2006), pp. 241–243.

50. Pamela M. Prah, "Dems Grab State Balance of Power," www.stateline.org/live/printable/story?contentId=156838; Eric Kelderman, "Democratic Wave Washes over Statehouses," www.stateline.org/live/printable/story?contentId=155730; (accessed January 16, 2003); "Democrats Make Major Gains in Nation's State Legislatures," www.ncsl.org/programs/press/2006/pr061108.htm (Accessed January 16, 2006).

51. Michael Janofsky, "Green Party in New Mexico Goes from Gadfly to Player," *New York Times* (July 19, 2002).

52. V. O. Key, Jr., *Southern Politics in State and Nation* (New York: Vintage Books, 1949), pp. 15–18, 298–311. For an analysis of Key's work, see *V. O. Key, Jr., and the Study of American Politics,* Milton C. Cummings, ed. (Washington, D.C.: American Political Science Association, 1988). David Mayhew's "Why Did V. O. Key Draw Back from His 'Have-Nots' Claim?" in the Cummings monograph is excellent.

53. Key, *Southern Politics,* pp. 307–310.

54. Thomas R. Dye, *Politics in States and Communities,* 7th ed. (Englewood Cliffs, N.J.: Prentice-Hall, 1991), p. 135.

55. Robert D. Brown, "Party Cleavages and Welfare Effort in the American States," *American Political Science Review* 89 (March 1995), pp. 23–33.

56. Diana Dwyre, Mark O'Gorman, Jeffrey M. Stonecash, and Rosalie Young, "Disorganized Politics and the Have-Nots: Politics and Taxes in New York and California," *Polity* 27 (Fall 1994), pp. 26–27.

57. James C. Garand, "Partisan Change and Shifting Expenditure Priorities in the American States, 1945–1978," *American Politics Quarterly* 13 (October 1985), pp. 370–371.

58. James E. Alt and Robert C. Lowery, "A Dynamic Model of State Budget Outcomes under Divided Partisan Government," *Journal of Politics* (November 2000), pp. 1062–1065.

59. Robert S. Erikson, Gerald C. Wright, and John McIver, *Statehouse Democracy: Public Opinion and Policy in the American States* (New York: Cambridge University Press, 1993).

60. Ibid., p. 103.
61. Morris Fiorina, *Divided Government,* 2d ed. (Boston: Allyn & Bacon, 1996), pp. 85–110.
62. Cynthia J. Bowling and Margaret R. Ferguson, "Divided Government, Interest Representation, and Policy Differences: Competing Explanations of Gridlock in the Fifty States," *Journal of Politics* 63 (February 2001), p. 187.
63. Laura A. van Assendelft, *Governors, Agenda Setting, and Divided Government* (Lanham, Md.: University Press of America, 1997), p. 202.
64. Robert C. Lowry, James E. Alt, and Karen E. Ferree, "Fiscal Policy Outcomes and Electoral Accountability in American States," *American Political Science Review* 92 (December 1998), pp. 759–774.
65. Jeffrey M. Berry, *The Interest Group Society,* 3d ed. (New York: Longman, 1997), p. 46.
66. *America's Civic Health Index: Broken Engagement,* a report by the National Conference on Citizenship, 2006, p. 34; http://casefoundation.cachefly.net/pdf/civic_health_summary.pdf (accessed February 3, 2007); Cliff Zukin, et al., *A New Engagement: Political Participation, Civic Life, and the Changing American Citizen* (New York: Oxford University Press, 2006), p. 61.
67. Clive S. Thomas and Ronald J. Hrebenar, "Who's Got Clout? Interest Group Power in the States," *State Legislatures* (April 1999), p. 31.
68. Clive S. Thomas and Ronald J. Hrebenar, "Interest Groups in the States," in *Politics in the American States,* 8th ed., Virginia Gray and Russell L. Hanson, eds. (Washington, D.C.: Congressional Quarterly Press, 2004), p. 121.
69. Alan Rosenthal, *The Third House,* 2nd ed. (Washington, D.C.: Congressional Quarterly Press, 2001), p. 174.
70. Ibid., pp. 129–130.
71. www.educationminnesota.org/index.cfm?page_id=4240
72. Sarah Laskow, *State Lobbying Becomes Billion-Dollar Business,* Center for Public Integrity, December 20, 2006, www.publicintegrity.org/hiredguns/report.aspx?aid=835. The source for the Texas lobbying example, which is referred to in the above article, is a report by Texans for Public Justice.
73. Thomas and Hrebenar, "Interest Groups in the States," pp. 114–115.
74. Lee Epstein, "Exploring the Participation of Organized Interests in State Court Litigation," *Political Research Quarterly* 47 (June 1994), pp. 341–348.
75. Brady Center to Prevent Gun Violence, "Indiana Court to Become First to Rule Gun Industry Shield Law Unconstitutional," www.bradycampaign.org/media/?pagename=release&release =830&printer_friendly=true.
76. Eric Adams, "State Rep. Tom Anderson Arrested on Seven Federal Charges," *Associated Content,* www.associatedcontent.com/pop_print.shtml?content_type=article&content_type_ id=99458.
77. Susan Biemesderfer, "Making Laws, Breaking Laws," *State Legislatures* (April 1991), p. 18.
78. Common Cause, *State Issue Brief: Lobby Disclosure Reform in the States* (Washington, D.C.: Common Cause, 1993), p. 2.
79. Beth A. Rosenson, *The Shadowlands of Conduct* (Washington, D.C.: Georgetown University Press, 2005), pp. 140–146.
80. Morehouse and Jewell, *State Politics, Parties, & Policy,* p. 88.
81. *The State of State Legislative Ethics: A Look at the Ethical Climate and Ethics Laws for State Legislators* (Denver, Colo.: National Conference of State Legislators, 2002), pp. 92–110.
82. Ginger Sampson and Peggy Kerns, *Gift Restrictions: Laws for Legislators—It's Not a Physics Lesson.* National Conference of State Legislatures, Center for Ethics in Government, Eye on Ethics, Briefing Papers on Important Ethical Issues, www.ncsl.org/programs/ethics/ legisbrief-gifts.
83. Rosenson, *Shadowlands,* p. 117.

84. Ibid., pp. 139–140.
85. Mary Curtis, "States Offer Grim Look at Curbing Corruption," *Los Angeles Times* (February 28, 2006), p. A9.
86. Peggy Kerns and Ginger Sampson, "Do Ethics Laws Work?" *State Legislatures* (July/August 2003), p. 43.
87. Christensen and Hogen-Esch, *Local Politics*, p. 241.
88. Ibid., p. 243.
89. Gregory E. McAvoy, *Controlling Technology: Citizen Rationality and the NIMBY Syndrome* (Washington, D.C.: Georgetown University Press, 1999), pp. 1–11.
90. Robert Lynd and Helen Lynd, *Middletown* (New York: Harcourt, Brace, and World, 1929), and Robert Lynd and Helen Lynd, *Middletown in Transition* (New York: Harcourt, Brace, and World, 1937).
91. Floyd Hunter, *Community Power Structure* (Chapel Hill: University of North Carolina Press, 1953).
92. Nelson Polsby, *Community Power and Political Theory* (New Haven, Conn.: Yale University Press, 1963).
93. Robert A. Dahl, *Who Governs?* (New Haven, Conn.: Yale University Press, 1961).
94. Lawrence J. R. Herson and John M. Bolland, *The Urban Web: Politics, Policy, and Theory,* 2nd ed. (Chicago: Nelson-Hall Publishers, 1998), pp. 179–180.

POLITICAL PARTICIPATION AND ELECTIONS

ARE YOU AN OPC?

OPC—that's short for an Online Political Citizen. Information technology is changing the way we live, and it may change how we participate in politics. OPCs are those who "use the Internet in a variety of ways to be politically involved,"[1] according to research sponsored by the Institute for Politics, Democracy & the Internet. Specifically, an OPC is a person who visited a Web site of a candidate or a political party early in the presidential election year of 2004, and participated in at least two additional activities such as donated money using the Internet to a political organization or candidate, visited a political discussion group, chat room or blog, or sent someone a political email. OPCs are still small in number; estimates are that they comprise about 7 percent of the general population. Their characteristics reflect the well-documented "digital divide"; they are younger, better educated, and have higher incomes than the general public; they also are more likely to be male and to be white. One might expect that OPCs are citizens who have always been interested in politics and they are simply using a new tool, the personal computer, as a means to participate. This is partially true, but a large number are attracted to politics for the first time. For example, 44 percent of the OPCs report almost no involvement in past political campaigns.

OPCs are "much more heavily involved in politics and civic life than the general public."[2] However, the political involvement of OPCs is not the same as other community leaders and opinion makers or, as they are called in this study, "influentials." OPCs are involved in political activities, but they tend to be those associated with the presidential election; they are less inclined to engage in local political or civic activities. It would seem natural that OPCs, especially as they grow older, would expand their interest in local politics and civic affairs. It is easy to see how the Internet could be valuable locally to communicate about community problems and mobilize concerned citizens. Still, much of local politics may best be accomplished by citizens skilled in interpersonal relations—whether it is presenting their views to a city council or persuading the president of a neighborhood association to run for mayor.

POINTS TO CONSIDER

- How can people participate in politics?
- What is the goal of a strong democracy?
- Discuss changes in voter registration procedures, especially those that affected the voting rights of African Americans, Hispanics, and other minority groups.
- What factors affect voter turnout in state elections?
- What are the important factors determining the winner of a gubernatorial election?
- How do judicial election campaigns differ from other campaigns?
- What do election campaigns cost?
- What is public financing of election campaigns and what factors determine its success?
- Highlight differences among the initiative, referendum, and recall.
- What are the pros and cons of the initiative process?

POLITICAL PARTICIPATION

Political participation is "actions through which ordinary members of a political system influence or attempt to influence outcomes."[3] For this definition, voting in elections is one example, but so are other acts such as contributing money to candidates or interest groups, signing petitions, protesting, and writing letters to government officials.

Within the past few years, political scientists have renewed their interest in another form of community involvement called civic engagement. **Civic engagement** refers to "participation aimed at achieving a public good, but usually through direct hands-on work in cooperation with others."[4] Examples of civic engagement are working together with someone or a group to solve a community problem, volunteering with an environmental organization, volunteering with an organization that helps people in need, and walking, running, or bicycling for a charitable cause. Civic engagement is not related directly to influencing government, but it can affect the quality of life in a community as much as many programs that are run by a government agency.

How Americans Participate

Much of what political scientists know about political participation and civic engagement is a result of **survey research,** which is a way of collecting information by asking a relatively small number of people that are representative of a larger population questions about their political attitudes or behavior.

Some of the best work in political science has focused on the topic of citizen participation, from Sidney Verba and Norman Nie's pioneering *Participation in America*[5] to the research of Cliff Zukin and associates recently published in *A New Engagement* in 2006. Figure 4-1 identifies a wide range of political and civic engagement activities, and the percentages show the level of participation by the American public during the previous twelve months, that is, twelve months before the time of the interviewing (2002). One activity not included in this figure is registering to vote, and it is the activity that has the highest level of participation, approximately 80 percent. Beyond registering to vote, participation drops dramatically; even the actual act of voting (on a regular basis) has a participation rate of just over half (51 percent). A few activities are in the 30 percent range, including consumer activism, which to be political in nature must be based primarily on an individual having policy or social concerns with a manufacturer or retailer. It is usually in the form of "boycotting," refusing to purchase a product to show disapproval, but also occurs as "buycotting," purchasing a product to show approval. Whether these activities are political is difficult to discern because it depends largely on an individual's motivation. A political motivation would be refusing to buy a manufacturer's products because of their environmental record, whereas refusing to buy because of product quality would not.[6] Trying to persuade others how to vote, charity fundraising, and participating actively in a group or association are done by one of every three citizens. A number of important means of participating are in the low teens, such as contacting a public official to ask assistance or express your opinion, contributing funds to a political campaign, and running, walking, or bicycling for charity fundraising. Coming in at the bottom is taking part in a demonstration or participating in door-to-door canvasing for a political or social group. Most observers conclude that, in the United States, participation, whether it is political or civic, is low.

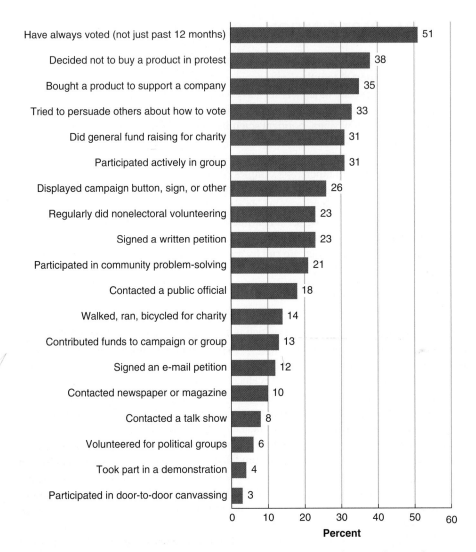

FIGURE 4-1 Political and Civic Engagement Activities During a Twelve-Month Period

Source: Cliff Zukin, Scott Keeter, Molly Andolina, Krista Jenkins, and Michael X. Delli Carpini, *A New Engagement: Political Participation, Civic Life, and the Changing American Citizen* (New York: Oxford University Press, 2006), p. 60.

Note: This figure is based on data from National Civic Engagement Survey I and is reproduced with permission of the Center for Information and Research on Civic Learning and Engagement (CIRCLE) at www.civicyouth.org.

Zukin and associates have two additional findings that should be mentioned briefly. The first is a typology of citizen involvement (Figure 4-2). One type is the "political specialist," who engages in two or more activities a year such as always voting and trying to persuade someone how to vote or displaying a bumper sticker or sign on behalf of a candidate. The second is the "civic specialist," who engages in two or more activities a year such as working with others to solve a community problem, raising money

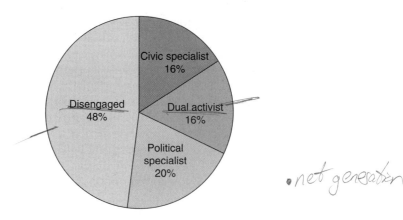

FIGURE 4-2 Types of Engagement among Americans

Source: Cliff Zukin, Scott Keeter, Molly Andolina, Krista Jenkins, and Michael X. Delli Carpini, *A New Engagement: Political Participation, Civic Life, and the Changing American Citizen* (New York: Oxford University Press, 2006), p. 64.

Note: This figure is based on data from National Civic Engagement Survey I and is reproduced with permission of the Center for Information and Research on Civic Learning and Engagement (CIRCLE) at www.civicyouth.org.

for a charity, or getting involved in similar nonpolitical activities. The third type of citizen is the "dual activist," who is engaged in both political and civic domains. Finally, there is the "disengaged"; at best these citizens may participate in one activity, at worst they simply do not participate.[7]

Second, Zukin and associates conclude, and other political scientists have also, that the so-called DotNet generation (those young adults born after 1976 and between the ages of 15 and 28) is not apathetic and disengaged, as they are frequently characterized. The truth is that young people today are less likely to engage in political activities but more likely to engage in civic activities. Activities such as voting, working in election campaigns, and being active in political parties are not a favored means of participation for young adults; they are more likely to be volunteering for nonpolitical organizations, raising money for charitable causes, and working informally with someone or a group to solve a problem in the community.[8]

Before leaving this overview of ways Americans participate in politics, a closer look at protest is required because controversy surrounds it as a means of political participation. Nonviolent protests such as marches, rallies, and demonstrations are protected by the First Amendment of the U.S. Constitution, and were especially prominent during the civil rights movement of the 1950s and 1960s. Specific causes of protests in urban areas have ranged from public housing conditions to police practices. Protests are aimed not only at decision makers but also at gaining support from public opinion, which may help influence those who make policies.

Protest also can be violent, as were the urban riots of the 1960s and the 1992 Los Angeles riot that occurred after a jury refused to find four police officers guilty of any wrongdoing for their beating of Rodney King while they were arresting him. Whether these urban riots are a form of political participation or are simply the work of habitual lawbreakers "who shoot, loot, and burn for strictly nonpolitical motives"[9] is still a hotly debated question. Although riots often have been touched off when seemingly routine contact between the police and African Americans went awry, the underlying cause of riots in several cities during the 1960s has been traced to long-standing racial discrimination and the resultant feeling of powerlessness on the part of inner-city African Americans. This is not to say that all rioters were politically motivated; certainly some rioters were participating for the possibility of stealing material goods.

Do political leaders respond to the demands of protestors? The answer is mixed. Of course, the civil rights movement is an example of the successful use of peaceful protest, especially demonstrations and marches, over a period of several years to achieve changes in laws. To be effective, protests must focus on specific policy goals that decision makers can act on rather than simply express general discontent.[10] After much debate, the U.S. Congress responded to the 1992 Los Angeles riots with financial assistance that was used to reopen destroyed businesses and provide summer jobs for youths. It also financed a Weed and Seed program that would "weed lawbreakers out of neighborhoods and seed these areas with enrichment services for children."[11] However, protests, especially those that are violent, always risk the possibility of creating a backlash against the actions and demands of protestors that reduces the likelihood they will achieve anything. Lawrence Herson and John Bolland conclude that the "lack of positive outcomes and the plethora of negative outcomes"[12] are the best way to describe the results of urban riots of the 1960s. Negative outcomes include increased police expenditures and the election in several cities of mayors who ran on law-and-order platforms.

Strong Democracy

The New England town meeting, citizens coming together to make decisions for the community, is the ideal of democratic decision making. Today, however, the size of most local governments and the complexity of issues they face make it impractical for everyone to come together at one time to make decisions. Nevertheless, a number of political scientists and governmental leaders think that ways must be found to increase citizen participation in government, that is, create what Benjamin Barber calls strong democracy.[13] They argue that this may not be possible in national and state politics because of problems of distance and size, but that it is possible in local governments. **Strong democracy** is the idea that citizenship involves people participating at least some of the time in the making of decisions that affect themselves and their community. The model would be public forums where people "could work with their neighbors to solve the problems of their community."[14]

Of course, the many demands on people's time lead one to question whether they would participate in these forums. Jeffrey Berry, Kent Portney, and Ken Thomson, after studying five cities, conclude that effective citizen participation can occur through neighborhood-based associations, containing 2,000 to 5,000 people, if they meet the criteria of breadth and depth. (These neighborhood associations would be more formal in terms of organization and function than those referred to in the context of local interest groups in Chapter 3.)

Breadth of participation is the extent to which every citizen is offered the opportunity to take part in the deliberations of their neighborhood association. This involves conducting an extensive outreach effort detailing information on the time and place of meetings and issues to be discussed. Efforts to keep citizens informed should be continuous, perhaps involving the publication of a monthly neighborhood newspaper describing the association's activities. This type of effort requires a commitment of financial resources and staff from the local government that the associations are a part of. Depth of participation is the extent to which citizens, working through associations, actually influence local governmental policies. Citizens should have a say, at least, in how land is used and how government funds are spent in their neighborhoods. Neighborhood assemblies, it is believed, "conducted as an open and ongoing forum for the discussion of a flexible and citizen generated agenda,"[15] can provide an institutional framework for effective citizen participation.

VOTING

Voter turnout varies a great deal over time and by the office that is on the ballot; nevertheless, it is still one of the most important acts of political participation. Sidney Verba, Kay Schlozman, and Henry Brady point to the vote as a unique political act because "casting a ballot is, by far, the most common act of citizenship in any democracy and because election returns are decisive in determining who shall govern."[16] However, before citizens can vote, they must register by filling out a voter registration application form for the local board of elections; this results in their names being placed on a list of eligible voters and their assignment to a polling place. This sounds simple enough, but voter registration procedures in the states have involved considerable controversy over the years.

African Americans and the Right to Vote

Historically, procedures and requirements in southern states made it extremely difficult for African Americans to register; in essence they discriminated against African Americans and other minority groups. Underlying this legal framework in most places in the South was the reality of threats and intimidation that prevented the vast majority of African Americans from even thinking about registering to vote. This has changed greatly since the mid-1960s. Sometimes states changed on their own; other times, only after being pressured by the federal government.

An example of a discriminatory voter registration requirement was the literacy test, which were initially adopted in the 1890s and became quite complex over the years by devising new ways to prevent African Americans from registering. Literacy tests frequently involved interpreting a section of the state constitution to the satisfaction of a local election official. Allowing these officials to determine whether an interpretation was correct or not gave them a way to refuse to register African Americans; all they had to say was that their interpretation was wrong. Provisions in the law allowed an official to read a section of the constitution to an illiterate person and, if they interpreted it to the satisfaction of the official, they would be allowed to register; this was a convenient procedure to register illiterate whites. Persons could also be prevented from registering if they failed a "good character" requirement, or be allowed to register if they passed this requirement. Citizenship tests that only constitutional scholars could pass were a requirement in some states.[17]

The civil rights movement in the 1960s was concerned about finding ways so African Americans could register to vote. In 1965 the need for federal action was dramatized when civil rights activists, marching for the right to vote in Alabama, were arrested and beaten by state troopers using nightsticks and tear gas. Federal action came quickly with the U.S. Congress adopting the **Voting Rights Act of 1965,** which suspended literacy tests as a requirement of registering to vote. The Voting Rights Act covered a county or state if it met the guidelines of a "triggering formula": (1) A literacy test was in use as of November 1, 1964, and (2) fewer than 50 percent of the eligible voters were registered or cast ballots in the 1964 presidential election. If a county or state met these conditions, and those in the South almost exclusively did, the U.S. attorney general was empowered to suspend the literacy tests and replace local registration officials with federal agents who would register voters under federal procedures. The act effectively ended literacy tests, and they were permanently banned nationwide in 1975. Because of eventual voluntary compliance in registering voters, federal registrars were sent to only a few counties in the South.

Another provision in the Voting Rights Act is Section 5, which has grown in importance over the years. This section provides for a procedure known as preclearance. **Preclearance** prohibits covered state and local governments from making any changes affecting voting unless they are approved by the U.S. attorney general or the U.S. District Court for the District of Columbia. Proposed changes are not approved if they deny or abridge the right to vote on account of race. This means that changes such as drawing new district lines for members of state or local legislatures, annexing additional land by a city that changes its racial composition, or changing the location of polling places have to be approved at the federal level before they can be implemented.[18]

The results of the Voting Rights Act are impressive: Nearly 1 million African Americans were added to voter registration lists in Deep South states. From 1964 to 1968, for example, the percentage of voting-age African Americans registered in Mississippi increased from 6.7 to 59.4. The U.S. Justice Department, charged with implementing the act, estimated that within five years after its passage as many African Americans had registered in Alabama, Mississippi, Georgia, Louisiana, North Carolina, and South Carolina as in the previous one hundred years.[19]

Voting Rights Today

The main provisions of the Voting Rights Act of 1965 were viewed originally as temporary but were extended by Congress, sometimes with important changes, in 1970, 1975, 1982, and most recently in 2006.

An important change was adopted in the 1975 amendments. Mexican Americans in southwestern states had suffered discrimination in their efforts to register and vote similar to, although not as severe as, that suffered by African Americans. And in the 1960s the **Chicano movement,** a "surge of militant activity among the younger generation of Mexican Americans that quickly spread throughout the Southwest,"[20] focused national attention on discrimination against Mexican Americans. As a result, coverage of the Voting Rights Act was extended to language minorities, such as Asian Americans, American Indians, Alaska natives, and Hispanic Americans. To be covered by the law, a language minority has to make up at least 5 percent of the voting-age population in a state or local jurisdiction, usually a county. In addition, election information including registration forms, voter information sample ballots, and actual ballots has to be available in the minority language.

Prior to the renewal of the Voting Rights Act in 1982, Congress debated whether those suing under the act had to prove that a defendant had intended to discriminate. Civil rights groups protested that intent would be difficult to prove and that, in any case, discrimination, even if it is not deliberate, still adversely affects African Americans, Hispanics, and other minorities. The 1982 amendments resolved this controversy by prohibiting any voting practice or procedure, regardless of intent, that results in discrimination. As a consequence, the Voting Rights Act today deals with subtle forms of discrimination such as minority vote dilution. **Minority vote dilution** occurs when election laws and racial bloc voting combine to keep minorities from winning elective positions. It has occurred in state and local governments throughout the United States, not just those in the South. Examples of minority vote dilution are especially evident at the local level where city or county councils use at-large elections (see Chapter 3). For example, if voting in a county with a population 51 percent white and 49 percent one or more minority groups is polarized—minority voters vote for minority candidates, and white voters vote for white candidates—100 percent of the council members will be white. All white candidates will be elected with 51 percent of the vote, and all minority candidates will lose, with 49 percent of the vote. Even though the minority population is almost as large as the white population, no minorities will be elected to the council. After being sued under the Voting Rights Act, many local governments with at-large elections and a history of no minorities running in or winning these elections have been forced to adopt single-member districts. These districts increase the likelihood of members of minority groups winning office because boundary lines are drawn so that the minority will be a majority of the voters in at least one or more districts.

The latest congressional debate over renewal of the temporary provisions of the Voting Rights Act included proposals that would have weakened it, but they were all defeated. The temporary provisions, Section 5, Section 203 (language minorities), and Sections 6 and 9 (federal observers), were all renewed. The title of this law has the names of three famous civil rights leaders: Fannie Lou Hamer, Rosa Parks and Coretta Scott King Voting Rights Reauthorization and Renewal Act of 2006.

Have voting rights changes significantly empowered minority groups? There is little doubt that the number of African Americans and Hispanics in elected local offices has steadily increased. For example, in 2002 close to 5,000 African Americans were serving as mayors and members of city or county councils, an increase of 55 percent since 1985. The number of Hispanics—the largest minority in the United States, who comprise 14 percent of the total population—in similar positions was just under 2,000 in 2002, an increase of almost 50 percent since 1985.

Still, these increases in officeholding, especially for Hispanics, do not indicate numerical equality or parity; that is, the proportion of minority officials in most local governments is less than the proportion of minorities in the population. Representation is improving, but recent studies show that **political incorporation,** where minorities are part of the dominant city policy making coalition on minority-related issues, is the exception rather than the rule.[21] Political scientist Clarence N. Stone has noted that greater representation by minorities has not meant either greater access to government for lower-class African Americans or that poor inner-city neighborhoods have benefited from new public works projects.[22]

Additional Changes in Voter Registration

Gradually, other registration requirements such as living in a state for at least one year and appearing in person at the election board's headquarters to register were changed. States changed residency requirements to only ten to thirty days before an election, and more than half the states adopted mail-in registration. A few states gave voters the opportunity to register when they obtain or renew their driver's license ("motor-voter" registration) or apply for certain types of public assistance such as food stamps and Medicaid (agency-based registration).[23] Although many states were easing registration procedures, Congress in 1993 enacted the **National Voter Registration Act (NVRA)** that required all states to adopt mail-in, "motor-voter," and agency-based registration procedures. In addition, state laws that purge voters, that is, cancel their registration solely for failure to vote at least once during a specified time, are prohibited. This act expanded federal control over voter registration.[24]

During 2003–04, state motor vehicle offices handled 33 percent of the 49.6 million registration applications or transactions processed nationwide; the next most popular way of taking care of registration transactions was through the mail, 32 percent of the total. Transactions include people registering to vote for the first time, changing their place of registration because they moved into a new county, or changing their name or local address.[25] States reported more than 174.8 million registered voters in 2004, 78.5 percent of the voting-age population.

What has been the impact of NVRA? Are more citizens registering to vote? And, as many of the advocates of NVRA predicted, are more people actually voting? Political scientists Robert D. Brown and Justin Wedeking have taken a close look at these questions. Even when other state characteristics that affect voter registration rates are taken into consideration, NVRA by itself has helped to increase voter registration rates. As one might expect, the greatest increase was in a majority of the states that did not have their own "motor-voter" laws prior to NVRA. Nevertheless, NVRA has not increased voter turnout. Brown and Wedeking emphasize that registration and voting are two separate processes and that the reason a person registers may not be enough of a reason to vote.[26] Completing a voter registration application at the DMV or MVA when you are renewing your driver's license is fairly easy; however, following an election campaign, deciding who to vote for and then actually voting is undoubtedly another level of motivation. Brown and Wedeking conclude that NVRA has created a "pool of individuals who have their tickets but have no desire to go to the game."[27] Clearly, registration is not the only hurdle to voting that must be surmounted. Still, given the millions of registration transactions that take place every year, it makes sense to make them as convenient as possible for citizens.

Six states have gone about as far as you can go in easing registration requirements: Idaho, Maine, Minnesota, New Hampshire, Wisconsin, and Wyoming allow Election Day registration (EDR); NVRA exempted EDR states from its coverage. Registration and voting become a one-step process completed at the same time. EDR was an important factor in Jesse Ventura's election as governor of Minnesota. Approximately 15 percent of the voters registered on Election Day, and many of them were new, young voters who voted overwhelmingly for Ventura.[28] A study of EDR states concludes that on average the voter turnout rate is 5 percent higher than in states that do not have a one-step process.[29] Nevertheless, concern about the potential for voting fraud has prevented most states from adopting it.

Does controversy still exist with voter registration today? Yes, debate over voter registration procedures continues. One side of the debate argues that even with the important changes in voter registration that have taken place, it could be easier and should be easier so that people will not be discouraged from registering because it takes too much time or involves too much paperwork. The other side argues that if voter registration is too easy it will allow voter fraud; that is, people who are not eligible will vote or people who are eligible will vote more than once. Although it is something of an oversimplification, the former position is labeled as supporting access to the ballot and the latter is viewed as supporting the integrity of the ballot. Proof of citizenship before a person can register to vote, a requirement being considered in a number of states, is a recent manifestation of the access/integrity debate. College students have presented another voter registration dilemma for state lawmakers. Should students be allowed to register in the communities where they are attending college? States can be classified in one of two ways in their approach to college-student voter registration:[30] **Restrictive states** have residency requirements that make it almost impossible for college students to register in their college communities. These states see a college residence as temporary for educational purposes only, not as an official residence. For all practical purposes, students must register where they lived before attending college. **Student choice states** allow college students to determine their own residency for registration purposes; they can register in their hometown or they can register where they are attending college. Approximately two-thirds of the states are student choice—a few by law but most through interpretation of laws by election officials. Political scientist Michael G. O'Loughlin concludes that student choice is the better option because "only by gaining local voting rights can students exercise their full rights as citizens"[31] and become effective participants in the community where they are living and attending college.

Voting Systems

A landmark in the history of elections in the United States occurred in the 2000 presidential election when questions were raised in Florida about the fairness of the election, especially the accuracy of the counting of votes. One fact this election brought to everyone's attention was that holding an election was not a simple event: More than 100 million voters cast ballots on over 700,000 voting machines in over 200,000 polling places that were managed by approximately 22,000 election officials and 1.4 million part-time Election Day workers.[32] Closer analysis revealed that the voting disaster in Florida could just as easily have happened in any number of states. The principal problem was with what election experts call **voting systems,** devices that are used for casting and tabulating ballots or votes.

What actually happened in Florida? Of the 6 million ballots that were cast in the presidential election, more than 175,000 ballots were "spoiled"; that is, they were rejected and not counted. Ballots were rejected because of "overvotes," where voters voted for more than one candidate for president, or "undervotes," where the voter's choice was not recorded. The common factor in the "spoiled" ballots is that the vast majority was cast on punch card voting systems that were used in a number of Florida counties. In this system, which came into use in the 1960s, voters marked their ballots by punching holes in paper cards. When the election was over and polling places closed, the cards were fed into computerized counting machines to tally the votes. The requirements of the punch card voting system and the large number of presidential and vice presidential candidates (a total of ten) that qualified for Florida's ballot caused problems with ballot design and instructions that led to confusion among a large number of voters. In Duval County, for example, the first page of the ballot listed the names of five presidential candidates and their running mates, and the second page had the names of the remaining five candidates and their running mates. The first page also had a printed instruction that read, "Turn page to continue voting." And that's exactly what many voters did, and in the process they voted for two presidential candidates and disqualified their ballot. Undervotes were caused when voters did not cleanly punch a hole in the card beside the name of the candidate they were voting for. If the hole isn't punched cleanly, a small piece of paper called a chad will remain. The counting machine will not read it, and the vote will be rejected. Overvotes in Florida numbered approximately 110,000, undervotes slightly over 60,000.[33]

Florida and a number of states acted quickly and established special commissions or committees to study voting procedures and determine what changes needed to be made; in the words of a Maryland committee, reforms had to be adopted to "ensure all votes are counted accurately and that voting is easily understood and as convenient as possible."[34] Florida was the first state to enact comprehensive reform, and the federal government soon followed when Congress passed and President George W. Bush signed into law the Help America Vote Act of 2002. The **Help America Vote Act (HAVA)** established the U.S. Election Assistance Commission to provide assistance to state and local government offices responsible for the administration of federal elections. One of the more important provisions of HAVA provided federal grant money to the states to assist in improving election administration, replace punch card voting systems, and improve access to polling places for persons with disabilities. Federal financial assistance was particularly important because the cost just for replacing punch card systems was high. [$100 million was the estimate for Los Angeles County, the nation's most populous voting jurisdiction.[35]] HAVA requires states to develop and maintain a single statewide voter registration list. This will eliminate county-maintained registration lists and should ensure a more accurate and up-to-date list of voters. As is often the case with federal laws, a few states on their own initiative made significant progress in reaching these requirements. Finally, HAVA establishes a Help America Vote College Program that encourages high school and college students to volunteer as poll workers on Election Day.

As frequently happens, efforts to solve a problem can create new and sometimes unforeseen problems. It was clear that punch card voting systems, widely used in many states and not just Florida, had to be replaced. Some states decided to adopt optical scan machines; voters indicate their choice by using a pencil to fill in a circle or complete an arrow that points to a candidate's name. Then they feed their ballots into a scanner that reads the ballots and tallies the votes. Other states moved to even more modern technology and chose **direct recording electronic systems (DREs),** which allow voters to make their choices by touching a screen (similar to an automated teller) or pushing a button. DREs have many advantages: They prevent overvotes, reduce undervoting by notifying a voter that he or she did not vote in a particular contest, and are more accessible to the visually impaired and disabled because of audio voting features and handheld voting devices. Unfortunately, the efficacy of DREs is now seriously questioned because a number of computer experts fear that the software that runs DREs could be tampered with and votes could be changed to give more votes to one of the candidates. A proposed solution is to have a voter-verified paper trail (VVPT); a printer would produce a paper copy of a voter's choices that would appear under a glass cover for inspection by the voter and then, if correct, would be automatically deposited in a box attached to the DRE.[36] States hope to have these problems resolved before the 2008 general election. Given the expense of the DREs and the paper trail problem, many states may simply adopt optical scanners, which are less expensive and automatically solve the paper trail problem.

Absentee and Early Voting

A single Election Day in November when hundreds of millions of Americans engage in a collective civic experience of casting their votes at their neighborhood school or a similar location may soon be a thing of the past, if it is not already. Political scientist John C. Fortier notes that in the 2004 presidential election, approximately 22 percent of the voters cast their ballot before Election Day; this is up from 14 percent in 2000 and from 5 percent in 1980.[37] Close to one in four voters is using an absentee ballot or is voting early. In **absentee voting,** individuals who will be away from their designated voting place on Election Day obtain a ballot from the local election office in advance of the election, mark it, and return it by mail. Absentee voting, which has a long history in the United States, was first used by some Union states during the Civil War; WWI and WWII allowed overseas military voting. Civilian absentee voting was gradually adopted by the states and was limited to individuals who were ill or would be out of town on business or for other reasons. California, in 1978, was the first to adopt a "no-excuses" absentee voting, which meant that anyone could ask for and receive an absentee ballot without offering any explanation as to why it was needed. Soon, over half the states followed this procedure. Oregon, after experimenting with vote-by-mail in a number of elections, changed in 1998 to a vote-by-mail system for all of its elections. In Oregon, ballots are mailed to all registered voters, who fill them out and return them by mail or drop them off at their local election office. Registered voters do not have to request ballots, and there are no polling places.[38] In **early voting,** citizens cast their votes in person in advance of Election Day at voting centers or a central election office. Citizens can vote as early as two weeks before the actual day of the election. Voting centers serve a fairly large geographic area and are not nearly as numerous as Election Day precinct voting places. Over half of the states allow early voting, Texas was the first, and absentee voting, in some form, is permitted in all fifty states. Participation varies by state, as can be seen in Table 4-1.

What has been the impact of increased absentee and early voting? Providing more than one day on which to vote makes voting more convenient. And this is important because national surveys indicate that citizens want voting to be as convenient as possible. Surveys also show that Oregonians are very happy with their vote-by-mail system, probably the ultimate in convenience.[39] If voting is more convenient, will more people vote? Generally, with the research available at this time, the answer is that turnout is not significantly increased; but the effect varies depending on the type of election. In high-profile

TABLE 4-1 Percentage of Total Ballots Cast by Absentee or Early Voting for Selected States, 2004		
State	Percent Absentee	Percent Early
Alabama	3.4	—
California	32.6	—
Colorado	27.9	19.2
Maine	10.7	6.7
Nebraska	13.4	—
New Mexico	20.1	30.5
Oregon	100.0	—
Oklahoma	4.3	5.8
Texas	2.6	47.7

Source: The authors compiled these percentages from several tables presented in John C. Fortier, *Absentee and Early Voting: Trends, Promises and Perils* (Washington, D.C.: AEI Press, 2006), pp. 25, 28, 29, 31.

— indicates no early voting permitted.

elections such as U.S. Senate or governor, there may be at best a small increase in voter turnout. The increase is among "sometime" voters—those who do not vote in every election; more convenient voting does not attract new voters. However, in low-profile elections such as local elections or ballot initiatives (discussed later in this chapter), the increase in turnout is larger, sometimes by 19 percentage points.[40] Overall, absentee and early voting has not given a large boost to turnout that some observers expected.

Fortier and other election analysts, who are probably in the minority, believe that in the next few years more and more states will rush to adopt absentee and early voting without weighing the benefits of a traditional polling place where a voter is properly identified by poll workers and is guaranteed a place to mark his or her ballot in secret and uninfluenced by others. Obviously, voters that vote early miss out on information about candidates and positions that may emerge in the last week or two before Election Day. Also being overlooked is the value, although it would be difficult to put an exact number on it, of a single Election Day and precinct voting as a "ritual of democracy that ties voters together as participants in a common act of governance."[41] Whether this symbolism is more important than convenience is rarely discussed.

Voter Turnout in Gubernatorial Elections

Voter turnout figures are calculated in a number of ways. A popular way is based on survey research: Respondents are simply asked to report their frequency of voting. The U.S. Bureau of the Census conducts this type of research every two years, but asks only about participation in national elections. For a number of reasons, voter turnout percentages from survey research are always slightly higher than the percentages arrived at by defining voter turnout as the percentage of the voting-age population that actually votes in an election—that is, the number of ballots counted by election officials divided by the number of a state's registered voters or voting-age population.

Table 4-2 shows voter turnout percentages in recent gubernatorial elections. A couple of methodological points: First, experts on voting statistics have refined their estimates of the number of individuals in the United States, who are eligible to vote. Prior to 2000, voter turnout was usually calculated with the voting-age population; most studies today use estimates of the voting-eligible population as the denominator. Political scientist Michael P. McDonald estimates the **voting-eligible population** for each state by taking the state's population aged eighteen and over and subtracting those who are not eligible to vote because they are noncitizens or ineligible felons who may be in prison or out of prison.[42] (State laws vary on how voting rights of felons can be restored.) Second, we are interested in looking at the level of participation. This means that voting-eligible population is a better denominator than registered voters because it provides a clearer idea of the level of participation. In all but a few states, if you are not registered, you cannot vote; it's not unusual to find 20 percent of a state's population is not registered to vote. Using this definition, turnout in recent gubernatorial elections has ranged from a low of just under 35 percent in Kentucky to a high of over 70 percent in New Hampshire. (For comparative purposes, remember that approximately 60 percent participation was reached in the 2004 presidential election.)

A close examination of Table 4-2 reveals several patterns:

1. The timing of elections is important for turnout. States that elect governors in the same years as presidents (2004) have higher turnout than states that elect governors in nonpresidential years. All but one of the states that held elections in 2004 had over 50 percent turnout, while only 20 percent of the states with elections in nonpresidential years reached that level. Presidential elections stimulate voter interest, increasing the number of people who go to the polls and the number of people who vote in governors' races.

2. The effect of presidential elections also can be found in New Hampshire and Vermont, where two-year gubernatorial terms allow elections to alternate between presidential and nonpresidential years. Both states have a much higher percentage of people voting for governor when they also are voting for president.

3. Although the relationship between voter turnout and region is not perfect, states in the South and Southwest have the lowest turnout, with midwestern and New England states having the highest turnout.

As noted in Chapter 1, political culture affects voter turnout, also. States with a moralistic culture consistently lead the nation in rates of turnout. Another factor that affects turnout is the closeness of the election; down-to-the-wire contests usually increase turnout.

Voter Turnout in Local Elections

Voter turnout is even lower in local (county and city) elections—usually less than 30 percent of the voting-eligible population. Surveys show that the decline of voter turnout over time is greater in local than in presidential elections. A variety of factors are responsible, including the lack of media attention paid to these elections, the absence of opponents to challenge incumbents in many races, and frequently the large number of positions that are filled by election. In most cases, there is little excitement because local officials deal

TABLE 4-2 Voter Turnout in Recent Gubernatorial Elections (Percentages)

2003	2004	2005	2006	
43.7 Louisiana	69.2 New Hampshire	41.6 New Jersey	59.6 Minnesota	42.9 Pennsylvania
43.1 Mississippi	65.8 Missouri	37.5 Virginia	57.8 South Dakota	41.5 Kansas
35.6 Kentucky	65.7 Washington		54.7 Vermont	40.9 New Mexico
	65.2 Vermont		53.0 Rhode Island	40.9 Tennessee
	64.0 North Dakota		52.8 Maine	40.7 California
	63.0 Delaware		52.8 Wisconsin	40.7 New Hampshire
	63.0 Montana		52.2 Michigan	40.0 Florida
	60.6 Utah		51.5 Oregon	39.8 Illinois
	58.2 North Carolina		51.4 Alaska	39.2 Arizona
	54.3 Indiana		49.4 Wyoming	38.6 Hawaii
	52.4 West Virginia		48.7 Massachusetts	37.4 Arizona
			48.3 Colorado	37.0 Alabama
			48.0 Maryland	36.6 Nevada
			47.4 Iowa	36.6 New York
			47.4 Ohio	35.3 Oklahoma
			46.3 Connecticut	34.7 South Carolina
			46.3 Nebraska	34.4 Georgia
			43.7 Idaho	30.9 Texas

Source: Compiled by the authors. Voting-eligible population for each state is from Michael P. McDonald's United States Election Project, *2006 Voting-Age and Voting-Eligible Population Estimates,* http://elections.gmu.edu/Voter_Turnout_2006.htm (accessed January, 19, 2007); votes cast in gubernatorial races are from http://uselectionatlas.org (accessed January 19, 2007).

largely with such noncontroversial issues as road repair and other basic services. In most small towns, officials avoid controversy and support the status quo. Campaigns are low-key events and center on name identification.

Nonpartisan elections, widely used at the local level, also lower voter turnout. This happens because the partisan identification of candidates that are displayed during the campaign and the party name on the election ballot lower the information costs of voting decisions by providing citizens with easily accessible information about candidates—whether they are Democrats or Republicans. And in most cities this information will provide voters with some ideas about the candidates' beliefs concerning the role of government. Also, some voters have feelings of loyalty to their party, and they will be motivated to support their party's candidates on Election Day. Brian Schaffner, Matthew Streb, and Gerald Wright, in a well-designed study, compared voter turnout in nonpartisan elections in Champaign, Illinois, to partisan elections in neighboring Urbana, Illinois. Both cities are in the same congressional district, so turnout in these two local elections was compared to turnout in a partisan congressional election. The results were very clear: Turnout in both cities was lower in the local elections than in the congressional, but turnout in Champaign dropped by 43 percent and in Urbana by only 33 percent. Turnout in the nonpartisan election dropped by an extra 10 percentage points.[43] In addition, without party labels incumbent candidates have an even greater electoral advantage. Schaffner, Streb, and Wright state that "without partisan cues voters rely on the next most obvious low cost voting cue—incumbency—which represents some combination of candidate name familiarity, less uncertainty about the candidate, and satisfaction with performance in office."[44]

A typical 30 percent voter turnout means that election outcomes can be determined by a little over 15 percent of the voting-eligible population. Given that those with low incomes are less likely to vote than those with higher incomes and more education, an upper-class elite often exercises great power in local elections.

ELECTION CAMPAIGNS

Running for Governor

State constitutional amendments that created four-year terms for governors and moved their election to the middle of the U.S. president's term have caused gubernatorial elections, and elections to other state offices, to become more autonomous affairs, that is, separate from the issues and personalities of presidential elections. These midterm elections have made it less likely that voters' evaluation of the parties' presidential candidates will affect their choice for governor. During the 1980s, for example, voters were prone to elect Republican presidents in presidential elections and Democratic governors two years later.[45]

Two midterm elections, however, are good examples of elections that lost any possibility of being autonomous from national events that were going against the Democratic Party in 1994, during President Clinton's first term, and against the Republican Party in 2006, during President Bush's second term. The voters' evaluations of the national scene in 1994 swept Republican congressional candidates to historic victories and were reflected in Republican gains in gubernatorial offices and even state legislative seats. In 2006 the

Democratic Party benefited from a national tide, electing more Democratic governors and state legislators. In these two elections, campaigning was a little easier for gubernatorial and state legislative candidates who belonged to the party that was benefiting from the national tide. (These elections were discussed in detail in Chapter 3.)

As with all elections, it is important to consider the effect of incumbency. Data gathered by Thad Beyle between 1970 and 2005 show that incumbent governors were eligible to seek another term in 76 percent of the elections. (Remember, most governors are limited to two four-year terms. See Chapter 6.) What happened in these elections? Basically, 78 percent of the incumbents decided to run, and 74 percent of the incumbents who decided to run were reelected.[46] These two percentages are not as high as those found for members of the U.S. House of Representatives, which are normally in the 80–90 percent range and sometimes even higher. Nevertheless, the percentages for governor are moderately high.

Incumbent reelection success for a shorter and more recent time period, between 2003 and 2006, is presented in Table 4-3. The percentage of incumbents eligible to run is 85 percent, higher than in the 35-year period for which Beyle collected data (85 percent versus 76 percent). The percentage of eligible incumbents who actually ran is almost identical to the earlier period (80 percent versus 78 percent); however, 83 percent were reelected, which is higher than the 74 percent reported by Beyle. Incumbents were very successful in 2006; no Democratic incumbents lost and only one Republican incumbent was defeated. But the high success rate of incumbents did not help the Republican Party because nine of the ten incumbents not running in the general election were Republicans, including those ineligible because of term limits. Along with the national tide, the lack of Republican incumbents on the ballot may also have helped the Democratic Party elect more of its candidates.

Peverill Squire and Christina Fastnow compared the election environment of incumbent governors and U.S. senators and concluded that it is different. Voters are more likely to know and have an opinion of their governor than of their senators. News about governors appears much more frequently in newspapers than news about senators. But better known does not translate into better liked: Governors receive less favorable job performance ratings than senators. Consequently, voters are more likely to vote for a challenger to an incumbent governor than for a challenger to an incumbent senator.[47]

TABLE 4-3 Incumbent Reelection Success in Gubernatorial Elections, 2003–2006

Year	Number of Races	Eligible to Run	Ran	Won
2006	36	31 (86%)	26 (84%)	25 (96%)
2005	2	1 (50%)	0	0
2004	11	11 (100%)	8 (73%)	4 (50%)
2003	3	1 (33%)	1	0
Totals	52	44 (85%)	35 (80%)	29 (83%)

Source: Data for 2003, 2004, and 2005 are from Thad Beyle, "Gubernatorial Elections, Campaign Costs and Power," *The Book of the States 2006* (Lexington, Ky.: Council of State Governments, 2006), p. 144. Data for 2006 were compiled by the authors from www.centerforpolitics.org/crystalball/2006/governor.

A recurrent question in the study of gubernatorial elections is the role of taxes in determining the outcome of the election. The specific question is this: Are candidates who raise taxes while they are in office punished by the voters, that is, do they lose votes in the next election? Obviously, it's possible to lose enough support among the voters to lose the election. Brian Stults and Richard F. Winters have taken a comprehensive look at this question of electoral retribution in gubernatorial elections from 1990 to 1998.[48] Conventional wisdom predicts that governors who raise taxes will be defeated at the next election. According to Stults and Winters, the picture is much more complicated than this. First, governors who raise state *sales* taxes are much more likely to lose support among the voters than governors who raise income taxes. (For a discussion of state taxes see Chapter 9.) The sales tax has "a unique ability to inspire voter ire" because it is levied on most purchases voters make and they are reminded daily of the increase.[49]

Another finding suggests that voter retribution is greater for *nonincumbent* gubernatorial candidates who belong to the same party as the governor who raised taxes than it is for the incumbents who actually raise taxes and then run for reelection. This relationship exists because many incumbents who raise taxes may decide not to run for reelection because they see their chances of success as being very low. Other incumbent governors will do the opposite. They take on the challenge of explaining to the voters why a tax increase was necessary and overcome or at least reduce its negative impact on electoral support. When an incumbent leaves the race and decides not to run, the candidate who is nominated is the target of greater electoral retribution. Party affiliation of candidates also has an effect, with voters showing greater displeasure toward Democratic candidates than Republican candidates. This may be because the Democratic Party is frequently viewed as the "tax and spend" party, but the evidence is not clear on this. Finally, in economic hard times governors may have to raise taxes to maintain programs and services, but it's not a reason that finds favor with the voters. Governors who raise taxes in hard times, especially the sales tax, face electoral retribution.[50]

Research by Thomas M. Carsey reminds us that gubernatorial elections are more than factors and variables. They involve many campaign decisions made by real candidates who are communicating with real voters about real issues, hoping to earn the support of a majority of them on Election Day. Carsey states that gubernatorial candidates can choose among three strategies regarding the information they communicate to voters. Briefly, the strategies are the following:

1. Candidates can change their own position on an issue that is salient to the voters by adopting a new position that is closer to the one held by most of the voters.
2. Candidates can try to persuade voters to change their position on a salient issue and to adopt the candidates' position.
3. Candidates can try to shift voters' attention to another issue that is more beneficial to them.[51]

Although candidates have used each strategy, Carsey believes that the third one is the best. The first strategy has problems. Candidates that change their position and move to where most of the voters are may end up losing their more partisan and ideological backers that want their candidate to stand for something, whether it be, for example, liberalism or conservatism. Also, candidates that change position usually are accused of flip-flopping on the issue. Voters wonder about the candidates' credibility. The second strategy of trying to convince voters to change their position and move closer to the candidate may occasionally work, but it usually won't because voters are being asked to admit that they have been mistaken in their thinking, something that is unlikely to happen during a campaign that lasts only a few months. But the third strategy, of trying to redefine the issues that are salient to the voters during the campaign, is an approach that avoids the pitfalls of the first two strategies. Carsey concludes:

> ... the campaign becomes a struggle between candidates providing information to voters as they try to define for voters the important issues in that particular election. One candidate might focus on economic concerns while the other stresses social issues. Which candidate wins will depend in part on who is better able to make their campaign theme more salient for voters.[52]

The 2002 gubernatorial election in Michigan is one for which this framework works well. The Republican nominee was Lieutenant Governor Dick Posthumus. His Democratic opponent was Jennifer M. Granholm, who was elected as Michigan's attorney general in 1998. Granholm's mix of "brains and movie-star looks" had propelled her to a strong lead over Posthumus in early polls. (Granholm is a Harvard Law School graduate and had spent several years in Los Angeles as an aspiring actress.) The Posthumus campaign tried to shift voters' attention from Granholm's personal characteristics by pointing to his twenty years of experience in Michigan government as better qualifying him to lead the state. His campaign accused Granholm of being light on substance and that the Democratic Party was running a "Spice Girls" ticket. Granholm countered with fifty-eight pages of position papers on her campaign's Web site and called for "new leadership" in the state after twelve years of Republican control of the governor's office.[53] Both candidates attempted to define the central campaign issues for the voters in ways that would benefit them; Granholm won the election and was reelected in 2006.

Running for the State Legislature

Every two years, upwards of 10,000 candidates may be running for approximately 5,000 seats in the lower houses of state legislatures, and as many as 2,600 candidates may be running for almost 1,300 seats in the state senates. Most have had a long-term interest in politics, and many come from politically active families. A study of legislative candidates found that almost half the candidates were "encouraged" to run; that is, they had been thinking of running when officials in the local party or local elected officials approached them, asking them to run. Approximately one-third of the candidates were "self-starters" who said that it was entirely their own idea to run. The smallest group of candidates was the "persuaded," who had not seriously thought about running until someone else suggested it to them.[54] Candidates frequently mention public service and, more than in the past, commitment to issues as reasons for running.[55] In almost all states, but especially large states where party control for a majority of legislative seats is close, parties have created legislative campaign committees. According to Gary Moncrief, Peverill Squire, and Malcolm Jewell, **legislative campaign committees** are controlled by legislative party leaders and provide financial support to both incumbent and nonincumbent candidates; they also are frequently active in recruiting candidates. These committees usually target districts, that is, identify districts that are crucial for the party to win and allocate most of their assistance to these districts. In addition, some legislative leaders have their own PACs that are used to support candidates.[56]

A study of ten states finds that close to half of the candidates are from broker careers; that is, they are in occupations that require them to negotiate, bargain, and persuade. Examples of such private careers are lawyers, teachers, real estate agents, and owners and operators of business establishments.[57] Candidates consciously weigh their opportunity costs. The risks, including some sacrifice of their private careers and of time spent with their families, are balanced against increases in social esteem and political influence. Of course, the opportunity costs include the chances of winning, the presence of an incumbent, and the financial cost of running a campaign.[58]

Individual campaigns differ greatly depending on the nature of the district and the strength of political parties. District size varies from about 846,000 people in California senate districts and 423,000 in California house districts to 16,000 in Wyoming senate districts and 3,000 in New Hampshire house districts. Of course, urban house districts are smaller geographically, whereas many rural senate districts are very large. The presence of professional political consultants in campaigns varies across the country. In the late 1990s, a survey of legislative candidates in a number of midsize to large states found that candidates are increasingly relying on campaign management services from professionals. In states with very large populations, such as California and New York, legislative campaigns are usually professionally managed and use new-style campaign techniques, including "wholesale" advertising through television and radio to reach large numbers of voters. State and local party organizations, where they are active, help by providing assistance in voter registration and get-out-the-vote drives.[59]

In many small to midsize states, however, legislative campaigns are still "retail" in nature; that is, they involve face-to-face contact between candidates and voters. With weak political parties and insufficient funds to hire professional campaign managers, candidates are pretty much on their own and need to develop a personal following that will volunteer for campaign work. Candidates will go door-to-door to drop off their campaign literature and meet voters. Mass advertising techniques include billboards, yard signs, and direct mail. Direct mail, usually done by a professional, is increasing in popularity because voters can be targeted according to their party affiliation, the frequency with which they vote, and when they registered to vote.

Political scientists value campaigns because they provide an opportunity, though not always fulfilled, for candidates to educate voters on the issues of the day. Tom Loftus, former speaker of the Wisconsin State Assembly, argues that campaigns, especially those involving face-to-face contact with the voters, also educate the candidate:

> All the handshaking, all the pleasantries exchanged, help make a politician representative. If you talk with people at their doors, on the threshold of their homes, and glimpse their families and perhaps their furniture and the pictures on the walls, you will begin to see their dreams realized and not realized, and you will begin to understand your prospective constituents.[60]

The number of members who leave a legislature at the end of their term and are replaced by newly elected members is called **membership turnover.** Turnover rates have been on a long-term decline in almost all states since the early 1960s; the fifty-state average per election in the 1990s was 23 percent in the senates and 25 percent in the lower houses.[61] A drop in the proportion of members who leave voluntarily—that is, simply decide not to run again, rather than being defeated in the primary or general election—is the most likely cause of this decline. Another trend is that the number of state legislative races that are contested by at least two candidates has been decreasing in a number of states. In many states, it is not unusual for 20 percent of the races to have only one candidate and be classified as uncontested elections.[62]

It must be kept in mind that political scientists emphasize the declining rates of turnover because historically they have been unusually high; for example, fifty years ago average senate turnover was 37 percent and house turnover was 41 percent. Today, even with a seemingly high percentage of members running for reelection and being reelected, there is a fair amount of turnover in most legislatures. (Whether it is too much or too little is the center of a debate between the supporters and opponents of term limits for state legislatures. See Chapter 5.) For example, if a state legislative chamber has 100 members and 80 percent run for reelection and 90 percent are reelected, there will be twenty-eight new members, that is, a membership turnover of 28 percent, which is still quite a few new members. In other words, if some members leave voluntarily, turnover rates can still be reasonably high even with a large percentage of incumbents being reelected.

Running for Judge

Two types of judicial elections can be found in the states: One is the type of election we usually think of in which citizens use their votes to fill an elected office in government, in this case a judge, by choosing from two or more candidates. The second type is a **retention election,** in which the name of an incumbent judge, whose term of office is about to expire, is placed on the ballot with no opposing candidate and voters decide whether the judge should be retained in office for another term. This section will not focus on retention elections but on those elections in which opposing candidates can appear on the ballot. (It is important to point out that the election of state judges is only one of several different methods of selecting judges. These methods are discussed in Chapter 7.)

Of all the election campaigns discussed in this chapter, the campaigns of those running to become judges have changed the most in the past few years. Earlier findings include the following: Judicial elections are almost invisible to voters and the media, voters have little information on the candidates, fewer voters vote in these contests than for other offices on the ballot and, if they vote, they often cannot remember who they voted for when asked by a survey research interviewer.[63] These conclusions are probably still true for elections to lower-level courts, but they no longer apply to election of judges to a state's highest court, usually called the court of appeals or supreme court. Two developments are important: The first development is federal court decisions declaring unconstitutional a variety of state laws and judicial ethics codes of the American Bar Association that regulate judicial campaigns. These regulations limited what candidates could say concerning their future conduct and actions in the courtroom. The most common limitation was that candidates could not make statements that indicate how they would decide on cases, issues, or controversies that were likely to come before the court. Many states went further and prohibited candidates from making "pledges or promises in office other than the faithful and impartial performance of the duties of the office."[64] A candidate for Minnesota's supreme court challenged Minnesota's version of these regulations. The U.S. Supreme Court in *Republican Party of Minnesota v. White* (2002)[65] ruled that Minnesota's "announce clause," which prohibited candidates from announcing their views on disputed legal or political issues, violated the First Amendment that guarantees freedom of speech. The Supreme Court also upheld a federal court of appeals decision, in another case from Minnesota, that removes other restrictions on judicial candidates; they can now attend political party conventions, seek party endorsements for their candidacy, and personally solicit campaign funds.[66] Rules prohibiting these activities also violated First Amendment free speech rights.

The second change in these elections is that they are becoming "nastier, noisier, and costlier."[67] This has been particularly noticeable in the past few years in Illinois, Kentucky, Ohio, and West Virginia. The elections have changed, in part, as the battle over the amount of money awarded in civil liability suits has grown more intense and spilled from the courtroom to the electoral arena. (See Chapter 7.) Personal injury lawyers are on one side and business groups, especially insurance companies, and their lawyers are on the other side. Both sides are seeking to elect judges who will be more likely to decide in their favor, and they are willing to spend hundreds of thousands of dollars in contributions to candidates' campaigns and in independent expenditures for expensive television advertising to help elect the candidates they are backing. Two Illinois Supreme Court candidates in the 2005 election raised a combined total of $9.3 million, exceeding by almost twice as much an earlier record set in Alabama. One of the big spenders is the Institute for Legal Reform, an affiliate of the U.S. Chamber of Commerce, which reportedly has spent $120 million in a four-year period; in 2004 it won every election it participated in.[68] Recently, in the state of Washington, which has nonpartisan judicial elections, one candidate benefited from $1.5 million in direct contributions to his campaign or from independent expenditures. Much of this money was from the Building Industry Association of Washington (BIAW), an organization of builders and developers that supports property rights and opposes government regulation. BIAW wanted to oust two incumbent judges who in several decisions had voted against the positions it favored. BIAW was less successful than the campaign forays by the Chamber of Commerce; two of the three candidates it backed lost the election.[69]

Many observers believe that the effect of these changes on judicial elections is negative. Large amounts of campaign spending, interest group activity, and candidates who speak more freely about their views on disputed legal or political issues may undermine the public's confidence in judicial decision making. Will the public still perceive judges as capable of approaching cases before them in a fair and impartial manner?[70]

Running for Mayor

Because of the great diversity of cities in terms of population, size, variety of ethnic groups, and economic vitality, it is difficult to generalize about mayoral campaigns. Obviously, running for mayor of Los Angeles and New York City is not the same as a campaign in small Town, U.S.A. Timing of local elections is different from federal and state elections. Local elections are usually held in odd-numbered years or in late spring of even-numbered years so that the contests will be decided on local issues and candidates. Another difference is whether elections are partisan or nonpartisan (see Chapter 3). New York has partisan elections and Los Angeles has nonpartisan; the dominant pattern is the latter with close to 70 percent of cities having nonpartisan elections. Political scientist Karen M.

Kaufmann also suggests that controversies surrounding local issues and candidates do not always fit into Democratic and Republican policy differences that are apparent at the national level. Group interests may be more important at the local level: Where will growth occur? Where will a new park be located? Will regulations on upkeep of rental housing be strictly enforced? Where will additional police patrols be assigned?[71]

Group interests and coalition building were apparent in mayoralty elections in Los Angeles in the 2001 and 2005 elections. With no incumbent running in 2001, a total of six candidates were on the ballot, and three were considered frontrunners in the nonpartisan primary: James Hahn, city attorney, with strong support in the African American community and from a popular political family; Steven Soboroff, a businessman with little political experience but well financed for the campaign and backed by a popular incumbent mayor; and Antonio Villaraigosa, former speaker of the California State Assembly, with support in the Latino community and among labor unions.[72] Voters were not focused on a single issue and in fact seemed rather satisfied with city affairs. (This was in drastic contrast to earlier elections that were racially polarized; for example, the 1993 election occurred shortly after the 1992 riots.) No candidate received a majority of the votes in the primary, necessitating a runoff election between the top two candidates, Villaraigosa (who finished first) and Hahn. Both candidates were liberals who identified with the Democratic Party and each had some support from white liberals, but Hahn had strong support among African Americans and Villaraigosa had strong support among Latinos. With these coalitions, the election would be decided by the candidate who could appeal to conservative whites; Hahn won, garnering close to 60 percent of the white vote and 54 percent of the total vote.

A rematch occurred in 2005, with Hahn and Villaraigosa again emerging as the top vote getters in the primary and facing each other in the runoff. But this time Villaraigosa was the winner (59 percent). Why this reversal? Hahn's four years as mayor had been lackluster, and Villaraigosa used the four years to build a broad-based coalition. He demonstrated his commitment to the city by running and winning a city council seat in 2003 and developed a stronger relationship with the African American community, especially younger leaders. Villaraigosa won majorities among Lations, whites, and African Americans, becoming Los Angeles's first Latino mayor since the nineteenth century.[73]

Mayoral candidates in large cities have been using new-style campaign techniques—polling, television advertisements, and direct mail—to communicate with voters. The hiring of professional political consultants to manage campaigns is common in big-city elections, also. Research by J. Cherie Strachan finds that old-style campaigning is being combined with the new style even in midsize cities (population ranging from 50,000 to 250,000). Old-style campaigning includes candidates and their volunteers going door-to-door, giving speeches to neighborhood groups, displaying yard signs, and running newspaper ads. One of the more popular new-style techniques in these races is that of direct mail.[74] (This technique is popular in state legislative races, also.) Today's direct mail is quite sophisticated and uses computer databases to target mailings to a candidate's campaign strategy by communicating specific messages to different groups of voters such as new voters, voters living in specific neighborhoods, registered independents, and voters registered with political parties.

Nonpartisan elections usually follow the pattern described above in Los Angeles: A primary election among several candidates is held and no candidate receives a majority of the votes, necessitating another two weeks of campaigning and a runoff election between the two candidates in the primary. The Center for Voting & Democracy advocates eliminating the runoff election by using a voting system called **instant runoff voting (IRV),** which allows voters to rank candidates in order of preference on a single ballot so that if no one has a majority, an "instant" runoff can occur. IRV is being considered in a number of cities and has been adopted by places as different as San Francisco and Burlington, Vermont. Here is how it works in Burlington, where it is used to elect the mayor: Voters mark their ballot (a mark-sense form) by filling in the first-choice "bubble" next to the name of their favorite candidate, then they fill in the second-choice "bubble" next to the name of their second favorite candidate, and so on. If there are five candidates on the ballot, voters can rank all five from most favorite to least favorite. (In San Francisco, voters can rank only their top three.) If a candidate receives a majority of the first-choice votes, he or she is the winner just as in a typical nonpartisan primary. If no one has a majority, the last-place candidate—the candidate who received the fewest first-choice votes—is declared defeated and all ballots are counted again. This time the second choice of voters who voted for the defeated candidate is counted. The process of eliminating the last-place candidate and recounting the ballots continues until one candidate receives a majority of the vote. The process sounds complicated, as critics often point out, but the system works as long as voters rank their preferences. And the need for a runoff election is eliminated.[75]

CAMPAIGN FINANCING

Cost of Campaigns

Of all state and local elections, gubernatorial races are the most expensive. Thad Beyle reports that total expenditures for electing governors between 2001 and 2004 were $1.14 billion. This marks a significant increase, over 60 percent, from the 1997–2000 period when $728 million was spent. As already noted in this chapter, one important cause of increased spending is the new-style campaigning, in which, as Beyle says, "The 'air-war' campaigns have replaced the 'ground-war' campaigns across the states."[76] On occasion, wealthy candidates can push up expenditures by spending large amounts of their own money. In 2002 a record $155 million was spent in the New York governor's race, reaching this level in large part because Thomas Golisano ran as an independent candidate spending $81 million of his own money.[77] Golisano lost. Candidates who spend their personal wealth are becoming more common. The Institute on Money in State Politics finds that in 2004, candidates gave themselves almost $43 million, 21 percent of the total raised by all gubernatorial candidates.[78]

Of course, the size of a state and whether or not an incumbent is on the ballot can affect the level of campaign spending. (State campaign finance laws, which will be discussed later in this chapter, also affect spending levels.) In 2004, in the small state of Vermont, the incumbent Republican governor was reelected with spending for all candidates totaling just over $1 million. Incumbent governors, because they make decisions that literally affect all interests, have no problem raising money. Challengers must overcome the name recognition and fundraising advantage that incumbents have. This may sound impossible, but if an incumbent's popularity is lagging and the race appears to be competitive, challengers can successfully raise large sums of money for their campaigns.

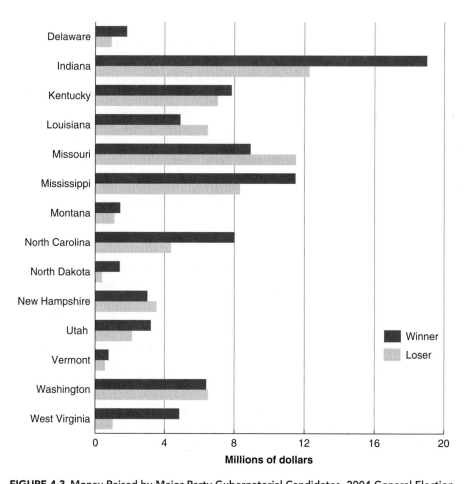

FIGURE 4-3 Money Raised by Major Party Gubernatorial Candidates, 2004 General Election

Source: Rachel Weiss, *State Elections Overview, 2004*, p. 7. The Institute on Money in State Politics. www.followthemoney.org/Research/index.phtml (accessed January 31, 2007). Used with permission of The Institute on Money in State Politics.

Yes, most of the time

Does the candidate who raises and spends the most money always win the election? Figure 4-3 shows the amount of money raised by major party candidates for the 2004 general election. The candidate who raises the most money usually wins; only three winning candidates in Figure 4-3 spent less money than their opponents, and in one state, Washington, candidates were almost equal in their spending. Money is important to campaigns but it does not guarantee victory.

State legislative candidates in the 2003 and 2004 general elections (over 11,000 candidates) raised $755 million for their campaigns. State-by-state variation is enormous, with heavily populated urban districts costing many times more than lightly populated rural districts. California assembly candidates averaged just over $400,000, and state senate candidates $555,000, in contributions. House candidates in states such as Maine, Montana, Vermont, and Wyoming raise less than $10,000 on average. Robert E. Hogan, examining legislative candidates in twenty-seven states, has identified several factors affecting campaign spending. Candidate-level factors such as being an incumbent, holding a leadership role in the legislature, and being a member of the legislative majority are associated with raising and spending more money. District-level factors, number of opponents in the primary, and a high rate of spending by the general election opponent also increase campaign spending; however, prior competitive elections in a district have a positive but weak effect on spending. Finally, the average campaign amount spent per voter—98 cents—is lowered by 18 cents if a state has public financing of elections.[79] (Public financing of elections will be discussed later in this chapter.)

Although contributions from individuals are still an important source of campaign funds, candidates also turn to other sources of money, typically to the business community (if they are Republicans) and labor unions or teachers' associations (if they are Democrats). Unlike federal elections, about half the states permit corporations to make campaign contributions directly from their profits. Many states allow labor unions to make contributions directly from their treasuries, also. Candidates use fundraising dinners and coffees and mail solicitations to raise money, especially in smaller states where campaigning is not as expensive.

As noted in Chapter 3, PACs have distributed greater and greater amounts of money to campaigns during the past twenty-five years. A study of state legislative candidates in several states found that on average, PAC contributions made up anywhere from 13 to 43 percent of the total funds candidates raised. PACs are particularly strong in Alabama, where there are over 650; two of the more active are A-VOTE PAC of the Alabama Education Association and ProgressPAC of the Business Council of Alabama. PACs can bring money quickly to a campaign; for example, during a two-month period in the final weeks before the primary in 2006, an incumbent Alabama state legislator received over $27,000 in contributions from twenty-eight PACs.[80]

Campaign Contributions: Disclosure and Limits

Efforts to regulate more closely the financing of campaigns originated as a response to a number of developments: the national Watergate scandal in the early 1970s, the public's view that politicians were too beholden to campaign contributions from special interests, and, occasionally, campaign financing scandals in individual states.

Disclosure laws, one of the first reforms adopted, require that candidates disclose the source of their campaign funds (contributions) and expenditures. With disclosure, the public can learn what interests are supporting a candidate before elections are held. If all contributors and the size of contributions are made public, ideally, voters have the opportunity to vote against a candidate who is receiving money from groups they don't support. Disclosure might even reduce the influence of special interests because candidates may not want to act in ways that appear to respond to interest groups that gave them money. All states have disclosure laws, but their quality varies. To be useful, disclosure reports must contain information on the amount of money contributed, the contributor's occupation, and his or her place of employment. Although some agencies responsible for collecting disclosure reports still hand-enter candidates' written information into a computer, most states have moved to electronic filing for candidates. Michael Malbin and Thomas Gais, in a major study of the real-world experience of state campaign finance reform, are skeptical that disclosure laws have achieved their goal. One problem is that the average voter will learn about the information only if it is reported by the news media, but very few newspapers have even one reporter analyzing rather complex campaign finance documents.[81]

Contribution limits are another way states regulate campaign financing. Thirty-six states have **contribution limits** that set a maximum on the amount of money individuals can contribute to candidates. These limits usually fall in the range of $1,000 to $5,000 per gubernatorial candidate per election and force candidates to raise smaller amounts of money from a greater number of people, reducing dependence on a few contributors that donate large sums. Limits are usually smaller for state legislative candidates. States that allow labor unions and corporations to make contributions usually place limits on them as well. PACs have similar limits on their contributions, and a few states have placed limits on the percentage of a candidate's contribution that can come from PACs. (Alabama is one of only a few states that have no limits on PAC contributions.) The latest regulation, adopted in over half of the states, places restrictions on giving and receiving campaign contributions while the state legislature is in session. In some states, the ban applies only to contributions by lobbyists; other states have a general ban on contributions.

How low can contribution limits be set? Could individuals be limited to contributing no more than $400 per statewide candidate per two-year election cycle, as was stated in Vermont's law? This question was decided in the Supreme Court case of *Randall v. Sorrell*.[82] The Court decided that Vermont's extremely low contribution limits could prevent candidates from raising enough funds to campaign effectively and for this reason were unconstitutional. Contribution limits are still constitutional, but if they are too low they may be unconstitutional.

Expenditure limits, or spending limits, place a ceiling on the total amount of money a candidate can spend campaigning for an elected office. With one exception, the Supreme Court has found expenditure limits unconstitutional. The Court concluded, in *Buckley v. Valeo*,[83] that candidates must spend money to communicate with voters and limiting how much money candidates spend violates the First Amendment. Expenditure limits are constitutional if they are optional; for example, candidates agree to limit their spending in exchange for an incentive to their campaign such as public funds. This will be discussed next when we consider public financing.

Public Financing of Campaigns

Public financing is the use of public funds, money collected by the state, to finance candidates' campaigns for elected offices such as governor or state legislator. It is a reform idea that has been adopted in fifteen states (and some cities) and is discussed on a fairly regular basis by other states. (A few states provide funds directly to political parties rather than individual candidates; this section focuses on states that have programs for candidates.) Many reasons are offered to support public financing; perhaps the most important is summarized by the Center for Governmental Studies:

> . . . escalating costs of running a political campaign and the growth of private money in the political system can distort the governmental process and lower the quality of a jurisdiction's legislation if politicians base their votes more on the wishes of their largest contributors than on the merits of the legislation.[84]

However, the use of public funds for political campaigns created quite a bit of controversy, and continues to do so today. Most states that adopted public financing early (late 1970s and early 1980s) relied on the voluntary participation of individual taxpayers; only a handful of states simply appropriated money from normal state revenues. The most popular voluntary method is an "add-on" tax, whereby a taxpayer donates, depending on the state, anywhere from $1 to $25; this adds to the taxes an individual must pay. Other states use the "tax checkoff," which allows voters to designate $1 to $5 of their taxes to public financing. The contribution is not added to their taxes but is taken out of what they already owe.

New Jersey adopted one of the first public financing laws in the nation. This law covers only gubernatorial candidates, but covers them in both primary and general elections. To qualify for public funds, a candidate must raise $300,000 (no single contribution can be larger than $3,000) from private sources; then he or she receives $2 in public funding for every $1 from private sources. By accepting public funds, candidates agree to expenditure limits. Candidates also are required to participate in two televised debates during the general election campaign. In the 2001 election, three candidates qualified for funding for the primary election and two qualified for the general election. Both of the general election candidates qualified for the maximum public funds they were entitled to: $5.6 million. Total expenditures for each candidate were limited to $8.4 million. Public financing in New Jersey has reduced the importance of special interest money and has encouraged candidates to run in the primary who might not have done so without the promise of public funds.[85] It should be noted that in states with public financing, candidates do *not* have to accept the money. If they choose, they can run their campaigns entirely from private contributions. And this happened in 2005 when two candidates used their personal wealth to finance their campaigns. Jon Corzine, who won the election, spent at least $43 million and his principal opponent, Douglas Forrester, spent $29 million. If they had accepted public financing, each candidate would have been limited to $14 million.

Public Financing Evaluated

Public financing laws are far from a universal success. Of course, public financing is not possible if funds are not available, and that is one of the problems. Another problem is that if candidates who accept public financing are required to adhere to unrealistically low expenditure limits, then they simply may decide that funding their campaigns from private sources with no expenditure limits is the wiser course. Public financing will not work if candidates refuse to participate. These problems and possible solutions will be reviewed below.

Taxpayer participation in the "add-on" tax and the "tax checkoff" is low. No "add-on" state has participation higher than 5 percent of its taxpayers; participation is higher in "tax checkoff" states, frequently approaching 20 percent. Massachusetts was one of the early states to provide public funding, but the "add-on" generated little revenue for the program. In 1994 a checkoff was adopted and taxpayer participation increased to about 10 percent, and the first time money was distributed to candidates was in the 1998 election. Since then, public funding in Massachusetts has been in disarray with the voters approving a new comprehensive program in 1998. The state legislature, which never funded this plan, eventually repealed it and enacted a more limited program.[86] These rates of participation mean that little money is raised to distribute to candidates, and until recently, only New Jersey and Minnesota were willing to use money from their general fund budgets to supplement taxpayer-designated funds. (Minnesota and New Jersey also use the "tax checkoff.")

Hawaii is a state that has actually raised a reasonable amount of money for public funding but has low expenditure limits. The Hawaii Election Campaign Fund had over $5 million at the time of the 2006 general elections. If candidates agree to expenditure limits for their campaigns, they can receive up to 30 percent of their total spending from the campaign fund. But the expenditure limits, or spending caps as they are sometimes called, are well below the amount of money needed to run a campaign and have any chance of winning. In 2004, in elections to Hawaii's lower house in the state legislature, average winning candidates spent $44,000 and the average losing candidate spent $21,000. Expenditure limits for candidates receiving public funds was from $12,000 to $20,000, depending on the number of voters in the district. In 2006 elections, only five of 182 candidates in the general election requested public funds, leading one observer of Hawaii's politics to conclude that few candidates want public funding "because it's tied to spending restrictions that are widely seen as a recipe for defeat."[87]

Within the past few years, several states have considered the latest ideas for public funding known as clean elections or clean money. **Clean election laws** provide candidates all of the funds necessary to run their campaigns if they agree to expenditure limits. Clean elections provide full public funding and differ from programs in Hawaii and New Jersey where public funds match private contributions to candidates. Maine, Arizona, and Connecticut have clean election funding programs for all statewide and state legislative candidates.[88] In 2006, voters in California defeated a clean election proposal that was on the ballot. Let's look at how clean elections work in Maine, the first state to adopt this plan. Candidates for a seat in the state senate, for example, are allowed to raise $1,500 from private sources—"seed money" as it's called. This "seed money" must include $5 donations from at least 150 people, and no single contribution can exceed $100. All qualifying candidates are given campaign funds for the primary and general elections based on the average amount spent in similar races in the two previous election cycles. Money for public financing comes from a Clean Election Fund, which receives money from three sources: qualifying contributions raised by candidates, "tax checkoff" on tax returns, and an appropriation from the state's general fund. Of course, candidates can finance their campaigns from private sources if they choose to. But the law has two additional provisions designed to discourage this: First, contribution limits are low, $250 per donor. (As of this writing, this limit for legislative candidates has not been found unconstitutional.) This means that a candidate will have to work hard to contact a large number of donors to obtain adequate campaign funds. Second, if publicly financed candidates are being outspent by privately financed candidates, they will receive funds to match the amount being spent by their opponents, up to double what they were initially authorized. Again, both of these provisions are designed to make public financing more attractive to candidates.

Minnesota's public financing system is worth taking a closer look at because it has been in existence longer than public financing systems in states that have recently adopted clean elections, and it is generally considered to be a model program. It provides partial public funding and its key elements are listed below:

1. Expenditure limits for candidates that accept public funds are higher than in most states and indexed to inflation.
2. Grants to candidates from the $5 checkoff are supplemented by money from the state treasury if the checkoff does not provide enough revenue.
3. Individuals who contribute to *publicly financed* candidates are eligible for state refunds of up to $50 for individuals and $100 per couple per calendar year.

Political scientist Kenneth Mayer's examination of public financing in Minnesota notes that participation is nearly universal for both incumbents and challengers. For example, in state senate races that Mayer studied, 98 percent of the general election candidates used public funds. He concludes that Minnesota's public financing of legislative races "can dramatically increase competition levels, by reducing incumbent fund-raising advantages and giving potential challengers an incentive to enter races."[89] Similar conclusions are found in Arizona and Maine, according to a more recent study by Mayer.[90]

It is ironic that public displeasure with candidates raising money from special interests has not produced public willingness to support a system of public financing based on relatively small contributions from all taxpayers. An average-size state with 1 million taxpayers and a $25 "tax checkoff" could raise $25 million a year, more than enough to finance gubernatorial elections every four years and perhaps state legislative elections as well.

INITIATIVE, REFERENDUM, AND RECALL

State and local governments differ from the federal government in that their constitutions or charters often permit the use of techniques of direct democracy known as the initiative, referendum, and recall. Although they were occasionally used in colonial America and their use can be traced back to ancient Greece, direct democracy in the United States is largely a product of the Progressive movement in the early twentieth century. As noted in Chapter 3, these reformers distrusted political machines and party bosses and wanted to have a way for citizens to directly check governmental corruption and incompetence.

Briefly stated, a **ballot measure** is a generic term that refers to anything on the ballot other than candidates for office. The initiative, referendum, and recall are ballot measures. More specifically, the **initiative** is a procedure whereby citizens can propose new laws or changes in state constitutions and determine by their votes in an election whether the proposal will be adopted. The **referendum** gives voters the opportunity to have the final say on a bill that their legislature already has approved. In both the initiative and referendum, proposed laws are actually placed on the ballot for voter approval. (The difference between a popular referendum and a legislative referendum will be explained soon.) The **recall** is a procedure to remove an elected public official from office before his or her term officially ends. States using these techniques today

TABLE 4-4 Initiative, Referendum, and Recall in the States

Initiative, Popular Referendum, and Recall	Initiative and Popular Referendum	Initiative	Popular Referendum	Recall	None
Alaska	Arkansas	Mississippi	Kentucky	Georgia	Alabama
Arizona	Florida		Maryland	Kansas	Connecticut
California	Illinois		New	Louisiana	Delaware
Colorado	Maine		Mexico	Minnesota	Hawaii
Idaho	Massachusetts			New Jersey	Indiana
Michigan	Missouri			Rhode	Iowa
Montana	Nebraska			Island	New
Nevada	Ohio			Wisconsin	Hampshire
North Dakota	Oklahoma				New York
Oregon	South Dakota				North
Washington	Utah				Carolina
	Wyoming				Pennsylvania
					South
					Carolina
					Tennessee
					Texas
					Vermont
					Virginia
					West Virginia

Sources: Compiled by the authors from the following: *I&R FactSheet,* Initiative and Referendum Institute, www .iandrinstitute.org/factsheets; National Conference of State Legislatures, "Recall of State Officials," www.ncsl.org/ programs/legismgt/elect/recallprovision.htm (accessed February 13, 2007).

Note: Maine, Massachusetts, and Mississippi use the indirect initiative only. The "None" category refers to states that do not have any form of the initiative, the popular referendum, or the recall. All states except Delaware use a legislative referendum for voting on proposed constitutional amendments.

are identified in Table 4-4. It's important to note two additional points: First, of the three, the initiative, because voters actually propose laws, receives the most attention from the public, the media, and academic researchers; it also will be the focus of this section. Second, the initiative, referendum, and recall are available in thousands of counties, cities, and towns and are actually used more frequently at the local level than at the state level; many states that do not have the statewide initiative allow its use at the local level.

What Kinds of Issues Are on the Ballot?

It has been just over 110 years since South Dakota became the first state to adopt the initiative procedure, and approximately 105 years since Oregon became the first state to have a statewide initiative on the ballot. During this time voters have decided the fate of slightly more than 2,200 initiatives. Over 50 percent of these initiatives have appeared on the ballots of just five states: Oregon (341), California (315), Colorado (196), North Dakota (175), and Arizona (165). Initiative activity also varies by decade. The last two decades of the twentieth century had high levels of usage, with a record high of 379 initiatives on the ballot during the 1990s.[91] The resurgence of interest in the initiative can be traced to California in 1978 when voters passed Proposition 13, which significantly reduced property taxes. (See Chapter 9.) This successful initiative was followed by similar measures in other states, demonstrating its effectiveness. Since 1990, voters have proposed and voted on the following:[92]

- Prohibit sport hunting of mountain lions (California, 1990, passed).
- Impose term limits for state legislatures (Oklahoma, 1990, passed).
- Allow physician-assisted suicide (Washington, 1991, failed; Michigan, 1998, failed).
- Impose "three strikes, you're out" sentences for major criminals (Washington, 1993, passed).
- Eliminate property tax exemptions for religious and nonprofit organizations (Colorado, 1996, failed).
- Permit use of marijuana for medicinal purposes (Arizona, 1996, passed).
- End racial preferences in state programs (California, 1996, passed).
- Decriminalize the use of marijuana (Alaska, 2000, failed).
- Pre-kindergarten learning opportunities (Florida, 2002, passed).
- Treatment instead of incarceration for nonviolent drug offenders (Ohio, 2002, failed).
- Define legal marriage as between one man and one woman (Oregon, 2004, passed).
- Require utilities to generate or purchase at least 10 percent of their electricity from renewable sources (Colorado, 2004, passed).

In the 2006 election, 204 statewide measures were on the ballots in thirty-seven states; seventy-six were placed on the ballot through the initiative process, making 2006 one of the busiest years for the initiative since it was first used. As in 2004, voters were asked to consider the question of gay marriage. Seven states approved constitutional amendments defining marriage as between a man and a woman. Arizona voters rejected, by a close vote, a ban on same-sex marriage, probably because this amendment went further than similar amendments by prohibiting state and local governments from offering health care benefits and legal status to heterosexual domestic partners (unmarried couples). Initiatives to increase the minimum wage were another popular issue, appearing on the ballots in six states; voters approved all of them. Ohio's minimum hourly wage was increased from $5.15 to $6.85, and it was indexed to inflation so that it will increase automatically as the cost of living increases. Voters in a number of states approved measures that would restrict local governments from taking private property for another private use. (For a fuller discussion of this eminent domain issue see Chapter 8.) Voters in Arizona, Nevada, and Ohio had to choose between "dueling initiatives" designed to restrict smoking in public places. Measures with strong restrictions were supported by health interest groups, while tobacco companies and their interest groups countered with proposals that contained a lot of exemptions and were generally less restrictive. In all three states, voters approved the more restrictive bans; proposals to increase the tobacco tax were defeated in California and Missouri, but passed in two other states.[93]

The Initiative Process

Two forms of the initiative are used in the states: The **direct initiative** allows voters to bypass the legislature and place proposals directly on the ballot. Citizens in twenty-one states can use the direct initiative to propose new laws and in eighteen states citizens can propose changes in the constitution. The vast majority of these states are located west of the Mississippi River, where political parties are weaker and nonpartisan good-government groups have been stronger.[94]

There are three stages in winning voter approval of a direct initiative. Political scientist Elisabeth Gerber classifies them as follows: drafting, qualifying, and campaigning.[95] In the drafting stage, a group of citizens research and write the proposed law that will appear on the ballot. Once the proposal is drafted it must be submitted to a state official, usually the secretary of state or attorney general, where it is reviewed and an official title and summary are written.

During the qualifying stage, supporters of the initiative must show support among the state's citizens; they do this by asking registered voters to sign petitions, which contain the official title and summary of the proposal. If a certain percentage of registered voters (usually about 10 percent) sign within a specified period of time (150 days in California, eighteen months in Wyoming), the proposal will be on the ballot in the following election. Laws regulating how petitions can be circulated are an important factor in determining the level of difficulty in using the initiative. A requirement that a person gathering signatures must actually witness each person signing the petition means that signature gathering will consume a large amount of time and money. The process is easier in states such as California, where signatures may be collected by mail, and in Washington, where petitions may be printed in newspapers. However, these methods are not trouble free because they frequently yield a high number of invalid signatures, that is, signatures of people who are not registered voters.[96]

If the initiative qualifies, the third stage is the campaign, the process of educating voters about the initiative and persuading them that they should vote for it. Of course, opponents will want to defeat it and they will try to convince voters to vote "no." Initiative campaigns differ from campaigns between candidates for elected offices in that there are *no limits* on the size of contributions that can be made to initiative campaign committees by individuals, corporations, labor unions, or interest groups; there are no limits on expenditures made by the campaign committee or by any group, either. The U.S. Supreme Court has ruled in a number of cases that any limits violate the First Amendment to the Constitution. A majority of the Court reasoned that the "risk of corruption perceived in cases involving candidate elections simply is not present in a popular vote on a public issue."[97] In other words, money in the form of large contributions could conceivably buy influence over what a candidate says and does, but this is not true in an election where a vote is being taken on ballot measures and large numbers of voters will decide the outcome with yes or no votes on the issues.

Another type of initiative is the **indirect initiative**, whereby a proposal with the required number of signatures must first be submitted to the legislature rather than going directly to the voters. If the legislature fails to act within a specified time, the proposal is then placed on the ballot for voter approval or disapproval. This procedure gives the legislature a chance to act, acknowledging its role in policy making. In Mississippi, if the legislature considers and amends an initiative, both the original initiative and the amended version are placed on the ballot. The indirect initiative is used in eight states, including five that also have the direct initiative. A total of seven states use the indirect initiative for statutes; two of these states also have the direct initiative.

The Referendum Process

Twenty-four states have a **popular referendum:** After voters gather the required number of signatures on petitions, a newly enacted law must win the approval of the voters at the next election. If the voters do not approve the law, it does not go into effect. The popular referendum, because of citizens signing petitions and citizens voting on a measure, is easily confused with the direct initiative. The important difference between the two is the source of the issue that appears on the ballot. With the direct initiative, a new law proposed by citizens is being voted on. With the popular referendum, the proposal being voted on is a law that was just approved by the legislature and signed by the governor.

The more common referendum procedure is the **legislative referendum,** whereby the legislature, after adopting a law, directs that it be placed on the ballot for final approval or disapproval by the voters. Some proposals, in a slight variation of the submission by the legislature process, may be required by state constitutions or local charters to go automatically to the voters. Examples are amendments to state constitutions and financial (tax and bond) issues.

The Recall Process

The recall is the least used, the least available, and, until the successful recall of California Governor Gray Davis in 2003, the least familiar of the three techniques of direct democracy. Eighteen state constitutions include a provision for the recall of their states' elected officials. These states tend to be the states that also have the initiative and referendum because the recall is also a product of the Progressive movement that was based, in part, on distrust of politicians. Generally, recalls occur more frequently, although they still are the exception rather than the rule, in local politics where the targets are mayors and members of city councils and school boards. It can be argued that the recall could impair the independence of the judiciary (see Chapter 7); nevertheless, a majority of these states allow the recall of judges. Prior to the recall of Gray Davis, only one governor had been recalled, Lynn Frazier of North Dakota in 1922. (Frazier, however, made a comeback shortly after he was recalled. North Dakota voters elected him to the U.S. Senate, where he served until he was defeated in a 1940 reelection bid.)

Supporters of a recall are required to gather signatures of registered voters on petitions that clearly call for the removal of an elected official. A signature requirement of 25 percent of the vote cast in the last election is fairly typical and is higher than the percentage needed for an initiative. Signatures must be gathered within a specified period of time, for example, ninety days. In California the signature requirement is only 12 percent and recall supporters have 160 days to circulate petitions; because of these lenient rules, California is one of the easiest states in which to attempt a recall.

If a sufficient number of signatures are collected, a special election is usually called. To remove the official from office, a majority of the voters must vote "yes." A successor may be chosen on the same ballot as the recall or in a subsequent special election. The former procedure was used in California, where voters first voted on the recall of Gray Davis and then voted for a new governor from among 135 candidates who qualified for the ballot! Arnold Schwarzenegger, of *The Terminator* and other movies, Cruz Bustamante, lieutenant governor of California, and Tom McClintock, a California state senator, were the only competitive candidates. The recall was approved with 55.4 percent of the vote, and Schwarzenegger won with 48.6 percent of the vote. If the recall had failed, the second vote would have had no meaning.

What are the grounds for recalling an elected official? A few states (e.g., Alaska, Georgia, and Minnesota) specify incompetence, neglect of duties, failure to perform duties prescribed by law, or violation of the oath of office. And some of these states provide for a court review to determine whether the allegations against an elected official satisfy the state's legal requirements for a recall election. Procedures in other states (e.g., California and Colorado) require that voters be informed through a "statement of reasons" for the recall, but do not identify the specific grounds that must be included in the statement. A majority of the recall states (e.g., Louisiana and Michigan) are completely open, requiring neither specific grounds nor a statement of reasons.[98]

In states where no specific grounds must be cited, a recall can be started by simple voter dissatisfaction with an elected official; however, even after the extensive national press coverage given to the California recall, it is important to remember that attempted recalls of state elected officials, as mentioned before, are still rare. Although no one is keeping track on a regular basis, one study found that between 1970 and 1995, only eleven recall elections of state officials were held in the entire country. (They were held in just five states: California, Wisconsin, Idaho, Michigan, and Oregon.) In eight of these elections, the officials lost their office (all were state legislators). In most cases it was not incompetence or wrongdoing that caused these successful recalls, but rather an official's position or vote on a controversial issue.[99]

Will the successful recall of Gray Davis be repeated in other states? Many political movements start in California and frequently spread across the nation, but this one has not. The factors leading to Davis's recall and the election of Arnold Schwarzenegger may not be easily duplicated in other states. Consider the following: First, Davis, for a number of reasons, including having to deal with the largest budget deficit among the fifty states, was unpopular with California voters. His job performance ratings were extremely low; at times the percentage of Californians giving him favorable approval ratings dipped into the low 20s. Second, opponents of Davis had ample money to finance the recall petition drive; Republican Congressman Darrell Issa used $1 million of his own money to bankroll the petition drive. Third, Schwarzenegger's candidacy offered voters an attractive nonpolitician to turn to; his candidacy probably made it much easier for voters to recall Davis.

The Direct Initiative Evaluated

One of the arguments for the direct initiative is that it is a way to counter the influence of special interests on legislators and to give citizens more control over the making of laws. However, some political scientists, journalists, and elected officials question whether today's practice of direct democracy is actually achieving these goals. To support their position they cite the fact that interest groups, not grassroots organizations composed of average citizens, are the dominant users of the initiative and referendum. Just organizing and financing a petition drive is expensive. Even a moderate-size state such as Oregon required 82,769 petition signatures for 2007 through 2010. Not an easy task for the most dedicated of volunteers! It is not hard to see why professional assistance might be needed. The amount of money spent to qualify initiatives for the ballot has increased dramatically, especially in California, where approximately 600,000 signatures are needed to place a proposed constitutional amendment on the ballot. A few years ago, $1 million would qualify a proposal, today it is between $2 million and $3 million. In 2005, supporters of several initiatives favored by Governor Schwarzenegger spent more than $3 million to collect the required number of signatures. Additional money is spent for media advertising to persuade voters to sign or not to sign petitions.[100] Of course, interest groups are well equipped with organizing skills and financial resources. And they do not have to know a lot about running an initiative campaign because they can hire "professional managers, petition circulators, media consultants, pollsters, direct-mail specialists and lawyers."[101] Paid petitioners frequently work with at least three separate initiatives, approaching citizens and asking them to sign as many as they agree with. Paid petition circulation is not new to the initiative process; it actually was used in Oregon in 1904 with the first state-level initiative in the United States. Petition circulators are paid for each signature they collect, sometimes up to $10 per signature.[102]

Several states—Idaho, Colorado, Mississippi, and Oregon—have tried to limit the practice of paid petition circulators, but until recently all efforts were ruled unconstitutional by the Supreme Court, including a law in Colorado that made it a felony to pay a person to collect signatures; the Court viewed this as placing a "severe burden" on speech. Oregon voters adopted in 2002 the Initiative Integrity Act, which prohibits paying petition circulators by the number of signatures they obtain on a petition. At least in lower federal courts, this has been upheld because it bans only a particular method of payment, not all payments.[103]

Evidence is strong that money is an important resource in getting initiatives on the ballot. However, an important question remains: Does the amount of money spent by supporters and opponents during the campaign stage determine whether initiatives are approved by the voters? Before looking at this question, it is important to note that in the hundred-year history of initiatives in the United States, voters approved less than half (41 percent) of the initiatives that actually made it to the ballot. Overall, the passage rate is not high. (Table 4-5 has more details on the number of initiatives proposed and passage rates.) One of the explanations for this low rate of passage is that if voters are uncertain of the likely policy consequences of an initiative, they tend to vote against it and it is defeated.[104] Research from Elisabeth Gerber examines more than 160 initiatives in several states, comparing the success of initiatives backed by economic interest groups and citizen interest groups. Economic groups such as trade associations and corporations have greater financial resources for campaign spending, but they are less successful than citizen interest groups such as the League of Women Voters and the Sierra Club in obtaining voter approval of proposals. About one-third of initiatives supported by economic interests are approved by the voters, compared to

TABLE 4-5 Statewide Initiative Passage Rates

	Number Proposed	Number Adopted	Passage Rate
DECADES WITH THE HIGHEST NUMBER OF BALLOT INITIATIVES			
1991–2000	389	188	48%
1911–1920	293	116	40%
1981–1990	271	115	42%
DECADES WITH THE LOWEST NUMBER OF BALLOT INITIATIVES			
1901–1910	56	25	45%
1961–1970	87	37	41%
1951–1960	114	45	39%
STATES WITH THE HIGHEST NUMBER OF BALLOT INITIATIVES IN NOVEMBER 2006			
Arizona	10	5	50%
Oregon	10	3	30%
California	8	2	25%
South Dakota	8	2	25%
Colorado	7	3	43%

Source: This table is modeled after a table by M. Dane Waters, "A Century Later—The Experiment with Citizen-Initiated Legislation Continues," in Everett Carll Ladd, ed., *America at the Polls, 1998* (Storrs, Conn.: The Roper Center for Public Opinion Research), p. 128. Table has been updated with information from *BallotWatch: Fall Ballot Measures 2006,* Report 2006 No. 3 (Los Angeles, Calif.: Initiative and Referendum Institute, 2006), and *BallotWatch: Election Results 2006,* Report 2006 No. 5 (Los Angeles, Calif.: Initiative and Referendum Institute, 2006), www.iandrinstitute.org.

one-half of those supported by citizen groups. However, economic interests are slightly more successful in defeating proposals they oppose.[105]

These groups are not the only actors in initiative politics; wealthy individuals have single-handedly put up the money for some ballot initiatives. Billionaire George Soros, an international financier-philanthropist, bankrolled the initiatives that legalized medical marijuana in Arizona and California. In 2006, California movie director and producer Stephen Bing, probably best known for *The Polar Express,* used close to $50 million of his personal funds to become the main force behind the campaign for Proposition 87. This initiative would have imposed a tax on oil production in the state to raise $4 billion to help develop alternative fuels.[106] Voters defeated Proposition 87. Other members of the "gazillionaire club" have not been successful in recent years—for example, Silicon Valley millionaire Ron Unz (public school instruction only in English, California) and founder of Amway Dick DeVos (school choice initiatives in Michigan). A recent twist is that elected officials occasionally become advocates of an initiative so they can associate their name with an initiative that appears to have great popular support, calculating that it may give their popularity a boost or help them in a reelection bid. Also, individuals who hope to be elected have used the process to gain statewide name recognition or build a reputation that legitimizes their interest in state policies to help in a later run for political office.

Similarly, in the 2004 presidential election, measures to ban same-sex marriages were on the ballots in many states and may have helped Republican candidates and even the presidential candidate, George W. Bush, who supported this ban. The Democratic Party hoped that minimum-wage initiatives in 2006 would help its candidates. This tactic rests on the belief that "high-profile, politically charged ballot propositions" will mobilize particular voters and influence voting decisions. For example, the minimum-wage initiative should mobilize a higher turnout of low-income workers and members of labor unions who also would be more likely to vote for Democratic candidates because they generally support the minimum-wage initiative. Although empirical research to document this relationship has been mixed, it has an intuitive appeal and has been named **ballot proposition spillover,** when ballot propositions influence candidate elections.[107]

There are also examples of private citizens who, through great determination, use the initiative process successfully. One such person is Helen Hill of Oregon, who ten years ago almost single-handedly won voter approval of Measure 58, which required the state to issue upon request an "unaltered, original and unamended certificate of birth" to any adopted person over 21. Although Hill was adopted, her primary motivation came from the fact that her father learned late in his life that he had been adopted, also. Hill's personal torment led her to use the initiative to seek a change in Oregon's adoption laws. Political scientist Richard Ellis calls Hill's story "a model citizen initiative."[108] Supporters of her proposal spent $17,000, raised from small contributions, and most of it went for a full-page newspaper ad in the *Oregonian*. Opposition to the proposal was neither well organized nor well financed. Still, even in this case money was important. During the crucial qualifying stage, Hill used some of the money she inherited from her father to hire a professional signature-gathering organization to complete the task of gathering the required number of signatures; this cost approximately $100,000,[109] well below the average cost but still a lot of money for a citizen.

Arguments over the direct initiative could easily fill a book of this size. Detractors argue that the average voter cannot be expected to read voter information pamphlets that sometimes total nearly one hundred pages (Arizona, 2004) and vote intelligently on as many as thirteen ballot propositions, including both initiatives and referendums (California, 2004). Richard Ellis says that the reason we elect political leaders is not to have them simply "mirror public preferences but to engage in reasoned debate about the public interest."[110] Advocates argue that citizens voting on public policy issues, actually making decisions, is what democracy is all about.[111] This may be one of those debates in which there is some truth on both sides. Certainly, representative government, in the form of legislatures, is needed. Citizens cannot be well informed on every issue and make all decisions required in today's complex world. On the other hand, citizen consideration of a reasonable number of initiatives during an election can give them a direct say in issues affecting their lives.

SUMMARY

American citizens can participate in politics in a number of ways—from voting to contacting public officials about a specific problem. Another form of participation is called civic engagement whereby citizens volunteer, for example, to work with others for a charitable cause in their community rather than trying to influence what their local government does. Advocates of strong democracy focus on ways of increasing citizen participation through neighborhood forums to solve at least some of the problems of their community.

Voter registration requirements that discriminated against minorities were eliminated by the Voting Rights Act of 1965 and subsequent amendments. The Voting Rights Act also prohibits more subtle forms of discrimination such as minority vote dilution. Although more African Americans and Hispanics are elected to state and local offices, it does not always follow that they dominate city policy making decisions on minority-related issues.

Even before the passage of the National Voter Registration Act, many states had made voter registration less burdensome by adopting mail and "motor-voter" procedures. States and the federal government have taken steps to improve voting systems and election administration after serious problems in the presidential election in Florida in 2000, although the current use of direct recording electronic systems (DREs) without a voter-verified paper trail is viewed as a potential problem. More and more citizens are casting votes in advance of Election Day through absentee or early voting. States that elect governors in presidential election years have higher turnout than those that do not. Local elections have lower turnout than state elections; and turnout is even lower if the elections are nonpartisan.

The advantage of holding state elections at a different time than presidential elections is that voters are less likely to be influenced by how they view the national political scene. However, the 1994 and 2006 midterm elections illustrate that it still is possible for national politics to affect state races.

Incumbent governors face a reelection environment that is less favorable than that of U.S. senators, but if they are eligible for reelection most of them will run and most will be reelected. How candidates define the issues for the voters is an important factor in determining who is elected governor.

Campaigns for a seat in the state legislature differ greatly because the size of legislative districts varies so much. States such as California and New York that have districts with a large population frequently have professionally managed campaigns; in most states, races are informal and involve face-to-face contact between candidates and voters, with only direct-mail advertising requiring an expert.

Judicial elections in which candidates oppose each other for the same judgeship have changed greatly in the last few years. Judicial candidates have been freed from regulations and ethics codes that limited what they could say about legal and political issues. Also, interest groups have contributed or spent large sums of money to defeat incumbent judges running for reelection who have made some decisions that the groups do not agree with.

Running for mayor in large cities involves new-style campaign techniques of professional consultants, polling, and television advertisements. Most cities have nonpartisan elections, and group interests and coalition building may be more important than political parties. Some modern campaign techniques, especially direct mail, have even found their way into midsize cities.

Political campaigns are increasingly expensive, especially in large states. Even before the start of this explosive growth, states attempted to regulate the influence of large financial contributors through laws that limited the size of contributions and required candidates to disclose information about the source of contributions and expenditures. Public financing of campaigns, which would reduce candidates' reliance on private contributors, had limited success in the past because sources of funding such as the "add-on" tax did not generate enough money, especially with campaign costs spiraling upward. Clean election laws are trying to correct this by tying candidates' acceptance of public funds to expenditure limits and using more reliable sources of revenue.

The initiative, referendum, and recall procedures allow citizens to propose laws, make decisions on laws that they or their legislatures have proposed, and remove elected officials from office before they have finished their terms. Progressive movement reformers hoped that these direct democracy techniques would be a way for ordinary citizens to enact laws without the influence of special interests that characterizes legislatures. It is clear that money is important in qualifying initiatives for the ballot; however, economic interest groups are less successful than citizen interest groups in obtaining voter approval for their proposals once they are on the ballot. In the hundred-year history of the initiative, voters have approved less than half of the initiatives that they voted on. The direct initiative has both strong supporters and critics.

KEY TERMS

political participation (p. 119)
civic engagement (p. 119)
survey research (p. 119)
strong democracy (p. 122)
Voting Rights Act of 1965 (p. 124)
preclearance (p. 124)
Chicano movement (p. 124)
minority vote dilution (p. 125)
political incorporation (p. 125)
National Voter Registration Act
 (NVRA) (p. 126)
restrictive states (p. 127)
student choice states (p. 127)
voting systems (p. 127)
Help America Vote Act (HAVA) (p. 128)
direct recording electronic systems
 (DREs) (p. 128)
absentee voting (p. 129)
early voting (p. 129)
voting-eligible population (p. 131)

legislative campaign committees (p. 136)
membership turnover (p. 137)
retention election (p. 138)
instant runoff voting (IRV) (p. 141)
disclosure laws (p. 143)
contribution limits (p. 144)
expenditure limits (p. 144)
public financing (p. 144)
clean election laws (p. 146)
ballot measure (p. 147)
initiative (p. 147)
referendum (p. 147)
recall (p. 147)
direct initiative (p. 150)
indirect initiative (p. 150)
popular referendum (p. 151)
legislative referendum (p. 151)
ballot proposition spillover (p. 155)

BRIEF COMPARISONS OF STATE/LOCAL DIFFERENCES

Issue	State Level	Local Level
Elections and voting	Midterm, partisan elections in most states. Voter turnout is in 40–59 percent range.	Elections, usually nonpartisan, are held at a variety of different times. Voter turnout is frequently under 30 percent.
Campaign financing	Excellent comparative studies. PACs play an important role. Public financing plans have been adopted in fifteen states, but are successful in only a few.	Few comparative studies. Little public financing. "Shoeleather" campaigns are still possible, but many are becoming more expensive and using new-style campaign techniques.
Direct democracy	Initiatives are regularly on the ballot in a few states such as Oregon, California, and Colorado. In many states, the referendum is used more frequently.	Initiative procedures are not as common as the other procedures. Referendums are used widely, especially for proposals for the construction of new public school building.

INTERESTING WEB SITES

www.azclean.org. The Clean Elections Institute advocates campaign finance reform and focuses on the progress of "clean election" laws, which have been adopted in Arizona and Maine and are under consideration in other states.

www.ballot.org and *www.iandrinstitute.org.* Good Web sites for the initiative and referendum. They have historical databases and lots of current information on what's happening with direct democracy in the states, with emphasis on the initiative.

www.civicyouth.org. Web site for the Center for Information and Research on Civic Learning and Engagement (CIRCLE). A great source for research on the civic and political participation of young Americans. Check out "Youth Voting" and "Volunteering/Community Service."

www.followthemoney.org. National Institute on Money in State Politics offers state-by-state information. Summaries of each state's campaign finance laws are available as well as information on how much money candidates received in campaign contributions and where it came from.

NOTES

1. Institute for Politics, Democracy & the Internet, *Political Influentials Online in the 2004 Presidential Campaign* (Washington, D.C.: George Washington University, Graduate School of Political Management, 2004), p. 11.
2. Ibid., p. 15.
3. Jack H. Nagel, *Participation* (Englewood Cliffs, N.J.: Prentice-Hall, 1987), p. 1.
4. Cliff Zukin, Scott Keeter, Molly Andolina, Krista Jenkins, and Michael X. Delli Carpini, *A New Engagement: Political Participation, Civic Life, and the Changing American Citizen* (New York: Oxford University Press, 2006), p. 51.
5. Sidney Verba and Norman H. Nie, *Participation in America: Political Democracy and Social Equality* (New York: Harper & Row, 1972).
6. Cliff Zukin, Scott Keeter, Molly Andolina, Krista Jenkins, Michael X. Delli Carpini, *A New Engagement: Political Participation, Civic Life, and the Changing American Citizen* (New York: Oxford University Press, 2006), pp. 77–81.
7. Ibid., pp. 63–65.
8. Ibid., pp. 188–190.
9. Lawrence J. R. Herson and John M. Bolland, *The Urban Web* (Chicago: Nelson-Hall Publishers, 1990), p. 171.
10. Terry Christensen and Tom Hoegen-Esch, *Local Politics: A Practical Guide to Governing at the Grassroots,* 2nd ed. (Armonk, N.Y.: M.E. Sharpe, 2006), pp. 253–254.
11. Dennis E. Gale, *Understanding Urban Unrest* (Thousand Oaks, Calif.: Sage Publications, 1996), p. 121.
12. Herson and Bolland, *Urban Web,* p. 172.
13. The term *strong democracy* is frequently found in the literature on citizen participation in the affairs of local communities. The idea is presented fully in Benjamin R. Barber, *Strong Democracy* (Berkeley: University of California Press, 1984).
14. Jeffrey M. Berry, Kent E. Portney, and Ken Thomson, *The Rebirth of Urban Democracy* (Washington, D.C.: Brookings Institution, 1993), p. 2.

15. Ibid., p. 270.
16. Sidney Verba, Kay Lehman Schlozman, and Henry E. Brady, *Voice and Equality: Civic Voluntarism in American Politics* (Cambridge, Mass.: Harvard University Press, 1995), p. 23.
17. V. O. Key, Jr., *Southern Politics in State and Nation* (New York: Alfred A. Knopf, 1949), pp. 556–577.
18. Chandler Davidson, "The Recent Evolution of Voting Rights Law Affecting Racial and Language Minorities," in *Quiet Revolution in the South*, Chandler Davidson and Bernard Grofman, eds. (Princeton, N.J.: Princeton University Press, 1994), p. 31.
19. Chandler Davidson, "The Voting Rights Act: A Brief History," in *Controversies in Minority Voting*, Bernard Grofman and Chandler Davidson, eds. (Washington, D.C.: Brookings Institution, 1992), p. 21.
20. Robert Brischetto, et al., "Texas," in *Controversies in Minority Voting*, Bernard Grofman and Chandler Davidson, eds. (Washington, D.C.: Brookings Institution, 1992), p. 241.
21. Rodney E. Hero, *Latinos and the U.S. Political Pluralism: Two-Tiered Pluralism* (Philadelphia, Pa.: Temple University Press, 1992), pp. 131–154; and Rodney Hero, *Latinos and U.S. Politics* (New York: HarperCollins, 1995), pp. 14–20. This term was first discussed by Rufus P. Browning, Dale R. Marshall, and David H. Tabb in *Protest Is Not Enough* (Berkeley: University of California Press, 1984). For African Americans, see www.census.gov/compendia/statab/tables/07s0403.xls; for Hispanics, see www.census.gov/compendia/statab/tables/07s0404.xls.
22. Clarence N. Stone, "Race and Regime in Atlanta," in Rufus P. Browning et al., eds., *Racial Politics in American Cities* (White Plains, N.Y.: Longman, 1991), pp. 125–139.
23. Frances Fox Piven and Richard A. Cloward, "Northern Bourbons: A Preliminary Report on the National Voter Registration Act," *PS: Political Science and Politics* 29 (March 1996), pp. 39–40. An "active"/"passive" classification of state mail-in and "motor-voter" laws, as they existed prior to the National Voter Registration Act, is contained in Stephen Knack, "Does 'Motor Voter' Work? Evidence from State-Level Data," *Journal of Politics* 57 (August 1995), pp. 800–801.
24. Richard G. Smolka and Ronald D. Michaelson, "Election Legislation, 1992–93," in *The Book of the States 1994–95* (Lexington, Ky.: Council of State Governments, 1994), pp. 204–208.
25. U.S. Election Assistance Commission, "The Impact of the National Voter Registration Act of 1993 on the Administration of Elections for Federal Office," www.eac.gov/NVRA-2004-Survey.htm#nvra12. See Tables 1, 2, and 3.
26. Robert D. Brown and Justin Wedeking, "People Who Have Their Tickets But Do Not Use Them," *American Politics Research* (July 2006), pp. 484–490. The effect of place of registration on voter turnout in the 1996 presidential election is described in Raymond Wolfinger and Jonathan Hoffman, "Registering and Voting with Motor Voter," *PS: Political Science and Politics* (March 2001), p. 89.
27. Ibid., p. 484.
28. Stephen I. Frank and Steven C. Wagner, *"We Shocked the World!" A Case Study of Jesse Ventura's Election as Governor of Minnesota* (New York: Harcourt College Publishers, 1999), pp. 6–7.
29. Mark J. Fenster, "The Impact of Allowing Day of Registration Voting on Turnout in U.S. Elections from 1960 to 1992," *American Politics Quarterly* 22 (January 1994), p. 84.
30. Michael G. O'Loughlin and Corey Unangst, *Democracy and College Student Voting*, 3rd ed., (Salisbury, Md.: Institute for Public Affairs and Civic Engagement, 2006), p. 13.
31. Ibid., p. 9.
32. Special Committee on Voting Systems and Election Procedures in Maryland, *Report and Recommendations* (February 2002), p. 4.

33. Of the numerous studies of what went wrong in Florida's 2000 election, one of the best is Dennis Cauchon and Jim Drinkard, "Florida Voter Errors Cost Gore the Election," *USA Today* (May 4, 2001), www.usatoday.com/news/washington/2001-05-10.

34. Special Committee, p. 55.

35. The Election Reform Information Project, "Ready for 2002, Forgetting 2000" (January 2000), pp. 8–12, www.wlwctionline.org/site/docs (accessed February 24, 2003).

36. Tova Andrea Wang, "Understanding the Debate Over Electronic Voting Machines" (New York: Century Fund, 2004), www.tcf.org/print.asp?type=PB&pubid=475.

37. John C. Fortier, *Absentee and Early Voting: Trends, Promises and Perils* (Washington, D.C.: AEI Press, 2006), p. 19.

38. Ibid., p. 14.

39. Ibid., p. 46.

40. Ibid., pp. 42–44.

41. Margaret Rosenfield, *All-Mail-Ballot Elections* (Washington, D.C.: National Clearing House on Election Administration, 1995), p. 39.

42. Detailed description of McDonald's procedures to estimate voting eligible population is available at http://elections.gmu.edu/voter_turnout.htm. U.S. Bureau of the Census estimates noncitizen population in each state as of 2000, and information on ineligible felons is from prison, parole, and probation reports of the U.S. Department of Justice.

43. Brian F. Schaffner, Matthew J. Streb, and Gerald C. Wright, "A Rule That Works: The Nonpartisan Ballot in State and Local Elections." Presented at the 1999 Annual Meeting of the Midwest Political Science Association, April 15–17, 1999, Chicago, Ill.

44. Brian F. Schaffner, Matthew Streb, and Gerald Wright, "Teams Without Uniforms: The Nonpartisan Ballot in State and Local Elections," *Political Research Quarterly* (March 2001), p. 25.

45. Mark E. Tompkins, "Have Gubernatorial Elections Become More Distinctive Contests?" *Journal of Politics* 50 (1988), pp. 192–205.

46. Thad Beyle, "Gubernatorial Elections, Campaign Costs and Powers," *The Book of the States 2006* (Lexington, Ky.: Council of State Governments, 2006), p. 143.

47. Peverill Squire and Christina Fastnow, "Comparing Gubernatorial and Senatorial Elections," *Political Research Quarterly* (September 1994), pp. 705–720.

48. Brian Stults and Richard F. Winters, "The Political Economy of Taxes and the Vote." Presented at the 2002 Annual Meeting of the Midwest Political Science Association, April 25–28, 2002.

49. Ibid., p. 10.

50. Ibid., p. 36.

51. Thomas M. Carsey, *Campaign Dynamics: The Race for Governor* (Ann Arbor: University of Michigan Press, 2000), p. 11.

52. Ibid., p. 15.

53. Paul West, "Michigan Woman's Star Rising on Political Stage," *Sun* (Baltimore), September 16, 2002, p. 1A.

54. Gary F. Moncrief, Peverill Squire, and Malcolm E. Jewell, *Who Runs for the State Legislature?* (Upper Saddle River, N.J.: Prentice-Hall, 2001), pp. 38–43.

55. Lillian C. Woo, "Today's Legislators: Who They Are and Why They Run," *State Legislatures* (April 1994), p. 29.

56. Moncrief, Squire, and Jewell, *Who Runs*, pp. 53–57.

57. Emily Van Dunk, "Who Runs for State Legislative Office? A Look at Candidates for Citizen and Professional Legislatures," presented at the 1994 Annual Meeting of the Midwest Political Science Association, April 14–16, Chicago.

58. Alan Rosenthal, *Legislative Life* (New York: Harper & Row, 1981), pp. 101–112.

59. Peter L. Francia, Paul S. Herrnson, John P. Frendreis, and Alan R. Gitelson, "The Battle for the Legislature: Party Campaigning in State House and State Senate Elections," in *The State of the Parties,* 4th ed., John C. Green and Rick Farmer, eds. (New York: Rowman & Littlefield Publishers, 2003), p. 189; Moncrief, Squire, and Jewell, *Who Runs,* p. 86.

60. Tom Loftus, *The Art of Legislative Politics* (Washington, D.C.: CQ Press, 1994), p. 10.

61. Keith E. Hamm and Gary F. Moncrief, "Legislative Politics in the States," in *Politics in the American States,* Virginia Gray and Russell L. Hanson, eds. (Washington, D.C.: CQ Press, 2004), p. 172.

62. Ibid., pp. 165–166.

63. Lawrence Baum, "Electing Judges," in *Contemplating Courts,* Lee Epstein, ed. (Washington, D.C.: CQ Press, 1995), pp. 33–36.

64. Brennan Center for Justice, "Republican Party of Minnesota v. White: What Does the Decision Mean for the Future of State Judicial Elections?" www.brennancenter.org/programs/prog (accessed March 4, 2002).

65. *Republican Party of Minnesota v. White,* 536 U.S. 765 (2002).

66. Elizabeth, Stawicki, "Ruling Ushers in New Era of Judicial Elections," Minnesota Public Radio, August 2, 2005, http://news.minnesota.publicradio.org/features/2005/08/02_stawickie_judicial (accessed January 20, 2007).

67. Roy A. Schotland, "Comment," *Law and Contemporary Problems* 61, no. 3 (Summer 1998), p. 150.

68. Zach Patton, "Robe Warriors," *Governing* (March 2006), www.governing.com/articles/3judges.htm (accessed January 20, 2007).

69. Gregory Roberts, "Special-Interest Money Fueling Judicial Races," *Seattle Post-Intelligencer* (September 15, 2006).

70. "A Brief History of Judicial Selection in State Courts," in Reports of the Task Forces of Citizens for Independent Courts, *Uncertain Justice: Politics and America's Courts* (New York: The Century Foundation, 2000), pp. 107–113.

71. Karen M. Kaufmann, *The Urban Voter: Group Conflict & Mayoral Voting Behavior in American Cities* (Ann Arbor: University of Michigan Voter, 2004), p. 3.

72. Ibid., p. 170.

73. Jill Lawrence, "L.A.'s Mayor-Elect Faces Challenges Head-On," *USA Today* (June 16, 2005), p. 15A; Harold Meyerson, "An Unlikely Ascent," *The American Prospect Online* (May 20, 2005), www.prospect.org/web/printfriendly-view.ww?id=9699.

74. J. Cherie Strachan, *High-Tech Grass Roots: The Professionalization of Local Elections* (New York: Rowman & Littlefield Publishers, 2003), pp. 31–32.

75. For more information on instant runoff voting, go to the Center for Voting and Democracy at www.fairvote.org. On Burlington's IRV, see www.burlingtonvotes.org.

76. Thad Beyle, "Gubernatorial Elections, Campaign Costs and Powers," *The Book of the States 2006* (Lexington, Ky.: Council of State Governments, 2006), p. 149. Beyle converts all expenditures to 2004 dollars, which controls for increases in the cost of living that occurs over time.

77. Ibid., pp. 147–149.

78. Rachel Weiss, *State Elections Overview: 2004,* Institute on Money in State Politics, p. 7, www.followthemoney.org/Research/index.phtml.

79. Robert E. Hogan, "The Costs of Representation in State Legislatures: Explaining Variations in Campaign Spending," *Social Science Quarterly* 81, no. 4 (December 2000), pp. 941–956.

80. William E. Cassie, Joel A. Thompson, and Malcolm E. Jewell, "The Pattern of PAC Contributions in Legislative Elections: An Eleven State Analysis." Presented at the Annual Meeting of the American Political Science Association, 1992, Chicago; "Report Says PACs Obscure millions in Contributions," *Decatur Daily News* (October 17, 2006), www.decaturdaily.com/decaturdaily/nes/061017/report.shtml; M. J. Ellington, "PACs Fill Garner's Campaign

Account," *Decatur Daily News* (June 4, 2006), www.decaturdaily.com/decaturdaily/news/060604/garner.shtml (accessed January 24, 2007).

81. Michael J. Malbin and Thomas L. Gais, *The Day After Reform: Sobering Campaign Finance Lessons from the States* (Albany, N.Y.: The Rockefeller Press, 1998), pp. 45–49.

82. *Randall v. Sorrell,* 548 U.S. 12.

83. *Buckley v. Valeo,* 424 U.S. 1 (1976).

84. Steven M. Levin, *Keeping It Clean: Public Financing in American Elections* (Los Angeles: Center for Governmental Studies, 2006), p. 3, www.cgs.org.

85. Herbert E. Alexander, *Reform and Reality: The Funding of State and Local Campaigns* (New York: The Twentieth Century Fund Press, 1999), pp. 30–32.

86. Mary M. Janicki, "Sources of Public Funding of Political Campaigns," OLR Research Report 99-R-1101 (Hartford, Conn.: Connecticut General Assembly, 1999), www.cga.ct.gov/ps99/rpt/olr/htm/99-r-1101.htm (accessed January 25, 2007).

87. Johnny Brannon, "Few Takers for 'Free' Public Campaign Money," *Honolulu Advertiser* (November 20, 2006), http://the.honoluluadvertiser.com/article/2006/Nov20/In/FP611200338.html (accessed January 28, 2007).

88. A good review of the current status of clean election reforms is in Levin, *Keeping It Clean.*

89. Kenneth R. Mayer, *Public Financing and Electoral Competition in Minnesota and Wisconsin* (Los Angeles: Citizens' Research Foundation, 1998), p. 12.

90. Kenneth R. Mayer, Timothy Werner, and Amanda Williams, *Do Public Funding Programs Enhance Electoral Competition?* Paper presented at the Fourth Annual Conference on State Politics and Policy, Kent State University, April 30–May 1, 2004.

91. Initiative and Referendum Institute, *Initiative Use* (Los Angeles: Initiative and Referendum Institute, 2006), p. 1, www.iandrinstitute.org/IRI%20Initiative%20Use%20(2006–11).pdf (accessed February 13, 2007).

92. Several reports on ballot measures that include summaries of the measures and election results are available from the Initiative and Referendum Institute at the University of Southern California. See www.iandrinstitute.org.

93. National Conference of State Legislatures, "Voters to Consider High Profile Ballot Measures" (Denver, Colo.: National Conference of State Legislatures, 2006), www.ncsl.org/programs/press/2006/pr060816ballot.htm; Ballot Initiative Strategy Center, "Trendlines 2006: What Is 2006 Really About?" (Washington, D.C.: Ballot Initiative Strategy Center, 2006), www.ballot.org; Initiative and Referendum Institute, "Ballotwatch: Election Results 2006" (Los Angeles: Initiative and Referendum Institute, 2006), www.iandrinstitute.org.

94. Charles M. Price, "The Initiative: A Comparative Analysis and Reassessment of a Western Phenomenon," *Western Political Quarterly* 28 (June 1975), p. 59.

95. Elisabeth R. Gerber, *The Populist Paradox: Interest Group Influence and the Promise of Direct Legislation* (Princeton, N.J.: Princeton University Press, 1999), pp. 38–44.

96. David Kehler and Robert M. Stern, "Initiatives in the 1980s and 1990s," in *The Book of the States 1994–95,* pp. 279–281.

97. *First National Bank of Boston v. Bellotti,* 435 U.S. 765 (1978), and *Citizens Against Rent Control v. City of Berkeley,* 454 U.S. 290 (1981). For a review of a number of important campaign finance cases, see L. Paige Whitaker, *Campaign Finance Regulation Under the First Amendment: Buckley v. Valeo and Its Supreme Court Progeny* (Washington, D.C.: Congressional Research Service, 2003).

98. Minnesota House of Representatives Research Department, *Recall of State Elected Officials: A Proposed Minnesota Constitutional Amendment* (October 1996), pp. 6–7, www.house.leg.state.mn.us/hrd/pubs/recall96.pdf (accessed March 12, 2003).

99. Ibid., p. 9.

100. John Wildermuth, "Special Election Push Costly for Governor, Foes" (May 4, 2005), www.sfgate.com/cgi-bin/article.cgi? (accessed February 16, 2007).

101. Martha Angle, "Initiatives: Vox Populi or Professional Ploy," *Congressional Quarterly Weekly Report* (October 15, 1994), p. 2982.

102. Andrew M. Gloger, *Paid Petitioners After Prete*, Report 2006-1 (Los Angeles: Initiative and Referendum Institute, 2006), p. 2.

103. Ibid., pp. 2–3.

104. Arthur Lupia and John G. Matsusaks, "Direct Democracy: New Approaches to Old Questions," *Annual Review of Political Science* (Palo Alto, Calif.: Annual Reviews, 2006), p. 471.

105. Elisabeth R. Gerber, *The Populist Paradox,* pp. 110–115.

106. Matthew Yi, "Filmmaker a Big Donor Behind the Scenes" (October 31, 2006), www.sfgate.com/cgi-bin/article.cgi? (accessed February 16, 2007).

107. Jeffrey R. Makin, *Are Ballot Propositions Spilling Over Onto Candidate Elections?* Report 2006-2 (Los Angeles: Initiative and Referendum Institute, 2006), p. 2.

108. Richard J. Ellis, *Democratic Delusions: The Initiative Process in America* (Lawrence, Kans.: University Press of Kansas, 2002), p. 14.

109. Ibid., pp. 8–9.

110. Ibid., p. 200.

111. Charles M. Price, "Direct Democracy Works," *State Government News* (June–July 1997), pp. 14–15, 35.

STATE AND LOCAL LEGISLATURES

BEGINNING A LEGISLATIVE CAREER

Stephanie Stuckey-Benfield is from a Georgia family that has a tradition of active involvement in politics; her grandfather was a state legislator and her father a U.S. congressman. Discussion of political issues at the dinner table, and almost any time, was not unusual as she was growing up. Certainly, there was a good chance she would want a political career.

After earning her bachelor's degree and law degree from the University of Georgia, she worked as an aide to a Georgia state senator and started networking in liberal social and political organizations in the Atlanta area. When a vacancy occurred in the legislative district she was living in, she decided to run. She won the Democratic primary election against one opponent and had no opposition in the general election. At the age of thirty-two, she became a member of the Georgia House of Representatives and has been reelected four times.

Stuckey-Benfield quickly adjusted to legislative life, finding an issue on which she could make a difference. With the state's major newspaper reporting that Georgia's high schools were funding boys' athletic programs at a much higher level than girls' athletic programs and that the schools could be sued for not complying with a federal law known as Title IX, she co-sponsored and negotiated approval of the Sports Equity Act of 2000. This law creates a framework to monitor high schools throughout Georgia to ensure they are complying with Title IX's requirement of equal opportunities for boys and girls to participate in athletic programs.

Stuckey-Benfield is at the beginning of a legislative career; she is dedicated to "twenty years on the job" and hopes to move into a leadership position such as chair of a major committee.[1] As will be discussed in this chapter, the idea of how long an individual should be a legislator is a central question that manifests itself in terms such as citizen legislature, professional legislature, and term limits.

POINTS TO CONSIDER

- What was the Reapportionment Revolution?
- Is gerrymandering widespread in the drawing of state legislative district lines?
- How do professional and citizen state legislatures differ?
- Compare the influence of committees and leaders in the state legislative lawmaking process.
- What are term limits and why are they a challenge to state legislatures?
- Why is membership turnover high on city councils?
- How are county governments organized?

STATE LEGISLATURES

Forty years ago, state legislatures were dominated by rural political interests and were described frequently as holdovers from the nineteenth century, when the public wanted a limited role for state government. A majority of the legislatures met every other year;

only twenty had annual sessions. They were frequently criticized, as one observer said, as "sometime governments: their presence is rarely felt or rarely missed."[2] Legislators spent more time back in their hometowns than in the state capital; it was a part-time job with minimal pay that individuals would decide to leave after one or two terms. Legislators had little legislative staff support and usually did not even have offices in the state capitol building.

Today, this description could not be further from the truth. State legislatures have undergone a dramatic transformation. Changes in representation have helped to elect more legislators who are from urban areas, more legislators who are women, and more legislators who are African American or Hispanic; in other words, legislators are more likely to reflect the characteristics of their state's citizens than in the past. Also, studies conducted by universities and the Citizens Conference on State Legislatures in the 1960s recommended significant reforms in legislative structure, including annual sessions, expanded staff support, and higher salaries for legislators.[3] The goal was to create legislatures whose members could devote full time to solving the complex problems of modern state government. Legislators would become policy experts, and state legislatures would take their rightful place in policy making as an equal to the executive branch. (The power of state governors is one of the topics in Chapter 6.)

Most states adopted all or at least some of these reforms, but by the 1990s the public seemed dismayed. Legislators were often viewed as more interested in advancing their own legislative careers than working for the interests of the people who elected them. The most visible manifestation of the public's mood was the term-limit movement that advocated limiting legislators to a few terms in office so that they would be more accountable to voters. Being a full-time legislator and staying in office for more than a couple of terms was no longer viewed as the ideal. If Stephanie Stuckey-Benfield had been elected in Arkansas, a state that adopted term limits, rather than Georgia, a state without term limits, she would have left office at the end of her third term in 2002, after serving only six years.

Apportionment and Districting

Before legislators can be elected, there must be districts containing voters they can represent. Creating legislative districts is accomplished through apportionment and districting. Some confusion exists in the meaning of these terms, so a brief definition of each is needed. **Apportionment** refers to how the number of seats in a legislative body is distributed within a state's boundaries. Historically, population and units of local government (such as counties) were the most important factors in apportionment. **Districting** is the process of drawing boundaries on a map that delineates the geographic areas—the districts—from which representatives will be elected. These are not terms we see in newspapers or hear on television every day. But they are used frequently after each federal decennial census (the next one is 2010), when states are required to *redistrict* their state legislatures using new population figures.[4]

The Reapportionment Revolution

Before 1962, state legislatures were described as malapportioned. Simply put, **malapportionment** meant that legislators from some districts represented more people than legislators from other districts. In part, this problem was caused by the legislatures' failure to change boundaries as population growth and shifts occurred; some state constitutions required redistricting on a regular basis, but these provisions were ignored. As a result, cities were underrepresented and legislatures were dominated by rural and small-town interests. Before 1962, for example, Alabama and Tennessee had not changed their apportionment or districting since 1901, and Vermont's house and senate had not changed since the adoption of the state constitution in 1793! Of the two legislative chambers, state senates were more malapportioned because representation in the senates frequently was apportioned to counties. In eight states, each county was guaranteed equal representation in the senate. This meant that counties, regardless of population, would have the same number of senators.

Illustrations of malapportionment could easily fill an entire book, but a few examples will do. Some legislative chambers were so malapportioned that the population represented by a majority of the legislators was only a fraction of the state's total population. In California, 10.7 percent of the state's population elected a majority of the members of the state senate: One senator represented 6 million people and another represented only 14,294 people. In Vermont, 11.9 percent of the state's population elected a majority of the members of the state's lower house: One representative served a district with twenty-four people and another served a district with 35,531 people! (Vermont was the only state that guaranteed to each town equal representation in the lower house.)

The federal courts were of no help to those who wanted states to reapportion. The Supreme Court ruled that malapportionment was a political question, meaning that change would have to come through the action of legislators themselves rather than by decisions from federal courts. This, of course, had the practical effect of producing no change as legislators were unlikely to risk voting themselves out of a job by adopting a new apportionment or districting plan.

In *Baker v. Carr*[5] (1962), however, the Supreme Court in a dramatic change ruled that federal courts have jurisdiction in cases challenging malapportionment. The Court concluded that malapportioned state legislatures could violate the equal protection clause of the Fourteenth Amendment. The reapportionment revolution was started. *Baker v. Carr* opened the floodgates, and suits challenging apportionment schemes that had been used for decades quickly appeared in every state. But it was not clear what would be acceptable to the Court. Would states be required to make extensive changes? In *Reynolds v. Sims*[6] (1964), the Court answered this question by ruling that both houses of the state legislatures must be apportioned on the basis of population—that is, "one person, one vote." The Court stated that "legislators represent people, not trees or acres." By including state senates, the Court rejected the use of the federal analogy as justification that one house of a state legislature, like the U.S. Senate, could be apportioned on the basis of geography or governmental units rather than population. The Court held that counties and cities within the states are not "sovereign entities" as are the states themselves; consequently, they are not entitled to representation. To summarize, the **Reapportionment Revolution** refers to the one-person/one-vote apportionment plan that the Supreme Court required for both houses of state legislatures. By 1968, every state had reapportioned/redistricted at least one house to meet the one-person/one-vote principle. This was followed very quickly with another round of redistricting after the

1970 census when every state had to again redistrict both houses to ensure they complied with one person/one vote with new population counts.

What were the effects of the Reapportionment Revolution? First, as expected, representatives from urban and especially suburban areas increased markedly. In some southern states where cities had been grossly underrepresented, urban representation increased by a factor of ten. These new legislators were younger, better educated, and had less political experience than those elected prior to reapportionment. There also was a significant increase in the number of African American legislators in both the North and the South. More recent research looks at reapportionment's effect on the Democratic and Republican Parties and finds that one party was not uniformly favored; this was contrary to the early prediction that the Democratic Party would benefit the most. The party that was most closely associated with urban interests in a particular state was the party that gained seats in the legislature, and this was not always the Democrats. In the North, it was the Democrats, but in the South it was the Republicans. In Florida, for example, the percentage of Republicans in the senate grew from 5 to 42 percent and in the house from 9 to 33 percent.[7]

Second, did the Reapportionment Revolution affect public policies? This is a more complicated question to answer. Obviously, many advocates of reapportionment at the time expected the adoption of polices that would be more favorable to urban areas and more liberal. Political scientist Timothy G. O'Rourke, in one of the early studies, was more cautious, reminding us that "reapportionment does not impinge on policy directly,"[8] but could initiate changes in the legislative process such as new members with different policy views than the members they replaced, which, in turn, could affect decisions made by committees and eventually policies passed by the legislature; in other words, with so many variables there was no guarantee of significant policy changes. Nevertheless, initial research findings showed that in states that were the most malapportioned, policies did change to favor urban areas. This was documented by examining how money was spent by the states and by legislators' perceptions of changes in policies.[9] A new and comprehensive look at this question provides additional evidence to support the conclusion that the Reapportionment Revolution did have a significant impact on policies. An examination of state financial assistance to counties before and after reapportionment discovers a clear pattern: As urban counties gained more legislators in the state capitals, they also gained a greater share of state funds. Stephen Ansolabehere, Alan Gerber, and Jim Snyder conclude: "Within 15 years of the *Baker* ruling, the doctrine of one-person, one-vote resulted in substantial equalization of the distribution of public funds within states."[10]

A final note on population equality: Although the Supreme Court demands almost exact population equality among congressional districts within a state, it has permitted greater flexibility in state legislative districts, generally allowing a maximum population deviation of 10 percent. This means, for example, that the smallest district in a state could be 4 percent smaller in population than the average district and the largest district could be 6 percent larger. In 2004, in a case from Georgia, the Supreme Court reminded those who draw state legislative districts that the court will not approve 10 percent deviation unless it is part of a "rational state policy"—for example, following traditional redistricting guidelines such as minimizing the crossing of local government boundaries or maintaining communities of interest. The reasons offered by the state of Georgia, which were principally political, were rejected and a redistricting plan with smaller deviations had to be devised.[11]

Legislative Redistricting Today

Although federal and state courts continue to be important actors in the redistricting process, it needs to be remembered that the responsibility of drawing district lines does not belong to the courts. In most states, it is the state legislature that must draw the new lines. As noted, this means that those who will be directly affected by where lines are placed also are the ones who draw them. Redistricting plans are contained in a bill and go through the normal legislative process of passage by both houses and approval of the governor before becoming law. This is done in the first or second year of each decade, as soon as population figures are available from the federal decennial census. However, before looking closer at how states actually redraw district lines, two more Supreme Court decisions must be discussed. One is concerned with political parties and the other with race.

Gerrymandering is the process of drawing district lines to gain as many legislative seats for a particular political party as is possible. Gerrymandering is most likely to occur when one party controls the redistricting process, that is, the governor's office and both houses of the legislature. With computer technology and sophisticated databases, creating districts nearly equal in population and still helping your party's candidates is not difficult. The Supreme Court ventured into the partisan gerrymandering question in *Davis v. Bandemer*[12] (1986). For the first time, the Court held that gerrymandering could violate the Constitution. However, this case, which involved the Indiana legislature, was not an unconstitutional gerrymander. Because the decision did not set definite guidelines for defining a gerrymander, it left the matter unclear. ***Davis v. Bandemer*** places a heavy burden of proof on those seeking to show that a particular gerrymander violates the Constitution.

Legislative redistricting plans also are subject to the Voting Rights Act of 1965 as amended. (See Chapter 4.) Plans that dilute the voting strength of minority groups are prohibited. To avoid court challenges after the 1990 census, most states with a substantial minority population drew a number of districts in which members of a minority group were in the majority. This is frequently referred to as "racial gerrymandering." The most interesting Supreme Court decision in the 1990s, *Shaw v. Reno*[13] (1993), involved not a state legislative redistricting plan but one the state of North Carolina had drawn for its twelve members of the U.S. House of Representatives. The ***Shaw v. Reno*** decision concludes that under certain conditions the creation of majority minority districts is a form of reverse discrimination and is unconstitutional. The Supreme Court did not say that all majority minority districts are unconstitutional. But if race is the sole factor in drawing a district's lines, and if other districting standards such as compactness and respect for local governmental boundaries are ignored, the district is probably unconstitutional. Several court cases followed that attempted to clarify the exact role of race in drawing district lines. The most important case again involved congressional districts in North Carolina. In ***Hunt (Easley) v. Cromartie***[14] (2001), the Supreme Court decided it is constitutional to concentrate African Americans, Hispanics, or other minorities in a district if it is done for political reasons. African Americans, who usually vote Democratic, could be concentrated in a majority-minority district if it was done to help elect a Democratic candidate. This is constitutional because the reason is political not racial; the goal is to create a Democratic legislative district.

Together, the fifteen-year-old *Davis* case and the more recent *Hunt* case were invitations for extensive partisan gerrymandering after the 2000 census, and that is what happened.[15] Redistricting of the Texas state legislature provides one of the best examples. The Texas legislature has the constitutional authority to draw new lines immediately following the release of census numbers. However, the Texas constitution also states that if the legislature is divided and cannot reach agreement, which happened in 2001, the task falls to a five-member Texas Legislative Redistricting Board. The members of the board include officials from the state's executive branch such as the attorney general and the lieutenant governor, and only one legislator, the Speaker of the Texas House of Representatives. In 2001 the board was composed of four Republicans and one Democrat, giving Republicans an opportunity for partisan gerrymandering. Figure 5-1 shows what happened to one district in the Texas House of Representatives. District 128, in Houston, elected a Democratic representative in the 2000 election; the Republican Party did not run a candidate. During the redistricting process, the geographic

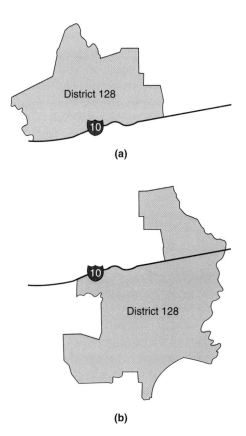

FIGURE 5-1 (a) Texas house district 128, 2000, before gerrymandering by Republican Party; (b) Texas house district 128, 2002, after gerrymandering by Republican Party.

Source: The map for 2000 is adapted from William Lilley, III, Laurence J. DeFranco, and William M. Diefenderfer, III, *The Almanac of State Legislatures* (Washington, D.C.: Congressional Quarterly, 1994), p. 287. Reproduced by permission of *Congressional Quarterly*. The map for 2002 is adapted from the Texas Legislative Council.

center of this district was shifted south of Interstate 10 to include more Republican voters. In the 2002 election, the Democratic incumbent decided not to run for reelection and district 128 elected a Republican. Three Houston-area districts with Democratic representatives were reconfigured to increase the likelihood that Republicans would be elected in 2002; Republicans were elected in two of the three.[16]

The final plans were approved on a 3–2 vote, and observers predicted that the Republican Party would expand its control in the senate and gain a majority in the house. The Mexican American Legal Defense and Educational Fund and other groups, including the Democratic Party, challenged the plan. The U.S. Justice Department, acting under the Voting Rights Act, requested changes in the House plan so as to improve Latino majorities in a few districts. When all was said and done, lower federal court judges approved the Legislative Redistricting Board's plan along with the Justice Department's changes.[17] After the 2002 election, Republicans increased their numbers in the 31-member senate from sixteen to nineteen and in the 150-member house from seventy-two to eighty-eight. This was the first time since 1870 that the Republican party in Texas controlled both houses of the legislature and the governor's office.[18]

California and New York reveal different redistricting outcomes. In California the Democratic Party controlled the governor's office and both houses of the legislature in 2001. Of course, the Democrats had an opportunity to draw new legislative maps to further their control of the legislature, but they took the unusual step of making a deal with the Republican Party. Democratic legislators agreed to forego drawing more Democratic-leaning districts and to draw lines that reflected the existing partisan makeup of the legislature. In other words, lines were drawn to preserve incumbents of both parties and to maintain the status quo. In exchange, Republican legislators agreed not to challenge the districting plan in the courts or through a referendum.[19] After the 2002 election, the Democrats actually lost two seats in the assembly (the lower house) and one seat in the senate. In the state of New York, three decades of divided control of the legislature have led to an arrangement whereby the district lines are drawn by the party with a majority in each house; the Democrats draw lines for the assembly and the Republicans draw lines for the senate. Then each house approves the work of the other, and the governor signs the bill. The governor has a small role or no role in this process. Drawing lines to protect incumbents (sometimes called "incumbent gerrymandering") is a frequent outcome when divided legislatures draw the lines. In 2002 it was estimated that more than 85 percent of New York's legislative districts gave one party (Democratic or Republican) at least 10 percent more voters than the other party.[20]

A few state constitutions place authority over legislative redistricting with a commission, not the legislature. States have various ways of selecting commission members and usually some of the members are legislators, but the legislature as an institution has no formal role to play in the process. Commissions tend to produce bipartisan gerrymandered plans that protect the incumbents of both parties.[21] An Apportionment Commission draws lines in New Jersey; it has ten members, five selected by the chairs of the Democratic and Republican Parties. If a majority of the commission members cannot agree on a plan, the chief justice of the Supreme Court of New Jersey appoints an eleventh member who becomes the tiebreaker. (It is important to note that not all commissions or boards have a bipartisan membership; some will have a membership that favors one party or another, and when this is the case the plans they create are usually partisan gerrymanders.)

Iowa has a unique approach. The Legislative Service Bureau, a nonpartisan legislative office, prepares a new districting plan following specific legal criteria; for example, districts should be composed of contiguous territory connected by roads and that the unity of county and city boundaries should be respected. Also, districts cannot be drawn to favor a political party or incumbent legislator; this means that information on party affiliation of registered voters, home addresses of incumbents, and election results cannot be used in drawing lines. The legislature, along with the governor, still retains approval, but in a series of steps. The first plan proposed by the bureau must be accepted or rejected by the legislature. If it is rejected, the bureau develops a second plan that again can be accepted or rejected. If it is rejected, a third plan is presented, which the legislature can accept, reject, or modify.[22] The advantage of this process is that the proposed plans carry some weight with the public and the news media because they come from a neutral office using neutral criteria to draw the lines. In addition, the majority party, or the majority party in cooperation with the minority party, would be subject to criticism for rejecting three plans only to end up writing and adopting their own. In 2001 the state senate rejected the bureau's first plan; however, the second plan was approved by the legislature and signed by the governor. Iowa's procedures, in fact, do not protect incumbent legislators; thirty-nine of one hundred house members and twenty-five of fifty senate members were placed in districts with at least one other incumbent; although an incumbent will run against another incumbent, other choices are available, including deciding not to run or moving to a nearby district where there is no incumbent legislator.[23]

In those states where the legislatures draw new district lines every ten years, there is always a fair amount of criticism of the way in which it is handled. In general, redistricting is criticized because it is perceived to be undemocratic, or at least unfair; as political scientist Michael P. McDonald says, "It provides politicians a chance to choose voters, rather than allowing voters to choose politicians."[24] But change is difficult; changing the redistricting process requires amending state constitutions, and legislatures are unlikely to approve proposing an amendment that takes redistricting out of their hands and gives it to someone else. Change is more likely, but certainly not easy, in states where voters can use the initiative process (see Chapter 4) to propose constitutional amendments. In the 2000 election, voters in Arizona passed an initiative that transferred redistricting from the legislature to the Arizona Independent Redistricting Commission (Proposition 106). This proposition also identified a number of criteria for the commission to follow in drawing new district lines; one of these criteria is to create competitive districts, as long as that does not hinder meeting other goals such as population equality, compactness, and contiguousness. Arizona may be the first state to recognize competitive districts as an explicit criterion for the redistricting process. More recently, California and Ohio voters defeated redistricting reform initiatives. The voters' decisions may come as a surprise, but political scientist Thomas E. Mann concludes that voters made the right decision because both initiatives were more "partisan power grabs" than real reform such as in Arizona.[25] Republicans were the likely beneficiaries in California and Democrats in Ohio. If it is a challenge to take the politics out of redistricting, it is also a challenge to take the politics out of improving the redistricting process. The League of Women Voters of the United States, its state leagues, and Common Cause are currently advocating redistricting reform.

A PROFILE OF LEGISLATORS AND LEGISLATURES

Legislators

For several decades, the state of Wisconsin after each general election has surveyed the members of the legislature to arrive at a demographic profile. Although Wisconsin may not be a typical state, its dedication to the collection of this information does give us an impression of whom we elect to represent us in state legislatures. The typical Wisconsin legislator is a male, fifty years of age, a full-time legislator with a college education, but this description conceals considerable variation in the background of Wisconsin's ninety-nine members of the lower house, which is called the assembly:

- Gender—73 men, 26 women.
- Age—average age is 50, with a range of 28 to 77 years; three members are in the 20 to 29 range and five are over 70.
- Occupation—a variety of occupations including 39 full-time legislators; 13 small business owners, 11 practicing attorneys, 9 farmers; other occupations are physician, realtor, civil engineer, labor arbitrator, and registered nurse.
- Education—70 members with a bachelor's or associate's degree; 34 went on to earn advanced degrees.
- Local government—41 served previously in a local elected office such as county board supervisor or city council member, school board member, or city mayor.
- Military service—19 members served in the U.S. armed services.
- Legislative staff—16 members worked previously for a member of U.S. Congress or the state legislature.[26]

Although most legislators are white males, the number of African American and women legislators has increased significantly since the 1970s. Today 23 percent of legislators are women, and slightly over 8 percent are African American. The number of women is five times as many as in the 1960s, and the number of African Americans has doubled since then. The increase in Hispanic legislators, now around 3 percent, has been gradual, although more substantial gains have been made in states with a large Hispanic population such as California, Florida, and Texas (Table 5-1).

TABLE 5-1 Top Five States for African American, Hispanic, and Women Legislators

African American	Percent	Hispanic	Percent	Women	Percent
Mississippi	29	New Mexico	41	Maryland	35
Alabama	26	California	23	Delaware	34
Maryland	23	Texas	20	Nevada	33
Georgia	22	Arizona	15	Vermont	33
Louisiana	21	Colorado	12	Washington	33

Source: National Conference of State Legislatures, "Legislator Demographics" (Denver, Colo.: National Conference of State Legislatures, 2007), www.ncsl.org/programs/legismgt/about/demographic_overview.htm (accessed February 19, 2007).

Basic Structure

With the exception of Nebraska, every state has a **bicameral** (two-house) legislature. Official names of the two houses are the senate and the house of representatives; however, in some states the lower house is called the assembly or the house of delegates.

The strong bicameral tradition originated when most legislatures in colonial America adopted the upper- and lower-house model of the British Parliament. The U.S. Constitution, of course, provides for two chambers, a House and Senate, and this has influenced the states. In the early years, many state legislatures included an economic class factor, in which extra property requirements were imposed for service in the upper chamber. Concern over a **unicameral** (one-house) legislature is reflected in John Adams's warning that "a single assembly is liable to all the vices, follies, and frailties of an individual; subject to fits of humor, starts of passion, flights of enthusiasms, partialities or prejudices, consequently productive of hasty results and absurd judgments."

It also is significant that separation of powers did not exist in early state governments. Governors had little power and often were appointed by the legislature. Legislatures exercised broad powers of economic management and occasionally even overrode the courts in some property-dispute cases. In such circumstances, a bicameral legislature offered greater protection against the abuse of power and undue influence by strong interest groups.

Nebraska adopted a unicameral legislature in 1934, largely due to the well-organized campaign by George Norris, a popular U.S. senator from Nebraska and important leader of the Progressive movement. (Nebraska also is the only legislature that elects its legislators on a nonpartisan ballot.) A study comparing the Nebraska and Minnesota legislatures concludes that the operating cost of Nebraska's unicameral legislature is considerably less than that of Minnesota's bicameral legislature. Although a number of factors contribute to this, it's clear that a smaller number of legislators (Nebraska's forty-nine senators versus Minnesota's sixty-seven senators and 134 representatives) and a consequently smaller legislative staff are important causes. To meet the criticism that two chambers are required to reduce the possibility of hasty consideration of bills, rules and procedures in Nebraska require lengthy and repeated consideration of bills during debate in the full senate. The process is described as "unusually full, exacting and methodical."[27] The case for unicameralism has been made at several state constitutional conventions during the past ten years. Although the idea appears logical to many academics and as a cost-savings measure should be attractive to citizens demanding more efficient and less costly government, arguments for unicameralism usually have failed to move politicians who fear radical change and the loss of a large number of legislative seats.

In 1999, Minnesota's governor, Jesse Ventura, proposed combining Minnesota's 134-seat house and 67-seat senate into a unicameral body of 135 members. Ventura argued that two houses cause too much partisan bickering and allow "legislators to duck accountability by saying that shortcomings were caused by members of the other house."[28] The proposed constitutional amendment, which also called for nonpartisan legislative elections, failed to pass the Minnesota legislature.

The number of members of state legislatures varies. The senates have the smaller membership, of course. The size of upper houses varies from twenty in Alaska to sixty-seven in Minnesota. New Hampshire has 400 members in its lower house who represent a total of 1.3 million people, while the California lower house has eighty members who represent more than 36 million people. In a majority of states (thirty), the lower house has 100 or more members, and in several others, the number is ninety-eight or ninety-nine. In thirty-four states, the upper house has at least thirty-five members.

Although most students of state government conclude that legislatures are too large, it is difficult to say what the ideal size should be because there are advantages and disadvantages to both large and small legislatures. Large bodies often become impersonal and more dedicated to staging debates than to taking action. On the other hand, in larger bodies the representational function, to be discussed shortly, is generally improved as legislators represent smaller numbers of people. There also is evidence that larger legislatures are more efficient because of their greater specialization in committees. A disadvantage of small legislatures is that members have a tendency to become too cozy in a kind of social club atmosphere. Moreover, racial and ethnic minorities are less likely to be represented among the members of small legislatures.

As a practical matter, the size of legislative bodies does not change very often. Nevertheless, marginal changes will occasionally be made to facilitate reapportionment and redistricting. Rhode Island reduced the size of the senate from fifty members to thirty-eight and the house from 100 to seventy-five. (This change took place in 2002, the first election after the census in 2000.)

Length of terms also varies among the states. The most common pattern is for representatives to serve two-year terms and senators four-year terms. Terms in the senate are usually staggered with half of the members elected every two years. Maryland is an exception to the normal pattern. In Maryland, all members of both houses, along with the governor, are elected for four-year terms at the same election; this provides voters the opportunity, if they desire, to vote in a large number of new faces in one single election.

Professional or Citizen or Hybrid?

The professional-citizen distinction is important in the study of state legislatures. Three factors distinguish professional from citizen legislatures: amount of time legislators spend on the job, salary legislators are paid, and size of the legislature's staff. Karl Kurtz, at the National Conference of State Legislatures, identifies three types of legislatures:[29]

> **Professional legislature.** Being a legislator is a full-time job, legislators receive a fairly high salary, and the legislature has a large staff.
>
> **Citizen legislature.** Being a legislator is considerably less than full time, legislators receive a lower salary, and the legislature has a small staff.
>
> **Hybrid legislature.** Legislators who fall in the middle in terms of the amount of time the job requires and the size of the staff and salary.

To some extent, these characteristics have developed from different conceptions of the important function of state legislatures. Advocates of professional legislatures want legislatures to "function as independent branches of government, capable of balancing the power of the executive branch and having the information necessary to make independent,

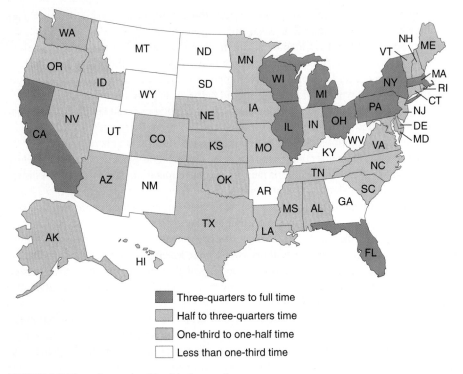

Three-quarters to full time

Half to three-quarters time

One-third to one-half time

Less than one-third time

FIGURE 5-2 Time demands of legislative work.

Source: Alan Rosenthal, Burdett A. Loomis, John R. Hibbing, and Karl T. Kurtz, *Republic on Trial: The Case for Representative Democracy* (Washington, D.C.: CQ Press, 2003), p. 73. Reprinted by permission of CQ Press.

informed policy decisions."[30] Supporters of citizen legislatures want legislatures that are closer to the people; that is, men and women leave their communities and full-time jobs for a couple of months to engage in public service as lawmakers in the state capital. In other words, one view emphasizes the legislature's power and independence and the other emphasizes the legislature's accountability to citizens. Kurtz compares all fifty state legislatures and finds that citizen legislatures are more common than professional legislatures, with most states falling into a hybrid or in-between category. Figure 5-2 is based on the amount of time required to serve in the legislature, probably the most important indicator of the citizen-professional dimension. The length of legislative sessions, the actual time legislators are in the state capital, varies greatly, from two months during a two-year period (Kentucky and Wyoming) to almost year-round (California and Massachusetts). But the job includes more than attending legislative sessions; for example, meeting with constituents—the people who live in their districts—is a year-round activity, and participating in committee meetings to study state problems during the interim is important in many states.[31] (The interim is the time period between official, regularly scheduled sessions.) Examples of professional, hybrid, and citizen legislatures are shown in Table 5-2.

TABLE 5-2 Diversity of State Legislatures			
	Professional	Hybrid	Citizen
State	New York	Maryland	Arkansas
Annual salary	$79,500	$40,500	$14,067
Amount of time	Three-quarters to full time	One-third to one-half time	Less than one-third time
Staff	3,428	965	493

Sources: Annual salaries are from *The Book of the States 2006* (Lexington, Ky.: Council of State Governments, 2006), pp. 84–85. Staff numbers are available from the National Conference of State Legislatures at www.ncsl.org/programs/legismgt/about/staffcount2003.htm.

In Figure 5-2, it is clear that a state's population affects whether its legislature is professional or citizen. California and New York, along with states in the Great Lakes region, have large populations. Time demands of legislative work are less than one-half time in states with smaller populations, especially those states in the Rocky Mountains and the South. Many of these states are classified as citizen legislatures. Hybrid states are found in all regions, especially in states whose population is medium-sized. Political culture is important, too. Southern states, with the exception of Florida, are absent from the professional category, even though Texas ranks second in population and Georgia and North Carolina are in the top twelve states. This is due in part to traditionalistic political cultures and a desire for limited government.

Large and diverse states probably need professional legislators who can devote full time or close to full time to the problems of governing, but small and medium-size states may get along fine with part-time legislators. And it is frequently argued today, as was already mentioned, that people who combine being a legislator for part of the year with another occupation will be more in touch with their constituents and better able to represent them. (The term-limit movement, which takes this argument even further, will be discussed later in this chapter.) The National Conference of State Legislatures concludes that the desire for more full-time, professional legislatures must be balanced with the benefits of part-time citizen bodies.[32]

Legislative Staff

If we asked you to guess the total number of staff members working in the legislatures in all fifty states, we are sure you would be way too low. The answer is 35,000. In 2003 this included 28,000 permanent or year-round staff and 7,000 session-only staff who worked when the legislature is actually in session. As can be seen in Table 5-3, permanent staff has grown dramatically between 1979 and 2003, by almost two-thirds, while session staff has decreased. Also, much of the growth, which was between 1979 and 1996, has slowed during the past few years. The importance of staff cannot be underestimated. A staffer quoted by Karl Kurtz sums it up by saying, "Legislative staff is the hidden engine that makes the legislature work."[33]

TABLE 5-3 Growth of Legislative Staff in U.S. State Legislatures					
Type of Staff	1979	1988	1996	2003	Net Change
Permanent	16,930	24,555	27,822	28,067	+11,137
Session-only	10,062	8,775	8,062	6,912	−3,150
Total	26,992	33,330	35,884	34,979	+7,987

Source: "StateStats: Legislative Staff Flourish over 30 years," *State Legislatures* (February 2004), p. 5.

Staff could be described in a number of ways, but an important distinction is between partisan and nonpartisan staff. **Partisan staff** works for the leaders of the legislative parties or for individual legislators and provides strategic or political advice on navigating the intricacies of the legislative process and on relations with the media. They also spend considerable time working with legislators' constituents. Legislative leaders' staff is an important communication link between the leaders and rank-and-file legislators. The Ohio General Assembly gives us some example of specific titles of these positions: Each senator has a legislative aide and an administrative assistant; the principal aide to the president of the senate is the senate chief of staff. In addition, partisan staff of the legislative majority party usually includes official parliamentary positions such as the chief administrative officer of the house or the senate clerk who are responsible for the smooth processing of legislation through their respective chambers. Many of these activities are associated with floor sessions when the entire membership of the house or senate meet, including introducing bills, referring bills to committees, preparing daily calendars, tracking amendments offered during debate, recording all daily actions in a journal, and making final copies of bills after they are amended and voted on.[34]

Nonpartisan staff was created to provide information and services to all members of the legislature without seeking to advance the interests of one party over another; in other words, it does not have its own policy agenda. Nonpartisan staff usually work out of a central office and frequently staff legislative committees. These nonpartisan offices go by different names including Legislative Service Commission (Ohio), Legislative Reference Bureau (Wisconsin), and Legislative Council (Texas).[35] Their services include bill drafting and research and bill analysis on bills that have been introduced. Generally, nonpartisan staffers are well educated; if not attorneys, they frequently have a master's degree in one of the social sciences such as economics or political science, or in business. Bill drafting, a rather technical venture, requires legal training and is usually in the purview of staff members who are attorneys. Much of the research can best be described as short-term research; in other words, it is a response to legislators' specific questions, for example: "How do other states spend the revenue that is produced by legalized lotteries?" Policy analysis of current issues or long-term research to anticipate new issues occurs much less frequently in state legislatures, although there are exceptions such as Kentucky's Long-Term Policy Research Center, which has looked at a variety of topics ranging from the impact of the shortage of nurses to factors affecting future environmental quality.[36]

FUNCTIONS OF STATE LEGISLATURES

Representation

What is representation? This deceptively simple question has been debated since the early beginnings of representative government. Edmund Burke, a member of the British House of Commons in the late eighteenth century, in a speech to the electors of Bristol, placed the controversy on the meaning of representation in what is now a classic formulation:

> Should (must) a representative do what his constituents want, and be bound by mandates or instructions from them; or should (must) he be free to act as seems best to him in pursuit of their welfare?[37]

Contemporary political scientists refer to this question as the mandate-independence controversy, or the delegate-trustee controversy. It has generated much research and debate. Alan Rosenthal, a prominent scholar of state legislatures, recently asked legislators in five states a very direct question: "If a constituency position on a bill were to come into conflict with your own views or judgments, which would generally prevail when you cast your vote?"[38] The responses (see Figure 5-3) are very clear with 59 percent choosing categories four and five, indicating that they would generally "vote according to own judgment." Only 20 percent would follow the views of their constituents rather than their own views.

Before concluding that most legislators are completely ignoring their constituents, several pieces of the puzzle of representation should be considered. On a number of issues during a legislative session, legislators may hear nothing from their constituents, so it's impossible to follow what does not exist. The issues are important to an interest group or two but not to most voters. On other issues, especially in districts that are demographically heterogeneous, constituency opinion may be divided, and the absence of a strong majority makes it difficult to say that there is a constituency opinion that may conflict with a legislator's own views. Nevertheless, each legislative session will have a few major issues that voters are interested in and have opinions on, and this is where there is potential for conflict between constituents and legislators. But there is not as much conflict as one might expect; on almost all of these issues, legislators claim that their views and constituency views are basically the same or, to a lesser extent, that there is no predominant constituency opinion. Only a small percentage of legislators, less than 20 percent, report that their views and constituency views are different.[39] In other words, legislators' views and constituency views are normally not in conflict; only infrequently do they actually have to choose between their views and the views of their

Vote constituency position	1	2	3	4	5	Vote according to own judgment
	6%	14%	21%	44%	15%	

FIGURE 5-3 Constituency Position versus Legislator's Own View or Judgment: Legislators from Five States.

Source: Alan Rosenthal, *Heavy Lifting: The Job of the American Legislature,* (Washington, D.C.: CQ Press, 2004), p. 44.

constituents. In addition, elections pose limits on legislators. "Elections are the mechanisms by which representatives are held accountable. If legislators stray too far afield, they risk challenge and defeat at the polls."[40]

Another aspect of representation is **constituency service,** which is helping out constituents on a variety of different concerns. Research by Lilliard Richardson finds that many legislators believe constituency service is the most important job they have; it helps in building trust with the public and is an important method of maintaining electoral support.[41] Examples of constituency service include obtaining a legislative resolution of congratulations for the local high school field hockey team that just won a state championship and sending copies of bills to interested constituents. Obtaining state funds for a new classroom building at a local community college, a new district court building, or a new highway bridge is also an example of constituency service. The most important kind of constituency service goes by the name of casework. **Casework** refers to requests from an individual who is having problems with state government, usually a department or agency in the executive branch. (It's not unusual for legislators to receive requests that are actually within the jurisdiction of a local government; when this happens, there is little they can do except to refer the person to an appropriate local government official.) Casework also covers a variety of subjects that range from constituent problems with driver's licenses or child support payments to state regulations for fertilizer runoff from farms. In most of these cases, there is little legislators can do themselves; rather, they will contact the appropriate administrative department or agency and request that it look into the problem. Sometimes a mistake is found and an earlier ruling that went against a constituent will be changed or modified; other times there is no mistake and no change in a decision. Either way, constituents have a favorable view of their legislators as trying to help. And it is not only constituents who approve of constituency service; legislators do also. According to Rosenthal, "Legislators want to have a sense of fulfillment in the jobs they do, and taking care of their constituents is a fulfilling activity."[42]

Policy Making

The most important function of the state legislature is to participate in making policy by passing laws. Any self-respecting legislature should not be content merely to deal with the governor's legislative program or routinely approve members' bills. It has a responsibility to initiate action and to deliberate on a wide variety of proposals dealing with the most important and controversial problems of the day, such as abortion, crime, gun control, welfare, and education, to name a few. In fact, legislators are confronted with issues that can range from the trivial (whether the ladybug should be designated the "state insect" in Ohio) to the enormously complex (annual general expenditures for the state of Texas in 2004 were close to $70 billion).

In reality, policy initiation, that is, priorities and ideas for legislation, remains largely in the hands of state governors. The lawmaking process is best for deliberation, discussion, marginal changes, and even the defeat of bills rather than the initiation of policy. Under the best of circumstances, legislators share their lawmaking power with the governor. More will be said of the governor's role in policy making and influence on the legislature in Chapter 6.

Over 100,000 bills are introduced in state legislatures during their regular sessions, but only a small percentage (less than 20 percent) actually become law. Minnesota is on the high side: More than 4,900 bills were introduced in 2005; 164 became law (less than 4 percent). Delaware, a much smaller state than Minnesota, had 546 bills introduced in the same year with 222 becoming law (40 percent). A state closer to the average is North Carolina where 2,903 bills were introduced and 463 became law (16 percent). A few states have adopted various rules to limit the number of bills that are introduced. One approach is to simply put a limit on the number of bills each legislator can introduce; in the Florida House of Representatives the limit is six bills. In Colorado the limit is five bills, but a Committee on Delayed Bills may grant permission for a legislator to exceed the limit. The idea behind these limits is to ensure that legislators have more time to consider important legislation by reducing what many observers consider to be superfluous bills that legislators introduce only because they please a constituent or an interest group. Others argue that these limits hinder members from carrying out their legislative responsibilities as they see fit.[43]

In general, all state legislatures follow a similar procedure for passing bills into laws. (Of course, in Nebraska bills are considered by one house.) Once a bill has been introduced in the upper or lower house, it is assigned to a committee. The committee holds public hearings, and then committee members meet to discuss and possibly amend the bill. If committee action is favorable, the bill is reported out and placed on the chamber's calendar.

The bill is then given a second reading on the floor (its introduction constitutes a first reading), following which there is debate, amendments are offered, and a vote is taken on passage. After a usual delay of one calendar day, a third reading occurs and a final vote is taken. If the vote is affirmative, the bill then moves to the other legislative chamber, where the process of committee and floor action is repeated. If the second chamber approves the bill without amendment, it goes to the governor for his or her signature. If the bill is approved in a different form by each house, a conference committee is appointed to work out an agreement, and both houses must approve the conference report before the bill is sent to the governor (Figure 5-4).

Legislative Oversight

With the growth of gubernatorial power and the expansion of state administrative bureaucracies, legislatures have struggled to find ways to check executive authority. Because their attention tends to be focused on immediate policy issues, legislators find it difficult to conduct long-range review of the executive branch. Generally, legislative oversight is review by the legislature of the performance of executive branch agencies in administering the laws and programs approved by the legislature. The purpose is to ensure that public services are delivered to citizens in an effective manner.

Legislative oversight takes many forms.[44] Constituents constantly ask legislators for help in dealing with state agencies, as mentioned earlier. In responding to a particular request, legislators may be prompted to review in more general terms how an agency is performing. In the budget process, several committees—appropriations, ways and means, and finance—review requests for money from state agencies, and this allows legislators to examine how well the agencies are performing. A majority of the states have enacted **"sunset laws,"** which call for the termination of executive branch agencies

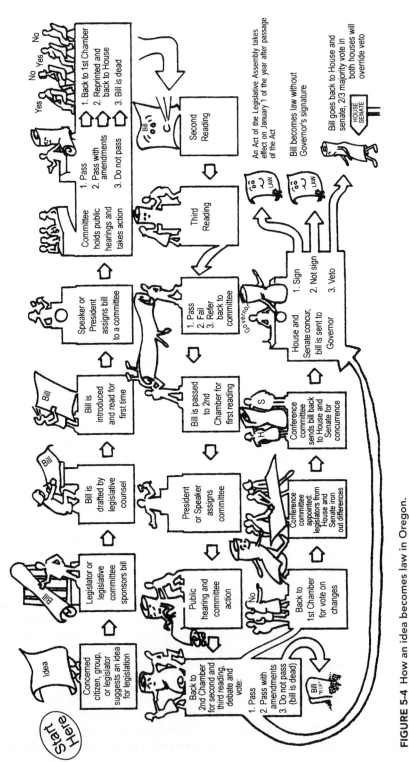

FIGURE 5-4 How an idea becomes law in Oregon.

Source: Oregon Legislative Assembly, "How an Idea Becomes Law: A Simplified View of the Oregon Legislative Process," www.leg.state.or.us/faq/lawprocs.pdf.

unless the legislature formally reviews and extends their programs. These reviews are required at regular intervals, in many states, every five years. Generally, the agencies that have been terminated have been minor and had lost their usefulness. Numerous other agencies have been consolidated or their authority and responsibilities clarified. A number of states have repealed or suspended their "sunset laws" because they required an excessive amount of time of both legislators and staff.

Today, almost every state legislature has a specific office—similar to the federal government's Government Accountability Office—that has primary responsibility for legislative oversight. These offices vary in their official names; in Illinois it is the Office of the Auditor General, Nebraska has the Legislative Program Evaluation Unit, and in Florida it is the Office of Program Policy Analysis and Government Accountability. These offices vary in size, organization, and activities; however, their focus is the same: to conduct research and produce reports that evaluate whether agencies are properly implementing government programs and to identify ways to improve these programs.[45]

LEGISLATIVE POLITICS

Committees

The state senates have approximately fifteen standing committees, and the lower houses have approximately twenty. (Standing committees are permanent committees that are created by a chamber's legislative rules.) These committees are established on a subject-matter basis to consider bills introduced by legislators and to monitor the activities of particular administrative agencies. The trend in recent years has been to reduce the number of committees. Nevertheless, a considerable range still exists among the states: Maryland is an example of a state with a few committees, eight in the senate and nine in the house; New York is on the high side with thirty-three in the senate and thirty-seven in the house. Joint committees, that is, members of both the senate and house serving on the same committees, can be found in Connecticut, Maine, and Massachusetts.

The actual influence committees have in determining the fate of bills varies among the states, and sometimes even between chambers in the same state. Committees have more influence in those states where the rules permit them to let bills die in committee without taking any action. This is the case for about 75 percent of the chambers; examples are Michigan, Ohio, and Rhode Island. In the remaining chambers, committees are required to report all bills referred to them, based on the belief that the full membership should have an opportunity to vote on proposed bills rather than allow bills to be bottled up in committee. Illinois has one of the weakest committee systems; committees are expected to ratify decisions made by the leadership and majority-party caucus (discussed below). On occasion, proposed bills have been placed on a "fast track" and were sent to a committee dominated by the leadership to ensure prompt action.[46]

Political Parties

A basic goal of political parties in a legislature is to produce the votes necessary to pass specific bills. However, the degree to which parties are successful in controlling their members' votes varies greatly among the states. In urban, industrial states with strong two-party systems, party control of voting behavior clearly is evident. Frequently, in these states, parties will caucus on a regular basis to determine a party position on various pieces of legislation and to mobilize support of its members for the party's position. In state legislatures, a **caucus** is the name given to a meeting of legislators who are members of the same political party. Daily caucuses occur in about 15 percent of the states, and about half the states have weekly caucuses.

Partisanship in voting on legislation, according to Sarah McCally Morehouse and Malcolm Jewell, is strongest where the Democratic and Republican parties "represent significantly different constituencies."[47] For example, in many states in the Northeast and Midwest, Democratic legislators are elected from working-class and some middle-class districts in urban areas, with a significant percentage of racial and ethnic minorities living in many of these districts. Republican legislators tend to be elected from higher income districts in suburban areas and from small-town and rural districts. Partisanship is particularly strong in Connecticut, Indiana, Illinois, Michigan, New York, and Pennsylvania, as well as California, Colorado, and Washington in the West. Partisanship is less important in most western states, for example, Montana and Oregon. Greater legislative partisanship is emerging in many southern states where the Republican Party is becoming more competitive and winning a larger share of seats in the legislature, for example, Florida, Georgia, and North Carolina. Research by Shannon Jenkins confirms the importance of constituency in voting on legislation by noting that legislators who represent people who make up the core constituencies in their party show more support for their party; and legislators who represent people who are atypical of their party's supporters are less likely to vote with their party. In other words, Democratic legislators with a high percentage of African Americans or Hispanics in their districts will have high support for their party; and Democratic legislators with a very small percentage of minority groups in their districts will tend to have lower support for their party. Of course, only a few Democratic legislators will be elected from these districts because they really are more typical of the Republican Party.[48]

Political parties do more than affect the voting behavior of legislators. The role of parties is particularly strong in the selection of legislative leaders, which we turn to next.

Leaders

In the lower house, a speaker, elected by a vote of the entire membership, is the presiding officer. Each party nominates its own candidate for speaker, and the nominee of the majority wins in a straight party-line vote. The speaker is the presiding officer *and* the effective leader of the majority party, even though the speaker's party has a position with the title of majority leader.

More than half of the state legislative chambers have an even number of members, and on occasion—about one chamber in every election year recently—a tie with an equal number of Democratic and Republican legislators winning office will occur. When this happens neither party has enough votes to elect the leaders. The usual solution is a negotiated agreement between the two parties to share power. Under one type of agreement the parties select co-leaders and committee co-chairs and alternate, sometimes daily, when they preside. Another approach is to divide power between the parties. One party selects the presiding officer, and members of the other party chair the most power-ful committees such as Appropriations and Ways and Means. These agreements, al-though not perfect, have prevented complete deadlock in the legislative process.[49] After a tie in the 2001 election in New Jersey, a power-sharing agreement provided for the rotation between the two parties at specified intervals of the senate presidency and committee chairs.

Identifying the most important leader in a state senate is more difficult than in the house. In over half of the states the lieutenant governor presides over the senate, following the federal arrangement whereby the vice president is the president of the Senate. Be-cause the voters elect the lieutenant governor, his or her influence in the senate is usually minimal, and the effective leader is the president pro tem, who is elected by the majority party. If the lieutenant governor has no constitutional responsibilities in the senate, the presiding officer is elected by the entire membership, usually in a party-line vote, and has the title of president of the senate.

How do these leaders affect the legislative process? Political scientists Malcolm Jewell and Marcia Whicker, in a major study of legislative leadership in the states, identify a number of roles:

- *Gatekeepers* in the lawmaking process who can use their power to delay or block the adoption of a proposed law.
- *Coalition builders* and *negotiators* who can put together majority support for a proposal that will determine whether it is enacted in the form it was introduced or becomes a "watered-down" version.
- *Communicators* who explain legislative intent to the public. By communicating their own interpretations of the how and why of new laws, they can aid public un-derstanding and acceptance.[50]

Legislative leaders have a considerable number of specific powers they can rely on in performing these roles. A major one is control over appointing legislators to commit-tees. This can be used to reward members who have been loyal to the leadership, assign-ing them to the more important committees. Committee assignments also have a policy dimension because leaders can appoint members to a committee who have policy views similar to theirs on bills that come before that committee. Leaders can also decide not to reappoint legislators to a committee, because most states do not have a written or un-written rule that gives legislators the right to reappointment.

Legislative leaders also appoint committee chairs. Because chairs owe their posi-tion to the leaders, they are much more likely to cooperate with them in speeding or slowing the movement of key bills through their committees and in keeping unwanted amendments from being adopted.[51] However, committees in state legislatures that are more professional usually have more influence in the legislative process. Lower turn-over allows members to stay on the same committees for a longer time and to develop expertise on bills that come before them. The same is true for committee chairs. When this happens, committees tend to become more independent of party leaders. Even though the leaders still control committee appointments, it may give them only "influ-ence over the broad direction in which the committee moves . . . the leader cannot solve differences over specific legislation by a constant threat to remove members from the committee."[52]

Generally, Jewell and Whicker conclude that legislative leadership style is changing. **Leadership style** is the extent to which leaders desire to control the behavior of other members and how they react to conflict. The command style of leadership is not as common as it used to be. Command-style leaders limit decision making to a single small group, minimize participation by rank-and-file legislators, and have a high need to control the behavior of others. Conflict is viewed as a challenge to their leadership. They are likely to use the threat of punishment (for example, removal from a committee) to pressure members to support the party line.

More prevalent today are the coordinating and consensus leadership styles. Coordinating-style leaders usually harmonize the decision making of various small groups of leaders. When conflict occurs, this type of leader tries to resolve it through negotiation and is more likely to use rewards rather than the threat of punishment. Rank-and-file legislators occasionally participate in decision making. Consensus-style leaders have a low need to control the behavior of others and use accommodation to resolve conflict. Rank-and-file legislators are encouraged to participate in decision making. Debate, discussion, and developing a consensus that a large number of party members can support replace the use of rewards and punishment to gain adherence to the party line.[53]

Another reason the consensus style is becoming prominent is that more women are moving into leadership positions and women are more likely to be consensus-style leaders. In 2005, four women were presiding officers: senate president in Colorado and Maine; house speaker in Oregon and Vermont. Overall, women held 13 percent of the leadership positions (including presiding officers and other positions such as majority and minority leaders) and 20 percent of the committee chairs. Women occupied at least one-fourth of the committee chair positions in ten states, including Colorado, California, Maine, and North Carolina.[54] Recall that 23 percent of all state legislators are women.

TERM LIMITS AND OTHER CHALLENGES TO STATE LEGISLATURES

State legislatures and representative democracy face a number of challenges today. One challenge is adjusting to the consequence of legislative term limits. The **term-limits movement** was a nationwide effort to limit the number of terms in office that state legislators could serve. Term limits were on the agenda in every state during the 1990s and were adopted by many. Another challenge is the public distrust of legislatures, and politics generally, which frequently reaches the level of cynicism. At least in part, public distrust was a major factor propelling the term-limits movement. (Limiting the terms for members of Congress was another goal of this movement; it was unsuccessful.) A third challenge comes from the techniques of direct democracy (see Chapter 4), especially when combined with the possibilities for political action that are presented by the Internet. Each of these challenges will be discussed below with special emphasis on term limits.

In 1990, term-limit initiatives were placed on the ballot and approved by voters in California, Colorado, and Oklahoma. Eventually, a total of twenty states adopted legislative term limits; at this time, fifteen states still have them (Table 5-4). Term limits usually were proposed through the initiative process, requiring voter initiation and approval, as amendments to state constitutions. Only Louisiana and Utah adopted term limits as

TABLE 5-4 States with Legislative Term Limits

State	Year Enacted	House Limit	House Impact Year	Senate Limit	Senate Impact Year	Nature of Limit
California	1990	6	1996	8	1998	Lifetime
Colorado	1990	8	1998	8	1998	Consecutive
Oklahoma	1990	12-year combined total for both houses. Impact year 2002.				Lifetime
Arizona	1992	8	2000	8	2000	Consecutive
Arkansas	1992	6	1998	8	2000	Lifetime
Florida	1992	8	2000	8	2000	Consecutive
Michigan	1992	6	1998	8	2002	Lifetime
Missouri	1992	8	2002	8	2002	Lifetime
Montana	1992	8	2000	8	2000	Consecutive
Ohio	1992	8	2000	8	2000	Consecutive
South Dakota	1992	8	2000	8	2000	Consecutive
Maine	1993	8	1996	8	1996	Consecutive
Louisiana	1995	12	2007	12	2007	Consecutive
Nevada	1996	12	2010	12	2010	Lifetime
Nebraska	2000	n/a		8	2006	Consecutive

Source: Information for this table is from National Conference of State Legislatures, www.ncsl.org/programs/legismgt/about/states.htm.

Note: Term limits in Maine were retroactive; the effective date was January 1, 1996, thus prior years of service counted for legislators who were serving when term limits were adopted.

statutory law, following the normal legislative process of approval by both the legislature and the governor. It's much easier to gain support from voters than it is from legislators; obviously, few legislators would approve limits on their terms that might force them from office before they are ready to leave.

Term limits adopted by Oklahoma voters are among the most restrictive, limiting a legislator during his or her lifetime to no more than twelve years of service in either or both houses. California law allows no more than six years in the assembly and eight years in the senate. In almost all states, terms served in the legislature prior to the adoption of the law did not count toward the number of allowable terms.

Although voters approved of term limits by overwhelming margins, among elected officials and political scientists, term limits had strong opponents as well as strong supporters. The supporters believed too many states had strayed from the ideal of the citizen legislature and that term limits would return them to that ideal. Mark Petracca, a political scientist and advocate of term limits, argued that individuals who believe their elected office is a profession or a career have a difficult time remaining in touch with the interests and values of the voters who elected them. Petracca states that "the professionalization of politics is incompatible with the essence of representative government";[55] it is incompatible because it distances legislators from the constituents they are supposed to serve. This creates a "culture of ruling" in state capitals that is based on the interaction of legislators with other legislators, lobbyists, and executive branch officials, all of whom are in the "business of regulating other people's lives or spending other people's money."[56] The professional legislature provided the means for members to become career legislators: longer sessions, higher salaries, and more staff and office space. Of course, legislators must be reelected or it is not a career, but this is not a problem, say the proponents of term limits, because PACs and other special interests provide ample campaign funds. This culture has a harmful impact because legislators are primarily interested in winning reelection. To do this they cater to interest groups and other special interests, and the interests of the voters they are elected to represent are forgotten.

Opponents argued that term limits violate one of the basic principles of democracy, that "the people choose their representatives and tell them when to leave."[57] People, not arbitrary limits, should make this decision. Aside from this normative argument, opponents stated that experienced legislators developed a knowledge of issues that frequently made them as much of an expert as, perhaps even more than, the governor and other members of the executive branch. This expertise helped the legislature make decisions independently, that is, without relying too much on the executive branch.

Arguments as to how term limits would affect the influence of interest groups were of particular importance, and here the two sides disagreed completely. Proponents argued that term limits would *reduce* the influence of special interests: Legislators, not planning on a legislative career, would have less interest in winning future elections and less interest in doing the bidding of special interests because they did not need a continuous supply of campaign funds. Opponents argued that special interests would be more influential under term limits: What would really happen is that legislators would have to rely on the lobbyists' knowledge of issues. Of course, their knowledge was always based on their clients' perspectives.[58] Thus, the influence of special interests would only increase.

Research on the actual effects of term limits is beginning to appear in the political science literature. A brief review of the findings will help to determine, although still somewhat tentatively, what changes have occurred in the real world of "termed" legislatures. One of the obvious findings is that membership turnover of legislators has increased. Over the past few decades, turnover rates were gradually decreasing in state legislatures (see Chapter 4); this trend has been reversed in term-limited states. In ten house chambers with term limits in effect, turnover rates from 1991 to 2000, compared to ten years earlier, increased by an average of 11.5 percent.[59] The increase was dramatic in a few states such as Michigan where it jumped to 60 percent in the house and 84 percent in the senate in 1998, the year limits were implemented. An anticipatory effect occurred in California with turnover increasing even before limits took effect; in other states, those that already had a fairly high turnover, the implementation of limits caused little change. But the general trend is clear: Membership turnover rates increased in term-limited states.[60]

Are term limits resulting in different types of people being elected to the legislature? Researchers working with the Joint Project on Term Limits have discovered no differences in the demographic characteristics of legislators that can be attributed to term limits. No differences were found in regard to family income, religious affiliation, or occupation. Term-limited legislators are no more likely to be women or minorities, and no more likely to be liberals or conservatives.[61] Equally important is that term-limited legislators are not serving a few terms in the legislature and then returning to their private-sector jobs. Richard J. Powell examined legislators who left office in 1998 because of term limits and discovered that more than half ran for another public office, and about half of those were elected. A few were candidates for the U.S. Congress, but many ran for local offices such as county or city councils and others moved into non-elective political positions such as an appointment within the executive branch.[62] The number of house members moving to the state senate also increased, especially in states that have the shortest term limits, six to eight years. And a new pattern was noted of members moving from the senate to the house, almost unheard of in states without term limits.[63] Jennifer Bowser, Keon Chi, and Thomas Little conclude that contrary to the hopes and expectations of advocates of term limits, "a new breed of diverse, citizen legislators"[64] has not appeared in termed legislatures.

Thad Kousser studied term limits in several states and suggests that the above findings do not mean that term limits have had no effect; rather, the effect may be somewhere else. And it could be with the larger number of new members each session and/or in the shorter time horizons that these legislators have; both are now a constant of legislative life in these states.[65] This broader line of inquiry is consistent with the opponents and supporters of term limits who predicted consequences beyond those mentioned above. For example, turnover can also be examined by looking at the tenure of legislative leaders, that is, the length of time they hold leadership positions. Prior to term limits, most of these positions were occupied by members who already had considerable experience as a legislator and then served as a leader for a number of additional years. This has changed radically with term limits. For example, average tenure of leaders in California before term limits was 9.5 years, after term limits it was only 2 years; in Maine it was 6.3 years before and 2.4 after.[66] And many legislators become leaders in their last legislative session before they are "termed out," which frequently results in members feeling they really don't have to cooperate with the leaders because they really are a "lame duck," a term used for politicians who are ineligible for reelection. Given these conditions, it is no surprise that the influence of leaders over the lawmaking process has declined in most term-limited states.[67]

John Carey and his colleagues used another approach and conducted a survey in 2006 to examine possible changes in legislators' attitudes. They discovered a "Burkean shift" among legislators in term-limited states. (See earlier discussion of representation in this chapter.) When legislators in both types of states are compared, term-limited legislators spend less time keeping in touch with their constituents, engage in less constituent service, and spend less time obtaining government money and projects for their districts. And on questions closely connected to Edmund Burke's philosophy, term-limited legislators are more likely to be concerned primarily with looking after the needs of the state as a whole than the district and more likely to follow their conscience when there is a conflict between what people in the district want and what their conscience thinks is best.[68] This is an unexpected finding to both sides in the term-limit debate.

At the institutional level, opponents of term limits predicted, and their view is supported, that the legislative branch would lose influence over policy making to the governor and executive branch. This has proved particularly true in the development of the state budget; legislative changes to the governor's budget proposal have declined significantly in term-limited states. The large number of legislators, and leaders, with shorter time in office means they also have less knowledge of budgets and less experience in challenging the governor's budget.[69] On the question of interest groups and lobbyists' influence in the legislative process the findings are somewhat surprising, certainly not expected by the opponents of term limits. Carey and his colleagues report that term limits have no measurable effect on legislators' perception of the extent of interest group influence in the legislative process and policy outcomes. They reason that lobbyists are advantaged because they have more policy knowledge on specific issues than inexperienced legislators; on the other hand, a fairly constant flow of new legislators disrupts the relationship between lobbyists and long-term incumbents and can reduce their influence.[70] Bowser states that new legislators "may share the general public's negative impression of lobbyists, viewing them as manipulators who are interested only in biasing public policy toward their own special interest."[71] Interest groups do not appear to have increased their influence in term-limited states compared to states without term limits.

On balance, what can be concluded about the effects of term limits? Membership turnover rates have increased, as term-limit supporters wanted, but there is no evidence of an increasing number of citizen legislators serving a few terms and then returning to private life; they leave the legislature but tend to move to different political careers. In addition, as legislators they are less attentive to their constituents, contrary to what term-limit supporters hoped for. The effect on the "culture of ruling" is problematic; turnover among legislative leaders is much higher, resulting in a decrease of the policy influence of legislatures, but increasing the influence of the governor and the executive branch. On the other hand, interest group influence does not appear to be any greater. Term-limit supporters may not have achieved everything they wanted, but from the perspective of term-limit opponents there is little positive. Citizens have lost some of their freedom to choose who represents them, and the lack of experienced legislative members and leaders has meant a legislative institution with less influence in policy making.

Constitutional challenges to state legislative term limits have been raised. In most cases, term limits have survived these challenges. The U.S. Supreme Court refused to hear a challenge to California's law. However, several state supreme courts found term limits unconstitutional. In Washington, the court's decision focused not on the substance of term limits but on the fact that they were adopted as an ordinary statute rather than an amendment to the state constitution. The court said that term limits are a qualification for office and, since qualifications for office are in the state constitution, they can be changed only through the constitutional amendment process. Six states have abolished legislative term limits (Table 5-5). Nebraska's Supreme Court also ruled against term limits in several decisions, but voters passed a new and constitutional version in 2000. In 2006, voters in Oregon rejected an initiative that would have reestablished term limits.

The legislative term-limits movement may have run its course (no state has adopted term limits since Nebraska's readoption in 2000), but generalized feelings of citizen dissatisfaction with government that it was based on have not gone away. Since the early 1970s, survey after survey has found distrust and lack of confidence in American political institutions, and these negative views of citizens are a challenge to state legislatures. For some, it raises a prior question: Is American politics really as terrible as the public perceives? The National Conference of State Legislatures and several well-known political scientists believe that many of these negative

TABLE 5-5 States That Adopted, Then Abolished Legislative Term Limits			
State	Year Enacted	Year Abolished	Abolished by . . .
Oregon	1992	2002	State supreme court
Utah	1992	2003	State legislature
Washington	1992	1998	State supreme court
Wyoming	1992	2004	State supreme court
Idaho	1994	2002	State legislature
Massachusetts	1994	1997	State supreme court

Source: Information for this table is from the National Conference of State Legislatures, www.ncsl.org/programs/legismgt/about/states.htm.

impressions are inaccurate. Alan Rosenthal, Karl Kurtz, John Hibbing, and Burdett Loomis have come forward to defend and explain how state legislatures and representative government work—in essence, they believe that a new "civic education" is required. Their approach is to compare public perceptions of state legislatures with the reality of the legislative process. For example, most people believe that a state's citizens "agree on what is right and necessary, so the legislature should just pass the laws that the people want."[72] But this view is not realistic because there is disagreement among citizens over what the most important problems facing a state or the nation are, and even more disagreement over the best way to solve these problems. We live in a diverse society with less agreement on issues than we think, and it is "the job of the legislature to resolve the clash of values, interests, and claims."[73]

A related public perception is that the "lawmaking process doesn't work well because of politics, unprincipled deal making and needless conflict." Rosenthal, Kurtz, Hibbing, and Loomis argue that this view is incorrect because the legislative process is normally not an orderly one; dissension, debate, and conflict, sometimes heated and intense, are a natural part of the process. To resolve the conflict, compromise is also part of the process; compromise is not the same as "selling out." It is unlikely that any group will get all of what it wants. We may not always like these decisions, "but we should understand why they came about and recognize that this frustrating process and these imperfect decisions are what democracy is all about."[74] Overall, these advocates of the importance of "civic education" want to communicate this idea: "Representative democracy does work—by no means perfectly, but reasonably well."[75]

A related challenge to state legislatures is the concept of direct democracy that we discussed in Chapter 4. Direct democracy, especially as embodied in the initiative process, allows citizens to propose laws and then decide their fate. With modern computer technology and the Internet, it is easy to imagine not only the gathering of initiative petition signatures but also voting on these initiatives by a simple keystroke from home computers. And why have elections on initiatives only once a year? Every week it would be possible for citizens to decide any number of issues affecting their state, county, and city. Elected representatives would be unnecessary; people would make their own decisions. An expanded system of direct democracy would replace legislative institutions that are the heart of representative government. There is no doubt that we will confront these questions, and probably sooner than many state government leaders and researchers expect.

But representative government has important advantages that should be weighed and considered. Political scientist Richard J. Ellis says it well:

> The point of having selected individuals study, discuss, and debate public policy in a face-to-face forum was that they might reach a judgment that was different from the opinion or prejudice with which they began. Expert testimony might lead them to revise their beliefs, or the intense pleas of affected groups might unsettle their convictions. The rival interests of other constituencies would need to be heard and considered; compromises would need to be reached.[76]

LOCAL LEGISLATURES

If it is dangerous to make generalizations about fifty state legislatures, the pitfalls clearly are multiplied when presenting an overview of close to 40,000 local legislatures found in counties, cities, townships, and towns. On two characteristics, however, local legislatures are different from their state counterparts: Local legislatures are *unicameral*. And membership in local legislatures is a part-time job with low salaries and minimal staff assistance, except in cities and counties with very large populations.

Counties

The **county** is a major unit of local government in the United States that exists as an agent for the state and as a unit of local governance. (Counties are called "parishes" in Louisiana and "boroughs" in Alaska.) There were 3,066 counties in 2007; thirty had a population of over 1 million and 677 had populations of less than 10,000. Loving County in Texas has a population of only sixty-seven people!

County governments are found in all states except Connecticut and Rhode Island. Counties have never been important in the New England states, where the town remains the basic unit of local government. The size and number of counties vary greatly. Delaware and Hawaii have only three counties each, whereas Texas has 254. San Bernardino County, California (20,000 square miles), is larger than Vermont and New Hampshire combined. Counties are the creatures of the state, and their existence often is spelled out in state constitutions. (Keep in mind that within most counties, there will be a number of cities and towns that provide general local government for people living within their boundaries; they may receive some services from the county, but most will come from the city or town.)

Counties traditionally have performed a limited number of state-mandated functions that included keeping records on property and statistics on people, maintenance of rural roads, administration of elections, and law enforcement. More recently, they have been given additional functions administering numerous federal and state programs such as child welfare, consumer protection, and economic development. Although counties have been the most important unit of government in rural areas, urban counties have been gaining significant authority. In some states, home-rule charters allow counties to perform functions that previously were city responsibilities. These include water supply, library services, sewage disposal, flood control, and management of airports. This has been especially true in southern states where counties traditionally have been more powerful than cities.[77] As will be discussed in Chapter 8, strong urban counties can serve as a kind of metropolitan government by providing a wide range of services traditionally associated with cities.

Counties that are neither urban nor rural—so-called 50-50 areas (they are fifty miles from a metropolitan area, and they have populations around 50,000)—are experiencing new demands from affluent families who are moving away from cities but still want many urban services.

Traditionally, counties have been governed by a **commission** that has both legislative and executive powers and is composed of three or five members elected by the voters. In a few states, such as Illinois and Wisconsin, there are large governing boards with ten or more members. Commissioners often share administrative duties with independently elected officials that include auditors, prosecutors, treasurers, and sheriffs. Commissioners' legislative functions include adopting a budget and setting tax rates. As executives, commissioners appoint some county employees and supervise delivery of county services. Although the Voting Rights Act has prompted more district elections in counties, the more common pattern is at-large election of commissioners.

The organization of county government has been criticized because the absence of a chief executive often has meant inadequate supervision and coordination of the numerous county departments. A system designed for rural, small-town America has not had the flexibility to adapt to the needs of urbanized, metropolitan populations.

Reformers have favored alternative forms of county government with appointed or elected executives. Change has come because the home-rule movement has allowed counties to pick among several types of structures that centralize administrative responsibility. One form of county government is the **commission-administrator;** the commissioners appoint an administrator who serves at the pleasure of the commission and is delegated a broad range of administrative responsibilities including hiring department heads and formulating annual budgets. Another form is the **council-executive,** which has two branches of government and a separation of powers; voters elect the executive and the council. Approximately 40 percent of the counties, especially those in urban areas, have adopted either one of these two forms of government. Administrators are sometimes called managers, chief administrative officers, or executive directors. Administrators' powers vary and include budget preparation, appointment of some department heads, and supervision of some departments. Executives who are elected by the voters have more substantial powers, which may include the ability to veto legislation approved by the county board. Typically, voters elect fewer county officials under this structure than under the commission form of government.

Cities

City councils vary in size: Cities with a large population also have larger councils. For example, cities with over 1 million people have councils with an average of thirty-three members, cities with 500,000 to 1 million people have an average of eleven council members, and cities between 50,000 to 99,999 have seven council members.[78] Members of larger councils are elected by districts, sometimes called wards. (The councils discussed in this section are associated with a type of local government known as a municipality. A **municipality** provides general government for a defined geographic area. The state grants it a charter that defines its powers, as explained in Chapter 1. A municipality can be a city, town, or village; however, "town" has a special meaning in the New England states and a few states in the Midwest. This will be explained below.)

Susan MacManus explains that council members must be both generalists and specialists because the issues that arise in communities vary widely: "land use, availability of housing and services, tax policy and tax rates, service delivery . . . , buildings and facilities, economic development, the environment, public safety, recreation, cultural opportunities, and more."[79]

A 2003 study by the National League of Cities presents information on individuals who were elected to city councils. Being a council member in a small city (25,000 to 69,999 residents) or medium-size (70,000 to 199,999 residents) city is a part-time job with a low salary. In small cities, the single largest percentage of annual salaries is in the $6,000 to $9,999 range; in medium cities the range that occurs most frequently is $10,000 to $14,999. Although salaries are low, council members report spending considerable time on council matters: twenty hours a week in small cities and thirty-two hours a week in medium cities. In large cities (200,000 residents and over), annual salaries are frequently $50,000 or greater and the job becomes full time with council members frequently working forty-eight hours a week.[80] City councils are becoming increasingly racially and ethnically diverse, with approximately 13 percent of the members (up from 7 percent in 1979) from various minority groups including African American, Hispanic, Asian, and Native American. Representation of minorities is greater in large cities because they usually are more ethnically diverse than smaller cities. Women make up 28 percent of city council members. Council members are well educated, with 75 percent having a college degree.[81] Much of the increase of minorities on councils has been caused by the change from at-large to single-member districts that were created as a result of the Voting Rights Act of 1965 and amendments that prohibited minority vote dilution (see Chapter 4).

When council members are part time, it is easier for the mayor or city manager to dominate their decision making. The degree of council participation in decision making is greatly affected by the form of city government (see Chapter 6). Councils are viewed as the most important source of policy initiation in cities with a council-manager form of government.[82] Where there is a weak-mayor system, the council will have considerable formal authority. In cities with strong mayors, the basic function of council members often is to act as representatives to bring complaints to the attention of city hall. In most cities, councils are passive and seldom act as policy innovators. Their most common role is to oppose rather than to propose policy.

A few large cities, Dallas, Los Angeles, New York, and Washington, D.C., have term limits for city council members, usually two terms, but they are the exception. Victor DeSantis and Tari Renner found that among cities with populations over 25,000, only 8.4 percent of cities reported having term limits.[83] Because of the higher rate of turnover for local officials, compared to state legislators, the drive for term limits for council members never attracted much support. Nearly half of the council members in the surveyed cities were in their first term. (And the average tenure for mayors was 5.4 years. The turnover of city managers was 29 percent in a one-year period.)

Primary cause of the high turnover rate is revealed in the National League of Cities study, which reports that in the year of its survey (2001) only a slight majority of council members indicated that they were planning to run for reelection. In other words, much of the turnover is voluntary. Why do so many members decide to leave? Although the most often cited reasons for running for the city council are "to serve city as whole" or "to serve my neighborhood," council members report quite a bit of frustration after they have been on the council for a while. The greatest source of frustration is conflict among council members themselves.[84] In the rather intimate setting of council meetings where the total membership may be seven or nine members, what begins as policy differences will end up taking the form of personal attacks or will be interpreted as personal attacks. And many council members find that rather than receiving personal satisfaction from serving their city or neighborhood, they have frustrating conflict, which they conclude is not worth the time away from family and the long hours. Why run again?

In small cities, council sessions may be once or twice a month, and in large cities, councils meet at least once a week. The use of committees and professional staff in large cities has been increasing because councils are facing more complex problems, but it is nowhere close to the level present in state legislatures. About one-half have committees and one-third have a professional staff. Staff are usually hired to serve the entire council, not individual committees or members. In the past, small-town councils, in particular, often resolved issues at an informal and private meeting before the scheduled session, and then voted unanimously in public sessions. State **"sunshine laws"** force councils to have open meetings on nearly all matters.

Townships and Towns

The **township,** basically a subdivision of a county, is a form of government found in Middle Atlantic and midwestern states. In much of the Midwest, townships were carefully laid out in six-mile squares, with 36 one-mile square sections. These surveyor's townships did not become political townships until later when local government was organized. As a result, all political townships are not neat six-mile squares. Midwest counties were designed so that no one would be more than a day's travelling time from the county seat, and the township hall was within an hour's buggy ride. Unlike towns, townships are primarily rural, not a combination of rural and urban areas. Townships also are not the principal unit of government in any state in which they are found. They exist throughout many states such as Ohio, Kansas, and Pennsylvania in the Midwest and Middle Atlantic, but only parts of other states such as Illinois and the Dakotas have townships. A few townships have annual meetings that are similar to New England town meetings, but most elect trustees to act as legislators, as well as administrators. Some elect a chief executive, commonly known as a supervisor. Many rural townships have transferred much of their authority (e.g., repair of roads and bridges) to counties.

In most midwestern states, all land area not incorporated into municipalities lies within the jurisdiction of townships. The township, typically with three elected trustees, may levy taxes and sue and be sued. In a few wealthy suburban areas (in Pennsylvania and Kansas, for example), townships have gained powers nearly equal to those of cities.

Township powers can grow as new businesses locate in unincorporated areas adjacent to cities and as the population of those areas increases.

Collectively, townships may have surprising political power in a state. When we consider that many midwestern counties are divided into more than a dozen townships, this means that some states have over 1,000 townships, with over 3,000 trustees. Because annexation presents a direct threat to their power, townships have lobbied in Ohio for a requirement that township land cannot be annexed without trustee approval. Of course, counties also have statewide organizations to lobby, and cities join state municipal leagues that present a unified effort to represent their interests in the state legislature.

The **town** continues to be the basic form of local government in New England states. In colonial America, a "town" included a village and surrounding farms. Over time, some New England urban areas have incorporated and withdrawn from towns, but towns as governmental units continue to be a combination of urban areas and the surrounding countryside. For example, New Hampshire has only ten counties and thirteen municipalities, but it has 221 towns. It is here, and in other towns in New England, that the fabled **New England town meeting** convenes annually and the assembled voters make decisions for their community. This is an example of true direct democracy, not representative democracy. The town meeting will levy taxes, determine how money will be spent, and elect next year's "selectmen" who will oversee the administration of the town's government.

Town meetings are frequently criticized for low citizen attendance, which averages 20 percent of the registered voters. Political scientist Frank M. Bryan, in a wide-ranging analysis and defense of town meetings, notes that the 20 percent figure is an average and that participation can be as high as slightly over 50 percent or as low as just under 5 percent.[85] One of the important factors affecting attendance is the size of the town; towns with smaller populations have higher participation than larger towns. The issues being considered at the meeting are the second factor, with controversial issues drawing greater attendance.[86]

SUMMARY

For state legislatures, the reapportionment revolution was a landmark event. Supreme Court decisions in the 1960s ruled that both the lower and the upper houses of state legislatures were to be apportioned on the basis of population. With the resulting shift in legislative power from rural to urban and suburban areas, many states began a process of professionalizing their legislatures. After each federal decennial census, new legislative district lines are drawn in the states. The only clear guideline is that districts must be substantially equal in population. Gerrymandering is widespread in the drawing of lines today, and efforts to improve the process are usually unsuccessful.

State legislators are usually white men, but the number of legislators who are women, African Americans, and members of other minority groups has increased substantially since 1975. As institutions, state legislatures are quite diverse. Some are professional and have longer sessions, higher salaries for their members, and a larger staff. At the other extreme are legislatures with short sessions, lower salaries, and a smaller staff; their members are usually called citizen legislators. Regardless of a legislature's size, partisan and nonpartisan staff are essential to the successful performance of its responsibilities.

State legislatures carry out a number of functions, including representation (individual legislators representing the interests of their constituents), lawmaking (making policy through the passage of laws), and legislative oversight (reviewing the performance of executive-branch agencies). Governors are important in lawmaking because they play a key role in the initiation of policies considered by the legislature.

Decision making in legislatures centers around committees, parties, and leaders. Leaders perform a number of roles and have powers such as control over the appointment of committee chairs that allow them to influence the making of decisions, even with the general decline in the strength of allegiance legislators have to their parties. Today's legislative leaders use a coordinating and consensus style of leadership more than a command style.

The term-limit movement of the 1990s, a manifestation of public dissatisfaction with government and career politicians, has limited the number of terms state legislators can serve in fifteen states. The effects of term limits are still unfolding, but there is little evidence that this reform has increased the presence of citizen-legislators in "termed" states; however, legislators pay less attention to their constituents, and the higher turnover of leaders has decreased the legislature's influence in the making of policy and increased that of the governor and the executive branch. Lack of public understanding of the legislative process and the use of the initiative are further challenges to state legislatures.

Generally, the most important local legislatures are city councils and county commissions. In most cities, being a council member is a part-time job, and the council is often dominated by the mayor or city manager. County commissioners have both legislative and executive responsibilities, and the latter frequently are shared with independently elected officials, such as the sheriff and engineers. The absence of a chief executive in county government is a frequent criticism. Almost half of the counties now have an elected chief executive or an appointed county administrator.

The town is an important unit of local government in New England. Many towns continue to have annual town meetings that serve as a legislative body and make decisions for the town. In many midwestern states, townships provide a few services for rural areas. Township trustees are elected by the voters to act as legislators and administrators.

KEY TERMS

apportionment (p. 166)
districting (p. 166)
malapportionment (p. 166)
Baker v. Carr (p. 167)
Reynolds v. Sims (p. 167)
Reapportionment Revolution (p. 167)
gerrymandering (p. 169)
Davis v. Bandemer (p. 169)
Shaw v. Reno (p. 169)
Hunt (Easley) v. Cromartie (p. 169)
bicameral (p. 174)
unicameral (p. 174)
professional legislature (p. 175)
citizen legislature (p. 175)
hybrid legislature (p. 175)
partisan staff (p. 178)
nonpartisan staff (p. 178)

constituency service (p. 180)
casework (p. 180)
"sunset laws" (p. 181)
caucus (p. 184)
leadership style (p. 186)
term-limits movement (p. 186)
county (p. 192)
commission (p. 193)
commission-administrator (p. 193)
council-executive (p. 193)
municipality (p. 194)
"sunshine laws" (p. 195)
township (p. 195)
town (p. 196)
New England town meeting (p. 196)

BRIEF COMPARISONS OF STATE/LOCAL DIFFERENCES

Issue	State Level	Local Level
Structural characteristics of legislatures	Bicameral (except Nebraska), larger number of members and committee system	Unicameral, smaller number of members, and usually no committee system
Degree of professionalization of legislatures	More likely to be viewed as full-time job, lower turnover, generally higher salaries	More likely to be viewed as part-time job, higher turnover, generally lower salaries
Legislative term limits	Adopted by close to one-third of the states	Not widely adopted, used by less than 10 percent of city councils

INTERESTING WEB SITES

The National Conference of State Legislatures in Denver, Colorado, maintains an excellent Web site at *www.ncsl.org*. Be sure to click on "State and Federal Issues" for reports on timely state issues and "Legislatures," where you can find a link to each state's legislature.

www.sllf.org/sllf.php/cat/1. Web site of the State Legislative Leadership Foundation; look at "Publications and Resources" for case studies of legislative leaders.

www.naco.org. The National Association of Counties maintains this site. It has all kinds of county information—issues to demographics—plus data on individual counties.

www.nlc.org/home. A comprehensive Web site on city issues sponsored by the National League of Cities. Basic information is available in "About Cities," and research reports on a variety of topics are found under "Resources for Cities."

NOTES

1. This case study is adapted from Ronald Keith Gaddie, *Born to Run: Origins of the Political Career* (Lanham, Md.: Rowman & Littlefield, 2003), pp. 103–117. Gaddie's excellent book describes eight personal histories of men and women who decided to run for the state legislature and were elected.
2. See John Burns, *The Sometime Governments* (New York: Bantam Books, 1971), p. 32.
3. Rich Jones, "State Legislatures," *The Book of the States 1994–95* (Lexington, Ky.: Council of State Governments, 1994), p. 98.
4. Newspaper and television reporters frequently use the term *redistricting* to refer to the drawing of new congressional district boundaries and *reapportionment* to refer to the drawing of new state legislative district boundaries. Although this usage is not exact, it conveniently distinguishes the two processes.
5. *Baker v. Carr*, 369 U.S. 186 (1962).

6. *Reynolds v. Sims,* 377 U.S. 533 (1964).

7. Timothy G. O'Rourke, "The Impact of Reapportionment on Congress and State Legislatures," in *Voting Rights and Redistricting in the United States,* Mark E. Rush, ed. (Westport, Conn.: Greenwood Press, 1998), p. 214; Nathaniel A. Persily, Thad Kousser, and Patrick Egan, "The Complicated Impact of One Person, One Vote on Political Competition and Representation," *North Carolina Law Review* 80 (May 2002), 1332–1340.

8. Timothy G. O'Rourke, *The Impact of Reapportionment* (New Brunswick, N.J.: Transaction Books, 1980), pp. 119–120.

9. O'Rourke, *Impact of Reapportionment;* David C. Saffell, "Reapportionment and Public Policies: State Legislators' Perspectives," *Policy Studies Journal* 9 (1980–1981), pp. 916–936.

10. Stephen Ansolabehere, Alan Gerber, and Jim Snyder, "Equal Votes, Equal Money: Court-Ordered Redistricting and Public Expenditures in the American States, *American Political Science Review* 96 (December 2002), p. 776.

11. *Cox v. Larios,* 542 U.S. 947 (2004); Ronald Weber, "State Legislative Redistricting in 2003–2004: Emerging Trends and Issues in Reapportionment," in *The Book of the States 2004* (Lexington, Ky.: Council of State Governments, 2005), pp. 120–121.

12. *Davis v. Bandemer,* 478 U.S. 109 (1986).

13. *Shaw v. Reno,* 509 U.S. 630 (1993); Two good studies of minority voting rights are Charles S. Bullock, III, "The Opening Up of State and Local Processes," in *American State and Local Politics: Directions for the 21st Century,* Ronald E. Weber and Paul Brace, eds. (New York: Chatham House Publishers, 1999), pp. 212–240; and Richard K. Scher, Jon L. Mills, and John J. Hotaling, *Voting Rights & Democracy: The Law and Politics of Districting* (Chicago: Nelson-Hall Publishers, 1997).

14. *Easley v. Cromartie,* 532 U.S. 234 (2001).

15. First attempts to present an overview of the post-2000 census redistricting can be found in Richard L. Engstrom, "The Post-2000 Round of Redistricting: An Entangled Thicket Within the Federal System," *Publius: The Journal of Federalism* (Fall 2002), pp. 51–70; and Ronald E. Weber, "State Legislative Redistricting in 2001–2002: Emerging Trends and Issues in Reapportionment," *The Book of the States 2001* (Lexington, Ky.: Council of State Governments, 2002), pp. 233–238.

16. Patty Reinert, "High Court Backs Texas Remap Plan; Hispanic Challenges Fail," *Houston Chronicle* (June 18, 2002), p. 1A, http://web.lexis-nexis.com (accessed March 25, 2003).

17. Laylan Copelin, "Districts Likely Set for 2002 Election: Federal Judges Largely Accept GOP-Backed Maps for Texas House, Senate," *Austin American Statesman* (November 29, 2001), p. A1, http://web.lexis-nexis.com (accessed March 25, 2003).

18. Tim Storey, "2002 State Legislative Elections," *Spectrum: The Journal of State Government* (Winter 2003), p. 9.

19. Steve Lawrence, "Davis Signs Bills Aimed at Status Quo in Legislature, Congress," Associated Press State & Local Wire (September 27, 2001), and Dan Walters, "A Self-Serving Redistricting Process," *Sacramento Bee* (October 19, 2001), p. B-9, http://web.lexis-nexis.com/universe (accessed March 25, 2003).

20. "Redistricting Disgrace; Governor Pataki Signs Off on a Plan That Serves the Interests of the Majority Parties," *Times Union* (Albany), April 24, 2002, p. A12, http://web.lexis-nexis.com/universe (accessed March 26, 2003).

21. An excellent analysis of redistricting in all fifty states is in Michael P. McDonald's "A Comparative Analysis of Redistricting Institutions in the United States, 2001–02," *State Politics & Policy Quarterly* 4 (Winter 2004), pp. 371–395.

22. Rex Honey and Douglas Deane Jones, "Iowa," in *Redistricting in the 1980's,* Leroy Hardy, Alan Heslop, and George S. Blair, eds. (Claremont, Calif.: Rose Institute of State and Local Government, 1993), pp. 97–102.

23. Mike Glover, "Moving Vans Fire Up After New Districts Approved," Associated Press State & Local Wire (June 20, 2001), http://web.lexis-nexis.com/universe (accessed March 28, 2003).

24. Michael P. McDonald, "United States Redistricting and the Decline of Competitive Congressional Districts." Paper presented at the George Mason Center for Public Choice, Fairfax, Virginia, April 2, 2003, p. 46.

25. Thomas E. Mann, "For Election Reform, a Heartening Defeat," *New York Times* (November 11, 2005), available at www.brookings.edu (accessed August 7, 2006), and Thomas E. Mann, "Redistricting Reform, *The National Voter* (June 2005), pp. 4–7.

26. "Profile of the 2005 Wisconsin Legislature," *Wisconsin Briefs* Brief 05-3, January 2005, Wisconsin Legislative Reference Bureau, pp. 2–3.

27. Tom Todd, "Nebraska's Unicameral Legislature: A Description and Some Comparisons with Minnesota's Bicameral Legislature," *Journal of the American Society of Legislative Clerks and Secretaries* (Spring 1998). AASLCS home page, www.ncsl.org/programs/legman/aslcs/cshome.htm (accessed March 25, 2003).

28. B. Drummond Ayres Jr., "Political Briefing. Ventura's Mission: Turning Two into One," *New York Times* (August 22, 1999), p. 22.

29. "NCSL Backgrounder: Full- and Part-Time Legislatures," National Conference of State Legislatures, www.ncsl.org/programs/press/2004backgrounder_fullandpart.htm (accessed August 10, 2006). An earlier version is Karl Kurtz, "Understanding Diversity of American State Legislatures," *Extension of Remarks* (June 1992), p. 3. Kurtz uses Red, White, and Blue as alternative names of the professional, hybrid, and citizen categories so as to avoid implying that one category is better than another.

30. Ibid.

31. Alan Rosenthal, Burdett A. Loomis, John R. Hibbing, and Karl T. Kurtz, *Republic on Trial: The Case for Representative Democracy* (Washington, D.C.: CQ Press, 2003), p. 72.

32. Karl Kurtz, "Understanding the Diversity of American State Legislatures," *Extension of Remarks* (June 1992), p. 3.

33. Karl T. Kurtz, "Strong Staff, Strong Institutions: Custodians of American Democracy," *State Legislatures* (July–August 2006), p. 28.

34. Ohio Legislative Service Commission, *A Guidebook for Ohio Legislators* (Columbus: Ohio Legislative Service Commission, 2005), pp. 85–89.

35. Tommy Neal, *Lawmaking and the Legislative Process: Committees, Connections and Compromises* (Phoenix, Ariz.: Oryx Press, 1996), pp. 23–27.

36. John A. Hird, *Power, Knowledge, and Politics: Policy Analysis in the States* (Washington, D.C.: Georgetown University Press, 2005), pp. 69–96.

37. Edmund Burke, quoted in Malcolm E. Jewell, *Representation in State Legislatures* (Lexington: University Press of Kentucky, 1982), p. 11.

38. Alan Rosenthal, *Heavy Lifting: The Job of the American Legislature* (Washington, D.C.: CQ Press, 2004), p. 43.

39. Ibid., pp. 44–46.

40. Alan Rosenthal, *The Decline of Representative Democracy: Process, Participation, and Power in State Legislatures* (Washington, D.C.: CQ Press, 1998), p. 25.

41. Lilliard Richardson, *Representation in State Legislatures,* Harry S. Truman School of Public Affairs, University of Missouri, 2004, www.truman.missouri.edu/ipp//Publications/briefs.html.

42. Rosenthal, *Heavy Lifting,* p. 33.

43. National Conference of State Legislatures, "Bill Introduction Limits," www.ncsl.org (accessed April 11, 2003).

44. Alan Rosenthal, "Legislative Oversight and the Balance of Power in State Government," *State Government* 56, no. 3 (1983), pp. 93–95.

45. National Legislative Program Evaluation Society, "Ensuring the Public Trust: How Program Policy Evaluation Is Serving State Legislatures" (July 2000), www.ncsl.org/program/nlpes.

46. Neal, *Lawmaking and the Legislative Process*, pp. 56–57; and Alan Rosenthal, *Representative Democracy*, pp. 141–145.

47. Sarah McCally Morehouse and Malcolm E. Jewell, *State Politics, Parties, & Policy*, 2d ed. (Lanham, Md.: Rowman & Littlefield, 2003), p. 227.

48. Shannon Jenkins, "Party Voting in State Legislatures," *Spectrum: The Journal of State Government* (Fall 2002), pp. 10–13.

49. National Conference of State Legislatures, "Legislative Deadlock: What If It Happens to You?" www.ncsl.org/programs/press/2000/tiedexpl.htm (accessed April 11, 2003).

50. Malcolm E. Jewell and Marcia Lynn Whicker, *Legislative Leadership in the American States* (Ann Arbor: The University of Michigan Press, 1994), pp. 58–59.

51. Ibid., pp. 89–95.

52. Ibid., p. 96.

53. Ibid., pp. 125–130.

54. Center for American Women and Politics, *Women State Legislators: Leadership Positions and Committee Chairs 2005* (New Brunswick, N.J.: Center for American Women and Politics, 2005), www.cawp.rutgers.edu (accessed February 22, 2007).

55. Mark P. Petracca, "The Poison of Professional Politics," Policy Analysis No. 151 (Washington, D.C.: CATO Institute, 1991), p. 4, www.cato.org/pub_display.php?pub_id=1011.

56. Edward H. Crane, "Six and Twelve: The Case for Serious Term Limits," *National Civic Review* (Summer 1991), pp. 252–253.

57. Cal Ledbetter, Jr., "Limiting Legislative Terms Is a Bad Idea," *National Civic Review* (Summer 1991), p. 244.

58. Charles Price, "Advocacy in the Age of Term Limits: Lobbying after Proposition 140," in *1994–1995 Annual California Government and Politics*, Thomas R. Hoeber and Charles M. Price, eds. (Sacramento, Calif.: California Journal Press, 1994), p. 56.

59. Jennifer Drage Bowser, Keon S. Chi, and Thomas H. Little, *Coping with Term Limits: A Practical Guide* (Denver, Colo.: National Conference of State Legislatures, 2006), p. 2.

60. Gary F. Moncrief, Richard G. Niemi, and Lynda W. Powell, "Time, Term Limits, and Turnover: Trends in Membership Stability in U.S. State Legislatures," *Legislative Studies Quarterly* (August 2004), p. 367.

61. John M. Carey, Richard G. Niemi, Lynda W. Powell, and Gary F. Moncrief, "The Effect of Term Limits on State Legislatures: A New Survey of the 50 States," *Legislative Studies Quarterly* (February 2006), pp. 113–117; www.lwv.org/AM/Template.cfm?Section=Home&template=/CM/HTMLDisplay.cfm&ContentID=3735; Bowser, Chi, and Little, *Coping with Term Limits*, p. 1.

62. Richard J. Powell, "The Unintended Effects of Term Limits on the Career Paths of State Legislators," in *The Test of Time: Coping with Legislative Term Limits*, Rick Farmer, John David Rausch, Jr., and John C. Green, eds. (Lanham, Md.: Lexington Books, 2003), p. 144.

63. Moncrief, Niemi, and Powell, "Time, Term Limits, and Turnover," p. 370.

64. Bowser, Chi, and Little, *Coping with Term Limits*, p. 1.

65. Thad Kousser, *Term Limits and the Dismantling of State Legislative Professionalism* (New York: Cambridge University Press, 2005), pp. 204–205.

66. Ibid., p. 91.

67. Jennifer Drage Bowser, "The Effects of Legislative Term Limits," in *The Book of the States 2005* (Lexington, Ky.: Council of State Governments, 2006), pp. 113–114.

68. Carey, et al., "Effect of Term Limits on State Legislatures," pp. 117–123.

69. Bowser, "Effects of Legislative Term Limits," pp. 4–5; Carey, et al., "Effect of Term Limits on State Legislatures," pp. 124–125.

70. Carey, et al., "Effect of Term Limits on State Legislatures," p. 124.
71. Bowser, "Effects of Legislative Term Limits," p. 6.
72. Alan Rosenthal, Karl T. Kurtz, John Hibbing, and Burdett Loomis, *The Case for Representative Democracy: What Americans Should Know About Their Legislatures* (Denver, Colo.: National Conference of State Legislatures, 2001), p. 18. Also see Rosenthal, Loomis, Hibbing, and Kurtz, *Republic on Trial*.
73. Rosenthal, Kurtz, Hibbing, and Loomis, *Case for Representative Democracy*, p. 18.
74. Ibid., p. 32.
75. Rosenthal, Loomis, Hibbing, and Kurtz, *Republic on Trial*, p. 215.
76. Richard J. Ellis, *Democratic Delusions: The Initiative Process in America* (Lawrence: University Press of Kansas, 2002), p. 200.
77. See David R. Berman, ed., *County Government in an Era of Change* (Westport, Conn.: Greenwood Press, 1993).
78. Evelina R. Moulder, *Profile of the City Council, 1996* (Washington, D.C.: International City/County Management Association, 1996).
79. Susan MacManus, "The Resurgent City Councils," in *American State and Local Politics: Directions for the 21st Century*, Ronald E. Weber and Paul Brace, eds. (New York: Chatham House, 1999), p. 181.
80. James H. Svara, *Two Decades of Continuity and Change in American City Councils* (Washington, D.C.: National League of Cities, 2003), p. 11.
81. Ibid., pp. 4–9.
82. Ibid, p. 50.
83. Victor S. DeSantis and Tari Renner, "Term Limits and Turnover Among Local Officials," in *The Municipal Yearbook 1993* (Washington, D.C.: International City/County Management Association, 1993), p. 36.
84. Svara, *Two Decades*, pp. 14–15, 33–34.
85. Frank M. Bryan, *Real Democracy: The New England Town Meeting and How It Works* (Chicago: University of Chicago Press, 2004), p. 73.
86. Ibid., pp. 233–236.

GOVERNORS, BUREAUCRATS, AND MAYORS

CRUSADING ATTORNEY GENERAL BECOMES GOVERNOR: A STEP UP?

After serving seven years as attorney general of New York, Democrat Eliot Spitzer was elected governor in 2006 with 69 percent of the vote—the largest share of the vote in the state's history.

A few months before the election, reporter Alan Greenblatt noted that Spitzer "has arguably been the most influential state official in the United States during the first decade of the twentieth-first century."[1] Then Greenblatt wondered if Spitzer would be giving up more power as attorney general than he would have elected governor.

As noted in Chapter 1, Spitzer crusaded against Wall Street economic interests and in favor of environmental and civil rights. As will be noted later in this chapter, attorneys general have the ability to pursue high-profile cases and use their subpoena power to get information, which can get them plenty of media attention. In Spitzer's case, his formal power was especially broad and because his state included the financial capital of the country, he could go after very big targets. Over the course of his time in office, Spitzer brought billions of dollars to the New York treasury and states around the country benefited economically from his legal victories.

Soon after he became attorney general in 1989, Spitzer says he realized that if Republicans in Washington were silly enough to give power away, he would take the opportunity to define and create an aggressive progressive agenda.[2] As Richard Nathan, co-director of the Rockefeller Institute of Government, notes, federalism is opportunistic—it can be pro-government and used to support public activism, or it can be used to further a conservative agenda to limit the role of government. Spitzer says he discovered federalism and became a "fervent federalist" when President Reagan came to office. As a result, as attorney general he became a leader in what Nathan refers to as a "new, new federalism" in which liberals have been able to pursue successfully an activist agenda in many states.

Will Spitzer be equally successful as governor? During the period that Spitzer was attorney general, George Pataki was the Republican governor of New York. Greenblatt points out that with the two houses of the legislature divided between Republicans and Democrats, Pataki had numerous vetoes overridden and his successes were limited. For the most part the governor got less press attention than did Spitzer.

Of course, Spitzer is aware of the potential problems he is likely to encounter as governor. He made fighting gridlock in the legislature a central feature of his campaign and he can expect strong opposition from Republicans, who still control the state senate. Still, his supporters point out that, as attorney general, Spitzer pursued issues that were available, at least in part, to all other attorneys general and that he will find opportunities to pursue new issues as governor.

POINTS TO CONSIDER

- Should governors' power of clemency be constitutionally restricted?
- How has the formal power of governors evolved over the past two hundred years?
- How does the formal power of governors differ among the fifty states?
- How does the personal power of governors compare with their formal power?

- What are some informal ways in which governors exercise control over legislatures?
- How has government benefited or suffered from the use of affirmative action?
- What are the goals of the "reinventing government" movement, what reforms are recommended to achieve these goals, and to what extent have states put these reforms into practice? What are its limitations?
- In what ways have the powers of statewide elected officials increased in recent years?
- Compare and contrast the roles of mayors in four different systems of municipal government.
- How can it be argued that a hybrid system of city government is the best of both worlds?
- What difference does it make to have significantly more women and minority mayors than was the case thirty years ago? What is the approach of "second-generation African American mayors"?

HISTORICAL DEVELOPMENT OF THE GOVERNOR'S OFFICE

When the early state constitutions were written, all governmental power was distrusted, but executives were particularly suspect because of the colonial experience under King George III of England. Consequently, the legislative branch dominated early state government. In most of the original states the legislature chose the governor. In all but three states, governors were limited to one-year terms and typically they were not in charge of state administrative agencies. Pennsylvania and Georgia had plural executives, that is, leadership by committee. In only one state did the governor have the veto power, and Virginia did not elect its governor until 1851.

During the **Jacksonian democracy era,** which began with the election to the presidency of Andrew Jackson in 1828, the prestige of chief executives was enhanced. Jacksonian democracy emphasized political and social equality, government by the "common man" over government by an aristocracy, that is, those who inherited their wealth and social position. Popular election was viewed as the best way to fill other executive offices, such as attorney general and treasurer. Pushed by the disclosure of legislative corruption and incompetence, states extended the terms of governors, usually to two years, and added the veto power. Toward the end of the nineteenth century, legislatures, responding to urban residents who were demanding more services, created new executive branch agencies. In New York, there were only ten state agencies in 1800; by 1900 the number had increased to eighty-one. Typically, these agencies were administered by boards and commissions, at least some of whose members were appointed by the legislature.[3] The executive branch of state government was becoming an administrative nightmare. As late as the 1980s, many governors lacked sufficient authority to manage state governments.

Many twentieth-century government reforms fall under the heading of **administrative efficiency,** meaning to centralize administrative authority and responsibility in the hands of one person—the governor. Boards and commissions were consolidated into a more manageable number of departments headed by a secretary appointed by the governor. Urbanization, the Great Depression, and the growth of federal programs administered by the states placed increasing burdens on state governments. To meet these responsibilities, governors have been given stronger budget authority and four-year terms. Changes were made by state constitutional conventions or by legislative action. Reapportionment reduced the influence of rural legislators, who historically were hostile toward executive authority. Another factor helping to strengthen the role of governors has been the general acceptance of the view that chief executives should maximize their powers in the manner of Franklin D. Roosevelt. The presidential model still continues to have a strong influence on people's willingness to support strong executive authority at the state level and on people's expectations that governors should be able to solve problems. Since the 1980s, the retreat of congressional policy making has resulted in a more dominant role for governors as policy makers, especially in the areas of health and welfare.

WHO BECOMES GOVERNOR?

The traditional image of the typical governor as a white male lawyer in his late forties is still fairly accurate, but it should not obscure the slowly increasing diversity of political leaders who are now becoming governors. Beginning in the twentieth century, several women were elected governor to succeed their husbands. But it was not until 1974 that a woman (Ella Grasso in Connecticut) was elected governor on her own. With the election of Alaska's first woman governor in 2006, twenty-two states have elected women governors. Arizona, whose incumbent governor is a woman, has elected three women, the most of any state. In 2006, five women incumbents were reelected governor. That brought the total of women governors to nine, the most at any time in the United States.

Since the mid-1970s an African American and three Hispanics have been elected governor. In 1996, Gary Locke of Washington became the first Asian American governor on the U.S. mainland. Hawaii has had three Asian American governors. Douglas Wilder, who served as governor of Virginia from 1989 to 1993, was the first African American governor. In 2006, Deval Patrick was elected governor of Massachusetts, becoming the second African American elected governor and ending sixteen years of Republican control of the governorship in a very Democratic state. Jerry Apodaca, Toney Anaya, and Bill Richardson in New Mexico and Bob Martinez in Florida are the only Hispanics to serve as governor since the mid-1970s. The major barrier faced by minority candidates for governor is that in no state do African Americans or Hispanics comprise more than 40 percent of the population.

In states with strong party organizations (e.g., Illinois and Massachusetts), a pattern of service in the state legislature or in another statewide elected position, such as attorney general, has been a common background for governors. Gubernatorial expert Thad Beyle notes that more than half the governors in office from 1900 to 2003 began their political careers as state legislators or in law enforcement.[4] Beyle found that 29 percent of lieutenant governors who ran for governor in the period 1977–2005 won, as did 25 percent of attorneys general. And about 12 percent of those elected had not held any elected position.[5] Beyle contends that governors who have worked their way up from local to statewide office are the most successful in office. In contrast to governors with limited political experience, these governors understand better how to form effective political alliances.

Because of limits on consecutive terms, an increasing number of former governors are among those running for governor. Although nearly all governors have had some previous experience in government, some, like Ronald Reagan and George W. Bush, were elected in their first try for public office. A measure of the increased status of governors is that since 1980 an increasingly larger number of people have left Congress to run for governor.

As noted in Chapter 4, in recent years about three-fourths of governors who were eligible for reelection decided to run and about three-fourths of them were successful. In the past twelve years only two incumbent governors have lost primary elections. Going into the 2006 elections, Republicans held twenty-eight of the nation's governorships. Democrats retained fourteen governorships, Republicans retained sixteen, one incumbent Republican (in Maryland) was defeated, and Democrats won five open elections. As a result, Democrats held a 28-22 advantage after the elections. Republicans had held a majority of the nation's governorships since 1994, winning about 60 percent of elections between then and 2005. As noted in Chapter 4, thirty-four states hold gubernatorial elections in the off-year between presidential elections. Because the governors of Vermont and New Hampshire serve two-year terms, their elections also are in the even-numbered off-year between presidential elections.

INSTITUTIONAL POWERS OF THE GOVERNOR

In a much-cited analysis of governors, political scientist Joseph A. Schlesinger studied formal gubernatorial powers and developed an overall measure of the relative power of governors in the fifty states.[6] **Institutional powers** are those powers that can be found in a state's constitution or statutes. The more important powers are those dealing with tenure potential, appointment of executive branch officials, control over preparing the budget, and ability to veto legislation.

Thad Beyle has updated and expanded Schlesinger's work on the formal powers of the governor.[7] Beyle includes the four powers discussed, adds two more—the number of separately elected officials in the executive branch and the party that controls the legislature—and then compares the *institutional* powers of the governors in all fifty states. States are rated on a scale of 1 to 5, with 5 representing governors who have the strongest power. The results, including an overall average for each state, are in Table 6-1.

The states where governors had the strongest formal powers in 2005, as measured on the Beyle scale, were West Virginia, New Jersey, and New York, all 4.1. Eight other states were nearly as strong. The weakest state was Vermont (2.5), with Rhode Island, New Hampshire, and Oklahoma slightly less weak. Beyle notes that the overall power of governors increased by 12.5 percent from 1960 to 2005. The largest gain (61 percent) was in veto power, as several governors gained the item veto. The largest decline (17 percent) was in party control over legislatures, largely due to Republican gains in southern state legislatures.

TABLE 6-1 Governors' Institutional Powers, 2005

State	SEP	TP	AP	BP	VP	PC	Total	Score
AL	1	4	3	3	4	2	17	2.8
AK	5	4	3.5	3	5	4	24.5	4.1
AZ	2.5	4	4	3	5	2	20.5	3.4
AR	2.5	4	3	3	4	2	18.5	3.1
CA	1	4	4	3	5	2	19	3.2
CO	4	4	3.5	3	5	2	21.5	3.6
CT	4	5	2.5	3	5	2	21.5	3.6
DE	2.5	4	3.5	3	5	3	21	3.5
FL	3	4	2.5	3	5	4	21.5	3.6
GA	1	4	2	3	5	4	19	3.2
HI	5	4	2.5	3	5	1	20.5	3.4
ID	2	4	2	3	5	5	21	3.5
IL	3	5	3	3	5	4	23	3.8
IN	3	4	2.5	3	2	4	18.5	3.1
IA	3	5	3	3	5	3	22	3.7
KS	3	4	3	3	5	2	20	3.3
KY	3	4	4	3	4	3	21	3.5
LA	1	4	3.5	3	5	4	20.5	3.4
ME	5	4	3.5	3	2	4	21.5	3.6
MD	4	4	2.5	5	5	2	22.5	3.8
MA	4	5	3.5	3	5	1	21.5	3.6
MI	4	4	3.5	3	5	2	21.5	3.6
MN	4	5	2.5	3	5	3	22.5	3.8
MS	1.5	4	2	3	5	2	17.5	2.9
MO	2.5	4	3	3	5	4	21.5	3.6
MT	3	4	3	3	5	3.5	21.5	3.6
NE	4	4	3	4	5	3	23	3.8
NV	2.5	4	3.5	3	2	3	18	3.0
NH	5	2	3	3	2	2	17	2.8
NJ	5	4	3.5	3	5	4	24.5	4.1
NM	3	4	3	3	5	4	22	3.7
NY	4	5	3.5	4	5	3	24.5	4.1
NC	1	4	3.5	3	2	4	17.5	2.9
ND	3	5	3.5	3	5	4	23.5	3.9
OH	4	4	3.5	3	5	4	23.5	3.9
OK	1	4	1	3	5	3	17	2.8
OR	2	4	3	3	5	3	20	3.3
PA	4	4	4	3	5	2	22	3.7
RI	2.5	4	3	3	2	1	15.5	2.6
SC	1	4	2	2	5	4	18	3.0
SD	3	4	3.5	3	5	4	22.5	3.8
TN	4.5	4	4	3	4	3	22.5	3.8

	SEP	TP	AP	BP	VP	PC	Total	Score
TX	2	5	1	2	5	4	19	3.2
UT	4	5	3	3	5	4	24	4.0
VT	2.5	2	3.5	3	2	2	15	2.5
VA	2.5	3	3.5	3	5	2	19	3.2
WA	1	5	3.5	3	5	4	21.5	3.6
WV	2.5	4	4	5	5	4	24.5	4.1
WI	3	5	2	3	5	2	20	3.3
WY	2	4	3.5	3	5	1	18.5	3.1
50-state average	2.9	4.1	3.1	3.1	4.5	3.0	20.7	3.5

Notes: SEP—Separately elected executive branch officials: 5 = only governor or governor/lieutenant governor team elected; 4.5 = governor or governor/lieutenant governor team, with one other elected official; 4 = governor/lieutenant governor team with some process officials (attorney general, secretary of state, treasurer, auditor) elected; 3 = governor/lieutenant governor team with process officials, and some major and minor policy officials elected; 2.5 = governor (no team) with six or fewer officials elected, but none are major policy officials; 2 = governor (no team) with six or fewer officials elected, including one major policy official; 1.5 = governor (no team) with six or fewer officials elected, but two are major policy officials; 1 = governor (no team) with seven or more process and several major policy officials elected. [Source: Council of State Governments (CSG), *Book of the States 2003* (2003): 201–206.]

TP—Tenure potential of governors: 5 = 4-year term, no restraint on reelection; 4.5 = 4-year term, only three terms permitted; 4 = 4-year term, only two terms permitted; 3 = 4-year term, no consecutive election permitted; 2 = 2-year term, no restraint on reelection; 1 = 2-year term, only two terms permitted. [Source: CSG, *The Book of the States 2003*, (2003): 183–184.]

AP—Governor's appointment powers in six major functional areas: corrections, K–12 education, health, highways/transportation, public utilities regulation, and welfare. The six individual office scores are totaled and then averaged and rounded to the nearest .5 for the state score. 5 = governor appoints, no other approval needed; 4 = governor appoints, a board, council, or legislature approves; 3 = someone else appoints, governor approves or shares appointment; 2 = someone else appoints, governor and others approve; 1 = someone else appoints, no approval or confirmation needed. [Source: CSG, *The Book of the States 2003* (2003): 201–206.]

BP—Governor's budget power: 5 = governor has full responsibility, legislature may not increase executive budget; 4 = governor has full responsibility, legislature can increase by special majority vote or subject to item veto; 3 = governor has full responsibility, legislature has unlimited power to change executive budget; 2 = governor shares responsibility, legislature has unlimited power to change executive budget; 1 = governor shares responsibility with other elected official, legislature has unlimited power to change executive budget. [Source: CSG, *The Book of the States 2003* (2003): 188–189, 392–393, and National Conference of State Legislatures, "Limits on Authority of Legislature to Change Budget" (1998).]

VP—Governor's veto power: 5 = governor has item veto and a special majority vote of the legislature is needed to override a veto (three-fifths of legislators elected or two-thirds of legislators present); 4 = has item veto with a majority of the legislators elected needed to override; 3 = has item veto with only a majority of the legislators present needed to override; 2 = no item veto, with a special legislative majority needed to override a regular veto; 1 = no item veto, only a simple legislative majority needed to override a regular veto. [Source: CSG, *The Book of the States 2003* (2003): 145–147, 188–189.]

PC—Gubernatorial party control: The governor's party—5 = has a substantial majority (75% or more) in both houses of the legislature; 4 = has a simple majority in both houses (under 75%), or a substantial majority in one house and a simple majority in the other; 3 = split control in the legislature or a nonpartisan legislature; 2 = has a simple minority (25% or more) in both houses, or a simple minority in one and a substantial minority (under 25%) in the other; 1 = has a substantial minority in both houses. [Source: NCSL Web page and report on the 2003 legislative elections.]

Total—sum of the scores on the six individual indices. Score—total divided by 6 to keep 5-point scale.

Source: Thad Beyle, December 31, 2004. Available at www.unc.edu/~beyle.

As we will see later in this chapter, there are several factors that allow governors with weak institutional powers to be strong leaders in their states. These include a range of personal powers, having both chambers of legislatures controlled by their party (party control is separated from institutional powers by some political scientists), and the governor's ability to respond well to crisis situations that are beyond his or her control.

Tenure Potential

As noted earlier in this chapter, governors historically had short terms of office. In ten of the original thirteen states, the governor was limited to a term of one year. And the others had two- and three-year terms. States moved first to two-year terms (by the 1840s) and gradually to four-year terms, which today can be found in forty-eight states. After Arkansas and Rhode Island switched to four-year terms, only New Hampshire and Vermont have two-year terms. As far as length of term is concerned, governors with four-year terms are high on tenure potential.

Another side of tenure potential is term limits, which has recently been an important issue with state legislators (see Chapter 5). Some states follow the model of the Twenty-second Amendment to the U.S. Constitution, which says that a person can be elected only twice to the presidency. In these states, governors can serve only two terms; for obvious reasons this type of term limitation is known as an absolute two-term limit. Other states limit the number of *consecutive* terms, usually two, so that it is possible to serve two four-year terms, leave the office for one term, and then serve another two terms. Only Virginia has a one-term limit. Overall, governors are relatively equal in tenure potential: Thirty-eight states have four-year terms and some form of restraint on reelection. Nine four-year-term states and the two states with two-year terms have no restraint of any kind on reelection. Of course, governors with four-year terms and no restraint on reelection have the highest tenure potential.

Tenure potential is a measure of the possible number of years a governor could stay in office. Why is tenure potential important to a governor's power? The ability to succeed oneself in office means that the governor will not become a **lame duck,** that is, have diminished power because he or she will soon leave office and cannot run again. Legislators cannot ignore a governor in the fourth year of his or her term if he or she may run for reelection and win and be around another four years. Shorter tenure lessens the ability of governors to attain leadership positions in groups such as the National Governors Association that can have an influence on public policy issues vital to the states. Also, a four-year term allows governors time to prove themselves: Policies enacted during their first two years (e.g., something controversial such as a tax increase) can be evaluated by reelection time two years later (whether any benefits have been produced by the tax increase).

In forty-nine states governors can have their terms ended by impeachment. Typically, the process is similar to presidential impeachment and removal, where action begins in the House and the Senate holds a trial in which a two-thirds vote is required for removal. Only four governors were impeached and removed in the twentieth century, the last in 1987 (Arizona). As we would expect, when threatened with impeachment or when facing criminal charges, several governors have resigned. The most recent was the governor of Connecticut, who was threatened with impeachment and resigned in 2004. Governors also can have their tenure ended by recall (see Chapter 4), but only two governors, including Gray Davis of California in 2003, have been recalled.

Appointing Power

Governors' **appointing power** is strongest when they alone can name people to head (usually called a secretary or director) the more important agencies in the executive branch such as corrections, public safety, education, agriculture, environment, and economic development. Appointive power diminishes when one or two houses of the legislature must approve appointments or if the appointment is made by a department director. If the position is elective or is filled by a board or commission, then the governor's formal power is reduced. As will be discussed later in this section, some states have a large number of separately elected state officials. This is why the governor of Texas ranks so low in appointive power. The reduction of separately elected officials was an ongoing reform in many states during the twentieth century. Even after widespread reform, most governors' power to appoint still falls in the middle of the Beyle scale.

Gubernatorial appointive power grew from weak beginnings, and it still varies greatly among states. There is variation not only among states but also within states. Even in states where the governor's appointing authority is strong, some appointments will need the approval of the senate and some will probably be made by a board or commission acting on its own.

A strong appointing power is important because governors free to appoint officials to top-level posts in the executive branch can select people whose political views are similar to theirs and who will feel a sense of obligation to the governor who appointed them. This will help a governor obtain action on his or her priorities. The downside of the power to appoint is that governors become responsible for the actions of their appointees. In nearly all administrations, governors, like presidents, are embarrassed (or worse) by the management mistakes or the ethical lapses of their appointees.

Budgetary Power

Early in the twentieth century, most states instituted an **executive budget.** This means that the governor and officials appointed directly by the governor have full responsibility to *prepare* the state budget. Governors' staffs almost always include a budget director and professional assistants. As noted, the budget staff reviews requests for funds from all state agencies and, with the governor exercising final approval, prepares a budget that is then acted upon by the legislature. In only about 10 states, including Texas, does the governor share responsibility for budget preparation with the state legislature or with other elected executive branch officials. In other states the governor's budget serves as the basis for legislative discussion.

Even when governors have strong formal powers, they find that their control does not give them complete discretion in proposing where money should be spent because more than 50 percent of the budget must provide funds for specific purposes (such as gasoline taxes for highway construction and maintenance). Also, the growth of federal mandates has limited states' ability to control their expenditures.

Only in West Virginia does the governor have full budget power, but most states have centralized budgets that give governors power to shift funds among departments, deny funds to some areas, and insert initiatives for new programs by identifying funds for them. Even as governors have gained budget authority, their power on the Beyle scale has declined since 1960 because many legislatures have gained unlimited power to change governors' proposed budgets.[8]

Veto Power

Governors are participants in the legislative process because they must sign bills passed by the legislature before they can become state law. After voters in North Carolina approved a veto referendum in 1996, all governors now have the power to veto legislation. Governors **veto** a bill by returning it to the legislature unsigned, along with their objections. The veto makes the governor a participant in the legislative process. If the legislature votes to override a veto, the bill becomes law without the governor's signature.

Budget problems, growing out of the Great Depression, brought an expansion of veto power that gave governors a way to avoid the difficult choice of accepting or rejecting an entire appropriations bill. The power of the **item veto** permits governors in forty-three states to veto individual items in appropriation bills. Several governors can exercise a conditional or **amendatory veto** in which they veto a bill but indicate what changes would make the bill acceptable to them. When governors, as in New Jersey and Illinois, have both an item veto and an amendatory veto, they are especially strong. Like the president, governors in fifteen states can use a **pocket veto:** They do not take any action on a bill near the end of a legislative session, and then if the legislature adjourns the bill is considered vetoed.

An extreme example of the veto power was found in Wisconsin where Republican Governor Tommy Thompson (1987–2001), taking literally his constitutional power to veto appropriation bills "in whole or in part," changed the meaning of sentences by vetoing words such as "shall" and "not." Thompson even struck out individual letters to make new words, and new laws. Local commentators labeled this the "Vanna White veto" (named after Vanna White, who appears on the television show *Wheel of Fortune*). During his first eight years in office, Thompson issued more than 1,500 partial vetoes. From 2003 to 2006, Governor Jim Doyle vetoed about one of every nine bills passed by the Wisconsin legislature. Curiously, no Wisconsin governor has had a veto overridden since 1985. In the early 1990s a federal court found the partial veto "quirky," but not unconstitutional. However, a constitutional amendment has somewhat lessened the veto power of the governor in Wisconsin.

As state legislatures have become stronger policy making bodies, able to challenge the governor on nearly every issue, the use of the item veto has increased. As a result, governors are more likely to veto bills to remove policy directives than to impose fiscal restraint. Overuse of the item veto can wreck havoc with legislative appropriations, and it greatly increases formal confrontations between governors and legislatures.

Typically, the governor's veto must be overridden by at least a two-thirds vote of the elected membership of both houses of the legislature (some states specify two-thirds of the members present on an override vote rather than elected membership). This means that the governor's veto will be sustained if he or she can persuade only a small percentage of the legislators in one house not to vote to override. A two-thirds vote is normally required to override an item veto.

In the 1990s governors vetoed about 4 percent of bills passed by legislatures and of those about 2 percent were overridden. Depending on the partisan makeup of the legislature, the nature of the state, and the attitude of the governor, the use of the veto varies greatly among the states. In the 1990s New Mexico's Republican governor Gary

Johnson vowed to veto any bill that increased the size of government. In one session Johnson vetoed 200 of 424 bills passed by the Democratic legislature.[9] Many of his vetoes were overridden and Johnson's tenure in office was largely ineffective. Still, he was reelected and left office in 2003 because of term limits. Governor Pete Wilson (1991–1999) of California vetoed about 20 percent of all bills sent to him and none was overridden. At the other extreme, in 1992–1993 the governor of Tennessee signed all bills sent to him.[10] In most states, if the governor's party has at least one-third of the seats, it is unlikely that vetoes will be overridden. As legislatures have become more assertive in the last 30 years, the percentage of vetoes overridden has increased.

Often a governor's threat of a veto can cause legislators to change the content of a bill before they finish acting on it. Unfortunately, no statistics are compiled on the number of times governors threaten to veto and with what success, but it is another tool a skillful governor can use to persuade legislators to modify bills so that they are more to the governor's liking. By threatening to use an item veto to block funds for a pet project of a legislator, the governor often can effectively pressure that member to support another of the governor's proposals or punish him or her for a previous vote.

Separately Elected Officials

Although states have steadily enacted reforms to reduce the number of separately elected officials, most continue to elect about a half dozen statewide officials plus the governor. These range from attorneys general in forty-three states to such positions as the heads of agriculture, education, and insurance in a few states. Problems arise when separately elected officials have partisan policy differences with the governor and choose to pursue their own agendas.

Only five states employ the presidential model in which only the governor and lieutenant governor are elected statewide. As with many other issues of gubernatorial power, the two newest states, Alaska and Hawaii, give their governor strong authority and follow the presidential model of statewide elections. At the other extreme, Beyle reports that in eight states, typically in the South, seven or more process and major policy officials are elected.

Party Control

Increasingly, voters have elected a governor of one party and the majority of at least one legislative chamber of the other party. Similar to politics at the national level, divided party control can lead to stalemated state government when, as noted, the governor's use of the veto increases. However, in most cases political scientists have found that divided government does not reduce legislative productivity.[11] However, as noted in Chapter 3, governors in divided states are less likely to pursue controversial issues. Voters seem to like the restraint that divided government brings. But divided government may affect the kind of legislation that is enacted. For example, a Democratic governor dealing with a Republican-controlled legislature is likely to be forced to compromise on some of his party's liberal principles.

Legislative expert Alan Rosenthal points out that while governors may have difficulty getting support from members of their own party, there often is a tendency to be loyal to the governor because an unpopular governor may cause voters to oppose legislators of his or her party.[12] As a result, governors may be able to lead their legislature even when members of their party dislike some of their proposals. As we would expect, governors are most successful when their party controls both chambers of the legislature and when there are a number of competitive districts in which their party's legislators cannot afford to lose votes. After the 2006 elections, Democrats controlled the executive and legislative branches in fifteen states, Republicans had united control in ten states, twenty-four states were split, and Nebraska has a nonpartisan legislature.

Of course, independent and third-party governors (as in Alaska, Connecticut, Maine, and Minnesota in the 1990s) always must deal with legislatures controlled by opposition political forces. Some of them, like Lowell Weicker of Connecticut (1991–1994) have been very effective legislative leaders. Others may be less adroit.

Following Ross Perot's bids for president in 1992 and 1996, Jesse Ventura ran for governor of Minnesota in 1998 on the Reform Party ticket. He was elected with 37 percent of the vote, getting strong support from young voters and those who previously had not been politically active. The colorful former professional wrestler had to deal with a legislature in which party control of the house and senate was split between Democrats and Republicans. Early in 2000 Ventura broke from the Reform Party to become an independent.

Few governors have been as critical of their legislators as Ventura, who once referred to Minnesota legislators as "gutless cowards." Ventura used his weekly radio program to go directly to the people and stir up dissatisfaction with the legislature. Still the governor's popularity steadily declined and Ventura chose not to run for reelection in 2002. Since the 2002 elections of a Republican in Minnesota and a Democrat in Maine, all governors have represented one of the two major parties.

There may be a tendency for "celebrity governors," who come into office without experience working with political parties, to play the "outside game" by going directly to the people. Arnold Schwarzenegger has used his celebrity status to threaten the California legislature, but he also has made efforts to negotiate with Democratic members of the legislature. However, in 2003 Schwarzenegger tried to bypass the Democratic-controlled legislature by supporting four initiatives that included placing severe spending limits on state government. All four failed and his approval rating dropped from 63 percent to 35 percent. Schwarzenegger responded with an apology to the people of California—"I didn't hear the majority of Californians when they were telling me they didn't like the special election. I barreled ahead anyway when I should have listened. I have absorbed my defeat and I have learned my lesson." The governor then set to work with the legislature supporting bills that raised the minimum wage and imposed strict standards for limiting greenhouse gases. He was reelected in 2006 with 56 percent of the vote.

Personal Power of Governors

Thad Beyle also has developed a five-point scale to measure the **personal power** of governors. This refers to personal attributes such as job performance and to situational factors such as the margin of victory by which the governor was elected. By their nature, personal power scores for any state change frequently and are more variable than institutional power scores.

The following are the four indicators of personal power that Beyle identifies.[13] First, the electoral mandate, or margin of victory, suggests that the larger the margin, the

TABLE 6-2 The Personal Powers of the Governors, 2005

State	EM	AL	PF	GP	GPP
Alabama	2	3	5	1	2.8
Alaska	5	3	5	2	3.8
Arizona	2	5	5	3	3.8
Arkansas	4	5	3	4	4.0
California	5	1	5	5	4.0
Colorado	5	5	3	5	4.5
Connecticut	1	3	5	5	3.5
Delaware	3	5	3	na	3.7
Florida	5	1	3	4	3.3
Georgia	3	3	5	3	3.5
Hawaii	3	2	5	4	3.5
Idaho	5	3	3	3	3.5
Illinois	4	3	5	4	4.0
Indiana	3	1	5	na	3.0
Iowa	4	5	5	4	4.5
Kansas	4	5	5	na	4.7
Kentucky	4	3	5	4	4.0
Louisiana	3	5	5	5	4.5
Maine	3	3	5	4	3.8
Maryland	3	3	5	4	3.8
Massachusetts	3	1	5	4	3.3
Michigan	3	5	5	5	4.5
Minnesota	4	3	5	4	4.0
Mississippi	4	1	5	na	3.3
Missouri	3	5	5	na	4.3
Montana	3	1	5	na	3.0
Nebraska	5	2	3	5	3.8
Nevada	5	1	3	4	3.3
New Hampshire	2	1	5	na	2.7
New Jersey	1	3	2	na	2.0
New Mexico	5	3	5	na	4.3
New York	5	3	5	3	4.0
North Carolina	5	5	3	4	4.3
North Dakota	5	1	5	5	4.0
Ohio	5	5	3	3	4.0
Oklahoma	2	3	5	na	3.3
Oregon	3	5	5	3	4.0
Pennsylvania	4	2	5	4	3.8
Rhode Island	4	1	5	5	3.8
South Carolina	4	3	5	na	4.0
South Dakota	5	3	5	5	4.5
Tennessee	3	2	5	5	3.8

(Continued)

TABLE 6-2 *(Continued)*					
State	EM	AL	PF	GP	GPP
Texas	5	5	5	2	4.3
Utah	5	1	5	na	3.7
Vermont	5	5	5	3	4.5
Virginia	3	1	1	4	2.3
Washington	2	5	5	na	4.0
West Virginia	5	5	5	na	5.0
Wisconsin	3	5	5	5	4.5
Wyoming	2	1	5	na	2.7
50-state average	3.6	3.1	4.5	3.9	3.8 [189.2]

Notes: EM—Governor's electoral mandate: 5 = landslide win of 11 or more points; 4 = comfortable majority of 6 to 10 points; 3 = narrow majority of 3 to 5 points; 2 = tight win of 0 to 2 points or a plurality win of under 50%; 1 = succeeded to office. [Source: Author's data, www.unc.edu/-beyle.]

AL—Governor's position on the state's political ambition ladder: 5 = steady progression; 4 = former governors; 3 = legislative leaders or members of Congress; 2 = substate position to governor; 1 = governorship is first elective office. [Source: National Governors' Association Web site, individual governors' Web sites in each state and author's data.]

PF—The personal future of the governor: 5 = early in term, can run again; 4 = late in term, can run again; 3 = early in term, term limited; 2 = succeeded to office, can run for election; 1 = late in final term. [Source: CSG, *The Book of the States 2004* (2004) and author's data.]

GP—Gubernatorial job performance rating in public opinion polls: 5 = over 60% positive job approval rating; 4 = 50–59% positive job approval rating; 3 = 40–49% positive job approval rating; 2 = 30–39% positive job approval rating; 1 = less than 30% positive job approval rating; na = no polling data available. [Source: Author's data.]

GPP—Governor's personal powers' index score, the sum of the scores for EM, AL, PF, GP divided by 4 and rounded to the nearest tenth, except for those states without a governor's job performance rating, for which the sum is divided by 3 and rounded to the nearest tenth.

Source: Thad Beyle, December 9, 2005. Available at www.unc.edu/-beyle.

stronger the governor will be. Second, position on the state's ambition ladder suggests that governors who have worked their way up by holding lower offices will be stronger because of their understanding of how to work with people in state government. Third, the personal future as governor suggests that governors serving early in their terms and/or those that can run again will be stronger than others at the ends of their terms. Fourth, governors with high performance ratings, as measured by how the public and those in government rate the governor, will be stronger. Regarding personal powers, there are many exceptions to the general rules, especially among the first three categories. For example, some governors with narrow margins of victory turn out to be much stronger leaders than those who won by a landslide.

As shown in Table 6-2, as of 2005, governors with the highest personal power scores were in West Virginia (5.0 on a scale of 1 to 5), Kansas (4.7), and six other states all with 4.5 scores. The lowest were in New Jersey (2.0), Virginia (2.3), Wyoming (2.7), and New Hampshire (2.7). When personal power scores were added to institutional power scores, the strongest governors were in West Virginia (9.1), South Dakota (8.3), and Iowa (8.2). The weakest were in New Hampshire (5.5), Virginia (5.5), and Alabama (5.6).

ROLES OF THE GOVERNOR

Chief Legislator

Identifying formal powers of governors is important, but it does not reveal what happens when men and women use these powers during their tenure, especially in their relationship with the legislative branch where only one of the formal powers—the veto—can be used directly. Also, lists of formal powers measure only *potential* effectiveness. Bad economic times, for example, may seriously limit the initiatives taken by a governor, even though he or she may have considerable formal power. But the most effective opposition to a governor's efforts to change policies resides right in the capitol building with the governor—the state legislature. Governors must persuade the legislature that what they want to accomplish is what the legislature, or at least a majority of its members, should want to accomplish also.

Like the president, governors bring a different political perspective to office than do legislators. Unlike individual legislators, governors represent the entire state and they are full-time public officials. Although power may be diffused among 100 legislators in most states, it is centralized in the governor.

Alan Rosenthal points out that a governor's style and techniques regarding how he or she deals with the legislature can impact greatly his or her effectiveness in dealing with the legislature.[14] Rosenthal says legislators like governors who provide access to them. Some governors have an open door policy that includes returning calls made to their residences. Of course, legislators like governors who reach out to them as they develop their agenda. Not surprisingly, legislators work best with governors they can trust when commitments are made early in the legislative process. As a final step, legislators want governors to share credit with them for developing policy. We might ask, as in any type of personal relationship, Why wouldn't governors want to do all these things? Why go out of your way to generate ill will? Most successful governors and mayors are able to overcome partisan and personal differences and work effectively with legislators.

State constitutions authorize governors to recommend measures to the legislature that they think should become law. This may seem to be rather innocuous, but it is the basis of the power of initiation. Initiation is the ability to set the policy agenda for the state, that is, to identify those issues that need to be addressed first. Governors begin the process of setting the agenda in their inaugural address, delivered at the start of their term. In this address, governors can set out broad themes and goals for their new administration and, because of media attention to the event, can communicate to the people. Annual **"state of the state" messages** from the governor to the legislature are more specific than inaugural addresses. These messages contain the governor's priorities for the upcoming legislative session and are referred to as the governor's legislative program. These proposals are general statements that will have to be drafted into bills and introduced by legislators, usually members of the leadership, and then considered by both houses. The fact that a bill is part of the governor's legislative program guarantees that it will receive serious consideration by the legislature and, in most cases, increases the likelihood that the bill will become law. Governors may also focus attention on a particular issue by calling the legislature into special session to deal with politically difficult problems. Because many legislatures meet for short regular sessions, the ability to call members back into session gives governors a means of exerting considerable pressure on legislators who are reluctant to face an issue.

Governors, such as George Pataki of New York, tend to be most effective when they limit the number of their legislative priorities. For example, each legislative session Zell Miller of Georgia (1991–1998) tried to present three or four proposals that had strong public support. In contrast, Mario Cuomo of New York proposed about 150 measures in 1989. Cuomo laid out an ambitious agenda and then abandoned it.[15]

Governors can influence the agenda through the creation of commissions or task forces to study a problem and make recommendations to solve it. Members of this type of commission are appointed by the governor and represent the governor's office and relevant interest groups. They may also contain key legislators and distinguished private citizens. Commission recommendations usually support the policy direction the governor wants to take: After all, it is the governor who created the commission. Because the commission works over several months, it is quite likely that it will attract media attention, which also may create some public support for its final product. In addition, members of the commission can be helpful in lobbying for legislative approval of the recommendations. The commission approach sounds easy, but it takes a skillful governor to balance the membership so that it is not viewed as a group that will simply get out the rubber stamp and "approve" everything the governor wants. If this is the case, the commission will be viewed as too one-sided, and it will be of little help in gaining legislative support of the governor's ideas. Rosenthal notes that commissions were popular in many public education reforms in the 1980s. Bill Clinton, as governor of Arkansas, used recommendations from a legislatively created committee on educational standards, chaired by his wife, Hillary Rodham Clinton, to pass a tax increase to pay for improvements in primary and secondary education.[16]

The power of publicity is similar to the power of initiation in that it sounds easy to do. Every governor should simply go directly to the public and, with public backing, get most everything he or she wants through the legislature. But it is not that easy, even if governors have the requisite communication skills. Rosenthal cautions that governors cannot "make use of this power on each and every issue; to do so would be self-defeating, for at some point they would no longer be taken seriously by the press or public."[17] Governors cannot continuously try to drum up public support and expect that the public will always respond. Still, governors are much more effective than legislators in getting media attention.

In a manner similar to the president, all governors are party leaders, though not in the sense that they occupy a formal position in their party's organization. Rather, they are the informal head of their party by virtue of the fact that they occupy the highest elected position in the state. At one time, governors working with the chairperson of their state party could maintain party discipline in the legislature through the use of patronage appointments to fill state jobs and the promise of help from the party in primary and general elections. But those days are long gone in most states: Patronage appointments are fewer, and candidates frequently run for the legislature without the help of anyone in their party. Still, certain political "plums," such as patronage jobs, awards of state contracts, and support for local projects, continue to be used by governors to get legislative votes for their proposals.

Many governors meet weekly or even daily with party leaders while the legislature is in session, and they often give special attention to individual legislators. In states where legislators are term limited, governors no longer have the advantage of dealing with house speakers and senate presidents who have acquired power by virtue of many years in their position and over the years have worked well with governors of both parties.

Chief of State

As chief of state, the governor performs a variety of ceremonial functions and acts as official spokesperson for the people of the state. Ceremonial functions include dedicating new highways and bridges, attending funerals and weddings, greeting distinguished visitors to the state capitol, proclaiming special days or weeks, and attending football games. Although much of this activity appears trivial and undoubtedly bores many governors, it does reap political rewards in terms of publicity and image building. Next to working with the legislature, ceremonial duties are the most time-consuming activity for most governors.

Governors act as economic advocates for their states, expending time and energy to lure business and manufacturing concerns from other states and to encourage plant investment from foreign corporations. At the urging of governors, legislatures have offered major economic concessions to foreign automobile manufacturers to build assembly plants in their states.

Following President Clinton's controversial pardons as he left office, there has been more scrutiny of gubernatorial clemency orders. Some 2,000 orders are issued annually by governors. They include **pardons** that release a person convicted of a crime from the legal penalties, and **commutations** that reduce the severity of punishment for a crime. Most of the controversial actions are done as governors prepare to leave office, and/or they involve clemency that appears to have been motivated by friendship or political advantage. Governor Ray Blanton of Tennessee granted about fifty pardons as he was leaving office, and several members of his staff were arrested for extortion before his successor was sworn in three days early. Governors in about two-thirds of the states have broad authority to issue pardons. In the other states gubernatorial power is shared with a state clemency board or exercised by a board whose members are appointed by the governor.

In 2003 outgoing Governor George Ryan of Illinois pardoned four condemned men outright and commuted the sentences of the remaining 164 men and four women on death row. Ryan was the fourth governor in American history to empty death row as he departed office, but the numbers involved in Illinois dwarfed all other clemency actions. In 2006 Ryan was sentenced to jail as part of a broad federal corruption case that was not related to his pardons. Among other charges, prosecutors said Ryan had put a "for sale" sign on his door. In return for political favors and state business, Ryan received money and other rewards totaling about $170,000.

Commander-in-Chief

Although governors do not command a navy with nuclear-powered submarines or an air force with intercontinental ballistic missiles, they do have a commander-in-chief role as head of their state's National Guard (formerly called the state militia) until it is called into service by the president. The U.S. Constitution provides for a cooperative system in which states appoint officers (the state adjutant general is their commander) and Congress organizes, arms, and finances the Guard. Since 1916, the former militias have been organized as an auxiliary of the regular army subject to substantial national control. As its civilian commander-in-chief, the governor may call the Guard into service for such emergencies as floods, tornadoes, or urban riots. In the case study for Chapter 1, we noted negotiations between Governor Arnold Schwarzenegger and the Bush administration to send California National Guard troops to help patrol the Mexican border.

The record of the Guard in responding to civil disturbances has ranged from adequate to disastrous. Prior to World War II, the Guard often was used brutally to break up racial disturbances, labor strikes, and prison riots. Since then, the most noteworthy incident occurred in 1970 when Ohio National Guardsmen killed four students and injured others in responding to a demonstration against the Vietnam War at Kent State University. On a more positive note, the Guard has been effective (often invaluable) when dealing with natural disasters. Also, after two days of rioting in Los Angeles in 1992, when the Los Angeles police clearly had lost control of the situation, Guardsmen were posted on nearly every corner, and looting quickly diminished. About 300 National Guard troops remained in New Orleans to help maintain order a year after Hurricane Katrina hit the city.

Although governors traditionally have acted as crisis managers responding to natural disasters and various challenges to law and order, concern about homeland security since 9/11 has put a new emphasis on that role. As with presidents, governors are expected to provide leadership in a crisis and, if they fail to respond effectively to disorder, it will mean a significant drop in public approval and often put their reelection in doubt.

Chief Administrator

As chief administrator, the governor is responsible for the management of all state administrative agencies. As noted, the governor's administrative authority in the early part of the twentieth century was not equal to the responsibility associated with a person who is a chief executive. Agencies in the executive branch were actually controlled by boards or commissions with several members. This meant that, if a governor wanted an agency to take some action, he or she would first have to convince the members of the board, because it was the board that had direct control over the agency's activities. This awkward administrative arrangement occurs less frequently today because administrative efficiency reforms have eliminated boards and commissions and reduced the number of agencies by consolidating them into a smaller number of departments. Nearly all states have a **cabinet** form of executive branch organization that concentrates authority and responsibility in the hands of the governor and creates a cabinet of department secretaries appointed by the governor who individually administer a department and collectively advise the governor. Cabinet size in 2006 ranged from seventy-five in New York to four in Florida.

Because of the increasing complexity of state government and the ever-broadening responsibilities of their office, governors have surrounded themselves with expanding numbers of staff personnel who provide both political and administrative assistance. In a large state a governor's staff of perhaps 100 people will include a press secretary, an executive secretary, a legal adviser, a speechwriter, a director of the budget, a commissioner of administration, and others assigned by the political party. Some staff will work as liaison with state, local, and federal agencies and as liaison to the state legislature to help guide the governor's program through the legislative process. Staff personnel tend to be young (in their thirties) and politically ambitious. Many are lawyers, and most staff members previously worked in the governor's campaign or in the campaigns of other candidates in their party.

In addition to serving in an administrative capacity, the governor's staff provides other more political services. The staff:

1. Serves as a research office to provide information and to help shape the governor's position on a wide range of policy issues
2. Serves as public relations specialists to do such things as write press releases and keep the governor posted on political developments that may affect how citizens perceive the governor
3. Handles the important tasks of answering the mail, controlling the governor's schedule, and determining who sees the governor

As with the president, the governor must guard against the dangers of an overprotective staff that isolates him or her from the world beyond the office. Reformers have often suggested that if governors would only adopt modern business management techniques, they would be able to manage public affairs much more effectively. However, this assumption overlooks some major differences between governors and private-sector chief executives. The governor's management task is much more difficult because the environment in which his or her decisions are made is more complex and less controllable. Even compared with large private businesses, the operations of states such as New York and California, or even Nebraska, are much more complex in terms of budget, number of personnel, and variety of functions.

Differences exist between managing state government and private enterprise that relate more directly to the political process. Governors must share power with legislative and judicial branches, and they must operate within a federal system in which the national government has substantial power. In addition, governors constantly keep in mind how management decisions might affect their future political aspirations.

ADMINISTRATION OF STATE AND LOCAL GOVERNMENT

As discussed in Chapter 1, the scope of state government activities has increased greatly during the twentieth century. As a result, state and local payrolls and numbers of employees now far outstrip those of the federal government. The number of state employees increased from less than 1 million in 1950 to 5.2 million in 2006 when there were 14.4 million local government employees and 2.8 million federal employees.

Employees of public agencies are part of what is commonly referred to as the **bureaucracy.** Bureaucracies are characterized as having a chain of command, with authority at the top of a hierarchy; a division of labor in which separate agencies perform specific tasks; and a set of formal rules that define how bureaucrats should respond in particular situations. The public (their customers) is to be treated in an impartial manner without political favoritism.

Bureaucrats are important because they implement policies that often have been approved by the legislature in skeletal form. As a result, bureaucrats have considerable discretion in the day-to-day administration of programs. This expansion of bureaucracy has placed increasing burdens of responsibility on governors and mayors, who historically have been denied strong powers as chief administrators. As noted, states have responded by giving governors control of budget preparation and the power to appoint and remove officials. In cities, charters have been amended to give mayors similar powers, and many cities have created the post of city manager.

Reorganization of Government

Despite changes, governors continue to be limited as administrators by the fragmented nature of state government. Most states failed to develop well-organized administrative structures because of the piecemeal growth of bureaucracy. As new functions were given to the states, the easiest response was to create a new state agency as visible proof to concerned citizens and interest groups that the state was "doing something" about the problem. Under these circumstances, the duties of each agency were not clearly defined, and the jurisdiction of new agencies often overlapped with that of already established agencies. Large cities had similar problems of fragmented organization. However, city reform came earlier than did state reform because of the adoption of strong-mayor–council and council-manager plans at the beginning of this century.

Because of the desire to take politics out of state government, many agencies were placed under the control of boards and commissions that acted independently of the governor. Agencies and departments performing similar tasks were nevertheless separated from one another with no one to serve as a coordinator. Communication between agencies was limited, and it was difficult for the governor or the legislature to know what the agencies were doing or who was responsible for their actions. Mergers were opposed by bureaucrats who sought to protect their jobs and by interest groups that were being aided by agencies they had helped create. At their peak in the 1950s, there were more than 100 boards, commissions, and departments in many states. There were even stories of dead men being appointed to serve on obscure boards.

The movement for administrative reform began in the 1890s but did not take hold in state government until after 1920, when administrative **reorganization** in Illinois under Governor Frank Lowden became known around the country. State reorganization commissions were appointed in several states, although there were few instances of substantial reform. The basic goal of the early reformers was to reduce the number of agencies and bring them more directly under the control of the governor. There was a general attempt to upgrade the bureaucracy by creating civil service commissions for merit appointment and by developing the executive budget. Following World War II and reform at the federal level, there was a revival of interest in structural reorganization. Now most governors can issue reorganization plans that take effect unless the legislature takes action to oppose them.

Since the mid-1970s, reorganization has been the most common response to correcting the problems of bureaucracy. Half the states completed major administrative overhauls from 1965 to 1990, some eliminating as many as 80 percent of their agencies.[18] Typically, states consolidate several similar agencies into one larger functional unit, such as transportation or welfare. The goal is to reduce duplication of services and to centralize administration in the hands of fewer department heads. In turn, governors are strengthened by giving them the power to appoint the heads of these reorganized superagencies. Reformers contend that these changes will produce more effective service delivery and that they will increase the accountability of bureaucrats to the public.

Because state administration is a highly politicized process, these apparently logical goals of centralization have met with strong resistance in virtually every state. Interest groups often prefer separation because of the strong control they have been able to maintain over state agencies. State legislators are able to use separate agencies to their political advantage, and they are inherently suspicious of moves to strengthen governors. Finally, by requiring specific allocation of matching funds to support categorical grants, federal grants-in-aid have encouraged the establishment of separate agencies.

Reorganization seldom has resulted in saving states money.[19] However, reorganizers argue that the main benefits will be more efficiency and more effective service delivery. Yet even here studies have shown that some services are provided best by small agencies in which a particular function is not subordinated to the main activities of the larger department. Even collegial administration (organizations headed by boards or commissions) may be as effective as single-headed departments. After his study of Texas, where collegial administration is very common, Charles Goodsell concluded that collegial administration has two major positive justifications.[20] It can improve the demographic and geographic representation of administration, and it has the ability to absorb political heat because of its representativeness. Goodsell believes that both legislators and career bureaucrats can "get off the hook" from constituent or interest group demands by referring critics to the independence of boards or commissions. Governors can sidestep attacks by arguing that a problem is out of their hands.

Clearly, reorganization does not always lead to greater efficiency or accountability. Centralization of authority may not work well for all organizations. Still, the extreme decentralization of state government, often bordering on chaos, has led to a lack of accountability, and to the extent that problems remain, good-government groups will continue to push for reorganization. Politically, it is in the best interest of governors to be able to consolidate their power through reorganization plans. Most academic observers conclude that the quality of administration has improved significantly, enabling states to respond to new demands placed on them by the devolution of authority from the national government.[21]

Richard Elling notes that government reorganization has been challenged by those who want to "reinvent government."[22] To them and other observers, reorganization is largely irrelevant to improving the delivery of government services. The problem, they say, is organization itself. The emphasis on hierarchy creates too many layers of government, which hinders communication and prevents flexible responses to new problems. As we will see later in this chapter, their recommendation is to replace bureaucratic government rather than to reform it.

Personnel Practices

The personnel systems of government agencies often affect their culture and expectations of employee behavior. Some agencies may discourage awarding middle-management positions to outsiders; others encourage transfers with experience in other types of organizations. When there is a strong preference to promote from within the agency, the bureaucrats who attain supervisory posts tend to be more rigid and less open to new ideas than are relative newcomers to the agency.

An agency's culture (and its policy orientation) is influenced by the **professional ideology** of its employees—that is, how they define their approach to the job in terms of their commitment to political neutrality and fairness in dealing with the public. For example, many social workers continue to place a strong emphasis on working with individual clients, whereas reformers contend that group political action is a more effective way to deal with the problems of the poor. In addition, professional codes of conduct may serve as a check on the abuse of administrative power.

As in any organization, newly hired employees in government undergo a period of socialization, in which they learn how they are expected to act within the framework of their agency's culture. Those who deviate from established norms usually encounter difficulty in working with their peers, and they may be denied promotions by their superiors. Although some agencies are program-oriented and encourage innovation, many are conservative and oppose change.

Personnel practices also include determining the kinds of people selected for government positions. Since the 1960s, the use of **affirmative action** programs has led to increased hiring of women and minorities in government agencies. Under affirmative action, special efforts are made to recruit, hire, and retain employees from groups of people that in the past have been discriminated against and have been underrepresented among government workers. The goal is to make the bureaucracy representative of the sexual, racial, and ethnic groups in the state or community. Greater diversity also has been achieved by gubernatorial appointments of women and minorities to top administrative posts.

In the past, ethnic background and/or political party connections played a major role in creating informal hiring qualifications that effectively screened applicants for jobs in many cities. This tended to exclude women and persons of color. Currently, although women and racial minority employees often are concentrated in certain areas such as social services, and they are less likely than white men to hold administrative posts, the percentage of women and minorities in government is significantly higher than in the private sector or in the federal government and the percentage of women administrators in state agencies is growing. Women administrators and women legislators in the states have had a similar pattern of growth from less than 5 percent in 1971 to 30 percent of agency heads and 22 percent of legislators in 2004.[23]

Merit Systems

The value of patronage began to decline as urban residents progressed to better paying jobs in private business and when the reform movement began to press for a **merit system** of civil service. Reformers argued that if workers were appointed by civil service commissions that developed competitive examinations, the system would be insulated from partisan politics and it would lead to "a competent corps of politically neutral civil servants."[24]

States moved slowly to implement civil service reform. It was not until the late 1930s that states were required by the federal government to put employees whose salaries were partially paid by federal grant funds under merit arrangements. Where machines remained in operation, cities moved even more slowly to institute merit appointment. Virtually all states have merit systems for at least 20 percent of their workers, and in nearly two-thirds of the states almost all workers are included.

Civil service systems have been broadly criticized in recent years. Although the bureaucratic model worked well to limit specific abuses before World War II, it has created new problems for contemporary government. In the 1930s government employees were not unionized, and courts had not acted to protect workers from wrongful discharge. Much of what civil service was designed to prevent has been ruled illegal or made unlikely to happen by collective bargaining agreements.

Management experts David Osborne and Ted Graebler contend that civil service rules can hamstring most personnel managers.[25] Unlike private businesses, where interviews and references are used to make hiring decisions, governments often must take the person with the highest score or one of the top three scorers on written examinations, even though they may otherwise be unsuited for the position. Because the process takes so long, the high scorers may accept another job during the six months or so that it takes between testing and hiring. Job classifications, which set pay levels, are determined by how long employees have worked, not by how well they have performed. When employees reach the top of their pay range, they cannot earn more money unless they are promoted into a new classification.

Osborne and Graebler also oppose merit pay systems, arguing that organizations should encourage employees to work together in teams and therefore should provide bonuses for quality group performance. To reward individuals with merit pay would be counterproductive.

Many civil service problems are being addressed by states and cities. The testing process has been streamlined. Questions have been revised to relate more closely to job skills, and departments have been given more freedom to choose among high-scoring candidates. Several states have established "broadband" job classifications in which hundreds of categories are greatly reduced with distinctions made between levels of expertise, or *bands*. As part of the reorganization process, management of the civil service system in most states has been shifted from semi-independent commissions to personnel departments whose heads are appointed by the governor. Similar to changes in the federal government, several states have established a senior executive level in which employees are given less job security but their pay and promotion are based on merit performance. Civil service systems have been abolished in some cities.

Several states have tried to abolish their civil service systems, but strong opposition from labor unions, as in Massachusetts, is a major reason why reform has failed. The most drastic change came when Georgia ended civil service for all employees hired after July 1, 1996. Governor Zell Miller pushed for the change as a way to make the governor more responsible to citizens.[26] The new system was designed to give more flexibility to hire and fire state workers and provide rewards for high-performance service. In 2001, Florida joined Georgia in eliminating most civil service protection for executive-branch employees. Texas has never had a centralized civil service system.

Collective Bargaining

As in the private sector, a group of government employees votes to unionize and usually affiliates with a national union through the process of **collective bargaining.**

The bargaining unit then negotiates a master contract that spells out such matters as pay, hours, fringe benefits, and grievance procedures. Most agreements stress seniority rights, meaning that longtime employees are protected from staff reductions. Evidence from across the country suggests that public employee unions have helped increase wages by 5 to 10 percent. As a result, in some states government workers are paid more than comparable workers in the private sector. They also have helped workers secure better health care and pension benefits. However, public employee unions present a potential threat to merit systems because of their emphasis on seniority. Moreover, their concern for job security may lead unions to oppose changes in personnel rules dealing with hiring and grievance procedures.

Unions often are blamed for protecting the incompetent. Although public employee unions clearly seek to protect job security, collective bargaining contracts explain only a small part of the problem as about 60 percent of state and local government workers, including teachers, are not members of unions. The major reason why it is difficult to fire public employees is that they are protected by a wide range of constitutional guarantees.[27] Often, management is at fault for failing to document an employee's performance, and there is good reason to guard against arbitrary or capricious decisions to fire people.

Only about 10 percent of government employees were unionized in 1960, but nearly one-third were members of collective bargaining units by the mid-1970s. About 60 percent of police were unionized by 1975. These increases occurred because of employee demand, weak employer resistance, the passage of protective legislation, and rulings from the Supreme Court supporting the right of government employees to join unions. Public unionization has leveled off since the mid-1970s as a result of changes in the distribution of public employees, more management resistance, and a decrease in inter-union competition in organizing campaigns. In the 1980s and 1990s public opinion turned against unions, and increasing use of privatization eliminated some public jobs.

Recently, union power has been growing in the Northeast and Midwest, where private-sector unions traditionally were strongest. As shown in Table 6-3, union membership by state and local workers is up significantly since 1997, while unionization has declined among federal government and private-sector workers. Indeed, state, county, and city workers stand as the last bastion of unionization in the United States.[28] Because twenty-seven states, mainly in the South and West, do not permit public employees to engage in collective bargaining, nearly all public employees who have a legal right to join a union have already done so. Seeking ways to expand their membership, some public-sector unions are trying to recruit individuals who do not work for the government, but whose salaries are supported largely by government contracts. These include large numbers of child care and health care workers. The most prominent public-sector unions are the National Education Association, the American Federation of Teachers, and the American Federation of State, County, and Municipal Workers, which ranks second behind the Teamsters as the largest labor union in the United States.

Although strikes by public employees are illegal in most states, job actions have occurred in many cities when groups such as firefighters and police officers have "sick-ins" (e.g., cases of the "blue flu") as a means of expressing their demands. In many cases, state law stipulates that public employee labor disputes must go to arbitration.

TABLE 6-3 U.S. Union Membership (in thousands)*						
	1997	1999	2001	2003	2005	% Change 1997–2005
State government employees	1,485	1,527	1,732	1,706	1,838	+28%
Local government employees	4,232	4,484	4,393	4,614	4,638	+9%
Federal government employees	1,030	1,047	1,037	1,004	954	−11%
Private-sector employees	9,363	9,419	9,113	8,452	8,255	−7%
All employees	16,110	16,477	16,275	15,776	15,685	−2%

*Government employees include teachers.

Source: Governing (June 2006), p. 34.

Budgeting

State budget preparations operate in a manner similar to the congressional process. They are executive-centered with responsibility for formulation fixed in an office of budget and management, whose head is appointed by the governor. Governors form a budget as a spending and policy document and send it to the legislature for review and adoption. Since the 1970s, legislatures, like Congress, have added staff and have used computerized information systems. Because of their skilled staff, many legislatures are able to develop independent sources of financial information.[29] As a result, appropriations committees and their subcommittees now are able to analyze governors' budgets much more carefully by using their own revenue projections. Hearings are held and negotiations proceed with the governor's office before the budget moves to the house and senate for approval. All states except Vermont require that their budget be balanced at some stage of its preparation or on final passage. Fifty years ago nearly all states prepared a biennial budget, but today thirty-eight states follow the national pattern of annual budgeting. Unlike the federal budget, where large items are budgeted in lump sums, most state budgets are written in specific, line-item form.[30]

Effective legislative or executive administrative oversight is strongly influenced by the type of budget process that the state employs. **Incremental budgeting**—the traditional system of using last year's figures as the basis for current calculations—provides little opportunity for overall review or program evaluation. Last year's figures were the result of previous political compromises. Agencies make requests for a few new programs, and they routinely overstate the amount of money they need. Governors make some cuts and legislators cut some more. As a result, old programs are seldom reviewed, little innovation occurs, legislators can point to their efforts to keep spending down, and agencies usually get about what they need to run their programs.

After experimenting with several budget reforms in the 1960s and 1970s aimed at correcting the problems of incremental budgeting, today nearly all states require some kind of **performance budgeting.** Governments first decide what they want to accomplish and then develop their budgets. Programs then are evaluated on the basis of work performance—are objectives being accomplished?—and on how efficiently services are being provided on a per-unit cost basis. This means the focus is on outcomes, or results, of programs. Traditionally, budgeting has focused on inputs—"how much money is spent, how many people are served, what services each person received."[31] This was done because it is much more difficult to measure results. Performance evaluation may also include the level of citizen satisfaction with the program—are streets clean, are people treated with respect by the police?

Urban Bureaucracy

So far we have focused on the administration of state government and the roles of governors and legislators. However, much of what was said about the nature of bureaucracy and about personnel practices applies equally to state and local governments. The leadership role of mayors is discussed at the end of this chapter.

As noted in Chapter 3, much of the impetus for reform and the move to bureaucratic government in the late nineteenth century was prompted by the abuses of urban political machines. However, we also have argued that the adoption of these reforms led to a number of unintended consequences, including an impersonal, middle-class bias in the delivery of government services. As a result, city residents found few bureaucrats who were responsive to their needs. Political scientist Theodore Lowi speaks of the "new machines"—powerful urban service bureaucracies protected by civil service rules, receiving substantial amounts of money from federal and state sources, and thus not responsible to elected city officials or to the general public.[32] This is part of picket fence federalism, discussed in Chapter 2.

Control of urban government also is made difficult because many street-level bureaucrats have broad discretion in how they perform their jobs. Contrary to what the hierarchical model suggests, people at the bottom of the bureaucracy—those who deal directly with the public—effectively make policy by deciding how public services will be dispensed. Bureaucrats often see clients in terms of group identification, but citizens seek personal attention to their problems.

The success of many urban programs rests with how well lower-level bureaucrats perform their jobs and how well their supervisors monitor their activities. Major problems include efficiency (how much it costs to produce a service), effectiveness (how well government is able to meet the objectives or goals of its programs), and equity (to what extent services are provided fairly to all residents).

As the number of city managers and strong mayors has grown, city budget making has become more executive-centered. As a result, the budget process in cities is similar to that at the state level—the mayor, or city manager, has a staff office that prepares the budget, the proposed budget is presented to the council for review, interest groups have an opportunity to comment on it, and finally the budget is enacted by the council. While the most common approach is incremental budgeting, many cities have been at the forefront of performance budgeting. As at the state level, city budgets must be balanced.

Criticism of service levels and budget procedures have led to a host of proposals for alternative ways to provide urban services. We turn to some of those in the next section.

Reinventing Government

David Osborne and Ted Graebler point out that the last times we "reinvented" government in the United States were during the Progressive era early in this century and again in the New Deal of the 1930s. Earlier we evaluated the impact of Progressive reforms on state and local government. Now that we are in a postindustrial, knowledge-based, global economy, Osborne and Graebler believe it is time to make major changes in government at all levels.[33] They use the term "entrepreneurial government" to describe a new model that uses resources in different ways to maximize productivity and effectiveness. In this new order, the bureaucratic model would be replaced by more flexible, responsive organizations that empower citizens rather than serve them.

Entrepreneurial governments, which are operating to various degrees in many cities across the country, function on the basis of several main principles. In their ideal form, entrepreneurial governments act in the following ways. They encourage competition among service providers by privatizing services or contracting them out. They empower citizens by encouraging them to take control of services through such means as public housing resident advisory boards, ballot initiatives, and community-oriented policing. They focus on outcomes by creating goals for government and measuring how well agencies perform their tasks. They treat citizens as valued customers with individual needs. They earn money by charging fees or by owning businesses, such as cable television systems. They anticipate problems, believing that an ounce of prevention is worth a pound of cure. For example, they believe that fire departments should be rewarded more for fire prevention than for their fast response time after a fire occurs.

Proponents of **reinventing government (REGO)** are critical of "orthodox" bureaucratic reorganization. They call for "flatter" bureaucracies in which the number of intermediate levels of organization between top management and street-level workers is substantially reduced.[34] At the same time, they want lower-level workers to have more freedom to make decisions without constant supervision. Managers should be hired on performance contracts. The belief is that if managers have more flexibility to improve services, they will be more responsive to consumers. REGO principles call for cutting red tape, putting customers first, empowering employees, and getting back to basics— "eliminate what we don't need."[35]

Of the many specific reforms advocated by REGO, the most commonly adopted in the 1990s were customer service training, strategic planning, and empowerment of lower-level personnel.[36] Observers have found that although support for REGO has declined since the late 1990s, it remains strong. Richard C. Kearney found the REGO is firmly established in American cities. Sixty-six percent of city managers in 2003 reported that they had asked their councils for funds to support contracting out, 71 percent had requested funds for customers service training, and 56 percent had requested funds for citizen surveys.[37] Kearney notes that recently government officials have switched to using such buzz words as "performance management" and "reengineering metrics" rather than "reinventing government."

A closely related approach is **Total Quality Management (TQM),** a business management philosophy identified with American W. Edwards Deming and first put into practice at Deming's direction by businesses in Japan. TQM stresses that the management process needs to be redesigned; the problem is not the workers, but the organizational structure. Major tenets of TQM include the following: The customer is the ultimate determiner of quality; quality results from people working together within systems, not from individual efforts; quality improvement requires effective worker participation; quality requires a total organizational commitment. TQM shares the reinventing government belief in flatter bureaucracies, but it is more supportive of the ability of bureaucracies to provide services. Some TQM principles have been implemented in a majority of the states.

Critics argue that since TQM was designed for routine manufacturing processes, it is much more difficult to apply to government services, which are very labor intensive. Unlike private businesses, it is not easy to identify who a government's customers are. For example, are the customers of an environmental protection agency the businesses it regulates or the groups that lobby for greater environmental protection? If it is both, then what weight should be assigned to each of their interests? The public wants clean air and water, but it also wants jobs and it wants to avoid inconvenient government regulation.

Many of the same criticisms apply to REGO in terms of the simplicity of a customer focus and the failure to recognize the benefits of hierarchical structures. In both cases, their benefits have been overstated and buzz words have been substituted for meaningful reform. Although few people would argue that long-term strategies for planning, outcomes-based budgeting, and citizen empowerment are bad, some programs have been reined in by politicians and voters who believe they have been carried to their illogical extremes. Innovation makes some people uncomfortable, and partisan political concerns may prevent otherwise rational budgeting changes from being implemented.

Privatization

The Progressives championed service delivery by bureaucracies as a means to eliminate the corruption of payoffs to political machines for contracts awarded by the city to private businesses and to ensure that everyone was treated the same, rather than given preferential attention because of political connections. As a result, we created a series of government monopolies—schools, garbage collection, utilities—to avoid waste and duplication.

Even when they are not conscious of reinventing government, many communities have discovered they can save money when private service providers compete for public business. As a result, **privatization** has become increasingly common since 1990. As explained by E. S. Savas, it can appear in several forms.[38] Perhaps the most familiar is contracting with private firms to perform a service previously done by government employees. In private business this is referred to as "outsourcing." Public-sector privatization includes managing prisons, providing janitorial services, operating homeless shelters, and collecting taxes. At the most extreme, a few newly incorporated cities have contracted out virtually all public services. Centennial, a city outside Denver that began its existence with 100,000 people, hired the management firm CH2M to staff all its departments except police and fire. Other than police and fire, the city has only four employees.

Privatization also includes contracting with not-for-profit agencies to provide a service such as meals-on-wheels, forming neighborhood security patrols, selling off publicly owned businesses, and giving housing vouchers to the poor. Because competition is central to the ideas of Osborne and Graebler, privatization has been strongly associated with the reinventing-government movement. In terms used by Osborne and Graebler, privatization separates steering from rowing in local government. Public officials set policy goals and monitor private providers of services (steer), and nongovernmental employees perform day-to-day tasks (row).

The increase in federal and state mandates is a major factor that has led cities to contract out for services. In particular, environmental mandates for such things as toxic waste cleanup require a level of technical expertise and the use of sophisticated equipment that often are beyond the capabilities of local governments.

Advocates of privatization, such as E. S. Savas, argue that it can substantially reduce service delivery costs. Political scientist James Q. Wilson agrees that private firms usually are more efficient, but he cautions that publicly owned utilities may have lower costs than private organizations.[39] Osborne and Graebler note that where private providers do not have to compete, they may be as inefficient as public monopolies.

Proponents contend that in addition to saving money, privatization is consistent with free market ideology, reduces the size of government, forces providers to be more responsive to customer needs, rewards innovation, avoids the rigidities of civil service, and introduces successful private management ideas to the public sector. Where public agencies have successfully competed for contracts against private businesses, the morale of public employees is greatly improved.

Opponents contend that when the costs of monitoring contracts are considered, service delivery may be more expensive under privatization (as much as 10 percent of the value of the contract). Contracting, they argue, encourages "lowballing," whereby private firms bid low and then raise their charges to cover the real costs of the service. When costs are lower, opponents believe it often is because providers cut corners in their services and pay workers lower salaries. There are concerns that private companies will not be sufficiently committed to affirmative action in hiring workers and that services may not be provided equitably to minority groups. Although encouraging competition sounds good, it often is difficult to find qualified providers of services when bids are requested. Of course, the traditional problems of corruption—bribery and kickbacks—continue to require close monitoring of contracts.

When law enforcement is privatized (see Chapter 7), there is special concern that civil liberties will be abused. Not surprisingly, public employee unions fear that privatization will lead to a loss of jobs and/or lower wages and benefits. In large cities, such as Chicago, African Americans have taken a substantial hit because they hold a disproportionately high percentage of service and maintenance jobs and those are the most likely to be privatized.[40] As under machine rule, there is still the danger of favoritism in awarding contracts.

Most of the pitfalls of privatization can be avoided by careful wording of contracts and by close supervision of the providers. For example, rather than automatically accepting the lowest bid, cities may use the "lowest responsible bid." City auditors' offices can ensure that bidding is truly competitive and can monitor contractors' performance. But, as noted, effective monitoring is expensive and time-consuming.

As in Phoenix, cities may wish to retain some public delivery of a service, such as garbage collection, even when the majority of the service is provided by private organizations. Contracts can encourage private companies to hire displaced city workers, or cities can assure public employees that they will not be laid off because of privatization. In a word, cities need to manage competition by defining clearly what they want done, by evaluating performance, and by penalizing those who do not provide services at the expected levels. As Chicago mayor Richard M. Daley stated, "People want services without higher taxes, and they don't care who gives it to them."

More than 90 percent of state agencies have privatized some of their services. The most frequently privatized services are custodial, food, clerical, and security. Increasingly, states also are privatizing the professional services of engineers and architects. While over 90 percent of privatization is done by contracting out, states also provide vouchers, especially for social services, and they enter into partnerships with private groups. Exclusive use of public employees is highest in providing public safety operations, such as fire and police, but contracts are used for every service that local governments perform.

E-Government

Just as the Internet has changed much of how private-sector business is transacted, so too has **e-government,** the delivery of public services on the Internet, changed the way in which residents interact with state and local governments. All states and about 90 percent of cities have some e-government operations. Commonly available state services online include tax preparation, vehicle registration, buying hunting and fishing licenses, and acquiring marriage licenses. In Florida the state maintains a Web site (FloridaCompareCare. gov) that tells people how the state's hospitals rank in terms of survival rates, protection against infection, and costs for procedures dealing with about a dozen health problems, such as coronary artery bypass surgery.[41] All states have online tourist sites.

Unlike some REGO fads, e-government services clearly are here to stay and will continue to increase in the future. They offer the same convenience advantages to residents as do online shopping services. They also encourage greater participation in government as individuals can e-mail messages to government officials and other interactive programs are available. In many states, Web sites are available in Spanish as well as in English.

Governing Magazine has a regular technology section that reports on state and local government technology innovation. Its annual *Source Book* ranks state Web sites and metropolitan-area wireless Internet access. In 2006 the top five state Web sites were in Utah, Maine, New Jersey, North Carolina, and Michigan. At the bottom were Louisiana, California, Alabama, Alaska, and Wyoming. Seattle, San Francisco, Austin, Portland (Oregon), and Toledo were listed as the "most wired" metropolitan areas. California led the nation with eleven metropolitan areas among the top 100 in the country for Internet access. Twelve rural states did not have any metropolitan area in the top 100.[42]

Problems involved with e-government include the fact that many people, especially the poor and elderly, do not have Internet access. A Pew survey in 2006 found that three-fourths of Americans reported that they had Internet access. Like all Internet use, there are concerns about security and privacy. While nearly all governments have Web sites, most are informational and not interactive. In many cases people can get a form online, but they have to mail it to a government office.

Nearly three-fourths of cities reported using GSIS (geographical information systems) in 2003.[43] This is a separate computer technology to create maps and display data to help analyze information. It is widely used by city planners.

STATEWIDE ELECTED EXECUTIVES

Unlike the national level, where the president and vice president are the only popularly elected officials, most states continue to fill several executive branch positions through election. Only three states—Maine, New Hampshire, and New Jersey—have a single statewide elected official, the governor. North Dakota has twelve and North Carolina and Florida each have ten. Regionally, the South has the most elected statewide officials. Many political scientists argue that the governor and lieutenant governor should be the only statewide elected executives. Electing more creates a **long ballot,** on which voters must vote for offices and candidates they know little about when electing a large number of officials. It also creates agencies that to some extent are independent of the governor because they also have their own executive who has been elected by the voters. Consequently, having a large number of separately elected officials (SEOs) is viewed as reducing a governor's influence in the executive branch. Brief descriptions of officials that are typically elected and their duties follow.

Lieutenant Governor

The basic responsibilities of the lieutenant governor are comparable to those of the vice president of the United States: to be first in line to succeed the governor in the event of the governor's death and in twenty states to be presiding officer of the state senate when it is in session (see Chapter 5). In the seven states that do not elect a lieutenant governor, the first in the line of succession usually is the secretary of state. New Jersey will elect its first lieutenant governor in 2009. Before approving the position of lieutenant governor, the president of the state's senate replaced a governor who left office and he or she continued to hold the senate leadership post while serving as governor. In Tennessee the speaker of the senate is given the title lieutenant governor.

When a governor is out of the state, many lieutenant governors become acting governor. This is an important difference with the vice presidency, because vice presidents do not become acting president when the president is out of the country. During this time, some of the lieutenant governors had signed bills into law, reviewed pending executions, and made other important decisions.

Still, the job of lieutenant governor will be determined largely by what the governor wants the lieutenant governor to do. Governors frequently consult their lieutenant governors when appointing administrators to head executive-branch agencies. Often they use lieutenant governors as policy advisers and occasionally as department heads. Since 9/11, several states have put their lieutenant governors in charge of homeland security. Utah abolished the position of secretary of state in 1980 and gave the duties to the lieutenant governor.

Perhaps the most powerful lieutenant governor is in Texas. There the lieutenant governor presides over the senate, appoints all committees, assigns all bills, and co-chairs the Legislative Budget Board.[44] During his first term in office, Republican Governor George W. Bush worked so cordially with Democratic Lieutenant Governor Bob Bullock that Bullock, who was retiring, endorsed Bush for reelection in 1998.

For a long time states elected governors and lieutenant governors separately, which meant that a governor might have to deal with a politically ambitious lieutenant governor of the opposite party. However, about half the states now have joint nomination and joint election of these two officials.

From 1980 to 2006, lieutenant governors were more likely than any other office-holders to become governor. In 2006 four sitting lieutenant governors ran for governor and all lost. However, three incumbent governors who had been lieutenant governor were reelected, and one other former lieutenant governor who was serving in Congress was elected governor in 2006. They joined four other governors not running for reelection, who were former lieutenant governors.

Attorney General

As the state's chief legal officer, the attorney general represents the state in legal disputes and serves as the legal adviser to the governor and other executive-branch employees. Curiously, in about half the states, the attorney general does not have to be a licensed attorney. Attorneys general are popularly elected in forty-three states, chosen by the governor in five states, chosen by the legislature in one state, and chosen by the state supreme court in one state. Although a part of the executive branch, they can become involved in battles with governors. An extreme example is when the attorney general of Arizona was a leader in the move to impeach Governor Evan Mecham in 1986–1987.

In most states, the attorney general is the second most powerful political figure in state office. His or her power stems in large part from the ability to initiate prosecution in well-publicized criminal and civil cases. In addition, when the governor, the legislature, administrative agencies, county attorneys, or city attorneys ask the attorney general for advice regarding an interpretation of state law, the attorney general's opinion generally has the force of law unless challenged in court. The attorney general's office is in charge of antitrust enforcement, consumer protection, data security, and the enforcement of state environmental laws.

In 1994, Mississippi Attorney General Mike Moore was the first to sue cigarette manufacturers under the then-novel strategy that the tobacco industry had unjustly benefited from his state's assumption of the costs for tobacco-related diseases and illnesses. So Mississippi sued to recover the Medicaid money spent on smoking-related health care costs. Other states' attorneys general joined Moore and a settlement was reached with tobacco companies in 1998 under which forty-six-states were to receive a total of nearly $250 billion over a 25-year period. Since then cigarette consumption in the United States has dropped by 20 percent and health improvements are beginning to be seen in men who were former smokers. Curiously, from 2000 to 2004 the federal government paid out $528 million in tobacco subsidies and then paid $10.1 billion to terminate the tobacco quota system for farmers.

As noted in the case study at the beginning of this chapter, New York Attorney General Eliot Spitzer's crusade against a variety of businesses helped lead to his election as governor in 2006. As attorney general, Spitzer was arguably the most powerful state official in the country. In 2006 three of four attorneys general running for governor were elected. In a reverse move, former California governor, secretary of state, and mayor of Oakland, Jerry Brown, was elected attorney general in 2006.

In many instances, the attorney general heads the largest law office in the state. This ability to appoint hundreds of young lawyers to serve in state government gives the attorney general a substantial power base should he or she choose to run for governor or senator after those attorneys have gained experience and moved into private practice around the state. Several attorneys general have gone on to become governors and well-known national political figures. They include Robert LaFollette of Wisconsin, Thomas Dewey of New York, and more recently Bill Clinton of Arkansas. Alberto Gonzales served as attorney general of Texas when George W. Bush was governor and as U.S. attorney general under President Bush.

Secretary of State

The duties of secretary of state are to keep records—such as the state constitution, constitutional amendments, legislative acts, and mortgages—and to supervise both federal and state elections. Secretaries of state are elected in thirty-five states and selected by either the governor or the legislature in twelve states; Alaska, Hawaii, and Utah do not have such a position. They receive statements of candidacy for public office, oversee the printing of ballots, and certify election results. Because secretaries of state are basically record keepers, many proposals call for the transfer of these duties to regular administrative departments.

Until 2000, being secretary of state was usually a low-profile position. But attention focused on the Florida presidential election and the partisan struggles over how ballots were to be counted and about who was eligible to vote made Secretary of State Katherine Harris a nationally known figure. Harris was elected to the U.S. House of Representatives in 2004, but lost a bid for the Senate in 2006. Controversy about voting procedures in the 2004 presidential election again put several secretaries of state in the news.

In 2006 twenty secretaries of state ran for some elective office while serving as their state's chief election officer. Obviously, this raised potential conflicts of interest. In Ohio, where the most serious allocations nationwide of voting mismanagement were raised in 2004, Secretary of State Kenneth Blackwell, running for governor, handed over some of his election duties to an aide. Blackwell was soundly defeated by Democratic U.S. Representative Ted Strickland.

Because of the new visibility of being secretary of state, the position has become more sought after by younger office seekers. An extreme example of past practice was Thad Eure of North Carolina, who retired in 1989 after fifty-two years in office.

Treasurer, Auditor, and Controller

A number of functions involving the handling of money generated from taxes are divided among several officials, and it is difficult to find more than a handful of states that do it the same way. State treasurers usually are responsible for tax collection, the safekeeping of state funds, and the actual spending of money. They manage college savings plans (529 plans) in every state. Treasurers are elected in thirty-seven states and chosen by the governor or legislature in twelve others. Texas and Minnesota eliminated the office in the 1990s.

Postaudit, a review after money is spent to see whether it was spent according to legislative intent and without corruption, is the responsibility of the state auditor. Auditors are elected in twenty-five states and chosen by the governor or legislature in others. In a few states, the auditor is called the controller. **Preaudit** is the approval of spending before it actually takes place and is normally done by the controller. The controller is elected in only nine states; appointment by an agency head (such as the department of finance) is becoming more common.

The treasurer, auditor, and controller will not be found in every state, but the functions they perform will be done by some office. The administrative efficiency school argues that all, or most, of these functions should be centralized in one office headed by a gubernatorial appointee. This would make the governor clearly responsible for performing these functions.

EXECUTIVES IN CITIES

Led by Progressive reformers seeking to rid cities of the corruption of political machines early in the twentieth century, many cities acted somewhat sooner than states to centralize authority and strengthen executive authority. However, many mayors continue to be limited by fragmented local organization. In addition, few mayors develop strong party organizations and must therefore depend on the strength of their personal appeal in providing political leadership. As state and federal funds support more local projects, mayors and local administrators are subjected to increased rules and regulations established by state legislators and by members of Congress.

Being the mayor in most large cities is a perilous job with constant political and economic pressure. Few mayors survive well enough to be successful in running for higher office. In small towns, mayors often are main-street merchants who lack the ambition to seek higher office. Even if they perform effectively, mayors often have difficulty becoming well known when seeking statewide office.

City executives function as part of four basic forms of government: weak-mayor–council, strong-mayor–council, council-manager, and commission.

FORMS OF CITY GOVERNMENT

Weak-Mayor–Council Plan

Until the 1870s, all American cities operated with **weak-mayor–council plans** of government. As with early state government, city government structure was strongly affected by skepticism about politicians and about government. As cities grew and demand for public services increased, it opened the way for political bosses (see Chapter 3) to assume power that was denied to mayors. Bosses and their machines were better able to coordinate the delivery of public services than were mayors of other cities who were hamstrung by a government structure that did not have a system of accountability. Starting in the 1880s, reform led to the creation of "strong-mayor" systems that centralized authority and were thought to be less likely to support political machines. Still, weak-mayor systems survive in many small towns and some medium-sized cities, especially in the South and West. In a few large cities with weak-mayor systems, individuals with strong personalities have been able to wield effective power as mayors.

In fact, any mayor's ability to move a city in his or her preferred direction may depend more on political skills and operating style than on formal power.

In a weak-mayor–council system, the council is both a legislative and an executive body (Figure 6-1). Council members appoint administrative officials; they make policy; they serve as ex officio members of boards; and they prepare the budget. The mayor is "weak" because of a lack of effective executive power. The authority to appoint is restricted, and the authority to remove often is altogether lacking. Often, the mayor cannot veto ordinances passed by the city council. In cities with weak mayors, no single person is charged with overall responsibility for government action. Other executive officials are independently elected (there is a long ballot that often is not understood by voters), and a number of boards and commissions are not controlled by the mayor. Because no one is in charge of the overall affairs of a city, voters do not know whom to blame when things go wrong. No one coordinates all public policies in a city, and no one can be held directly accountable when there are service breakdowns.

The weak-mayor system does have some advantages. City departments are free to act without undue political pressure from the mayor. If voters are concerned about the misuse of executive power, the weak-mayor system creates strong checks by the council and by independent boards.

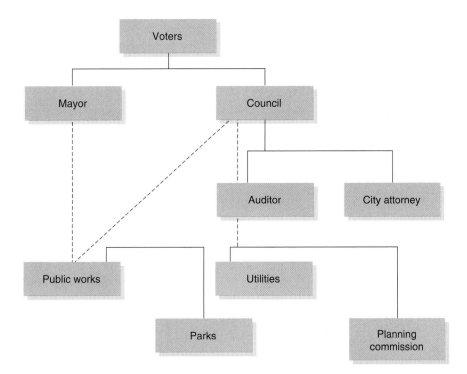

FIGURE 6-1 Hypothetical weak-mayor–council plan. Council has both legislative and executive authority. Council must consent to mayor's appointments of department heads. Mayor's power of removal restricted. Council has primary control over the budget. Some department heads are appointed directly by council.

Strong-Mayor–Council Plan

Under the **strong-mayor–council plan,** there is a short ballot. The mayor controls the budget, has broad power to appoint and remove city officials, and can veto ordinances passed by the council. Strong mayors are directly elected by the voters and usually have four-year terms with the possibility of reelection (Figure 6-2). The council confirms appointments, and it usually controls the appropriations process. Like that of most governors, the mayor's legal position provides a firm base for political leadership, and the mayor is constantly in the limelight. In most cities the "strong" mayor is, in fact, a compromise between a weak and a very strong system.

This plan is used in most large cities where a complex administrative structure requires firm leadership and direction and is most commonly found in New England and the Midwest. Most cities with more than 1 million population have a strong-mayor–council system. Problems arise when voters expect too much from the mayor and find it easy to blame that individual for whatever goes wrong in the city. Often, those politicians who are effective campaigners lack the administrative skills to manage the day-to-day affairs of a large city. To offset this shortcoming of the system, many cities with strong mayors have established the position of **chief administrative officer (CAO).** Appointed by the mayor, this professional person is given broad authority to manage the financial affairs of the city. In a few cities the CAO is a permanent position that carries over from one administration to another. In most cases, it is subject to appointment by the mayor. In New York City the mayor selects several deputy mayors who function

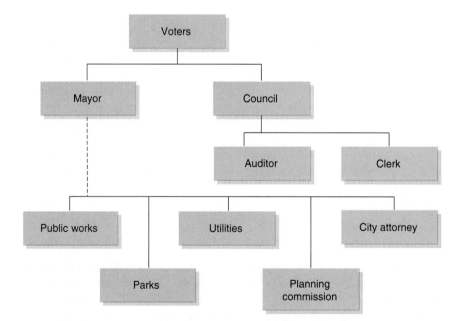

FIGURE 6-2 Hypothetical strong-mayor–council plan. Mayor has strong administrative authority. Mayor appoints and dismisses department heads. Mayor prepares the budget. Short ballot.

according to the CAO concept. About three-fourths of all municipal systems of government report having a CAO.

As with governors, "strong" formal powers do not guarantee that mayors will be effective leaders in their cities. They need to have personal leadership capabilities, and even the strongest mayors usually lack some formal powers that they would like to have in an ideal situation. Mayors need to build networks of support in order to compete with private economic power in their cities and to deal effectively with strong government bureaucracies. Likewise, mayors with weak formal power may be "strong" leaders because they are carefully tuned in to the political environment of their cities. This means that to be recognized as the political leader of his or her city, a mayor must exercise power beyond what is provided in the city charters.

Council-Manager Plan

The council-manager plan originated early in the twentieth century as part of the Progressive movement. Reformers sought to eliminate corruption from city hall by removing administration from partisan politics. Their answer was to replace the mayor with a professional administrator appointed by the council. Among the early city reformers was Richard S. Childs, who founded the national short-ballot organization in 1909. A short ballot implied consolidation of elected offices, and in many cases, plans calling for a city manager were accompanied by the initiation of nonpartisan elections, civil service systems, and the short ballot. To reformers, the city manager was viewed as a "business director" and the city council as a "corporate board of directors."

Under most council-manager plans, the manager is in charge of personnel matters, prepares the budget, and oversees the day-to-day operations of city departments. The final budget and any policy recommendations made by the manager must be approved by the council. In many cases, managers have assumed more of a policy making role for themselves. As a result, patterns of liberal or conservative policy solutions often can be associated with particular managers. While it has been widely assumed that under the original model, managers were to avoid being policy advocates, many academics believe that the early reforms intended power to be shared between council members and managers. At the same time, council members often intervene in adminstrative decesions.[45]

In 1914 Dayton, Ohio, was the first city of substantial size to adopt the council-manager plan. By 1918 there were nearly 100 cities with managers, and counties began to adopt the system in the 1930s. Small towns often have found it too expensive to hire a full-time manager, and in many large northern cities the council-manager system has been opposed by strong labor unions and minority groups, who often believe the manager has a pro-business bias.

Susan McManus and Charles Bullock report that 59 percent of cities had a council-manager system in 2001, up by 10 percent from 1981.[46] Seventy percent of cities with populations between 50,000 and 249,000 had managers. Among cities over 250,000, about 40 percent had managers. At the other extreme, 42 percent of cities with populations between 2,500 and 4,999 had managers. The council-manager system dominates in the Pacific Coast states (82 percent of cities) and the South Atlantic states (75 percent). Managers are likely to be found in newer, fast-growing cities, with mobile populations. This includes many suburban communities across the country.

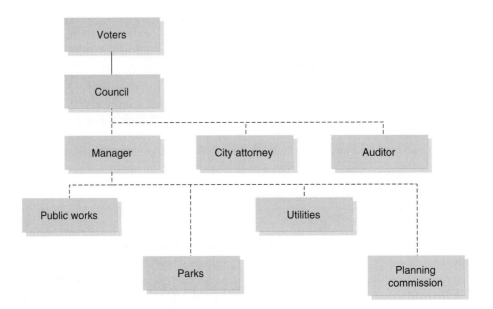

FIGURE 6-3 Hypothetical council-manager plan. Usually small council (5–7 members). Often nonpartisan elections. Council members make policy and oversee city administration. Full-time professional manager. Budget prepared by the manager. Mayor usually has only ceremonial power.

Until recently, Phoenix, Dallas, and San Diego were the largest cities with managers. In 2004 voters in San Diego approved a change to a mayor-council system, while in 2005 voters in Dallas rejected such a change. About a dozen cities, including Cincinnati, Oakland, and Richmond, have switched from managers to mayors in the last ten years. On the other hand, in 2004 El Paso switched from a strong mayor to a city manager. Although several big cities have switched from managers to mayors, overall the number of cities with managers keeps growing every year.

In most cases a small council elected at large hires a manager (Figure 6-3). In the past, managers often were civil engineers. Now they are likely to be people trained in public administration. The manager serves at the pleasure of the council in a relationship similar to that of a superintendent of schools and the board of education. In the past, a mayor often was selected from among the council members to perform ceremonial duties. Now there is an elected mayor in over half the cities with a manager. As will be discussed later, many of these cities have given increased power to the mayor, such as preparing the budget.

Currently, about 15 percent of managers are women, up from 1 percent in 1974. The conventional wisdom has been that there is high turnover among managers, but recent survey show the median tenure is nearly seven years.[47] Tenure is shortest in small cities where managers often are looking to move up to better paying positions. Greater job security and more involvement in the policy making process may affect the kinds of people attracted to what once was a transitory profession.

Although some reformers have overstated the impact of the manager system (in particular, they fail to understand that "politics" cannot be eliminated and that the struggle for power will not disappear once partisan labels are removed), it has provided efficient, accountable government in many cities. Weaknesses stem from the nature of individual managers—it is difficult to attract competent, experienced people, and the manager must maintain a middle-of-the-road position in which he or she avoids, on the one hand, setting policy and, on the other hand, simply running errands for the council.

Some managers have had a tendency to become very closely identified with business and professional interests in their community. Because of this perceived bias, organized labor in many cities has opposed the creation of a manager plan. There has also been opposition from African Americans and other minorities who believe their interests will be better served in nonreformed cities where the mayor's office may be more responsive to citizen demands. This has led to increasing the authority of mayors and the election of council members by district in several cities with managers.

Commission Plan

The impetus for the commission plan was a storm that virtually destroyed Galveston, Texas in 1900. So many people were killed that attempts were made to bury people at sea. But bodies washed back on shore and increased the threat of disease.[48] Martial law was declared to stop looting. In response to the crisis, commissioners were appointed to run the city. This became the model for a new form of municipal government.

A **commission plan** has several (usually three to nine) commissioners, elected at large, who exercise both legislative and executive authority. The commissioners are organized as heads of various city departments (public works, parks, finance), and they also act collectively to pass ordinances and control spending (Figure 6-4). Often a mayor is selected from among the commissioners, but his or her duties are largely ceremonial.

at large - all at one time

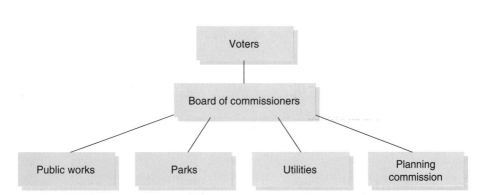

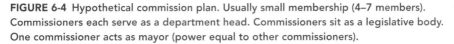

FIGURE 6-4 Hypothetical commission plan. Usually small membership (4–7 members). Commissioners each serve as a department head. Commissioners sit as a legislative body. One commissioner acts as mayor (power equal to other commissioners).

After its initiation in Galveston in 1901, use of the commission plan spread quickly, and by 1917 it was in operation in about 500 cities. Dallas, Houston, and Fort Worth were among the first cities that had commissions, and several other big cities, including Pittsburgh and Buffalo, adopted the plan early in the twentieth century. As recently as 1970, about 200 cities had commission forms of government. The *Municipal Year Book* reports that fewer than fifty cities have commission governments and nearly all of them have populations under 25,000. Portland, Oregon, is the largest city that has a commission form of government. In 2007 voters, by a 3 to 1 margin, defeated an initiative that would have centralized power with the mayor and ended the city's 92-year-old unique, convoluted commission-mayor system. In most states there are no city commissions at all. Even Galveston now has a council-manager form of government. The Voting Rights Act has made the commission form with its at-large voting an endangered species of city government.

The commission plan has many disadvantages. Because it does not provide for separation of powers, it places little control on spending and administration. In most cities it is difficult to attract top-quality persons to serve as commissioners, and thus government business often is in the hands of amateurs. Without a chief executive, it is difficult to pinpoint responsibility. The small size of the commission does not foster debate and criticism, and it encourages a fraternity of tolerance. City commissioners often practice a mutual hands-off policy from one another's functional areas, and each moves in his or her own direction without overall coordination. The commission has become nearly extinct because of the fundamental flaws noted above and the rise of the city manager form of government as the reform of choice beginning in the 1920s.

Hybrid System

As we have noted in describing mayors and managers, over a period of about twenty years the two systems have adopted many of the characteristics of the other. Seeking to improve management productivity, both strong- and weak-mayor systems have added a chief administrative officer, whose job is similar to a manager's, and they have added civil service protection. On the other hand, manager cities have adopted characteristics of mayor-council systems in order to improve political responsiveness and leadership capabilities. Many manager cities have moved to the direct election of a mayor, who in some cases can veto council-passed ordinances, prepare the budget, and even nominate the manager. They also have changed to council members chosen by districts.

H. George Frederickson, Gary Alan Johnson, and Curtis Wood refer to this as a newly merged **hybrid system** that combines characteristics of mayor and manager systems as creating the "adapted city." They found that often citizens voted in incremental steps over several years to merge the two systems because they wanted the advantages of direct neighborhood representation and assignment of political responsibility to a mayor, but they also wanted a merit-based administration that operated relatively free of partisan political concerns.[49] In most cases, hybrid systems appear to be functioning as residents expected. Often there is a sense of teamwork between mayors and managers, and in many cases CAOs are persons who formerly were city managers.

THE ROLES OF MAYORS

Mayors, like governors and presidents, play a variety of roles. As the ceremonial head of the city, mayors greet distinguished visitors to the city, attend endless rounds of dinners, and issue proclamations. These activities help give mayors visibility, and they build up political goodwill. As chief administrators, mayors oversee the work of city employees and prepare an executive budget. They may be limited in this function, however, by the presence of independent boards and commissions and other officials who are separately elected. And like governors the mayors can be classified as "strong" or "weak," depending on the nature of their city's charter. As chief legislators, strong mayors exercise strong control over the agenda considered by the council, and they can veto ordinances passed by the council. Increasingly, mayors act as chief city ambassador, devoting a great deal of time to meetings at the state capital and in Washington. Many cities have full-time lobbyists in Washington, and others act through the United States Conference of Mayors and the National League of Cities.

Typically, being mayor is a difficult job because many mayors lack the ability to veto council ordinances, to appoint department heads, and to prepare budgets. Often their pay is low and they lack staff assistance. In many large cities, especially in the Northeast and Midwest, declining populations and high levels of poverty put severe financial restraints on the ability of mayors to maintain basic levels of public services.

As a result, the power of mayors, even more than the power of the governor, rests in their ability to persuade through the use of public relations approaches, the mass media, and bargaining among various urban interests. If mayors are effective persuaders, they can overcome many of the handicaps of weak formal authority, as did Richard Lee of New Haven, Connecticut. In a classic study of political power, Lee was described as "not [being at] the peak of a pyramid but rather at the center of intersecting circles."[50] He rarely commanded. He negotiated, cajoled, exhorted, beguiled, charmed, pressed, appealed, reasoned, promised, insisted, demanded, even threatened; but he most needed support from other leaders who simply could not be commanded. Because the mayor did not dare command, he had to bargain.

Minority and Women Mayors

Minority mayors constitute an increasingly large category of individuals who, although they have different styles of leadership, face similar problems. Since 1980, African Americans have served as mayors of many of the nation's largest cities—Atlanta, Baltimore, Chicago, Cleveland, Dallas, Denver, Detroit, Houston, Kansas City, Los Angeles, Memphis, Minneapolis, New Orleans, New York, Philadelphia, St. Louis, San Francisco, Seattle, and Washington, D.C. In 2005 several cities, including Buffalo and Cincinnati, elected their first African American mayors. In Atlanta, Mayor Shirley Franklin, an African American, was easily reelected.

The first generation of African American mayors, led by Carl Stokes in Cleveland and Richard Hatcher in Gary, Indiana, both elected in 1967, served in predominantly African American cities. The major focus of their administrations was the **"political incorporation of blacks."**[51] That is, they sought to use city government as a means to empower African Americans and other minorities in the political and civic life of their communities. Most studies of cities with first-generation African American mayors have found that after their election African Americans have gotten more municipal jobs and African American contractors have benefited from affirmative action programs to award city contracts to minority businesses.[52] In particular, this can be seen in Detroit where longtime mayor Coleman Young began a policy of giving preferential treatment to local businesses over firms outside the city.

The second generation of African American mayors includes several elected in cities such as Dallas, Denver, Houston, Minneapolis, San Francisco, and Seattle, where African Americans make up less than one-third of the population. In fact, the majority of African Americans elected mayor since the early 1980s have done so in places where blacks comprise less than half the population.[53] Cities in western states with reformed government structures have had less difficulty electing African Americans than have those in the East with a history of machine politics.

In predominantly white cities, African American mayoral candidates obviously must forge coalitions to get the support of white voters. Once in office, their goals tend to focus more on broad economic development, rather than on African American incorporation. This means that race is deemphasized in election campaigns, as well as in governing. Even in predominantly African American cities, such as Detroit and Cleveland, successful second-generation mayoral candidates have de-racialized their campaigns and then altered the focus of their administrations.

In virtually all cities, once African American mayors are in office they need to work with the predominantly white business community to further economic development for African Americans. Some African-American mayors find it difficult to maintain an effective balance between catering to their electoral constituency and forging alliances with upper-class white bankers and merchants. If they seem to be working too closely with the white business community, they are criticized by African Americans for "selling out." If they alienate the white business establishment, African American mayors risk even more white businesses moving out of their cities. As in Detroit, affluent white suburbs have prospered since the 1980s, while the city has continued to lose people and jobs.

Facing population flight to the suburbs, rising poverty, and a declining tax base, commentators as early as 1969 began to refer to the "hollow prize" inherited by black mayors.[54] Just when blacks began to get elected mayor, their cities seemed to be crumbling. Considering the continuing encirclement of minority central cities by white suburbs and the isolation of cities with black mayors, Neil Kraus and Todd Swanstrom conclude that the "hollow prize problem will only worsen." John Harrigan and Ronald Vogel note that in many large cities, "Even if every city government position were filled by an African American and even if the maximum number of development dollars were spent on rebuilding downtowns, the central-city government left on its own still would not have the resources to end the poverty of the large underclass."[55]

After electing African American mayors in the 1980s, several cities, including Gary, Indiana, Oakland, New York, Chicago, and Los Angeles, elected white mayors in the 1990s. In Chicago the first African American mayor, Harold Washington, was elected in 1983. in 1989 Richard M. Daley, son of the legendary Mayor Richard J. Daley, was elected mayor and he has been reelected five times. In each election, Daley has overwhelmed African American opponents in a city where in 2000 whites composed about 31 percent of the city's population, African Americans 36 percent, and Hispanics 26 percent.

A few predominantly Hispanic large cities, mainly in Texas and Florida, have elected Hispanic mayors. Occasionally, as in Denver and San Diego, predominantly Anglo cities have elected Hispanic mayors. Hispanics are much less segregated than African Americans, and their relatively greater population dispersion lessens their potential for political power in American cities. Only in San Antonio, El Paso, and Miami do Hispanics constitute more than half the population in cities with populations over 300,000. Laredo, Texas, with a population of about 175,000, is 95 percent Hispanic, and it has had Hispanic mayors since 1988.

Although mayors of big cities have overwhelmingly been Democrats—virtually all African American and Hispanic mayors have been Democrats—an interesting feature of the 1990s was the election of white, Republican mayors in the nation's two largest cities, New York and Los Angeles. In New York City, Rudolph Giuliani, the Republican mayor for much of the 1990s, was replaced by Michael Bloomberg in 2001 when Giuliani was term limited. Bloomberg, who earlier had switched from being a Democrat, was easily reelected in 2005 and then changed to an Independent in 2007. In 2005 Antonio Villaraigosa became the first Hispanic mayor of Los Angeles since 1872. In the primary, Villaraigosa finished ahead of the white incumbent mayor, James Hahn, and the African American former chief of police. Then he got 59 percent of the vote in a run-off against Hahn. Hispanics make up about 48 percent of the population of Los Angeles, but just a quarter of its voters. In Los Angeles and in many other cities, Hispanics face an extra burden of winning votes from African Americans, who have been used to dominating political coalitions of color. By about 2025, Hispanics are expected to outnumber Hispanics by 2 to 1 in the United States.

A third change has been the election of increasing numbers of women mayors, including several African Americans. Since 1979, women have been elected mayor in such widely dispersed big cities as Chicago, San Francisco, San Diego, Fort Worth, Portland, Minneapolis, Cleveland, Houston, Pittsburgh, Washington, D.C., Salt Lake City, and Las Vegas. Still, there are relatively few women mayors of large cities. In 2007 there were women mayors in 35 of the 243 cities with populations over 100,000 and of the nation's 100 largest cities, 12 had women mayors. One explanation for the fact that there are proportionately fewer women mayors of big cities than there are women governors is that while women often serve as city council members they lack administrative experience at the local level. In contrast, several women governors have held statewide administrative positions.[56]

Paralleling the experience of African Americans in cities with African American mayors, research shows that the election of women mayors has led to more jobs for women in the municipal workforce. Being mayor of a large city seldom offers long-term job security, regardless of race or gender. Kathy Whitmore was reelected mayor of Houston five times, but Jane Byrne in Chicago, Sharon Pratt Kelly in Washington, D.C., and Jane Campbell in Cleveland served only one term after being unable to respond effectively to the problems facing their cities. Contrary to long-held "conventional wisdom," women mayoral candidates appear to be able to raise money and get newspaper endorsements at about the same rate as men.

SUMMARY

The roles played by governors parallel those of the president. A governor acts as chief of state, commander in chief, chief legislator, and chief administrator. The formal (constitutional) powers of governors, including tenure potential, appointment, budgeting, and veto, all have been increased since the 1950s. Although governors increasingly have had to deal with legislatures controlled by the opposition party, they have become effective policy leaders. In addition, the personal power of governors often is equally important for their success as legislative leaders.

As chief administrators, governors have been given expanded authority to prepare budgets and appoint department heads, but they are hindered as managers by the existence of independent boards and commissions and by personnel practices, such as merit systems and collective bargaining contracts.

Many cities, states, and counties have instituted reforms aimed at "reinventing government," to improve efficiency and service delivery. Techniques include privatization and entrepreneurial activities. In addition, the delivery of more services online (e-government) is changing the way residents interact with state and local governments.

Cities have moved from weak-council plans to strong-mayor–council and council-manager plans in their attempts to centralize power. Managers often are found in newer, suburban communities. Increasingly, city manager and mayor-council systems have taken on each other's characteristics to form a new hybrid type of city government.

The number of women and minority mayors has increased substantially since the 1960s, but minorities may find they have won a "hollow prize," and relatively few women have been elected mayor of large cities. In several cases, African Americans have been elected mayor in predominantly white cities and Republicans have won in predominantly Democratic cities.

KEY TERMS

Jacksonian democracy era (p. 205)
administrative efficiency (p. 205)
institutional powers (p. 207)
tenure potential (p. 210)
lame duck (p. 210)
appointing power (p. 210)
executive budget (p. 211)
veto (p. 212)
item veto (p. 212)
amendatory veto (p. 212)
pocket veto (p. 212)
personal power (p. 214)
state of the state message (p. 217)
pardons (p. 219)
commutations (p. 219)
cabinet (p. 220)
bureaucracy (p. 221)
reorganization (p. 222)
professional ideology (p. 224)
affirmative action (p. 224)

merit system (p. 224)
collective bargaining (p. 225)
incremental budgeting (p. 227)
performance budgeting (p. 228)
entrepreneurial government (p. 229)
reinventing government (REGO) (p. 229)
Total Quality Management (TQM) (p. 229)
privatization (p. 230)
e-government (p. 232)
long ballot (p. 233)
postaudit (p. 235)
preaudit (p. 236)
weak-mayor–council plan (p. 236)
strong-mayor–council plan (p. 238)
chief administrative officer (CAO) (p. 238)
council-manager plan (p. 239)
commission plan (p. 241)
hybrid system (p. 242)
political incorporation of blacks (p. 243)

BRIEF COMPARISONS OF STATE/LOCAL DIFFERENCES

Issue	State Level	Local Governments
Evolution of executive power	Substantially stronger gubernatorial authority since the 1960s	Change from weak to strong mayors, to commissions, to managers, to CAOs, and to hybrid systems
Extent of executive power	Governors' ability to veto, appoint a cabinet, prepare budgets is extensive	"Weak" mayors, manager-council, and commission systems all lack central executive authority, but power has become more centralized
Party control	Governors often have to operate with divided party control of state government	Mayors often operate in cities with nonpartisan elections
Separately elected officials	Governors must deal with several separately elected statewide officials, but pick their own cabinets	In most cases, mayors do not face separately elected city officials, but they share power with council members and managers
Administration	Governors are limited by civil service rules and by public unions	Mayors are limited by civil service rules and by public unions
Reinventing government and TQM	Implemented "flatter" bureaucracies and budget reforms	Implemented entrepreneurial enterprises, customer satisfaction measures, such as surveys of service quality

INTERESTING WEB SITES

www.nga.org. An easy to use site sponsored by the National Governors' Association, a bipartisan organization of the nation's and U.S. territories' governors. Go to the bottom of the page and click on "Governors" to find access to biographies, summaries of state-of-the-state addresses; be sure to click on "Inside the Governor's Office."

For a partisan look at governors, go to *www.democraticgovernors.org* and *www.rga.org*.

www.icma.org. The International City/County Managers Association Web site is excellent. Current topics are easily accessible from the home page. Also go to the "Browse by Topic" pull-down menu and check out "Council Manager Form of Government," "Career Resources," "Ethics," among others.

www.nasbo.org. Web site of the professional association of the chief financial advisers to the nation's governors, National Association of State Budget Officers. Online reports that focus on the budgeting process and expenditures are available.

www.usmayors.org. The United States Conference of Mayors maintains this nonpartisan Web site. "Meet the Mayors" and "Mayoral Elections Database" are good resources. At the bottom of the page, click on "U.S. Mayor Newspaper" for links to articles about what mayors are doing in a number of cities.

NOTES

1. Alan Greenblatt, "Spitzer's Gamble," *Governing* (August 2006), p. 15.
2. Richard P. Nathan, "There Will Always be a New Federalism," *Journal of Public Administration Research and Theory* (2006), www.rockinst.org.
3. Larry Sabato, *Goodbye to Good-Time Charlie: The American Governorship Transformed*, 2d ed. (Washington, D.C.: Congressional Quarterly Press, 1983), pp. 5–7.
4. Thad Beyle, "The Governors," in *Politics in the American States*, 8th ed. Virginia Gray and Russell L. Hanson, eds. (Washington, D.C.: Congressional Quarterly Press, 2004), p. 196.
5. Thad Beyle, "Gubernatorial Elections, Campaign Costs, and Powers," *Book of the States 2006* (Lexington, Ky.: Council of State Governments, 2006), p. 145.
6. Joseph A. Schlesinger, "The Politics of the Executive," in *Politics in the American States*, 2d ed., Herbert Jacob and Kenneth N. Vines, eds. (Boston, Mass.: Little, Brown, 1971), pp. 222–234.
7. Beyle, "The Governors," pp. 210–218.
8. Beyle, "The Governors," p. 215.
9. Alan Rosenthal, *Heavy Lifting: The Job of the American Legislature* (Washington: Congressional Quarterly Press, 2004), p. 175.
10. Beyle, "The Governors," p. 216.
11. David R. Mayhew, *Divided We Govern: Party Control, Lawmaking, and Investigations* (New Haven, Conn.: Yale University Press 1991).
12. Rosenthal, *Heavy Lifting*, pp. 179–180.
13. Beyle, "The Governors," pp. 205–210.
14. Rosenthal, *Heavy Lifting*, pp. 186–188.
15. Alan Rosenthal, *The Decline of Representative Democracy* (Washington, D.C. Congressional Quarterly Press, 1998), p. 295.
16. Alan Rosenthal, *Governors and Legislatures: Contending Powers* (Washington, D.C.: Congressional Quarterly Press, 1990), pp. 110–112.
17. Ibid., pp. 26–27.
18. Richard C. Elling, "Administering State Programs: Performance and Politics," in *Politics in the American States*, 8th ed., Virginia Gray and Russell L. Hanson, eds. p. 268.
19. James K. Conant, "In the Shadow of Wilson and Brownlow: Executive Branch Reorganization in the States, 1965–1987," *Public Administration Review* (September–October 1988), p. 895.
20. Charles T. Goodsell, "Collegial State Administration: Design for Today?" *Western Political Quarterly* (September 1981), pp. 455–460.
21. Cynthia J. Bowling and Deil S. Wright, "Public Administration in the Fifty States: A Half-Century Administrative Revolution," *State and Local Government Review* (Winter 1988), pp. 52–64.
22. Elling, "Administering State Programs," p. 268.
23. Christine Kelleher, et al., "Women in State Governments: Trends and Issues," *Book of the States 2006* (Lexington, Ky.: Council of State Governments, 2006), p. 414.
24. Elling, "Administering State Programs," p. 272.

25. David Osborne and Ted Graebler, *Reinventing Government* (Reading, Mass.: Addison-Wesley, 1992), p. 125.

26. Jonathan Walters, "Who Needs Civil Service?" *Governing* (August 1997), p. 18.

27. Jonathan Walters, "The Fine Art of Firing the Incompetent," *Governing* (June 1994), p. 36.

28. Jonathan Walters, "Solidarity Forgotten," *Governing* (June 2006), p. 32.

29. Rosenthal, *Governors and Legislatures,* p. 141.

30. Richard F. Winter, "The Politics of Taxing and Spending," in *Politics in the American States*, 7th ed., Virginia Gray, et al., eds, (Washington, D.C.: Congressional Quarterly Press, 1999), p. 335.

31. Osborne and Graebler, *Reinventing Government,* p. 349.

32. Theodore Lowi, "Machine Politics—Old and New," *Public Interest* (Fall 1967), p. 86.

33. Osborne and Graebler, *Reinventing Government,* Preface.

34. Jonathan Walters, "Flattening the Bureaucracy," *Governing* (June 1996), pp. 20–24.

35. Joel A. Aberbach and Bert A. Rockman, "Reinventing Government: Problems and Prospects." Paper presented at the Annual Meeting of the Midwest Political Science Association (April 1999), p. 6.

36. Jeffery F. Brudney and Deil S. Wright, "Revisiting Administrative Reform in the American States: The Status of Reinventing Government in the 1990s," *Public Administrative Review* (May–June 2002), p. 357.

37. Richard C. Kearney, "Reinventing Government and Battling Budget Crises: Manager and Municipal Government Actions in 2003," *Municipal Year Book 2005* (Washington, D.C.: International City/County Management Association, 2005), pp. 28–29.

38. E. S. Savas, *Privatization: The Key to Better Government* (Chatham, N.J.: Chatham House, 1987), p. 3. Also see E. S. Savas, *Privatization and Public-Private Partnerships* (Chatham, N.J.: Chatham House, 2000).

39. James Q. Wilson, *Bureaucracy: What Government Agencies Do and Why They Do It* (New York: Basic Books, 1989), pp. 350–351.

40. Charles Mahtesian, "Taking Chicago Private," *Governing* (April 1994), p. 31.

41. Penelope Lemov, "A Dose of Transparency," *Governing* (September 2006), p. 50.

42. *Governning State & Local Source Book 2006* (Washington, D.C.: Congressional Quarterly Press, 2006), pp. 98–99.

43. David Coursey, "E-Government Trends, Benefits, and Challenges," *Municipal Year Book 2005* (Washington, D.C.: International City/County Management Association, 2005), p. 20.

44. Jonathan Walters, "The Taming of Texas," *Governing* (July 1998), p. 20.

45. John J. Harrigan and Ronald K. Vogel, *Political Change in the Metropolis,* 7th ed. (New York: Longman, 2003), p. 90.

46. Susan A. McManus and Charles S. Bullock, III, "The Form, Structure, and Composition of America's Municipalities in the New Millennium," *Municipal Year Book 2005* (Washington, D.C.: International City/County Management Association, 2005), p. 5.

47. David N. Ammons and Matthew J. Bosse, "Tenure of City Managers: Examining the Dual Meanings of 'Average Tenure'" *State and Local Government Review,* no. 1 (2005), pp. 61–71.

48. Russell D. Murphy, "Commission Government," in *Encyclopedia of Urban America,* Neil Larry Shumsky, ed. (Santa Barbara, Calif.: ABC-CLIO, 1998), 193.

49. H. George Frederickson, Gary Alan Johnson, and Curtis Wood, "The Changing Structure of American Cities: A Study of Diffusion of Innovation," *Public Administration Review* (May–June 2004), pp. 328–329. These authors' views are summarized in *The Adopted City: Institutional Dynamics and Structural Change* (Armonk, N.Y.: M. E. Sharpe, 2004).

50. Robert A. Dahl, *Who Governs? Democracy and Power in an American City* (New Haven, Conn.: Yale University Press, 1961), p. 204.

51. This term was first discussed by Rufus P. Browning, Dale R. Marshall, and David H. Tabb in *Protest Is Not Enough* (Berkeley: University of California Press, 1984).
52. See Peter K. Eisinger, "Black Mayors and the Policy of Racial Advancement," in *Culture, Ethnicity, and Identity,* William C. McReedy, ed. (New York: Academic Press, 1983), pp. 95–109.
53. Rob Gurwitt, "Black, White, and Blurred," *Governing* (September 2001), p. 20.
54. Neil Kraus and Todd Swanstrom, "Minority Mayors and the Hollow Prize Problem," *PS: Political Science and Politics* (March 2001), pp. 99–104.
55. Harrigan and Vogel, *Political Change in the Metropolis,* p. 129.
56. Alan Greenblatt, "City Hall Ceiling," *Governing* (December 2006), pp. 18–20.

chapter
7

COURTS, POLICE, AND CORRECTIONS

THE WORST JUDGES MONEY CAN BUY

CA**S E**
STUDY
As we will see in the chapter, while there may not be a *best* way to select state judges, there is a *worst* way and several states, led by Texas and Ohio, have found it. That way is an election process with partisan identification of candidates who rely on large contributions from lawyers and potential litigants to fund million-dollar campaigns.

"Shopping for justice" by former Congress member Tom DeLay in 2005 drew national attention to the judicial selection in Texas. In the months immediately preceding the prosecution of DeLay on charges of receiving illegal campaign contributions, several judges were replaced or recused themselves from hearing the case because they had made campaign contributions to Democratic or Republican candidates. It raised the question "Can a partisan Republican defendant appear to get a fair trial from a Democratic judge, as revealed by the political contributions the judge made?"[1]

Traditionally, concern has been on money that judges receive. A 1998 study found that seven Texas Supreme Court judges elected between 1994 and 1998 had raised $9.2 million, with 40 percent coming from groups with cases before the court. The survey found that nearly half the judges believed the money had influenced their decisions.

A recent study by the *New York Times* found that over a twelve-year period Ohio Supreme Court justices had routinely heard cases after receiving money from one of the parties involved or from groups filing briefs.[2] Justice Terrence O'Donnell, who raised more than $3 million for his 2006 reelection campaign, was found to have voted 91 percent of the time in favor of his contributors. *New York Times* researchers found that often Ohio Supreme Court justices had taken money from parties *after* arguments in court and *before* decisions were made. O'Donnell was reelected with 59 percent of the vote.

Texas is one of ten states with partisan judicial elections. In Ohio, general elections are nonpartisan, but judicial primaries are partisan so that party affiliations of candidates are well known. The *New York Times* study showed that business groups carefully screened candidates in Ohio to decide who they would support.

The traditional pay-for-justice systems in many states have been exacerbated by recent U.S. Supreme Court decisions that permit judicial candidates personally to solicit campaign funds from litigants and lawyers and to engage in other partisan political activities. Later we will examine some other judicial selection processes that seek to promote fair and impartial justice.

POINTS TO CONSIDER

- Examine the way in which state courts are organized and the functions performed by courts at each level.
- How have courts been reformed since the 1970s? Why is change resisted?
- Compare the methods by which state judges are selected. What are the effects of each system on the kinds of judges selected? How should selection systems be changed?
- What has been the relationship between the Supreme Court and state courts since the 1960s?
- What are the major theories for the decrease in crime in recent years?
- What is community policing and how well does it work?

- Why have prison populations increased as crime has decreased?
- Should prisons return, at least in part, to concern about rehabilitating inmates?
- Why do so many more executions take place in southern states than in all other regions of the country?
- Which alternatives to imprisonment are likely to be the best substitutes for time spent behind bars?
- What has been the impact of new technology on fighting crime? What problems does it create?
- How much are Americans willing to sacrifice individual rights in order to feel more secure from criminals and terrorists?

State courts deal with those issues that most directly affect people's everyday lives. Most criminal cases are decided in state courts because most crimes are violations of state laws. Virtually all cases dealing with domestic relations—divorce, adoption, child custody—are heard by state courts. Questions of property ownership, contracts, zoning, wills and estates, and automobile accidents all originate in state courts. Yet most people do not know the names of their local judges, and they cannot identify any recent opinion of their state's supreme court.

Over 96 million cases are filed in state courts each year. This represents about 99 percent of all litigation in the United States. About two-thirds of all state cases involve traffic offenses. Of the remaining one-third, about half are criminal cases and half are civil cases. A substantial proportion of state litigation deals with economic issues, such as government regulation of utilities, workers' compensation, and zoning.

The legal system of the United States is complicated by a federal structure that permits a variety of laws and courts, rather than specifying a unified plan. Throughout the country, state law is the basic law. In the United States, federal law is drafted for specific purposes and **common law** is interpreted individually by each state. Common law is judge-made law that originated in England from decisions shaped according to existing custom. Decisions were reapplied in similar situations (precedents) and, over a period of time, became common to the nation. Both state and federal courts are bound by state law unless a state statute has been superseded by federal law or is in conflict with the Constitution.

The system is made even more complex by the dual nature of state and federal courts. Unlike many other federal systems, in the United States both the states and the federal government have a complete set of trial and appellate courts. Although federal courts are concerned only with cases that raise federal issues (i.e., involve the interpretation of federal laws or the U.S. Constitution), the jurisdiction of state and federal courts occasionally overlaps. In some civil suits this gives plaintiffs the choice of initiating action in a state or federal court, and in some criminal cases it means the defendant may be tried in both state and federal courts. State courts are inferior to federal courts in the sense that decisions of state supreme courts can be reviewed and overturned by the U.S. Supreme Court. State supreme courts decide thousands of cases each year, and only a fraction of 1 percent are reviewed by the U.S. Supreme Court.

As we will see in this chapter, there have been significant organizational reforms in state court systems since the mid-1970s and many states have changed the ways in which they select judges. Most states have adopted reforms to help them manage greatly increased caseloads. These include greater use of computers; alternative resolutions to disputes, such as mediation and arbitration; and the use of magistrates, who are local attorneys given judicial authority to hear less important cases. Still, judges, lawyers, and organizations that frequently appear in court have vested interests they want to protect and they often resist changes.

STATE COURT ORGANIZATION AND MANAGEMENT

The historical development of state court systems is strikingly similar to the development of state and local bureaucracy as discussed in Chapter 6. In the nineteenth century, the forces of urbanization and industrialization created a myriad of social and economic problems. Crowded cities led to increases in crime and juvenile delinquency and to the breakup of families. Landlord-tenant relations caused conflicts that were resolved by lawsuits. Questions of employer liability for personal injury and property damage opened new areas in the law. The use of automobiles created traffic law problems; and, of course, accident claims placed a heavy burden on local courts.

The response of many states was to create new courts, just as new boards and commissions were added to cope with regulatory problems. As with the bureaucracy, courts expanded in an unplanned manner. Their jurisdiction often overlapped, and each court acted independently of others. As an example, in the early 1930s there were 556 independent courts in Chicago, of which 505 were justices of the peace who completed for business.[3] New courts included those for juvenile and family relations, small claims, traffic, and, more recently, illegal drugs. Each court had its own rules of procedure, and the nature of decisions varied among courts with similar jurisdiction. As with state administrative structures, much of the history of twentieth-century court organization can be written in terms of reform attempts to unify and streamline complex state court systems.

At the extremes, some states have fully consolidated their courts, and others continue to operate very complex, fragmented court systems. Iowa (Figure 7-1) represents a state that has streamlined its court system to a very basic form. In contrast, New York (Figure 7-2) has thirteen sets of courts. Although many states have simplified their court systems, typically several different types of trial courts remain at the state level.

Court organization is important because it affects access to the legal system and it helps determine the nature of judicial decisions. Justice delayed is justice denied, and the efficient operation of state courts, with the speedy resolution of legal matters, has broad consequences for society.

Trial Courts

Trial courts of limited or specialized jurisdiction hear less serious criminal and civil cases. Municipal courts, for example, often are limited to **criminal misdemeanors,** for which the punishment is a fine or jail sentence of less than one year. In **civil cases** relating to the private rights of individuals, these courts hear cases involving limited amounts of money. In specialized courts only certain parties, such as juveniles or drug abusers, appear. When cases are appealed from these courts, a new trial is held (*trial de novo*) without reference to the first proceeding.

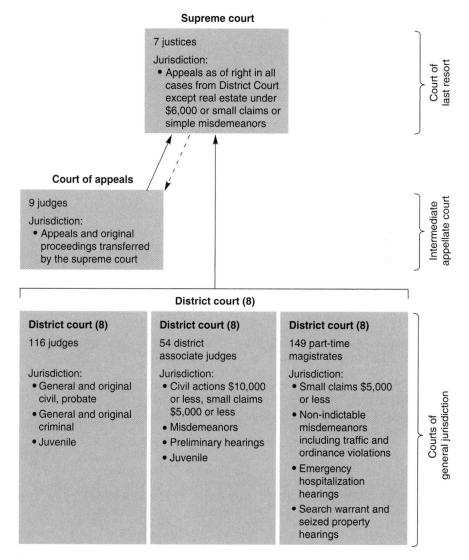

Supreme court

7 justices Jurisdiction: • Appeals as of right in all cases from District Court except real estate under $6,000 or small claims or simple misdemeanors	Court of last resort

Court of appeals

9 judges Jurisdiction: • Appeals and original proceedings transferred by the supreme court	Intermediate appellate court

District court (8)

District court (8)	District court (8)	District court (8)	
116 judges Jurisdiction: • General and original civil, probate • General and original criminal • Juvenile	54 district associate judges Jurisdiction: • Civil actions $10,000 or less, small claims $5,000 or less • Misdemeanors • Preliminary hearings • Juvenile	149 part-time magistrates Jurisdiction: • Small claims $5,000 or less • Non-indictable misdemeanors including traffic and ordinance violations • Emergency hospitalization hearings • Search warrant and seized property hearings	Courts of general jurisdiction

FIGURE 7-1 Iowa court structure, 2007.

Source: Directory of State Court Clerks and County Courthouses, 2007 edition (Washington, D.C.: CQ Press, 2007), p. 82.

Trial courts of general jurisdiction hear serious criminal cases (felonies) and serious civil cases in which there are no limits on the amount of money being sought. In most states, these courts are at the county level, or circuit courts may extend over two or more counties. In the few states that do not have courts of limited jurisdiction, courts of general jurisdiction handle all litigation.

In most states minor trial courts are highly decentralized. There are many municipal courts in urban areas and a variety of county courts in rural areas. Then there are separate trial courts to perform specific judicial functions, such as small claims or juvenile crime.

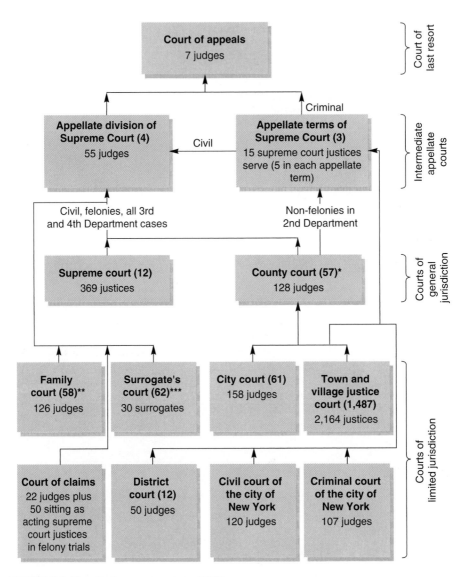

FIGURE 7-2 New York court structure, 2007.

Source: Directory of State Court Clerks and County Courthouses, 2007 edition (Washington, D.C.: CQ Press, 2007), p. 180.

Only a few states have a single, unified set of minor courts. However, states are moving toward court systems that are more simplified. While many states, such as New York, continue to have a large number of specialized courts with their own procedures, some of them have centralized their court systems under an administrative judge who controls caseloads, makes staff assignments, and determines budgets. A majority of states have assumed all or most of funding of court systems. Often it is the office of the chief justice that assigns retired judges to help manage caseloads and is responsible for disciplining attorneys and judges.

Both lawyers and judges are divided in their support for court reform. Defendants' lawyers and their business clients tend to prefer streamlined systems that they believe are more efficient and better serve their interests. Plaintiffs' lawyers tend to oppose reform, believing they can use their knowledge of more complex systems to win cases. Appellate judges prefer unified court systems, but trial judges often see their jobs threatened by reform.[4]

"Justice" in minor trial courts often is quick and routine. Defendants appear, they plead guilty or **no contest (nolo contendere),** a fine is set, and the court proceeds to the next case. When defendants plead "no contest," it is in effect an admission of guilt without stating so formally. The defendant does not contest the charges but does not admit civil liability. This can be very important in traffic accidents where a civil suit for monetary damages may follow the criminal traffic violation. Although penalties technically are the same as for a plea of guilty, judges may be more lenient when defendants throw themselves on the mercy of the court and explain the circumstances leading to their arrest.[5]

Major trial courts handle felony criminal cases and civil cases involving large amounts of money. Because felony cases place the strongest demands on trial courts, the large increase in criminal filings since 1980 has made effective case management critical if courts are to function well with limits on new personnel. Most often major trial courts—known as district courts, superior courts, or common pleas courts—are established at the county level. Although they are less fragmented than minor trial courts, major trial courts typically have divisions to hear such specialized cases as divorce proceedings and probate of wills. As noted, when cases are appealed from municipal courts, they usually are retried in a major trial court. Less than 5 percent of decisions are appealed from major trial courts, and thus for most litigants they are, in fact, courts of first and last resort.

Appellate Courts

Early in the twentieth century most states had only a supreme court to which all cases were appealed. In 2006, thirty-nine states had intermediate **courts of appeal** to deal with the increased volume of cases. Those states without intermediate appeals courts all are geographically small or they have small populations. Some states have one appellate court; in other states there are several regional appellate courts. In a few states, intermediate appellate courts are divided between criminal and civil divisions. Even where these intermediate courts do exist, some cases proceed directly from trial courts to the state supreme court. Appellate court judges usually sit in panels of three to hear cases. Parties to suits (litigants) are successful if they can convince at least two judges that their arguments are correct. In a majority of cases, appeals are mandatory, meaning that intermediate court of appeals judges can exercise little control over their docket. In some states, intermediate courts of appeal publish few of their opinions and judges often let other colleagues speak for them with little review of the opinion.[6]

All states have a supreme court that hears appeals from intermediate courts of appeal and, occasionally, hears appeals directly from major trial courts. State supreme courts have from five to nine justices, who generally sit *en banc* (all together) to hear cases (Table 7-1). Although the highest court in most states is called the supreme court,

TABLE 7-1 State Courts of Last Resort

State or Other Jurisdiction	Name of Court	Justices Chosen(a)				Chief Justice	
		At Large	By District	No. of Judges (b)	Term (in years) (c)	Method of Selection	Term of Office for Chief Justice
Alabama	S.C.	✓		9	6	Popular election	6 years
Alaska	S.C.	✓		5	10	By court	3 years (d)
Arizona	S.C.	✓		5	6	By court	5 years
Arkansas	S.C.	✓		7	8	Popular election	8 years
California	S.C.	✓		7	12	Appointed by governor	12 years
Colorado	S.C.	✓		7	10	By court	Indefinite
Connecticut	S.C.	✓		7	8	Legislative appointment (e)	8 years
Delaware	S.C.	✓		5	12	Appointed by governor, with consent of Senate	12 years
Florida	S.C.	(f)		7	6	By court	2 years
Georgia	S.C.	✓		7	6	By court	4 years
Hawaii	S.C.	✓		5	10	Appointed by governor, with consent of Senate (g)	10 years
Idaho	S.C.	✓		5	6	By court	4 years
Illinois	S.C.		✓	7	10	By court	3 years
Indiana	S.C.	✓		5	10(h)	Judicial nominating commission appointment	5 years
Iowa	S.C.	✓		7	8	By court	8 years
Kansas	S.C.	✓		7	6	Rotation by seniority	Indefinite
Kentucky	S.C.		✓	7	8	By court	4 years
Louisiana	S.C.		✓	7	10	By seniority of service	Duration of service
Maine	S.J.C.	✓		7	7	Appointed by governor	7 years
Maryland	C.A.		✓	7	10	Appointed by governor	Indefinite

State	Court					Method of selection	Term
Massachusetts	S.J.C.	✓		7	To age 70	Appointed by governor (j)	To age 70
Michigan	S.C.	✓		7	8	By court	2 years
Minnesota	S.C.	✓		7	6	Popular election	6 years
Mississippi	S.C.	✓	✓	9	8	By seniority of service	Duration of service
Missouri	S.C.	✓		7	12	By court (k)	2 years
Montana	S.C.	✓		7	8	Popular election	8 years
Nebraska	S.C.	✓	✓ (l)	7	6(m)	Appointed by governor from Judicial Nominating Commission	Duration of service
Nevada	S.C.	✓		5	6	Rotation	2 years
New Hampshire	S.C.	✓		5	To age 70	Appointed by governor with approval of elected executive council	To age 70
New Jersey	S.C.	✓		7	7 (n)	Appointed by governor, with consent of Senate	Duration of service
New Mexico	S.C.	✓		5	8	By court	2 years
New York	C.A.	✓		7	14	Appointed by governor from Judicial Nomination Commission	14 years
North Carolina	S.C.	✓		7	8	Popular election	8 years
North Dakota	S.C.	✓		5 (o)	10	By Supreme and district court judges	5 years (p)
Ohio	S.C.	✓		7	6	Popular election	6 years
Oklahoma	S.C.	✓	✓	9	6	By court	2 years
	C.C.A.			5	6	By court	2 years
Oregon	S.C.	✓		7	6	By court	6 years
Pennsylvania	S.C.	✓		7	10	Rotation by seniority	Duration of term
Rhode Island	S.C.	✓		5	Life	Appointed by governor from Judicial Nominating Commission (i)	Life
South Carolina	S.C.	✓		5	10	Legislative election	10 years

(Continued)

TABLE 7-1 *(Continued)*

State or Other Jurisdiction	Name of Court	Justices Chosen (a)		No. of Judges (b)	Term (in years) (c)	Chief Justice	
		At Large	By District			Method of Selection	Term of Office for Chief Justice
South Dakota	S.C.		✓(q)	5	8	By court	4 years
Tennessee	S.C.	✓		5	8	By court	4 years
Texas	S.C.	✓		9	6	Partisan election	6 years
	C.C.A.	✓		9	6	Partisan election	6 years (r)
Utah	S.C.	✓		5	10 (s)	By court	4 years
Vermont	S.C.	✓		5	6	Appointed by governor from Judicial Nomination Commission, with consent of Senate	6 years
Virginia	S.C.	✓		7	12	Seniority	Indefinite
Washington	S.C.	✓		9	6	By court	4 years
West Virginia	S.C.A.		✓	5	12	Rotation by seniority	1 year
Wisconsin	S.C.	✓		7	10	Seniority	Until declined
Wyoming	S.C.	✓		5	8	By court	At pleasure of court
Dist. of Columbia	C.A.	✓		9	15	Judicial Nominating Commission appointment	4 years
Puerto Rico	S.C.	✓		7	To age 70	Appointed by governor, with consent of Senate	To age 70

Key:
S.C.—Supreme Court
S.C.A.—Supreme Court of Appeals
S.J.C.—Supreme Judicial Court

C.A.—Court of Appeals
C.C.A.—Court of Criminal Appeals
H.C.—High Court

(a) See Chapter 5 table "Selection and Retention of Judges," in *The Book of the States 2006,* for details.

(b) Number includes chief justice.

(c) The initial term may be shorter. See Chapter 5 table "Selection and Retention of Judges," in *The Book of the States 2006,* for details.

(d) A justice may serve more than one term as chief justice, but may not serve consecutive terms in that position.

(e) Governor nominates from candidates submitted by Judicial Selection Commission.

(f) Regional (5), Statewide (2), Regional based on District of Appeal.

(g) Judicial Selection Commission nominates.

(h) Initial two years; retention 10 years.

(i) With House and Senate confirmation.

(j) Chief Justices are appointed, until age 70, by the Governor with the advice and consent of the Executive (Governor's) Council.

(k) Selection is typically rotated among the judges.

(l) Chief justice chosen statewide; associate judges chosen by district.

(m) More than three years for first election and every six years thereafter.

(n) Followed by tenure.

(o) A temporary court of appeals was established July 1, 1987 to exercise appellate and original jurisdiction was delegated by the supreme court. This court does not sit, has no assigned judges, has heard no appeals and is currently unfunded.

(p) Or expiration of term, whichever is first.

(q) Initially chosen by district; retention determined statewide.

(r) Presiding judge of Court of Criminal Appeals.

(s) Initial three years; retention 10 years.

Source: National Center for State Courts, February 2006. *The Book of the States 2006* (Lexington, Ky.: Council of State Governments, 2006), pp. 242–243.

in a few states it is referred to as the court of appeals, supreme judicial court, or, as in New York, supreme court of appeals (see Figure 7-2). Oklahoma and Texas have separate courts of last resort for criminal and civil cases. Although state supreme courts do not have as much discretion over which cases to hear as the U.S. Supreme Court, their discretion is so broad that most appeals are rejected.

An ultimate power for state supreme courts and for the U.S. Supreme Court is the ability to declare legislative acts unconstitutional. The use of **judicial review** by state supreme courts—that is, to overrule, declare unconstitutional, acts passed by state legislatures—is about as frequent as it is for the U.S. Supreme Court to overrule acts passed by Congress.[7] Political scientist Henry Glick points out that the percentage of challenged state laws declared unconstitutional varies greatly among state supreme courts.

Like the U.S. Supreme Court, state supreme courts schedule oral arguments and then meet in private conference to decide cases. Unlike the U.S. Supreme Court, in many state supreme courts opinion assignments are made on a rotating basis among the justices, and this reduces the power of the chief justice. Chief justices in both systems are one among equals in deciding cases, but they may play a dominant role in leading the discussion of cases in conference, and they also have special administrative powers over their court system.

In contrast to the U.S. Supreme Court, there are relatively few dissents among judges in state supreme court decisions. Several factors help explain this apparent lack of conflict. First, legal tradition supports unanimity to present clear policy guidelines. Second, some courts assign one judge to research the case and write the opinion. In such circumstances, the other judges are likely to concur, because they have not paid close attention to the case. Moreover, because of the nature of their interaction in a small group setting, with as few as five justices, there is a need to maintain congenial personal relations.

Because the U.S. Constitution often is vague about the nature of governmental power, the U.S. Supreme Court must interpret what it means and this gives the Court substantial power. As noted in Chapter 1, state constitutions are more detailed and therefore more specific than the U.S. Constitution. Still, state supreme court judges exercise considerable discretionary power because state provisions often become outdated and the large number of amendments causes state constitutions to contain inconsistent and contradictory statements.

In states with intermediate appellate courts, supreme courts have more discretion to decide what cases they will hear. State court expert Henry R. Glick notes that when supreme court justices have more control to select cases they believe are important, it gives them more time to consider legal concepts and write opinions.[8] This often means they play a strong role as policy makers in a manner similar to the U.S. Supreme Court justices.

In contrast to legislators, judges are more likely to be drawn from a homogeneous upper-class or middle-class background, which means they tend to share similar perspectives on many legal issues. Because of a variety of reasons, including open discrimination, until the 1980s there were few women or minority lawyers and proportionally even fewer women or minority judges. By 2000, one-fourth of state supreme court justices were female, compared to 3.1 percent in 1980.[9] Racial composition also changed significantly from 0.6 percent nonwhite in 1980 to 11.6 percent in 2000. There were only two African American justices on all state supreme courts in 1980. In 2000, women were represented on forty-nine of the fifty-two state high courts, and there was at least one racial minority on twenty-six of the high courts.

Political scientists have documented some connection between judges' race and gender, plus party affiliation and religion, and the nature of their decisions. However, there is disagreement about the strength of those connections. The presence of minority and women justices clearly speaks to the representativeness of courts and access to them by all groups of society.

Court Unification

The structure of state courts can have an important political impact on a variety of groups. Particularly in urban areas, courts have massive backlogs of cases, a situation that directly influences the administration of justice. Since the mid-1960s, the number of cases filed and disposed of has increased by 1,000 percent. Because they are unable to make **bail** (money or credit deposited with the court to get an arrested person temporarily released on the assurance that he or she will appear for trial), large numbers of people charged with crimes, but assumed innocent until proven guilty, are forced to spend months in county jails waiting for their cases to appear on the court calendar. Forced to exist in overcrowded, outdated facilities, many prisoners have suffered physical hardships, and a variety of suits have been initiated by civil liberties groups to force improvements in jail conditions. These same groups have protested against the bail system, which forces indigents to await trial in jail, and they have complained vigorously about judicial sentencing practices in which different penalties, ranging from probation to several years in prison, are given to individuals who have committed similar offenses. The backlog of cases also has led to the widespread use of plea bargaining (discussed in the following section).

In most states, the variety of courts operating under different rules of procedure within a single county results in confusion and unequal application of the law. The quality of "justice" may depend largely on how successful attorneys are in steering cases to courts presided over by judges who are likely to share their perspectives. Trial judges function independently of one another, and there are few effective controls that can be applied to them by appellate courts.

Faced with such a situation, reformers have called for an integrated system in which the number of separate courts would be greatly reduced and the problem of overlapping jurisdiction eliminated. Reformers would place all judges under the general supervision of the chief justice of their state in order to ensure uniform practices and standards of conduct.

Only a few states have consolidated their court system into a single set of courts that handle all trial court litigation. Most continue to have a number of specialized courts with their own procedures. As noted, New York has thirteen kinds of trial courts. States have been more successful in centralizing or unifying their court system under an administrative judge than in consolidating their courts.[10] A majority of states have assumed all or most of the funding of court systems. Only a few states, such as Hawaii, have consolidated *and* centralized their courts.

There is little pattern to which states have unified courts. Unified and decentralized systems occur in all regions and in large and small states. However, unified control by the supreme court tends to be strongest in the western states.

In addition to streamlining the structure of courts, unified judicial systems include centralizing authority with the state supreme court to budget for all courts; to manage the caseload of courts statewide, including the use of retired judges; and to be responsible for disciplining attorneys and judges. In such cases, the chief justice becomes an administrator responsible for the operation of courts across the state.

Reform is difficult to accomplish because traditional court practices benefit groups, such as lawyers and political parties, that have substantial political influence. Opposition also comes from legislators and judges who believe their existing power would be diminished by the elimination of the current maze of courts and the independence it provides to local judges. In some states, reformers have given up trying to change the way in which judges are selected in order to get agreement first on court unification.

Proponents of consolidation argue that fragmented court systems are inefficient and that overlapping court jurisdiction often is confusing. Opponents counter that it is desirable for courts to have the flexibility to adapt to unique needs of the local area. Proponents of centralized control contend that when each court makes its own procedural rules, "justice" may vary greatly among courts that are independent of each other. State supreme court justices favor centralization because it increases their power, but local judges and government officials want to maintain community control.

Political scientist Lawrence Baum concludes that court unification may not produce the benefits its proponents proclaim.[11] Even in consolidated systems, individual courts and judges may retain substantial autonomy and efficiency may be more closely related to the work habits of individual judges than to court structure. If cases are disposed of more quickly, it may be at the expense of careful review. Many people believe that courts *should* be influenced by external politics to maintain public accountability. Although nearly all state court systems have become more unified in recent years, no state's system is totally unified, and it is unlikely that major changes will occur in the near future.

Access to Courts and Court Management

As noted above, court reform efforts during most of the twentieth century centered on reorganization, or structural reform of state systems. More recently, the focus has shifted to include ensuring racial, ethnic, income, and gender access to courts. Too often people are effectively denied access because of legal costs. Many states do not require public defender systems statewide. Even when they exist, public defender offices often are underfunded, and budgets for paying court-appointed counsel have been cut. Most researchers conclude that public defenders are more effective than court-appointed attorneys, who may have little criminal court experience. In general, however, defending the poor is not a high priority for state and local governments. The United States is the only Western democracy in which civil litigants are not guaranteed legal counsel.

In addition to issues dealing with legal counsel, states have taken a number of other steps to improve access to courts in both criminal and civil proceedings. These include training and certifying court interpreters for those with limited English skills;

enforcement of the Americans with Disabilities Act, by applying it to litigants, witnesses, jurors, and spectators; examination of racial, ethnic, and gender bias in the courts; the use of alternative dispute resolution, such as mediation and arbitration; the expansion of night courts; the availability of day care; and the creation of family courts. Family courts consolidate all matters concerning families—divorce, child custody, adoption, and domestic violence—into a single court. Improving access, of course, increases the caseloads of courts that are already crowded.

Access to crowded courts in civil matters is increasingly aided by the use of mediation and arbitration. These and other forms of alternative dispute resolution are less costly and complex than court procedures, and they can be tailored to the specific needs of the participants.

In **mediation** an impartial third party assists the disputants in reaching a voluntary settlement. Usually the process is nonadversarial, meaning that there is no attempt to determine right or wrong, but instead the parties seek to reach a mutual agreement among a selection of alternative solutions. **Arbitration** calls for one or more persons to hear the arguments in a dispute, review the evidence, and reach a decision, or award. The parties agree ahead of time to be bound by the decision. Arbitration is often used in labor disputes. More recently, court-annexed arbitration has been used in which judges refer civil suits to private arbitrators, who render prompt decisions. If the losing party does not accept the arbitrator's decision, a trial can be held in the regular court system. In a similar process, a few cities have moved lesser criminal cases to special judges who settle disputes without a jury.

Professional management has been introduced into most state court systems. This includes the use of court administrators and improved budget procedures. Better management can improve access to courts by shifting many routine functions away from downtown court buildings and neighborhood facilities. The National Center for State Courts has developed a set of measures, known as CourTools, to give court administrators a way to evaluate court performance.[12] Measures include "access to fairness"— accessibility of courts and how well people are treated—and speed and efficiency. This system of evaluation is being used in county courts in Arizona and California.

Recently, both federal and state governments have become much more concerned about the security of courthouses, as well as the security of judges and their families. David Rottman notes, "For the nation's courts, 2005 was a year of living dangerously."[13] In Chicago, the husband and mother of a federal judge were murdered by a litigant whose claim the judge had dismissed. In an Atlanta courthouse, a defendant grabbed the gun of a sheriff's deputy and killed the judge and a court reporter. The life of a Florida trial judge was threatened by people upset with his ruling in the Terri Schiavo end-of-life case. As a result of these and other incidents, security has been tightened in courthouses and judges have asked for personal protection.

TRIAL COURT PROCEDURES

As presented in movies and on television, the commonly accepted view of the administration of justice is that of the classic adversary system in which the attorney battles valiantly on behalf of his or her clients. There is always a jury, a narrow-minded prosecutor, and a white-haired judge who wields even control as the attorneys take turns objecting to the irrelevant, immaterial, and leading questions of their worthy opponent. In such a setting, justice always triumphs as the defendant is exonerated and the guilty person is dramatically exposed. In fact, however, most legal issues are settled without a trial when the defendant pleads guilty and the judge issues a sentence.

Plea Bargaining

Only about 10 percent of all criminal cases come to trial. Most are settled in pretrial negotiations among the defendant, the prosecutor, and the judge. This arrangement—**plea bargaining**—in which the defendant pleads guilty in return for a reduced charge and, most likely, a less severe penalty, is dominated by the prosecutor. Defense attorneys typically approach prosecutors to see what kind of bargain they can reach. Because prosecutors and defense attorneys know more about the details of a case, judges often defer to them for factual information and sentencing guidelines. As we would expect, cases most likely to be bargained are those where there is strong evidence against the defendant and the charges are not serious.[14] Still, prosecutors may not want to bargain some cases where they are very confident they will win at trial.

Plea bargaining is a common practice because it appears to benefit each of the interested parties. Defendants plead guilty because they receive a reduction of charge (e.g., from aggravated murder to manslaughter); a reduction in length of sentence; a chance for probation; or some combination of these agreements that results in softening the potential damage of the original charge. Prosecutors seek to avoid time-consuming trials, and they also wish to keep their conviction rates high. In some cases, the prosecutor may have obtained evidence illegally or may wish to protect informants by keeping them from taking the witness stand; he or she is therefore willing to trade a trial with its doubtful outcome for the sure thing of a guilty plea to a reduced charge. Attorneys for both sides like pretrial settlements because they can control the flow of information. Witnesses are not questioned, and they are not subject to the strict rules of trial procedure. Judges, concerned with avoiding delay and backlogs, encourage plea bargaining as a speedy way to dispose of cases. The police benefit because they do not have to appear in court as witnesses during their off-duty hours. Plea bargaining also helps the police "clear" cases and therefore bolsters their image as successful crime fighters. This was acknowledged as a judicial fact of life by the U.S. Supreme Court in *Santobello v. New York* (1971). Although the *Santobello* decision recognizes the need for plea bargaining, it also requires that judges make sure that defendants understand the agreements.

Plea bargaining is a quick and efficient means of disposing of legal disputes. Given the existing structure of the courts and the limited number of judges, the legal system in most states would rapidly break down if even half the criminal defendants pleaded not guilty and demanded a jury trial. At the present time, many defendants are convinced that they will be in for a rough time if they do not cooperate with the police and plead guilty rather than having their cases come to trial.

Plea bargaining has been going on for more than one hundred years. Surprisingly, it is not a technique that developed in response to a heavy criminal caseload in big cities. Evidence suggests that heavy caseloads do not cause plea bargaining.[15] Plea bargaining is widespread in rural counties that have low crime rates, and in some cities with heavy caseloads it is used relatively little. Researchers suggest that the use of plea bargaining is closely tied to the closeness of interaction among members of the courtroom work group—judges, lawyers, and prosecutors.[16] Because these officials often work closely together for a year or more, personal relations develop and they seek more informal solutions for cases. Pretrial settlements in civil cases are a product of the same circumstances that lead to plea bargaining in criminal cases. In both situations, settlement helps courtroom work groups achieve several goals. As James Eisenstein and Herbert Jacob show, plea bargaining reduces uncertainty for all parties, it helps maintain the cohesion of the work group, and it makes the court look good to the general public by showing that it can dispose of cases quickly and that "justice" is done. In other words, criminals are caught and punished.

In spite of its appealing characteristics, plea bargaining has many disturbing consequences. In plea bargaining, the procedures are invisible and informal. Records are not kept of conversations, and decisions seldom are reviewed by higher courts to determine whether the defendant really was guilty as charged. There is a strong potential for coercion as the prosecutor pressures the defendant. Illegally obtained evidence that might be held inadmissible in a court is never questioned. Often the unsuspecting defendant is simply advised by his or her court-appointed attorney to plead guilty, thereby saving the attorney time and allowing him or her to collect an easy fee. Some bargains appear to be too lenient and thus benefit criminal defendants. In other instances, defendants risk much harsher sentences if they insist on their right to go to trial, and thus they may accept a plea bargain even when the case against them is relatively weak.

Given the broad criticism against plea bargaining, it is not surprising that there have been calls to abolish it. Indeed, some state and local governments have experimented with strict limits on plea bargaining. However, most have reinstated it rather quickly. As noted, close-knit courtroom work groups encourage plea bargaining, and in most cases it is clear that the defendant is guilty. Several states and the federal government have passed laws requiring mandatory sentencing for certain crimes. This eliminates plea bargaining in those instances. However, prosecutors often refuse to charge defendants with crimes that require a mandatory sentence because it limits their power to bargain.

Juries

The Sixth Amendment grants the right to a jury trial in state criminal proceedings, but this right does not extend to defendants charged with misdemeanors or to defendants in juvenile court proceedings.

A group of potential jury persons (a *venire*) is selected by lot, usually from voting lists or drivers' licenses. These people are called into court as jury cases arise and are examined (*voir dire*) regarding their qualifications to return an impartial verdict in the case at hand. Jurors must be residents of the state in which the trial is taking place, and most states have a literacy requirement.

Traditionally, *state trial juries,* known as **petit juries,** were composed of twelve persons who were required to reach unanimous verdicts in criminal cases. Although most states continue those practices, and they are used in all federal court trials, several states use six- or eight-person juries for all but capital (death penalty) offenses. In all but two of those states, unanimous verdicts are required. In several states, twelve-person juries can convict with less than unanimous verdicts. In most states, juries in civil cases are not required to be unanimous. The U.S. Supreme Court has held that the Seventh Amendment's right to a jury trial in civil cases does not apply to state courts.

States also use **grand juries,** which are bodies of twelve to twenty-five members whose purposes are inquisitorial and accusatorial. The grand jury meets in secret and decides by a majority vote. If the grand jury believes the prosecutor has produced enough evidence to proceed to trial, it issues an indictment. Because grand juries are expensive and time-consuming, they have been abolished in many states.

Charges have been made that the jury system underrepresents minorities. Because African Americans and Hispanics are less likely than whites to be registered to vote, driver's license lists are increasingly used to pick jury members. However, these lists tend to underrepresent older persons, and many who live in large urban areas do not have driver's licenses. Minorities also may be disadvantaged by changes in trial location. In the highly publicized Rodney King trial in 1992 there was a change of venue from Los Angeles, where his alleged beating by police took place, to the nearly all-white suburb of Simi Valley, where it was unlikely there would be any African American jurors. In 1986 (*Batson v. Kentucky*) the Supreme Court held that prosecutors may not use their peremptory challenges (whereby potential jury members may be rejected without any reason, as contrasted with dismissal "for cause" whereby attorneys have reason to believe a potential juror may be biased) to exclude members based on race. In 1994 this ruling was extended to prevent exclusion based on gender in *J.E.B. v. Alabama*. Critics of six- and seven-person juries contend that they are more likely than twelve-member juries to exclude minorities and they are less likely to have a minority point of view.[17]

In spite of the importance attached to the jury system, it is not employed as often as one might expect. In some jurisdictions, as many as 90 percent of all people charged with criminal offenses plead guilty. Of those going to trial, roughly half opt to have their cases heard by a judge. Fewer than 10 percent nationwide of those charged with a criminal offense demand a jury trial.

Compared with judge-tried cases, jury trials are longer, cost more, and involve more people. Most research indicates that judge and jury decisions are remarkably similar. A classic study of the American jury system found that judges agreed with jury verdicts 80 percent of the time. When there was disagreement, the jury tended to be more lenient than the judge and more willing to consider a social, as opposed to a strictly legal, definition of guilt.[18]

JUDICIAL SELECTION

The way in which state court systems function is influenced strongly by the quality of judicial personnel. In turn, the type of judge presiding in courtrooms across the country is influenced by the ways in which judges are selected. Judicial selection is a highly political process that directly affects the interests of the most powerful partisan forces in states and communities. Political parties use judgeships as a source of patronage. Lawyers and their bar associations are very much involved in the selection process. Not only are the judgeships themselves prized positions, but judges are able to spread the patronage further by assigning counsel in criminal cases, by naming administrators of estates where a will does not exist, and by appointing numerous minor court officials.

TABLE 7-2 Principal Methods of Judicial Selection for State Courts

Partisan Election	Nonpartisan Election	Legislative Appointment	Gubernatorial Appointment	Merit Plan
Alabama	Arkansas	South Carolina	California	Alaska
Illinois	Georgia	Virginia	Maine[a]	Arizona
Louisiana	Idaho		New Hampshire[b]	Colorado
New York[a]	Kentucky		New Jersey	Connecticut
North Carolina	Michigan			Delaware
Pennsylvania	Minnesota			Florida
Tennessee	Mississippi			Hawaii
Texas	Montana			Indiana
West Virginia	Nevada			Iowa
	North Carolina			Kansas
	North Dakota			Maryland
	Ohio			Massachusetts
	Oregon			Missouri
	Washington			Nebraska
	Wisconsin			New Hampshire[b]
				New Mexico
				New York[a]
				Oklahoma
				Rhode Island
				South Dakota
				Utah
				Vermont
				Wyoming

Source: Council of State Governments, *The Book of the States 2006* (Lexington, Ky.: Council of State Governments, 2006). Based on data on pp. 251–254.

[a]New York: partisan election for trial judges; merit selection for appellate judges

[b]New Hampshire: state constitution calls for appointment by governor, but governor has created a merit selection commission

Each of the thirteen original states selected judges by either legislative or gubernatorial appointment. By the 1830s the popular democracy movement associated with Andrew Jackson began pushing states to elect judges. The concurrent rise of political parties meant that the selection and recruitment of judges were done by powerful new political party leaders in many large cities.[19] The Progressive movement, early in the twentieth century, reacted against political parties by moving to nonpartisan judicial elections. A feeling of dissatisfaction with both election and appointment of judges led the American Judicature Society, founded in 1913, to propose a plan in which judicial nominating commissions would recommend judicial candidates to governors. From this came the merit system, first used in Missouri in 1940.

Several selection systems are currently used by the fifty states—election, appointment by governors, appointment by legislatures, merit plans, and various combinations of these basic plans (Table 7-2). About a dozen states use one system for trial judges and another for appellate judges, and there may be special systems for minor trial judges. Currently, over thirty states use a merit system to select judges at least at one court level or to fill midterm vacancies. Trial judges are more likely to be elected than are appellate judges. There are so many variations of the basic systems that virtually no two states have the same methods of judicial selection. Still, there are considerable similarities among all five basic systems.

Election continues to be the most popular way of selecting judges. Judges are on the ballot along with a variety of other officials, and parties participate by endorsing candidates and managing nominations. Even when nonpartisan systems are used, parties often play a dominant role. In Ohio, for example, judges are chosen in nonpartisan general elections, but partisan primaries are conducted in which judges' party affiliations are clearly stated. Partisan election (election by party label) is most likely to occur in the South. In most cases judicial elections are nearly invisible to voters. Often they are held at odd times during the year and voter turnout is lower than in legislative and gubernatorial elections.

In many instances, judges resign before their term of office expires. This allows the governor to make an interim appointment. Typically, incumbent judges stand an excellent chance of being reelected. In addition to low turnout, often there are no opposition candidates in judicial elections.

In four states, the governor appoints some judges in a manner similar to the presidential selection of federal judges. Usually the legislature confirms the appointment, and a strong role is played by interest groups to influence nominations. In a few states, the legislature appoints judges. In those cases, the governor often plays a major role in controlling the legislature's choices and most judges are former state legislators.

Merit Systems

Most states adopting new plans of judicial selection since the 1930s have chosen some form of *merit system*. These plans, which have many variations, are based on a selection process first instituted by California in 1934 and made popular by Missouri in 1940. The goal of merit plans is to remove judicial selection from the influence of partisan politics and to select judges on the basis of ability, in large part as determined by lawyers and sitting judges.

The **Missouri Plan** operates as follows. Whenever a judicial vacancy arises, the governor appoints an individual from a list of acceptable names submitted by a commission. There are three commissions in Missouri to nominate judges for three types of courts. The commissions are composed of lawyers, ordinary citizens, and a sitting judge. The lawyers are elected by all the lawyers in the court's district; the lay citizens are appointed by the governor; and the judge is the presiding judge of the court of appeals in that area. States employ a variety of methods to select members of the nominating commissions. In their quests to create impartial commissions, some states have devised very complex selection systems. Then there are a variety of ways to select the commission chair.

After a judge has served for a period of time, his or her name appears on the ballot and the voters check yes or no. If the vote is no, the selection process begins again. If the vote is yes, the judge's name will appear on future ballots, again without an opponent, and the voters will decide whether they wish the judge to remain in office. In a few states, judges run in competitive, partisan retention elections.

In California the governor appoints all supreme court and court of appeals justices. These appointments must be approved by the Committee on Judicial Appointments, which is composed of several judges and the state attorney general. Following appointment, California uses merit-retention elections for appellate judges, similar to those in Missouri. Trial court judges are selected by nonpartisan election.

Contrary to the arguments of good-government groups, most studies indicate that merit plans do *not* produce judges who differ substantially from those who are elected or appointed. They have not had better legal qualifications nor have they decided cases in a noticeably different manner from judges selected by other methods. In the most comprehensive review of the Missouri Plan, the authors note that "governors have used their appointments to reward friends or past political supporters and have implemented the plan very largely from a personal and political viewpoint."[20]

Turnout usually is low in retention elections, and few judges have been voted out of office in states with merit plans. In California, no judge had been voted out of office since the plan was implemented in 1934 until chief justice Rose Elizabeth Bird and two justices were overwhelmingly denied reconfirmation in 1986.

Particularly when considering the results of California retention elections in the 1980s and early 1990s, it was easy to conclude that if interest groups targeted judges for defeat, it would be difficult for judges to defend themselves. However, across the country *fewer* judges were defeated in the 1990s than in the past and voter participation increased.[21]

Merit systems do not remove partisan considerations from the judiciary, nor do they make judicial elections different from elections for other public offices. For example, the 1986 judicial retention election in California was as high-spending and personally contentious as any gubernatorial partisan election.

In the 1980s, voters in several states defeated proposals to move to merit systems of judicial selection, and there have been few proposals for change since then. In general, the proponents and opponents of merit selection among the states have been similar. Proponents include various good-government groups, such as the League of Women Voters; bar associations; and business groups. Opponents include trial lawyers, labor unions, and minorities. Political parties often are split on merit selection depending on how they have fared under an electoral system.[22]

Judicial Elections

We have seen that in practice most judges selected by merit plans enjoy a lifetime of service, although they are subject to periodic approval at the polls. As noted in Chapter 4, incumbent judges usually face little opposition. Often lawyers are reluctant to challenge sitting judges, and low-level campaigns favor incumbents running against challengers who are not well known to the general public. Incumbent judges are even less likely to be defeated in nonpartisan elections where party identification cannot be used as a voting clue. When incumbents are defeated, oftentimes there have been allegations of immoral conduct or incompetence that have been played up by the local media.

Recently, judicial elections have become more visible, more competitive, and more partisan. As noted in the chapter case study, multimillion-dollar judicial campaigns are common in several states. Because individuals are unlikely to make contributions to judicial campaigns, groups with vested interests in court decisions are likely to make large contributions to candidates they believe will issue decisions favorable to them. Big spending, especially for television ads, makes judicial races more visible to the public, but it may not make them more competitive when incumbent judges raise much more money than their challengers. Only a handful of states have public funding systems for judicial elections.

Traditionally, judicial codes of ethics and state laws have restricted campaign practices. Nearly 90 percent of all state judges face election, either directly or in retention elections. Campaign restrictions included bans on candidates giving their personal opinions on policy issues. As a result, voters often were frustrated by campaigns that centered around candidates' past experiences and vague claims that they would be "fair, but tough" when dealing with criminal defendants. As noted in Chapter 4, recent litigation in several federal and state courts has led to changes that allow judicial candidates to engage in partisan political activities, including personally soliciting funds from lawyers and litigants. In 2006 the U.S. Supreme Court refused to review a circuit court decision that struck down a large portion of Minnesota's code of judicial conduct.

As in Texas, where it is said that judges "swing the gavel with one hand and take money with the other," getting a fair trial may be increasingly rare in high-profile cases across the country. Tom DeLay is not the only litigant with the means to shop for a sympathetic judge.

Regardless of the method of selection, partisan politics plays a major role in the selection of judges. Even in Missouri, governors have appointed most judges from their own party. In nonpartisan elections, parties are usually active in primary elections, and they are often directly involved in general elections. Interest groups are active participants in every selection plan. Governors tend to draw a high percentage of their appointments from current and past members of the state legislature. Under both partisan and merit systems, judges seem equally objective and equally attuned to popular sentiment in their states.

Unlike federal judges, few state judges are given life tenure in a single appointment and few states give their governors sole power to appoint judges. For appellate courts, the typical length of a term is five to twelve years. Generally, terms of trial judges are shorter, averaging four to eight years. Long terms are believed to be beneficial because they help ensure judicial independence.

Minority lawyers and politicians prefer that judges be elected from small, single-member districts where it is more likely that a majority of voters will be minorities than is the case in at-large districts that compose an entire city or county. Their position has been helped by the Supreme Court's rulings in *Clark v. Roemer* (1991) and in *Chisom v. Roemer* (1991) that provisions of the Voting Rights Act of 1982 are applicable to judicial elections because judges, like legislators, serve as "representatives" of the people. Governors making interim appointments in states with judicial election systems may select minorities as a means of getting the support of those communities in upcoming elections.

State court systems also have been politicized by state legislators seeking to prevent courts from reviewing some laws they have passed. This is referred to as "court stripping."[23] For example, in 2005 some legislatures tried to prevent their state courts from hearing and deciding challenges to school funding plans. In 2006 there were initiatives in several states aimed at punishing judges for being out of step with partisan political views.

Discipline and Removal of Judges

All appellate judges serve for at least six years. Terms range up to fourteen years (in New York). In Rhode Island, judges have life appointments, and in a few states appointment is to age seventy. Only in rare instances have judges been removed, or even disciplined, during their term in office. Nearly all states have constitutional provisions for impeachment, but the process (which involves securing valid signatures on petitions and holding trials) is time-consuming and very expensive. Few judges have been impeached and removed from office. Seven states permit judicial recall; but even fewer judges have been recalled than have been impeached.

Not only are these traditional means of removal time-consuming and costly, but they also are often perceived as overly harsh penalties for the alleged offenses. As a result, judges with serious problems frequently escape removal because voters or legislatures are reluctant to take such drastic action. Occasionally, judges resign when threatened with impeachment.

A more practical solution to dealing with problems of judicial incompetence or unethical behavior has been the creation of judicial tenure commissions composed of lawyers, judges, and citizens. They investigate complaints, hold hearings, and impose penalties ranging from temporary suspension to removal. More than thirty states have judicial commissions. Most are patterned after the California Commission of Judicial Performance, which was established in 1960 when voters approved a constitutional initiative. The California Commission has nine members: five judges, two attorneys, and two citizens. The commission investigates complaints against judges, and, if the allegations have merit, it seeks voluntary compliance through a confidential proceeding with the judge. If the problem cannot be resolved in this way, the commission schedules a hearing and then it can recommend dismissal. Dismissal of a judge must be approved by the state supreme court.

About three-fourths of states have a mandatory retirement age, usually seventy, for judges. This is aimed at lessening problems associated with senile judges. As we might expect, judges are convicted of many of the same crimes that legislators commit— accepting bribes, drunk driving, and drug abuse. Often this leads to resignation, imprisonment, or election defeat.

FEDERAL-STATE COURT RELATIONS

We have noted that overwhelmingly litigation in the United States takes place in state courts. Although decisions of state supreme courts may be appealed to the United States Supreme Court, if the case does not raise a substantial federal question or if it has been decided on independent state grounds, the U.S. Supreme Court will not review it.[24] This means that very few state cases are reviewed by the Supreme Court.

In the 1950s and 1960s, the liberal Warren Court overturned a number of state court decisions dealing with school desegregation, rights of criminal defendants, and legislative reapportionment. Since the 1970s, a more conservative Supreme Court has been less intrusive in state judicial affairs. As noted in Chapter 2, since the early 1990s the Court has overturned several laws passed by Congress that were found to infringe on the power of state government.

Under a doctrine known as **new judicial federalism,** state supreme courts have relied on their state constitutions to become independent policy makers, handing down decisions that differ from those of the U.S. Supreme Court and its interpretation of the U.S. Constitution. Evidence of the new judicial federalism can be seen in the decisions of courts across the country in several areas of policy making. These include rights of criminal defendants and privacy issues.

However, Henry R. Glick cautions against overstating the frequency with which state courts make use of state constitutions to support their decisions. He notes that "state supreme courts rely on state constitutions as the sole basis of their decisions in one-sixth or fewer of their cases involving state legislation, preferring mostly U.S. Supreme Court precedents or a combination of state and national constitutions in these cases."[25] When they do rely on state constitutions, Glick finds that state supreme courts often interpret rights in ways similar to the U.S. Supreme Court. He notes that most states have conservative political environments and only a relatively few liberal states have been leaders in the new judicial federalism.

Supreme courts around the country have ruled against their states' funding systems for education. A decade after the Supreme Court upheld Georgia's anti-sodomy law in *Bowers v. Hardwick* (1986), the Georgia supreme court overturned the law as a violation of individual rights in its state constitution. Based on rights provided in their states' constitutions, some state courts have rejected Supreme Court rulings dealing with obscenity, gay rights, and rights of criminal defendants.

Historically, the U.S. Supreme Court has gotten support of national officials by imposing the agenda of Congress and the president on states that have tried to block its implementation. In doing so, the Supreme Court has used its power of judicial review to overrule state laws on the grounds that they violate the U.S. Constitution in over 1,000 cases. This compares to about 150 federal cases that have struck down congressional and presidential actions.

Supreme Court oversight often has been used to keep states and regions whose partisan character was contrary to the national majority in line with national policy. For example, in the mid-twentieth century the Supreme Court ruled against various means of resistance to civil rights laws by southern states. In such circumstances the Supreme Court is said to interpose with a "friendly hand" to support national officials and also to exercise its independent power of judicial review.[26]

FIGHTING CRIME

Overwhelmingly, crime control in the United States is the responsibility of states, counties, and cities. The relatively small federal involvement is reflected by statistics that show that New York City's 37,000 sworn police officers are about triple the number of

FBI special agents. About 95 percent of all crime occurs within the jurisdiction of state and local governments. Nearly 90 percent of the money spent to fight crime and house prisoners comes from state sources.

Like other policy making areas we have discussed, crime and corrections reflect the interaction of officials at all levels of governments. Although cities bear the greatest burden of fighting crime, federal, state, and county governments all are involved in passing laws, appropriating money, and making rulings that affect crime fighting at the street level as well as correctional facilities from city jails to maximum security state prisons. Under the Law Enforcement Assistance Administration, created in the late 1960s, and legislation passed in the 1990s, hundreds of millions of dollars were given to local governments to build prisons and hire thousands of police officers. Under the George W. Bush administration, federal funding to hire police officers virtually ended.

The crime rate in the United States remained fairly steady through the first half of the twentieth century. Then it tripled from 1960 to 1980. Many plausible reasons were given for the increase—demographic (more young men aged 18 to 24 who are responsible for a majority of all violent crimes), economic (a downturn in the 1970s meant fewer jobs were available), and an increase in drug abuse. However, economists Steven D. Levitt and Stephen J. Dubner believe that the main cause of the rise in crime was due to "lenient justice," meaning shorter prison sentences.[27] In part, they argue, politicians became softer on crime because they did not want to appear to be racist. The crime rate leveled off in the early 1980s and then increased later in the decade.

With the rise in violent crime, politicians increasingly tried to use the rising crime rate and subsequent fear of crime to their advantage. State legislators passed bills calling for stricter criminal penalties and mayors tried to instill in their police departments a zero-tolerance for crime. The death penalty was restored in most states and prison populations grew exponentially. Between 1980 and 2000 there was a fifteen-fold increase in the number of people sent to prison for drug charges. Sociologists and political scientists developed a multitude of theories to explain why crime was rising, and they proposed an equally large number of solutions to combat the crime problem.

Beginning in 1992, the crime rate steadily decreased throughout the decade. Rates dropped in every region of the country and in all categories of violent crime as well as burglary and theft. Declines were most significant in the nation's largest cities where crime rates have been the highest. By 2000, the murder rate was at its lowest level since 1966. Rates of violent crimes had declined almost 50 percent since the early 1990s and were the lowest since the government began tracking the crime rate in 1973. Since 2000, there have been minor fluctuations in the rate of crime. By 2005, overall violent and property crime reached a 32-year low, although gun violence increased. About 16,000 Americans are murdered each year, mostly by young people with guns. The trend upward continued in 2006, with increases of about 2 percent in the rates of murder and all violent crimes. In 2006, the overall crime rate was highest in Dallas, Houston, Phoenix, and San Antonio.

The obvious question put to experts in the field of law enforcement has been, Why did violent crime decrease so dramatically? A related question is how to keep the crime rate stable since it may be unrealistic to expect further decreases. Many of the responses have been just the reverse of earlier responses by experts as to why crime increased in the 1970s and 1980s—proportionately fewer young males, economic recovery, and decline of the crack cocaine trade. Also noted has been the fact that by 2000 over 2 million Americans were in prison where, of course, they were not committing street crimes.

Another answer that seemed to explain the significant decline of crime in New York City particularly well was better policing and more police officers on the street. New York City added about 13,000 officers in the 1990s, equal to the entire Chicago police force and nearly 50 percent more officers than the Los Angeles police force. New York City has assigned about 1,000 police officers to counter intelligence since 9/11.

New York City also adopted the **"broken windows" theory of fighting crime.** As presented by political scientist James Q. Wilson and criminologist George Kelling, this theory contended that to a large extent crime was the result of disorder.[28] The authors recommended, and New York City put into operation, a policy of cracking down on seemingly minor crimes, such as graffiti, which if left unpunished would lead to a general breakdown of order in a community. As the chief of the NYPD said in the mid-1990s, "If you peed on the street, you were going to jail." In his best-selling book, *The Tipping Point, New Yorker* staff writer Malcolm Gladwell argues that an epidemic, in this case crime, can be tipped, or reversed, by tinkering with small details.[29] And in New York City the small details were responding to minor criminal violations.

New York City also implemented a program known as CompStat, which is a computerized mapping method of identifying criminal hot spots in the city and then dispatching extra police to the area. Many other cities have implemented this program. With that and other police strategies in place, crime has continued to drop in New York City even though several other large cities have seen increases in recent years. With the city's population up 125,000 since 2001, crime in 2006 was down 25 percent. Even with a planned increase of 800 officers in 2006, the NYPD was down by about 4,000 officers from its peak of 40,800 in 2000.[30]

In the face of widely accepted "conventional wisdom" explanations for falling crime rates in New York City and across the country, economists Steven Levitt and Stephen Dubner beg to differ. In their best-selling book, *Freakonomics,* they contend that longer prison sentences and the legalization of abortion decades before the crime drop in the 1990s were the major reasons for the so-called miracle in New York City. Levitt and Dubner agree that the addition of more police and a reduction of the crack cocaine epidemic also contributed to the crime drop in New York City in the 1990s. But these were secondary factors. They contend that longer prison sentences obviously kept potential criminals in jail and that this accounts for about one-third of the drop in crime in the 1990s.[31] Of course, imprisonment comes at a significant cost of about $25,000 per year, per inmate.

More controversial is their contention that the legalization of abortion in New York City in 1970 *(Roe v. Wade* followed in 1973) was the single most important cause of the reduction in crime. Levitt and Dubner state that living in poverty and living in single-parent households are the strongest predictors that children will become criminals. Since abortions reduced the number of children at risk of becoming criminals—poor women and unmarried teenagers were disproportionately likely to have abortions after 1973—the crime rate declined. The authors recognize that this "unintended benefit" of abortion is "jarring" for liberals and conservatives to discover.[32] But as John Tierney says about the abortion theory, versus the tipping point theory, "The ideas that make us comfortable are the ones to be aware."[33]

In a series of academic papers written in 2006 and 2007, economist Rick Nevin contended that the biggest factor contributing to the drop in crime in New York City and across the nation in the 1990s was an effort decades earlier to reduce exposure to lead poisoning. Nevin's curious conclusions are based on scientific studies that have linked exposure to lead in young children to violent behavior as they get older. Nevin's data show similar associations in nine other countries. Unlike the theory of Levitt and Dubner regarding the impact of abortion on crime rates, Nevin's theory also explains the rise of crime in the 1980s and earlier fluctuations in the rate of crime.

Curiously, even as crime rates decreased, *fear* of crime, perhaps heightened by watching local television news, remained high. This helps explain why state legislators and judges continue to find it politically advantageous to be seen as "tough on crime."

Regardless of what causes an individual to perform criminal acts, we can strongly associate violent criminal behavior with young males: Half of the crimes on the annual *Uniform Crime Reports* are committed by males under the age of twenty. Except for larceny-theft, where they constitute about 30 percent of all arrests, women make up less than 15 percent of the arrests for all other *UCR* crimes, and only about 7 percent of all prisoners in the United States are women (this is up from 4 percent in 1981). Arrest rates in cities with populations over 100,000 are nearly double those in rural areas.

There are several reasons why we should be cautious when reading crime statistics. First, the *Uniform Crime Reports*—the major source of national crime statistics, published by the FBI—covers only four types of violent crime (assault, murder, rape, and robbery) and four types of property crime (arson, burglary, larceny, and motor vehicle theft). Most white-collar crimes are omitted. Second, many crimes are not reported to the police. Third, police reports to the FBI may underestimate the amount of crime to make local departments look better. And fourth, although most murders and motor vehicle thefts are reported, other crimes, for various reasons, are vastly underreported to the police. In 2006 about 53 percent of violent crimes and 60 percent of property crimes were never reported to the police. Many victims do not report crimes to the police because they do not think the police can solve cases, or they don't think crimes are important enough to report, or the crimes (often assault or rape) have been committed by a relative or friend, or the victim fears retaliation from gang members.

As indicated in Table 7-3, the crime rate varies by a factor of about 3 among the states. In general, New England states have the lowest crime rate. As we would expect, the five states with the least crime are small, rural, and predominantly white. But New York, New Jersey, and Pennsylvania are among the ten states with the least crime. Seven of the ten states with the most crime are in the South and Southwest, but Washington and Oregon, states with few minorities, are among those with the most crime. Many "conventional wisdom" beliefs about crime are not supported by these statistics. For example, in urban, racially mixed New Jersey (where gambling is legal in Atlantic City) the crime rate is much lower than in rural, predominantly white Utah. The state with the highest percentage of African Americans (Mississippi) ranks twenty-sixth in the rate of crime.

The murder rate is much higher in the South than in any other part of the country, a pattern that has been true as long as records have been kept. The lowest murder rates are in New England and Upper Midwest states. Without the South, the U.S. murder rate would not differ greatly from the rate in other democratic nations. Traditional attitudes stemming from slavery, rural isolation, and a historic sense of personal honor seem to account for the especially high murder rates in Louisiana, Mississippi, and Alabama. However, there has been a significant decline in the murder rate in all regions of the country, including the South, since the 1990s.

TABLE 7-3 State Crime and Murder Rates per 100,000 Population, 2001

	Crime Rate*			Murder Rate**	
Rank	State	Rate	Rank	State	Rate
1	Arizona	5,844.6	1	Louisiana	12.7
2	South Carolina	5,289.0	2	Maryland	9.4
3	Washington	5,193.0	3	New Mexico	8.9
4	Louisiana	5,048.9	4	Mississippi	7.8
5	Hawaii	5,047.2	5	Nevada	7.4
6	Texas	5,034.5	6	Arizona	7.2
7	Tennessee	5,001.7	7	Georgia	6.9
8	Oregon	4,929.6	7	South Carolina	6.9
9	Florida	4,891.0	9	California	6.7
10	New Mexico	4,885.0	10	Arkansas	6.4
11	Nevada	4,822.5	10	Michigan	6.4
12	Oklahoma	4,742.6	12	Missouri	6.2
13	Georgia	4,721.4	12	North Carolina	6.2
14	North Carolina	4,608.0	14	Illinois	6.1
15	Arkansas	4,512.1	14	Texas	6.1
16	Alabama	4,451.6	16	Tennessee	5.9
17	Missouri	4,394.0	17	Kentucky	5.7
18	Kansas	4,348.0	18	Alabama	5.6
19	Maryland	4,340.7	18	Alaska	5.6
20	Utah	4,321.6	20	Florida	5.4
21	Colorado	4,292.8	21	Oklahoma	5.3
22	Alaska	4,017.3	22	Pennsylvania	5.2
23	Ohio	4,015.0	22	Virginia	5.2
24	California	3,970.8	24	Indiana	5.1
25	Nebraska	3,829.3	25	New York	4.6
26	Mississippi	3,773.6	26	Kansas	4.5
27	Delaware	3,732.3	26	New Jersey	4.5
28	Illinois	3,729.0	26	Ohio	4.5
29	Indiana	3,723.0	29	Colorado	4.4
30	Wyoming	3,563.9	30	West Virginia	3.7
31	Michigan	3,547.8	31	Montana	3.2
32	Minnesota	3,308.6	32	Washington	3.1
33	Montana	3,230.0	33	Wisconsin	2.8
34	Iowa	3,176.2	34	Connecticut	2.6
35	Rhode Island	3,131.5	34	Hawaii	2.6
36	Idaho	3,039.3	34	Massachusetts	2.6
37	Virginia	2,952.2	34	Vermont	2.6
38	Massachusetts	2,918.5	38	Oregon	2.5
39	Connecticut	2,913.5	39	Rhode Island	2.4
40	Wisconsin	2,872.7	40	Nebraska	2.3
41	Pennsylvania	2,826.1	40	South Dakota	2.3
42	New Jersey	2,784.9	42	Idaho	2.2
43	Kentucky	2,782.6	42	Minnesota	2.2

44	West Virginia	2,777.4	42	Wyoming	2.2
45	New York	2,640.2	45	Delaware	2.0
46	Maine	2,513.1	46	Utah	1.9
47	Vermont	2,420.2	47	Iowa	1.6
48	New Hampshire	2,207.1	48	Maine	1.4
49	South Dakota	2,105.0	48	New Hampshire	1.4
50	North Dakota	1,996.0	48	North Dakota	1.4
District of Columbia		6,230.3	District of Columbia		35.8

*Includes murder, rape, robbery, aggravated assault, burglary, larceny-theft, and motor vehicle theft.
**Includes non-negligent manslaughter.

Source: State Rankings 2006 (Lawrence, Kans.: Morgan Quitno Press), pp. 28 and 35, www.morganquitno.com.

POLICE ACTIVITIES AND ORGANIZATION

Police make arrests for only about 20 percent of the most serious crimes that are reported to them. However, in millions of cases where arrests are made, the crimes are processed as misdemeanors. Thousands more are turned over to juvenile authorities. Millions of urban burglaries are reported to the police largely for insurance purposes, and in most cases there is little hope that arrests will be made. Because urban police are so overworked and because often there are no credible witnesses, in many cases no one seriously expects the police to make arrests.

In routine patrolling and in responding to calls, police have unusually broad **discretionary authority.** Working alone or in pairs, police officers operate with little direct supervision from police administrators when deciding how to respond to possible crimes. James Q. Wilson notes that police discretion is inevitable, "partly because it is impossible to observe every public infraction, partly because many laws require interpretation before they can be applied at all, partly because the police can sometimes get information about serious crimes by overlooking minor crimes, and partly because the police believe that public opinion would not tolerate a policy of full enforcement of all laws all the time."[34] This means that the discretionary authority of police often is of greater importance than department manuals and official policy statements in affecting the day-to-day operations of the police.

One of the results of having so much discretionary authority is that police often decide to handle situations informally, rather than strictly enforcing the law. For example, police may choose to issue a warning instead of an arrest for possession of certain controlled substances. The ways in which police exercise discretion may depend on the background and personality of the officer, the characteristics of suspects (if they are belligerent or if their style of dress is offensive, they are more likely to be arrested), and the nature of the offense. Laws relating to many "victimless" offenses, such as gambling, often are regarded by police as just "part of the landscape" and ignored.[35]

Law enforcement takes up only about 10 percent of police time. Most of their shifts are devoted to service (responding to motor vehicle accidents or directing traffic) and to peacekeeping (intervening in family disputes, quieting noisy parties). Of course, if police in cruisers were not "doing nothing," they would not be able to respond quickly to emergencies.

Police discretionary activity and the allocation of their time among the three basic functions noted are influenced by department policy. Some departments target certain kinds of crime to be enforced, some emphasize the service function, and some reduce discretion by keeping in close communication with officers. In turn, department policy may be strongly associated with the style of the department.

Prior to the reform era of the early twentieth century, many police departments were controlled by urban political machines. As a result, law enforcement was applied unevenly across communities. Even where political machines did not exist, corruption was widespread in police departments. Corruption peaked during the 1920s when prohibition was in effect. In many cities, near the turn of the century, a **watchman style** of police behavior emphasized maintenance of order in public places, rather than law enforcement. Police were poorly paid, locally recruited, and minimally trained in virtually all cities and towns.[36]

Political reformers (see Chapter 3) sought to cut the political ties of many police departments. Beginning in the 1920s, the so-called **professional movement in policing** stressed a formal, hierarchical organization (command structure) and emphasized fighting crime over other police services. To correct problems associated with the watchman style, many police departments went to the opposite extreme of enforcing all laws in a very legalistic approach to the job of law enforcement. This corresponded with changes in technology—automobiles, radios, new forensic techniques—that altered the ways in which police solved crimes. Police were evaluated by such means as the percentage of crimes solved and response time to calls for assistance. Later, these departments embraced the use of helicopters and SWAT forces.

Beginning in the 1970s, criminologists seriously questioned the organization of police departments because it was not effective at preventing crime or limiting disorder. They proposed that the mission of police departments change from solving crimes to preventing crime. To do this would require changes in both the goals and organization of police departments. Criminologists contended that departments should switch to problem-solving policing that would deal with the underlying social problems that cause crime.

It should be noted that not all police departments adopted the legalistic model. In many middle-class communities (often suburban), police departments adopted a **service style** in which serious crimes were treated seriously, but minor infractions, particularly when they involved juveniles, were handled more informally. In the suburban communities where a service style continues to be used, police are courteous, well-paid, and well-trained.

With crime rates escalating in the 1980s, many observers concluded that the professional model was not working. Aggressive police tactics associated with these departments raised serious concerns about the protection of individual rights, and such tactics were not preventing crime. People in most large cities felt increasingly unsafe.

Change came in the form of a return, in part, to a much earlier style of policing whereby officers walked a beat and got to know their neighborhoods. While there were some experiments with this approach as early as the mid-1960s, it wasn't until the early 1990s that many communities across the country began to implement **community policing.** Elements of community policing include the creation of substations across cities, foot patrols, frequent meetings between police and neighborhood residents, and keeping police on the same beats for longer periods of time.[37] A major goal of these departments is to be proactive, rather than simply responding to emergency calls (see the discussion of reinventing government in Chapter 6). In terms of organizational change, more responsibility is directed to the lower ranks as departments become less hierarchical. In turn, residents are given more responsibility to prevent and solve crimes on their own.

The use of community policing was given a lot of credit for the drop in crime in Boston in the 1990s and in several large cities across the country. Then crime began to rise in Boston and, as we have noted, it continued to decline in New York City where implementation of the "broken windows" approach stressed strict enforcement of the law and did not include a strong emphasis on community policing. Moreover, several big cities that had made virtually no reforms in their police departments saw crime decrease in the 1990s. All of this caused people to wonder how important the role of the police is to fighting crime. As we have noted, Levitt and Dubner give relatively little weight to the "tipping point" argument, or to any police strategies, to explain the decline in crime.

Community policing continues to be practiced in many cities, where it is part of the "reinventing government" emphasis on giving citizens some control over public safety and creating anticipatory government. Still, criticism often remains strong. Most fundamentally, it is argued by some police officials and academics that the term *community policing* is ambiguous because "community" is difficult to define. In addition, it is difficult to measure "citizen satisfaction" with any style of policing, and some police officials have reservations about how much citizens want to be engaged in patrolling their own neighborhoods. As a practical matter, the traditional police subculture that is committed to arrests and crime fighting has made community policing difficult to implement in many cities. At the same time that police departments tout their commitment to interacting with residents at the neighborhood level, nearly 90 percent of all departments have created SWAT teams, up from about 60 percent in 1982. This suggests that aggressive law enforcement has not been abandoned.

Every state except Hawaii has a law enforcement agency known as the *state police*, the state highway patrol, or, as in Texas, the Rangers. In a quarter of the states, the responsibility of this central police force is limited to highway duties. In the other states, law enforcement responsibilities include aiding local police in making arrests and controlling riots. In 2005 state police forces ranged in size from 126 in North Dakota to 6,678 in California. In Delaware they make up about one-third of all sworn officers. In several other states the state police comprise less than 5 percent of all police officers.

Traditionally, the county sheriff has been a central figure in American law enforcement. In addition to making arrests, the sheriff maintains the county jail and serves summonses and warrants. In every state except Rhode Island, which does not have counties, the sheriff is elected. Although sheriffs continue to play a major role in rural counties, municipal police forces have assumed most of the sheriff's law enforcement duties in urban areas. However, sheriffs' offices have become very professionalized in many suburban areas where smaller communities may contract with the county for law enforcement service. On the average, about 60 percent of state law enforcement personnel are municipal police, 30 percent work at the county level, and 10 percent work at the state level.

CORRECTIONS

Sentencing Philosophies

The history of prisons in the United States shows that we have gone through a great variety of stages, seeking ways to further public safety and punish offenders. Over the years government officials have followed five basic philosophies to help justify the choice of sentences and to help define the purpose of incarceration.

First, **retribution,** the most ancient goal of sentencing, suggests that offenders deserve punishment and that it is proper for society to seek vengeance for crimes that are normally offensive. In earlier societies punishment often was certain, quick, and brutal, even for what appears now to be a minor offense. Nowadays, long terms of imprisonment are justified by saying the offenders got what was coming to them.

Second, **deterrence** contends that certain, swift punishment of convicted criminals will cause other people not to commit crimes. Because imprisonment is thought to be an especially effective deterrence, this philosophy is compatible with incapacitation.[38] To the extent that crime rates have continued to rise as prison sentences have gotten longer, there are serious questions raised about their deterrent effect. In particular, there has been a long-standing debate (discussed later in this chapter) about the deterrent effect of the death penalty for the crime of murder. Many criminologists argue that it is *certainty,* more than severity of punishment, that deters crime.[39] And as noted, most crimes in the United States go unreported or no arrest is made.

Third, **rehabilitation** became the goal of prison reformers in the 1930s, and it dominated prison philosophy into the 1970s. Rehabilitation was applied to youthful offenders and to adult offenders by Pennsylvania Quakers in the late eighteenth century, but retribution soon came to be the primary goal of adult sentencing in the United States.

As the term *corrections* suggests, rehabilitation seeks to change individual behavior, to make offenders see the evil of their ways, and to prepare them for a productive life outside prison. For those sentenced to prison, there is an emphasis on psychological counseling, education, and job training. It was recommended that prisons should be smaller and should be located close to cities so that family visits would be more frequent. After release, rehabilitation called for halfway houses and more parole officers to better supervise the reentry of former prisoners into society. Psychology offered the opportunity to treat offenders at various stages and to "cure" them of their criminal tendencies.

Of course, the basic test of rehabilitation is how well ex-prisoners behave after their release from prison. The answer is not well. About two-thirds of inmates who have committed felonies return to prison within three years of their release. Instead of rehabilitation, imprisonment seemed more likely to serve as a training ground for future criminal behavior. With the crime rate soaring, longer sentences neither deterred crime nor rehabilitated criminals. However, some observers point out that when prisoners attend vocational training classes or take college courses, they are much less likely to return to a life of crime. Yet education programs have been reduced in response to a change in the philosophy of incarceration, as well as to cuts in state budgets.

In response to these realities and in reaction to increased fear of crime, the dominant sentencing philosophy switched to a fourth philosophy, **incapacitation.** This calls for separating people from society, often by long, or at least certain, prison sentences. It is argued that to the extent criminals are taken off the streets, they will not be endangering lives and property. Incapacitation differs from retribution to the extent that its primary objective is not punishment. For example, a convicted criminal can be incapacitated by house arrest using electronic monitoring devices. The period 1980 to 1995 is sometimes referred to as the "warehousing era" of incarceration because so many people were locked up and little effort was made to rehabilitate prisoners.

Since around 1995 there has been broad support for the idea that prisoners are receiving their "just desserts." That is, imprisonment is fully deserved and it is a proper consequence considering what convicted criminals have done. Acting under this approach, several states have abolished **parole** (early supervised release from prison) and even instituted chain gangs, where prisoners wear black-and-white striped uniforms and do such work as road repairs.[40]

More recently, a fifth philosophy, **restoration,** has emerged. While traditional sentencing punishes offenders, restoration refers to the healing of all parties. It includes support for victims' compensation and seeking input from the community to determine appropriate service projects for those released from prison.

Characteristics of Prisoners

The number of sentenced prisoners under federal and state jurisdiction remained remarkably constant, near 200,000, from 1920 to 1970, and then a sharp increase began in the mid-1970s. Even as crime has declined since the early 1990s, the prison population has continued to grow. State prisons held about 685,000 prisoners in 1990 and about 1.5 million in 2005. In addition, over one-half million people were on parole. The rate of incarceration in 2005 for federal and state prisons was 488 per 100,000 population. This was up from 411 in 1995.

Among all prisoners in the United States, about 62 percent are racial or ethnic minorities. Women comprised 7 percent of federal and state inmates, and they accounted for nearly one in four arrests in 2005. Much of the recent increase in the number of women inmates is attributed to drug offenses, specifically, methamphetamine. Oklahoma and Mississippi, which had the highest rates per capita of imprisonment for women in 2005, incarcerated about ten times as many women as did Massachusetts and Rhode Island, which had the lowest rates per capita of imprisonment for women in that year. Although longer sentences are creating older inmates and a much higher percentage of middle-aged inmates, those 65 and older are less than 2 percent of the prison population.

As incarceration rates soared in the 1990s, one effect was to reduce the stigma of imprisonment and its deterrent power on African American and Hispanic males. An estimated 20 percent of black men in their late twenties were in prison in 2005, compared to 3.7 percent of Hispanic males and 1.7 percent of white males in their late twenties. When so many young men are locked up, the social stigma of being in jail is reduced. Minority children are growing up with few male role models, and this has had a broad-based effect on their communities.

As shown in Table 7-4, the incarceration rate varies greatly among the states. In general, southern states have the highest rates, whereas New England and North Central

TABLE 7-4 State Prisoner Incarceration Rate, 2004*

Rank	State	Rate	Rank	State	Rate
1	Louisiana	816	27	Wyoming	389
2	Texas	694	28	Indiana	383
3	Mississippi	669	29	Connecticut	377
4	Oklahoma	649	30	Oregon	365
5	Georgia	574	31	North Carolina	357
6	Alabama	556	32	Illinois	346
7	South Carolina	539	33	New York	331
8	Missouri	538	34	Hawaii	329
9	Arizona	534	35	Pennsylvania	329
10	Arkansas	495	36	Kansas	327
11	Delaware	488	37	New Mexico	318
12	Florida	486	38	New Jersey	306
13	Michigan	483	39	Iowa	288
14	Nevada	474	40	West Virginia	277
15	Virginia	473	41	Washington	264
16	California	456	42	Utah	246
17	Idaho	454	43	Vermont	233
18	Colorado	438	44	Massachusetts	232
19	Tennessee	437	45	Nebraska	230
20	Montana	416	46	North Dakota	195
21	Kentucky	412	47	New Hampshire	187
22	Maryland	406	48	Rhode Island	175
23	South Dakota	399	49	Minnesota	171
24	Alaska	398	50	Maine	148
25	Ohio	391		District of Columbia**	NA
26	Wisconsin	390			

*National rate = 432 state prisoners per 100,000 population, as of December 31, 2004. Includes only inmates sentenced to more than one year. Does not include federal incarceration rate of 54 prisoners per 100,000 population. State and federal combined incarceration rate is 486 prisoners per 100,000 population.

**Responsibility for sentenced felons in D.C. was transferred to the Federal Bureau of Prisons in 2001.

Source: State Rankings 2006 (Lawrence, Kans.: Morgan Quitno Press, p. 58, www.morganquitno.com.)

states have relatively few people in prison. Although the rate of incarceration correlates reasonably well with the crime rate (see Table 7-3), several states, such as Oklahoma and Mississippi, rank much higher in rates of incarceration than in rates of crime. Nearly one-third of all the nation's state prisoners are in three states: California, Texas, and Florida. Much of the disparity in rates of imprisonment can be explained by differences in culture among the states: great variations in degrees of punitiveness, or the willingness to punish people.

We have noted that since the mid-1990s the prison population has continued to grow as crime rates have declined. In large part, this is because many states had approved longer minimum sentences for a variety of crimes and had ended parole. Arrests for drug-related crimes were especially high in the 1980s, and state legislators responded to the public's demand to get tough on criminals by requiring that convicted felons serve a higher percentage of their prison terms. In some states, citizen initiatives required mandatory sentencing. Curiously, drug use declined in the 1990s, but arrests remained high and those convicted got long terms of imprisonment.

Among other reasons for the increase in prison populations are laws enacted in the 1980s and 1990s, such as "three strikes" and "truth in sentencing," that restricted early release by not permitting shorter sentences for good behavior. Following the kidnapping and murder of twelve-year-old Polly Klaas in 1993, California passed its three-strikes law, which requires a sentence of twenty-five years to life for a criminal's third felony conviction. Since then, over half the states plus Congress have passed similar laws. The California law is the most extreme because it allows misdemeanor crimes to be included if they are the third offense. Reviewing two similar cases from California in 2003, the Supreme Court in a 5–4 vote upheld the California law. Writing for the majority in both cases, Justice O'Connor stressed the long criminal histories of both defendants and noted that the Supreme Court had a "long tradition of deferring to state legislatures" on sentencing guidelines. Dissenters on the Court stressed that the sentences (in one instance the defendant's third strike was shoplifting $153 worth of videos and his penalty was fifty years in prison) were "grossly disproportionate" to the crimes. Critics of three-strikes laws have pointed to the high cost of enforcement. There are more trials because no one pleads guilty on a third offense, and these laws keep inmates in prisons for long periods of time. Moreover, there is evidence that some district attorneys have chosen to prosecute fewer misdemeanors and focus on serious three-strike defendants.

A major turning point in sentencing occurred during 2003 when about half the states passed laws eliminating some of their mandatory minimum sentences and restoring early release for parole. Even many conservative legislators concluded that the existing laws were too harsh and too costly. Faced with budget deficits and rising prison populations, *New York Times* reporter Fox Butterfield noted, legislators decided it was more effective to be smart on crime instead of tough on crime.[41] Several states eased "truth in sentencing" laws. Criminologists long have pointed out that it is not the *severity* of punishment, but the *certainty* of punishment that deters crime.

Alternatives to Imprisonment

As we would expect, states have had to build more facilities to house the growing number of prisoners and spend more money on corrections. In 2004, states spent over $56 billion on corrections, up by $2 billion from 2003. Prison spending accounts for about 7 percent of all state spending. Per capita corrections spending is highest in Alaska, and California spends more than twice as much on corrections as any other state.[42]

To keep costs down, states have built larger prisons (with up to 5,000 inmates each) that house a wide range of prisoners, from the least to the most dangerous. To help satisfy conflicting political demands to put more people in jail and to keep down state expenditures, many new prisons have a harsh environment—gray walls, no windows, stainless steel tables, and high-voltage wire fences that eliminate the need for patrol. Touch the fence and you're dead.[43] Inmates of several of these new "supermax" prisons have filed lawsuits alleging abusive treatment and racial discrimination.

Perhaps the most popular (and the most controversial) way to reduce the costs of incarceration is to privatize prisons. Although private prisons were used in colonial America, tales of prisoner abuse led to public management of virtually all prisons and jails until the idea was revived in the 1980s. However, state prisons have a long history of contracting out such services as food and psychological testing to private business. Some large businesses, including Corrections Corporation of America, run prisons in several states. Private prisons hold nearly 6 percent of all state prisoners. They are operated in over thirty states, with Texas having the largest number of privately run prisons.

As discussed in Chapter 6, advocates of all types of privatization argue that public services can be produced more efficiently and at lower cost by private industry. Managing some services, such as trash collection, can be evaluated on a cost-efficiency basis. However, running prisons raises more complex issues, including how to ensure the humane treatment of prisoners, how to guard against the possibility of prison contractors keeping inmates in jail longer so that they can make more money, and how to assess legal liability when inmates bring lawsuits. Of course, state on-site supervision of prisons and careful wording of contracts could prevent more obvious abuses. Moreover, the record in many states shows public management has produced overcrowded prisons, delayed construction of new facilities, poorly maintained buildings, and physical abuse of prisoners. Privately managed prisons have benefited from state and federal mandates to reduce prison overcrowding.

Some critics charge that the widespread privatization of juvenile criminal facilities, such as group homes, has led to longer periods of custody and less emphasis on rehabilitation than in traditional public institutions.

States have sought various other ways to reduce the costs of incarceration. At the most extreme in terms of public safety, several states, including Oregon, have used early-release programs to create space in prisons. Other states release prisoners into a system of intensive probation, with close supervision by parole officers, or halfway houses that help former prisoners reenter society. Even Texas, perhaps the most hard-nosed of states, has decided to require probation and treatment, not imprisonment, for first-time offenders caught with small amounts of illegal drugs. Many states use a kind of house arrest in which offenders are monitored by electronic devices on their ankles. Fines may be an effective way to punish nonviolent first-time offenders. Several states have used **alternative sentencing** to create programs that divert convicted criminals, often drug users, out of the prison system into community-based treatment centers.

A number of states have used **boot camps** to scare young offenders straight. These camps are based on the military model of discipline and rigorous physical training. Inmates who accept the regimen are released in a relatively short time, while others are transferred to the regular prison system if they are noncooperative or if they choose to leave the boot camp. Because of charges of physical abuse, several states have ended their boot camps. What began as a popular program in the 1970s to get tough with juvenile offenders has become a vehicle for reconsidering the entire juvenile detention system. For example, Illinois operates several small, campus-like facilities around the state that focus on education and group counseling to change behavior.

The Commission on Safety and Abuse in America's Prisons released a report in 2006 saying that prisons are failing on so many fronts, if they were public schools we would shut them down. The report highlighted violence in prisons caused, in large part, by crowding and idleness and high rates of disease. It noted that the rising use of high-security segregation units leads to violence in prisons and **recidivism,** that is, released prisoners who return to criminal behavior after release. The report said that prisoners often are released from solitary confinement directly to the street.

Considering that 5 percent of the U.S. population accounts for 25 percent of the world's prison population and that American crime rates remain very high compared to those of other Western democracies, there is a movement across the country to scale down prison populations. As we have noted, many states are trying to do that by providing alternative forms of sentencing.

CAPITAL PUNISHMENT

The ultimate penalty, of course, is death. This ancient punishment has a brutal history. In biblical Israel, criminals were stoned to death. In Rome, beheading was the preferred method of death, although arsonists were burned and slaves were strangled.[44] In the Dark Ages those suspected of committing certain crimes were submerged in cold water or placed in boiling oil. Early in the nineteenth century 160 crimes were punishable by death in England. The guillotine was invented in France as an efficient way of beheading criminals. In the United States electrocution replaced hanging early in the twentieth century as the most common form of capital punishment. More recently, lethal injection has become the most widely authorized form of execution among the states.

The Role of the Supreme Court

From 1930 to 1967 about 3,800 persons were executed in the United States. Executions were halted in 1967 by an order of the U.S. Supreme Court as it waited to decide pending cases challenging the constitutionality of the death penalty. The Supreme Court's 1972 decision in *Furman v. Georgia* effectively struck down the way in which the death penalty was administered in thirty-seven states. The majority (5–4) ruled that the Georgia statute, which allowed the jury to decide guilt or innocence and at the same time assign a sentence in capital cases, permitted an arbitrary and capricious application of the death penalty. The Court's decision in *Gregg v. Georgia* two years later upheld the use of the death penalty as modified by the state of Georgia. Based on the Court's 7–2 opinion in *Gregg,* death penalty statutes are constitutionally acceptable if there is a two-stage process in which the jury first considers whether the defendant is guilty of murder and then at a sentencing stage the same jury considers any **aggravating** or **mitigating circumstances.** The jury must find the defendant guilty beyond a reasonable doubt of at least one aggravating circumstance, such as that the offense was committed for hire, in order to impose the death penalty. Then the state supreme court must review the death sentence. Mitigating circumstances, such as lack of a criminal record or a mental condition, are used to support a lesser penalty.

Following *Furman* and *Gregg,* the Supreme Court held that mandatory death sentences for certain crimes are unconstitutional and that capital punishment for rape is excessive. Later, however, a more conservative Court made it easier for states to execute convicted murderers by supporting the death penalty for persons as young as sixteen years old and for those who are mentally retarded. In addition, the Rehnquist Court limited the number of prisoner petitions from those sentenced to death, and it permitted victim impact studies at the time of sentencing to help determine the defendant's "blameworthiness."

Two decisions in 2002 restricted the use of the death penalty. In *Ring v. Arizona* the Court struck down laws in five states that had permitted judges alone, not juries, to decide the imposition of capital punishment. In all other types of crimes it is almost always the judge who sets the sentence. In *Atkins v. Virginia* the Court held that the Eighth Amendment bars the execution of the mentally retarded. At the time, seventeen of the thirty-eight states that imposed the death penalty banned executing the mentally retarded.

In an Ohio murder case decided in 2007, the Supreme Court made it easier for the prosecution to remove potential jurors in murder trials who express ambivalence about the death penalty. However, the conservative block that was the majority in most of the 2006–07 term's criminal opinions did not prevail in four opinions that limited the use of the death penalty in Texas. Included was *Panetti v. Quarterman* (2007), in which the Supreme Court held that the Fifth Circuit had employed an improperly restrictive test when it rejected Scott Panetti's claim of mental competency. That supported earlier Supreme Court rulings limiting execution of the mentally ill.

State Responses

Although some states did not restore the death penalty after the Supreme Court permitted it in 1976, most states rewrote their laws to comply with the *Furman* decision. Thirty-seven states and the federal government had capital punishment statutes in 2007. The last state to restore the death penalty was New York, in 1995. After the law was passed, no one was executed and in 2004 the New York Court of Appeals held the law unconstitutional. The death penalty has not been reinstated in New York. Because of legal restrictions, imposition of the death penalty is time-consuming, costly, and seldom applied.

In 2005, sixty persons were executed in sixteen states. Of those, nineteen were in Texas. Several states with capital punishment have not executed anyone since it was reinstated in 1976. As shown in Figure 7-3, the number of persons under sentence of death in 2004 declined for the fourth consecutive year. Since 1976, more than half of those sentenced to death have been white, but the African American percentage is much higher than their percentage of the total U.S. population. Of those executed in 2005, forty-one were white and nineteen were black. In 2004, fifty-two women, of a total of 3,314 persons, were under sentence of death. One woman was executed in 2005.[45]

In recent years nearly 90 percent of all executions have been in southern states. One explanation for this regional pattern is that southern appellate judges play the key role, seldom granting appeals from death row inmates and not having reservations about imposing the death penalty. Judges in the South are more likely than in other regions to run for political office and being tough on crime helps them. Moreover, we have noted cultural differences by region that influence patterns of imprisonment.

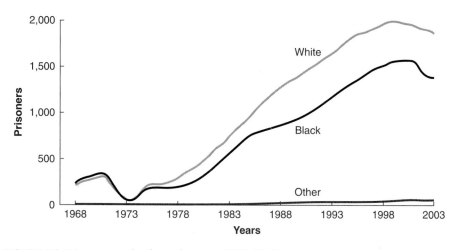

FIGURE 7-3 Prisoners on death row by race, 1968–2004.

Source: U.S. Department of Justice, Bureau of Justice Statistics, www.ojp.usdoj.gov/bjs (revised on February 2, 2006).

The number of state executions since *Furman v. Georgia* peaked at ninety-nine in 1999 and dropped to its lowest level (sixty) in a decade in 2005. After holding steady at about 300 each year through the 1990s, the number of death sentences has dropped steadily since 1999. In large part, increased reluctance to seek the death penalty stems from the reactions of prosecutors to reports from several states showing that DNA evidence has exonerated persons sentenced to death.[46] In addition, a study by law professor Brandon Garrett, to be published in 2008, showed that about 200 other innocent people serving time for non-murder offenses had been cleared by DNA evidence.[47] Reluctance to impose the death penalty also comes from evidence that, for various reasons, a substantial number of people are wrongfully convicted. Garrett found that false identification by eyewitnesses was the leading cause of wrongful convictions. Incorrect forensic evidence, especially hair analysis, was the second most common cause. Although any wrongful conviction is a serious matter, trial mistakes in capital punishment cases obviously can be fatal.

The first death-row inmate to be exonerated because of DNA evidence was released from prison in 1993. As of 2007, fourteen people on death row had been exonerated because of DNA evidence. Thirteen of them had been convicted for rape/murder. In most violent crimes, including murder, biological evidence is not available to help prove innocence. It seems likely that thousands of people are serving long sentences for various crimes they did not commit, but there is little hope that DNA evidence can be found to clear them. In 2000 Governor George Ryan of Illinois declared a moratorium on executions after thirteen innocent persons were discovered on the state's death row. Since then, governors in several other states have temporarily suspended capital punishment and federal executions were put on hold.

Race and the Death Penalty

The fact that about 40 percent of all persons who have been executed are African American has led many to oppose capital punishment on the grounds that it is inherently unfair. Just before his retirement in 1994, Justice Harry Blackmun cited racial inequities as a major reason for his opposition to capital punishment in any circumstances. In 1987 the Supreme Court refused to strike down Georgia's system of sentencing, even though a study showed that African Americans in Georgia who killed whites were four times more likely to receive the death sentence than African Americans who killed other African Americans (*McCleskey v. Kemp*). David C. Baldus and colleagues, in the most authoritative study of racial factors in capital punishment, concluded that racial disparities are due more to the *race of the victim* than to the race of the murderer. When the victim is white, the likelihood that the death penalty will be imposed is more than double than when the victim is African American.[48] Before 2003, Texas had not executed a white person for killing an African American for nearly a century.

An American Bar Association study reported in 2006 showed that a defendant's race, quality of legal representation, and geography have more of an effect on death sentencing than do the facts of cases.[49] Often, African Americans are victims of all three factors. Half of all executions since 1980 have been in Texas and Virginia.

NEW DIRECTIONS IN THE CRIMINAL JUSTICE SYSTEM

Since the early 1970s, computers have become an important part of all police departments, including those in small towns and rural counties. This followed the creation of the Law Enforcement Assistance Administration in 1968, whose tasks included technological assistance to state and local governments to aid their fight against crime. Computers have given police easy access to nationwide crime information, and they permit checks on stolen vehicles through machines installed in patrol cars. Police can use large computer databases to cross-reference information and to identify suspects. For example, computer models can be used to track the activities of gang members.

Computers can be used in training programs, including shoot/no-shoot decisions and police pursuit driving simulations. And they can be used to generate psychological profiles and in crime scene analysis. Forensic animation, in which computers simulate criminal activity, is useful in both training and crime-solving. Computer imaging can be especially helpful in updating photographs of children who have been missing for several years.

In the previous section we noted the use of DNA evidence to exonerate defendants in capital crimes. Only a few human cells from hair or blood samples are needed to identify suspected criminals. Beginning in the 1980s, DNA was largely seen as a benefit to defendants. Prosecutors often opposed it and several courts denied requests for DNA testing. But it increasingly has been used by prosecutors to secure convictions. DNA can look at decades-old evidence and accurately identify suspects. Other recently developed forensic tools can lift latent fingerprints, and computer imaging can expand partial fingerprints that previously could not be used as evidence.

Typically, state statutes of limitation to prosecute crimes are three to five years, except for murder, for which no limits exist. The use of improved technology is leading some criminologists to suggest that time restrictions for other felonies should be eliminated because the prosecution can produce accurate evidence connecting persons to crimes in the distant past. Author/lawyer Scott Turow cautions against removing statutes of limitation because it is difficult to recapture nuances of past events, such as changes in community expectations and the nature of victim consent.[50]

There is increasing concern about **biocrime**—the use of chemicals and toxins to inflict damage, particularly if used by terrorists—and about **cybercrime**—crime committed through computer technology. Fighting these kinds of crime requires technically sophisticated responses by law enforcement.

Criminologist Frank Schmallenger highlights several new crime-fighting ideas that are still largely in the development stage.[51] They include "radar flashlights" that allow police to "see through walls" and remote video inspection systems that transmit images of drivers, vehicles, and passengers to an inspector many miles away. These and various ways in intercepting electronic communication raise serious concerns about protecting First Amendment rights from "supersnoop" technologies that listen, record, and photograph.

SUMMARY

States typically have three-tiered court systems composed of fragmented trial courts, intermediate courts of appeal, and a supreme court. State supreme courts hear and decide cases in ways similar to the U.S. Supreme Court, but they often differ in that the power of state chief justices is less and there are fewer dissenting opinions.

Court reform has centered on consolidating and centralizing state trial and appellate courts. While there is more administration centralizing in most states, various parties resist changes that threaten their vested interests.

Criminal procedures are strongly influenced by plea bargaining, in which all interested parties seem to benefit. The prevalence of plea bargaining is affected by the cohesiveness of courtroom work groups, whose members seek to reduce uncertainty and avoid time-consuming trials.

Academics have devoted a great deal of time to studying procedures by which judges are selected—election, appointment, and merit. Their conclusions are that the method of selection has, at best, a limited impact on the quality of judges and the nature of their opinions. But when there are elections, serious questions are raised about the influence of campaign contributions on the fairness of judicial opinions. Recently, changes in judicial codes of conduct have permitted candidates to campaign in partisan ways. Courts have politicized in other ways as legislators seek ways to control judicial decision making.

While much has been said about a "new judicial federalism" in which state courts rely more on state constitutions and act contrary to the U.S. Supreme Court, most state courts tend to interpret individual rights in a manner similar to the U.S. Supreme Court. It appears that the impact of a new judicial federalism has been overstated.

A variety of theories have been put forth to help explain the decline in crime since the early 1990s. While most of them have some validity, it may be that access to abortion and high rates of imprisonment account for most of the decline.

Criminologists continue to struggle with the mystery of why crime increases and why it decreases in different places and at different times. Various explanations, from the state of the national economy to police strategies, including community policing and "quality of life" enforcement, are explored.

On the job, police have an unusually high amount of discretion. Police behavior can be influenced by the type of organizational structure of their departments. Police departments across the country implemented various styles of community policing to bring police and residents closer together to fight crime.

Despite the decline in crime, longer and more certain prison sentences have resulted in growing prison populations. To cope with this increase, states have built new, large prisons, and recently they have been using more alternatives to incarceration, such as house arrest and supervised probation.

Support for capital punishment, permissible in thirty-seven states, has been declining, in part, due to the use of DNA evidence that has exonerated several prisoners on death row. As with crime rates and rates of imprisonment, southern states have much higher rates of capital punishment than other states.

Crime fighting has been aided by the use of increasingly sophisticated technology, including a wide variety of computer applications. As more invasive devices become operational, they raise increasing questions about the need to protect individual liberty.

KEY TERMS

common law (p. 253)
trial courts of limited jurisdiction (p. 254)
criminal misdemeanors (p. 254)
civil cases (p. 254)
trial courts of general jurisdiction (p. 255)
no contest (nolo contendere) (p. 257)
major trial courts (p. 257)
courts of appeal (p. 257)
judicial review (p. 262)
bail (p. 263)
mediation (p. 265)
arbitration (p. 265)
plea bargaining (p. 266)
petit juries (p. 267)
grand juries (p. 268)
Missouri Plan (p. 270)
new judicial federalism (p. 274)
"broken windows" theory of fighting crime (p. 276)

discretionary authority (p. 279)
watchman style (p. 280)
professional movement in policing (p. 280)
service style (p. 280)
community policing (p. 280)
retribution (p. 282)
deterrence (p. 282)
rehabilitation (p. 282)
incapacitation (p. 282)
parole (p. 283)
restoration (p. 283)
alternative sentencing (p. 286)
boot camps (p. 286)
recidivism (p. 287)
aggravating circumstances (p. 287)
mitigating circumstances (p. 287)
biocrime (p. 291)
cybercrime (p. 291)

BRIEF COMPARISONS OF STATE/LOCAL DIFFERENCES

Issue	States	Local Governments
Judicial selection	Appellate judges often selected by merit systems	Trial judges tend to be elected, often on nonpartisan ballots
Judicial philosophy	Appellate judges issue written opinions; may have discretion over which cases they hear	Trial judges deal with narrow issues and seldom give innovative decisions
Law enforcement personnel	State police are relatively small in number and in some states are limited to highway duties	Municipal and county police comprise about 90 percent of total law enforcement personnel
Correctional facilities	Prisons house convicted felons	Jails house those arrested and awaiting trial or convicted offenders serving short-term sentences

INTERESTING WEB SITES

www.ajs.org. Web site of the American Judicature Society, a nonpartisan organization interested in judicial independence, ethics, and selection. AJS is a strong advocate of merit selection of judges. Many articles from the journal, *Judicature,* are online.

www.ncsconline.org. The National Center for State Courts is an independent, nonprofit organization with the goal of improving the administration of justice through leadership and services to state courts. "Court Web Sites" and "CourTopics: State Links" access general and state-specific information. Also, under "NCSC Projects," "Center for Jury Studies" reports on an important but neglected responsibility of citizenship.

www.ojp.usdoj.gov/bjs. The Bureau of Justice Statistics, part of the U.S. Department of Justice, has an extensive Web site. Click on "Courts & Sentencing," then "Court Organization" to access "State Court Organization 2004," a detailed examination of state courts.

www.fbi.gov. At the FBI's Web site, click on the lefthand side, click on "Use Our Resources," then "For Researchers," then "Crime Stats" to access *Uniform Crime Report* to view the latest crime statistics.

NOTES

1. Ralph Blumenthal, "DeLay Case Turns Spotlight on Texas Judicial System," *New York Times* (November 8, 2005), p. A19.
2. Adam Liptak and Janet Roberts, "Campaign Cash Mirrors a High Court's Rulings," *New York Times* (October 1, 2006), pp. 1, 20.
3. Henry R. Glick and Kenneth N. Vines, *State Court Systems* (Englewood Cliffs, N.J.: Prentice-Hall, 1973), p. 25.
4. Henry R. Glick, "Courts: Politics and the Judicial Process," in *Politics in the American States,* 8th ed., Virginia Gray and Russell L. Hanson, eds. (Washington, D.C.: Congressional Quarterly Press, 2004), p. 236.
5. Henry J. Abraham, *The Judicial Process,* 7th ed. (New York: Oxford University Press, 1998), p. 149.
6. Henry R. Glick, *Courts, Politics, and Justice*, 3d ed. (New York: McGraw-Hill, 1993), p. 338.
7. Ibid., pp. 371–372.
8. Glick, "Courts: Politics and the Judicial Process," p. 238.
9. Chris W. Bonneau, "The Composition of State Supreme Courts 2000," *Judicature* (July-August 2002), p. 28.
10. Lawrence Baum, *American Courts,* 4th ed. (Boston: Houghton Mifflin, 1998), p. 50.
11. Ibid., pp. 53–54.
12. Zach Patton, "Judging the Judges," *Governing* (October 2006), p. 42.
13. David Rottman, "The State of Courts in 2005: A Year of Living Dangerously," *Book of the States 2006* (Lexington, Ky.: Council of State Governments, 2006), p. 237.
14. Glick, *Courts, Politics, and Justice*, pp. 230–231.
15. Ibid., p. 232.
16. See James Eisenstein and Herbert Jacob, *Felony Justice* (Boston: Little, Brown, 1977).
17. Kathleen Sylvester, "Putting the Jury on Trial," *Governing* (March 1993), pp. 40–41.
18. Harry Kalven and Hans Zeizel, *The American Jury* (Boston: Little, Brown, 1966).
19. Anthony Champagne and Judith Haydel, eds., *Judicial Reform in the States* (Lanham, Md.: University Press of America, 1993), p. 6.

20. Richard A. Watson and Ronald G. Downing, *The Politics of Bench and Bar: Judicial Selection under the Missouri Nonpartisan Court Plan* (New York: Wiley, 1969), pp. 338–339.
21. Traciel V. Reid, "The Politicization of Retention Elections," *Judicature* (September–October 1999), pp. 68–77.
22. See Champagne and Haydel, *Judicial Reform in the States,* p. 185.
23. Rottman, "The State of Courts in 2005." p. 237.
24. David M. O'Brien, *Constitutional Law and Politics,* vol. 1, 5th ed. (New York: W. W. Norton, 2003), p. 753.
25. Glick, "Court: Politics and the Judicial Process," p. 256.
26. Keith E. Whittington, "Interpose Your Friendly Hand: Political Support for the Exercise of Judicial Review by the United States Supreme Court," *American Political Science Review* (November 2005), p. 594.
27. Steven D. Levitt and Stephen J. Dubner, *Freakonomics* (New York: Harper Collins, 2005), p. 122.
28. James Q. Wilson and George Kelling, "Broken Windows," *Atlantic Monthly* (March 1982), p. 29–38.
29. Malcolm Gladwell, *The Tipping Point* (New York: Little, Brown, 2002), pp. 150–151.
30. Jim Rutenberg and Sewell Chan. "In a Shift, New York Says It Will Add 800 Officers," *New York Times* (March 22, 2006), p. A23.
31. Levitt and Dubner, *Freakonomics,* p. 124.
32. Ibid., p. 141.
33. John Tierney, "The Miracle That Wasn't," *New York Times* (April 16, 2005), p. A13.
34. James Q. Wilson, *Varieties of Police Behavior* (New York: Atheneum, 1973), p. 7.
35. Frank Schmallenger, *Criminal Justice Today,* 8th ed. (Upper Saddle River, N.J.: Pearson, 2005), p. 252.
36. Wilson, *Varieties of Police Behavior,* chap. 5.
37. Peter Burns and Matt Thomas, "Fear and Loathing in Five Communities: The Impact of Community Policing." Paper presented at the annual meeting of the Midwest Political Science Association (April 15–17, 1999), p. 3.
38. Schmallenger, *Criminal Justice Today,* p. 454.
39. James Q. Wilson, *Thinking about Crime* (New York: Basic Books, 1975), pp. 174–175.
40. Schmallenger, *Criminal Justice Today,* p. 554.
41. Fox Butterfield, "With Cash Tight, States Reassess Long Jail Term," *New York Times* (November 10, 2003), p. A1.
42. *Governing Source Book 2006* (Washington, D.C.: Congressional Quarterly Press, 2006), p. 66.
43. Penelope Lemov, "Roboprison," *Governing* (March 1995), pp. 24–29.
44. Herbert A. Johnson, *History of Criminal Justice* (Cincinnati: Anderson, 1988), p. 36.
45. All death penalty statistics are from U.S. Department of Justice, Bureau of Justice Statistics, www.ojp.usdoj.gov/bjs (revised February 2, 2006).
46. Liz Hallovan, "Pulling Back from the Brink," *U.S. News & World Report* (May 8, 2006), pp. 36, 37.
47. Adam Liptak, "False Conviction Study Points to the Unreliability of Evidence," *New York Times* (July 23, 2007), pp. 1, 10.
48. David C. Baldus, George Woodworth, and Charles A. Pulaski, Jr., "Monitoring and Evaluating Contemporary Death Sentencing Systems: Lessons from Georgia," *University of California Davis Law Review* (Summer 1985), pp. 1375–1407.
49. Liz Halloran, "Pulling Back from the Brink," *US News & World Report* (May 8, 2006), p. 37.
50. Scott Turow, "Still Guilty After All These Years," *New York Times* (April 8, 2007), sec. 4, p. 11.
51. Schmallenger, *Criminal Justice Today,* p. 772.

chapter

8

SUBURBS, METROPOLITAN AREAS, AND RURAL COMMUNITIES

LOCAL GOVERNMENT COOPERATION IN IOWA

In 2005 Governor Tom Vilsak concluded that Iowa simply had too many local governments—99 counties, about 3,000 cities and towns, and a bunch of special districts. He proposed to reduce the overall number to about fifteen by roughly following the boundaries of community colleges across the state.[1] Vilsak did not believe the state government could or should force consolations, but he thought it could provide sufficient inducements to affect mergers. Not surprisingly, the plan didn't work.

As we will see later in this chapter, consolidated city-county governments, which would create the most revolutionary change in the local government landscape, seldom are welcomed by residents of the area, regardless of where they live. In 2005, voters rejected a merger between Des Moines, the largest city in Iowa, and Polk County.

But just because voters in Polk County rejected the most extreme form of consolidation didn't mean they were not open to other means of cooperation with neighboring communities.

As Alan Greenblatt explains, Vilsak's fundamental point—that there are redundant layers of local government in the state—has been widely accepted in Iowa. As a result, his failed plan for mass mergers has become the catalyst for incremental changes across the state as officials find new ways to cooperate.

For example, the city of Des Moines and Polk County jails have consolidated their buildings and operations. A new regional transit authority has been established in Polk County, and several task forces are meeting to discuss ways in which city-county responsibilities can be shared. They may not be saving a lot of money, but services are provided more efficiently.

In other parts of Iowa, countywide planning and zoning have been implemented. Nearly a thousand agreements for cooperation are contracted among local governments each year, and the number of informal agreements is much larger. Several police and sheriff departments have merged.

Traditionally, school consolidation has been extremely difficult in states with many small towns. Iowa has about 390 school districts, and local football and basketball teams provide a centerpiece for community involvement and local pride. Iowa hasn't seen a change in that mindset, but Adams County, with 4,400 people and seven school districts, is considering merging all other public services.

The accumulated effect of little mergers across Iowa is changing the way communities view each other and the way they provide services.

POINTS TO CONSIDER

- Why has urban sprawl occurred? What are its consequences?
- How do cities and suburbs differ from each other?
- What is the myth of the suburban monolith?
- Why did outer suburban and rural voters support Republican candidates so strongly prior to 2006? Why did both groups change their voting behavior in 2006?
- Why has city-county consolidation been very difficult to achieve? Is it a goal worth pursuing for most counties?

- Should states and cities limit growth? What are some "smart growth" strategies?
- How has zoning adversely affected cities? How should zoning rules be changed?
- Have state legislators overacted to *Kelso v. New London*?
- Would you want to live in a town designed by the New Urbanists?
- How have large food producers and fast-food retailers affected rural/small-town America? What can be done to improve the situation?

Throughout this book we have discussed a variety of urban issues—the reform movement, the nature of community power, and the roles of interest groups, mayors, and council members. We now turn our attention beyond central city limits to look at politics in suburbs, small towns, and rural areas. The 1920 census showed that the United States had changed from a predominantly small-town, rural society in the nineteenth century to a predominantly urban society. As noted in Chapter 1, urbanization of the United States has increased to the point where currently over 80 percent of Americans live in metropolitan statistical areas (MSAs).

Clearly, we have become a largely urbanized people. Yet more people live *outside* central cities than within them. The 1970 census showed that for the first time in U.S. history more than half the population of metropolitan areas was suburban. Moreover, because MSAs include whole counties adjacent to a central city or contiguous cities of 50,000 people, many residents of MSAs actually live in small towns that are not suburban, or they live in rural areas. Of course, nearly 20 percent of Americans live outside MSAs.

Our primary concern in this chapter is to examine politics in suburbia to see how it differs from big-city politics and to see how suburban communities interact with each other. The prevailing view of the suburbs in the 1950s was that they were a homogeneous group of bedroom communities whose white, upper- and middle-class residents voted Republican and limited their concern for social issues to their local schools.[2] This picture was oversimplified even in the 1950s, and suburbs have become increasingly diverse. By the 1970s the idealized version of these communities differed greatly from reality. After examining contemporary suburban life, we will look at ways in which metropolitan areas are attempting to create order where literally hundreds of overlapping governments have fragmented the political process. Then we will travel farther away from central cities to examine life in small-town and rural America.

URBAN SPRAWL: CAUSES AND EFFECTS

As political scientists John Harrigan and Ronald Vogel note, central cities could have grown by annexing areas on their fringes where population was growing.[3] Instead, cities became surrounded by autonomous suburban communities whose residents sought the advantages of a small-town setting close to the economic and cultural opportunities of the central city. As recently as 1950, 70 percent of metropolitan area populations lived in central cities. In 2000, just over 70 percent lived *outside* central cities in the nation's twenty-five largest metropolitan areas. An even higher percentage of voters and the overwhelming majority of elites now reside in suburbs. In addition, most metropolitan residents work in suburban areas.

The mobility afforded by widespread automobile ownership after World War II and the construction of new highways helped to accelerate suburban growth. A host of federal government policies—including the interstate highway system, lower-interest home loans insured by the Federal Housing Administration, tax codes that permitted deductions for home mortgage interest, and grants to build hospitals and sewerage plants—encouraged Americans to move to the suburbs in the 1950s.

The Nature of Suburbs

An increasing trend since the 1980s has been the expansion of **satellite (or edge) cities** on the fringes of metropolitan areas.[4] Although cities such as West Palm Beach (Miami), Scottsdale (Phoenix), and White Plains (New York) are related to the central city, they are employment centers in their own right and often have downtowns and cultural complexes that are quite separate from the core city. The newest edge cities are characterized by low-density, heavily landscaped office campuses, and they are located adjacent to large upper-middle and high-income housing tracts. Always moving farther from the central city, new edge cities, such as Plano, Texas, on the Dallas Tollway, are located several miles beyond the last generation of edge cities.[5]

Growth continues beyond edge cities in so-called **edgeless cities,** which Robert E. Lang, director of the Metropolitan Institute at Virginia Tech, describes as "a form of sprawling office development that does not have the density or cohesiveness of edge cities but accounts for two-thirds of office space found outside downtowns.[6] Lang notes that it is important to follow office space because that is where most job growth occurs, which has a major impact on sprawl and transportation analysis. *New York Times* columnist David Brooks refers to these areas as "exurbia." They include communities such as those stretching from Orlando to Tampa that have little contact with urban life.

Earlier decisions made by private businesses also facilitated population movement away from central cities. Faced with labor unrest near the end of the nineteenth century, many businesses relocated their plants to the suburbs as a way to isolate workers and to control union activities. Credit institutions often practiced **redlining,** in which they refused to make loans for construction in certain parts of cities they considered too risky. Depressed areas of cities grew worse as new or rehabilitated housing was not funded. The lack of acceptable central city housing led to the exodus of the middle class to the suburbs as government policy made it easier for them to buy houses.

Often these privately made decisions were strongly influenced by racial factors. Redlining made it nearly impossible for many African Americans to get home loans. As more African Americans and Hispanics moved into northern cities after World War II, residential segregation increased. Jobs, shops, and sports stadiums moved to the suburbs and minorities were left behind. In the suburbs, open space was lost to sprawl and exclusionary zoning (discussed later in the chapter) often served to limit housing opportunities for *all* low-income people.

As people have moved farther away from the central city, urban sprawl has created **fragmented government** over which there often is little or no coordination or control by a central agency (see Table 8-1). The New York City metropolitan area, for example, extends over more than thirty counties in three states and contains more than 23 million people. There are nearly 2,200 separate government units, including over 700 special

TABLE 8-1 Political Fragmentation in the 25 Largest Metropolitan Areas

Metropolitan Area	Counties	Municipalities and Townships	Total Local Governments	Local Governments per 100,000 Residents	Population Living in Central City (%)
Pittsburgh	6	412	418	17.7	14.8
Minneapolis– St. Paul	13	331	344	12.3	22.4
St. Louis	12	300	312	12.2	13.8
Cincinnati	13	222	235	12.2	18.0
Kansas City	11	171	182	10.6	34.6
Cleveland	8	259	267	9.2	17.1
Philadelphia	14	428	442	7.4	24.7
Milwaukee	5	108	113	6.9	36.1
Chicago	13	554	567	6.6	31.7
Detroit	10	325	335	6.2	18.4
Boston	14	282	296	5.1	9.6
Dallas	12	184	196	4.2	23.1
Portland	8	79	87	4.1	23.2
New York	27	729	756	3.8	37.3
Atlanta	20	107	127	3.5	11.4
Denver	7	67	74	3.2	21.9
Houston	8	115	123	2.8	41.1
Seattle	6	88	94	2.8	15.9
Tampa	4	35	39	1.8	13.0
San Francisco	10	104	114	1.7	11.1
Miami	2	55	57	1.6	10.5
Phoenix	2	32	34	1.2	42.1
Los Angeles	5	177	182	1.2	23.0
San Diego	1	18	19	0.7	43.7
Washington, D.C.	33	125	158	2.2	17.1

Source: Myron Orfield, *American Metropolitics: The New Suburban Reality* (Washington, D.C.: Brookings Institution Press, 2002), pp. 132, 134.

districts that are responsible for providing a single service. Even though population growth in metropolitan New York has increased less than 10 percent since 1970, the amount of developed land in the area has increased over 60 percent. The Chicago metropolitan area contains more than 1,100 governmental units. Phoenix in 1940 had a population of 65,000 within a ten-square-mile area. Currently the city has a population of 1.4 million in a 475-square-mile area. In addition, suburban sprawl has led to the expansion of Tempe, Mesa, Paradise Valley, and other new cities in the Phoenix metropolitan area.

David Rusk, former mayor of Albuquerque, notes that 56 percent of Americans lived in 168 "old metropolitan areas" in 1950.[7] The central cities in these metropolitan areas had about 60 percent of the region's population. By 1990, 66 percent of Americans lived in the old metropolitan areas, but their central cities contained only one-third of the regional population. In addition, Rusk identifies another 152 "young metropolitan areas" that had developed, mainly in the South and West, by 1990. Largely because of annexation, their central cities were able to capture much of the area's growth, and as a result they had about 62 percent of the metropolitan population. Rusk reports that the total population of all metropolitan areas increased by 128 percent from 1950 to 1990, while their land area increased by 181 percent.

In 1950 the 172 metropolitan areas in the United States had a population of 85 million, or 56 percent of the total population of the country. In 2000 there were 331 metropolitan areas with 226 million people, or 80 percent of the total population. The ten largest metropolitan areas had a population of about 89 million.

The fragmentation of metropolitan government makes it extremely difficult to establish responsibility for metropolitan area policy. In addition, public services suffer because small units are unable to provide many specialized services; there is duplication of services when many governments independently operate facilities such as sewage disposal and water plants; and it is difficult to deal with the many problems—pollution, mass transit, crime, traffic congestion—that extend over several community boundary lines. Affluent suburbs can spend vast sums for education, but central cities face a declining tax base and an increasing demand for services. Property tax *rates* may be higher in a central city than in its more affluent suburbs. At the same time, many suburban governments need to spend relatively little money for crime control or public health. The low-density development of suburbs tends to drive up the cost of infrastructure development and repair.

Fragmentation has numerous other consequences. Significant racial imbalance occurs because outer-ring suburbs remain predominantly white, whereas the central city and, increasingly, inner-ring suburbs have large African American and Hispanic populations. Suburban land-use regulations drive up the cost of new construction, and this leads to a shortage of housing in central cities when low-income persons are forced to stay within city limits. Suburbs that restrict the growth of *all* types of housing units force development on the suburban fringe, thus adding to the existing urban sprawl. Suburbs that restrict growth push development out farther, and this destroys more green space.[8] In several cases, large, fragile environments are endangered by overdevelopment. These include Chesapeake Bay and large parts of the arid Southwest. For example, more than 80 percent of the population of Arizona lives in the Sonoran Desert, where most areas get less than ten inches of rain a year.

There have been both push and pull effects regarding patterns of residence. Suburbs have "pulled" residents out of cities with their promise of a better life, but residents of central cities have also been "pushed out" because of a variety of city problems. Migrants from large cities most often mention crime as their major reason for leaving. Rundown schools, drugs, pollution, high taxes, and the rising cost of living are other factors that push people to the suburbs. As the percentage of African Americans and Hispanics has increased in central cities, a clear undercurrent of racism also has influenced whites to flee to predominantly white suburbs. In large cities, people also sense a loss of community feeling and often find it difficult to participate in government decision making.

The movement of racial minorities to inner-ring suburbs has led to resegregation by race as whites move farther away in the metropolitan area. Until 1990, there was general agreement among academics that when a community's African American population approaches 20 to 30 percent, whites begin to move out in substantial numbers (the **tipping point** has been reached). In the 1990s, political scientist Andrew Hacker suggested that white exodus can begin much earlier, when the African American population is as low as 10 percent.[9]

When middle-class families and industry leave, the city's tax base shrinks, and this occurs at a time when welfare, police, and public health expenses are increasing. Yet great private wealth remains in the nation's largest cities. Cities continue to attract unskilled workers who seek better lives. But, unlike the early twentieth-century immigrants, today's urban poor find few unskilled jobs, and union control of apprenticeship programs makes it difficult to acquire trade skills. In addition, young blacks are particularly frustrated and alienated when they encounter a substantial gap between real and anticipated social and economic gains. Inner-city neighborhoods continue to deteriorate, even as downtown development projects create spectacular new buildings. For example, in 2006 the poverty rate in Cleveland was about 33 percent, the highest of any major city in the country, despite the construction of new sports facilities and downtown office buildings several years earlier. Like Detroit, there is a wide economic gap between Cleveland and its suburbs. The poverty rate for metropolitan Cleveland (14 percent) was very close to the national average.

Still, there is increasing evidence to indicate that life in cities has actually improved. In places such as Boston and Baltimore, middle-class people have returned to live in the city, and new shopping areas such as Boston's Quincy Market are flourishing. The Society Hill–Market Street East area in Philadelphia is another example of a successful renewal effort. Cincinnati has banned new surface parking lots downtown, and its city planning department has several full-time employees working on historical preservation. Downtowns are being preserved in virtually all cities. This is in contrast to the mid-1960s, when some 1,600 federally supported urban renewal projects in 800 cities often were bulldozing historic neighborhoods. Federal tax laws now encourage preservation, and cities are putting a priority on downtown development. Unfortunately, as upscale renovation has lured white suburbanites back to inner cities, the increased costs have driven African Americans and Hispanics to other urban neighborhoods.

Most large cities have experienced significant white flight since the mid-1970s, resulting in increasing concentration of Hispanics and African Americans in inner cities while many suburbs remain predominantly white. Overwhelmingly, African Americans are likely to live in metropolitan areas. The 2000 census showed that for the first time non-Hispanic whites were a minority of the total population living in the nation's 100 largest cities. Seventy-one of the 100 largest cities lost white population in the 1990s. At the same time, those cities had a 43 percent increase in Hispanic residents. Chicago gained 208,000 Hispanics and had its first overall population gain since 1950. Detroit lost 53 percent of its white population in the 1990s and saw its total population drop below 1 million for the first time since 1920. By 2005 Detroit had a population of 887,000, down from its peak of over 1.8 million in 1950. The city is about 82 percent black. The Detroit metropolitan area has the largest percent black population in the United States (25 percent), but because of the extremely high black population in the central city, the metropolitan area is among the most segregated in the country.

Although suburbs remain mostly white, there has been a substantial departure of middle- and working-class minority persons from cities since the 1980s. For example, in the 1980s and 1990s the population of Washington, D.C., declined by nearly 200,000, and the loss of African American households was nearly three times as great as for whites. Hispanic and Asian American suburbanization has occurred at even higher rates than for African Americans across the country. Circles of African American–majority suburbs exist around Washington, Atlanta, St. Louis, Los Angeles, and Chicago. Minorities leaving central cities cite the same reasons as whites for their flight to suburbs—crime, quality of life, property values, and schools.

While the number of all-white suburbs is diminishing, many suburbs are becoming predominantly white. In suburban Detroit, Livonia was 96.5 percent white in 2000 and Warren was 93.3 percent white. The most racially segregated suburban area in the United States is on Long Island, New York. David Rusk blames its segregation on a mixture of tax, zoning, housing, and education policies that result from Long Island's "frustrating maze of little-box governments; 109 villages, towns, and cities; and 129 school districts."[10] At the other extreme, so-called disaster suburbs such as East St. Louis, Illinois, and Compton, California, are nearly all minority and very poor.

In general, suburbs have not provided a supportive environment for women. When women were more likely to stay home with their children in the 1950s, they often were isolated in suburban communities without public transportation. Although suburbs have become more gender diverse, with more widows, singles, and divorcées, many communities still provide little support for independent women. Divorced women with children often are frustrated by the lack of public transportation and affordable housing.[11]

In addition to socioeconomic differences, political differences between central cities and suburbs can be identified. From our understanding of socioeconomic factors and their relationship to party identification (see Chapter 3), we would expect cities to be strongly Democratic and suburbs to be strongly Republican. In fact, cities, with their concentrations of union members, ethnic minorities, and African Americans, historically have supported the Democratic Party in national and local elections. New York City has cast a majority of its votes for every Democratic presidential candidate since Thomas Jefferson. St. Louis has not had a Republican mayor since 1945. However, New York City and Los Angeles elected Republican mayors in the 1990s and New York City elected another Republican mayor in 2002 and 2006. However, New York City voters have continued to elect Democrats to other local, state, and national offices. Several other large cities—including Cleveland, Indianapolis, Minneapolis, and San Diego—have elected Republican mayors in recent years. Although predominantly white, upper-class suburbs on the outer ring of metropolitan areas support Republican candidates in state and national elections, overall, as we will see in the following section, suburbs are much more politically competitive than conventional wisdom has suggested.

As we will also discuss in the next section, suburban variety extends to voting patterns, where working-class inner suburbs have supported Democrats and more distant (and more exclusive) suburbs have strongly supported Republicans. Still, in the fourteen presidential elections from 1952 through 2004, only in 1964 (Lyndon B. Johnson) did a Democrat win more than half the suburban vote. In 2004 President Bush carried 97 of the nation's 100 fastest-growing counties, while following a strategy devised by presidential adviser Karl Rove to appeal to voters in the exurbs.

In 2006 the national Democratic and Republican Parties both focused their attention to what were perceived to be suburban swing voters. Democrats sensed the opportunity to win votes in close-in suburbs, with their increased numbers of racial and ethnic minorities, singles, and retired people and where they had gained 58 percent of the presidential vote in 2004. Republicans continued to focus on outer suburbs and exurbs, hoping to build on their success in 2004. There was a rough calculation that at each smaller increment of urban population, George W. Bush had received a higher proportion of the vote. The advantage for Democrats is that in the fifty largest metropolitan areas only about 5.6 million live in the exurbs.[12]

In May 2006, a Gallup Poll showed George W. Bush with a 29 percent approval rating among suburban voters. In November, unhappiness with the president and the war in Iraq led to the defeat of Republicans in several suburban congressional districts across the country. For example, a ten-term Republican was defeated in suburban Philadelphia and a ten-term Republican lost in Connecticut. In Florida the incumbent Republican lost in a suburban district north of Miami where 37 percent of the people were older than 65. A Democrat was elected in a district composed of affluent suburbs north of Denver, in large part because well-educated voters were put off by the rise of social conservatives in the Republican Party. Overall, the suburban vote for House Democrats increased by 8.2 percent from 2004. In much of the country, voters seemed to be more concerned with education, safety, and the environment than with so-called culture war issues, such as abortion and same-sex marriage.

Having noted differences, and some similarities, between cities and suburbs, we need to point out that in many ways cities and suburbs are growing more alike.[13] Inner suburbs resemble central cities in terms of greater ethnic diversity, deteriorating infrastructure, and high crime. Many central cities are attracting increasing numbers of prosperous, well-educated people to redeveloped areas where lofts and condos have replaced warehouses and factories.[14] Many downtowns have changed from being predominantly business centers to places with lifestyle amenities. Even in the outer suburbs, residents are commuting to other suburbs. Many suburbs have downtowns and a sense of community identity. However, this sense of cultural identity is missing in the exurbs, where the population is so dispersed that social conditions seem unlikely to change in the near future.

Suburban Variety

Just as central cities exist along a continuum from those that are weak or declining, such as Detroit and Cleveland, to those that are strong and gentrifying, such as Seattle and Phoenix, we can identify great variety among suburbs. Former Minnesota state legislator and scholar Myron Orfield attacks the "myth of the suburban monolith" by describing three main categories of suburbs that are emerging in metropolitan areas across the country.[15]

Forty percent of the population in metropolitan areas live in what Orfield calls **"at-risk" suburbs.** Some of them are older, inner-ring communities that have been bypassed by metropolitan growth. Others are located on the outer ring of metropolitan areas where there is a transition from rural to suburban. In addition to having some incorporated communities, fringe areas in many regions, such as Atlanta, contain large tracts of unincorporated territory that have high rates of poverty. At-risk suburbs lack a viable business district, and they often share many of the same economic and social problems of central cities. Many inner-ring at-risk suburbs, such as those around Chicago, are even more racially segregated than their central cities.

About one-quarter of the population of metropolitan areas live in **"bedroom-developing" suburbs.** These communities resemble the 1950s view of the "typical" suburb. Their predominantly white population, living in newer houses, has the most school-aged children of any communities in the region. Because they often lack an adequate tax base, these suburbs face fiscal pressures to build roads and sewer systems and to construct and maintain schools.

Less than 10 percent of the population of metropolitan areas live in suburbs that Orfield calls **"affluent job centers."** These are the edge cities we discussed earlier. With abundant office space, they have more jobs than bedrooms. For these communities, urban sprawl is advantageous. Still, problems exist. Many workers cannot afford local housing, there is traffic congestion, and it is difficult to resist pressures to develop open space.

Orfield has a series of color-coded maps that clearly show the mix of communities in several metropolitan areas.[16] For example, the San Francisco region has large expanses of at-risk, low-density, unincorporated areas on its fringes, and it has an inner ring of at-risk, segregated suburbs near Oakland. Affluent communities are dominant in Santa Clara County, which is at the southeast corner of the region.

Orfield also shows that suburbs are much more politically complex than they have been portrayed in the suburban monolith model. His computer-generated mapping of the twenty-five largest metropolitan areas (home to 46 percent of the nation's population) has produced some surprising results. Orfield found that in 1998 state legislative seats were evenly split between Democrats and Republicans. Many of the country's swing districts, those with no permanent allegiance to either major party, are in the suburbs.[17] Orfield suggests that characterizing suburban women as "soccer moms" misses the suburban reality. Although residents of affluent job centers often vote Republican, the overwhelming number of suburban residents live in at-risk and bedroom-developing suburbs, and it is these swing voters that Orfield believes will play the pivotal role in determining the outcome of upcoming American elections. As we noted earlier, suburban voters in 2006 were instrumental in the defeat of several long-serving Republicans. Clearly these same districts will be crucial in the 2008 presidential and congressional elections.

THE POLITICS OF METROPOLITAN CONSOLIDATION

Differences in the political, social, and economic composition of cities and suburbs have a direct effect on public policy. In many instances, people have moved to suburbs to escape the problems of central cities or, increasingly, to escape the problems of inner-ring suburbs. They do not want to contribute tax dollars to help solve other people's social problems. Meanwhile, cities must respond to a host of pressing issues even as their revenue base declines.

As we would expect, city-suburb differences also have a major impact on the fate of proposals for consolidation of metropolitan governments. As we noted in the case study for this chapter, in most instances, consolidation plans are opposed by both city and suburban officials, who seek to maintain their community's autonomy and their personal political power. Of the two groups, those in suburbs have been the most opposed to unification. However, the support of residents of central cities also has waned.

With population of the central cities declining, metropolitan government would come to mean control by white, middle-class suburbanites. The liberal coalitions of labor and African Americans that control many city governments would stand to lose considerable power if their political strength were diluted in a metropolitan area. From our earlier discussion of fragmented government, it seems as though most academics view sprawl and fragmentation as creating a host of efficiency problems, whereas most residents view it as a desirable feature of grassroots democracy, making government more responsive to local concerns.[18]

African Americans and labor leaders usually oppose consolidation for reasons that are more political, social, and psychological than economic. They contend that the existence of many local governments helps increase citizen *access* to decision making, which produces a greater sense of community and personal effectiveness in dealing with smaller units of government. In such a situation, a variety of groups have the opportunity to make their views heard and to affect public policy.

Fragmentation benefits white, upper-class suburbanites because it allows them to isolate themselves from the problems of cities and to maintain school assignments based strictly on place of residence. In a time when there is strong sentiment for less government, suburban residents may not place a high priority on improved service delivery. Few are likely to believe that metropolitan government, or any government, would improve service and most fear it would increase taxes. Evidence from metropolitan areas where consolidation has occurred—Miami and Nashville—shows that expenditures have risen. In fact, many suburban residents use few government services. They live in gated communities, protected by private security; their garbage is picked up by private providers; and their children attend private schools.

Among academics, those who support the **public choice theory** argue that metropolitan area residents are best served by a fragmented system in which various communities can offer different sets of services that appeal to various tastes of citizens.[19] Public choice theorists contend that those citizens who are willing to pay more for certain services, such as education and recreation, can choose to live in certain communities and those who prefer lower taxes and fewer services can live elsewhere. This is comparable to a free marketplace where consumers shop for the best products at the most appropriate price. As in business, it is contended that competition among suburban communities will lead to innovation and a greater incentive to produce government services more efficiently. Public choice advocates contend that some services can be provided more economically by smaller units of government and that in other cases cooperative metropolitan arrangements can be made. They believe that, as in the economic marketplace, competition among cities will lead them to provide high-quality services with relatively low taxes as a means to attract new residents and businesses.

Robert Bruegmann, a professor of art history and urban planning, argues that sprawl is a good thing because it has allowed people to do what they want—own a house with a yard in a community with good schools and nearby recreational activities. In effect, Bruegmann contends, the American middle-class can do what previously was available only to the rich.[20]

Critics of public choice theory respond that, although this model might work for those free to move within the metropolitan area, many people do not have the ability to "vote with their feet." Family, finances, and jobs may greatly reduce the mobility of many residents. Of course, this is particularly true for the poor and for minorities. Even if people were relatively free to move, it might result in isolated suburbs pursuing narrow goals to benefit their own residents with little concern for resolving areawide problems. They note that there is little evidence that competition among cities leads to improved service levels. In fact, competition may increase disparities as rich communities invest in facilities that attract upscale residents and poor communities only get poorer.

Those in favor of consolidation are most likely to be business and professional people whose perspective is similar to that of early twentieth-century urban reformers. These groups fear that as the central cities are abandoned by the middle class, the poor and less well educated will gain undue political influence. They also believe that metropolitan government would be more efficient because it could achieve the economies of large-scale operations and provide improved public services.

State politics expert Neal R. Peirce argues that metropolitan areas have become **citistates** that are regional in scope, with economic connections among individual cities. He contends that standing alone even large cities cannot compete well.[21] To compete in a world economy where cities outside the United States have more extensive metropolitan government, Peirce strongly urges residents of metropolitan areas to work together politically to serve their common economic interests.

"Mega cities," or "megalopolises," are other terms used to describe the clusters that operate as giant cities with a flow of goods, services, and people among individual cities. Robert E. Lang and Dawn Dhavale identify ten "megapolitan areas" that extend across thirty-five states and contain two-thirds of the U.S. population.[22] Their growth has been aided by interstate highways that, for example, have connected Portland, Oregon, with Seattle and Phoenix with Tucson.

Contrary to conventional wisdom, some supporters of consolidation argue that it will help minorities. They note that, although African Americans and Hispanics often constitute a majority of voters in large cities, those cities have such weak tax bases that it is nearly impossible for them to respond effectively to the needs of the minority community. These reformers advocate a district system of election in which minority groups would be directly represented in an areawide government. W. W. Herndon, the long-time African American mayor of Memphis, has been the only mayor of one of the country's fifty largest cities to strongly advocate city-county consolidation. Mayor Herndon believes that Memphis will continue to struggle economically as its suburbs capture most of the region's growth. He also believes that by 2010 African Americans will comprise a majority of the entire county's population. In Louisville, the sixty-fifth city in the country in 2000, successful consolidation with Jefferson County in 2002 was led by Mayor Jerry Abramson. Having been term-limited as mayor of Louisville, Abramson was easily elected to the new office of metropolitan mayor. Then he was reelected in 2006. Overnight, Louisville became the nation's twenty-third largest city. In part, the sense of gaining national importance helped voters support consolidation.

Plans for Metropolitan Cooperation

Because opposition to consolidation is so widespread and is based on so many different rationales, it is not surprising that proposals to establish metropolitan governments have failed nearly 75 percent of the time they have been brought before the voters. However, a metropolitan area need not make the move from extreme fragmentation to rigid consolidation in one giant step. There are several intermediate options available, such as annexation, special districts, and councils of government. Federalism expert David B. Walker outlines seventeen approaches to regional service problems, ranging from those that are the most politically feasible and least controversial to those, such as city-county consolidation, that have relatively little likelihood of being adopted.[23] We need to remember that, even though comprehensive consolidation of municipalities in metropolitan areas is rare, other approaches are relatively easy to accomplish, and consequently, they are found in most metropolitan areas. As noted in the case study, many communities in Iowa use mechanisms such as interlocal agreements because they appeal to values of reciprocity, cooperation, and old-fashioned good neighborliness.

Among the "easiest" to adopt regional approaches to service delivery, Walker includes informal cooperation between two local jurisdictions; interlocal service contracts between two or more local jurisdictions; and joint power agreements in which two or more jurisdictions agree to plan, finance, and deliver a service. About two-thirds of the states permit **extraterritorial powers** in which cities can exercise some regulatory power outside their boundaries in unincorporated areas. This might include zoning and subdivision regulation. In Texas, cities have extraterritorial powers that extend five miles from their corporate limits. As we will see later, this power makes cities "elastic" because they can prevent new incorporation on their borders and later annex territory.

The following plans are included in Walker's categories of "middling" and "hardest" approaches to metropolitan cooperation.

Annexation

Throughout the nineteenth century, most growth in metropolitan areas occurred through **annexation,** in which a city extends its boundaries by absorbing adjacent land. Because annexation was so common, there was little of the suburban fringe fragmentation that marks present-day metropolitan areas. For example, Philadelphia used annexation to expand from two square miles to 136 square miles in 1854, and the city's boundaries have not expanded since then.[24] In 1898 New York City expanded its territory sixfold by adding Brooklyn. By the early 1900s opposition to annexation developed, and large cities in the East and Midwest became surrounded by incorporated suburban communities. Suburban residents wanted to be isolated from large immigrant populations in central cities, and many state legislatures changed annexation laws to require approval by voters in the area to be annexed and by voters in the city.

Annexation has continued to be a useful tool of big-city growth in many southern and southwestern states. In part, this is because in some states—Arizona, Missouri, North Carolina, Oklahoma, Texas, Tennessee, and Virginia—land may be annexed by action of the city alone or by judicial procedures. Often annexation occurs because the owner of a large tract of land wants to develop it and wants city services, such as water and sewers. Texas permits each city to annex up to 10 percent of its territory without any voter approval. In about a dozen states, municipalities are permitted by law to veto the incorporation of new jurisdictions forming just outside their boundaries. In over half the states, approval is required by those in the area to be annexed. Often approval also is required by the residents in the larger community.

In Oklahoma, Oklahoma City has annexed more than 500 square miles of territory since 1959, and Tulsa added 116.8 square miles in a single annexation in 1966. The largest city in area outside Alaska, where three city-county consolidated areas have over 1,000 square miles, is Jacksonville, Florida. City-county consolidation in 1967 gave Jacksonville 774 square miles. Since 1950, Houston has annexed land to grow from 160 to 580 square miles, and Phoenix grew from 17.1 square miles in 1950 to 475 square miles in 2005. Because of its aggressive annexation, Houston still has nearly one-half the population of its metropolitan area. When city-county consolidations are *not* considered, Oklahoma City, with 607 square miles, is the largest city in land area. Houston is second, and Los Angeles (469 square miles) is third. All cities with the largest land areas are in the West and Southwest where most of their growth occurred after World War II and there was little opposition from neighboring cities to annexation. In contrast, most older eastern cities are quite small: Boston has forty-eight square miles, Pittsburgh fifty-six square miles.

Aggressive annexations can lead residents in outlying areas to incorporate new cities in self-defense. Most states require voter approval to create new incorporations, and they set a minimum population that the area must have. In some states the minimum is as low as 300 people. Some new suburban cities are incorporated with very large populations. For example, the largest new cities in the 1990s were Federal Way, Washington (67,535), Lake Forest, California (56,065), and Lakewood, Washington (55,937). Washington, California, Utah, and Florida accounted for 80 percent of the national population in new incorporated municipalities in the 1990s. The largest newly incorporated city in United States history was created in 2001 when voters in Arapahoe County, Colorado, approved Centennial, with a population of 104,000 spread across thirty-six square miles of suburban Denver.

In a few cases, cities detach property from their boundaries. For example, Oklahoma City detached thirty square miles during the 1980s and is still **overbounded**—that is, large amounts of virtually uninhabited land remain within the corporation.

Large annexations have declined since the 1980s.[25] Many southern cities have annexed as much land as they can manage, and new laws in Texas and other states have made annexation more difficult. In some cases, unincorporated areas get services from county governments and no longer look to central cities to provide them. The largest annexation in the 1990s occurred in the South, where cities gained 17.8 percent more land area by annexations. The least land gained was in the East, where, following a long trend, annexations added 3.3 percent more land to cities and most of that was due to a reclassification of five Massachusetts towns as cities.[26] Cities that added the most population by annexation were San Antonio (125,692) and Charlotte (112,103). In North Carolina, land can be annexed without the owner's consent and cities can veto the incorporation of new municipalities adjacent to their boundaries.

Annexation is viewed as a means by which metropolitan areas can eliminate some conflicts of authority, avoid duplication of services, and promote more orderly growth. As noted, cities annex land undergoing development to control that development or protect the environment. Opposition comes from suburbanites who fear higher taxes and wish to remain independent of the central city. In some cases, cities may simply add to their problems by annexing areas that lack a strong tax base and are in need of costly services such as roads, water, and sewers. Often these fringe areas have not imposed any zoning laws, and thus they present special development problems to city administrators.

Many large cities—such as Boston, Chicago, Detroit, Minneapolis, and Pittsburgh—long ago became encircled by incorporated areas and have been unable to expand their boundaries. For them, annexation presents no solution to their metropolitan problems. In the Los Angeles area, for example, Beverly Hills continues to resist the annexation efforts of Los Angeles, which completely encircles that affluent suburb. Los Angeles annexed land from 1910 to 1919 to expand its territory fourfold. Pittsburgh is surrounded by nearly two hundred municipalities, and there are nearly one hundred municipalities in St. Louis County. Although some central cities are able to coerce annexation by withholding services such as water to independent suburbs, cities in most states cannot force annexation against the wishes of suburban residents. In addition, some of the largest metropolitan areas, including New York City, Philadelphia, Chicago, and St. Louis, extend into two or more states, and of course no central city can annex land outside its state's boundaries. Five cities (Detroit, San Diego, El Paso, Brownsville, and Laredo), have boundaries that adjoin urban areas outside the United States.

Special Districts

A politically inoffensive way of providing services on a metropolitan-wide or intermunicipal level is to create a special district government. **Special districts** most often perform a single function and they are appealing because they are superimposed on the existing structure of government and leave municipal boundaries untouched. As a result, suburbs receive the services they need without losing their independence. Special districts also have the advantage of bypassing taxation or debt limitations imposed on local units by state law. About half of all existing special districts have been created for fire protection, soil conservation, water, and drainage. Others provide sewer, recreation, housing, and mosquito-control services. Since 1942, the number of special districts has grown from 8,000 to nearly 36,000 (although school districts may be classified as special districts, they are considered separately by the Bureau of the Census). Recently there has been a significant increase in the number of special districts on the fringes of metropolitan areas. Often in the Southwest these special districts provide a variety of services to suburban residents and become a kind of junior city.[27] Later the area may be annexed by the central city.

Special districts are established under state law and usually require voter approval. In most states, they are governed by a small board, which has taxing and bonding authority. Board members are most often chosen indirectly, rather than being elected directly by popular vote.

In spite of their wide appeal, special districts have many problems. Governing boards have low voter visibility, and in most cases there is little citizen access to their decision making. One result is that contractors and others doing business with special districts (lawyers, bankers, real estate agents) often operate behind the scenes to their own economic advantage. Special districts are frequently established to meet short-range goals. Once created, they lessen the likelihood that long-range planning will be accomplished to meet problems at their most fundamental levels. Because 90 percent of special districts perform only a single function, coordination of government services is made more difficult and district administrators often view public policy from the narrow perspective of what benefits them without considering the overall needs of their community. Special districts usually encompass only a few municipalities within a metropolitan area, so they cannot be viewed as a suitable substitute for metropolitan government.

In addition to local special districts, there are regional districts that are areawide organizations, usually set up by state law. These include the Chicago Metropolitan Sanitary District, the Bay Area Rapid Transit District (San Francisco area), and the Port Authority of New York and New Jersey. These large units require special action by state legislatures, and because of their size they can become very expensive and quite independent of municipal and county governments.

Councils of Government

Councils of government (COGs) are voluntary regional associations of local governments in a metropolitan area that are concerned about a broad range of problems, such as water supply, transportation, sewers, and airports. Each local government is represented in the COG by its own elected officials. Operating roughly like the United Nations, COGs meet to discuss problems, exchange information, and make policy proposals. COGs usually conceive comprehensive plans for metropolitan development, but they do not have the ability to enforce their rulings on communities that oppose their recommendations.

The first COG was created in Detroit in 1954. In the 1960s federal policy (Model Cities Act of 1966) strongly encouraged COGs by requiring local applications for federal funds to be reviewed by a regional agency. By the mid-1970s there were 650 COGs and over forty federal programs to promote regional planning and coordination. The regional review requirement was removed by the Reagan administration in the 1980s as the political base of the Republican Party moved to the Sunbelt and suburbs. As a result, COG activity declined in the 1980s, but it expanded with federal help in the 1990s.

COGs are not governments because they can only make recommendations and hope for voluntary compliance by member governments. Their weaknesses include a tendency to concentrate on less controversial physical problems, such as sewers and water supply, and to avoid more controversial socioeconomic problems, such as racism and poverty. Their authority is very limited, since they can seldom compel participation or compliance with decisions. Since COGs are voluntary organizations, members can withdraw if they wish. Because COG officials also are employed by local governments in the area, there often is conflict among them based on their municipal alliance. In some instances COG membership has been roughly proportional to the population of constituent governments, but other COGs have one-vote-per-government systems. In the former, smaller suburbs are disadvantaged; in the latter the political power of central cities is weakened.

Two-Tier Government

Two-tier government is a type of metropolitan government that meets the desire of local governments to maintain their identity within a metropolitan area. A federal relationship is established between cities and a metropolitan government similar to the relationship between the states and the national government. In this arrangement, areawide functions are assigned to the metropolitan government, and local functions remain with existing municipalities. The existing communities retain their own form of government.

In the United States, Metro Miami–Dade County is the only two-tier system. Elsewhere, such a system has operated in Toronto, Winnipeg, Berlin, and London. The Toronto plan was approved in 1954 by action of the province of Ontario, not the local voters. Under

Toronto's federation plan, local governments maintain their existence and a regional government is responsible for issues that affect the metropolitan area. In 1997 the federation plan was replaced by a more unified arrangement. The city of Toronto and five suburbs were merged into a unitary government, but Toronto's outer suburbs kept their own identity.[28]

Metro Dade has helped bring about improved mass transit and land-use planning. But it has not been able to control sprawl in the south Florida area that extends beyond Dade County into parts of three other counties. Nearly half the population of Dade County lives in unincorporated areas, so for them there is only one tier (Metro Dade) of government.

In Miami after World War II, residents were confronted with a host of problems stemming from accelerated growth. In 1957 the voters of Dade County were asked by the Florida legislature to approve a two-tier form of government.[29] Approval came by a slim margin with only 26 percent of those eligible registered to vote. The proposal was supported by the Miami business community, the newspapers, and such good-government groups as the League of Women Voters. Opposition came chiefly from various local public officials and from the wealthier suburbs, such as Surfside and Miami Beach. In metropolitan Miami the usual opponents of unification—organized labor, political parties, and minority groups—all lacked effective organization. As in Jacksonville, the electorate consisted of a large percentage of newcomers to the community. Such a situation is unlikely to exist in any of the older cities of the Midwest or Northeast.

Under a federal-type structure, the twenty-six cities in the metropolitan Dade County area kept control of many local functions, including garbage pickup, street maintenance, and police and fire protection. The reorganized county government, with commissioners and a newly created manager, was given control over countywide services such as mass transit and water pollution.

Since 1957, Miami and Dade County have experienced a huge gain in population, with Hispanics (largely Cuban) making up about two-thirds of the population of the city of Miami. After African Americans and Hispanics filed suit, charging that the at-large election system diluted their power on the nine-member Metro commission, a federal district court ordered a change to elections by districts, which led to a significant increase in the number of Hispanics on the commission. In 2007, Dade County voters approved a strong-mayor proposal that was pushed by the mayor, but opposed by all thirteen commissioners. Although 57 percent of voters approved the issue, turnout was only 14 percent. The mayor will have control of the budget and oversee the county's 30,000 employees, including some sixty department heads.

Three-Tier Government

Three-tier government place a regional government on top of municipalities and counties, with the regional government having substantial authority. There are only a few examples of this form of government, with the most prominent being in metropolitan Portland, Oregon, and in Minneapolis–St. Paul.

The Twin Cities Metropolitan Council was created by the state legislature in 1969 to act as a planning, coordinating, and review agency for the region. The council's seventeen members, appointed by the governor, are nonpartisan and represent geographical districts in the metropolitan area. A bill passed by the Minnesota legislature in 1997 calling for council members to be directly elected was vetoed by the governor. The governor also appoints the head of Met Council. It remains responsible to the legislature, which can change its recommendations. Both Governor Jesse Ventura and his successor, Tim Pawlenty, have argued that the Met Council should give more autonomy to local governments. Despite his criticism of the council, Ventura placed the council chair on his cabinet.

Although the council is not a metropolitan government, it does oversee sewers, highways, transit, parks, and airports in a seven-county area that had more than 300 governments, including 130 incorporated suburbs, with little cooperation between them before 1969. The council supervises metropolitan public policy making through its control of the capital budgets of the operating agencies that provide metropolitan services. Because of its broad authority and taxing power, Met Council differs from most councils of government. Although it does not operate public services, it has the power to overrule municipalities, counties, and special districts in its area. Met Council also oversees a tax base–sharing program created by the state legislature to deal with the problem of some communities developing faster than others and creating wide financial gaps between those communities with new businesses and industry and those with declining tax bases. Forty percent of the net value of new construction in the metro area is placed in a fund and redistributed to all communities in the region according to their population and need.

Met Council has several powers, such as the ability to levy property taxes and to issue bonds, that most regional organizations across the country lack. But it has been bypassed in making several important decisions, including the decision to build a domed stadium in downtown Minneapolis and a World Trade Center building. Although the state legislature gave the council new responsibilities in the 1990s, it refused to approve direct election of council members.

The most ambitious regional authority is the Metropolitan Service District (Metro) for Portland, Oregon, which runs the zoo, the convention center, and the performing arts center and directs regional land use and transportation for twenty-four cities and three counties. Metro originated from a federal planning grant in the mid-1970s. A 65-member citizens' committee studied proposals for regional government and recommended the plan to the Oregon legislature with the provision that it be submitted to area voters. As in the Twin Cities, a Portland COG had existed for several years before the new government was approved by Portland area voters and the Oregon legislature in 1978. Metro has a paid, elected executive officer and seven elected council members who are paid an annual salary. Before 1993 they were paid only a per diem allowance. Under a new charter approved in 1993, Metro has increased planning powers and can impose taxes without voter approval. Metro's achievements include land-use planning and environmental protection. It is responsible for setting the urban growth boundary in metropolitan Portland that seeks to control sprawl. Still, many policy areas in the region are not dealt with by Metro, and sprawl has continued as the urban boundary has been extended. The regional transit system has not been extended across the Columbia River to Vancouver, Washington.

Regional government created by popular vote succeeded in Portland, but failed in Tampa, Denver, and Rochester, which had similar federal grants. Its original approval by Portland voters was due in large part to Oregon's strong tradition of citizen participation. Still, Metro remains largely unknown to most residents in greater Portland. Few know who their Metro councilor is.

City-County Consolidation

The most serious attempts at establishing metropolitan government in the United States have come in the form of merging a county and its cities into a single governmental unit. Although proposals have been introduced in many cities, **city-county consolidation** has been successful in only a few large metropolitan areas—Louisville, Nashville, Jacksonville, Lexington, and Indianapolis. Voters in Oakland, St. Louis, Portland, Pittsburgh, Memphis, Albuquerque, and Tampa have rejected city-county consolidation referenda. Compared with the other methods of integration, consolidation minimizes more completely the duplication of services and makes possible metropolitan-wide planning and administration. In each instance where such a proposal has been adopted, however, some public services continue to be administered by local units of government whose identities have remained intact. Because many metropolitan areas extend beyond a single county, city-county consolidation offers few possibilities to the nation's largest cities.

In the nineteenth and early twentieth centuries, state legislatures mandated city-county consolidation in New Orleans (1805), Boston, Philadelphia, San Francisco, New York, Denver, and Honolulu (1907). City-county consolidation was common in the nineteenth century, but no consolidations occurred from 1908 until 1947 when voters in Baton Rouge/East Baton Rouge Parish in Louisiana approved a referendum. This was the beginning of consolidations via referenda. Five city-county consolidations were approved in the 1960s, and from 1970 through 2000 voters approved referenda for fourteen consolidations. All but two (one in Montana and one in Kansas) were in southern states, with Georgia the leader. Since 1968 there have only been two mergers in big cities, Jacksonville and Louisville, that were approved by voters. Success has come in medium-sized (150,000 to 800,000) metropolitan areas and in small, rural western parts of the United States. No consolidated government has ever changed back to its separate forms.

City-county consolidation activity was unusually high in the 1990s. Wayandotte County and Kansas City, Kansas, consolidated in 1997 and consolidations were studied or proposed in four other Kansas counties. Still, most attempts in the 1990s to consolidate cities and counties, including Des Moines, Iowa, and Spokane, Washington, failed. Political scientists Suzanne Leland and Christopher Cannon speculate that the increase in consolidation activity was due in large part to the devolution of responsibilities to states and localities and the decline of many inner cities.[30] Residents don't want tax increases and yet they don't want to see public services cut. When some cities have difficulty providing adequate services, reformers argue that voters should approve consolidation as a means to improve government efficiency and reduce metropolitan fragmentation. Still, as noted in the case study, consolidation most often is viewed as too extreme. But discussion about consolidation, as in Iowa, may lead to the adoption of other, less intrusive forms of cooperation among local governments.

Over forty cities operate independently of any county and perform both city and county functions. They include all forty-one cities in Virginia, plus Baltimore, St. Louis, and Carson City, Nevada.

In most cases, proponents of consolidation have been successful only after long battles in which ultimate victory was achieved with the help of unusual political circumstances. Prior political corruption helped gain approval of reform in Jacksonville, Florida, after there were grand jury charges of graft and corruption and the city-county schools lost their accreditation. In metropolitan Nashville, suburban voters feared an aggressive annexation policy waged by the mayor of Nashville.

In 1969, Indianapolis became the first northern city to become part of a city-county consolidation. It is significant that approval came by state legislative action without a popular vote by the residents of Marion County. UNIGOV (as the consolidation is named) operates under a single mayor and a 29-member council. To a large extent, its creation was made possible because of Republican control of the appropriate state legislative committees and the political leadership of Richard Lugar, the Republican mayor of Indianapolis and currently Indiana's senior U.S. senator. Approval of UNIGOV also was aided by the preservation of most suburban and county offices as well as special service and taxing districts within the county. Three small municipalities and sixteen townships in Marion County chose not to be included in the consolidated government. As in Nashville and Jacksonville, a large council, elected in a combination of at-large and single districts, provides representation for a wide range of groups within Marion County. Republicans controlled UNIGOV, winning all mayoral elections until 2000 and often electing at least twenty members of the council.

Many existing governments have remained separate under UNIGOV. School districts continue to maintain their boundaries, and the county, suburban cities, and special districts continue to elect officials and operate as legal entities. Thus the degree of unification is less than that under most other city-county consolidations.

As political scientist James H. Seroka notes, because of the small number of city-county consolidations, it is difficult to make generalizations about why cities and counties join together.[31] As we have noted, in some cases, such as Jacksonville, political crisis has aided the cause of consolidation. Seroka notes that the role played by local elites in successful consolidations has varied from support to opposition to indifference. Consolidation seems more likely to occur in states where the legal framework is supportive and in counties with relatively few municipalities. As we would expect, the absence of strong racial and economic divisions within the county is helpful. In many cases, the first attempts at consolidation have failed and support has grown over time. So there needs to be a long-term commitment among proponents of consolidation.

Proponents have the challenge of responding to the reality that there is not strong evidence that consolidation would bring direct benefits, such as saving money through economies of scale, improved economic development, or more efficient service delivery. In fact, with larger bureaucracies, cost may go up and residents may feel less connected to their local government.

Elastic Cities

Former mayor of Albuquerque David Rusk has calculated a "point of (almost) no return" for cities.[32] This point comes when a city's population has declined 20 percent from its peak, when minority population of the city is at least three times the percentage of minorities in its suburbs, and when per capita income in the city has fallen below 70 percent of that of its suburbs. Cities in this category include Detroit and Cleveland, with several other inelastic cities moving in that direction. David Rusk notes that unlike the 1980s when all cities that had passed his "point of no return" declined even further, in the

1990s a few cities on the endangered list improved. The most dramatic turnaround was Chicago, where the city-suburban income gap closed because of improvements in housing and employment in the city. As a result, Rusk now has a set of characteristics of cities that place them *almost* beyond the point of no return.

Rusk says that playing the "inside game," which included federal programs such as enterprise zones and community development block grants, did not work in troubled cities.[33] He notes that "gimmicks" such as new convention centers also have not helped turn cities around.

If large cities in the Northeast and Midwest cannot grow by annexation, and if they are unable to consolidate with their counties, what hope is there that they will benefit from the growth occurring just beyond their limits in the suburbs? Rusk's answer is that cities need to switch to playing the "outside game." That is, by building coalitions with older suburbs (the "at-risk" communities we noted earlier), business organizations, and various nonprofit organizations, central cities should put pressure on state legislators to initiate regional solutions to their problems. As Rusk sees it, "State legislatures *must* serve as regional policy bodies because they are the only ones that can."[34] Without a regional government, such as the Twin Cities Metropolitan Council, which was created by the Minnesota legislature, no group speaks for the entire region.

Myron Orfield contends that it is essential for central cities to build coalitions with their suburbs.[35] Among the many bills introduced by Orfield to deal with metropolitan area problems were those calling for the direct election of Metropolitan Council members and calling on suburbs to provide low- and moderate-income housing.

Rusk points out that almost *all* metropolitan areas have grown since 1950. Surprisingly, the Detroit metropolitan area grew by 40 percent from 1950 to 2000, even as the city lost about 1 million people. Although inelastic cities, such as Detroit and Cleveland, have lost population, **elastic cities,** such as Houston (area in square miles up 237 percent since 1950) and Columbus, Ohio (up 385 percent), have greatly increased their populations (Tables 8-2 and 8-3). From 2000 to 2006, Detroit and Cleveland continued to lose population, while Houston and Indianapolis gained population. Elastic cities are able to "capture" suburban growth, usually by annexation, and increase in population. As a result, most elastic cities are doing well financially, even though they may be in modest-income areas, and many point-of-no-return cities are doing poorly, even though some are in wealthy areas. Elastic cities are much less racially segregated (only 30 percent of Houston's 2000 population was African American) than inelastic cities (80 percent of Detroit's 2000 population was African American) because their central cities are not hemmed in by predominantly white suburbs. Compared to elastic cities, inelastic cities have less job creation, and there is a greater income disparity between them and their suburbs.

PLANNING

Many early American cities, with Savannah, Georgia, as a prime example, were carefully plotted and still retain much of their distinctive original design. Most nineteenth-century cities in the Midwest and West were "new towns." As such, the layout of streets, the location of parks, and the placement of businesses were planned in detail. However, as

TABLE 8-2 Elastic Cities Expand Their City Limits; Inelastic Cities Do Not

	City Area (square miles)		Percentage Change	
Central City	1950	2000	1950–2000	1990s
Houston, Tex.	160	579	262%	7%
Detroit, Mich.	139	139	0	0
Columbus, Ohio	39	210	434	10
Cleveland, Ohio	75	78	3	1
Nashville, Tenn.	22	473	2051	0
Louisville, Ky.	40	62	56	0
Indianapolis, Ind.	55	361	555	0
Milwaukee, Wis.	50	96	92	0
Albuquerque, N. Mex.	48	181	277	37
Syracuse, N.Y.	25	25	0	0
Madison, Wis.	15	69	346	19
Harrisburg, Pa.	6	8	29	0
Raleigh, N.C.	11	115	942	30
Richmond, Va.	37	60	62	0

Source: David Rusk, *Cities without Suburbs,* 3d ed. (Baltimore: Johns Hopkins University Press, 2003), p. 18.

TABLE 8-3 Elastic Cities Gain Population; Inelastic Cities Lose Population

	City Population			
	1950 (or peak*)	2000	Percentage Change	
			1950–2000	1990s
Houston, Tex.	596,163	1,953,631	228%	20%
Detroit, Mich.	1,849,568	951,270	−49	−8
Columbus, Ohio	375,901	711,470	89	12
Cleveland, Ohio	914,808	478,403	−48	−5
Nashville, Tenn.	174,307	545,524	213	7
Louisville, Ky.	390,639	256,231	−34	−5
Indianapolis, Ind.	427,173	781,870	83	7
Milwaukee, Wis.	741,324	596,974	−19	−5
Albuquerque, N. Mex.	96,815	448,607	363	17
Syracuse, N.Y.	220,583	147,306	−33	−10
Madison, Wis.	96,056	208,054	117	9
Harrisburg, Pa.	89,544	48,950	−45	−7
Raleigh, N.C.	65,679	276,093	320	33
Richmond, Va.	249,332	197,790	−21	−3

Source: David Rusk, *Cities without Suburbs,* 3d ed. (Baltimore: Johns Hopkins University Press, 2003), p. 29.

*Peak population: Louisville and Milwaukee in 1960; Richmond in 1970.

city populations rapidly expanded, growth was largely unplanned. Thus by the 1880s, many large cities were crowded, dirty, and unhealthy. The same reform movement that brought changes to the structure and operation of city government (see Chapter 6) also reinstituted planning to beautify cities.

The results of the "city beautiful" movement were especially impressive in Chicago where, after much of the city was leveled in the 1871 fire, a grid system was developed from coordinates downtown. Every eight blocks is one mile and every four blocks in any direction is a wider, commercial street. Many of the suburbs, such as Skokie, continued the numerical system. If you fly into Midway Airport at night you can see the grid pattern, with intense lights every half mile reflecting commercial areas. You can see the grid as you approach O'Hare International Airport, but the newer suburbs have not continued the grid, favoring wavy cul-de-sac patterns—the price of "progress."

Planners created master plans for the overall development of cities to serve as guides to government officials and private business. Comprehensive planning goes far beyond concern early in the twentieth century for a set of maps and land-use guidelines. Planners now consider such matters as population projections, transportation, and sociocultural patterns. In most larger cities there is a planning commission, made up of businesspeople and other residents, and a city planner who reports to the mayor or city manager. Often the layout of suburbs has been designed by real estate developers. After incorporation, suburbs may develop a master plan and set up planning offices that are similar to those in central cities. Even most relatively small cities now have planning offices and economic development offices.

We have noted that regional planning is directed by COGs in most metropolitan areas. Seattle and Portland serve as top-of-the-line models for managing regional growth. Both employ regional zoning powers to draw urban boundaries as a means to control sprawl. In essence, they are calling for denser living inside prescribed boundaries. Although sprawl has been contained in the Portland area, the metropolitan population increased by more than 250,000 from 1980 to 2000. Housing prices have risen and developers have pushed for boundary extensions. Metropolitan Council officials respond that while sprawl has been largely uncontrolled in cities such as Denver and Phoenix, housing prices there have risen as much as in Portland.

Oregon has had statewide land-use planning since 1973. Outside of Portland it is managed by county governments. Curiously, the original plan was pushed by conservative Republican legislators, not liberal environmentalists from Portland.[36] Farmers were watching their fields get paved over by urban sprawl and they wanted it to stop. Oregon has protected more farm land than any other state, but resentment grew as protected farm and forest land forced urban growth to stay within boundaries and people were not able to sell their property to developers. In 2004 overwhelming passage of Measure 37 gave people who owned land before restrictions went into effect the right to get a waiver of the law, or a cash settlement from the county if they could show that legal restrictions had reduced the value of their property. Because of the potential expense, counties routinely have waived the regulations, opening the way to development. In 2006 several other western states approved similar measures.

In 1997 Maryland became the first state to use the power of state government to manage growth. Its **"smart growth"** program decrees that state funding for infrastructure will not go to support projects outside designated growth areas. As Myron Orfield notes, "Smart growth planning accepts that growth is inevitable and even desirable—if it is correctly and intelligently done."[37] Smart growth strategies include managing growth, as in Portland, Oregon, by creating urban growth boundaries; preserving agricultural land and open space; and using higher density design for city housing. New Jersey has developed a "Blueprint for Intelligent Growth" with a map that translates all the state's written environmental rules into visual form.

Many communities across the country used the initiative process to limit growth in the 1990s. Throughout the twentieth century, zoning was the most common way for cities, especially suburbs, to limit growth.

Zoning

Zoning ordinances divide a community into districts (residential, industrial, light industrial, commercial, recreational) and prescribe the uses that can be made of the land in each zone. They help maintain property values by separating commercial activities from residential neighborhoods and protecting the environment. Such ordinances are enforced by a building inspector, and a zoning board is created to make exceptions to rules or amend their provisions. In many cities, zoning ordinances have been enacted too late, after commercial and industrial establishments had already misused the land. Zoning ordinances that prescribe the height of buildings or the amount of land necessary for home construction have the effect of keeping minority groups out of upper-class suburbs. Since New York City adopted the first zoning ordinance in 1916, all major cities except Houston have enacted some form of zoning. Still, Houston controls development by a comprehensive planning commission, and a majority of surrounding counties have zoning.[38] Since 1926 the Supreme Court consistently has upheld the legality of zoning ordinances as part of governments' police powers.

A particularly controversial use of zoning is when it is used to *exclude* lower-income persons from suburban communities. Zoning can exclude economic groups of people by setting minimum lot sizes and by prohibiting apartments of a certain size or, in extreme cases, prohibiting all apartment buildings. Suburbs also may exclude people through subdivision infrastructure costs that are assessed to builders and passed on to home buyers. As noted, fragmented communities encourage racial and economic segregation. Smaller communities tend to promote uniformity, not diversity, and they make areawide planning very difficult. As housing costs have soared since the 1980s, even middle-income white people find themselves effectively shut out of many suburban communities. This remains true despite the drop in housing prices in 2007.

Even in the absence of metropolitan government, some state legislatures, as in Connecticut, have enacted **inclusionary zoning** to force developers to include affordable housing in a mix of new homes. The New Jersey Supreme Court ruled in 1975 that all zoning regulations in Mount Laurel were invalid because they failed to provide a range of density levels and building types. The court used a "fair share" concept regarding the location of multifamily housing as well as of houses on small lots. Later the New Jersey Supreme Court imposed an affirmative duty on communities to provide affordable housing. Responding to strong suburban opposition, the New Jersey legislature passed a law that weakened the definition of "affordable housing" and allowed suburbs to rezone as little as possible.

In 1977 the U.S. Supreme Court ruled that communities are not required to alter zoning laws to provide housing for low-income families. The case involved Arlington

Heights, a Chicago suburb, and its refusal to rezone a vacant property surrounded by single-family homes to permit construction of a federally subsidized townhouse development. In supporting the Arlington Heights board of trustees, the Court reasoned that predominantly white communities do not have to make special allowances for integration unless there is proof of purposeful racial discrimination. Thus a zoning ordinance was upheld, even though it resulted in a racially disproportionate impact. Two Supreme Court decisions in 1987 overturned no-growth measures that limited land use, supporting the argument that property cannot be taken by local government without fair compensation paid to its owners.

Zoning has limited the construction of multifamily housing in many suburbs. Coupled with the steep increase in the cost of housing, this has forced families to move to the exurban fringe of metropolitan areas. As noted earlier, this kind of sprawl has a number of undesirable consequences, including the loss of a sense of community and a breakdown of family life for people who spend nearly four hours a day commuting in their cars.

Widespread opposition has developed against zoning laws that were written shortly after World War II. That was a time when a new generation of urban planners started to use zoning as a means to determine what urban neighborhoods should look like after massive urban renewal bulldozed buildings.[39] New zoning codes created more distance between residential, commercial, and industrial uses. Pedestrians were discouraged as planners tried to create a suburban experience that they thought people wanted in cities.

New Urbanists, such as James H. Kunster, call for an end to existing zoning codes and propose such changes as combining residential and commercial buildings, making streets narrower to discourage automobiles and encourage pedestrians, and bringing back public space in the form of numerous small parks.[40]

Architects and planners Andres Duany and Elizabeth Plater-Zybeck are responsible for several New Urbanist developments, such as Seaside and Celebration in Florida. These communities encourage people to walk and interact with their neighbors by the placement of shops in town squares and by the construction of mixed-income houses set on small lots with front porches instead of garages that face the street. Celebration also micromanages the lives of its residents down to the level of telling them what color curtains (white) they can hang in their windows. Seaside, which has served as the model for new communities across the country, is showing signs of aging and also has been affected by beach erosion.

Governor Haley Barbour of Mississippi has supported New Urbanist concepts to construct more compact communities in much of southern Mississippi that was damaged by Hurricane Katrina. "The goal," says Barbour, "is to build the coast back like it can be, rather than simply like it was." New Urbanist principles have been used to build suburban communities and to design urban public housing in cities such as Chicago, Atlanta, and Baltimore.

Eminent Domain

All state constitutions have provisions similar to the statement in the Fifth Amendment of the U.S. Constitution that says, "nor shall any property be taken for public use, without just compensation." The power of **eminent domain** allows state and local governments to "take" (purchase at a fair price) private property that they intend for "public use." When owners of private property have refused to sell it to governments, traditionally they have used their power of eminent domain to set a "fair" price and "take" it from the owners. Most often the purposes have been to build roads, bridges, public buildings, or parks. As such, eminent domain has been a useful tool to assist public planning and development.

In 1954 the Supreme Court said governments could condemn and then take homes and stores in "blighted areas" for redevelopment. This helped eminent domain become a major tool for urban renewal projects in the 1960s. Soon local governments began to seize homes of unwilling sellers in order to make the property available to private developers who would build facilities that would provide jobs and and/or increase tax collections. This led to protests by property owners across the country and to legal action charging that the takings were not being done for a "public purpose," that is, to create things that the general public would use.

In *Kelso v. New London* (Connecticut) the Supreme Court in 2005 upheld the right of a city to condemn an unblighted working-class neighborhood to provide space for private developers to construct upscale condominiums. Writing for a five-person majority, Justice Stevens said, "Promoting economic development is a traditional and long accepted function of government." He noted that city councils and state legislatures should be given "broad latitude in determining what public needs justify the use of the takings power." In dissent, Justice O' Connor said it is "likely" the beneficiaries of the decision will be people "with disproportionate influence and power in the political process, including large corporations and development firms."

Public reaction to the decision was overwhelmingly negative. In response, state legislators across the country rushed to curtail governments' ability to condemn land. In fact, Justice Stevens's opinion expressed sympathy for homeowners, adding that ". . . nothing in our opinion precludes any state from placing further restrictions on its exercise of the takings power." In 2006 initiatives limiting the power of eminent domain were approved in nine of the twelve states where they were on the ballot. They received 86 percent approval in New Hampshire and South Carolina. By 2007, thirty-eight states, including Connecticut, had adopted measures to limit the power of eminent domain.

While the *Kelso* opinion supported power that local governments already were using, the political reality has been that in most cases local officials do not want to incur the wrath of voters by approving the aggressive use of eminent domain. The National League of Cities continues to support the use of eminent domain as a means for improving neighborhoods and supporting economic development projects. Many observers believe that states have overreacted to *Kelso v. New London*. Still, the ability of a local government to take a house in which the owners have lived for many years becomes a very emotional issue. In 2007 the Supreme Court declined to revisit the use of eminent domain in an economic development case from Port Chester, New York.

RURAL AND SMALL-TOWN AMERICA

Moving beyond the city limits of suburbs, we come to rural America. Although the Bureau of the Census defines **rural** as the population outside incorporated or unincorporated places with more than 2,500 people and/or outside urbanized areas, few people living in communities of 5,000 or 15,000 and located outside metropolitan areas think of themselves as urban. There is general agreement that small-scale, low-density settlements are "rural,"[41] and the study of rural America includes "small towns" with as many as 25,000 people.[42] Even following the census definition, the United States is more rural than we commonly perceive it. For example, nearly half the counties in Ohio, New York, and Pennsylvania in 2000 had less than 50,000 population and were officially designated as nonmetropolitan, or rural. Across the country, three-fourths of the nation's counties are rural and nearly 80 percent of the nation's land area is located in rural areas. Still, there has been a significant change since 1910 when 62 percent of Americans lived in communities with populations of 10,000 or less. In 2000, it was about 15 percent.

Although urban-rural differences may be declining nationally as a result of such factors as cable television, access to interstate highways, the use of computers, and increased population mobility, many government officials believe that such differences are the biggest dividing line in their state's politics. For example, in Oregon, which is divided east from west by the Cascade Mountains, major differences of opinion are evident on such issues as taxation, land use, the environment, government regulation, and gay rights.[43]

As newspaper reporter Foster Church points out, rural Oregonians are distrustful of government at a distance, and they are especially fearful of state- or federal-imposed environmental regulations that can affect their livelihood. Living in homogeneous communities, rural Oregonians often appear less tolerant of diverse lifestyles than do urban dwellers.

Given this set of opinions, it is not surprising that rural areas for the past fifty years have consistently supported Republican candidates. In 2004 they voted for George W. Bush by a margin of nearly 20 percent. Although they comprise less than 20 percent of the nation's population, rural voters were a key factor in the 2000 and 2004 presidential elections, casting critical Republican votes in swing states such as Ohio, Missouri, and Tennessee.

Before the 2006 congressional elections, presidential adviser Karl Rove predicted that the Republican Party would maintain control of the House and Senate. While we would expect Rove to be publicly optimistic, his prediction was based on the belief that white, conservative, small-town voters would continue to vote Republican. Rove knew not only that those voters had responded conservatively to issues such as abortion, same-sex marriage, gun control, and terrorism in recent elections, but also that Republican-controlled redistricting after 2000 had increased the power of small-town/rural voters in many states.[44]

As noted earlier, rural voters supported Republican candidates in 2006 at a significantly lower rate than in 2004. The Iraq War and the Representative Mark Foley scandal pushed many rural voters to support Democratic candidates. In addition, the Democratic Party recruited moderate candidates to run in rural districts and states with large rural populations. In Missouri the Democratic winner for governor in a very close race focused strongly on small-town voters.

Although rural and farming are not synonymous, a romanticized view of rural America plotted with family-owned farms continues to influence public policy. Legislators are led to believe that if they improve farm life, they will improve rural life. In fact, farming constitutes less than 2 percent of the national economic activity and labor force. Farmers make up less than 8 percent of the *rural* population, and the majority of the income among farm families comes from nonfarm employment. There are more prison inmates than farmers in the United States.

Agribusiness increasingly dominates, with 20 percent of farms producing 85 percent of the U.S. agricultural output. Eric Schlosser's best-selling book, *Fast Food Nation,* chronicles how powerful restaurant chains have been able to affect farmers and small towns (plus, of course, influence the nation's eating habits). For example, Schlosser notes that three potato producers control 80 percent of the market for French fries and set potato prices for farmers. As a consequence, Idaho has lost half its potato farmers in the past thirty years.[45] Four meatpacking firms slaughter about 85 percent of the nation's cattle. Packing plants have moved from large cities to small towns in the Midwest and Rocky Mountain West where, says Schlosser, their Mexican workers have created the first migrant *industrial* workforce in American history. Tyson Corporation manufactures half of all McNuggets and micromanages the raising of chickens in which farmers exist as virtual serfs.

Yet the growth of corporate farming only serves to make the family farmer a more sympathetic figure to legislators and the general public. Although state legislatures make tax and growth decisions to prevent development of agricultural land, farm policy—price support and acreage allotments—is made by Congress.

From 1930 to 1970, rural populations grew very slowly and from 1940 to 1970 most nonmetropolitan counties lost population. Then in the 1970s a rural turnaround occurred in which the nonmetropolitan population gain exceeded the metropolitan gain for the first time in at least 150 years. In the 1980s, the farm crisis, a drop in rural manufacturing, and an urban revival led to a loss of population (about 1.4 million) in the majority of nonmetropolitan counties. Rural population rebounded in the early 1990s as three-quarters of the nonmetropolitan counties gained people—a net in-migration of 3.5 million people in all rural counties during the 1990s. In 2001 and 2002, rural population grew at an annual rate of 0.6 percent, down from an annual rate of 0.9 percent in the same nonmetropolitan counties in the 1990s. The annual metropolitan area rate of growth in 2001 and 2002 was 1.25 percent. Currently about 50 million live in rural areas.

There are several explanations for the recent trends in rural population.[46] In the 1970s the "period effect" of an energy crisis caused many older, less energy-efficient manufacturing plants in cities to close down and many people moved out of cities. We have noted the reasons for a population decline in the 1980s. In the 1990s, several factors can be cited to explain rural growth. These include new manufacturing plants, new prisons, and an influx of retirees.[47]

Beginning in 1994–1995, rural population growth steadily decreased annually until, as we noted, there were small increases at the turn of this century. Demographers cite national prosperity in the late 1990s and a decrease in the inflow of people from metropolitan places for the slump in rural population growth. Nearly three-quarters of nonmetropolitan residents live in micropolitan areas based around cities with populations between 10,000 and 49,000 (see Chapter 1).

As noted in Chapter 1, there has been substantial growth in rural areas of Colorado, Idaho, and Utah. A significant proportion of that growth has been from white people moving to small towns and rural areas, particularly on the fringes of large cities. Demographer Kenneth M. Johnson, cited by Alan Ehrenhalt, refers to a "selective deconcentration of the American population," in part caused by the fact that new technology allows young professionals to work from their homes in any part of the country. There is a particular attraction to those small towns with cultural (universities) and/or recreational (ski resorts) assets.

Where population has increased, many rural governments must deal with the replacement of aging infrastructure and the need to spend more money for education. In addition, new residents expect the same quality of services, such as medical care and garbage pickup, that they had in urban places. And there is more pressure on state government to preserve farmland. For new residents, growth may destroy the "rural way of life" that enticed them to move. As landscapes and farm land are threatened by development, some rural Montanans are considering zoning entire counties.

Of course, other rural areas continue to lose population. These tend to be where economies are still strongly linked to farming and mining. In some of those places, people have been moving out and there are more deaths than births. Counties losing population are most likely to be found in a line moving north to south from North Dakota through northern Texas. And one of the nation's poorest regions extends from western Texas to the San Joaquin Valley in California.

Earlier we contrasted the roles of council members in cities with their small-town counterparts. Clearly, there are many differences in towns of part-time versus full-time mayors and council members. In small towns with growing populations, part-time government officials may be overwhelmed with demands for services that their new, former urban residents want. Having moved in search of lower taxes, many of the new residents also expect the same quality of public services they enjoyed when they lived in cities. Unplanned small-town residential expansion increasingly resembles suburban sprawl into the countryside with new houses adjacent to farm fields. New residents then discover the reality of fertilizers, dust, and early morning noise.

In many sparsely populated southern and western states the county is the only form of local government. As noted in Chapter 5, townships are a common form of rural government in the Midwest and Northeast. They are less common in the West because the population of many areas has been too low to support them. Although some rural townships fund roads, parks, and even schools, most have lost power as county or regional governments have assumed more of their traditional duties.

Rural special districts, especially for electrification and soil conservation, have greatly increased in number since the mid-twentieth century. At the same time, thousands of rural school districts across the country have been consolidated into areawide or single-county districts.

Many poor rural areas share a surprisingly large number of similarities with the nation's inner-city neighborhoods.[48] Both have steadily lost population since 1950. Education, transportation, and health care problems in these "other Americas" are equally severe. Rural America has a greater concentration of poor people than does urban America. One-fifth of rural children live in poverty. As noted earlier, people in rural areas have become increasingly dependent on their own form of federal welfare, after having long criticized the residents of urban ghettos for their lack of personal initiative.

At the other extreme, those rural areas with the greatest growth resemble the suburbanization process that began in the 1950s.[49] As we have noted, just as technological and communications innovations have led businesses to move to suburban locations, more recent innovations have encouraged the movement of people to nonmetropolitan areas. People moved to the suburbs seeking more space and improved lifestyles, and now they are moving to rural areas for the same reasons—with the added bonus of a significantly lower cost of living beyond the suburbs.

SUMMARY

Although urban sprawl has been developing for nearly a century, it is largely a post–World War II phenomenon. The movement of people and businesses away from central cities has been aided by federal government policies, private business decisions to relocate, and the social problems of cities. The results are politically fragmented metropolitan areas and a concentration of racial minorities in central cities.

Contrary to the myth that there is a bland sameness to virtually all suburbs, the new suburban reality is that suburbs differ economically, socially, and politically. One categorization identifies at-risk suburbs, bedroom-developing suburbs, and affluent job center suburbs. At-risk suburbs exist on the edge of central cities and at the edge of metropolitan areas. Contrary to conventional wisdom, suburban areas often elect Democratic candidates.

In response to increased metropolitan fragmentation, a host of cooperative solutions have been tried. They range from those that are relatively easy to implement, such as joint power agreements, to "middling" approaches, such as annexation and councils of government, to the difficult, such as city-county consolidation, as well as two-tier and three-tier systems. Although city-county consolidation has been opposed by both suburban and central city residents, many urbanists contend that cities must be "elastic" if they are to grow in population and to prosper. David Rusk believes that central cities must build coalitions with their suburbs and that state legislatures must serve as regional policy bodies if meaningful cooperation is to occur within metropolitan areas. In many cases there is significant informal cooperation among local governments.

Zoning was the most common technique by which urban planners attempted to design cities in the twentieth century. Recently, however, zoning has been strongly criticized by the New Urbanists, who want to create more livable cities by mixing neighborhood uses rather than separating uses. The power of eminent domain has been a useful tool for urban planning, but the Supreme Court decision in *Kelso v. New London* in 2005 has created a public outcry against alleged abuses of the "takings" power.

Beyond suburbs, 20 percent of Americans live in small towns and rural areas. Although rural population has declined significantly since World War II, there was a marked upturn in the early 1990s as new technology allowed young professionals to work from home in any part of the country. This trend was particularly strong in the states of the Rocky Mountain West that attracted both young workers and retirees. Although rural Americans are distrustful of distant state government and are opposed to intervention in their affairs by city people, they share a surprisingly large number of social and economic problems with the residents of central cities. In 2006 Democrats and Republicans identified rural/small-town voters as key to their overall success. For various reasons, rural residents were much more likely to vote for Democrats in 2006 than in 2004, and this helped the Democratic Party gain control of Congress and add several governorships.

KEY TERMS

satellite (or edge) cities (p. 298)

edgeless cities (p. 298)

redlining (p. 298)

fragmented government (p. 298)

tipping point (p. 301)

at-risk suburbs (p. 303)

bedroom-developing suburbs (p. 304)

affluent job centers (p. 304)

public choice theory (p. 305)

citistates (p. 306)

extraterritorial powers (p. 307)

annexation (p. 307)

overbounded (p. 308)

special districts (p. 309)

councils of government (COGs) (p. 310)

two-tier government (p. 310)

three-tier government (p. 311)
city-county consolidation (p. 313)
elastic cities (p. 315)
smart growth (p. 325)
zoning (p. 318)

inclusionary zoning (p. 318)
New Urbanists (p. 319)
eminent domain (p. 319)
rural (p. 320)

INTERESTING WEB SITES

www.metroresearch.org. This is the Web site of the Metropolitan Area Research Corporation (MARC), a nonprofit organization specializing in geographic information systems (GIS) and demographic research. Click on "Reports & Maps," then "The Struggle to Grow Equitably: Taxes and Races in America's Regions" for maps of socioeconomic, fiscal capacity, race, and land-use trends in 100 metropolitan areas. An excellent site.

www.narc.org. The National Association of Regional Councils is a nonprofit membership organization serving the interests of regional councils and metropolitan planning organizations. Click on "Development," "Environment," "Homeland Security," or "Transportation" for information from a regional perspective.

www.smallcommunities.org/ncsc. The National Center for Small Communities Web site has limited online resources and is oriented to leaders of small communities, but is worth a glance.

www.smartgrowth.org. Web site of Smart Growth Network. Go to "About Smart Growth," and click on "Smart Growth Principles" or "Smart Growth Issues" for details on smart growth planning and development.

NOTES

1. Alan Greenblatt, "Little Mergers on the Prairie," *Governing* (July 2006), p. 49.
2. For a look at the classic sociological studies of the 1950s, see David Riesman, *The Lonely Crowd* (Garden City, N.Y.: Doubleday, 1956); and William H. Whyte, *The Organization Man* (Garden City, N.Y.: Doubleday, 1959).
3. John J. Harrigan and Ronald K. Vogel, *Political Change in the Metropolis,* 7th ed. (New York: Longman, 2003), p. 234.
4. Joel Garreau, *Edge City: Life on the New Frontier* (New York: Doubleday, 1991).
5. David Rusk, *Inside Game Outside Game* (Washington, D.C.: Brookings Institution Press, 1999), pp. 96–97.
6. Robert E. Lang, *Edgeless Cities: Exploring the Elusive Metropolis* (Washington, D.C.: Brookings Institution Press, 2003), p. 1.
7. Rusk, *Inside Game Outside Game,* p. 67.
8. Bernard H. Ross and Myron A. Levine, *Urban Politics: Power in Metropolitan American,* 7th ed. (Belmont, Calif.: Thomson Wadsworth, 2006), pp. 365–366.
9. Andrew Hacker, *Black and White, Separate, Hostile, Unequal* (New York: Ballantine, 1992), pp. 35–38.
10. Bruce Lambert, "Study Says Long Island Is the Most Racially Segregated Suburb in the U.S.," *New York Times* (June 5, 2002), p. A21.

11. Ross and Levine, *Urban Politics,* pp. 339–345.
12. Timothy Egan, "'06 Race Focuses on the Suburbs, Inner and Outer," *New York Times* (June 16, 2006), pp. A1, A22.
13. Otis White, www.governing.com (June 2, 2005).
14. Alan Ehrenhalt, "Return to Center," *Governing* (August 2004), p. 6.
15. Myron Orfield, *American Metropolitics: The New Suburban Reality* (Washington, D.C.: Brookings Institution Press, 2002), pp. 28–46.
16. Ibid., following p. 48.
17. Ibid., p. 157.
18. James H. Seroka, "City-County Consolidation: Gaining Perspective on the Limits of Our Understanding," *State and Local Government Review* 37, no. 1 (2005), p. 72.
19. Vincent Ostrom, Charles Tiebout, and Robert Warren, "The Organization of Government in Metropolitan Areas." *American Political Science Review* (December 1961), pp. 831–842. This is the classic work connecting public choice theory to urban politics.
20. See Robert Bruegmann, *Sprawl: A Compact Theory* (Chicago: University of Chicago Press, 2005).
21. Neal R. Peirce with Curtis W. Johnson and John S. Hall, *Citistates: How Urban America Can Prosper in a Competitive World* (Washington, D.C.: Seven Locks Press, 1993), p. x.
22. See Robert E. Lang and Dawn Dhavale, *Beyond Megalopolis: Exploring America's New 'Metropolitan' Geography* (Blacksburg, Va.: Metropolitan Institute, 2005).
23. David B. Walker, "Snow White and the 17 Dwarfs: From Metropolitan Cooperation to Governance," *National Civic Review* (January/February 1987), pp. 14–27. Also see Walker, *The Rebirth of Federalism* (Chatham, N.J.: Chatham House, 1995), pp. 272–281.
24. Ross and Levine, *Urban Politics,* p. 422.
25. Ross and Levine, *Urban Politics,* pp. 423–424.
26. Roger Johnson, Mac Perry, and Lisa Lollock, "Annexation and Population in American Cities, 1990–2000, *Municipal Year Book* (Washington, D.C.: International City/County Management Association, 2004), pp. 3–5.
27. Ross and Levine, *Urban Politics,* p. 419.
28. Ibid., pp. 392–393.
29. See Edward Sofen, *The Miami Metropolitan Experiment,* 2d ed. (Garden City, N.Y.: Doubleday, 1966).
30. See Suzanne Leland and Christopher Cannon, "Metropolitan City-County Consolidation: Is There a Recipe for Success?" Paper presented for the Annual Conference of the Midwest Political Science Association in Chicago (April 1997).
31. Seroka, "City-County Consolidation," p. 72.
32. David Rusk, *Cities Without Suburbs,* 3d ed. (Baltimore: Johns Hopkins University Press, 2003), pp. 78–83.
33. Rusk, *Inside Game Outside Game,* chs. 2 and 3.
34. Ibid., p. 247.
35. Harrigan and Vogel, *Political Change in the Metropolis,* p. 307.
36. Rusk, *Inside Game Outside Game,* p. 155.
37. Orfield, *American Metropolitics,* p. 115.
38. Ross and Levine, *Urban Politics,* p. 357.
39. Alan Ehrenhalt, "The Trouble With Zoning," *Governing* (February 1998), p. 29.
40. James H. Kunster, *Home From Nowhere: Remaking Our Everyday World for the 21st Century* (New York: Simon and Schuster, 1996).
41. David W. Sears and J. Norman Reid, "Rural Strategies and Rural Development," *Policy Studies Journal* (1992), p. 215.

42. Alvin D. Sokolow, "Small Local Governments as Community Builders," *National Civic Review* (1989), pp. 362–370.

43. Foster Church. "County Consequences," *The Oregonian* (July 11, 1993), p. 1.

44. Brian Mann, "Winning Small," *New York Times* (November 2, 2006), p. A27.

45. Eric Schlosser, *Fast Food Nation* (New York: Houghton Mifflin, 2001), p. 122.

46. Kenneth M. Johnson, "The Rural Rebound," *PRB Reports on America* (Washington, D.C.: Population Reference Bureau, 1999), pp. 10–11.

47. Alan Ehrenhalt, "Small-Town Prophets," *Governing* (November 2001), p. 8.

48. See Oska Gray Davidson, *Broken Heartland: The Rise of America's Rural Ghetto* (New York: Free Press, 1990).

49. Johnson, "The Rural Rebound," p. 17.

chapter

9

FINANCING STATE AND LOCAL GOVERNMENT

TABOR—TAXPAYER'S BILL OF RIGHTS— IN COLORADO

If you were to ask the first fifty people you see at your favorite shopping mall their opinion of taxes, they would surely say that they do not like to pay taxes and that the taxes they do pay are too high. Nevertheless, almost everyone likes the services state and local governments provide, which, of course, are paid for from tax revenues. The question of taxes in state and local politics—and national politics, too—causes one to focus on fundamental questions such as: What services should government provide? Who should be taxed to pay for services? What kind of taxes should be used to raise revenue? As will be seen in this chapter, to ensure low taxes has been the goal of a number of political movements, most recently Americans for Tax Reform and Americans for Limited Government. Influential conservative leaders including Grover Norquist, Dick Armey, and Howard Rich are active in these organizations. Their goal is to make government so small, by lowering spending, that they can "drown government in a bathtub." And TABOR, they believe, is one way to accomplish this.[1]

TABOR started in Colorado in 1992 when voters approved a state constitutional amendment that limited state government spending to an annual adjustment that equaled percentage growth in population plus the inflation rate. A unique provision of TABOR required that tax dollars collected in excess of this spending limit be returned to the taxpayers. In addition, any new tax or increase in a tax rate must be approved by the voters, not just the legislature and the governor. Initially, rapid population growth and a growing economy provided state government adequate revenue to provide services and over $3 billion in "TABOR refunds" to taxpayers. To reduce state revenue surpluses, the legislature reduced personal income and sales tax rates. TABOR seemed to work until a downturn in the economy, the recession of 2001, reduced state tax revenues and forced legislators to make hundreds of millions of dollars in budget cuts. Even as the economy recovered, TABOR restrictions continued to limit how quickly revenues increased, which resulted in a budget crisis and a difficult choice: Either cut spending for services below what citizens of Colorado had come to expect or find a way to ask voters to increase tax revenues. In 2005, Republican Governor Bill Owens and the legislature reached a bipartisan compromise to solve the crisis. They proposed a five-year suspension of "TABOR refunds," allowing the state to retain tax collections above current spending limits. These funds were to be used for K–12 education, higher education, health care, and transportation—the services that had been hardest hit by budget cuts. Because of TABOR, this proposal had to be submitted as Referendum C to Colorado voters in the 2006 election; it was approved by a vote of 52 percent in favor and 48 percent against.[2]

POINTS TO CONSIDER

- Compare the growth of state and local government expenditures to that of federal government expenditures.
- What services do state and local expenditures provide?
- How do the principal sources of revenue for state governments differ from those for local governments?
- What are nontax sources of revenue?

- How and why have state governments become involved in gambling activities?
- What are the criteria for a "good tax"?
- Compare short-term and long-term revenue problems.

HOW MUCH?

State and Local Expenditures

How much money do state and local governments raise and spend? This simple question is not as easy to answer as it might seem. The most accurate picture of spending can be found by examining **direct general expenditures,** a rather complicated name that requires some explanation. The word general means that almost all expenditures are covered; a few are excluded, such as spending on unemployment and workers' compensation, which are financed by government-mandated employer and employee contributions. Direct refers to expenditures that are actual payments, that is, money paid to government employees, to contractors that governments buy things from, or to beneficiaries of government programs. Another important term is **intergovernmental expenditures,** which are transfer payments from one level of government to another and are particularly difficult to sort out in arriving at how much money state and local governments spend. (See Chapter 2.) It is important to note that these payments are not counted as spending by the government that transfers the funds. These transfer payments become a source of revenue for the government that receives the money and expenditures for the level of government that uses it to make actual payments. Intergovernmental expenditures are an important part of state government spending because states not only receive federal grants and frequently pass the money on to local governments, but also have their own programs that transfer funds to local governments.

Direct general expenditures in 2004 for state and local governments totaled $1.9 trillion. Dollars per capita (for each person in the United States) are a little easier to comprehend; state government expenditures in 2004 were $2,788 per capita and for local governments $3,685. Expenditures by the federal government were $2.3 trillion for the same year, including almost $406 billion in grants to state and local governments.[3]

The real growth of expenditures can be identified in Figure 9-1 where they are viewed as a percentage of the gross domestic product (GDP), that is, the total output of goods and services produced inside the United States. The federal government's share is large but has changed little over the years, staying just shy of 20 percent. State and local government expenditures show substantial growth, from almost 6 percent of the GDP in 1952 to 10 percent in 1972, an increase of more than 60 percent!

Limitations on Raising Revenue

In their attempts to raise revenue, state and local governments are affected by a number of factors, most fundamentally, by the level of wealth and personal income within their boundaries. Unless poor states and communities increase tax rates to unbearable levels, they simply cannot raise sufficient revenue to provide services comparable to those in

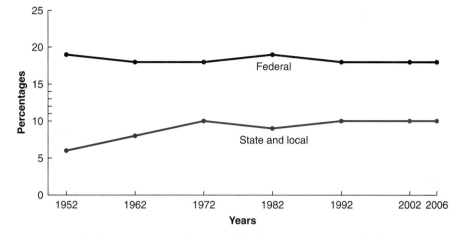

FIGURE 9-1 Federal government and state and local government expenditures as a percentage of GDP, selected years.

Source: Executive Office of the President of the United States, *Historical Tables, Budget of the United States Government, Fiscal Year 2008* (Washington, D.C.: U.S. Government Printing Office, 2007). pp. 314–315.

affluent areas. This is a particularly important problem in large cities and will be discussed later in this chapter.

State and local governments also have constitutional limits on taxation. The U.S. Constitution prohibits interference with federal operations by states through taxation, and it protects interstate commerce from direct taxation or undue interference by the states. It also prohibits states from taxing exports and imports without the consent of Congress. Perhaps of more importance are state constitutions, which frequently restrict taxing authority by exempting certain kinds of property and by defining the kinds of taxes that can be imposed.

The most serious limitations are placed on local governments, which have only those powers of taxation that state constitutions have granted them. State constitutions prescribe what taxes local governments may impose, they often establish the amount of taxation, they specify procedures of tax administration, and they outline the purposes for which tax revenues may be used. The only exceptions are in a few states where constitutions contain home-rule clauses (see Chapter 1) giving cities a general grant of power to levy taxes.

TABOR, the subject of this chapter's case study, is a recent example of efforts in almost every state to adopt some version of **TELs** (tax and expenditure limitations), which place limits on the size of revenue or expenditure increases of state and local governments. The National Conference of State Legislatures estimates that thirty states have TELs, which usually are in the form of restrictions on expenditures. Expenditure increases are linked to growth in personal income or a growth index related to the expansion of the economy. How restrictive these laws are varies from state to state. Delaware has a fairly easy to live with restriction that requires appropriations to be limited to 98 percent of the annual revenue estimate. In Washington, spending increases are tied to the rate of inflation and population growth, a much more restrictive limit than Delaware's. About half of the states with TELs have another constraint on raising taxes: supermajority voting rules in their state legislatures. This means a majority of three-fifths or even three-fourths of the membership in both chambers is needed to pass a new tax or an increase in a current tax. A few states (Colorado, Missouri, and Washington) have the additional requirement that all new taxes or tax increases over a certain amount are to be approved by the voters before they can be implemented.[4]

WHERE DOES THE MONEY GO?

Table 9-1 presents an overview of thirteen major functions on which state and local governments spend the most money. The biggest expenditure item is for elementary and secondary education. The operation of public schools consumes over 25 percent of state and local spending. The other education category—higher education, which refers to publicly operated universities, colleges, and community colleges—accounts for 10 percent of total expenditures. These two categories taken together make up almost 37 percent of state and local expenditures. The second biggest item, 17.6 percent, is for public welfare. This includes, for example, income support payments to the poor and payments made directly to doctors and hospitals for providing medical care for the poor and elderly. Health expenditures include public health research, immunization programs, and maternal and child health programs, and amount to slightly over 3 percent of expenditures.

Although Table 9-1 presents state and local spending together, this does *not* mean that both levels spend equally across all of these functions. State governments, through

TABLE 9-1 Major Direct General Expenditures by State and Local Governments, 2004

Function	Expenditure (in billions)	Percent
Elementary and secondary education	$505.0	26.5
Public welfare	335.3	17.6
Higher education	194.2	10.2
Highways	118.2	6.2
Hospitals	96.6	5.1
Interest on general debt	81.7	4.3
Police protection	69.7	3.7
Health	63.1	3.3
Corrections	56.5	3.0
Sewerage and solid waste management	55.9	2.9
Natural resources, parks and recreation	53.8	2.8
Housing and community development	37.2	2.0
Fire protection	28.3	1.5
Other	207.7	10.9
Total	1,695.5	100.0

Source: "Table 1. State and Local Government Finances by Level of Government and by State: 2003–04," www.census.gov/govs/estimate/02uss1_1.html (accessed March 13, 2007).

Note: Expenditures include federal grants-in-aid to state and local governments.

the operation of state prisons, spend two-thirds of the total that is spent on corrections. On the other hand, local governments are primarily responsible for police protection and spend over 85 percent of these funds. Eighty-five percent of higher education expenditures are made by state government, only 15 percent by local government. A good example of the use of intergovernmental revenue is in elementary and secondary education spending. More than 50 percent of the money spent by local school districts is actually money that is transferred to them from the state and even the federal government.

WHERE DOES THE MONEY COME FROM?

Intergovernmental expenditures are an important source of revenue, but the taxing policies of state and local governments generate the vast majority of their revenues (often referred to as "own source" revenue). This comes from taxes such as the income tax (both individual and corporate), the sales tax, the property tax, and nontax revenue such as user charges and state-operated or state-regulated gambling activities. Before examining these taxes in some detail, we will look at their relative importance in generating revenues.

Figure 9-2 shows the principal revenues for state governments over the years. The corporate income tax and the sales tax have declined in importance since 1952. At that

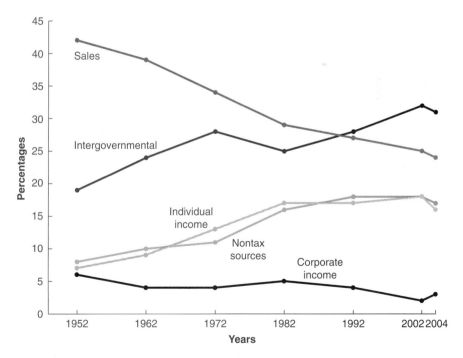

FIGURE 9-2 State general revenues by principal sources, 1952–2004 (in percentages).

Source: Percentage calculations for 2004 were made by the authors from data in "Table 1. State and Local Government Finances by Level of Government and by State: 2003–04," *www.census.gov/govs/estimate/02ussl_1.html* (accessed March 13, 2007). Percentages for early years were calculated from data in various editions of U.S. Bureau of the Census, *Statistical Abstract of the United States.*

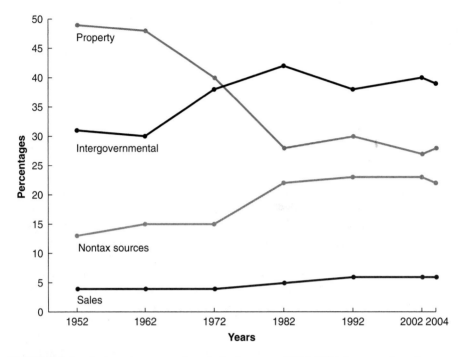

FIGURE 9-3 Local general revenues by principal sources, 1952–2004 (in percentages).

Source: Percentage calculations for 2004 were made by the authors from data in "Table 1. State and Local Government Finances by Level of Government and by State: 2003–04," *www.census.gov/govs/estimate/0400s100ussl.html* (accessed March 13, 2007). Percentages for early years were calculated from data in various editions of U.S. Bureau of the Census, *Statistical Abstract of the United States.*

time almost half of state revenues came from the sales tax. In terms of proportion of total revenues, the individual income tax and nontax sources have increased the most, with the former having more than a two-fold increase. Intergovernmental revenue, of which 94 percent comes from the federal government, has become more important—in fact, even more important than the sales tax in recent years. Overall, in terms of own source revenue, the sales tax is still dominant, 8 percentage points ahead of the individual income tax and nontax sources.

Figure 9-3 has information on principal revenue sources for local governments. Note first of all that two of the taxes that are important to state governments, individual and corporate income taxes, are missing when we look at local governments. These taxes are rarely used at the local level, at least in part because they are so heavily used by the federal and state governments. The proportion of revenue from property taxes has decreased dramatically, although it is still the most important own source revenue. Nontax sources have increased significantly; the local sales tax has also, but it still represents a relatively small contribution to the total picture, only 6 percent. In 2004 intergovernmental revenue, from both the federal and state governments, provided the largest proportion of revenue to local governments, 39 percent.

It is easy to see that the use of particular kinds of taxes follows a pattern in which the national government relies heavily on the income tax, state governments rely on the sales tax, and local governments depend on the property tax. John R. Bartle, an expert on state and local finance, states, however, that at the local government level, "an important shift is occurring from the property tax towards income and sales taxes, and especially non-tax sources."[5]

Property Tax

In most states, the **property tax** is a tax on what is termed real property, that is, land and the buildings on it. The property tax is almost exclusively a local tax and the county treasurer usually administers it. It is a fairly complicated process that includes assessment of property values, determination of tax rates (millage), tax computation, and tax collection. A market approach is frequently used to assess the value of real property. In this approach, a local assessor periodically evaluates all property in a neighborhood by using the value of property that has been recently sold. Assessors must develop and maintain detailed records of each property. One economist describes the market approach as "similar to neighbors estimating the current market value of their homes based on the sale price of a home on the same street."[6] Tax rates, set by local government officials, are sometimes expressed in mills; a mill is one-thousandth of a dollar. Thus, if a house and the land it is on are assessed at $100,000 and the mill rate is 20, the tax will be $2,000 ($100,000 × 0.020). This rate is frequently reported as $2.00 per $100 of assessed valuation.

A whole class of property, owned by charitable and nonprofit organizations, is exempt from the property tax. Exempt organizations include churches, synagogues, mosques, charities, colleges, and universities. The value of this exempt property nationwide is approximately $990 billion, or 7 percent of total real estate values; lost property tax revenue is estimated as high as $13 billion. Voluntary payments in lieu of taxes (PILOTs) are sometimes made by exempt organizations, but they fall far short of the loss in revenue.[7]

General Sales Tax

Mississippi, in 1932, shortly after the start of the Great Depression, became the first state to use a general sales tax. The property tax was the mainstay of state and local government revenue at that time, but during the Depression incomes fell more rapidly than the taxes on the property people owned and many simply could not pay.[8] During the first three years of the Great Depression, incomes fell by 33 percent and unemployment was at 25 percent. Foreclosures to pay property taxes were common, but unpopular. Consequently, twenty-two states, looking for other sources of revenue, quickly followed Mississippi's lead and adopted the sales tax before the end of 1938. During the 1940s and 1950s, ten more states decided to use a sales tax; and in the 1960s, with state governments facing increased responsibilities, eleven states adopted it. Vermont was the last (1969). Currently, only five states—Alaska, Delaware, Montana, New Hampshire, and Oregon—do not use it.

The **general sales tax** is levied on retail sales, and today the state tax rate ranges from a low of 2.9 percent (Colorado) to a high of 7 percent (Mississippi, New Jersey, Rhode Island, and Tennessee). Over half of the states have a sales tax rate at 5 percent or higher. An important element in the sales tax is the tax base, that is, what is actually taxed. The sales tax does not apply to the sale of all goods and services. For example, most states do not tax the sale of food in grocery stores or prescription drugs, and a few even exempt clothing. (However, most states do tax the purchase of nonprescription drugs.) Services are another area that is not usually taxed by states; this includes legal, accounting, and management consulting services as well as barber and beauty services.[9]

More than thirty states authorize local governments to use the sales tax, and about 6,400 do. (This seems like a lot, but remember that close to 40,000 general-purpose local governments are found in the United States.) Of course, the local tax is added on to the state sales tax so local government rates tend to be low, usually 1 or 2 percent. For example, a person making a purchase in Kansas City, Kansas (in 2007), paid 5.3 percent state sales tax, 1.0 percent county tax, and 1.25 percent city tax, for a total tax of 7.55 percent. The state sales tax in California is 6.00 percent, with a statewide local tax rate of 1.25, making a total tax rate of 7.25. In a number of large cities, including Chicago, Dallas, Los Angeles, New Orleans, New York, and Seattle, the combined state and local sales tax rate is over 8 percent.[10]

Income Tax

Forty-three states have a personal income tax, and forty-five have a corporate income tax. Wisconsin was the first state to adopt an income tax, in 1911, two years before the federal government enacted its income tax. Although eight states adopted the income tax shortly after Wisconsin, it wasn't until the Great Depression that it was adopted by a large number of states (sixteen). Beginning in 1961, another eleven states added the income tax; New Jersey was the last (1976). The seven states without an income tax are Alaska, Florida, Nevada, South Dakota, Texas, Washington, and Wyoming. (New Hampshire and Tennessee limit the income tax to dividend and interest income only.)

The **income tax** is levied on individual and corporate income and almost never taxes total income but, rather, what is called taxable income, the amount left after exemptions, adjustments, and credits have been subtracted.[11] State income tax rates are typically much lower than federal rates. A few states have a "flat tax," which means the rate is the same without regard to income level; Colorado's rate is 4.63 percent, and Pennsylvania's is 3.07 percent. Although most state income taxes are graduated—that is, the rate of taxation increases as income increases—the rate of increase and the maximum rate vary from state to state but are much less than those in federal tax schedules. The tax rate for Iowa is one of the most graduated; it begins at 0.36 percent and increases to 8.98 percent; this top rate is paid on incomes of $60,436 and higher. Many states have tax rates that range from 2 percent to 7 percent.[12]

Wisconsin also was the first state to tax the income or profits of corporations; this tax was adopted at the same time as the personal income tax. As other states adopted the personal income tax, they also adopted the corporate income tax because it was politically impossible to tax personal income and not tax corporate income. Tax rates on corporate income are usually flat and the rate is frequently around 7 percent; however, the amount of revenue produced for the states is relatively low, as noted earlier (see Figure 9-2.) Corporations in Arkansas have avoided paying their state's corporate income tax, or reduced the size of their payment, by setting up subsidiaries of their corporations in states with lower or no income tax.[13] David Brunori, a lawyer who specializes in tax issues, suggests that good tax planning by tax lawyers, along with tax breaks that states give to corporations to encourage economic development, keep the revenue generated from this tax lower than it could be.[14]

Approximately 3,800 local governments in thirteen states also tax income, with especially heavy use in Pennsylvania (where almost all school districts and municipalities use it). Rates tend to be low, 1 or 2 percent.

Other Taxes

All states place an **excise tax,** sometimes called a selective sales tax, on particular commodities such as cigarettes, alcoholic beverages, and gasoline. Taxes on cigarettes and alcoholic beverages are often called sin taxes because they tax products that many people consider if not sinful at least harmful. The idea is that taxing these products will raise revenue and may help to diminish consumption. The median tax on a pack of cigarettes is 80 cents; South Carolina has the lowest at 7 cents and New Jersey the highest at $2.57. Alcoholic beverages are usually taxed on a per-gallon basis. Tax on beer, for example, ranges from 2 cents a gallon in Wyoming to $1.07 a gallon in Alaska.

The cigarette tax has been increased with unusual frequency in recent years—in more than forty states since 2002, and a number of these states have increased it more than once. Proposals in a few state legislatures in 2007 would increase the tax by close to $1 a pack and use the revenues to provide health insurance to state residents who cannot afford to buy it on their own. Legislation introduced in Wisconsin would provide health insurance to most of the state's 250,000 uninsured. Tobacco lobbyists argue that smokers have paid enough in cigarette taxes and that these large increases are discriminatory against a minority group; in many states the price of a pack of cigarettes is over $4.[15]

The tax on gasoline is considered a benefit tax in that there is a relationship between public service benefits received and taxes paid. Gasoline taxes are used to finance the construction and maintenance of highways, so people who use the highways the most will pay a greater share. Alaska has the lowest tax at 8 cents per gallon and Washington the highest at 34 cents. During the 1920s and early 1930s, prior to the adoption of the general sales tax, selective sales taxes brought in about 28 percent of state tax revenue (over 50 percent of this amount was from the gasoline tax).[16]

A variety of other taxes are levied—on admissions to entertainment events, inheritances family members receive, and stock transfers, for example. In states that have valuable natural resources—such as coal, oil, natural gas, and timber—a **severance tax** often is levied on their extraction and removal. Although about two-thirds of the states employ some form of severance tax, a few states account for most of the severance tax revenue. In Alaska, with large oil and natural gas production, the severance tax provides almost 50 percent of state revenues; and it is equally important in Wyoming with oil, gas, and coal being taxed. New Mexico receives approximately 16 percent of its revenues by taxing, in addition to oil and natural gas, the extraction of "hard-rock minerals" including coal and copper.

Nontax Sources

User Charges

A **user charge** (or user fee) is defined as "a payment to government for a specific good, service, or privilege."[17] The definition implies that the payment will equal the actual cost of the service, but that's not always the case. Both state and local governments levy user charges. At the local level, user charges are various and include fees paid for the following: rides on subways and buses, trash collection, police services at special events, and water and sewerage systems. One user charge imposed by many local governments is the impact fee, a one-time fee paid by real estate developers to cover at least part of the cost of extending water and sewer lines and building streets for a new housing development. A significant user charge among state governments is the tuition and fees students pay, frequently with the help of their parents, to attend public-supported colleges and universities.[18] Other familiar charges are tolls for highways and bridges and fees to enter parks and other recreational areas.

Gambling

Ten years ago, the National Gambling Impact Study Commission observed the following:

> The most salient fact about gambling in America . . . is that over the past 25 years, the United States has been transformed from a nation in which legalized gambling was a limited and a relatively rare phenomenon into one in which legalized gambling is common and growing.[19]

If this was a good description in 1999, it is even truer today. How much money do Americans wager in legalized gambling? Some reports say the answer is hundreds of billions of dollars a year; the American Gaming Association (AGA), a trade association for commercial casinos, says it is much less. The AGA agrees that the total amount of money wagered is in the hundreds of billions; however, much of that money is returned to players as "winnings." Thus, the term **gross gaming revenue** refers to the amount wagered minus "winnings." Using this measure, Americans spent (or lost) in 2005 more than $80 billion gambling in horse racing, lotteries, commercial and Indian reservation casinos, and charitable bingo, among others. With a total U.S. population of just over 300 million, this represents approximately $267 for every person. More money is spent in commercial casinos and state-operated lotteries than in other forms of legalized gambling. (Please note that the AGA and other supporters of what has traditionally been called gambling prefer to use the term *gaming*.) For example, in 2005 there were 455 commercial casinos, almost half located in Nevada; their gross gaming revenue was just over $30 billion, a total that has almost doubled since 1995. Almost $17 billion of this amount was spent for employee salaries and benefits and taxes.[20]

Although there are a number of causes for this dramatic change, there is little doubt that state governments played an important role. The continuing anti-tax mood during the last two decades of the twentieth century, combined with occasional downturns in the economy that reduced state revenues, forced more and more states to turn to state-operated lotteries as a source of revenue. Between 1982 and 1992 the number of states with lotteries increased from fifteen to thirty-six. Today, forty-two states operate lotteries; North Carolina, Oklahoma, and Tennessee were the last states to adopt lotteries. The District of Columbia also operates a lottery. (See Figure 9-4.) Alabama voters defeated a lottery referendum in 1999 (54 percent against, 44 percent in favor), even though it had the strong support of Governor Don Siegelman.

Lotteries are not new in the United States; in fact, they were used in colonial times and during the nineteenth century, but scandals and unethical practices brought federal and state controls. After 1894, when the federal government banned interstate lotteries,

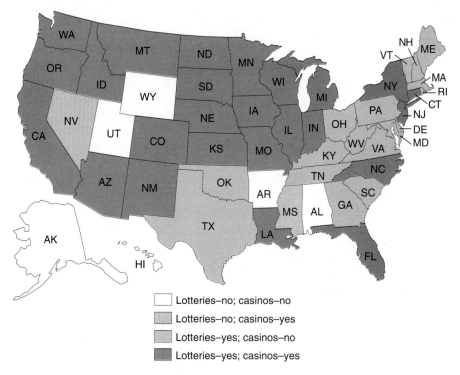

FIGURE 9-4 Gambling in the states, 2006.

Source: States that have lotteries are listed at http://en.wikipedia.org/wiki/Lotteries_in_the_United_States; information on casino gambling in the states is from *2006 State of the States: The AGA Survey of Casino Entertainment* (Washington, D.C.: American Gaming Association, 2006), p. 4. www.americangaming.org/survey/index.cfm (accessed March 21, 2006).

Note: States with casinos may have commercial casinos only, Native-American-owned casinos only, or both. States with slot machines at horse racing tracks ("racinos") are not classified as casinos here because they do not have the full range of games normally associated with casinos such as blackjack and roulette.

no legal lotteries existed in the United States until New Hampshire, hoping to avoid the adoption of a general sales tax, instituted a state-operated lottery in 1964. New York followed a few years later.[21] But it was New Jersey (1971)—by lowering the price of tickets, increasing the number of ticket outlets, giving somewhat better odds, and aggressively marketing the game—that is credited with designing a lottery that proved popular with the public and created more revenue for the state than expected.[22]

In 2004, $45 billion was spent on lottery tickets alone; $27 billion was returned to the players as "winnings," $3 billion of this total was spent for lottery administration, and $15 billion went to the state governments as revenue.[23] This is a considerable amount of money, but how much does it contribute to a state's total revenue picture? In 2004, lottery revenues averaged only 2.2 percent of the fifty-state total for own source revenue. The range among the states is from a low of 0.6 percent (Minnesota and Montana) to a high of 8.7 percent (West Virginia).[24] For most states, lottery revenues are not a big part of the revenue picture; still, if it were not available, the money would have to come from some form of taxation.

When states adopt a lottery, the revenues frequently are earmarked for popular programs such as education. Critics contend that the earmarking of revenues is something of a shell game because legislatures often reduce general revenue funds to these programs as soon as they start receiving lottery revenues. In other words, rather than becoming additional funding, lottery revenues become a substitution, more or less dollar for dollar, allowing for a reduction in general fund support. The state of Georgia, which adopted a lottery in 1994, tried to avoid this problem by mandating that lottery revenue should pay for new programs—the HOPE (Helping Outstanding Pupils Educationally) college scholarships, prekindergarten classes, and technology in the classrooms—that were being funded for the first time. Political scientist Thomas P. Lauth and Mark D. Robbins conclude that, in fact, Georgia has been reasonably successful in using lottery revenue as additional funding because of earmarking and a budget process that is "transparent." The Georgia constitution was amended so that these revenues were separately accounted for in the governor's annual budget, and the governor was required to make specific recommendations as to their use.[25] Although Oklahoma and Tennessee followed the Georgia model, lottery revenues are more often used for substitution of existing funding than for new or additional funding.

Recently, many states have moved beyond lotteries to casino gambling (see Figure 9-4). Nevada was the first to legalize casinos (1931); four decades later (1971), New Jersey did the same. No other state legalized casinos until the 1990s when they were legalized in state after state. By 1999, casinos operated in twenty-six states, including states where casinos are on land controlled by American Indian tribes. The development of Indian casinos is an important factor in the expansion of casinos in the 1990s, along with a strong economic recession (1991–92) that forced states to look for new sources of revenue.

How tribes obtained authority to open casinos is an interesting story involving the legal relationship among tribes, the states, and the federal government. Generally, federal and tribal laws, not laws of state governments, control the affairs of American Indians. Indians "retain important sovereign powers over their members and their territory," subject to the powers of the federal government.[26] In several states during the 1980s, tribes started offering high-stakes bingo games and card clubs where draw poker was played, even though these games were not explicitly allowed by the laws of the state. This obvious conflict with state law resulted in a U.S. Supreme Court case, *California v. Cabazon Band of Mission Indians* (1987). The Court ruled against California's attempt to regulate the gambling activities of the Cabazon and Morongo Bands because it infringed on the authority of tribal governments.[27] It was now clear that gambling would expand on reservations. Many observers, knowing the desperate economic conditions on Indian reservations, supported this decision because it offered a way to bring much needed economic development; still, there would have to be some regulatory oversight. In 1988, Congress passed and President Reagan signed into law the **Indian Gaming Regulatory Act (IGRA),** which established the National Indian Gaming Commission and tried to clarify the regulatory relationship between the states and tribes for various types of gambling. For casino-style games, tribes and states must negotiate agreements that describe the games that will be played and how they will be regulated. Within a few years of enacting the IGRA, there were more than 150 state-tribal agreements (or compacts) in almost half of the states.[28] Today, more than 400 tribal casinos operate in twenty-eight states, with the largest number in Oklahoma and California.

States rushed to casino gambling not only because of additional tax revenue but also in the hope that it would be an economic development tool that would create jobs for workers who would build and operate the casinos. Every time a state considers authorizing casinos, there is a heated debate over their economic benefits and costs.

The state of Nevada is often described as an example of the benefits of a gambling industry. Tourism is the mainstay of the Nevada economy and visitors to casinos come to gamble. Approximately 85 percent of Nevada's gambling revenue comes from out-of-state tourists. Recent estimates are that Nevada's 52 million tourists spend $12 billion a year.[29] The state tax on gambling receipts generates enough revenue so that Nevada does not need an income tax. Can Nevada's success be duplicated? It is clear that in economically depressed communities there are some benefits in terms of increased employment and income and increased tax revenues. For example, a few Indian tribes have had considerable success, notably the Mashantucket Pequot Indians who own and operate the Foxwoods Resort Casino in Connecticut, which recently had an annual gross gaming revenue of $1.6 billion. Unfortunately, it is difficult to measure the social costs of legalized gambling, that is, the effects on individuals, families, and communities. These costs may be considerable and need serious discussion before states or communities permit casino gambling. For example, bankruptcies in Iowa increased at a rate significantly above the national average after the introduction of casinos. And the cost to individuals and families when gambling becomes addictive is only beginning to be examined. Research sponsored by the National Gambling Impact Study Commission estimates that in any given year there are 2 million adults in the United States who are pathological gamblers.[30]

Just as the expansion of gambling activities seemed to peak, a downturn in the national economy in 2002–03, accompanied by a drop in state revenues, caused many states to consider a number of options to help balance their budgets. The expansion of slot machines, now called video lottery terminals (VLTs) at racetracks, was particularly popular, leading to the term "racinos." Gambling critics dislike VLTs because they are believed to be particularly addictive, but states see them as a source of instant revenue, and they have been taxed at rates as high as 50 percent.[31] Interstate competition is a new factor pushing states to allow "racinos" or other forms of casino-type gambling. Many state policy makers are increasingly coming to the conclusion that if their state's citizens are going to play the slots or engage in other forms of gambling they might as well do it inside their home state, rather than boarding a bus and traveling to neighboring states. In other words, policy makers decide they need to keep spending on gambling inside their state and within the state tax system; it's a defensive move.[32] This happened in New York and Pennsylvania. Pennsylvania's recently adopted law allows up to 61,000 slot machines, primarily at racetracks, but also at slot casinos and resorts.

Critics of legal gambling realize that it's unlikely to go away; many are now proposing that states attempt to regulate its negative effects, such as requiring truth-in-advertising rules for lottery ads, especially emphasizing the odds of winning, which are very low. Another proposal is that states should require casinos to make investments not just in the gambling hall but also in resort development such as hotels, shops, restaurants, and other recreational facilities. This type of investment would have a greater impact on the local economy by boosting tourism, which would provide more jobs.[33] An emerging problem is that legalized gambling, especially with slot machines, is becoming so widespread today that some observers wonder if we are not reaching a gambling saturation point. In terms of boosting an area's economy, gambling is most successful when tourists come into a state or community and spend their money—and spend lots of it (Nevada is the classic example). If gambling facilities are close by and are used only by local citizens, they are simply an alternative way for locals to spend their money, and there is little positive change to the economy or the government's revenues. In terms of many private businesses, a "cannibalizing" effect can occur: "By competing for, and often winning, much of a limited market, gambling operations can hurt local firms, ultimately driving them out of business."[34]

IS THERE A GOOD TAX?

Criteria

Public finance experts have established a number of criteria for a "good tax": sufficiency, stability, simplicity, and fairness. **Sufficiency** means that state and local taxes must raise enough revenue to fund the programs and policies that citizens want. **Stability** refers to raising a consistent amount of revenue over time, that is, few fluctuations from year to year. **Simplicity** denotes the ease and cost of administering and collecting the tax. **Fairness** reflects the idea that taxes should be equitable.[35] Two of these criteria—simplicity and fairness—will be discussed in more detail here. Let's look at fairness first.

Fairness is based on value judgments and, according to David Brunori, arriving at a consensus on how to achieve it through policy decisions is "perhaps more than any other aspect of sound tax policy . . . subject to substantial disagreement."[36] Many tax experts argue that an important component of fairness is **vertical equity;** that is, taxes should be related to an individual's ability to pay. Another way of putting this is that taxes should be progressive; as income increases, the tax paid as a percentage of income also increases. By way of example, a person with an annual income of $60,000 should be taxed at a 7 percent rate, paying $4,200 in taxes; and a person with an annual income of $30,000 should be taxed at a 3 percent rate, paying $900 in taxes. Not everyone agrees with the progressive concept. Opponents argue that taxes should be proportional. Everyone should be taxed at the same rate, let's say 5 percent. The person with an income of $60,000 would pay $3,000 in taxes and the person making $30,000 would pay $1,500. Most tax experts agree that taxes should not be regressive. A regressive tax is one that taxes those with lower incomes at a higher rate than those with higher incomes. Continuing with our example, this would mean that those with $60,000 incomes would be taxed at 3 percent (paying $1,800 in taxes) and those with $30,000 incomes would be taxed at 7 percent (paying $2,100 in taxes). No state income tax system is set up this way! However, because state and local governments use a mix of taxes in collecting revenues it is possible, in the total tax system, for some taxes to be more regressive than others.[37]

The tax that might earn a failing grade on simplicity is the property tax. All taxes involve some administrative costs, but the record keeping on each property, the hiring and training of assessors, the periodic reassessments, and the handling of appeals make the property tax an expensive tax to administer. Keep in mind that this process is normally not centralized in a single large office at the state capital but is being carried out in all of the counties in a state.

How fair are the state sales and income taxes? On this criterion, the sales tax is probably the most controversial. Critics argue that the sales tax is regressive because lower-income individuals pay a larger percentage of their income in sales taxes than do middle- and upper-income individuals. However, most states exempt from the sales tax items that people must have, such as food, prescription drugs, and medical services. This means that the sales tax does not take as large a share of money from low-income persons than it otherwise would. These exemptions reduce the regressive nature of the sales tax, making it only moderately regressive.[38] Approximately one-third of the states (Alabama, Connecticut, Georgia, North Carolina, and the District of Columbia) have instituted **sales tax holidays** that provide a temporary sales tax exemption on certain items for a specific period of time. These holidays usually occur during a few days in August, the traditional back-to-school shopping period, and exempt clothing, shoes, and school supplies, sometimes even personal computers. As to the fairness of the state income tax, most observers would agree that it is moderately progressive.[39] Although some states have a flat tax rate, which is also called proportional, most states have at least a few tax rates with at least small differences between the lowest and the highest rates.

Although economists debate the fairness of the property tax,[40] it is clear that the public views it as the "worst tax," that is, the least fair. A 2006 national survey by the Tax Foundation reports that among state and local taxes the local property tax is selected as the "worst tax" by 39 percent of the respondents, followed by the state income tax with 20 percent.[41] Why is the property tax perceived as unfair? One reason is that the value of an individual's home is not always tied to his or her annual income. For example, people may live in areas that are growing rapidly, so their property values are increasing dramatically, along with their property taxes, even though their incomes may be increasing modestly at best. Of course, when people retire, their incomes usually drop, but their property values and taxes may continue to increase. Another reason, not necessarily linked to fairness, is that the property tax is a highly visible tax. Homeowners receive a bill from the city or county once a year and suffer "sticker shock" when they see they owe $2,000 or more, exceeding any single tax payment they make.[42] (Paying is a little easier for those who are buying their home because banks and lending companies usually add to the monthly mortgage payment an amount of money that over twelve months will yield enough to pay their property taxes.)

The Property Tax Revolt

Public dissatisfaction with the property tax was particularly acute in California during the 1970s when real estate values doubled and, for many homeowners, property tax bills skyrocketed, sometimes as much as 20 to 30 percent per year.[43] The ensuing property tax revolt was truly a landmark event that quickly affected taxation policies in almost every state and still affects California's politics today. Howard Jarvis, using California's initiative process, led a campaign that succeeded in placing **Proposition 13,** a tax-reduction measure, on the 1978 ballot. With a $7 billion surplus in the state's treasury, voters did not believe dire warnings of cuts in services if Proposition 13 passed. Labor unions, teachers, public employees, the League of Women Voters, and most elected officials urged a no vote, but Proposition 13 passed with nearly 70 percent support in a high turnout election. It had three main provisions:

- It limited property taxes to 1 percent of assessed value.
- It "rolled back" assessed values of all property to 1975 assessments. Annual updating increases were limited to no more than 2 percent per year. However, any change of ownership triggers reappraisal based on current value, usually the purchase price, which results in an increase in taxes for the new owner.
- It prohibited the state from raising any state taxes to make up for lost revenue unless the new taxes are approved by a two-thirds vote of the legislature.

The passage of Proposition 13 led to a flurry of tax-cutting activity in more than half the states from 1978 to 1980. Eighteen states approved limitations on taxes and expenditures (TELs, as we called them earlier). The most extreme limits were approved in Massachusetts, Minnesota, and Idaho. Massachusetts voters approved a ballot measure referred to as Proposition 2½, which limited taxes to 2.5 percent of assessed value and annual increases in assessment to 2.5 percent.

Initially the impact of Proposition 13 was what its supporters wanted; property tax bills declined significantly, and because of the state's budget surplus most public services remained about the same. When the surplus disappeared in the early 1980s, revenue problems began to emerge and continue to plague the state periodically.[44] As a result, there were cuts in many state programs and communities began to impose user charges for many services. Also, the provision in Proposition 13 that allows property to be reappraised to current market value only when it is sold means that new property owners may pay taxes as much as ten times higher than those of people who have been living in similar houses for years. This system of reappraisal (or reassessment) also benefits big business and large landowners because their holdings are sold less frequently.[45]

Many states, rather than taking the extreme approach of adopting a Proposition 13 equivalent, opted for enacting limited property tax relief laws. Economists Arthur O'Sullivan, Terri Sexton, and Steven Sheffrin define property tax relief as any "measure that reduces property taxes below what they otherwise would be."[46] The principal types are homestead exemptions and circuit breakers; both target specific homeowners. **Homestead exemptions,** used in forty-four states and the District of Columbia, are aimed at people who own their home and also are elderly, disabled, or have low incomes. The exemptions exclude from taxation a certain amount of the assessed value of their home. The exemption amount is subtracted from the assessed value of the property before the amount of tax is calculated. **Circuit breakers,** used in thirty-four states and the District of Columbia, limit the percentage of a homeowner's income that can be taken in property taxes. As with the homestead exemption, this program is designed to prevent senior citizens on fixed retirement incomes and low-income households from having to sell their homes because of higher and higher property taxes. The name circuit breaker is appropriate because when an individual's property tax exceeds a certain point relative to income, this program "breaks" the load of higher taxes.[47]

BORROWING AND DEBT POLICIES

When state and local governments wish to finance major capital spending such as building highways or schools, they usually must borrow money. Borrowing to meet current expenses is discouraged, although it does occur. Long-term borrowing for permanent improvements is standard procedure. Because of unsound financial management in the nineteenth century, state constitutions place narrow limits on borrowing. Limits are placed on the amount of debt that can be incurred, and borrowing decisions frequently are made by the voters in referendums, rather than by legislators.

Older cities in the Northeast tend to have more debt than other cities because of the variety of services they provide and their deteriorating financial base. State debt occurs because capital spending necessitates borrowing. States and cities are rated by private agencies, and if they have low ratings (based on their financial condition), they must pay higher rates of interest. Debt also exists because states form government corporations to finance public works projects, and these corporations can borrow money in excess of state constitutional limits.

To pay for capital improvements, which may involve tens of millions of dollars, governments issue bonds **General-obligation bonds** are backed by the full faith and credit of the issuing government. In approving this kind of bond, the government agrees to increase taxes to pay the interest and ultimately to retire the bond. **Revenue bonds** are supported by the income from a project such as a toll road. In most cases, voter approval is not needed to issue revenue bonds, and the bonds can often be used to extend the total debt of a government beyond constitutional limits. Generally, both types of bonds are attractive investments, especially to wealthy investors, because the interest they pay is exempt from the federal and state income taxes. Because revenue bonds are somewhat more risky than general-obligation bonds, they usually pay a slightly higher rate of interest.

THE OUTLOOK FOR REVENUES

Short-Term Problems

State and local government revenues are affected by the economic cycle of growth and recession. Periods of economic growth cause an increase in revenue, especially for state governments that rely on the sales and income taxes that result in increased revenue collections when more people are working and spending money. The period of the late 1990s through the first few years of the 2000s is a particularly good example of how the health of the economy affects state finances and is worth examining closely. As the twentieth century came to an end, the national economy was strong and state finances were remarkably healthy. The fifty states had a total surplus in

1999 of $33 billion. Governors and legislators were faced with the question of what to do with budget surpluses. They decided on a number of actions:

- Twenty states cut taxes to reduce excess revenues.
- Seventeen states made deposits to their "rainy day" funds. (These are funds that can be used when state revenues are not as plentiful.)
- Thirteen states targeted certain programs for extra funding.
- Thirteen states funded capital construction projects, rather than borrowing money.[48]

But just a couple of years later, economic conditions were not as good and state (and local) government revenues fell with a vengeance. The relationship between the performance of the economy and state tax revenues can be seen in Figure 9-5; changes in revenue per capita rather closely follow changes in economic growth. The recession that started in the spring of 2001 was different from the previous two in that the drop in tax revenues (−7.4 percent) was much greater than the negative change in economic growth (−0.7 percent). Analysts suggest that this "super-sized" drop in revenues was caused primarily by a decline in income tax collections that occurred when investors could no longer realize capital gains from selling stocks; dramatic stock market price increases not only stopped but they dropped precipitously.[49] (Capital gains—money earned from selling stocks at a higher price than an investor originally bought them for—are reported as income on state tax returns.)

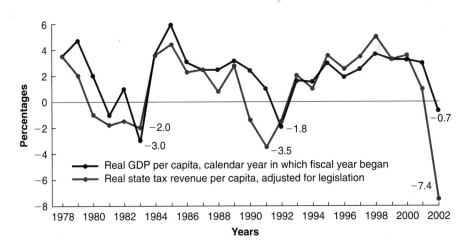

FIGURE 9-5 Comparison of decline in state revenues during three economic recessions: 1980–82, 1990–91 and 2001–02.

Source: Donald J. Boyd and Nicholas W. Jenny, "State Fiscal Crisis Far Worse Than Economy Would Suggest," The Rockefeller Institute State Fiscal News (May 2003), p. 1, fiscal@rockinst.org (accessed May 13, 2003). Reprinted with permission from The Nelson A. Rockefeller Institute of Government.

Note: "Adjusted for legislation" means that any legislative changes in tax policy that affected revenue collections have been controlled for. "Fiscal year" refers to a financial accounting period of one year, which does not necessarily begin on January 1. State government fiscal years usually begin on July 1 and end on June 30.

State political leaders were facing the worst budget deficits in over fifty years. The $33 billion surplus of 1999 had turned into a $37 billion deficit in 2002, with similar deficits predicted for at least the next couple of years. As was mentioned in Chapter 6, however, unlike the federal government, state governments cannot run a deficit in their operating budgets. In all states but Vermont, constitutional or statutory language requires balanced budgets.

How did state governors and legislators react to this latest economic downturn and unbalanced budgets? Did they reduce spending? Or did they raise taxes? States did both, depending on individual state circumstances. Some specific ideas are offered by Nicholas W. Jenny and Richard P. Nathan, policy analysts at the Rockefeller Institute of Government; the ideas are arranged, more or less, from the "least painful" to the "most painful":[50]

- Use reserve funds such as "rainy day" funds and refinance debt that would lower interest payments. (Remember, states usually have a capital budget from which they borrow money [incur debt] to buy land, construct buildings, and purchase major equipment.)
- Defer spending and accelerate revenue collections.
- Implement hiring freezes.
- Raise "sin taxes" and close tax loopholes.
- Implement across-the-board or targeted spending cuts.
- Freeze planned tax cuts and spending increases.
- Increase major taxes and adopt substantial spending cuts.

Twenty-nine states implemented across-the-board or targeted budget cuts; higher education budgets were one of the favorite targets. Political leaders know that colleges and universities can increase tuition and fees to make up some of the reduction. Although specific amounts vary, usually no agency is spared, including corrections, Medicaid, and state aid to primary and secondary education. Many of the steps taken to balance state budgets had a negative effect on local governments because the amount of their state financial aid may be cut. Fifteen states took the "most painful" step and enacted significant tax increases, increasing tax revenues by at least 1 percent of general fund expenditures. Four states increased their sales tax rate; in Indiana the increase was from 5 to 6 percent. The most popular tax increase was on cigarettes; Pennsylvania more than tripled its tax per pack, from 31 cents to $1.00, bringing in an extra $570 million in 2003.[51]

Some states used the pressure of budget problems to look for ways to do things more efficiently. Virginia Governor Mark Warner (2001–05), an ex-telecommunications executive, developed plans to merge all information technology workers into a single agency by eliminating three existing agencies and consolidating others. The new agency would buy and maintain the state's "high-tech infrastructure" and in the process save the state $100 million a year.[52]

It is important to note that governors also resorted to what are called "gimmicks," that is, policies that provided a "one-shot injection of revenue or one-time savings on expenditures."[53] Examples include delaying state aid payments to local governments and school districts and delaying state payments to pension funds. Not all of these gimmicks are harmful, but some are. Delaying payments to pension funds means that payments will have to be made later; the payment is simply shifted to future taxpayers.

To be sure, economic cycles will always be with us, and recessions will cause revenue shortfalls. "Rainy day" funds can help to provide some extra money during a recession, but political leaders will be confronted with difficult decisions of cutting spending and increasing taxes to maintain balanced budgets. Fortunately, economic downturns do not last forever, and by 2005 state tax revenue grew by 10.7 percent—the strongest growth in almost fifteen years.[54]

Long-Term Problems

Some specialists on state taxes see a long-term problem with state tax systems; they refer to it as a structural deficit. A **structural deficit** exists when money produced by the tax system is insufficient "to maintain existing level of services."[55] Changes in the American economy have affected, in particular, that mainstay of state taxes, the sales tax. Two examples will help to explain this.

It has been widely reported that the strength of the American economy is less in the manufacturing of tangible goods and more in the production of services. The service sector is the fastest growing sector of the American economy. However, the general sales tax, as has been noted, primarily taxes the purchase of tangible goods, not services. During the past sixty years, services have grown from 41 percent of household consumption to 58 percent. The Federation of Tax Administrators estimates that there are 168 services that could be taxed. Services provided by accountants, attorneys, doctors, and engineers are the most frequently mentioned examples, but others include barber/beautician, health club, janitorial, lawn care and landscaping, and pool cleaning services. Dial-up Internet access, broadband Internet access, direct satellite TV, and architectural services were recently added to the list of services that could possibly be taxed. Only two states—Hawaii and New Mexico—tax roughly the entire list of services; most states tax only a few.[56] It's difficult for states to expand the taxing of services because this is always viewed as a tax increase, and some of the affected groups such as doctors and lawyers are influential interest groups. A comprehensive approach that broadened the sales tax base to include all services and at the same time lowered the tax rate might be successful. The Center on Budget and Policy Priorities recommends that states adopt a comprehensive range of services, excluding only those items that would be extremely unpopular with the public to tax such as education, health care, insurance, and funeral services. Estimates are that a majority of states would increase their annual sales tax revenues by 25 to 30 percent, among all fifty states the total would be approximately $57 billion per year.[57]

Another example deals with changes in the way people shop and buy things. Retail sales through mail-order catalogs, the Home Shopping Network, and the rapid growth of sales over the Internet (e-commerce) have a negative effect on tax collections. Of course, there is little doubt that e-commerce business in the near future will be larger than anything previously achieved by "remote sellers." Whether state "A" can require remote sellers in state "B" to collect sales taxes on items sold to citizens in state "A" is a complex constitutional and administrative problem. The U.S. Supreme Court in *Quill Corp. v. North Dakota*[58] decided that remote sellers were not obligated to collect and remit taxes on sales made to citizens in other states. There was an exception: If a remote seller has a physical presence or nexus (for example, another store or even a warehouse) in the same state as a consumer purchasing an item from the remote seller, then the remote seller is required to collect and remit those taxes. And consumers in states where the remote seller does not have a nexus are to calculate and remit at the end of the year taxes owed to their home states on items that were purchased from remote sellers. (How many times have you done this?) Of course, most citizens are unaware of this requirement, and states have no real way to enforce it.

This is a continuing issue for the National Conference of State Legislatures (NCSL) and the National Governors Association (NGA), in particular, because large amounts of tax revenue are being lost. Estimated revenue loss in 2008 for untaxed e-commerce was $17.8 billion and $15.9 billion for catalog and television sales, for a total of more than $33 billion.[59] As a practical matter, at the present time it would be difficult for remote sellers to collect sales taxes from all consumers because approximately 7,500 taxing jurisdictions (state and local governments) often define and tax the same products differently. For example, a marshmallow may be a food in one state and not taxed, but candy in another state and taxed. It's almost impossible for businesses selling to customers nationwide to keep track of what's what in the various taxing jurisdictions. But with the considerable loss in revenue and the concern that local retail stores were being treated unfairly (their customers cannot evade the sales tax), state political leaders active in NCSL and NGA cooperated in a major project to bring uniformity to the forty-five different sales and use tax systems.[60] The result was the **Streamlined Sales and Use Tax Agreement (SSUTA),** which simplifies and modernizes sales tax collection and administration and provides a way that online and other remote sellers can collect sales taxes on customers who do not live in their state. By the start of 2007, twenty-one states have adopted uniform tax laws and are official members of this agreement; however, they can only encourage, not require, online and other out-of-state retailers to collect these taxes. An Amazon.com executive stated that his company had no intention of collecting taxes for SSUTA; he argued that the system still was not simple and still was not fair.[61] Whether or not SSUTA will achieve its objective is an open question. Only the federal government, the Congress, or the Supreme Court, because they have power over commerce between the states, could require remote sellers to collect and remit taxes on out-of-state buyers.

The implications of this discussion of long-term financial problems are summarized nicely by David Brunori: "Perhaps the problem is not so much with raising taxes as with reforming a system that, in the modern economy, is not designed to bring in enough revenue."[62]

The Revenue Dilemma of Cities

Local governments are not immune to revenue problems, and this is especially true in large, central cities (population of 500,000 or more) that are surrounded by suburbs. No one can help but notice the differences between life in the cities and life in the suburbs, and most people with at least moderate financial resources conclude that they would rather live in the suburbs than the central cities. The percentage of the U.S. population living in these cities declined from 15.5 percent to 12.7 percent between 1970 and 2000. More important than this decline is the fact that residents of large cities who have not moved to the suburbs tend to be poor; from 1970 to 1997, nearly 6 million middle- and high-income families left the cities. During most of the 1990s, median household income

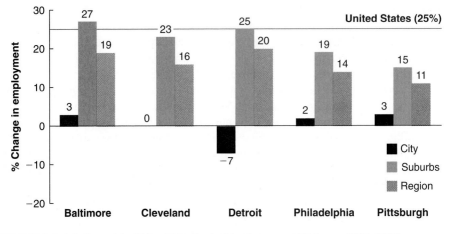

FIGURE 9-6 Job Growth in Older Cities in the Northeast and Midwest, 1991–2001.

Source: PolicyLink, *A Data Profile of Older Core Cities*, www.policylink.org/Research/OlderCoreCities/DataProfile.pdf (accessed March 28, 2007). Reprinted wih permission of Radhika K. Fox, Associate Director, PolicyLink.

in central cities was approximately one-third less than suburban incomes. These differences tend to be the greatest in older cities of the Northeast and Midwest. For example, the 1999 median household income in Philadelphia was only 65 percent of the median income for the surrounding region, $30,700 versus $47,500; and Cleveland was only 60 percent of its surrounding region ($25,900 versus $42,000). Job growth is slower in central cities than in the surrounding suburbs and region, also. During a ten-year period, national employment grew by 25 percent but barely budged in the cities identified in Figure 9-6; job growth was much higher in the suburbs of these cities, and in two of them it was at or above the national average.[63] Central cities also have more problems, such as higher crime rates and a declining infrastructure that require higher expenditures by their governments. The resulting higher taxes are another reason for businesses and residents to move to the suburbs, where taxes are usually lower, which further reduces the cities' tax base and increases the likelihood that taxes will be raised.

If taxes are not raised, then the quality of services declines. Because of a wider array of problems, cities have less money to spend on elementary and secondary schools; education expenditures consume "about half of most suburban budgets, but rarely more than a third of most central cities."[64] Many are caught in a downward spiral that can be reversed only by increased financial assistance from the federal and state governments or arrangements that would allow central cities to share in their suburbs' tax base.[65] (See Chapter 8 for a more complete discussion of cities and suburbs.)

Solving long-term financial problems of state and local governments in the twenty-first century will not be easy. The "reinventing government" approach (see Chapter 6) may yield more efficient delivery of services, but it will not solve structural deficit problems and lack of revenue in many cities. Extraordinary political leadership will be required to modernize tax systems to do away with structural deficits and find revenue for cities that have a shrinking tax base.

SUMMARY

State and local governments spend a great deal of money ($1.9 trillion in 2004), and their share of total government spending has increased in the last few decades. Almost one-third of these expenditures is used to finance the public school system (elementary and secondary education, as well as higher education). Other significant expenditure items are public welfare, health and hospitals, and highways.

Intergovernmental funds are an important source of revenue for both state and local governments. In terms of their own taxes, the sales tax is the most important source of revenue for state governments, and the property tax is the most important source for local governments. Both of these taxes have been declining in their percentage contribution to state and local treasuries over the past few decades, and user charges have been growing in importance. In their search for new revenues, more states are operating lotteries. Casino gambling, which is regulated by states or Indian tribal governments, has spread rapidly. Potential social costs of legalized casinos are frequently pushed aside in the search for new tax revenues and the promise of economic development and jobs.

The public gives low ratings to the property tax because many property owners doubt its fairness, one of the criteria used to evaluate different kinds of taxes. Public dissatisfaction has manifested itself in a number of ways, from California's Proposition 13 to the adoption in most states of property tax relief laws, which reduce property taxes through homestead exemptions and circuit breakers.

Short-term changes in state and local tax revenues are influenced by the state of the economy; a weak economy or one in recession reduces tax revenues, and strong economic growth increases revenues. In either period, political leaders are faced with decisions concerning the level of government services that should be provided and how much their citizens should pay in taxes. State governments and many local governments are experiencing structural deficits whereby existing tax systems will not generate sufficient revenue to maintain services that citizens expect. Major challenges in the next few years will be to change state tax systems so that they reflect the move from a manufacturing to a service economy and to find a way to fund services in large cities that have an inadequate tax base.

KEY TERMS

direct general expenditures (p. 330)
intergovernmental expenditures (p. 330)
TELs (p. 331)
property tax (p. 335)
general sales tax (p. 335)
income tax (p. 336)
excise tax (p. 337)
severance tax (p. 337)
user charge (p. 337)
gross gaming revenue (p. 338)
California v. Cabazon Band of Mission Indians (p. 340)
Indian Gaming Regulatory Act (IGRA) (p. 340)

sufficiency (p. 342)
stability (p. 342)
simplicity (p. 342)
fairness (p. 342)
vertical equity (p. 342)
sales tax holidays (p. 343)
Proposition 13 (p. 344)
homestead exemptions (p. 344)
circuit breakers (p. 344)
general-obligation bonds (p. 345)
revenue bonds (p. 345)
structural deficit (p. 348)
Streamlined Sales and Use Tax Agreement (SSUTA) (p. 349)

BRIEF COMPARISONS OF STATE/LOCAL DIFFERENCES

Issue	State Level	Local Level
Principal expenditures	Higher education, public welfare, and corrections	Elementary and secondary schools and police protection
Principal own source revenue	Sales tax	Property tax
Long-term revenue problems	Structural deficits	Inadequate tax base in large cities

INTERESTING WEB SITES

www.rockinst.org. This is the Web site of the Nelson A. Rockefeller Institute of Government in Albany, New York. Click on "State and Local Finance" for analysis of revenues and expenditures. This is a great Web site for information on a variety of state and local issues; for example, explore "Higher Education" and "Welfare and Jobs."

www.census.gov. This site provides detailed information on revenues and expenditures from the U.S. Census Bureau. Click on "Government" and you will find a list of reports for state and local governments generally, for specific states, and even public school systems. (These reports are not up to the minute; for example, 2006 data should be available in 2008.)

www.taxadmin.org. Web site of the Federation of Tax Administrators. Click on "State Comparisons" for the details of each state's tax system such as tax rates, tax collections, amnesty programs, sales tax holidays, and more.

NOTES

1. Pamela M. Prah, "Anti-tax Ballot Box Revolt Stifled," www.stateline.org/live/printable/story?contentId=149788 (accessed March 19, 2007). Ballot Initiative Strategy Center, "Trendlines 2006," www.ballot.org/index.asp (accessed October 8, 2006).
2. National Conference of State Legislatures, "Talking Points on TABOR," www.ncsl.org/programs/fiscal/taborpts.htm (accessed March 19, 2007). An excellent source for information on TABOR and Referendum C is The Bell Policy Center at www.thebell.org.
3. State and local expenditures for FY 2003–04 are from "Table 1. State and Local Government Finances by Level of Government and by State: 2003–04," www.census.gov/govs/estmate/0400ussl_1.html (accessed March 13, 2007). Federal expenditures are from U.S. Bureau of the Census, *Statistical Abstract of the United States, 2007,* "Table 460. Federal Budget Outlays by Type: 1990 to 2006" and "Table 421. Federal Grants-in-Aid to State and Local Governments: 1990 to 2006," www.census.gov/compendia/statab (accessed March 19, 2007). Per capita calculations are based on an estimated U.S. population in 2004 of 294 million.
4. National Conference of State Legislatures, "State Tax and Expenditure Limits," www.ncsl.org/programs/fiscal/telsabout.htm (accessed March 19, 2007); also see Michael J. New,

"Limiting Government through Direct Democracy: The Case of State Tax and Expenditure Limitations," *Policy Analysis* (Washington, D.C.: Cato Institute, 2001), pp. 5–6.

5. John R. Bartle, "Trends in Local Government Taxation in the 21st Century," *Spectrum: The Journal of State Government* (Winter 2003), p. 26.

6. Henry J. Raimondo, *Economics of State and Local Government* (New York: Praeger Publishers, 1992), p. 138.

7. David Brunori, *Local Tax Policy: A Federalist Perspective* (Washington, D.C.: Urban Institute Press, 2003), pp. 63–64.

8. *Local Revenue Diversification: Local Sales Taxes* (Washington, D.C.: Advisory Commission on Intergovernmental Relations, 1989), 3; J. Richard Aronson and John L. Hilley, *Financing State and Local Governments* (Washington, D.C.: Brookings Institution, 1986), p. 94.

9. Raimondo, *Economics,* pp. 168–171.

10. Bartle, "Trends in Local Government Taxation," p. 27.

11. Ronald John Hy and William L. Waugh, Jr., *State and Local Tax Policies: A Comparative Handbook* (Westport, Conn.: Greenwood Press, 1995), p. 36.

12. Income tax rates, sales tax rates, and other tax rates discussed in this section can be found at "State Comparisons" on the Federation of Tax Administrators Web site, www.taxadmin.org (accessed March 20, 2007).

13. Wesley Brown, "Corporate Income Dwindles as Companies Shift Tax Burden," May 2, 2003, www.nwaonline.net (accessed May 5, 2003).

14. David Brunori, *State Tax Policy: A Political Perspective* (Washington, D.C.: Urban Institute Press, 2001), pp.109–113.

15. Richard Wolf, "States Consider Tobacco Tax Hikes," *USA Today* (February 27, 2007), www.usatoday.com/news/nation/2007-02-26-tabacco-tax_x.htm (accessed March 20, 2007).

16. Aronson and Hilley, *Financing,* p. 43.

17. Raimondo, *Economics,* p. 206.

18. Aronson and Hilley, *Financing,* p. 157.

19. *National Gambling Impact Study Commission, Final Report,* 1-1, 1999, www.ngisc.gov.

20. American Gaming Association, "Fact Sheets: Gaming Revenue: 10-year Trends," www.americangaming.org/Industry/factsheets/statistics (accessed March 21, 2007).

21. John L. Mikesell and C. Kurt Zorn, "State Lotteries as Fiscal Savior or Fiscal Fraud," *Public Administration Review* (July/August 1986), p. 311.

22. Frederick D. Stocker, "State-Sponsored Gambling as a Source of Public Revenue," *National Tax Journal* 25 (September 1972), p. 437; Raimondo, *Economics,* p. 212.

23. *Statistical Abstract of the United States, 2007,* "Table 438. Gross Revenue from Parimutuel and Amusement Taxes and Lotteries by State: 2002 to 2004," www.census.gov/compendia/statab/2007edition.html (accessed March 22, 2007).

24. Mary Edwards, *State and Local Revenues Beyond the Property Tax* (Cambridge, Mass.: Lincoln Institute of Land Policy, 2006), p. 35, www.lincolninst.edu/subcenters/TFDP/materials/edwards-revenue.pdf.

25. Thomas P. Lauth and Mark D. Robbins, "The Georgia Lottery and State Appropriations for Education: Substitution or Additional Funding?" *Public Budgeting & Finance* (Fall 2002), pp. 89–100.

26. Office of Tribal Justice, U.S. Department of Justice, *Department of Justice Policy on Indian Sovereignty,* www.usdoj.gov/otj/sovtrbtxt.htm, p. 2 (accessed May 10, 2003).

27. *California v. Cabazon Band of Mission Indians,* 480 U.S. 202 (1987).

28. Roger Dunstan, *Gambling in California,* "Indian Gaming," pp.1–11, California Research Bureau, CRB-97-003, January 1997, www.library.ca.gov/CRB/97/03/Chapt4.html (accessed May 10, 2003).

29. See "Industry Information: State Information: Statistics: Nevada," www.americangaming.org/Industry/state/statistics.cfm?stateid=9 (accessed March 22, 2007).

30. *Gambling Impact,* pp. 7–19.
31. Clyde Haberman, "The Inverse of A.T.M. Is V.L.T.," *New York Times* (May 13, 2003); Alex Berenson, "The States Bet Bigger on Betting," *New York Times* (May 18, 2003), www.nytimes .com (accessed May 18, 2003).
32. Ian Pulsipher, "Counting on Gambling," *State Legislatures* (February 2005), pp. 24–25.
33. John Lyman Mason and Michael Nelson, *Governing Gambling* (New York: Century Foundation Press, 2001), pp. 24–28, 52–55.
34. Pulsipher, "Counting on Gambling," pp. 25–26.
35. Brunori, *State Tax Policy,* pp. 13–27.
36. Ibid., p. 19.
37. An excellent analysis of the tax systems in each of the fifty states can be found in "The Way We Tax," *Governing* (February 2003), pp. 20–97.
38. Raimondo, *Economics,* p. 180.
39. Ibid., pp. 200–201.
40. See Raimondo, *Economics,* pp. 152–156, for a discussion of two different views of the fairness of the property tax.
41. Tax Foundation, "2006 Annual Survey of U.S. Attitudes on Tax and Wealth," www .taxfoundation/files/survey_topline-20060405.pdf (accessed March 23, 2007).
42. Brunori, *Local Tax Policy,* p. 58.
43. Arthur O'Sullivan, Terri A. Sexton, and Steven M. Sheffrin, *Property Taxes and Tax Revolts: The Legacy of Proposition 13* (New York: Cambridge University Press, 1995), p. 2.
44. Michael A. Shires, *Patterns in California Government Revenues Since Proposition 13* (San Francisco: Public Policy Institute of California, 1999), www.ppic.org/content/pubs/report/ R_399MSR.pdf (accessed March 23, 2007).
45. Terry Christensen and Tom Hogen-Esch, *Local Politics: A Practical Guide to Governing at the Grassroots* (Armonk, N.Y.: M. E. Sharpe, 2006), p. 290.
46. Sullivan, Sexton, and Sheffrin, *Property Taxes,* p. 26.
47. Ibid., pp. 26–27.
48. National Conference of State Legislatures, *State Budget & Tax Actions, 1999: Preliminary Report,* www.ncsl.org./programs/fiscal/presbta99.htm.
49. Donald J. Boyd and Nicholas W. Jenny, "State Fiscal Crisis Far Worse Than Economy Would Suggest: Huge Drop in Capital Gains, Other Investment Income Likely to Blame," *The Rockefeller Institute State Fiscal News* (May 2003), pp. 1–4, www.rockinst.org.
50. Nicholas W. Jenny and Richard P. Nathan, "Sizing Up the Shortfalls: The States in Straits," *Government Finance Review* (April 2003), p. 13, www.rockinst.org (accessed May 14, 2003).
51. Nicholas W. Jenny, "2002 Tax and Budget Review and 2003 Budget Preview," *State Fiscal Brief* (March 2003), pp. 2–3, www.rockinst.org.
52. Jason White, "Budget Crisis Spurs Innovation, Reform," *Stateline.org,* www.stateline.org (accessed March 28, 2003).
53. Steven D. Gold, "A Framework for Viewing State Policies," in *The Fiscal Crisis of the States,* Steven D. Gold, ed. (Washington, D.C.: Georgetown University Press, 1995), p. 47.
54. Nicholas W. Jenny, "Solid Footing for State Finances: Fiscal Year 2005 Tax Revenue Summary," *State Fiscal Brief* (March 2006), p. 1, http://rfs.rockinst.org/exhibit/9047/Full%20Text/ SFB75.pdf (accessed March 24, 2007).
55. Gold, "Framework," p. 43.
56. Ray Scheppach, "Silver Lining in State Fiscal Crisis?" *Stateline.org,* www.stateline.org (accessed May 4, 2003).
57. Michael Mazerov, *Expanding Sales Taxation of Services: Options and Issues* (Washington, D.C.: Center on Budget & Policy Priorities, 2003), pp. 3–4, www.cbpp.org/3-24-2003sfp.htm (accessed March 31, 2007).

58. *Quill Corp. v. North Dakota,* 504 U.S. 298 (1992).
59. "Streamlined Sales Tax Agreement Goes Into Effect," *State Legislatures* (December 2005), p. 5.
60. A use tax is similar to a sales tax and the two terms are frequently mentioned together; it is a tax on items that are used in one state but were purchased in another state. As mentioned in the text, this tax usually is not paid by consumers; however, there are exceptions. For example, let's say that you buy a car in a state that borders your home state because the neighboring state does not have a sales tax. When you bring your car home and register it, you will have to pay a use tax on the car because it will be used in your home state.
61. Robert Tanner, "States Expand Push for Sales Taxes on Internet Purchases," *USA Today* (October 31, 2005), www.usatoday.com/tech/news/techpolicy/2005-08-31-internet-taxes_x.htm.
62. David Brunori, "Sticking to Principles," *Governing* (February 2003), http://governing.com/gpp/2003/gp3brun.htm (accessed on March 27, 2007).
63. Radhika K. Fox, Sarah Treuhaft, and Regan Douglass, *Shared Prosperity, Stronger Regions: An Agenda for Rebuilding America's Older Core Cities* (Oakland, Calif.: PolicyLink, 2005), www.policylink.org/Research/OlderCoreCities/DataProfile.pdf.
64. Peter D. Salins, "Metropolitan Areas: Cities, Suburbs, and the Ties That Bind," in *Interwoven Destinies: Cities and the Nation,* Henry G. Cisneros, ed. (New York: W. W. Norton & Company, 1993), p. 158.
65. Carol O'Cleireagain, "Cities' Role in the Metropolitan Economy and the Federal Structure," in *Interwoven Destinies: Cities and the Nation,* Henry G. Cisneros, ed., pp. 176–183.

STATE AND LOCAL POLICY MAKING

Conflict and Accommodation

THE POLITICS OF WIND

Wind generating electricity, an alternative source of energy. What could be better? Renewable energy. No carbon dioxide emissions that cause global warming. Reduced dependence on oil from the Middle East. What an easy decision! Who could possibly oppose wind power?

A project proposed in 2001 by a private development company, Cape Wind Associates, to build the first offshore wind farm in the United States in the waters off Cape Cod, Massachusetts, has generated considerable controversy, to say the least. And a final decision is unlikely for the next couple of years. The Cape Wind project would consist of 130 wind turbines in a 25-square-mile area, five miles offshore in Nantucket Sound. The wind turbines, over 400 feet high, would be placed 600 to 900 yards apart. Electricity generated would provide close to 80 percent of Cape Cod's electricity needs.[1] Cape Wind would appear to be a state and local decision, but the location of the wind farm places it in water under federal jurisdiction, requiring federal approval as well. Before construction can proceed, permission is required from close to twenty local, state, and federal agencies, and may even face more challenges in state or federal courts.

The three levels of decision making provide opponents numerous opportunities to defeat Cape Wind. And there are opponents. The supporters of Cape Wind describe their opponents as wealthy and powerful families who own mansions along the coast of Nantucket Sound and don't want their views and sailing spoiled by 130 wind turbines. The outspoken opposition of Massachusetts Senator Edward Kennedy and his nephew Robert F. Kennedy, Jr., is frequently cited as an example of wealthy opponents. Hyannis Port, home of the historic Kennedy Compound, would be within approximately eight miles of the wind farm.[2] But on closer look, opposition was broader based than this and included many Cape Cod residents. Members of a local interest group, the Alliance to Protect Nantucket Sound, predict that the wind farm will have a negative effect on the area's major industries, which are tourism and fishing; they also believe the farm's location near a major shipping lane creates a navigational hazard and that the 100-foot blades of the turbines pose a risk to migratory birds. Nationally, well-known environmental groups are divided on this project; for example, Greenpeace USA and World Wildlife Fund support it, and the Massachusetts Audubon Society and Natural Resources Defense Council oppose it.

As of this writing, Cape Wind has been approved by the state of Massachusetts. The Supreme Judicial Court upheld a decision by the state's Energy Facilities Siting Board, permitting construction of transmission lines to bring electricity to shore. The board's decision was appealed in the courts by the Alliance to Protect Nantucket Sound. Also, the state's Environmental Affairs secretary approved the wind-farm developer's environmental impact statement, stating that it complies with environmental laws and that the project's environmental benefits will offset its negative impact. At the federal level, Congress authorized the Interior Department's Minerals Management Service (MMS) to be the lead agency in reviewing proposed offshore wind farms. It will complete review of Cape Wind sometime in 2008. (The MMS also supervises offshore oil drilling.) Finally, the U.S. Coast Guard has authority to mandate changes in the wind farm, if it concludes that the farm poses navigational hazards.[3]

POINTS TO CONSIDER

- Compare federal, state, and local roles in public schools.
- What are the three general categories of social welfare programs?
- What are the basic features of the Personal Responsibility and Work Opportunity Reconciliation Act? What is its impact?
- Describe incentives that state and local governments use to attract businesses.
- How do state and local governments contribute to homeland security?
- What is the negative side of incentives?
- How are state governments important in global warming policies?
- What is civic environmentalism?

State and local government is the subject of this book; however, as the case study illustrates, the complex policy making process in the United States normally involves all three levels of government: federal, state, and local. Generally, the process is one of continual conflict and accommodation between various groups and levels of government, resulting in incremental change in policies. Radical change in policies is unusual. The media tend to focus on the activities of the federal government, but that doesn't mean that it is always the dominant actor in policy making. Five policy areas will be examined in this chapter: homeland security, education, welfare, economic development, and environmental protection. At first glance, homeland security would seem to be a federal responsibility with little for state and local governments to do, but nothing could be further from the truth. Education policy is an area in which local governments have been preeminent until just recently; now both the federal and state governments are playing more important roles. Welfare policy is one of the most complicated in terms of sharing power; however, with changes in federal welfare laws the influence of the states has grown in the past few years. Economic development policy is controlled by state and local governments, without any federal interference. Finally, the federal government has the strongest voice in environmental protection, but the influence of state governments, especially in global warming, is generally greater than most citizens realize.

HOMELAND SECURITY

Discussion of the concept of homeland security in the United States began in the late 1990s; however, it did not receive much attention by the public, even among those citizens who follow politics closely. The U.S. Commission on National Security/21st Century (chaired by two former U.S. senators, Gary Hart and Warren Rudman, and usually referred to as the Hart-Rudman Commission) warned in 1999 that "America will become increasingly vulnerable to hostile attack on our homeland, and our military superiority will not entirely protect us. . . . Americans will likely die on American soil, possibly in large numbers."[4] Of course, the 9/11 terrorist attacks on the World Trade Center in New York City and the Pentagon in Washington, D.C., immediately pushed homeland security to the top of the political agenda. A **Department of Homeland Security (DHS),** created by Congress in 2002, merged twenty-two federal agencies into one cabinet-level department "to provide the unifying core for the vast national network of organizations and institutions involved in efforts to secure our nation."[5] The Federal Emergency Management Agency (FEMA) and the Transportation Security Administration (TSA) are two of the better known agencies that are now part of DHS. DHS has a broad mission; a few of its more important tasks are listed below.

- Prevention—Detect, deter, and mitigate threats to the U.S. homeland.
- Protection—Safeguard the American people and their freedoms, critical infrastructure, property, and the nation's economy from acts of terrorism, natural disasters, or other emergencies.
- Response—Lead, manage, and coordinate the national response to acts of terrorism, natural disasters, or other emergencies.
- Recovery—Lead national, state, local, and private-sector efforts to restore services and rebuild communities after acts of terrorism, natural disasters, or other emergencies.[6]

But what is the exact role of state and local governments? Political scientists Susan Clarke and Erica Chenoweth believe state and local governments are as important as the federal government:

> Regardless of the national character of homeland security policy, the reality is that all terrorism is local. Ultimately so are all security initiatives. Paradoxically, the greater the national security threats, the more important the local role in the United States.[7]

Of course, identifying appropriate federal, state, and local roles is nothing new, nor is it easy, for American federalism. (See Chapter 2.) Immediately after 9/11, the national role was seen as preventing attacks, and state and local governments were viewed as being responsible for "consequence mitigation," that is, the first responders, with responsibility to deal with the damage and chaos of an actual attack and to lessen the loss in lives and property. This provides a fairly clear separation of responsibilities, but some experts, such as Michael O'Hanlon, argue that state and local governments should be more active in prevention. He believes that local police, especially in the nation's largest cities, which are the most likely targets of terrorist attacks, need stronger intelligence (gathering and analyzing information) and counterterrorism operations.[8] However, only one city, New York, has a counterterrorism unit in its police department. Created shortly after 9/11, it runs extensive intelligence operations within the city and even has intelligence officers stationed overseas. When terrorists attacked a train in Madrid, Spain, in 2004, the New York Police Department was the first foreign law-enforcement agency on the scene.[9] According to a National Governor's Association survey, state homeland security directors are not satisfied with the quality of intelligence on possible domestic terrorist activities that they receive from the federal government; they favor the development of state intelligence "fusion centers" where local, state, and federal officials would work closely.[10] Political scientist Kiki Caruson and her associates contend that homeland security requires a new focus on regionalism, that is, structures between the single state capital and the hundreds of local governments within a state. (The concept of regionalism is discussed in Chapter 8.) In a study of Florida, which has seven domestic security task force regions, they found "the regional approach offers a way to harness resources spread across jurisdictions."[11]

Almost exactly four years after 9/11, Hurricane Katrina made landfall in the Gulf Coast states of Louisiana, Mississippi, and Alabama. It was the most severe natural

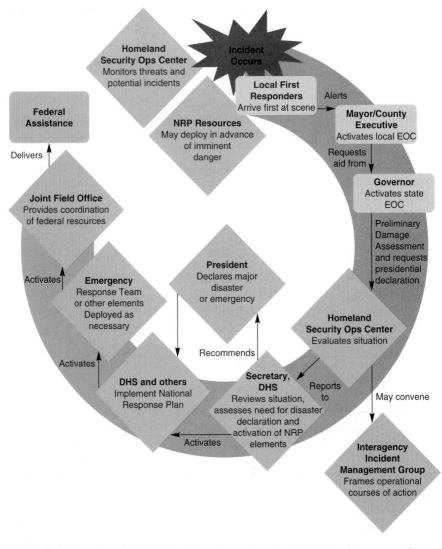

FIGURE 10-1 Overview of initial federal involvement under the National Response Plan.

Source: U.S. Department of Homeland Security, *National Response Plan* (December 2004), p. 93, www.dhs.gov/xprepresp/committees/ editorial_0566.shtm.

disaster to hit the United States in at least a century. It was far larger than earlier weather-related events such as Hurricane Andrew in 1992 and Missouri River floods in 1993. Significant effects from Katrina covered an area of 100,000 square miles, approximately the size of Britain, resulting in the deaths of more than 1,800 people and $80 billion in property damage. Conditions in New Orleans were particularly catastrophic when water from a storm surge, along with high winds and rain, overtopped and breached levees, causing flooding in large parts of the city. An incomplete evacuation in advance of the storm left thousands of people stranded in apartments and houses with the elderly and ill trapped in hospitals and nursing homes. Almost everyone was criticized for an inadequate response to this crisis—local officials and state officials—and at the national level FEMA was singled out for the strongest disapproval. Public management researchers Herman Leonard and Arnold Howitt agree that failures of individuals and agencies were apparent at all levels, but they conclude that the dismal response to Katrina was "a story of failures of systems and of failures to construct systems in advance that would have permitted and helped to produce better performance and outcomes."[12]

Federalism, by separating levels of government, becomes one of the principal challenges to meet in designing a unified system that can meet Katrina-sized disasters. Characteristics not usually associated with federalism—direction, cooperation, coordination, and integration—are crucial to responding effectively to disasters we have encountered in the first decade of the twenty-first century. More coordinated planning has resulted in the adoption of a National Response Plan. (This plan was approved eight months before Katrina.) The **National Response Plan (NRP)** "establishes a single, comprehensive approach to domestic incident management to prevent, prepare for, respond to, and recover from terrorist attacks, major disasters, and other emergencies."[13] (See Figure 10-1.) Leonard and Howitt suggest that an important factor that will determine the effectiveness of the NRP in a real crisis will be whether or not first responders and managers have participated in enhanced training and exercise opportunities so that they can practice and execute these plans.[14] This includes federal, state, and local governments.

EDUCATION

The U.S. Constitution makes no direct reference to schools and education, but state constitutions almost always specify that education is the responsibility of state government. The constitution of Maryland, for example, declares that the legislature shall "establish throughout the State a thorough and efficient system of Free Public Schools, and shall provide by taxation, or otherwise for their maintenance." All states have statutes detailing the organizational structure of public education, and they delegate considerable control over elementary and secondary education to local school districts.[15] Since the 1980s, however, state government has been increasing its influence on elementary and secondary school policies. State government's importance in providing higher education has grown so much since World War II that today's state universities and colleges rival the prestige of once-dominant private institutions.

Education is a gigantic enterprise. In the fall of 2005, 72.1 million persons were enrolled in elementary and secondary schools and colleges in the United States. About 4.4 million teachers were employed, and administrative and support staff totaled 5.0 million.[16] Before looking at recent education reform issues, a brief description of the traditional roles of the three levels of government is needed.

Local Government's Traditional Role

Boards of education in local school districts make many decisions concerning the operations of public schools. Ninety percent of the more than 15,000 school districts in the United States are classified as **independent school districts,** meaning they are administratively and financially independent of other units of local government. The school board can levy taxes, usually with voter approval, spend money, and hire a superintendent and teachers. In addition, the board oversees the actual operation of schools within its district, but "independent" does not mean that it can do anything it wants. Its policies must be consistent with state and federal laws.

School board members in independent school districts are elected directly by the voters, usually on nonpartisan ballots, in elections held at different times from the more publicized elections for state offices. As a result, school board elections usually have low voter turnout and can be dominated by single-issue groups whose educational concerns may be limited to school policies on sex education or AIDS.[17]

Dependent school districts lack sufficient autonomy in budgetary matters to be considered as a separate government. The school board, even if the voters elect its members, reports to another unit of local government such as a mayor or county council. This board has no taxing authority; therefore, the governmental unit it reports to must approve its budget. The board may or may not have authority to appoint the superintendent, and even if the board does, it may be influenced by the mayor or other political leaders.

In one of the few comprehensive studies of school districts, Michael Berkman and Eric Plutzer point out that the creation of school districts independent of municipal governments with a governing board elected by the voters was one of several Progressive movement reforms to challenge the extensive corruption of political machines that was present in turn-of-the-century cities.[18] (See Chapter 3.) Recently, however, a growing dissatisfaction with low-performing public schools, especially in large cities, has caused some present-day reformers to advocate that a single official needs to be in charge and accountable for improving schools. In what is referred to as **mayoral takeover,** mayors are granted authority to appoint school board members rather than continuing election by the voters. Mayoral takeover has occurred in Boston, Chicago, New York City, and Washington, D.C., among others. Has it worked? A study by two educational researchers states that the purpose of mayoral takeover is "to bring about major restructuring in the ways schools are managed and governed."[19] Although it is too early for well-supported conclusions, early findings indicate that mayoral takeover is associated with greater per-pupil expenditures in important categories such as instruction. Spending on the school system's "central office" has not increased, perhaps indicating greater management efficiency as well. Student achievement trends are described as meriting "cautious optimism"; some districts improved, some leveled off, and some even declined in a few subjects. The most positive finding on achievement is that the lowest performing schools were achieving gains greater than district averages, indicating that mayors may be targeting resources to these schools.[20]

State Government's Traditional Role

With thousands of school districts, it is easy to lose sight of the fact that school districts work within policies established by state government. Aside from education policy making responsibilities of governors and legislatures, forty-nine states have a state board of education that is part of the executive branch and is responsible for the general supervision of elementary and secondary education within the state.[21] The governor usually appoints members of these boards, but voters elect them in a few states. As with local school boards, members serve without salary and are not professional educators.

State boards of education appoint the state school superintendent, although in some states he or she will be elected by the voters or appointed by the governor. The state superintendent is important in determining educational policy and heads a state department of education that averages about three hundred employees.

Traditional activities at the state level have involved teacher certification and standards for the instructional program. All states have regulations governing teacher certification, that is, how a person becomes qualified to teach, and administer these regulations directly.[22] Frequently, states approve teaching programs at colleges and universities, and graduates of these programs are automatically certified. State legislatures delegate the writing of standards for the instructional program to state boards of education. Minimum standards, which must be followed by local school boards, may be established for curriculum, instructional materials, promotion, and graduation requirements.[23]

Federal Government's Traditional Role

The federal role in education is based on the Congress and president making laws and also on decisions by the Supreme Court. In 1979 a separate Department of Education was created in the executive branch; prior to that there was a Division of Education and even earlier an Office of Education, both housed within a department that had broader responsibilities than just education.

Although our emphasis is on education policy making at the state and local levels, the federal government plays an important role. Early examples are the Morrill Act (1862), which helped states establish colleges of agricultural and mechanical education (the forerunners of many of today's large state universities), and the Smith-Hughes Act (1917), which provided matching funds to assist states in establishing vocational education programs.

Still, it is the **Elementary and Secondary Education Act of 1965** that significantly extended the federal government's role. The most important component of this law, commonly referred to as Title I, provided federal funds to local school districts ($1.06 billion the first year) that had large numbers of children from low-income families. (Children from low-income families are likely to enter school not prepared to learn and have difficulty making normal progress.) Money also was provided for library resources, textbooks, and other instructional materials.[24]

The federal government's impact on schools is more obvious in the adoption of national policies than in the number of federal tax dollars transferred to the states. A few examples are listed:

■ The U.S. Supreme Court decision of *Brown v. Board of Education* (1954) declared racially segregated public schools unconstitutional.

■ Title IX of the Education Amendments of 1972 forbids sex discrimination in schools receiving federal financial assistance. As a result, courses designed for one sex have been eliminated and the number of girls' athletic programs has increased.

■ The Education for All Handicapped Children Act of 1975 (frequently referred to as Public Law 94-142) requires schools to provide appropriate public education for handicapped children that meets their special needs.

- In *Davis v. Monroe County Board of Education* (1999), the Supreme Court held that schools can be sued if they are "deliberately indifferent" to student-on-student sexual harassment.
- In *Board of Education v. Earls* (2002), the Supreme Court ruled to allow random drug tests for all middle and high school students participating in extracurricular activities. The ruling greatly expanded the scope of school drug testing, which previously had been allowed only for student athletes.

All of these federal-level policies have had a tremendous impact on public schools.

School Financing

When it comes to revenues for operating public schools, the dominance of state and local governments over the federal government is clear (Figure 10-2). State government's share has gradually increased, and in 2002–03 was 49 percent of total revenues. The local share, which was close to 60 percent in 1951–52, has declined to 43 percent. The federal government's contribution has never been particularly large; it peaked at just under 10 percent in 1971–72 and has declined to just under 8 percent since.

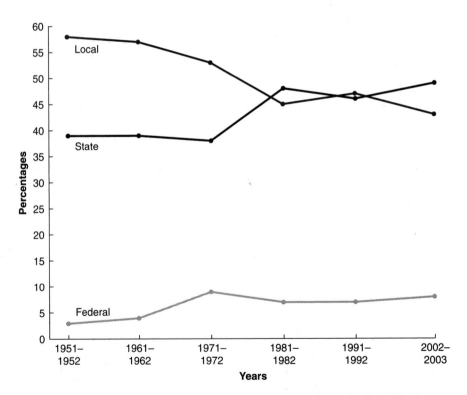

FIGURE 10-2 Sources of funds for public elementary and secondary schools, 1951–52 to 2002–03.

Source: U.S. Department of Education, National Center for Education Statistics, *Digest of Education Statistics, 2005*, http://nces.ed.gov/programs/digest/d05/tables.

The pattern of state-local financing varies greatly among the states. At the extremes, the state of Hawaii finances 90 percent of the cost of public education and North Carolina finances over 60 percent, whereas in Illinois and Pennsylvania the state share is 33 percent and 37 percent, respectively. In general, political culture is the strongest indicator of the degree of state control.[25] The traditionalistic southern states have a history of more centralized or state control of education. In contrast, the moralistic states of the Upper Midwest have stressed local control and financing of schools.

Local school districts depend on property taxes as their primary source of local revenue. As was noted in Chapter 9, the amount of revenue the property tax raises depends to a great extent on the value of property, or the tax base, in the school district. This can result in **funding inequities,** creating "rich" school districts and "poor" school districts literally existing alongside each other within the same state. Districts with valuable residential, commercial, and industrial property have a rich tax base and can easily raise money to finance higher expenditures than districts with a low-valued tax base. African American school children in inner cities and white school children in rural communities live in districts that tend to have schools supported by low-valued tax bases.

Ohio provides an example. In 1997, in rural Eastern Local School District, local property taxes raised $1,082 per student; in wealthy Upper Arlington, a suburb of Columbus, local property taxes provided $6,705! Even with federal and state aid Upper Arlington spent $10,000 per student and Eastern spent only $6,000 per student. Although many factors affect student learning, there is little doubt that the funding inequality between the two districts is important in explaining Upper Arlington's success in meeting twenty-five of Ohio's twenty-seven academic performance standards while Eastern met only fourteen.[26]

Inequities in school district funding have caused considerable political controversy. Some educators argue that the kind of education children receive should not depend on the tax base of their school districts; all children should have an opportunity to an equal education. The other side argues that effort to equalize school funding is a "Robin Hood" approach, taking money from rich areas of the state and giving it to poor areas, and will result in a leveling down of schools. This debate has flowed into the court system, as do many issues in American politics. A national right to equalized funding for education was denied by the U.S. Supreme Court in *San Antonio Independent School District v. Rodriguez* (1973). In upholding the Texas school finance system, the Court concluded that education is not a fundamental right protected by the Constitution. (This opinion overturned a lower federal court ruling that the Texas system of school finance did violate the equal protection clause of the Fourteenth Amendment because it discriminated against less wealthy districts. In the San Antonio area, the most affluent school district spent nearly twice as much per year, per pupil, as the poorest district.)

It seemed that this decision would end legal challenges to inequities in school funding, but nothing is further from the truth. Justice Thurgood Marshall, writing for the Court's minority in the *Rodriguez* case, suggested in a footnote that the unsuccessful plaintiffs might pursue their claims in state courts.[27] Plaintiffs took this advice and turned to state courts, using as the basis for their suits provisions in state constitutions concerning the state government's responsibility to educate its citizens. Over the years, suits have been filed in forty-five states. Plaintiffs won in twenty-six states, including Alabama, New Jersey, and New Hampshire; and lost in sixteen states, including

Georgia, Oklahoma, and Virginia. New challenges are pending in many states where plantiffs previously lost. Even where legal challenges have not been successful, many states have adopted legislation to reduce school-district financial disparities by reducing reliance on the local property tax to fund schools.

It takes a number of years for these cases to work their way through the state court system, and if a state's highest court rules in favor of the plaintiffs, it can take additional years finding a legislative agreement to implement the decision. New York may be a little extreme, but it is not entirely atypical. The first challenge to school funding inequities in the state of New York, initiated in 1978, failed as the court of appeals, New York's highest court, concluded that inequities did exist, but the state constitution did not require equal funding. The court recognized, however, that the constitution did guarantee the right to a "sound basic education." After considerable legal wrangling during the 1990s, another case went to trial and the plaintiffs won, only to have the decision overturned by an inter-mediate-level appeals court, ruling that an eighth-grade education was all that was guar-anteed by the constitution. Of course, this resulted in an appeal to the court of appeals. In 2003 the plaintiffs finally succeeded and the court's decision required the state of New York to implement major school funding and accountability reforms; a sound basic edu-cation was defined as a meaningful high school education providing its graduates with skills and knowledge to "function productively" in the twenty-first century.[28] But not until 2007 did the state legislature and the newly elected governor, Eliot Spitzer, agree on a plan that satisfied the court's decision. Key elements include the following:

- Changes in the formula so that distribution of state education aid will be on the basis of the financial need of school districts. This will result in a significant in-crease in aid to New York City school districts, up to an additional $3 billion in the next four years.
- To ensure accountability, school districts receiving increases of 10 percent or $15 million in state aid must develop a comprehensive plan for how they will spend the money and implement their educational programs. These accountability mea-sures are a critical part of ensuring that the new money is spent effectively.
- New York City is required to develop a plan for reducing class sizes over five years.[29]

After years of legal and political debate, the case of *Campaign for Fiscal Equity v. State* was settled.[30]

Do Public Schools Provide a Quality Education?

Widespread concern for the quality of education in the United States started with a 1983 report from the National Commission on Excellence in Education titled *A Nation at Risk: The Imperative for Educational Reform*. In dramatic language the report said: "If an unfriendly foreign power had attempted to impose on America the mediocre educa-tional performance that exists today, we might well have viewed it as an act of war. As it stands, we have allowed this to happen to ourselves."[31]

During the ensuing years, national concern with education has not lessened. A study commissioned by the Hoover Institute at Stanford University, which updates *A Nation at Risk,* argues that the "tide of mediocrity remains high."[32] For example, SAT scores have improved since 1982, but they are still below their 1970s level; students do no more homework than they did in 1982; and in global comparisons, U.S. students still fail to score among the top nations. Fewer teachers are specialized in the subject areas they teach than in 1983, and the school year is seven days shorter than it was in the 1970s—other indicators that the quality of education has not changed.[33] Not all professional educators or citizens would agree with this assessment. Most would agree, however, that there is a serious "achievement gap" between schools that produce lower performing students and schools that produce higher performing students.

Education Reforms

All levels of government have been active in debating and adopting educational reforms, but it is state governments that seized the initiative, at least initially. State politicians have the authority to reduce financing inequities between districts, and they have been sensitive to the demand for accountability, that is, the belief that schools should be held responsible for graduating students who have the reading, writing, and calculating skills needed in today's workplace.[34] By the end of the 1980s, nearly all states had tightened curriculum requirements and increased teachers' salaries; many adopted merit pay that allows larger raises for exceptional teachers. New standards such as a minimum grade point average and minimum scores on standardized tests were adopted for college students seeking to enter the teaching profession.

In the 1990s, some states—Alabama, Kentucky, Ohio, and Washington, for example—adopted "comprehensive statewide reforms," in which specific goals for student performance are identified, curriculum frameworks to achieve the goals are supported by the state, and tests are developed and administered to measure whether the goals are being met. Teachers and administrators in successful schools would be rewarded, and those in failing schools would be given assistance or may even be penalized.[35] In a short period of time, these ideas were accepted by nearly all states and became known as a standards-based accountability system. Simply put, in a **standards-based accountability system** the state emphasizes student achievement by setting goals in the form of standards and creates a statewide assessment plan to measure the academic performance of students, schools, and districts. The state also decides what sanctions or rewards will be provided to schools based on performance or improvement—or the lack of it—over time.[36]

Many educators and political leaders, notably President George W. Bush and his brother Jeb Bush, governor of Florida (1999–2007), have advocated more radical reforms under the label of **school choice,** meaning that parents and their children could choose any school, public or private, to attend. (In practice, parents would be given a voucher, that is, a certificate which they could use to pay for the education of their children at a school of their choice.) This market-oriented reform, its advocates contend, would force schools to compete for students. To engage in this competition, public school principals and teachers would be given more freedom to design their own curriculum and teaching strategies. To attract students, schools would have to establish a record demonstrating that their students actually learn. The frequently cited teacher's expression to an uncooperative student that "I get paid, whether you learn this or not" would no longer be true because if a school's students are not performing, its enrollment will drop. And just like a business in the economic marketplace, a school could fail and the principal and teachers would be out of their jobs. Schools, it is hoped, will compete on the basis of quality.[37]

Objections to school choice are many. Some critics do not want any public money going to private schools. Others wonder where the "good" schools would come from, especially in big cities where the quality of public schools is uniformly low. Starting a new school, finding and renovating a building, hiring teachers and administrators, and buying supplies cannot be done overnight.[38]

The first *statewide* plan for school choice, as opposed to limited plans adopted in a few cities, uses vouchers and evolved from a campaign promise made by Jeb Bush when he was running for governor in 1998. A year later the Florida legislature approved Bush's A+ Education Plan, a comprehensive reform package that included expanded testing of students, no social promotion, higher teacher standards, and grading of schools based on the test scores of their students. The voucher program, known as "opportunity scholarships," worked this way: If a school receives a grade of "F" for two years within a four-year period, parents can transfer their child from that school to a private school and the state will give them a voucher worth up to $4,000 to help pay the tuition.[39] Over 700 students were attending private schools with opportunity scholarships when, in 2006, the Florida Supreme Court declared the plan unconstitutional because it violated Florida's constitution, which requires "a uniform, safe, secure and high-quality system of free public schools."[40] Still, school vouchers have strong supporters working for their consideration in a number of states. The cities of Cleveland and Milwaukee operate voucher programs, and Utah recently adopted a statewide program.

A slightly different approach to school reform is the charter school movement; the first charter school opened in Minnesota in 1992. **Charter schools** receive public finds and are operated by independent groups under contract with a local school board or the state for a specified period of time. Even though they receive public funds, they are exempt from most state and local regulations that govern public schools. For example, charter schools can decide how to use their time during the school day and how to choose their teachers rather than following the rules of the school district.[41] The idea is that educational innovation and improvement, which will improve student performance, will be greater where there is less regulation. And if that's not the case, their charter will not be renewed. Forty states and the District of Columbia have laws that allow charter schools, and more than 3,900 such schools serving nearly a million students. Paul Hill, director of the Center on Reinventing Public Education, argues that state laws authorizing charter schools frequently have tilted the playing field against charter schools, making it difficult for them to succeed. For example, in some states funding for charter schools is only 75 percent of the money public schools receive on a per-student basis.[42] Charter schools are small, most enrolling fewer than 250 students; public school enrollment is more than 530 students per school. Although charter schools in a few states enroll a higher percentage of minority students, in most states racial composition is similar to statewide averages. Charter schools tend to have fewer students with disabilities; however, they have a slightly higher percentage of students from low-income families, and the percentage of limited-English-proficient students is similar to that of public schools.[43]

Is there evidence that voucher programs or charter schools improve student performance? Generally, debate surrounding school choice has been so heated that much of the research has been used to buttress the views of choice supporters or opponents. Findings from objective studies have been mixed. Political scientist Paul Peterson, looking at the Milwaukee Parental Choice Program, states that voucher revenues have helped

Catholic and Lutheran private schools to "stabilize their operations and enhance their facilities,"[44] and that voucher students attending these secondary schools had higher graduation rates than students attending public high schools. On the other hand, a number of new schools attracted students even though the schools were of questionable quality. The National Assessment of Educational Progress, using data from 2003, and in one of the few comprehensive studies, found that students in charter schools scored slightly lower in reading tests (approximately five points) and six points lower in math than students in public schools.[45] Although it is always easier to call for more research, this would seem to be an area in which it is truly needed before we can make conclusions concerning the success of school choice.

A renewed interest in education by the federal government started in 1989 when President George H. W. Bush convened the President's Education Summit at the University of Virginia. This conference led to the adoption of national goals, including: All children will start school ready to learn; high school graduation rates will be at least 90 percent; students will demonstrate competence in a challenging curriculum; and schools will be safe, disciplined, and alcohol- and drug-free. President Clinton and Congress affirmed these goals in two new laws; the most important one was the Improving America's Schools Act (IASA) of 1994, which was actually a reauthorization and revision of the Elementary and Secondary Education Act mentioned earlier. In IASA, the federal government moved from encouraging state educational reform to achieve these goals to general requirements that states had to comply with to continue to receive federal funds. The federal government was now "investing in standards and assessments as a means to hold schools more accountable for the performance of its [sic] students."[46] Of course, many states had already moved in this direction.

When President George W. Bush took office in 2001, education was one of his top priorities. His proposal for education reform built on IASA and his own experiences as governor of Texas. The bill that Congress passed and President Bush signed into law is called the **No Child Left Behind Act of 2001 (NCLB).** This law requires states to do more in reforming their educational systems and to ensure, as the name of the law implies, that no child will be left behind. Some of the requirements of NCLB that the states must follow are listed below.[47]

- Expand the scope and frequency of student testing.
- Guarantee that every teacher is qualified in his or her subject area.
- Test students annually in grades 3–8 in mathematics and reading or language arts.
- Demonstrate adequate yearly progress (AYP) in raising the percentage of students proficient in reading and math.
- Demonstrate AYP in narrowing the test-score gap between advantaged and disadvantaged students.

If schools fail to meet these standards, the state is allowed to replace all or most of the school staff, extend the school day or year, change the curriculum, or restructure the school and reopen it as a charter school.[48] NCLB also increases federal funding to public schools by approximately 24 percent. (Keep in mind that the federal share is very low to begin with.) NCLB increases funding in several areas, including K–3 reading programs and before- and after-school programs, and provides states with greater flexibility to use federal funds as they see fit. Of course, the states have many new requirements to follow.

The implementation of NCLB has created considerable controversy during the past few years. (NCLB is up for reauthorization in the U.S. Congress in 2007.) Many states resented the intrusion of the federal government into a policy area that was viewed as the primary responsibility of state and local government. Educators particularly disliked requirements to administer the annual reading and math tests that are part of the state's assessment and accountability system to students with disabilities and students who are learning English. In addition, almost all state officials claimed that NCLB was an unfunded mandate (see Chapter 2); the increase in federal funds was not nearly enough to cover items such as creating and improving testing systems and contracting for supplemental services (tutoring, for example). State and local funds had to be used to meet federal requirements. On the positive side, curriculum and instruction are more aligned with standards and assessment, student achievement on state tests is rising, and greater efforts have been made to improve curriculum, staffing, and leadership at low-performing schools.[49]

Higher Education

In response to growing demand for higher education, state support for colleges and universities has expanded greatly since World War II. In 1947, about half of all college students were enrolled in state institutions. By 1968, the figure had risen to 71 percent, and in 2004 over 75 percent. Increased student demand has meant expanded facilities on existing campuses, the creation of new colleges, and a tremendous increase in the number of community colleges. This, of course, was accomplished by a vast expenditure of state funds. Between 2000 and 2012, college enrollment is projected to grow from 15 million to almost 18 million students because the traditional college-age population (18–24) will grow by 15 percent during this time period. At present, roughly two-thirds of high school graduates attend college compared to only 45 percent in 1960.

The quality of public institutions of higher learning improved significantly during the last half of the twentieth century. The University of California (especially at Berkeley and Los Angeles) and other major state-supported universities stand on an equal footing with the best private institutions in their states. Several states have established "centers of excellence" at their major universities, and special funds have been created to hire eminent scholars.

Unlike the administration of elementary and secondary schools, state control of colleges is much more diverse. In some states, such as Wisconsin, there is a single governing board for all public universities; in other states, such as Illinois, there are several university systems and several boards. In most cases the governor appoints board members, although they are popularly elected in a few states.

State- and local-appropriated funds account for approximately two-thirds of the general operating expenses of public colleges; of course, the exact amount varies from state to state. States that appropriate less money charge their students higher tuition (Figure 10-3). A geographic pattern of state aid to public colleges is not readily apparent, although the northeastern states rank very low in appropriations per student, in part because well-established private institutions continue to dominate there. Massachusetts has made a determined effort to upgrade its state system of higher education.

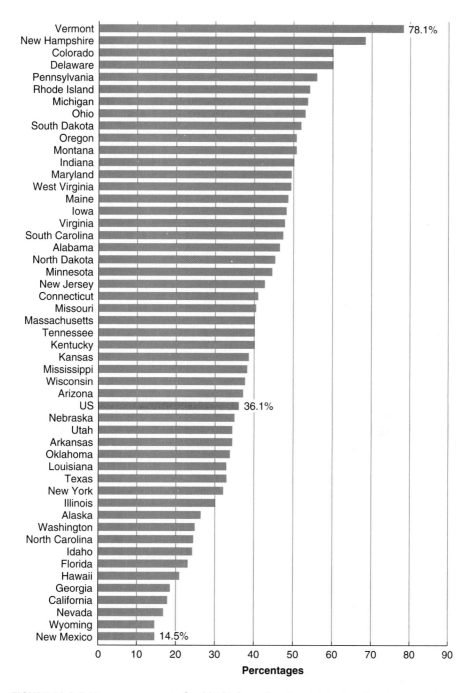

FIGURE 10-3 Tuition as a percent of public higher education total educational revenue by state, 2006.

Source: State Higher Education Executive Officers, *State Higher Education Finance: FY 2006*, p. 30, www.sheeo.org/finance/shef_fy06.pdf. Reprinted with permission of the State Higher Education Executive Officers.

Note: Tuition revenue as used by SHEEO is net—that is, tuition and fees minus state-funded student financial aid.

Community colleges receive appropriated monies from both state and local governments. Community colleges are strong competitors with four-year institutions for state funds because they are popular with state legislators who like the emphasis on technical and vocational education. In addition, community colleges provide an inexpensive way for students to complete their first two years of college close to home before transferring to a four-year institution to complete a bachelor's degree.

Most states give some form of financial assistance to private colleges or to students who are legal residents attending in-state private colleges. Only three states—Arizona, Nevada, and Wyoming, states with few private colleges—do not. Among the more generous states, New York and Illinois have programs for students attending private colleges, and they also make per capita payments to private colleges.

States have developed innovative plans to help parents finance their children's college education. Almost half of the states have prepaid tuition plans that can be purchased in monthly payments by parents while their children are growing up. These plans lock in today's tuition rates. States also have college savings plans (usually called 529 plans, a name derived from Internal Revenue Code Section 529) in which parents can save money that is exempt from federal taxes, and frequently from state taxes.

Affordability of both private and public higher education is a continuing issue in the states. From 1995 to 2005, average tuition and fees, after adjusting for inflation, rose 36 percent at private four-year colleges and universities, 51 percent at public four-year institutions, and 30 percent at community colleges. State funding fell to its lowest level in over two decades.[50] In all states, students and their families are required to pay more of their income to complete four years of undergraduate education and achieve a bachelor's degree. Studies by the National Center for Public Policy and Higher Education report that only a few states offer both low-priced colleges and substantial financial aid targeted to low-income students. Considerable variations exist among the states; for example, the proportion of family income required to pay for higher education at public four-institutions in New Jersey has increased from 24 percent to 37 percent, with similar increases in most states. Among the fifty states, only California, Colorado, Illinois, and Virginia offer both low-cost colleges and high-levels of need-based financial aid.[51]

Concern over accountability, which has been around for years in elementary and secondary schools, has reached higher education. Governors and state legislators are asking questions about the efficiency and productivity of colleges and universities. Much of the concern is over program duplication and faculty workload. Legislators in Ohio questioned, for example, whether their state really needed thirteen Ph.D. programs in history. Faculty workload, in terms of the amount of time spent in the classroom, is a perennial issue. Many citizens and legislators actually believe that a professor who teaches four three-hour courses is working only twelve hours a week. Of course, the time involved in preparing lectures, grading papers and exams, meeting with students, attending committee meetings, and doing research more than fills a forty-hour week. Upon reflection, government officials usually agree that faculty members are not slackers. A more serious issue is how faculty members divide their time between their two most important duties: teaching and advising undergraduate students and doing research. State legislators think professors are spending too much time on research and not enough in the classroom. Legislation has been introduced in a number of states that would increase the amount of time faculty spend on undergraduate education.[52] Public colleges and universities are being forced to prove they are using taxpayer funds wisely.

SOCIAL WELFARE

What is social welfare? **Social welfare** refers to governmental policies "that directly affect the income, services, and opportunities available to people who are aged, poor, disabled, ill, or otherwise vulnerable."[53] Historically, local governments provided services to the poor, but the federal government moved in strongly beginning in 1935. In the 1980s, states started playing a greater role that culminated in 1996 when Congress passed and President Clinton signed into law a major welfare reform bill. Social welfare policy making illustrates better than most other policy areas the complex interrelationships that can occur among levels of government in the United States.

Major Policies

Social services, social insurance, and public assistance are the three general categories of social welfare policy.[54] **Social services** are provided to those with special needs. Examples are day care, job training, mental health care, and vocational rehabilitation.

Social insurance programs are designed to prevent poverty and are financed by contributions from employees and employers. Employees are then entitled to benefits regardless of their personal wealth. One of the best-known programs in this category is unemployment compensation, sometimes called unemployment insurance, which provides benefits to regularly employed persons who become involuntarily unemployed and are able and willing to accept suitable employment in another job when one is available.[55] In other words, it provides some income to those who are temporarily unemployed. Wisconsin, in 1932, established the first unemployment compensation program in the United States. The Social Security Act, signed into law by President Franklin Roosevelt in 1935, did not establish one national unemployment compensation program but contained a tax incentive to encourage states to establish and administer their own programs, which the states did. Although there are general federal guidelines that a state must follow, they have some leeway in creating their own unemployment compensation programs. State programs are financed by taxes paid by employers and collected by the states. (The money, however, is deposited in the unemployment trust fund in the U.S. Department of Treasury.) States determine the amount and duration of benefits, establish eligibility requirements, take claims, and pay benefits. The federal government requires that states operate programs that are "fairly administered and financially secure"[56] and offer other services, such as job counseling and placement. Occasionally, during a recession, Congress will authorize and help finance extended benefits for the unemployed who have exhausted benefits under state programs.

Unemployment compensation, even in a fairly strong economy, is a large program. In 2005 the weekly average number of insured unemployed persons was 2.7 million, receiving an average weekly benefit payment of $267 for an average of fifteen weeks; benefits totaled $31.2 billion.[57]

Public assistance programs pay benefits out of general-revenue funds to people who meet a legal definition of being poor. These programs have been contentious political issues at the local, state, and federal levels, and it is these programs that politicians and voters think of when the word *welfare* is used. Examples are food stamps, Medicaid, and the most widely known, and now defunct, Aid to Families with Dependent Children (AFDC).

Congress passed and President Lyndon Johnson signed into law the Food Stamp Act in 1964. **Food stamps** are designed to improve nutrition in low-income families. More than unemployment compensation, this is truly a federal program. Food stamps are coupons that can be redeemed at grocery stores for food. The federal government pays for the entire cost of the coupons and shares the cost of administering the Food Stamp Program with the states. The Department of Agriculture and state and local welfare offices administer the Food Stamp Program, following national eligibility standards and benefit levels. States have much less discretion with this program but are involved in administering it because they certify an individual's eligibility. The average monthly number participating in the Food Stamp Program in 2005 was 23.9 million, and food stamp expenditures were $24.6 billion.

Medicaid, established in Social Security amendments of 1965, provides health care services for persons who have low incomes and limited resources. Children and their mothers, the disabled, and the elderly are the main beneficiaries of Medicaid. Federal and state governments share its cost, which in 2003 totaled $233.2 billion. Overall, the federal government pays approximately 55 percent of the cost; however, a state's average per capita income level determines its share. States that have a lower per capita income pay a smaller share than states with a higher per capita income. The federal share has varied from a high of 76 percent in Mississippi to a low of 50 percent in eleven states. More than 50 million persons received health care services through Medicaid in 1999. Within broad federal guidelines, each state establishes eligibility standards, type of services covered, and the rate of payment for services by health care providers, which is usually below what is charged other patients. In terms of social welfare policies, Medicaid is the most expensive program in the United States, and its cost has been increasing rapidly, posing a difficult problem for states at a time of stable or declining revenues.[58]

Even though a new federal law overhauling welfare eliminated the Aid to Families with Dependent Children (AFDC) program, it needs to be described briefly because it served as a flash point in the welfare reform debate of the 1990s. AFDC, which originated in the Social Security Act of 1935, provided cash assistance to poor families with only one parent so that children could continue to be cared for in their own homes.[59] In its next to last year of operation, 1996, the average monthly number of families on AFDC was about 4.2 million, and the average monthly payment per family was $383. The federal government paid about 55 percent of total AFDC spending; the remainder came from the states.

The public's perception of AFDC was not only that it supported people who should be working but also that many women had children simply to receive benefits. Critics of the program pointed to children born to unmarried teenagers who then became dependent on AFDC rather than completing school and finding a job. Many of these popular perceptions were not entirely accurate. For example, teenage mothers made up only 8 percent of AFDC parents. But there was enough truth in the perceptions that they fueled a national debate on reforming the AFDC program.

Ending Welfare as We Know It

"Ending welfare as we know it" expressed the sentiment of many voters and political leaders during the 1990s. Political scientists Lyke Thompson and Donald Norris put the problem into perspective:

> [Welfare] is a solution to the problem of poverty, but it is also a persistent problem in it-self. For welfare is an inadequate response to the problem of poverty; it is perceived to neither increase income enough to end poverty nor encourage its recipients to stand up and leave it on their own. It invites reform.[60]

The road to reform actually started when a few states decided to take advantage of an obscure provision in the 1962 amendments to the Social Security Act. This provision, known as **Section 1115 waivers,** allowed states to experiment with welfare reform through "demonstration projects." States interested in demonstration projects had to obtain a Section 1115 waiver from the U.S. Department of Health and Human Services. States were not encouraged to apply for waivers until the Reagan administration, and they did not appear in any great numbers until the Bush and Clinton administrations.[61] Although the waiver process was slow and cumbersome, by 1995 over fifty demonstration projects were operating in twenty-seven states. These waivers allowed states to try things that federal rules would normally prohibit. Wisconsin with seven projects and Illinois with six were early leaders among the states. Wisconsin, under Republican Governor Tommy Thompson, initiated a number of unusual stipulations for welfare recipients, including "learnfare," which tied a parent's AFDC grant to children's school attendance, and "bridefare," which paid the recipient more if she married. Wisconsin Works, W-2 as it was known, was a more comprehensive program than other program in that it moved welfare recipients to jobs.[62]

State reform efforts were important but represented incremental change when compared to the welfare reform bill approved by Congress and signed into law by President Clinton. This law, the **Personal Responsibility and Work Opportunity Reconciliation Act of 1996,** eliminated AFDC and with it the sixty-year-old federal guarantee of welfare checks for low-income mothers. The most important goal of the act was to end welfare dependence by promoting job preparation and work. **Temporary Assistance for Needy Families (TANF),** a block grant of $2.3 billion annually, replaced AFDC. As with all block grants, the states were given more discretion in program design and implementation. For example, states could decide the following:

- What families to help and benefits they will receive.
- Whether to adopt financial rewards and/or penalties to encourage recipients to work.
- Whether to allow the provision of services through contracts with charitable religious or private organizations.

However, some federal strings were attached. For example, states must achieve minimum work participation rates among those receiving aid, and states must require unwed mothers under eighteen to live in an adult-supervised setting in order to receive aid. The most significant federal requirement is that of a "lifetime time limit"; that is, individuals can receive TANF support for only five years during their entire lifetime.[63]

Journalist Jeffrey Katz summarized the meaning of this new law when he said that state and local governments will "now shoulder most of the responsibilities . . . of turning welfare offices into job placement centers and moving people from welfare to work."[64]

What has been the impact of a decade of welfare reform? The principal effects are summarized below:

- Welfare caseloads declined dramatically. Between 1996 and 2002, the number of families receiving cash benefits dropped from 4.6 million under AFDC to 2.1 million under TANF. The share of eligible families enrolled in these programs dropped from 80 percent to 49 percent.
- Participation in work or participation in activities to prepare for work increased significantly. The number of welfare recipients working during the preceding twelve months rose from 31 percent (1997) to 44 percent (1999), falling to 39 percent in a tougher job market in 2002.
- As caseloads declined, states shifted resources from benefit payments to "work support" funding such as child care, transportation, and tax credits to support work and family independence.
- TANF recipients can increase their families' income by working part time and still receive TANF benefits.
- Welfare "leavers," those who leave TANF and enter the workforce, are usually in low-wage jobs, with an hourly wage around $8; they are less likely to return to TANF if they receive some government support such as child care assistance.[65]

Although most observers believe that considerable progress has been made in reducing welfare dependency, The Urban Institute's Assessing the New Federalism Project is more cautious:

> Yet work is not enough: The ability of parents in 11 million low-income working families to provide for their children's basic needs remains precarious. Whether the yardsticks are poverty and low income on federal guidelines or food or housing insecurity, many families work long hours and still can't satisfy basic economic needs. The lack of access to health care intensifies the stress and risk.[66]

Health insurance, or the lack of it, has been a staple topic in American politics for decades. Many individuals and families are covered by insurance where they work, with most of the cost being paid by the employer and a smaller premium paid by the employees. Those who are 65 and over receive substantial coverage from Medicare. The poor are covered by Medicaid. A small percentage of the adult population purchases health insurance on its own. Still, according to the Census Bureau's 2005 Current Population Survey (CPS), there were 45.8 million uninsured individuals, or 15.7 percent of the civilian non-institutionalized population. The uninsured tend to have low incomes but usually not low enough to qualify for Medicaid; half of the uninsured are below 200 percent of the federal poverty level, which at the time of this survey was $18,620 for a single individual and $37,700 for a family of four. The uninsured are more likely to be young, 21 percent of the uninsured are under 18 and 63 percent are under 34. Young adults 18 to 34 are disproportionately uninsured relative to their presence in the overall population.

At the national level, universal health insurance plans are talked about and written about, but no serious attempt to enact such a plan has occurred since President Bill Clinton's failed effort in 1993. However, in 1997 Congress did enact an important policy when it passed the **State Children's Health Insurance Program (SCHIP),** a partnership between federal and state governments to provide health insurance to low-income children under the age of 19 and who are not eligible for Medicaid. Today, state programs cover more than 6 million children. From almost all observers, SCHIP has been declared a success. States like the program's flexibility, which allows them to determine to a large extent the structure of their own program and eligibility requirements. For example, Maryland covers families earning up to 200 percent of the federal poverty level at no charge to the families, and children from families earning up to 300 percent of the poverty level pay approximately $50 per month.[67]

The most significant step toward universal coverage was taken by Massachusetts in 2006 when the legislature passed and Governor Mitt Romney signed into law the Massachusetts Health Care Reform Plan. It was expected to cover over 90 percent of the state's 600,000 uninsured residents. The law has a unique "pay-or-play" approach for individuals. Uninsured residents who are not eligible for Medicaid and do not have insurance through their employers will be required to buy health insurance or pay a penalty. The first-year penalty is the loss of a tax exemption worth about $150; penalties become stiffer after the first year. To make insurance more affordable, a new program, Commonwealth Care, was created; for example, subsidized policies will be offered to individuals and families who earn between 100 percent and 300 percent of the federal poverty level. For those who do not qualify for subsidized coverage, the Commonwealth Health Insurance Connector, a new state agency, will guide individuals and small businesses to certified insurance policies. Individuals will be able to buy coverage from the connector using pre-tax dollars. This should lower costs by pooling purchasing power and sharing overhead costs. Insurers also are encouraged to offer low-cost, limited-benefit plans to people aged 19 to 26, the age group likeliest not to have coverage.[68] More than twenty states are now considering some form of universal coverage. Of course, developing and adopting this type of reform is a major accomplishment, and lobbying by insurance companies, physicians, and experts on both sides is intense; nevertheless, implementation is sure to be no easy task. Leif Haase, a researcher at the Century Foundation, notes a particular dilemma with the Massachusetts Health Care Reform Plan: Will policies with adequate coverage be offered at a price that individuals can afford? Or will a reasonable price provide skimpy benefits and high deductibles and be of little use?[69]

ECONOMIC DEVELOPMENT

At first glance, economic policy appears to be completely dominated by the federal government. After all, state and local governments do not have an equivalent of the Federal Reserve Board that sets interest rates. States cannot constitutionally carry budget deficits that could help stimulate their economies during a recession. Governors and mayors cannot sign free trade agreements with other nations such as the one President Bush signed with Australia in 2004 that eliminates almost all tariffs on U.S. exports to

Australia. Eliminating these tariffs, according to government officials, will increase the export of U.S. manufactured goods to Australia by nearly $2 billion per year and create new jobs for American workers. It is true that the federal government is a dominant actor in economic policy, but state and local governments play an important role in their own economies.

At various times in American history, states have taken an active role in stimulating economic growth. Perhaps the best known period is the early nineteenth century when state governments financed a transportation network, especially canals, that opened up states in the interior of the country (Illinois, Indiana, and Ohio) to trade with the Northeast and South. The state of New York spent $7 million to build the Erie Canal, the most successful of many similar ventures by state governments.[70]

In the early part of the twentieth century, a few states moved to protect their workers by establishing minimum labor standards and providing unemployment insurance and workers' compensation programs. Southern states, beginning in the 1930s, adopted policies to diversify their agricultural economies by attracting northern industry. Mississippi created the Balance Agriculture with Industry program, which lured companies from the North by offering tax incentives and low labor costs.[71]

During the post–World War II period, a vibrant American economy dominated the world for at least twenty-five years, economic growth was reasonably widespread within the United States, and generally there was little state intervention to promote economic growth. The fact that investment decisions were made by private businesses free to locate in any state was of little importance. During the 1980s and 1990s, however, increasing economic competition from abroad and slow growth in the national economy created a situation where "state effort to sustain growth could be instrumental for economic progress."[72] State governors now rank economic development as important as more traditional state issues, such as education, welfare, and highway construction and maintenance.

Location Incentives and Bidding Wars

The demand for businesses that provide factory or service jobs exceeds the supply, resulting in competition between state and local governments. To win this competition, they have adopted a **maintenance/attraction strategy,** which offers businesses incentives to maintain existing industries where they are or to induce out-of-state businesses to relocate or build branch plants within their boundaries.[73]

An example of this approach is the use of **tax incentives,** which give tax breaks to recruit and retain businesses. The nature of this incentive varies from state to state; North Carolina offers a $2,800 income tax credit for every new manufacturing job created above a threshold of nine. The creation of specific jobs is only one item that qualifies for tax breaks. Others include the purchase of equipment and machinery, raw materials used in manufacturing, and money spent on research and development. The total number of different tax incentives offered is over fifteen, although not all of them are used by every state.[74]

Local governments frequently exempt a new business from the local property tax for a number of years, an incentive known as tax abatement. Property tax abatement is the most popular incentive used by local governments. Gaining in popularity is another incentive called tax increment financing (TIF). A geographic area within a city must be designated as a TIF district; with this designation the city improves the district with site clearance, utility installation, and street construction, and also offers subsidized financing to encourage businesses to locate there. Money is borrowed for the improvements and is paid back from future growth in property tax revenues that the improved district generates. If everything works as planned, this development will pay for itself and the money will not have to be taken from current local budgets.[75]

Financial incentives are low-interest loans that have the backing of state or local governments. More than forty states offer loans for plant construction, purchasing equipment, existing plant expansion, and establishing plants in areas of high unemployment. Both tax and financial incentives lower a business's costs, which should translate into increased sales and profits. Generally, states in the South have the highest number of incentives to attract businesses.

Unfortunately, today's global economy, in which jobs can move abroad almost as easily as they move from state to state, has intensified competition. States and communities are now putting together **customized incentives,** a package of a large number of firm-specific incentives used to recruit a major new business or retain an existing one. Customized incentives are usually associated with a bidding war whereby one state after another ups the ante, hoping to win a new automobile manufacturing plant or an equivalent prize. Journalist George Hohmann has called automobile plants the "big enchilada" in state economic development efforts.[76]

DaimlerChrysler's announcement in 2002 that it planned to build a manufacturing plant, this one for Dodge Sprinter vans, set off a round of bidding wars in southern states. (Foreign car makers appear to like the South because of low-cost, non-union labor.)[77] South Carolina's legislature passed a bill allowing it to borrow more money for economic development, including $110 million for DaimlerChrysler. Florida lawmakers approved new worker training funds and a corporate tax cut. A news reporter in Louisiana wondered why state officials did not make an effort to bring the plant to Louisiana. At the same time, Arkansas legislators debated whether, in a tight budget year, money should go to public schools or economic development by pursuing a new Toyota automobile plant.[78] The state of Georgia, with a $320 million incentives package, was the eventual winner of the plant; unfortunately for Georgia, the proposed plant was put on hold and was never built. Eventually, DaimlerChrysler converted a facility it owned in South Carolina; even this came with incentives such as reduced costs in shipping parts from Germany through the port of Charleston and tax credits for each new employee hired.[79]

The details of an incentives package put together by Mississippi officials to attract a Toyota plant to Tupelo are probably typical. It is a big plant located on a 1,700-acre site. It will cost $1.3 billion and will build 150,000 Highlander crossover utility vehicles annually when it opens in 2010, and it will employ 2,000 workers at $20 per hour after three years on the job. The state of Mississippi's incentive package totaled $323.9 million, including $50 million for site preparation, $57 million for offsite roads, $20 million for offsite rail infrastructure, $44 million for utilities, and $80 million for employee training.[80]

It's not clear if the high cost of incentives has peaked, but some observers are questioning whether the economic benefits a state and its citizens receive from acquiring a new facility actually outweigh the costs. States are being cautioned that before offering an expensive package of incentives they should look at it from the perspective of cost-benefit analysis. But this is hardly an exact science. In the case of the Toyota plant, what benefits does it offer the state of Mississippi and its citizens? Of course, the principal benefit is that new jobs are created.

What are the costs of incentives for states and their citizens? A number of costs such as those in Mississippi that involved purchasing the site and conducting training sessions are an exact amount of money that is easily known. And taxes not collected because of various tax breaks can be estimated with some reliability. However, development impact costs are usually ignored or seriously underestimated. Research on the relationship between job growth and population growth shows that many of the newly created jobs go to new residents who, if not for the presence of a new plant, would be living someplace else. And new residents require "new schools, wider roads, extra police and other governmental expenses that come with population growth."[81] Because costs are particularly difficult to estimate, states and communities should be careful in offering incentive packages that exceed a realistic appraisal. One has to wonder about the long-term benefits of 210 jobs at a $600 million Google "server farm" that received $260 million in tax abatements and grants from the city of Lenoir, Caldwell County, and the state of North Carolina. The city and county have forgiven 100 percent of Google's business property taxes and 80 percent of its real estate taxes for the next thirty years.[82]

Head-to-head competition in the bidding wars has increased in intensity and is frequently being called an "economic civil war" between states and communities. In addition, it is increasingly clear that businesses are playing one state or community against another, trying to get the best deal they can. For example, Marriott International threatened to move its headquarters from Montgomery County, Maryland, to Virginia. Before negotiations with both states were finished, Marriott executives decided to stay in Maryland and asked Virginia officials to keep their decision confidential so that they could negotiate the best possible incentives package with Maryland, which amounted to $44 million in state and county grants and tax breaks and Marriott's promise to add 700 jobs.[83] As in most wars, ethics are too easily set aside by the participants.

Some state leaders have called for a truce. The National Governors Association has adopted voluntary guidelines that encourage governors to improve the general business climate in their states rather than use customized incentives packages. Under these guidelines, incentive packages would be used primarily to encourage investment in economically depressed areas.[84] Still, in these bidding wars no political leader appears willing to "disarm unilaterally," for fear of losing a new plant to a neighboring state or city. Illinois and other states have adopted "clawback" provisions that require companies to repay the state for incentives if they decide to leave. Illinois legislators were outraged with Motorola when it decided to close a nine-year-old cell phone plant after the state had provided $36 million in tax credits and road improvements.[85] Finally, the question of state incentives such as tax exemptions and tax credits was challenged in federal courts. Plaintiffs in *DaimlerChrysler Corp. v. Cuno*,[86] Ohio and Michigan citizens, argued that tax incentives offered to DaimlerChrysler to expand its operations in Toledo violated the U.S. Constitution's Commerce Clause because it "coerced" business to expand locally rather than out-of-state. The Supreme Court failed to decide on the central question raised in this case, but decided that the plaintiffs did not have standing in this case, meaning that they should not have sued because they could not demonstrate that they would suffer sufficient harm from Ohio's incentives policies.

Alternative Approaches

A few states are trying a different approach to promote economic development by developing "new growth opportunities for local entrepreneurs and businesses."[87] Political scientist John Jackson calls this a **creation strategy** that relies on increasing the availability of capital for entrepreneurs, educating the workforce, and promoting innovation.[88] This approach may help take states out of the bidding wars because political leaders will focus on their state's economy as it is, evaluating strengths and weaknesses, establishing economic goals, and building on economic strengths. In Pennsylvania, Ben Franklin Technology Partners (BFTP) assists emerging technology enterprises by ensuring they have access to the "resources they need to become more efficient, more competitive and more successful in the global marketplace." Recently, BFTP awarded a $300,000 grant to Pittsburgh-based Concurrent EDA, a fledgling business that is developing software tools to help in the design and production of microchips for today's electronic necessities.[89]

Another manifestation of this strategy is to concentrate on cluster-based economic development. The idea is that government development policies should focus on creating and enhancing regional **clusters of innovation,** which are "fast-growing groups of businesses that share markets, labor, new ideas, and products."[90] A classic example of such a cluster is the Research Triangle Park located in North Carolina between Duke University in Durham, North Carolina State University in Raleigh, and the University of North Carolina at Chapel Hill. It is famous for its world-class research centers, which today total over 130 research and development organizations ranging from environmental sciences to pharmaceuticals. South Carolina is working to develop an automotive cluster with an International Center for Automotive Research at Clemson University and a BMW assembly plant in the Greenville-Spartanburg area. Many states are promoting the biotechnology field in the hopes of developing a cluster; a few states, including California, New Jersey, and Maryland, are using state funds to support controversial embryonic stem cell research. Federal funding for this research is very restricted. Another area of interest is renewable energy, with several states funding research on ethanol.

According to the National Governors Association, most cluster development initiatives include the following:

- Promote research by encouraging partnerships and leveraging public funds to attract private investment;
- Build a skilled workforce by providing training and education to meet industry needs;
- Support entrepreneurs by providing incentives for job creation.[91]

David Osborne, who specializes in strategic management, suggests that in today's world of high-tech industries and global competition, states must have, among other characteristics, a skilled, educated workforce, an intellectual infrastructure of first-rate universities and research facilities, and an attractive quality of life.[92] In other words, the expenditure of public revenues on traditional government functions is important in the long run in determining a state's or a community's economic prosperity.

ENVIRONMENTAL PROTECTION

Prior to the first Earth Day in 1970, environmental protection was primarily a state and local responsibility. In the late nineteenth century, Chicago and Cincinnati had laws regulating smoke emissions, and the first state law regulating air quality was passed in Ohio about the same time. In 1952, Oregon was the first state to pass statewide air pollution legislation and to establish an air pollution control agency. Generally, however, state and local governments paid little attention to environmental protection. Increased public concern about the issue caused the federal government to assume a leadership role in the early 1970s that led to the passage of two significant laws: the Clean Air Act of 1970 and the Federal Water Pollution Control Act of 1972 (usually called the Clean Water Act). Both laws, which have been amended several times since their adoption, are basic to environmental protection today. The federal government, with increasing public concern over the quality of the environment, has passed additional environmental laws in the last thirty years and, to the casual observer, appears to be the major source of initiatives to improve the environment. But we should not conclude that states have been doing nothing. In fact, in the last few years many states and communities have been extraordinarily active.

The Role of State Governments

For the past several years, the most important environmental problem has been that of global warming. We could infer, with the word *global,* that state governments in the United States would seldom discuss this issue and would seldom make any policy decision that would be effective. Nothing could be further from the truth. Barry Rabe, who studies environmental policy, reminds us that if the fifty states of the U.S.A. were separate sovereign nations, thirteen would rank among the world's top forty in terms of greenhouse gas emissions, with Texas in seventh place, ahead of the United Kingdom.[93] Clearly, state decisions can be important. Before looking at the states, a quick review of this issue and the federal government's response is necessary. **Global warming** is the warming of the Earth's atmosphere from the presence of higher levels of carbon dioxide that are caused by the burning of fossil fuels, especially coal, oil, and gasoline. The resulting climate change, it is believed, will cause rising sea levels, permafrost thawing in Alaska, more extreme weather events, and altered patterns of agriculture. Under President George W. Bush, the federal government has maintained a policy of disengagement on global warming.[94] The Bush administration called for more research and voluntary reductions in emissions of "greenhouse" gases, and withdrew from international negotiations on the Kyoto Protocol, which specifies mandatory reductions in greenhouse gas emissions. In part, it has been a leadership vacuum at the federal level that has allowed many states to act.

A recent example of state initiatives is found in a U.S. Supreme Court case, *Massachusetts v. Environmental Protection Agency* (2007); as the name implies, Massachusetts and several other states and cities sued the federal government's major administrative agency responsible for protecting the environment. The dispute was over whether or not carbon dioxide could be regulated by the Environmental Protection Agency. The EPA decided that it could not regulate greenhouse gas emissions because the Clean Air Act did not authorize their regulation and, even if it had the authority, a causal link between these emissions and global warming was not firmly established. It was this decision that was challenged, and the several states and cities that brought the suit won. The Supreme Court, in a 5–4 decision, held that the EPA has the statutory basis to regulate air pollutants that can "reasonably be anticipated to endanger public health or welfare." The Court went on to say that the only way the EPA could decide not to regulate was if it determines that greenhouse gases "do not contribute to climate change or if it provides some reasonable explanation as to why it cannot or will not exercise its discretion to determine whether they do."[95] Although the effect of this decision is not evident at this writing, it seems safe to predict that EPA will have to act to regulate greenhouse gases.

But have states acted in a direct way to reduce greenhouse gases? It is one thing to sue the federal government for not acting and something else for states to decide to act on their own. Barry Rabe, in a comprehensive examination of states and climate change policies, has developed an elaborate classification based on an evaluation of their efforts. These are the more important ones:

- Prime-time states—These states recognize global warming and climate change as an environmental threat and have adopted a number of different programs that establish greenhouse gas reduction as a state policy. New Jersey, for example, announced a Sustainability Greenhouse Gas Action Plan in 2000 to reduce emissions below 1990 levels through energy conservation, new technologies, and pollution prevention, among others.[96]
- Opportunistic states—Programs to reduce greenhouse gases have been adopted in these states, but they are primarily seen as opportunities for economic development and less about alleviating climate change as an environmental problem. For example, Nebraska's agricultural economy, if policies created a "carbon market," could increase the income of farmers by changing farming practices so that more carbon is stored in the soil. The economic development side is also apparent in a statement by Massachusetts Governor Deval Patrick: "I don't just want wind farms. I want companies that build turbines. I want hybrid-vehicle companies to consult us on conservation strategies. I want companies that design solar panels."[97]
- Stealth states—These states adopt policies similar to opportunistic states, but political leaders steer clear of saying they are acting to reduce greenhouse gases. Major constituencies in stealth states do not believe global warming is an important problem, and they would work to defeat programs that were so labeled. Texas is a case in point where state laws are encouraging the generation of electricity from renewable energy sources. In 1999, Governor George W. Bush and the Texas legislature did not officially say they were acting to reduce greenhouse gases, only that they wanted to diversify the state's sources of electricity.[98]
- Hostile or indifferent states—These states see reducing greenhouse gases unilaterally as a threat to the health of their state's economy. Major industries in these states generate large amounts of greenhouse gases, directly or indirectly. Examples are West Virginia, a major source of coal for coal-burning electric power plants, Ohio with a number of large coal-burning plants, and Michigan with large automobile manufacturing plants.

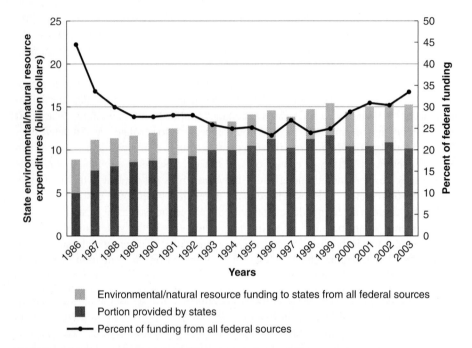

FIGURE 10-4 Trends in state environmental and natural resource spending, 1986–2003.

Source: R. Steven Brown and Michael J. Keifer, "ECOS Budget Survey: Budgets Are Bruised, but Still Strong," *ECOStates* (Summer 2003), p. 13, www.ecos.org/files/892_file_2003BudgetsArticle.pdf. Reprinted with permission of the Environmental Council of the States.

Although not all states are on the cutting edge, Rabe concludes that states "have clearly picked up the pace in climate change policy, as measured by the number of new initiatives, their range of coverage, and the rigor with which they attempt to achieve significant reductions."[99] Certainly, in the past ten years, states have accomplished more than the federal government.

Funding for environmental protection and natural resources comes from both federal and state governments. Federal funds (EPA and natural resources) peaked in the mid-1980s. In 1986, states spent a total of $8.7 billion, with $3.86 billion (44 percent) coming from the federal level. Between 1986 and 2003, state spending more than doubled and federal funding to states increased slightly. In 2003, states spent more than twice as much ($10.1 billion) as they received from the federal level ($5 billion).[100] (See Figure 10-4. Please note that these dollar figures are adjusted for increases in the cost of living to the year 2003.) A few states, such as Arizona, found innovative ways to fund environmental programs. Arizona enacted a $1.50 surcharge on annual motor vehicle registrations to provide money for air pollution control improvements.

Civic Environmentalism

Environmental protection is frequently thought of in terms of command and control regulation, that is, "rules of behavior that are applied to specific individuals or organizations through an enforcement process."[101] A different approach is offered in **civic environmentalism,** a movement to mobilize the efforts of local citizens to improve environmental quality. It is a bottom-up approach to environmental protection. A leading expert on civic environmentalism, DeWitt John, has identified the "unfinished business" in environmental protection and the use of nonregulatory tools as two of the key components of civic environmentalism.

First, unfinished business refers to those pollution issues that have not always received adequate attention and need the involvement and cooperation of large numbers of citizens to solve. A classic example is **nonpoint pollution,** pollution that comes from many sources such as fertilizer runoff from hundreds of farms and can cover a large area. (Point pollution comes from a single, easily identifiable source such as a smokestack.) Another example of unfinished business is pollution prevention, trying to prevent at least some pollution before it occurs rather than trying to clean up after it happens. Likely candidates are homeowners who overfertilize their yards and flower gardens and backyard mechanics who change their cars' oil and do not dispose of it properly.

Nonpoint pollution has been an important issue in Iowa, where large quantities of herbicides and chemical fertilizers are used to increase corn yields. Iowans took steps to reduce the use of these chemicals, thereby protecting the drinking water supply from contamination. Florida's Governor Lawton Chiles (1991–98) led the way in negotiating an end to a three-year battle between local, state, and federal officials over water quality in the Everglades. The result was an agreement on initial plans to protect and restore the Everglades. In Colorado, the state's Public Utilities Commission made a commitment to energy conservation by encouraging "demand-side" management from companies generating electric power. (Reducing demand for electricity reduces the amount of electricity produced, which reduces pollution from the generation of electricity, especially from coal-fired electric power plants.) Demand-side management means utility companies encourage consumers to take measures to use less electricity, which they would normally see as counter to their interests because less consumption could reduce company profits.[102]

Second, civic environmentalism makes extensive use of nonregulatory tools, such as educating the public at large about environmental concerns, technical assistance, and grants along with tax credits and loans to correct pollution problems. The Groundwater Protection Act in Iowa emphasized educating farmers about new ways of cultivating and rotating crops as well as reduced use of chemicals. Funds were provided to help farmers pay for improvements that would reduce chemical pollution of waters. This nonregulatory approach may be better than command-and-control regulation when there are a large number of polluters (90 percent of Iowa is farmland and there are 100,000 farmers) and when it is difficult to monitor how much pollution each individual contributes such as in groundwater contamination.[103]

Civic environmentalists do not want the regulatory processes of federal and state governments out of the picture completely. They see the bottom-up approach as a complement to current laws and regulations.

SUMMARY

Homeland security, "efforts to secure our nation," may appear to be the exclusive responsibility of the federal government, but all acts of terrorism or natural disasters are local. Local governments as first responders must deal with the initial consequences of a terrorist attack and should play an important role along with the federal government in preventing attacks. Responding to Hurricane

Katrina-sized disasters requires advance planning and coordination of all three levels of government.

Providing elementary, secondary and higher education is a major government function. Historically, elementary and secondary education policy has been made by more than 15,000 local school districts, within the general guidelines of state boards of education, governors, and legislators.

School funding inequities and public concern over the quality of education in public schools have caused the federal government and especially state governments to become more active participants in the making of education policy. States are assuming a larger role in financing school systems. State court rulings have required many states, including New York, to adopt major reforms to eliminate funding inequities and improve the management and quality of public schools. Almost all states are adopting more laws and regulations that school districts must follow. For example, many states established specific goals for student performance and developed tests that measure whether the goals are met. The charter school movement advocates the creation of new schools that are financed by public funds but are independent of the rules and regulations that govern traditional public schools. School choice, a more radical reform proposal than the charter school movement, is being discussed. The federal government, through the No Child Left Behind Act of 2001, sets new requirements for educational reform that states must meet.

States have played an important role in meeting the demand for higher education by creating public two- and four-year colleges and universities. Although state funds on the average account for about 36 percent of the revenue of public higher educational institutions, the amount of state support and student tuition varies considerably from state to state. The quality of public higher education is frequently praised, but critical questions dealing with efficiency and productivity have been raised recently.

The federal government is the principal developer and funder of social welfare programs. But state and local governments are important because they assist in financing and play a meaningful role in their administration. Social services, such as day care, and social insurance programs, such as unemployment compensation, are much less controversial than public assistance programs that pay benefits to people who meet a legal definition of poor. In 1996, Congress passed a welfare reform law called the Personal Responsibility and Work Opportunity Reconciliation Act, which eliminated the politically unpopular Aid to Families with Dependent Children and established a goal of ending welfare dependence by promoting job preparation and work. The welfare caseload has dropped dramatically, but debate continues as to whether or not welfare "leavers" are moving out of poverty. The large number of Americans who are not covered by health insurance is an emerging welfare issue. A new program funded by federal and state governments covers children of low-income families who are not eligible for Medicaid. Massachusetts has taken a significant step toward universal health coverage for its residents.

State and local governments adopt economic development policies to encourage business investment in their particular state or community. The traditional approach is the maintenance/ attraction strategy that uses a variety of tax and financial incentives to attract new businesses and keep those that they have. Increasing competition for private investment, especially large automobile manufacturing plants, has caused bidding wars between states. However, development impact costs, which are usually ignored by state and local officials, sometimes exceed economic benefits of a new manufacturing plant. A newer approach, called a creation strategy, provides resources for existing local entrepreneurs and businesses to develop new products or processes that have the potential for growth.

In environmental protection, state governments are leaders in adopting policies and programs to reduce greenhouse gas emissions that cause global warming; the federal government has done little on this important issue. This is contrary to the usual pattern of environmental protection whereby the federal government develops policies and state governments are primarily involved in funding, monitoring, and enforcing them. Civic environmentalism is a bottom-up approach to improving the environment through the efforts of local citizens.

KEY TERMS

Department of Homeland
  Security (DHS) (p. 358)
National Response Plan (NRP) (p. 361)
independent school districts (p. 361)
dependent school districts (p. 362)
mayoral takeover (p. 362)
Elementary and Secondary Education Act
  of 1965 (p. 363)
funding inequities (p. 365)
standards-based accountability system
  (p. 367)
school choice (p. 367)
charter schools (p. 368)
No Child Left Behind Act of 2001 (NCLB)
  (p. 369)
social welfare (p. 373)
social services (p. 373)
social insurance (p. 373)
public assistance (p. 373)

food stamps (p. 374)
Medicaid (p. 374)
Section 1115 waivers (p. 375)
Personal Responsibility and Work
  Opportunity Reconciliation Act of
  1996 (p. 375)
Temporary Assistance for Needy Families
  (TANF) (p. 375)
State Children's Health Insurance Program
  (SCHIP) (p. 377)
maintenance/attraction strategy (p. 378)
tax incentives (p. 378)
financial incentives (p. 379)
customized incentives (p. 379)
creation strategy (p. 381)
clusters of innovation (p. 381)
global warming (p. 382)
civic environmentalism (p. 384)
nonpoint pollution (p. 385)

BRIEF COMPARISONS OF STATE/LOCAL DIFFERENCES

Issue	State Level	Local Level
Education	Growing influence in policies and funding. However, states must follow the federal government's NCLB Act.	Influence in policies and funding is still important, but has been declining in recent years.
Welfare	Expanded policy role under federal government's TANF program.	Administer welfare programs.
Economic development	Aggressive competition for new businesses using tax and financial incentives.	Aggressive competition for new businesses using tax abatements and tax increment financing.
Environmental protection	Initiating programs to reduce greenhouse gases and important in funding and implementing federal laws.	Provide services such as water, disposal of solid waste, and sewage treatment according to federal and state guidelines.

INTERESTING WEB SITES

http://movingideas.org. The Moving Ideas Network provides access to ideas and resources from leading progressive research and advocacy institutions.

www.heritage.org. This is the Web site of the Heritage Foundation, a research and educational institute whose mission is to formulate and promote conservative public policies.

www.ecos.org. The Environment Council of the States' Web site describes the role of state governments in environmental protection. Great site; click on almost anything for useful information.

NOTES

1. Pam Belluck, "Plan for Wind Farm off Massachusetts Clears State Hurdle," *New York Times* (March 31, 2007), www.nytimes.com/2007/03/31/us/31wind.html (accessed April 5, 2007).
2. Michael Shellenberger and Ted Norhaus, "Arctic Battle Should Move to Hyannis Port," *San Francisco Chronicle* (December 21, 2005), www.sfgate.com/cgi-bin/article.cgi?file=/c/a/2005/12/21 (accessed April 5, 2007).
3. Rick Klein, "Congress Reaches Pact on Wind Farm," *Boston Globe* (June 22, 2006), www.boston.com/news/nation/washington/articles/2006/06/22 (accessed April 4, 2007); Stephanie Ebbert, "Cape Wind Moves on to Federal Review After State OK," *Boston Globe* (March 31, 2007), www.boston.com/news/local/massachusetts/articles/2007/03/31 (accessed April 4, 2007).
4. U.S. Commission on National Security/21st Century (1999) as quoted in Annette D. Beresford, "Homeland Security as an American Ideology: Implications for U.S. Policy and Action," *Journal of Homeland Security and Emergency Management* 1, no. 3 (2004), p. 6, www.bepress.com/jhsem/vol1/iss3/301.
5. Department of Homeland Security, *Strategic Plan—Securing Our Homeland* (February 2004), www.dhs.gov/xabout/strategicplan/index.shtm (accessed April 16, 2007).
6. Ibid.
7. Susan E. Clarke and Erica Chenoweth, "The Politics of Vulnerability: Constructing Local Performance Regimes for Homeland Security," *Review of Policy Research* 23, no. 1 (2006), p. 95.
8. Michael O'Hanlon, "The Role of State and Local Governments in Homeland Security," written testimony for the Senate Committee on Homeland Security and Governmental Affairs, July 14, 2005.
9. Council on Foreign Relations, Eben Kaplan, "New York Spurs Counter-Terrorism Efforts" (February 2007), www.cfr.org/publication.12312 (accessed April 2, 2007).
10. NGA Center for Best Practices, Issue Brief, *2006 State Homeland Security Directors Survey: New Challenges, Changing Relationships* (April 2006), pp. 6–7, www.nga.org/center, (accessed April 2, 2007).
11. Kiki Caruson, Susan A. MacManus, Matthew Kohen, and Thomas A. Watson, "Homeland Security Preparedness: The Rebirth of Regionalism," *Publius* (Winter 2005), pp. 167–168.
12. Herman B. Leonard and Arnold M. Howitt, "Katrina as Prelude: Preparing for and Responding to Katrina-Class Disturbances in the United States—Testimony to U.S. Senate

Committee, March 8, 2006," *Journal of Homeland Security and Emergency Management* 3, no. 2 (2006), p. 3.

13. Department of Homeland Security, *Quick Reference Guide for the National Response Plan* (May 22, 2006), p. 1, www.dhs.gov/xlibrary/assets/NRP_Quick_Reference_Guide_5-22-06.pdf (accessed April 18, 2007).

14. Arnold M. Howitt and Herman B. "Dutch" Leonard, "Katrina and the Core Challenges of Disaster Response," *Fletcher Forum of World Affairs* 30, no. 1 (2006), p. 221.

15. Roald F. Campbell and others, *The Organization and Control of American Schools* (Columbus, Ohio: Merrill Publishing Company, 1990), p. 50.

16. *Digest of Education Statistics, 2001* (Washington, D.C.: National Center for Education Statistics, 2002), http://nces.ed.gov/pubs2002/digest2001/introduction.asp.

17. Jacqueline P. Danzberger and Michael D. Usdan, "Strengthening a Grass Roots American Institution: The School Board," in *School Boards: Changing Local Control,* Patricia F. First and Herbert J. Walberg, eds. (Berkeley, Calif.: McCutchan Publishing Corporation, 1992), pp. 98–99.

18. Michael B. Berkman and Eric Plutzer, *Ten Thousand Democracies: Politics and Public Opinion in America's School Districts* (Washington, D.C.: Georgetown University Press, 2005), pp. 3–5.

19. Kenneth K. Wong and Francis X. Shen, "When Mayors Lead Urban Schools: Toward Developing a Framework to Assess the Effects of Mayoral Takeover of Urban Districts." Paper prepared for School Board Politics Conference, Program on Education Policy and Governance, Harvard University, October 15–17, 2003, p. 2.

20. Ibid., pp. 31–32.

21. Campbell and others, *Organization and Control,* p. 81.

22. Ibid., p. 93.

23. Ibid., pp. 91–92.

24. The U.S. Department of Education's Office of Elementary and Secondary Education has information on current programs and funding at its Web site: www.ed.gov/offices/OESE.

25. Frederick M. Wirt, "Does Control Follow the Dollar? School Policy, State-Local Linkages, and Political Culture," *Publius* 10 (1980), pp. 69–88.

26. "School-Funding Deadline Looms for Ohio," *USA Today* (June 20, 2001), www.usatoday.com/news/nation/june01/2001-06-11-ohio-school (accessed May 29, 2003).

27. William J. Fowler, "Introduction to Achieving Equity in School Finance, Overview," http://nces.ed.gov/edfin/litigation/introduction (accessed May 23, 2003).

28. Jessica Wolff and Joseph Wardenski, "The School Funding Victory," *Gotham Gazette* (June 27, 2003), www.gothamgazette.com/article/education (accessed April 25, 2007).

29. "Litigation into Law and Public Engagement into Policy: *CFE* Money Flowing to New York Districts This Year" National Access Network, www.schoolfunding.info/news/policy (accessed April 25, 2007).

30. This ruling, issued in 2003, is available at www.cfequity.org/CFEIIdecision.pdf.

31. National Commission on Excellence in Education, *A Nation at Risk* (Washington, D.C.: Department of Education, 1983), p. 5.

32. Majorie Coeyman, "Twenty Years After 'A Nation at Risk'" *Christian Science Monitor* (April 22, 2003), www.csmonitor.com/2003/04p13s02-lepr.html (accessed May 29, 2003).

33. Ibid.

34. Campbell and others, *Organization and Control,* p. 82.

35. Paul T. Hill, *Reinventing Public Education* (Santa Monica, Calif.: Rand, 1995), pp. 75–78.

36. National Conference of State Legislatures, "Education Policy Issues: Accountability, Standards, and Assessments," www.ncsl.org/programs/educ/ahomepage.html (accessed May 27, 2003).

37. A concise statement of the market-based approach to education can be found in John E. Chubb and Eric A. Hanushek, "Reforming Educational Reform," in *Setting National Priorities: Policy for the Nineties,* Henry J. Aaron, ed. (Washington, D.C.: Brookings Institution, 1990), pp. 213–247.

38. Hill, *Reinventing Public Education,* pp. 82–83.

39. Diane Rado, "Bush Signs, Defends Voucher Bill," *St. Petersburg Times* (June 22, 1999), p. 1A; Mike Clary, "Florida to Be First to Launch Statewide School Vouchers," *Los Angeles Times* (April 29, 1999), p. A1.

40. Greg Toppo, "Florida Supreme Court Strikes Down School Vouchers," *USA Today* (January 5, 2006), www.usatoday.com/news/nation/2006-01-05-florida-school-vouchers (accessed April 25, 2007).

41. Paul T. Hill and Robin J. Lake, *Charter Schools and Accountability in Public Education* (Washington, D.C.: Brookings Institution Press, 2002), pp. 4–5.

42. Paul T. Hill, "Introduction," in *Choice with Equity: An Assessment of the Koret Task Force on K–12 Education,* Paul T. Hill, ed. (Stanford, Calif.: Hoover Press, 2002), pp. 1–4.

43. National Conference of State Legislatures, "Education Program, Charter Schools," www.ncsl.org/programs/educ/charter.htm.

44. Paul E. Peterson, "School Choice in Milwaukee Fifteen Years Later," in *Charter Schools against the Odds: An Assessment of the Koret Task Force on K–12 Education,* Paul T. Hill, ed. (Stanford, Calif.: Hoover Press, 2006), p. 87. Peterson's analysis is based largely on an excellent series of newspaper articles in 2005 by Alan J. Borsuk, Sarah Carr, and Leonard Sykes, Jr., "Lessons from the Voucher Schools: How Is Milwaukee's Experiment to Expand School Choice for Low-Income Students Faring 15 Years Later?" *Milwaukee Journal Sentinel,* www.jsonline.com/story/index.aspx?id=333146&format=print.

45. Henry Braun, Frank Jenkins, and Wendy Grigg, *A Closer Look at Charter Schools Using Hierarchical Linear Modeling,* (NCES 2006–460), (Washington, D.C.: U.S. Department of Education, Institute of Educational Sciences, National Center for Education Statistics), http://nces.ed.gov/nationsreportcard/pubs/studies/2006460.asp.

46. National Conference of State Legislatures, Education Program Education Issues, "NCLB History," www.ncsl.org/programs/educ/NCLBHistory.html (accessed May 27, 2003).

47. Education Commission of the States, Issue Site: No Child Left Behind, www.ecs.org (accessed June 2, 2003).

48. NCSL, "NCLB History."

49. Center on Education Policy, *Ten Big Effects of the No Child Left Behind Act on Public Schools* (2006), www.cep-dc.org/nclb/NCLB-TenBigEffects.pdf (accessed April 28, 2007).

50. U.S. Department of Education, *A Test of Leadership: Charting the Future of U.S. Higher Education* (2006), p. 10, www.ed.gov/about/bdscomm/list/hiedfuture/index.html.

51. National Center for Public Policy and Higher Education, "Measuring Up 2002: The State-by-State Report Card for Higher Education: Affordability," http://measuringup.highereducation .org/2002/Affordability.cfm; Justin Pope, "Study Faults Most States on Higher Education Affordability," *Boston Globe* (September 7, 2006), www.boston.com/news/articles/2006/09/07.

52. Charles Mathesian, "Higher Ed: The No-Longer-Sacred Cow," *Governing* 8 (July 1995), pp. 20–26.

53. Diana M. DiNitto, *Social Welfare: Politics and Public Policy,* 4th ed. (Needham Heights, Mass.: Allyn & Bacon, 1995), p. 3.

54. Ibid., pp. 3–4.

55. "Unemployment Insurance," *Social Security Bulletin* 56 (Winter 1993), p. 19.

56. Ibid.

57. www.socialsecurity.gov/policy/docs/statcomps/supplement/2006/9a.html (accessed May 1, 2007).

58. www.cms.hhs.gov/home/medicaid.asp (accessed May 1, 2007).

59. DiNitto, *Social Welfare,* p. 167.

60. Donald F. Norris and Lyke Thompson, eds., *The Politics of Welfare Reform* (Thousand Oaks, Calif.: Sage Publications, 1995), pp. 3–4.

61. Kitty Dumas, "States Bypassing Congress in Reforming Welfare," *Congressional Quarterly Weekly Report* (April 11, 1992), pp. 951–952; "Welfare by Waiver," *Public Welfare* (Winter 1995), p. 4.

62. Jason DeParle, "Getting Opal Caples to Work," *New York Times Magazine* (August 24, 1997), pp. 33–61.

63. Vee Burke, CRS Report for Congress, *The New Welfare Law: Temporary Assistance for Needy Families,* Congressional Research Service, The Library of Congress, 1997.

64. Jeffrey L. Katz, "After 60 Years, Most Control Is Passing to States," *Congressional Quarterly Weekly Report* (August 3, 1996), p. 2196.

65. The Urban Institute, "A Decade of Welfare Reform: Facts and Figures" (June 2006), www.urban.org/UploadedPDF/900980_welfarereform.pdf.

66. Olivia A. Golden, *Assessing the New Federalism: Eight Years Later* (Washington, D.C.: The Urban Institute, 2005), p. 43.

67. Vanessa Sumo, "Weekly Update: Where to, SCHIP?" *Region Focus* (April 25, 2007), www.richmondfed.org/publications/economic_research/region_focus/weekly_update/index.cfm.

68. Anna C. Spencer, "Massachusetts Going for Full Coverage," *State News State Health Notes* 27, no. 465 (2006), www.ncsl.org/programs/health/shn/2006/sn465.htm.

69. Leif Wellington Haase, "The Massachusetts Universal Coverage Plan: Raising the Curtain," The Century Foundation News & Commentary (April 17, 2007), www.tcf.org/print.asp?type=NC&pubid=1554.

70. Paul Brace, *State Government and Economic Performance* (Baltimore, Md.: Johns Hopkins University Press, 1993), p. 19.

71. Ibid., pp. 24–25.

72. Ibid., p. 31.

73. John E. Jackson, "Michigan," *The New Economic Role of American States,* R. Scott Fosler, ed. (New York: Oxford University Press, 1988), pp. 105–111.

74. The Council of State Governments, "State Business Incentives," *State Trends and Forecasts* 3 (June 1994), p. 3.

75. Richard D. Bingham, "Economic Development Policies," in *Cities, Politics and Policy: A Comparative Analysis,* John P. Pelissero, ed. (Washington, D.C.: CQ Press, 2003), pp. 248–251.

76. George Hohmann, "Competition for Toyota Plants Is Intense," *Charleston Daily Mail* (March 1, 2007), www.dailymail.com/story/Business/George+Hohmann (accessed May 1, 2007).

77. Stewart Yerton, "Louisiana May Pass on Bidding for Plant: DaimlerChrysler to Pick Site in 2003," *Times-Picayune* (August 2, 2002), p. 1, http://web.lexis.com/univ.

78. Melissa Nelson, "Legislators Consider Possible Incentive Packages," Associated Press State and Local Wire (December 4, 2002), http://web.lexis.com/univ.

79. Shannon Cavanaugh, "Sprinting Ahead," *Charleston Regional Business Journal* (December 12, 2005), www.charlestonbusiness.com (accessed May 2, 2007).

80. James R. Healey, "Toyota to Build Mississippi Plant," *USA Today* (March 5, 2007), www.usatoday.com/money/autos/2007-02-27-toyota-plant_x.htm (accessed May 1, 2007).

81. Jay Hancock, "Officials Base Subsidies on Flawed Model," *Baltimore Sun* (October 12, 1999), p. 9A.

82. Ann Markusen, "Better Deals for State and Local Economic Development," *Employment Research* (April 2007), p. 4, www.upjohninst.org/publications/newsletter (accessed May 1, 2007).

83. Jay Hancock, "Marriott Used Virginia as Ruse to Raise Maryland Bid," *Baltimore Sun* (March 27, 1999), p. 1A.
84. Council of State Governments, "State Business," pp. 18–19.
85. Christopher Swope, "Economic Development: States Tighten Up Tax Lures," *Governing* (May 2003), p. 80.
86. The U.S. Supreme Court decision of *DaimlerChrysler v. Cuno* can be found at www .supremecourtus.gov/opinions/05slipopinion.html.
87. Virginia Gray and Peter Eisinger, *American States and Cities* (New York: HarperCollins Publishers, 1991), p. 286.
88. Jackson, "Michigan," pp. 105–111.
89. www.benfranklin.org.
90. NGA Center for Best Practices, Issue Brief, *Enhancing Competitiveness: A Review of Recent State Economic Development Initiatives—2005* (May 2006), p. 1.
91. For an overview of "clusters of innovation," see NGA Center for Best Practices and Council on Competitiveness, *Innovation America: Cluster-Based Strategies for Growing State Economies* (2006), www.ngaorg/files/pdf/0702innovationclusters.pdf.
92. David Osborne, *Laboratories of Democracy* (Boston: Harvard Business School, 1990), pp. 4–11.
93. Barry Rabe, "Second Generation Climate Policies in the American States: Proliferation, Diffusion, and Regionalization," *Issues in Governance Studies* 6 (August 2006). Washington, D.C.: Brookings Institution.
94. Ibid.
95. Rebecca Cho and Jennifer Koons, "Medill—On the Docket: *Massachusetts, et. al. v. Environmental Protection Agency, et. al.*," http://docket.medill.northwester.edu/archives/003742print.php (accessed May 5, 2007).
96. Barry Rabe, *Statehouse and Greenhouse: The Emerging Politics of American Climate Change Policy* (Washington, D.C.: Brookings Institution, 2004), pp. 116–118.
97. Eric Kelderman, "Greenhouse-Gas Limits Gain Steam in States," *Stateline.org.* (May 1, 2007), www.stateline.org (accessed May 1, 2007).
98. Rabe, *Statehouse and Greenhouse,* pp. 49–51.
99. Ibid., p. 21.
100. R. Steven Brown and Michael J. Keifer, "ECOS Budget Survey: Budgets Are Bruised, but Still Strong," *ECOStates* (Summer 2003), pp. 10–11, www.ecos.org/files/892_file_ 2003BudgetsArticle.pdf (accessed May 5, 2007).
101. DeWitt John, *Civic Environmentalism: Alternatives to Regulation in States and Communities* (Washington, D.C.: CQ Press, 1994), p. 309.
102. Ibid., pp. 259–270.
103. Ibid., p. 10.

Appendix

INFORMATION ON STATES

State Fast Facts

State	Nickname	Capital	Population*	Area**
Alabama	Heart of Dixie	Montgomery	4,557,808	52,419
Alaska	The Last Frontier	Juneau	663,661	663,267
Arizona	Grand Canyon State	Phoenix	5,939,292	113,998
Arkansas	The Natural State	Little Rock	2,779,154	53,179
California	Golden State	Sacramento	36,132,147	163,696
Colorado	Centennial State	Denver	4,665,177	104,094
Connecticut	Constitution State	Hartford	3,510,297	5,543
Delaware	First State	Dover	843,524	2,489
Florida	Sunshine State	Tallahassee	17,789,864	65,755
Georgia	Peach State	Atlanta	9,072,576	59,425
Hawaii	Aloha State	Honolulu	1,275,194	10,931
Idaho	Gem State	Boise	1,429,096	83,570
Illinois	Land of Lincoln	Springfield	12,763,371	57,914
Indiana	Hoosier State	Indianapolis	6,271,973	36,418
Iowa	Hawkeye State	Des Moines	2,966,334	56,272
Kansas	Sunflower State	Topeka	2,744,687	82,277
Kentucky	Bluegrass State	Frankfort	4,173,405	40,409
Louisiana	Pelican State	Baton Rouge	4,523,628	51,840
Maine	Pine Tree State	Augusta	1,321,505	35,385
Maryland	Free State	Annapolis	5,600,388	12,407
Massachusetts	Bay State	Boston	6,398,743	10,555
Michigan	Great Lake State	Lansing	10,120,860	96,716
Minnesota	North Star State	St. Paul	5,132,799	86,939
Mississippi	Magnolia State	Jackson	2,921,088	48,430
Missouri	Show Me State	Jefferson City	5,800,310	69,704
Montana	Treasure State	Helena	935,670	147,042
Nebraska	Cornhusker State	Lincoln	1,758,787	77,354
Nevada	Sagebrush State	Carson City	2,414,807	110,561
New Hampshire	Granite State	Concord	1,309,940	9,350
New Jersey	Garden State	Trenton	8,717,925	8,721
New Mexico	Land of Enchantment	Santa Fe	1,928,384	121,590
New York	Empire State	Albany	19,254,630	54,556
North Carolina	Tar Heel State	Raleigh	8,683,242	53,819
North Dakota	Peace Garden State	Bismarck	636,677	70,700

(Continued)

State Fast Facts *(Continued)*

State	Nickname	Capital	Population*	Area**
Ohio	Buckeye State	Columbus	11,464,042	44,825
Oklahoma	Sooner State	Oklahoma City	3,547,884	69,898
Oregon	Beaver State	Salem	3,641,056	98,381
Pennsylvania	Keystone State	Harrisburg	12,429,616	46,055
Rhode Island	Ocean State	Providence	1,076,189	1,545
South Carolina	Palmetto State	Columbia	4,255,083	32,020
South Dakota	Mount Rushmore State	Pierre	775,933	77,117
Tennessee	Volunteer State	Nashville	5,962,959	42,143
Texas	Lone Star State	Austin	22,859,968	268,581
Utah	Beehive State	Salt Lake City	2,469,585	84,899
Vermont	Green Mountain State	Montpelier	623,050	9,614
Virginia	Old Dominion	Richmond	7,567,465	42,774
Washington	Evergreen State	Olympia	6,287,759	71,300
West Virginia	Mountain State	Charleston	1,816,856	24,230
Wisconsin	Badger State	Madison	5,536,201	65,498
Wyoming	Equality State	Cheyenne	509,294	97,814

* *2005 Census resident population estimates.*
***Total of land and water area in square miles.*

Source: Kathleen O'Leary Morgan and Scott Morgan, eds., *State Rankings 2006,* 17th ed. (Lawrence, Kans.: Morgan Quitno Press, 2006), p. vi.

Date Each State Admitted to Statehood*

	ALPHA ORDER			RANK ORDER	
Rank	State	Date of Admission	Rank	State	Date of Admission
22	Alabama	December 14, 1819	1	Delaware	December 7, 1787
49	Alaska	January 3, 1959	2	Pennsylvania	December 12, 1787
48	Arizona	February 14, 1912	3	New Jersey	December 18, 1787
25	Arkansas	June 15, 1836	4	Georgia	January 2, 1788
31	California	September 9, 1850	5	Connecticut	January 9, 1788
38	Colorado	August 1, 1876	6	Massachusetts	February 6, 1788
5	Connecticut	January 9, 1788	7	Maryland	April 28, 1788
1	Delaware	December 7, 1787	8	South Carolina	May 23, 1788
27	Florida	March 3, 1845	9	New Hampshire	June 21, 1788
4	Georgia	January 2, 1788	10	Virginia	June 26, 1788
50	Hawaii	August 21, 1959	11	New York	July 26, 1788
43	Idaho	July 3, 1890	12	North Carolina	November 21, 1789
21	Illinois	December 3, 1818	13	Rhode Island	May 29, 1790
19	Indiana	December 11, 1816	14	Vermont	March 4, 1791
29	Iowa	December 28, 1846	15	Kentucky	June 1, 1792
34	Kansas	January 29, 1861	16	Tennessee	June 1, 1796
15	Kentucky	June 1, 1792	17	Ohio	March 1, 1803
18	Louisiana	April 30, 1812	18	Louisiana	April 30, 1812

Date Each State Admitted to Statehood* *(Continued)*

Rank	State	Date of Admission	Rank	State	Date of Admission
	ALPHA ORDER			RANK ORDER	
23	Maine	March 15, 1820	19	Indiana	December 11, 1816
7	Maryland	April 28, 1788	20	Mississippi	December 10, 1817
6	Massachusetts	February 6, 1788	21	Illinois	December 3, 1818
26	Michigan	January 26, 1837	22	Alabama	December 14, 1819
32	Minnesota	May 11, 1858	23	Maine	March 15, 1820
20	Mississippi	December 10, 1817	24	Missouri	August 10, 1821
24	Missouri	August 10, 1821	25	Arkansas	June 15, 1836
41	Montana	November 8, 1889	26	Michigan	January 26, 1837
37	Nebraska	March 1, 1867	27	Florida	March 3, 1845
36	Nevada	October 31, 1864	28	Texas	December 29, 1845
9	New Hampshire	June 21, 1788	29	Iowa	December 28, 1846
3	New Jersey	December 18, 1787	30	Wisconsin	May 29, 1848
47	New Mexico	January 6, 1912	31	California	September 9, 1850
11	New York	July 26, 1788	32	Minnesota	May 11, 1858
12	North Carolina	November 21, 1789	33	Oregon	February 14, 1859
39	North Dakota	November 2, 1889	34	Kansas	January 29, 1861
17	Ohio	March 1, 1803	35	West Virginia	June 20, 1863
46	Oklahoma	November 16, 1907	36	Nevada	October 31, 1864
33	Oregon	February 14, 1859	37	Nebraska	March 1, 1867
2	Pennsylvania	December 12, 1787	38	Colorado	August 1, 1876
13	Rhode Island	May 29, 1790	39	North Dakota	November 2, 1889
8	South Carolina	May 23, 1788	39	South Dakota	November 2, 1889
39	South Dakota	November 2, 1889	41	Montana	November 8, 1889
16	Tennessee	June 1, 1796	42	Washington	November 11, 1889
28	Texas	December 29, 1845	43	Idaho	July 3, 1890
45	Utah	January 4, 1896	44	Wyoming	July 10, 1890
14	Vermont	March 4, 1791	45	Utah	January 4, 1896
10	Virginia	June 26, 1788	46	Oklahoma	November 16, 1907
42	Washington	November 11, 1889	47	New Mexico	January 6, 1912
35	West Virginia	June 20, 1863	48	Arizona	February 14, 1912
30	Wisconsin	May 29, 1848	49	Alaska	January 3, 1959
44	Wyoming	July 10, 1890	50	Hawaii	August 21, 1959

*First thirteen states show date of ratification of Constitution.

Source: State Rankings 2006, p.1.

State Population—Rank, Percent Change, and Population Density: 1980 to 2004

[As of April 1, except 2004 as of July 1. Insofar as possible, population shown for all years is that of present area of state. Minus sign (−) indicates decrease.]

State	RANK				PERCENT CHANGE			POPULATION PER SQUARE MILE OF LAND AREA[1]		
	1980	1990	2000	2004	1980–1990	1990–2000	2000–2004	1990	2000	2004
United States	(X)	(X)	(X)	(X)	9.8	13.1	4.3	70.3	79.6	83.0
Alabama	22	22	23	23	3.8	10.1	1.9	79.6	87.6	89.3
Alaska	50	49	48	47	36.9	14.0	4.5	1.0	1.1	1.1
Arizona	29	24	20	18	34.8	40.0	12.0	32.3	45.2	50.5
Arkansas	33	33	33	32	2.8	13.7	3.0	45.1	51.3	52.9
California	1	1	1	1	26.0	13.6	6.0	191.1	217.2	230.1
Colorado	28	26	24	22	14.0	30.6	7.0	31.8	41.5	44.4
Connecticut	25	27	29	29	5.8	3.6	2.9	678.5	702.9	723.2
Delaware	47	46	45	45	12.1	17.6	6.0	341.0	401.1	425.1
District of Columbia	(X)	(X)	(X)	(X)	−4.9	−5.7	−3.2	9,884.4	9,316.4	9,015.0
Florida	7	4	4	4	32.7	23.5	8.8	239.9	296.4	322.6
Georgia	13	11	10	9	18.6	26.4	7.8	111.9	141.4	152.5
Hawaii	39	41	42	42	14.9	9.3	4.2	172.6	188.6	196.6
Idaho	41	42	39	39	6.7	28.5	7.7	12.2	15.6	16.8
Illinois	5	6	5	5	(Z)	8.7	2.4	205.6	223.4	228.7
Indiana	12	14	14	14	1.0	9.7	2.6	154.6	169.5	173.9
Iowa	27	30	30	30	−4.7	5.4	1.0	49.7	52.4	52.9
Kansas	32	32	32	33	4.8	8.5	1.7	30.3	32.9	33.4
Kentucky	23	23	25	26	0.7	9.6	2.6	92.8	101.7	104.4
Louisiana	19	21	22	24	0.4	5.9	1.0	96.9	102.6	103.7
Maine	38	38	40	40	9.2	3.8	3.3	39.8	41.3	42.7
Maryland	18	19	19	19	13.4	10.8	4.9	489.1	541.9	568.7
Massachusetts	11	13	13	13	4.9	5.5	1.1	767.4	809.8	818.4
Michigan	8	8	8	8	0.4	6.9	1.8	163.6	175.0	178.0

State									
Minnesota	21	20	21	21	7.4	12.4	3.7	55.0	61.8	64.1
Mississippi	31	31	31	31	2.2	10.5	2.0	54.9	60.6	61.9
Missouri	15	15	17	17	4.1	9.4	2.8	74.3	81.2	83.5
Montana	44	44	44	44	1.6	12.9	2.7	5.5	6.2	6.4
Nebraska	35	36	38	38	0.5	8.4	2.1	20.5	22.3	22.7
Nevada	43	39	35	35	50.1	66.3	16.8	10.9	18.2	21.3
New Hampshire	42	40	41	41	20.5	11.4	5.2	123.7	137.8	144.9
New Jersey	9	9	9	10	5.2	8.6	3.4	1,044.5	1,134.4	1,172.8
New Mexico	37	37	36	36	16.3	20.1	4.6	12.5	15.0	15.7
New York	2	2	3	3	2.5	5.5	1.3	381.0	401.9	407.2
North Carolina	10	10	11	11	12.8	21.3	6.1	136.2	165.2	175.3
North Dakota	46	47	48	48	-2.1	0.5	-1.2	9.3	9.3	9.2
Ohio	6	7	7	7	0.5	4.7	0.9	264.9	277.3	279.8
Oklahoma	26	28	28	28	4.0	9.7	2.1	45.8	50.3	51.3
Oregon	30	29	27	27	7.9	20.4	5.1	29.6	35.6	37.4
Pennsylvania	4	5	6	6	0.2	3.4	1.0	265.1	274.0	276.8
Rhode Island	40	43	43	43	5.9	4.5	3.1	960.3	1,003.2	1,034.2
South Carolina	24	25	26	25	11.7	15.1	4.6	115.8	133.2	139.4
South Dakota	45	45	46	46	0.8	8.5	2.1	9.2	9.9	10.2
Tennessee	17	17	16	16	6.2	16.7	3.7	118.3	138.0	143.2
Texas	3	3	2	2	19.4	22.8	7.9	64.9	79.6	85.9
Utah	36	35	34	34	17.9	29.6	7.0	21.0	27.2	29.1
Vermont	48	48	49	49	10.0	8.2	2.1	60.8	65.8	67.2
Virginia	14	12	12	12	15.8	14.4	5.4	156.3	178.8	188.4
Washington	20	18	15	15	17.8	21.1	5.3	73.1	88.6	93.2
West Virginia	34	34	37	37	-8.0	0.8	0.4	74.5	75.1	75.4
Wisconsin	16	16	18	20	4.0	9.6	2.7	90.1	98.8	101.4
Wyoming	49	50	50	50	-3.4	8.9	2.6	4.7	5.1	5.2

X Not applicable.

Z Less than 0.05 percent.

[1] Persons per square mile were calculated on the basis of land area data from the 2000 census.

Source: U.S. Census Bureau, *Statistical Abstract of the United States: 2006,* 125th ed. (Washington, D.C., 2006), p. 22.

	Personal Income (in millions)	Personal Income Rank	Personal Income Per Capita	Per Capita Rank	Gross State Product (in millions)	GSP Per Capita	GSP Per Capita Rank
Alabama	$ 132,796	24	$29,136	41	$ 149,796	$32,866	45
Alaska	23,634	47	35,612	16	39,872	60,079	2
Arizona	179,765	21	30,267	38	215,759	36,327	39
Arkansas	74,687	33	26,874	48	86,802	31,233	48
California	1,338,181	1	37,036	11	1,621,843	44,886	12
Colorado	177,025	22	37,946	8	216,064	46,314	9
Connecticut	167,858	23	47,819	1	194,469	55,400	3
Delaware	31,265	44	37,065	10	54,354	64,437	1
Florida	590,954	4	33,219	23	674,049	37,889	33
Georgia	282,347	12	31,121	35	364,310	40,155	20
Hawaii	44,044	40	34,539	19	53,710	42,119	18
Idaho	40,241	42	28,158	44	47,178	33,012	44
Illinois	461,014	5	36,120	14	560,236	43,894	13
Indiana	196,160	16	31,276	33	238,638	38,048	30
Iowa	95,858	30	32,315	28	114,291	38,529	28
Kansas	90,126	31	32,836	25	105,448	38,419	29
Kentucky	118,998	26	28,513	42	140,359	33,632	43
Louisiana	112,275	28	24,820	50	166,310	36,765	37
Maine	41,300	41	31,252	34	45,070	34,105	41
Maryland	233,874	14	41,760	4	244,899	43,729	14
Massachusetts	283,391	11	44,289	2	328,535	51,344	5
Michigan	335,164	9	33,116	24	377,895	37,338	34
Minnesota	191,830	17	37,373	9	233,292	45,451	11
Mississippi	73,955	34	25,318	49	80,197	27,454	50
Missouri	185,026	20	31,899	30	216,069	37,251	35
Montana	27,497	45	29,387	39	29,851	31,903	47
Nebraska	59,124	36	33,616	20	70,263	39,950	22

Nevada	86,650	32	35,883	15	110,546	45,778	10
New Hampshire	50,312	38	38,408	6	55,690	42,513	17
New Jersey	381,595	7	43,771	3	430,787	49,414	7
New Mexico	53,308	37	27,644	46	69,324	35,949	40
New York	779,941	2	40,507	5	963,466	50,038	6
North Carolina	265,296	13	30,553	37	344,641	39,690	24
North Dakota	19,988	49	31,395	32	24,178	37,975	32
Ohio	372,332	8	32,478	26	442,440	38,594	27
Oklahoma	104,060	29	29,330	40	120,549	33,978	42
Oregon	116,889	27	32,103	29	145,351	39,920	23
Pennsylvania	433,752	6	34,897	18	487,169	39,194	26
Rhode Island	38,907	43	36,153	13	43,791	40,691	19
South Carolina	120,639	25	28,352	43	139,771	32,848	46
South Dakota	24,530	46	31,614	31	31,066	40,037	21
Tennessee	185,488	19	31,107	36	226,502	37,985	31
Texas	742,074	3	32,462	27	982,403	42,975	15
Utah	69,299	35	28,061	45	89,836	36,377	38
Vermont	20,764	48	33,327	22	23,134	37,130	36
Virginia	290,511	10	38,390	7	352,745	46,613	8
Washington	222,643	15	35,409	17	268,502	42,702	16
West Virginia	49,445	39	27,215	47	53,782	29,602	49
Wisconsin	185,821	18	33,565	21	217,537	39,294	25
Wyoming	18,731	50	36,778	12	27,422	53,843	4
D.C.	30,270	—	54,985	—	82,777	150,361	—
U.S.	10,251,639	—	34,586	—	12,402,967	41,844	—

Source: U.S. Bureau of Economic Analysis, 2005 (personal income) & 2005 (GSP) estimate. *State and Local Sourcebook 2006.* Supplement to *Governing,* p. 5.

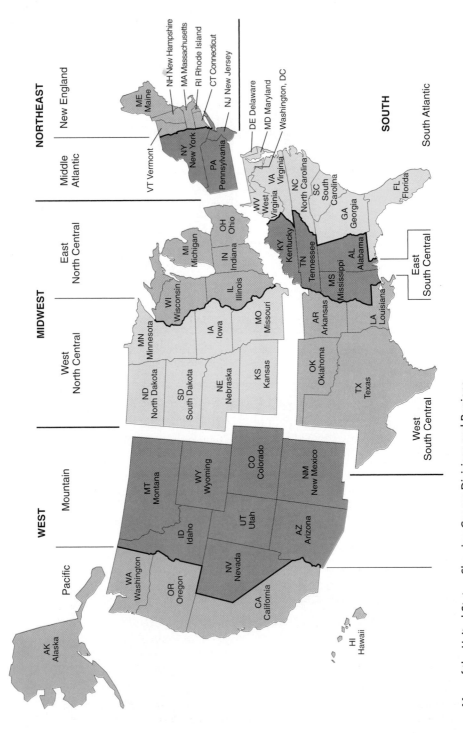

Map of the United States, Showing Census Divisions and Regions

Source: U.S. Census Bureau, *Statistical Abstract of the United States*, 125th ed. (Washington, D.C., 2006), inside cover.

Index